ESSAYS on the GITA

SRI AUROBINDO

SANAGE
PUBLISHING HOUSE

Paperback: 978-936205702-0
Hardback: 978-936205953-6
eBook: 978-936205944-4

Printed by:

Sanage Publishing House LLP
Mumbai, India

sanagepublishing@gmail.com

Sri Aurobindo (born Aurobindo Ghose; 15 August 1872 – 5 December 1950) was an Indian philosopher, yogi, maharishi, poet, and Indian nationalist. He was also a journalist, editing newspapers such as Bande Mataram. He joined the Indian movement for independence from British colonial rule, until 1910 was one of its influential leaders, and then became a spiritual reformer, introducing his visions on human progress and spiritual evolution.

His main literary works are The Life Divine, which deals with the philosophical aspect of Integral Yoga; Synthesis of Yoga, which deals with the principles and methods of Integral Yoga; and Savitri: A Legend and a Symbol, an epic poem.

Publisher's Note

The first series of Essays on the Gita appeared in the monthly review Arya between August 1916 and July 1918. It was revised by Sri Aurobindo and published as a book in 1922.The second series appeared in the Arya between August 1918 and July 1920. In 1928 Sri Aurobindo brought out an extensively revised edition in book form. For the present edition, the text has been thoroughly checked against all previous editions and against the manuscripts of the revised Arya.

CONTENTS

Sri Aurobindo in Pondicherry, c. 1915

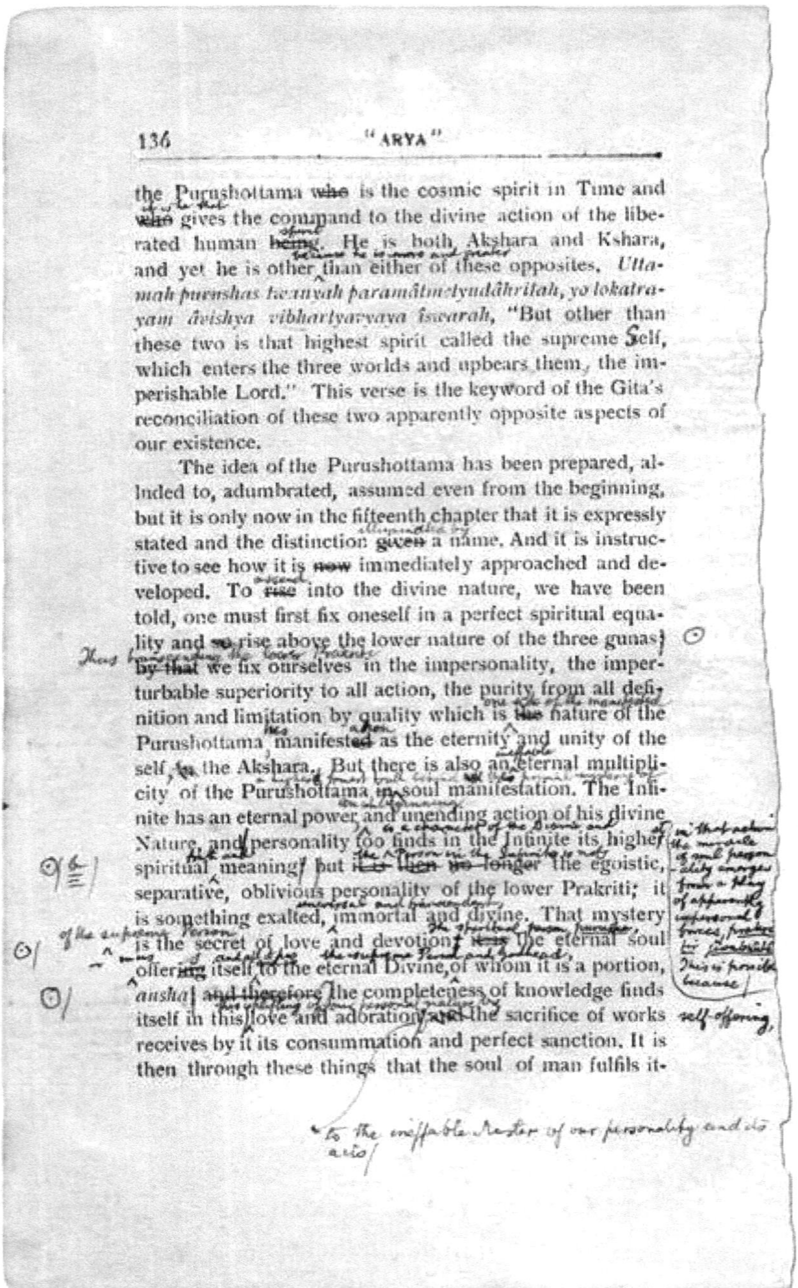

the Purushottama who is the cosmic spirit in Time and who gives the command to the divine action of the liberated human being. He is both Akshara and Kshara, and yet he is other than either of these opposites. *Uttamah purushas tvanyah paramâtmetyudâhritah, yo lokatrayam âvishya vibhartyavyaya îswarah,* "But other than these two is that highest spirit called the supreme Self, which enters the three worlds and upbears them, the imperishable Lord." This verse is the keyword of the Gita's reconciliation of these two apparently opposite aspects of our existence.

The idea of the Purushottama has been prepared, alluded to, adumbrated, assumed even from the beginning, but it is only now in the fifteenth chapter that it is expressly stated and the distinction given a name. And it is instructive to see how it is now immediately approached and developed. To rise into the divine nature, we have been told, one must first fix oneself in a perfect spiritual equality and so rise above the lower nature of the three gunas; by that we fix ourselves in the impersonality, the imperturbable superiority to all action, the purity from all definition and limitation by quality which is the nature of the Purushottama manifested as the eternity and unity of the self, in the Akshara. But there is also an eternal multiplicity of the Purushottama in soul manifestation. The Infinite has an eternal power and unending action of his divine Nature, and personality too finds in the Infinite its higher spiritual meaning; but it is then no longer the egoistic, separative, oblivious personality of the lower Prakriti; it is something exalted, immortal and divine. That mystery is the secret of love and devotion; it is the eternal soul offering itself to the eternal Divine, of whom it is a portion, *ansha*; and therefore the completeness of knowledge finds itself in this love and adoration and the sacrifice of works receives by it its consummation and perfect sanction. It is then through these things that the soul of man fulfils it-

A page of the Arya as revised by Sri Aurobindo

First Series

I

OUR DEMAND AND NEED FROM THE GITA

The World abounds with scriptures sacred and pro-fane, with revelations and half-revelations, with religions and philosophies, sects and schools and systems. To these the many minds of a half-ripe knowledge or no knowledge at all attach themselves with exclusiveness and passion and will have it that this or the other book is alone the eternal Word of God and all others are either impostures or at best imperfectly inspired, that this or that philosophy is the last word of the reasoning intellect and other systems are either errors or saved only by such partial truth in them as links them to the one true philosophical cult. Even the discoveries of physical Science have been elevated into a creed and in its name religion and spirituality banned as ignorance and superstition, philosophy as frippery and moonshine. And to these bigoted exclusions and vain wranglings even the wise have often lent themselves, misled by some spirit of darkness that has mingled with their light and overshadowed it with some cloud of intellectual egoism or spiritual pride. Mankind seems now indeed inclined to grow a little modester and wiser; we no longer slay our fellows in the name of God's truth or because they have minds differently trained or differently constituted from ours;

we are less ready to curse and revile our neighbour because he is wicked or presumptuous enough to differ from us in opinion; we are ready even to admit that Truth is everywhere and cannot be our sole monopoly; we are beginning to look at other religions and philosophies for the truth and help they contain and no longer merely in order to damn them as false or criticize what we conceive to be their errors. But we are still apt to declare that our truth gives us the supreme knowledge which other religions or philosophies have missed or only imperfectly grasped so that they deal either with subsidiary and inferior aspects of the truth of things or can merely prepare less evolved minds for the heights to which we have arrived. And we are still prone to force upon ourselves or others the whole sacred mass of the book or gospel we admire, insisting that all shall be accepted as eternally valid truth and no iota or underline or diaeresis denied its part of the plenary inspiration.

It may therefore be useful in approaching an ancient Scripture, such as the Veda, Upanishads, or Gita, to precisely indicate the spirit in which we approach it and what exactly we think we may derive from it that is of value to humanity and its future. First of all, there is undoubtedly a Truth one and eternal which we are seeking, from which all other truth derives, by the light of which all other truth finds its right place, explanation, and relation to the scheme of knowledge. But precisely for that reason it cannot be shut up in a single trenchant formula, it is not likely to be found in its entirety or in all its bearings in any single philosophy or scripture or uttered altogether and forever by any one teacher, thinker, prophet, or Avatar. Nor has it been wholly found by us if our view of it necessitates the intolerant exclusion of the truth underlying other systems; for when we reject passionately, we mean simply that we cannot appreciate and explain. Secondly, this Truth, though it is one and eternal, expresses itself in Time and through the mind of man; therefore, every Scripture must necessarily contain two elements, one temporary, perishable, belonging to the ideas of the period and country in which it was produced, the other eternal and im-perishable and applicable in all ages and countries. Moreover, in the statement of the Truth the actual form given to it, the system and arrangement, the metaphysical and intellectual mould, the precise expression used must be largely subject to the mutations of Time and cease to have the same force; for the human intellect modifies itself always; continually dividing and putting together it is obliged to shift its divisions continually and to rearrange its syntheses; it is always leaving old expression and symbol for new or, if it uses the old, it so changes its connotation or at least its exact content and association that we can never be quite sure of understanding an ancient book of this kind precisely in the sense and spirit it bore to its contemporaries. What is of entirely permanent value is that which besides being universal has been experienced, lived, and seen with a higher than the intellectual vision.

I hold it therefore of small importance to extract from the Gita its exact metaphysical connotation as it was understood by the men of the time, — even if that were accurately possible. That it is not possible, is shown by the divergence of the original commentaries which have been and are still being written upon it; for they all agree in each disagreeing with all the others, each finds in the Gita its own system of metaphysics and trend of religious thought. Nor will even the most painstaking and disinterested scholarship and the most luminous theories of the historical development of Indian philosophy save us from inevitable error. But what we can do with profit is to seek in the Gita for the actual living truths it contains, apart from their metaphysical form, to extract from it what can help us or the world at large and to put it in the most natural and vital form and expression we can find that will be suitable to the mentality and helpful to the spiritual needs of our present-day humanity. No doubt in this attempt we may mix a good deal of error born of our own individuality and of the ideas in which we live, as did greater men before us, but if we steep ourselves in the spirit of this great Scripture and, above all, if we have tried to live in that spirit, we may be sure of finding in it as much real truth as we are capable of receiving as well as the spiritual influence and actual help that, personally, we were intended to derive from it. And that is after all what Scriptures were written to give; the rest is academical disputation or theological dogma. Only those Scriptures, religions, philosophies which can be thus constantly renewed, relived, their stuff of permanent truth constantly reshaped and developed in the inner thought and spiritual experience of a developing humanity, continue to be of living importance to mankind. The rest remain as monuments of the past but have no actual force or vital impulse for the future.

In the Gita there is very little that is merely local or temporal and its spirit is so large, profound, and universal that even this little can easily be universalized without the sense of the teaching suffering any diminution or violation; rather by giving an ampler scope to it than belonged to the country and epoch, the teaching gains in depth, truth, and power. Often indeed the Gita itself suggests a wider scope that can in this way be given to an idea in itself local or limited. Thus it dwells on the ancient Indian system and idea of sacrifice as an interchange between gods and men, — a system and idea which have long been practically obsolete in India itself and are no longer real to the general human mind; but we find here a sense so entirely subtle, figurative and symbolic given to the word "sacrifice" and the conception of the gods is so little local or mythological, so entirely cosmic and philosophical that we can easily accept both as expressive of a practical fact of psychology and general law of Nature and so apply them to the modern conceptions of interchange between life and life and of ethical sacrifice and self-giving as to widen and deepen these and cast over them a more spiritual aspect and the light of a profounder and more far-reaching Truth. Equally the idea of action according to the Shastra, the fourfold order of society, the allusion to the relative position of the four orders or the comparative spiritual disabilities of Shudras and women seem at first sight local and temporal, and, if they are too much pressed in their literal sense, narrow so much at least of the teaching, deprive it of its universality and spiritual depth and limit its validity for mankind at large. But if we look behind to the spirit and sense and not at the local name and temporal institution, we see that here too the sense is deep and true and the spirit philosophical, spiritual, and universal. By Shastra we perceive that the Gita means the law imposed on itself by humanity as a substitute for the purely egoistic action of the natural unregenerate man and a control on his tendency to seek in the satisfaction of his desire the standard and aim of his life. We see too that the fourfold order of society is merely the concrete form of a spiritual truth which is itself independent of the form; it rests on the conception of right works as a rightly ordered expression of the nature of the individual being through whom the work is done, that nature assigning him his line and scope in life according to his inborn quality and his self-expressive function. Since this is the spirit in which the Gita advances its most local and particular instances, we are justified in pursuing always the same principle and looking always for the deeper general truth which is sure to underlie whatever seems at first sight merely local and of the time. For we shall find always that the deeper truth and principle is implied in the grain of the thought even when it is not expressly stated in its language.

Nor shall we deal in any other spirit with the element of philosophical dogma or religious creed which either enters into the Gita or hangs about it owing to its use of the philosophical terms and religious symbols current at the time. When the Gita speaks of Sankhya and Yoga, we shall not discuss beyond the limits of what is just essential for our statement, the relations of the Sankhya of the Gita with its one Purusha and strong Vedantic colouring to the non-theistic or "atheistic" Sankhya that has come down to us bringing with it its scheme of many Purushas and one Prakriti, nor of the Yoga of the Gita, many-sided, subtle, rich and flexible to the theistic doctrine and the fixed, scientific, rigorously defined and graded system of the Yoga of Patanjali. In the Gita the Sankhya and Yoga are evidently only two convergent parts of the same Vedantic truth or rather two concurrent ways of approaching its realization, the one philosophical, intellectual, analytic, the other intuitional, devotional, practical, ethical, synthetic, reaching knowledge through experience. The Gita recognizes no real difference in their teachings. Still less need we discuss the theories which regard the Gita as the fruit of some particular religious system or tradition. Its teaching is universal whatever may have been its origins.

The philosophical system of the Gita, its arrangement of truth, is not that part of its teaching which is the most vital, profound, eternally durable; but most of the material of which the system is composed, the principal ideas suggestive and penetrating which are woven into its complex harmony, are eternally valuable and valid; for they are not merely the luminous ideas or striking speculations of a philosophic intellect, but rather enduring truths of spiritual experience, verifiable facts of our highest psychological possibilities which no attempt to read deeply the mystery of existence can afford to neglect. Whatever the system may be, it is not, as the commentators strive to make it, framed, or intended to support any exclusive school of philosophical thought or to put forward predominantly the claims of any one form of Yoga. The language of the Gita, the structure of thought, the combination and balancing of ideas belong neither to the temper of a sectarian teacher nor to the spirit of a rigorous analytical dialectics cutting off one angle of the truth to exclude all the others; but rather there is a wide, undulating, encircling movement of ideas which is the manifestation of a vast synthetic mind and a rich synthetic experience. This is one of those great syntheses in which Indian spirituality has been as rich as in its creation of the more intensive, exclusive movements of knowledge and religious realization that follow out with an absolute concentration one clue, one path to its extreme issues. It does not cleave asunder but reconciles and unifies.

The thought of the Gita is not pure Monism although it sees in one unchanging, pure, eternal Self the foundation of all cosmic existence, nor Mayavada although it speaks of the Maya of the three modes of Prakriti omnipresent in the created world; nor is it qualified Monism although it places in the One his eternal supreme Prakriti manifested in the form of the Jiva and lays most stress on dwelling in God rather than dissolution as the supreme state of spiritual consciousness; nor is it Sankhya although it explains the created world by the double principle of Purusha and Prakriti; nor is it Vaishnava Theism although it presents to us Krishna, who is the Avatara of Vishnu according to the Puranas, as the supreme Deity and allows no essential difference nor any actual superiority of the status of the indefinable relation-less Brahman over that of this Lord of beings who is the Master of the universe and the Friend of all creatures. Like the earlier spiritual synthesis of the Upanishads this later synthesis at once spiritual and intellectual avoids naturally every such rigid determination as would injure its universal comprehensiveness. Its aim is precisely the opposite to that of the polemist commentators who found this Scripture established as one of the three highest Vedantic authorities and attempted to turn it into a weapon of offence and defence against other schools and systems. The Gita is not a weapon for dialectical warfare; it is a gate opening on the whole world of spiritual truth and experience and the view it gives us embraces all the provinces of that supreme region. It maps out, but it does not cut up or build walls or hedges to confine our vision.

There have been other syntheses in the long history of Indian thought. We start with the Vedic synthesis of the psychological being of man in its highest flights and widest rangings of divine knowledge, power, joy, life, and glory with the cosmic existence of the gods, pursued behind the symbols of the material universe into those superior planes which are hidden from the physical sense and the material mentality. The crown of this synthesis was in the experience of the Vedic Rishis something divine, transcendent, and blissful in whose unity the increasing soul of man and the eternal divine fullness of the cosmic godheads meet perfectly and fulfil themselves. The Upanishads take up this crowning experience of the earlier seers and make it their starting point for a high and profound synthesis of spiritual knowledge; they draw together into a great harmony all that had been seen and experienced by the inspired and liberated knowers of the Eternal throughout a great and fruitful period of spiritual seeking. The Gita starts from this Vedantic synthesis and upon the basis of its essential ideas builds another harmony of the three great means and powers, Love, Knowledge, and Works, through which the soul of man can directly approach and cast itself into the Eternal. There is yet another, the Tantric,[1] which though less subtle and spiritually profound, is even more bold and forceful than the synthesis of the Gita, for it seizes even upon the obstacles to the spiritual life and compels them to become the means for a richer spiritual conquest and enables us to embrace the whole of Life in our divine scope as the Lila[2] of the Divine; and in some directions it is more immediately rich and fruitful, for it brings forward into the foreground along with divine knowledge, divine works and an enriched devotion of divine Love, the secrets also of the Hatha and Raja Yogas, the use of the body and of mental askesis for the opening up of the divine life on all its planes, to which the Gita gives only a passing and perfunctory attention. Moreover, it grasps at that idea of the divine perfectibility of man, possessed by the Vedic Rishis but thrown into the background by the intermediate ages, which is destined to fill so large a place in any future synthesis of human thought, experience, and aspiration.

---

1 All the Puranic tradition, it must be remembered, draws the richness of its contents from the Tantra.

2 The cosmic Play.

We of the coming day stand at the head of a new age of development which must lead to such a new and larger synthesis. We are not called upon to be orthodox Vedantins of any of the three schools or Tantrics or to adhere to one of the theistic religions of the past or to entrench ourselves within the four corners of the teaching of the Gita. That would be to limit ourselves and to attempt to create our spiritual life out of the being, knowledge, and nature of others, of the men of the past, instead of building it out of our own being and potentialities. We do not belong to the past dawns, but to the noon's of the future. A mass of new material is flowing into us; we have not only to assimilate the influences of the great theistic religions of India and of the world and a recovered sense of the meaning of Buddhism, but to take full account of the potent though limited revelations of modern knowledge and seeking; and, beyond that, the remote and dateless past which seemed to be dead is returning upon us with an effulgence of many luminous secrets long lost to the consciousness of mankind but now breaking out again from behind the veil. All this points to a new, a very rich, a very vast synthesis; a fresh and widely embracing harmonization of our gains is both an intellectual and a spiritual necessity of the future. But just as the past syntheses have taken those which preceded them for their starting point, so also must that of the future, to be on firm ground, proceed from what the great bodies of realized spiritual thought and experience in the past have given. Among them the Gita takes a most important place.

Our object, then, in studying the Gita will not be a scholastic or academical scrutiny of its thought, nor to place its philosophy in the history of metaphysical speculation, nor shall we deal with it in the manner of the analytical dialectician. We approach it for help and light and our aim must be to distinguish its essential and living message, that in it on which humanity has to seize for its perfection and its highest spiritual welfare.

II

THE DIVINE TEACHER

The Peculiarity of the Gita among the great religious books of the world is that it does not stand apart as a work by itself, the fruit of the spiritual life of a creative personality like Christ, Mahomed or Buddha or of an epoch of pure spiritual searching like the Veda and Upanishads, but is given as an episode in an epic history of nations and their wars and men and their deeds and arises out of a critical moment in the soul of one of its leading personages face to face with the crowning action of his life, a work terrible, violent and sanguinary, at the point when he must either recoil from it altogether or carry it through to its inexorable completion. It matters little whether or no as modern criticism supposes, the Gita is a later composition inserted into the mass of the Mahabharata by its author in order to invest its teaching with the authority and popularity of the great national epic. There seem to me to be strong grounds against this supposition for which, besides, the evidence, extrinsic or internal, is in the last degree scanty and insufficient. But even if it be sound, there remains the fact that the author has not only taken pains to interweave his work inextricably into the vast web of the larger poem but is careful again and again to remind us of the situation from which the teaching has arisen; he returns to it prominently, not only at the end but in the middle of his profoundest philosophical disquisitions. We must accept the insistence of the author and give its full importance to this recurrent preoccupation of the Teacher and the disciple. The teaching of the Gita must therefore be regarded not merely in the light of a general spiritual philosophy or ethical doctrine, but as bearing upon a practical crisis in the application of ethics and spirituality to human life. For what that crisis stands, what is the significance of the battle of Kurukshetra and its effect on Arjuna's inner being, we have first to determine if we would grasp the central drift of the ideas of the Gita.

Very obviously a great body of the profoundest teaching cannot be built round an ordinary occurrence which has no gulfs of deep suggestion and hazardous difficulty behind its superficial and outward aspects and can be governed well enough by the ordinary everyday standards of thought and action. There are indeed three things in the Gita which are spiritually significant, almost symbolic, typical of the profoundest relations and problems of the spiritual life and of human existence at its roots; they are the divine personality of the Teacher, his characteristic relations with his disciple and the occasion of his teaching. The teacher is God himself descended into humanity; the disciple is the first, as we might say in modern language, the representative man of his age, closest friend and chosen instrument of the Avatar, his protagonist in an immense work and struggle the secret purpose of which is unknown to the actors in it, known only to the incarnate Godhead who guides it all from behind the veil of his unfathomable mind of knowledge; the occasion is the violent crisis of that work and struggle at the moment when the anguish and moral difficulty and blind violence of its apparent movements forces itself with the shock of a visible revelation on the mind of its representative man and raises the whole question of the meaning of God in the world and the goal and drift and sense of human life and conduct.

India has from ancient times strongly held a belief in the reality of the Avatara, the descent into form, the revelation of the Godhead in humanity. In the West this belief has never really stamped itself upon the mind because it has been presented through exoteric Christianity as a theological dogma without any roots in the reason and general consciousness and attitude towards life. But in India it has grown up and persisted as a logical outcome of the Vedantic view of life and taken firm root in the consciousness of the race. All existence is a manifestation of God because He is the only existence, and nothing can be except as either a real figuring or else a figment of that one reality. Therefore, every conscious being is in part or in some way a descent of the Infinite into the apparent finiteness of name and form. But it is a veiled manifestation and there is a gradation between the supreme being[1] of the Divine and the consciousness shrouded partly or wholly by ignorance of self in the finite. The conscious embodied soul[2] is the spark of the divine Fire and that soul in man opens out to self-knowledge as it develops out of ignorance of self into self-being. The Divine also, pouring itself into the forms of the cosmic existence, is revealed ordinarily in an efflorescence of its powers, in energies and magnitudes of its knowledge, love, joy, developed force of being,[3] in degrees and faces of its divinity. But when the divine Consciousness and Power, taking upon itself the human form and the human mode of action, possesses it not only by powers and magnitudes, by degrees and outward faces of itself but out of its eternal self-knowledge, when the Unborn knows itself and acts in the frame of the mental being and the appearance of birth, that is the height of the conditioned manifestation; it is the full and conscious descent of the Godhead, it is the Avatara.

The Vaishnava form of Vedantism which has laid most stress upon this conception expresses the relation of God in man to man in God by the double figure of Nara-Narayana, associated historically with the origin of a religious school very similar in

---

1 para bhava.
2 dehī
3 vibhutī.

its doctrines to the teaching of the Gita. Nara is the human soul which, eternal companion of the Divine, finds itself only when it awakens to that companionship and begins, as the Gita would say, to live in God. Narayana is the divine Soul always present in our humanity, the secret guide, friend and helper of the human being, the "Lord who abides within the heart of creatures" of the Gita; when within us the veil of that secret sanctuary is withdrawn and man speaks face to face with God, hears the divine voice, receives the divine light, acts in the divine power, then becomes possible the supreme uplifting of the embodied human conscious-being into the unborn and eternal. He becomes capable of that dwelling in God and giving up of his whole consciousness into the Divine which the Gita upholds as the best or highest secret of things, uttamam rahasyam. When this eternal divine Consciousness always present in every human being, this God in man, takes possession partly[4] or wholly of the human consciousness and becomes in visible human shape the guide, teacher, leader of the world, not as those who living in their humanity yet feel something of the power or light or love of the divine Gnosis informing and conducting them but out of that divine Gnosis itself, direct from its central force and plenitude, then we have the manifest Avatar. The inner Divinity is the eternal Avatar in man; the human manifestation is its sign and development in the external world.

When we thus understand the conception of Avatarhood, we see that whether for the fundamental teaching of the Gita, our present subject, or for spiritual life generally the external aspect has only a secondary importance. Such controversies as the one that has raged in Europe over the historicity of Christ, would seem to a spiritually-minded Indian largely a waste of time; he would concede to it a considerable historical, but hardly any

4 Chaitanya, the Avatar of Nadiya, is said to have been thus partly or occasionally occupied by the divine Consciousness and Power.

religious importance; for what does it matter in the end whether a Jesus son of the carpenter Joseph was actually born in Nazareth or Bethlehem, lived and taught and was done to death on a real or trumped-up charge of sedition, so long as we can know by spiritual experience the inner Christ, live uplifted in the light of his teaching and escape from the yoke of the natural Law by that atonement of man with God of which the crucifixion is the symbol? If the Christ, God made man, lives within our spiritual being, it would seem to matter little whether or not a son of Mary physically lived and suffered and died in Judea. So too the Krishna who matters to us is the eternal incarnation of the Divine and not the historical teacher and leader of men.

In seeking the kernel of the thought of the Gita we need, therefore, only concern ourselves with the spiritual significance of the human-divine Krishna of the Mahabharata who is presented to us as the teacher of Arjuna on the battlefield of Kurukshetra. The historical Krishna, no doubt, existed. We meet the name first in the Chhandogya Upanishad where all we can gather about him is that he was well known in spiritual tradition as a knower of the Brahman, so well-known indeed in his personality and the circumstances of his life that it was sufficient to refer to him by the name of his mother as Krishna son of Devaki for all to understand who was meant. In the same Upanishad we find mention of King Dhritarashtra son of Vichitravirya and since tradition associated the two together so closely that they are both of them leading personages in the action of the Mahabharata, we may fairly conclude that they were actually contemporaries and that the epic is to a great extent dealing with historical characters and in the war of Kurukshetra with a historical occurrence imprinted firmly on the memory of the race. We know too that Krishna and Arjuna were the object of religious worship in the Pre-Christian centuries; and there is some reason to suppose that they were so in connection with a religious and philosophical tradition from which the Gita may have gathered many of its elements and even the foundation of its synthesis of knowledge, devotion and works and perhaps also that the human Krishna was the founder, restorer or at the least one of the early teachers of this school. The Gita may well in spite of its later form represent the outcome in Indian thought of the teaching of Krishna and the connection of that teaching with the historical Krishna, with Arjuna and with the war of Kurukshetra may be something more than a dramatic fiction. In the Mahabharata Krishna is represented both as the historical character and the Avatar; his worship and Avatarhood must therefore have been well established by the time—apparently from the fifth to the first centuries B.C.—when the old story and poem or epic tradition of the Bharatas took its present form. There is a hint also in the poem of the story or legend of the Avatar's early life in Vrindavan which, as developed by the Puranas into an intense and powerful spiritual symbol, has exercised so profound an influence on the religious mind of India. We also have in the Harivansha, an account of the life of Krishna, very evidently full of legends, which perhaps formed the basis of the Puranic accounts.

But all this, though of considerable historical importance, has none whatever for our present purpose. We are concerned only with the figure of the divine Teacher as it is presented to us in the Gita and with the Power for which it there stands in the spiritual illumination of the human being. The Gita accepts the human Avatarhood; for the Lord speaks of the repeated, the constant[5] manifestation of the Divine in humanity, when He the eternal Unborn assumes by his Maya, by the power of the infinite Consciousness to clothe itself apparently in finite forms, the conditions of becoming which we call birth. But it is not this upon which stress is laid, but on the transcendent, the cosmic and the internal Divine; it is on the Source of all things and the Master of all and on the Godhead secret in man. It is this internal divinity who is meant when the Gita speaks of the doer

5 bahuni me vyatıtani janmani . . . sambhavami yuge yuge.

of violent Asuric austerities troubling the God within or of the sin of those who despise the Divine lodged in the human body or of the same Godhead destroying our ignorance by the blazing lamp of knowledge. It is then the eternal Avatar, this God in man, the divine Consciousness always present in the human being who manifested in a visible form speaks to the human soul in the Gita, illumines the meaning of life and the secret of divine action and gives it the light of the divine knowledge and guidance and the assuring and fortifying word of the Master of existence in the hour when it comes face to face with the painful mystery of the world. This is what the Indian religious consciousness seeks to make near to itself in whatever form, whether in the symbolic human image it enshrines in its temples or in the worship of its Avatars or in the devotion to the human Guru through whom the voice of the one world-Teacher makes itself heard. Through these it strives to awaken to that inner voice, unveil that form of the Formless and stand face to face with that manifest divine Power, Love and Knowledge.

Secondly, there is the typical, almost the symbolic significance of the human Krishna who stands behind the great action of the Mahabharata, not as its hero, but as its secret centre and hidden guide. That action is the action of a whole world of men and nations, some of whom have come as helpers of an effort and result by which they do not personally profit, and to these he is a leader, some as its opponents and to them he also is an opponent, the baffler of their designs and their slayer and he seems even to some of them an instigator of all evil and destroyer of their old order and familiar world and secure conventions of virtue and good; some are representatives of that which has to be fulfilled and to them he is counsellor, helper, friend. Where the action pursues its natural course or the doers of the work have to suffer at the hands of its enemies and undergo the ordeals which prepare them for mastery, the Avatar is unseen or appears only for occasional comfort and aid, but at every crisis his hand is felt, yet in such a way that all imagine themselves to be the protagonists and even Arjuna, his nearest friend and chief instrument, does not perceive that he is an instrument and has to confess at last that all the while he did not really know his divine Friend. He has received counsel from his wisdom, help from his power, has loved, and been loved, has even adored without understanding his divine nature; but he has been guided like all others through his own egoism and the counsel, help and direction have been given in the language and received by the thoughts of the Ignorance. Until the moment when all has been pushed to the terrible issue of the struggle on the field of Kurukshetra and the Avatar stands at last, still not as fighter, but as the charioteer in the battle-car which carries the destiny of the fight, he has not revealed Himself even to those whom he has chosen.

Thus, the figure of Krishna becomes, as it were, the symbol of the divine dealings with humanity. Through our egoism and ignorance we are moved, thinking that we are the doers of the work, vaunting of ourselves as the real causes of the result and that which moves us we see only occasionally as some vague or even some human and earthly fountain of knowledge, aspiration, force, some Principle or Light or Power which we acknowledge and adore without knowing what it is until the occasion arises that forces us to stand arrested before the Veil.

And the action in which this divine figure moves is the whole wide action of man in life, not merely the inner life, but all this obscure course of the world which we can judge only by the twilight of the human reason as it opens up dimly before our uncertain advance the little span in front. This is the distinguishing feature of the Gita that it is the culmination of such an action which gives rise to its teaching and assigns that prominence and bold relief to the gospel of works which it enunciates with an emphasis and force we do not find in other Indian Scriptures. Not only in the Gita, but in other passages of the Mahabharata we meet with

Krishna declaring emphatically the necessity of action, but it is here that he reveals its secret and the divinity behind our works.

The symbolic companionship of Arjuna and Krishna, the human, and the divine soul, is expressed elsewhere in Indian thought, in the heavenward journey of Indra and Kutsa seated in one chariot, in the figure of the two birds upon one tree in the Upanishad, in the twin figures of Nara and Narayana, the seers who do tapasya together for the knowledge. But in all three it is the idea of the divine knowledge in which, as the Gita says, all action culminates that is in view; here it is instead the action which leads to that knowledge and in which the divine Knower figures himself. Arjuna and Krishna, this human and this divine, stand together not as seers in the peaceful hermitage of meditation but as fighter and holder of the reins in the clamorous field, in the midst of the hurtling shafts, in the chariot of battle. The Teacher of the Gita is therefore not only the God in man who unveils himself in the word of knowledge, but the God in man who moves our whole world of action, by and for whom all our humanity exists and struggles and labours, towards whom all human life travels and progresses. He is the secret Master of works and sacrifice and the Friend of the human peoples.

III

THE HUMAN DISCIPLE

Such then is the divine Teacher of the Gita, the eternal Avatar, the Divine who has descended into the human consciousness, the Lord seated within the heart of all beings, He who guides from behind the veil all our thought and action and heart's seeking even as He directs from behind the veil of visible and sensible forms and forces and tendencies the great universal action of the world which He has manifested in His own being. All the strife of our upward endeavour and seeking finds its culmination and ceases in a satisfied fulfilment when we can rend the veil and get behind our apparent self to this real Self, can realize our whole being in this true Lord of our being, can give up our personality to and into this one real Person, merge our ever-dispersed and ever-converging mental activities into His plenary light, offer up our errant and struggling will and energies into His vast, luminous and undivided Will, at once renounce and satisfy all our dissipated outward-moving desires and emotions in the plenitude of His self-existent Bliss. This is the world-Teacher of whose eternal knowledge all other highest teaching is but the various reflection and partial word, this the Voice to which the hearing of our soul has to awaken.

Arjuna, the disciple who receives his initiation on the battlefield, is a counterpart of this conception; he is the type of the struggling human soul who has not yet received the knowledge but has grown fit to receive it by action in the world in a close companionship and an increasing nearness to the higher and divine Self in humanity. There is a method of explaining the Gita in which not only this episode but the whole Mahabharata is turned into an allegory of the inner life and has nothing to do with our outward human life and action, but only with the battles of the soul and the powers that strive within us for possession. That is a view which the general character and the actual language of the epic does not justify and, if pressed, would turn the straightforward philosophical language of the Gita into a constant, laborious and somewhat puerile mystification. The language of the Veda and part at least of the Puranas is plainly symbolic, full of figures and concrete representations of things that lie behind the veil, but the Gita is written in plain terms and professes to solve the great ethical and spiritual difficulties which the life of man raises, and it will not do to go behind this plain language and thought and wrest them to the service of our fancy. But there is this much of truth in the view, that the setting of the doctrine though not symbolical, is certainly typical, as indeed the setting of such a discourse as the Gita must necessarily be if it is to have any relation at all with that which it frames. Arjuna, as we have seen, is the representative man of a great world-struggle and divinely guided movement of men and nations; in the Gita he typifies the human soul of action brought face to face through that action in its highest and most violent crisis with the problem of human life and its apparent incompatibility with the spiritual state or even with a purely ethical ideal of perfection.

Arjuna is the fighter in the chariot with the divine Krishna as his charioteer. In the Veda also we have this image of the human soul and the divine riding in one chariot through a great battle to the goal of a high-aspiring effort. But there it is a pure figure and symbol. The Divine is there Indra, the Master of the World of Light and Immortality, the power of divine knowledge which descends to the aid of the human seeker battling with the sons of falsehood, darkness, limitation, mortality; the battle is with spiritual enemies who bar the way to the higher world of our being; and the goal is that plane of vast being resplendent with the light of the supreme Truth and uplifted to the conscious immortality of the perfected soul, of which Indra is the master. The human soul is Kutsa, he who constantly seeks the seer-knowledge, as his name implies, and he is the son of Arjuna or Arjuni, the White One, child of Switra the White Mother; he is, that is to say, the sattwic or purified and light-filled soul which is open to the unbroken glories of the divine knowledge. And when the chariot reaches the end of its journey, the own home of Indra, the human Kutsa has grown into such an exact likeness of his divine companion that he can only be distinguished by Sachi, the wife of Indra, because she is "truth-conscious". The parable is evidently of the inner life of man; it is a figure of the human growing into the likeness of the eternal divine by the increasing illumination of Knowledge. But the Gita starts from action and Arjuna is the man of action and not of knowledge, the fighter, never the seer or the thinker.

From the beginning of the Gita this characteristic temperament of the disciple is clearly indicated, and it is maintained throughout. It becomes first evident in the manner in which he is awakened to the sense of what he is doing, the great slaughter of which he is to be the chief instrument, in the thoughts which immediately rise in him, in the standpoint and the psychological motives which make him recoil from the whole terrible catastrophe. They are not the thoughts, the standpoint, the motives of a philosophical or even of a deeply reflective mind or a spiritual temperament confronted with the same or a similar problem. They are those, as we might say, of the practical or the pragmatic man, the emotional, sensational, moral and intelligent human being not habituated to profound and original reflection or any sounding of the depths, accustomed rather to high but fixed standards of thought and action and a confident treading through all vicissitudes and difficulties, who now finds all his standards failing him and all the basis of his confidence in himself and his life shorn away from under him at a single stroke. That is the nature of the crisis which he undergoes.

Arjuna is, in the language of the Gita, a man subject to the action of the three gunas or modes of the Nature-Force and habituated to move unquestioningly in that field, like the generality of men. He justifies his name only in being so far pure and sattwic as to be governed by high and clear principles and impulses and habitually control his lower nature by the noblest Law which he knows. He is not of a violent Asuric disposition, not the slave of his passions, but has been trained to a high calm and self-control, to an unswerving performance of his duties and firm obedience to the best principles of the time and society in which he lived and the religion and ethics to which he was brought up. He is egoistic like other men, but with the purer or sattwic egoism which regards the moral law and society and the claims of others and not only or predominantly his own interests, desires, and passions. He has lived and guided himself by the Shastra, the moral and social code. The thought which preoccupies him, the standard which he obeys is the dharma, that collective Indian conception of the religious, social, and moral rule of conduct, and especially the rule of the station and function to which he belongs, he the Kshatriya, the high-minded, self-governed, chivalrous prince and warrior and leader of Aryan men. Always following this rule, conscious of virtue and right dealing he has travelled so far and finds suddenly that it has led him to become the protagonist of a terrific and unparalleled slaughter, a monstrous civil war involving all the cultured Aryan nations which must lead to the complete destruction of the flower of their manhood and threatens their ordered civilization with chaos and collapse.

It is typical again of the pragmatic man that it is through his sensations that he awakens to the meaning of his action. He has asked his friend and charioteer to place him between the two armies, not with any profounder idea, but with the proud intention of viewing and looking in the face these myriads of the champions of unrighteousness whom he has to meet and conquer and slay "in this holiday of fight" so that the right may prevail. It is as he gazes that the revelation of the meaning of a civil and domestic war comes home to him, a war in which not only men of the same race, the same nation, the same clan, but those of the same family and household stand upon opposite sides. All whom the social man holds most dear and sacred, he must meet as enemies and slay, — the worshipped teacher and preceptor, the old friend, comrade and companion in arms, grandsires, uncles, those who stood in the relation to him of father, of son, of grandson, connections by blood and connections by marriage,— all these social ties have to be cut asunder by the sword. It is not that he did not know these things before, but he has never realized it all; obsessed by his claims and wrongs and by the principles of his life, the struggle for the right, the duty of the Kshatriya to protect justice and the law and fight and beat down injustice and lawless violence, he has neither thought it out deeply nor felt it in his heart and at the core of his life. And now it is shown to his vision by the divine charioteer, placed sensationally before his eyes, and comes home to him like a blow delivered at the very centre of his sensational, vital, and emotional being.

The first result is a violent sensational and physical crisis which produces a disgust of the action and its material objects and of life itself. He rejects the vital aim pursued by egoistic humanity in its action, —happiness and enjoyment; he rejects the vital aim of the Kshatriya, victory and rule and power and the government of men. What after all is this fight for justice when reduced to its practical terms, but just this, a fight for the interests of himself, his brothers, and his party, for possession and enjoyment and rule? But at such a cost these things are not worth having. For they are of no value in themselves, but only as a means to the right maintenance of social and national life and it is these very aims that in the person of his kin and his race he is about to destroy. And then comes the cry of the emotions. These are they for whose sake life and happiness are desired, our "own people". Who would consent to slay these for the sake of all the earth, or even for the kingdom of the three worlds? What pleasure can there be in life, what happiness, what satisfaction in oneself after such a deed? The whole thing is a dreadful sin,—for now the moral sense awakens to justify the revolt of the sensations and the emotions. It is a sin, there is no right nor justice in mutual slaughter; especially are those who are to be slain the natural objects of reverence and of love, those without whom one would not care to live, and to violate these sacred feelings can be no virtue, can be nothing but a heinous crime. Granted that the offence, the aggression, the first sin, the crimes of greed and selfish passion which have brought things to such a pass came from the other side; yet armed resistance to wrong under such circumstances would be itself a sin and crime worse than theirs because they are blinded by passion and unconscious of guilt, while on this side it would be with a clear sense of guilt that the sin would be committed. And for what? For the maintenance of family morality, of the social law and the law of the nation? These are the very standards that will be destroyed by this civil war; the family itself will be brought to the point of annihilation, corruption of morals and loss of the purity of race will be engendered, the eternal laws of the race and moral law of the family will be destroyed. Ruin of the race, the collapse of its high traditions, ethical degradation, and hell for the authors of such a crime, these are the only practical results possible of this monstrous civil strife. "Therefore," cries Arjuna, casting down the divine bow and inexhaustible quiver given to him by the gods for that tremendous hour, "it is more for my welfare that the sons of Dhritarashtra armed should slay me unarmed and unresisting. I will not fight."

The character of this inner crisis is therefore not the questioning of the thinker; it is not a recoil from the appearances of life and a turning of the eye inward in search of the truth of things, the real meaning of existence and a solution or an escape from the dark riddle of the world. It is the sensational, emotional and moral revolt of the man hitherto satisfied with action and its current standards who finds himself cast by them into a hideous chaos where they are in violent conflict with each other and with themselves and there is no moral standing-ground left, nothing to lay hold of and walk by, no dharma.[1] That for the soul of action in the mental being is the worst possible crisis, failure and overthrow. The revolt itself is the most elemental and simple possible; sensationally, the elemental feeling of horror, pity, and disgust; vitally, the loss of attraction and faith in the recognized and familiar objects of action and aims of life; emotionally, the recoil of the ordinary feelings of social man, affection, reverence, desire of a common happiness and satisfaction, from a stern duty outraging them all; morally, the elementary sense of sin and hell and rejection of "blood-stained enjoyments"; practically, the sense that the standards of action have led to a result which destroys the practical aims of action. But the whole upshot is that all-embracing inner bankruptcy which Arjuna expresses when he says that his whole conscious being, not the thought alone but heart and vital desires and all, are utterly bewildered and can find nowhere the dharma, nowhere any valid law of action. For this alone he takes refuge as a disciple with Krishna; give me, he practically asks, that which I have lost, a true law, a clear rule of action, a path by which I can again confidently walk. He does not ask for the secret of life or of the world, the meaning and purpose of it all, but for a dharma.

Yet it is precisely this secret for which he does not ask, or at least so much of the knowledge as is necessary to lead him into a higher life, to which the divine Teacher intends to lead this

---

1 Dharma means literally that which one lays hold of and which holds things together, the law, the norm, the rule of nature, action, and life.

disciple; for he means him to give up all dharmas except the one broad and vast rule of living consciously in the Divine and acting from that consciousness. Therefore, after testing the completeness of his revolt from the ordinary standards of conduct, he proceeds to tell him much that has to do with the state of the soul, but nothing of any outward rule of action. He must be equal in soul, abandon the desire of the fruits of work, rise above his intellectual notions of sin and virtue, live and act in Yoga with a mind in Samadhi, firmly fixed, that is to say, in the Divine alone. Arjuna is not satisfied: he wishes to know how the change to this state will affect the outward action of the man, what result it will have on his speech, his movements, his state, what difference it will make in this acting, living human being. Krishna persists merely in enlarging upon the ideas he has already brought forward, on the soul-state behind the action, not on the action itself. It is the fixed anchoring of the intelligence in a state of desireless equality that is the one thing needed. Arjuna breaks out impatiently,—for here is no rule of conduct such as he sought, but rather, as it seems to him, the negation of all action,—"If thou holdest the intelligence to be greater than action, why then dost thou appoint me to an action terrible in its nature? Thou bewilderest my understanding with a mingled word: speak one thing decisively by which I can attain to what is the best." It is always the pragmatic man who has no value for metaphysical thought or for the inner life except when they help him to his one demand, a dharma, a law of life in the world or, if need be, of leaving the world; for that too is a decisive action which he can understand. But to live and act in the world, yet be above it, this is a "mingled" and confusing word the sense of which he has no patience to grasp.

The rest of Arjuna's questions and utterances proceed from the same temperament and character. When he is told that once the soul-state is assured there need be no apparent change in the action, he must act always by the law of his nature, even if the act itself seem faulty and deficient compared with that of another law than his own, he is troubled. The nature! but what of this sense of sin in the action with which he is preoccupied? is it not this very nature which drives men as if by force and even against their better will into sin and guilt? His practical intelligence is baffled by Krishna's assertion that it was he who in ancient times revealed to Vivasvan this Yoga, since lost, which he is now again revealing to Arjuna, and by his demand for an explanation he provokes the famous and oft-quoted statement of Avatarhood and its mundane purpose. He is again perplexed by the words in which Krishna continues to reconcile action and renunciation of action and asks once again for a decisive statement of that which is the best and highest, not this "mingled" word. When he realizes fully the nature of the Yoga which he is bidden to embrace, his pragmatic nature accustomed to act from mental will and preference and desire is appalled by its difficulty and he asks what is the end of the soul which attempts and fails, whether it does not lose both this life of human activity and thought and emotion which it has left behind and the Brahmic consciousness to which it aspires and falling from both perish like a dissolving cloud?

When his doubts and perplexities are resolved and he knows that it is the Divine which must be his law, he aims again and always at such clear and decisive knowledge as will guide him practically to this source and this rule of his future action. How is the Divine to be distinguished among the various states of being which constitute our ordinary experience? What are the great manifestations of its self-energy in the world in which he can recognize and realize it by meditation? May he not see even now the divine cosmic Form of That which is actually speaking to him through the veil of the human mind and body? And his last questions demand a clear distinction between renunciation of works and this subtler renunciation he is asked to prefer; the actual difference between Purusha and Prakriti, the Field, and the Knower of the Field, so important for the practice of desireless action under the drive of the divine Will; and finally, a clear statement of the practical operations and results of the three modes of Prakriti which he is bidden to surmount.

To such a disciple the Teacher of the Gita gives his divine teaching. He seizes him at a moment of his psychological development by egoistic action when all the mental, moral, emotional values of the ordinary egoistic and social life of man have col-lapsed in a sudden bankruptcy, and he has to lift him up out of this lower life into a higher consciousness, out of ignorant attachment to action into that which transcends, yet originates and orders action, out of ego into Self, out of life in mind, vitality and body into that higher nature beyond mind which is the status of the Divine. He has at the same time to give him that for which he asks and for which he is inspired to seek by the guidance within him, a new Law of life and action high above the insufficient rule of the ordinary human existence with its endless conflicts and oppositions, perplexities and illusory certainties, a higher Law by which the soul shall be free from this bondage of works and yet powerful to act and conquer in the vast liberty of its divine being. For the action must be performed, the world must fulfil its cycles and the soul of the human being must not turn back in ignorance from the work it is here to do. The whole course of the teaching of the Gita is determined and directed, even in its widest wheeling's, towards the fulfilment of these three objects.

IV

THE CORE OF THE TEACHING

We know the divine Teacher; we see the human disciple; it remains to form a clear conception of the doctrine. A clear conception fastening upon the essential idea, the central heart of the teaching is especially necessary here because the Gita with its rich and many-sided thought, its synthetical grasp of different aspects of the spiritual life and the fluent winding motion of its argument lends itself, even more than other scriptures, to one-sided misrepresentations born of a partisan intellectuality. The unconscious or half-conscious wresting of fact and word and idea to suit a preconceived notion or the doctrine or principle of one's preference is recognized by Indian logicians as one of the most fruitful sources of fallacy; and it is perhaps the one which it is most difficult for even the most conscientious thinker to avoid. For the human reason is incapable of always playing the detective upon itself in this respect; it is its very nature to seize upon some partial conclusion, idea, principle, become its partisan and make it the key to all truth, and it has an infinite faculty of doubling upon itself so as to avoid detecting in its operations this necessary and cherished weakness. The Gita lends itself easily to this kind of error because it is easy, by throwing particular emphasis on one of its aspects or even on some salient and emphatic text and putting all the rest of the eighteen chapters into the background or making them a subordinate and auxiliary teaching, to turn it into a partisan of our own doctrine or dogma.

Thus, there are those who make the Gita teach, not works at all, but a discipline of preparation for renouncing life and works: the indifferent performance of prescribed actions or of whatever task may lie ready to the hands, becomes the means, the discipline; the final renunciation of life and works is the sole real object. It is quite easy to justify this view by citations from the book and by a certain arrangement of stress in following out its argument, especially if we shut our eyes to the peculiar way in which it uses such a word as sannyasa¯, renunciation; but it is quite impossible to persist in this view on an impartial reading in face of the continual assertion to the very end that action should be preferred to inaction and that superiority lies with the true, the inner renunciation of desire by equality and the giving up of works to the supreme Purusha.

Others again speak of the Gita as if the doctrine of devotion were its whole teaching and put in the background its monistic elements and the high place it gives to quietistic immergence in the oneself of all. And undoubtedly its emphasis on devotion, its insistence on the aspect of the Divine as Lord and Purusha and its doctrine of the Purushottama, the Supreme Being who is superior both to the mutable Being and to the Immutable and who is what in His relation to the world we know as God, are the most striking and among the most vital elements of the Gita. Still, this Lord is the Self in whom all knowledge culminates and the Master of sacrifice to whom all works lead as well as the Lord of Love into who's being the heart of devotion enters, and the Gita preserves a perfectly equal balance, emphasizing now knowledge, now works, now devotion, but for the purposes of the immediate trend of the thought, not with any absolute separate preference of one over the others. He in whom all three meet and become one, He is the Supreme Being, the Purushottama.

But at the present day, since in fact the modern mind began to recognize and deal at all with the Gita, the tendency is to subordinate its elements of knowledge and devotion, to take advantage of its continual insistence on action and to find in it a scripture of the Karma yoga, a Light leading us on the path of action, a Gospel of Works. Undoubtedly, the Gita is a Gospel of Works, but of works which culminate in knowledge, that is, in spiritual realization and quietude and of works motived by devotion, that is, a conscious surrender of one's whole self-first into the hands and then into the being of the Supreme, and not at all of works as they are understood by the modern mind, not at all an action dictated by egoistic and altruistic, by personal, social, humanitarian motives, principles, ideals. Yet this is what present-day interpretations seek to make of the Gita. We are told continually by many authoritative voices that the Gita, opposing in this the ordinary ascetic and quietistic tendency of Indian thought and spirituality, proclaims with no uncertain sound the gospel of human action, the ideal of disinterested performance of social duties, nay, even, it would seem, the quite modern ideal of social service. To all this I can only reply that very patently and even on the very surface of it the Gita does nothing of the kind and that this is a modern misreading, a reading of the modern mind into an ancient book, of the present-day European or Europeanized intellect into a thoroughly antique, a thoroughly Oriental and Indian teaching. That which the Gita teaches is not a human, but a divine action; not the performance of social duties, but the abandonment of all other standards of duty or conduct for a selfless performance of the divine will working through our nature; not social service, but the action of the Best, the God-possessed, the Master-men done impersonally for the sake of the world and as a sacrifice to Him who stands behind man and Nature.

In other words, the Gita is not a book of practical ethics, but of the spiritual life. The modern mind is just now the European mind, such as it has become after having abandoned not only the philosophic idealism of the highest Graeco-Roman culture from which it started, but the Christian devotionalism of the Middle

Ages; these it has replaced by or transmuted into a practical idealism and social, patriotic, and philanthropic devotion. It has got rid of God or kept Him only for Sunday use and erected in His place man as its deity and society as its visible idol. At its best it is practical, ethical, social, pragmatic, altruistic, humanitarian. Now all these things are good, are especially needed at the present day, are part of the divine Will or they would not have become so dominant in humanity. Nor is there any reason why the divine man, the man who lives in the Brahmic consciousness, in the God-being should not be all of these things in his action; he will be, if they are the best ideal of the age, the Yugadharma, and there is no yet higher ideal to be established, no great radical change to be effected. For he is, as the Teacher points out to his disciple, the best who has to set the standard for others; and in fact, Arjuna is called upon to live according to the highest ideals of his age and the prevailing culture, but with knowledge, with understanding of that which lay behind, and not as ordinary men, with a following of the merely outward law and rule.

But the point here is that the modern mind has exiled from its practical motive-power the two essential things, God or the Eternal and spirituality or the God-state, which are the master conceptions of the Gita. It lives in humanity only, and the Gita would have us live in God, though for the world in God; in its life, heart, and intellect only, and the Gita would have us live in the spirit; in the mutable Being who is "all creatures", and the Gita would have us live also in the Immutable and the Supreme; in the changing march of Time, and the Gita would have us live in the Eternal. Or if these higher things are now beginning to be vaguely envisaged, it is only to make them subservient to man and society; but God and spirituality exist in their own right and not as adjuncts. And in practice the lower in us must learn to exist for the higher, in order that the higher also may in us consciously exist for the lower, to draw it nearer to its own altitudes.

Therefore, it is a mistake to interpret the Gita from the standpoint of the mentality of today and force it to teach us the disinterested performance of duty as the highest and all-sufficient law. A little consideration of the situation with which the Gita deals will show us that this could not be its meaning. For the whole point of the teaching, that from which it arises, that which compels the disciple to seek the Teacher, is an inextricable clash of the various related conceptions of duty ending in the collapse of the whole useful intellectual and moral edifice erected by the human mind. In human life some sort of a clash arises fairly often, as for instance between domestic duties and the call of the country or the cause, or between the claim of the country and the good of humanity or some larger religious or moral principle. An inner situation may even arise, as with the Buddha, in which all duties have to be abandoned, trampled on, flung aside in order to follow the call of the Divine within. I cannot think that the Gita would solve such an inner situation by sending Buddha back to his wife and father and the government of the Sakya State or would direct a Ramakrishna to become a Pundit in a vernacular school and disinterestedly teach little boys their lessons or bind down a Vivekananda to support his family and for that to follow dispassionately the law or medicine or journalism. The Gita does not teach the disinterested performance of duties but the following of the divine life, the abandonment of all dharmas, sarvadharmān, to take refuge in the Supreme alone, and the divine activity of a Buddha, a Ramakrishna, a Vivekananda is perfectly in consonance with this teaching. Nay, although the Gita prefers action to inaction, it does not rule out the renunciation of works, but accepts it as one of the ways to the Divine. If that can only be attained by renouncing works, and life and all duties and the call is strong within us, then into the bonfire they must go and there is no help for it. The call of God is imperative and cannot be weighed against any other considerations.

But here there is this farther difficulty that the action which

Arjuna must do is one from which his moral sense recoils. It is his duty to fight, you say? But that duty has now become to his mind a terrible sin. How does it help him or solve his difficulty, to tell him that he must do his duty disinterestedly, dispassionately? He will want to know which is his duty or how it can be his duty to destroy in a sanguinary massacre his kin, his race, and his country. He is told that he has right on his side, but that does not and cannot satisfy him, because his very point is that the justice of his legal claim does not justify him in supporting it by a pitiless massacre destructive to the future of his nation. Is he then to act dispassionately in the sense of not caring whether it is a sin or what its consequences may be so long as he does his duty as a soldier? That may be the teaching of a State, of politicians, of lawyers, of ethical casuists; it can never be the teaching of a great religious and philosophical Scripture which sets out to solve the problem of life and action from the very roots. And if that is what the Gita has to say on a most poignant moral and spiritual problem, we must put it out of the list of the world's Scriptures and thrust it, if anywhere, then into our library of political science and ethical casuistry.

Undoubtedly, the Gita does, like the Upanishads, teach the equality which rises above sin and virtue, beyond good and evil, but only as a part of the Brahmic consciousness and for the man who is on the path and advanced enough to fulfil the supreme rule. It does not preach indifference to good and evil for the ordinary life of man, where such a doctrine would have the most pernicious consequences. On the contrary it affirms that the doers of evil shall not attain to God. Therefore, if Arjuna simply seeks to fulfil in the best way the ordinary law of man's life, disinterested performance of what he feels to be a sin, a thing of Hell, will not help him, even though that sin be his duty as a soldier. He must refrain from what his conscience abhors though a thousand duties were shattered to pieces.

We must remember that duty is an idea which in practice rests upon social conceptions. We may extend the term beyond its proper connotation and talk of our duty to ourselves, or we may, if we like, say in a transcendent sense that it was Buddha's duty to abandon all, or even that it is the ascetic's duty to sit motionless in a cave! But this is obviously to play with words. Duty is a relative term and depends upon our relation to others. It is a father's duty, as a father, to nurture and educate his children; a lawyers to do his best for his client even if he knows him to be guilty and his defence to be a lie; a soldiers to fight and shoot to order even if he kill his own kin and countrymen; a judges to send the guilty to prison and hang the murderer. And so long as these positions are accepted, the duty remains clear, a practical matter of course even when it is not a point of honour or affection and overrides the absolute religious or moral law. But what if the inner view is changed, if the lawyer is awakened to the absolute sinfulness of falsehood, the judge becomes convinced that capital punishment is a crime against humanity, the man called upon to the battlefield feels, like the conscientious objector of today or as a Tolstoy would feel, that in no circumstances is it permissible to take human life any more than to eat human flesh? It is obvious that here the moral law which is above all relative duties must prevail; and that law depends on no social relation or conception of duty but on the awakened inner perception of man, the moral being.

There are in the world, in fact, two different laws of conduct each valid on its own plane, the rule principally dependent on external status and the rule independent of status and entirely dependent on the thought and conscience. The Gita does not teach us to subordinate the higher plane to the lower, it does not ask the awakened moral consciousness to slay itself on the altar of duty as a sacrifice and victim to the law of the social status. It calls us higher and not lower; from the conflict of the two planes, it bids us ascend to a supreme poise above the mainly practical, above the purely ethical, to the Brahmic consciousness. It replaces the conception of social duty by a divine obligation. The subjection to external law gives place to a certain principle of inner self-determination of action proceeding by the soul's freedom from the tangled law of works. And this, as we shall see,—the Brahmic consciousness, the soul's freedom from works and the determination of works in the nature by the Lord within and above us,—is the kernel of the Gita's teaching with regard to action.

The Gita can only be understood, like any other great work of the kind, by studying it in its entirety and as a developing argument. But the modern interpreters, starting from the great writer Bankim Chandra Chatterji who first gave to the Gita this new sense of a Gospel of Duty, have laid an almost exclusive stress on the first three or four chapters and in those on the idea of equality, on the expression kartavyam karma, the work that is to be done, which they render by duty, and on the phrase "Thou hast a right to action, but none to the fruits of action" which is now popularly quoted as the great word, mahav¯akya¯, of the Gita. The rest of the eighteen chapters with their high philosophy are given a secondary importance, except indeed the great vision in the eleventh. This is natural enough for the modern mind which is, or has been till yesterday, inclined to be impatient of metaphysical subtleties and far-off spiritual seeking's, eager to get to work and, like Arjuna himself, mainly concerned for a workable law of works, a dharma. But it is the wrong way to handle this, Scripture.

The equality which the Gita preaches is not disinterested-ness, —the great command to Arjuna given after the foundation and main structure of the teaching have been laid and built, "Arise, slay thy enemies, enjoy a prosperous kingdom," has not the ring of an uncompromising altruism or of a white, dispassionate abnegation; it is a state of inner poise and wideness which is the foundation of spiritual freedom. With that poise, in that freedom we have to do the "work that is to be done," a phrase which the Gita uses with the greatest wideness including in it all works, sarvakarman¯i, and which far exceeds, though it may include, social duties or ethical obligations. What is the work to be done is not to be determined by the individual choice; nor is the right to the action and the rejection of claim to the fruit the great word of the Gita, but only a preliminary word governing the first state of the disciple when he begins ascending the hill of Yoga. It is practically superseded at a subsequent stage. For the Gita goes on to affirm emphatically that the man is not the doer of the action; it is Prakriti, it is Nature, it is the great Force with its three modes of action that works through him, and he must learn to see that it is not he who does the work. Therefore the "right to action" is an idea which is only valid so long as we are still under the illusion of being the doer; it must necessarily disappear from the mind like the claim to the fruit as soon as we cease to be to our own consciousness the doer of our works. All pragmatic egoism, whether of the claim to fruits or of the right to action, is then at an end.

But the determinism of Prakriti is not the last word of the Gita. The equality of the will and the rejection of fruits are only means for entering with the mind and the heart and the understanding into the divine consciousness and living in it; and the Gita expressly says that they are to be employed as a means as long as the disciple is unable so to live or even to seek by practice the gradual development of this higher state. And what is this Divine, whom Krishna declares himself to be? It is the Purushottama beyond the Self that acts not, beyond the Prakriti that acts, foundation of the one, master of the other, the Lord of whom all is the manifestation, who even in our present subjection to Maya sits in the heart of His creatures governing the works of Prakriti, He by whom the armies on the field of Kurukshetra have already been slain while yet they live and who uses Arjuna only as an instrument or immediate occasion of this great slaughter. Prakriti is only His executive force. The disciple has to rise beyond this Force and its three modes or gunas; he has to become trigunatita. Not to her has he to surrender his actions, over which he has no longer any claim or "right", but into the being of the Supreme. Reposing his mind and understanding, heart and will in Him, with self-knowledge, with God-knowledge, with world-knowledge, with a perfect equality, a perfect devotion, an absolute self-giving, he has to do works as an offering to the Master of all self-energizing's and all sacrifice. Identified in will, conscious with that consciousness, That shall decide and initiate the action. This is the solution which the Divine Teacher offers to the disciple.

What the great, the supreme word of the Gita is, its mahavakya, we have not to seek; for the Gita itself declares it in its last utterance, the crowning note of the great diapason. "With the Lord in thy heart take refuge with all thy being; by His grace thou shalt attain to the supreme peace and the eternal status. So have I expounded to thee a knowledge more secret than that which is hidden. Further hear the most secret, the supreme word that I shall speak to thee. Become my-minded, devoted to Me, to Me do sacrifice and adoration; infallibly, thou shalt come to Me, for dear to me art thou. Abandoning all laws of conduct seek refuge in Me alone. I will release thee from all sin; do not grieve."

The argument of the Gita resolves itself into three great steps by which action rises out of the human into the divine plane leaving the bondage of the lower for the liberty of a higher law. First, by the renunciation of desire and a perfect equality works have to be done as a sacrifice by man as the doer, a sacrifice to a deity who is the supreme and only Self though by him not yet realized in his own being. This is the initial step. Secondly, not only the desire of the fruit, but the claim to be the doer of works has to be renounced in the realization of the Self as the equal, the inactive, the immutable principle and of all works as simply the operation of universal Force, of the Nature-Soul, Prakriti, the unequal, active, mutable power. Lastly, the supreme Self has to be seen as the supreme Purusha governing this Prakriti, of whom the soul in Nature is a partial manifestation, by whom all works are directed, in a perfect transcendence, through Nature. To him love and adoration and the sacrifice of works have to be offered; the whole being has to be surrendered to Him and the whole consciousness raised up to dwell in this divine consciousness so that the human soul may share in His divine transcendence of Nature and of His works and act in a perfect spiritual liberty.

The first step is Karma yoga, the selfless sacrifice of works, and here the Gita's insistence is on action. The second is Jnana yoga, the self-realization and knowledge of the true nature of the self and the world; and here the insistence is on knowledge; but the sacrifice of works continues, and the path of Works becomes one with but does not disappear into the path of Knowledge. The last step is Bhakti yoga, adoration and seeking of the supreme Self as the Divine Being, and here the insistence is on devotion; but the knowledge is not subordinated, only raised, vitalized, and fulfilled, and still the sacrifice of works continues; the double path becomes the triune way of knowledge, works and devotion. And the fruit of the sacrifice, the one fruit still placed before the seeker, is attained, union with the divine Being and oneness with the supreme divine nature.

V

KURUKSHETRA

Before we can proceed, following in the large steps of the Teacher of the Gita, to watch his tracing of the triune path of man,—the path, which is that of his will, heart, thought raising themselves to the Highest and into the being of that which is the supreme object of all action, love, and knowledge, we must consider once more the situation from which the Gita arises, but now in its largest bearings as a type of human life and even of all world-existence. For although Arjuna is himself concerned only with his own situation, his inner struggle and the law of action he must follow, yet, as we have seen, the particular question he raises, in the manner in which he raises it, does really bring up the whole question of human life and action, what the world is and why it is and how possibly, it being what it is, life here in the world can be reconciled with life in the Spirit. And all these deep and difficult matter the Teacher insists on resolving as the very foundation of his command to an action which must proceed from a new poise of being and by the light of a liberating knowledge.

But what, then, is it that makes the difficulty for the man who has to take the world as it is and act in it and yet would live, within, the spiritual life? What is this aspect of existence which appalls his awakened mind and brings about what the title of the first chapter of the Gita calls significantly the Yoga of the dejection of Arjuna, the dejection and discouragement felt by the human being when he is forced to face the spectacle of the universe as it really is with the veil of the ethical illusion, the illusion of self-righteousness torn from his eyes, before a higher reconciliation with himself is effected? It is that aspect which is figured outwardly in the carnage and massacre of Kurukshetra and spiritually by the vision of the Lord of all things as Time arising to devour and destroy the creatures whom it has made.

This is the vision of the Lord of all existence as the universal Creator but also the universal Destroyer, of whom the ancient Scripture can say in a ruthless image, "The sages and the heroes are his food and death is the spice of his banquet." It is one and the same truth seen first indirectly and obscurely in the facts of life and then directly and clearly in the soul's vision of that which manifests itself in life. The outward aspect is that of world-existence and human existence proceeding by struggle and slaughter; the inward aspect is that of the universal Being fulfilling himself in a vast creation and a vast destruction. Life a battle and a field of death, this is Kurukshetra; God the Terrible, this is the vision that Arjuna sees on that field of massacre.

War, said Heraclitus, is the father of all things, War is the king of all; and the saying, like most of the apophthegms of the Greek thinker, suggests a profound truth. From a clash of material or other forces everything in this world, if not the world itself, seems to be born; by a struggle of forces, tendencies, principles, beings it seems to proceed, ever creating new things, ever destroying the old, marching one knows not very well whither,— to a final self-destruction, say some; in an unending series of vain cycles, say others; in progressive cycles, is the most optimistic conclusion, leading through whatever trouble and apparent confusion towards a higher and higher approximation to some divine apocalypse. However that may be, this is certain that there is not only no construction here without destruction, no harmony except by a poise of contending forces won out of many actual and potential discords, but also no continued existence of life except by a constant self-feeding and devouring of other life. Our very bodily life is a constant dying and being reborn, the body itself a beleaguered city attacked by assailing, protected by defending forces whose business is to devour each other: and this is only a type of all our existence. The command seems to have gone out from the beginning, "Thou shalt not conquer except by battle with thy fellows and thy surroundings; thou shalt not even live except by battle and struggle and by absorbing into thyself other life. The first law of this world that I have made is creation and preservation by destruction."

Ancient thought accepted this starting-point so far as it could see it by scrutiny of the universe. The old Upanishads saw it very clearly and phrased it with an uncompromising thoroughness which will have nothing to do with any honeyed glosses or optimistic scuttling's of the truth. Hunger that is Death, they said, is the creator and master of this world, and they figured vital existence in the image of the Horse of the sacrifice. Matter they described by a name which means ordinary food and they said, we call it food because it is devoured and devours creatures. The eater eating is eaten, this is the formula of the material world, as the Darwinians rediscovered when they laid it down that the struggle for life is the law of evolutionary existence. Modern science has only rephrased the old truths that had already been expressed in much more forcible, wide, and accurate formulas by the apophthegm of Heraclitus and the figures employed by the Upanishads.

Nietzsche's insistence upon war as an aspect of life and the ideal man as a warrior,—the camel-man he may be to begin with and the child-man hereafter, but the lion-man he must become in the middle, if he is to attain his perfection,—these now much-decried theories of Nietzsche have, however much we may differ from many of the moral and practical conclusions he drew from them, their undeniable justification and recall us to a truth we like to hide out of sight. It is good that we should be reminded of it; first, because to see it has for every strong soul a tonic effect which saves us from the flabbiness and relaxation encouraged by a too mellifluous philosophic, religious or ethical sentimentalism, that which loves to look upon Nature as love and life and beauty and good, but turns away from her grim mask of death, adoring God as Shiva but refusing to adore him as Rudra; secondly, because unless we have the honesty and courage to look existence straight in the face, we shall never arrive at any effective solution of its discords and oppositions. We must see first what life and the world are; afterwards, we can all the better set about finding the right way to transform them into what they should be. If this repellent aspect of existence holds in itself some secret of the final harmony, we shall by ignoring or belittling it miss that secret and all our efforts at a solution will fail by fault of our self-indulgent ignoring of the true elements of the problem. If, on the other hand, it is an enemy to be beaten down, trampled on, excised, eliminated, still we gain nothing by underrating its power and hold upon life or refusing to see how firmly it is rooted in the effective past and the actually operative principles of existence.

War and destruction are not only a universal principle of our life here in its purely material aspects, but also of our mental and moral existence. It is self-evident that in the actual life of man intellectual, social, political, moral we can make no real step forward without a struggle, a battle between what exists and lives and what seeks to exist and live and between all that stands behind either. It is impossible, at least as men and things are, to advance, to grow, to fulfil and still to observe really and utterly that principle of harmlessness which is yet placed before us as the highest and best law of conduct. We will use only soul-force and never destroy by war or any even defensive employment of physical violence? Good, though until soul-force is effective, the Asuric force in men and nations tramples down, breaks, slaughters, burns, pollutes, as we see it doing today, but then at its ease and unhindered, and you have perhaps caused as much destruction of life by your abstinence as others by resort to violence; still you have set up an ideal which may someday and at any rate ought to lead up to better things. But even soul-force, when it is effective, destroys. Only those who have used it with eyes open, know how much more terrible and destructive it is than the sword and the cannon; and only those who do not limit their view to the act and its immediate results, can see how tremendous its after-effects are, how much is eventually destroyed and with that much all the life that depended on it and fed upon it. Evil cannot perish without the destruction of much that lives by the evil, and it is no less destruction even if we personally are saved the pain of a sensational act of violence.

Moreover, every time we use soul-force we raise a great force of Karma against our adversary, the aftermovements of which we have no power to control. Vasishtha uses soul-force against the military violence of Vishwamitra and armies of Huns and Shakas and Pallavas hurl themselves on the aggressor. The very quiescence and passivity of the spiritual man under violence and aggression awakens the tremendous forces of the world to a retributive action; and it may even be more merciful to stay in their path, though by force, those who represent evil than to allow them to trample on until they call down on themselves a worse destruction than we would ever think of inflicting. It is not enough that our own hands should remain clean and our souls unstained for the law of strife and destruction to die out of the world; that which is its root must first disappear out of humanity. Much less will mere immobility and inertia unwilling to use or incapable of using any kind of resistance to evil, abrogate the law; inertia, tamas, indeed, injures much more than can the rajasic principle of strife which at least creates more than it destroys. Therefore, so far as the problem of the individual's action goes, his abstention from strife and its inevitable concomitant destruction in their more gross and physical form may help his own moral being, but it leaves the Slayer of creatures unabolished.

For the rest the whole of human history bears witness to the inexorable vitality and persistent prevalence of this principle in the world. It is natural that we should attempt to palliate, to lay stress on other aspects. Strife and destruction are not all; there is the saving principle of association and mutual help as well as the force of dissociation and mutual strife; a power of love no less than a power of egoistic self-assertion; an impulse to sacrifice ourselves for others as well as the impulse to sacrifice others to ourselves. But when we see how these have actually worked, we shall not be tempted to gloss over or ignore the power of their opposites. Association has been worked not only for mutual help, but at the same time for defence and aggression, to strengthen us against all those attacks or resists in the struggle for life. Association itself has been a servant of war, egoism, and the self-assertion of life against life. Love itself has been constantly a power of death. Especially the love of good and the love of God, as embraced by the human ego, have been responsible for much strife, slaughter, and destruction. Self-sacrifice is great and noble, but at its highest it is an acknowledgment of the law of Life by death and becomes an offering on the altar of some Power that demands a victim in order that the work desired may be done. The mother bird facing the animal of prey in defence of its young, the patriot dying for his country's freedom, the religious martyr, or the martyr of an idea, these in the lower and the superior scale of animal life are highest examples of self-sacrifice, and it is evident to what they bear witness.

But if we look at after results, an easy optimism becomes even less possible. See the patriot dying in order that his country may be free and mark that country a few decades after the Lord of Karma has paid the price of the blood and the suffering that was given; you shall see it in its turn an oppressor, an exploiter and conqueror of colonies and dependencies devouring others that it may live and succeed aggressively in life. The Christian martyrs perish in their thousands, setting soul-force against empire-force that Christ may conquer, Christianity prevail. Soul-force does triumph, Christianity does prevail but not Christ; the victorious religion becomes a militant and dominant Church and a more fanatically persecuting power than the creed and the empire which it replaced. The very religions organize themselves into powers of mutual strife and battle together fiercely to live, to grow, to possess the world.

All which seems to show that here is an element in existence, perhaps the initial element, which we do not know how to conquer either because it cannot be conquered or because we have not looked at it with a strong and impartial gaze so as to recognize it calmly and fairly and know what it is. We must look existence in the face if our aim is to arrive at a right solution, whatever that solution may be. And to look existence in the face is to look God in the face; for the two cannot be separated, nor the responsibility for the laws of world-existence be shifted away from Him who created them or from That which constituted it. Yet here too we love to palliate and equivocate. We erect a God of Love and Mercy, a God of good, a God just, righteous and virtuous according to our own moral conceptions of justice, virtue, and righteousness, and all the rest, we say, is not He or is not His, but was made by some diabolical Power which He suffered for some reason to work out its wicked will or by some dark Ahriman counterbalancing our gracious Or-muzd or was even the fault of selfish and sinful man who has spoiled what was made originally perfect by God. As if man had created the law of death and devouring in the animal world or that tremendous process by which Nature creates indeed and preserves but in the same step and by the same inextricable action slays and destroys. It is only a few religions which have had the courage to say without any reserve, like the Indian, that this enigmatic World-Power is one Deity, one Trinity, to lift up the image of the Force that acts in the world in the figure not only of the beneficent Durga, but of the terrible Kali in her blood-stained dance of destruction and to say, "This too is the Mother; this also known to be God; this too, if thou hast the strength, adore." And it is significant that the religion which has had this unflinching honesty and tremendous courage, has succeeded in creating a profound and wide-spread spirituality such as no other can parallel. For truth is the foundation of real spirituality and courage is its soul. **Tasyai satyam ayatanam**.

All this is not to say that strife and destruction are the alpha and omega of existence, that harmony is not greater than war, love more the manifest divine than death or that we must not move towards the replacement of physical force by soul-force, of war by peace, of strife by union, of devouring by love, of egoism by universality, of death by immortal life. God is not only the Destroyer, but the Friend of creatures; not only the cosmic Trinity, but the Transcendent; the terrible Kali is also the loving and beneficent Mother; the lord of Kurukshetra is the divine comrade and charioteer, the attracter of beings, incarnate Krishna. And whithersoever he is driving through all the strife and clash and confusion, to whatever goal or godhead he may be attracting us, it is—no doubt of that—to some transcendence of all these aspects upon which we have been so firmly insisting. But where, how, with what kind of transcendence, under what conditions, this we have to discover; and to discover it, the first necessity is to see the world as it is, to observe and value rightly his action as it reveals itself at the start and now; afterwards the way and the goal will better reveal themselves. We must acknowledge Kurukshetra; we must submit to the law of Life by Death before we can find our way to the life immortal; we must open our eyes, with a less appalled gaze than Arjuna's, to the vision of our Lord of Time and Death and cease to deny, hate, or recoil from the universal Destroyer.

VI

MAN, AND THE BATTLE OF LIFE

THUS, if we are to appreciate in its catholicity the teaching of the Gita, we must accept intellectually its standpoint and courageous envisaging of the manifest nature and process of the world. The divine charioteer of Kurukshetra reveals himself on one side as the Lord of all the worlds and the Friend and omniscient Guide of all creatures, on the other as Time the Destroyer "arisen for the destruction of these peoples." The Gita, following in this the spirit of the catholic Hindu religion, affirms this also as God; it does not attempt to evade the enigma of the world by escaping from it through a side-door. If, in fact, we do not regard existence merely as the mechanic action of a brute and indifferent material Force or, on the other hand, as an equally mechanical play of ideas and energies arising out of an original Non-Existence or else reflected in the passive Soul or the evolution of a dream or nightmare in the surface consciousness of an indifferent, immutable Transcendence which is unaffected by the dream and has no real part in it,—if we accept at all, as the Gita accepts, the existence of God, that is to say of the omnipresent, omniscient, omnipotent, yet always transcendent Being who manifests the world and Himself in the world, who is not the slave but the lord of His creative Consciousness, Nature or Force (Maya, Prakriti or Shakti), who is not baffled or thwarted in His world-conception or design by His creatures, man or devil, who does not need to justify Himself by shifting the responsibility for any part of His creation or manifestation on that which is created or manifested, then the human being has to start from a great, a difficult act of faith. Finding himself in a world which is apparently a chaos of battling powers, a clash of vast and obscure forces, a life which subsists only by constant change and death, menaced from every side by pain, suffering, evil and destruction, he has to see the omnipresent Deity in it all and conscious that of this enigma there must be a solution and beyond this Ignorance in which he dwells a Knowledge that reconciles, he has to take his stand upon this faith, "Though Thou slay me, yet will I trust in Thee." All human thought or faith that is active and affirmative, whether it be theistic, pantheistic, or atheistic, does in fact involve more or less explicitly and completely such an attitude. It admits and it believes: admits the discords of the world, believes in some highest principle of God, universal Being or Nature which shall enable us to transcend, overcome or harmonize these discords, perhaps even to do all three at once, to harmonize by overcoming and transcending.

Then, as to human life in its actualities, we have to accept its aspect of a struggle and a battle mounting into supreme crises such as that of Kurukshetra. The Gita, as we have seen, takes for its frame such a period of transition and crisis as humanity periodically experiences in its history, in which great forces clash together for a huge destruction and reconstruction, intellectual, social, moral, religious, political, and these in the actual psychological and social stage of human evolution culminate usually through a violent physical convulsion of strife, war or revolution. The Gita proceeds from the acceptance of the necessity in Nature for such vehement crises and it accepts not only the moral aspect, the struggle between righteousness and unrighteousness, between the self-affirming law of Good and the forces that oppose its progression, but also the physical aspect, the actual armed war or other vehement physical strife between the human beings who represent the antagonistic powers. We must remember that the Gita was composed at a time when war was even more than it is now a necessary part of human activity and the idea of its elimination from the scheme of life would have been an absolute chimera. The gospel of universal peace and goodwill among men—for without a universal and entire mutual goodwill there can be no real and abiding peace—has never succeeded for a moment in possessing itself of human life during the historic cycle of our progress, because morally, socially, spiritually the race was not prepared and the poise of Nature in its evolution would not admit of its being immediately prepared for any such transcendence. Even now we have not actually progressed beyond the feasibility of a system of accommodation between conflicting interests which may minimize the recurrence of the worst forms of strife. And towards this consummation the method, the approach which humanity has been forced by its own nature to adopt, is a monstrous mutual massacre unparalleled in history; a universal war, full of bitterness and irreconcilable hatred, is the straightway and the triumphant means modern man has found for the establishment of universal peace! That consummation, too, founded not upon any fundamental change in human nature, but upon intellectual notions, economic convenience, vital and sentimental shrinking's from the loss of life, discomfort, and horror of war, effected by nothing better than political adjustments, gives no very certain promise of firm foundation and long duration. A day may come, must surely come, we will say, when humanity will be ready spiritually, morally, socially for the reign of universal peace; meanwhile the aspect of battle and the nature and function of man as a fighter have to be accepted and accounted for by any practical philosophy and religion. The Gita, taking life as it is and not only as it may be in some distant future, puts the question how this aspect and function of life, which is really an aspect and function of human activity in general, can be harmonized with the spiritual existence.

The Gita is therefore addressed to a fighter, a man of action, one whose duty in life is that of war and protection, war as a part of government for the protection of those who are excused from that duty, debarred from protecting themselves and therefore at the mercy of the strong and the violent, war, secondly and by a moral extension of this idea, for the protection of the weak and the oppressed and for the maintenance of right and justice in the world. For all these ideas, the social and practical, the moral and the chivalrous enter into the Indian conception of the Kshatriya, the man who is a warrior and ruler by function and a knight and king in his nature. Although the more general and universal ideas of the Gita are those which are the most important to us, we ought not to leave out of consideration altogether the colouring and trend they take from the peculiar Indian culture and social system in the midst of which they arose. That system differed from the modern in its conception. To the modern mind man is a thinker, worker or producer and a fighter all in one, and the tendency of the social system is to lump all these activities and to demand from each individual his contribution to the intellectual, economical, and military life and needs of the community without paying any heed to the demands of his individual nature and temperament. The ancient Indian civilization laid peculiar stress on the individual nature, tendency, temperament and sought to determine by it the ethical type, function, and place in the society. Nor did it consider man primarily as a social being or the fullness of his social existence as the highest ideal, but rather as a spiritual being in process of formation and development and his social life, ethical law, play of temperament and exercise of function as means and stages of spiritual formation. Thought and knowledge, war and government, production and distribution, labour and service were carefully differentiated functions of society, each assigned to those who were naturally called to it and providing the right means by which they could individually proceed towards their spiritual development and self-perfection.

The modern idea of a common obligation in all the main

departments of human activity has its advantages; it helps to greater solidarity, unity, and fullness in the life of the community and a more all-round development of the complete human being as opposed to the endless divisions and over-specialization and the narrowing and artificial shackling of the life of the individual to which the Indian system eventually led. But it also has its disadvantages and in certain of its developments the too logical application of it has led to grotesque and disastrous absurdities. This is evident enough in the character of modern war. From the idea of a common military obligation binding on every individual to defend and fight for the community by which he lives and profits, has arisen the system by which the whole manhood of the nation is hurled into the bloody trench to slay and be slain, thinkers, artists, philosophers, priests, merchants, artisans all torn from their natural functions, the whole life of the community disorganized, reason and conscience overridden, even the minister of religion who is salaried by the State or called by his function to preach the gospel of peace and love forced to deny his creed and become a butcher of his fellowmen! Not only are conscience and nature violated by the arbitrary fiat of the military State, but national defence carried to an insane extreme makes its best attempt to become a national suicide.

Indian civilization on the contrary made it its chief aim to minimize the incidence and disaster of war. For this purpose, it limited the military obligation to the small class who by their birth, nature and traditions were marked out for this function and found in it their natural means of self-development through the flowering of the soul in the qualities of courage, disciplined force, strong helpfulness, and chivalrous nobility for which the warrior's life pursued under the stress of a high ideal gives a field and opportunities. The rest of the community was in every way guarded from slaughter and outrage; their life and occupations were as little interfered with as possible and the combative and destructive tendencies of human nature were given a restricted field, confined in a sort of lists so as to do the minimum amount of harm to the general life of the race, while at the same time by being subjected to high ethical ideals and every possible rule of humanity and chivalry the function of war was obliged to help in ennobling and elevating instead of brutalizing those who performed it. It must be remembered that it is war of this kind and under these conditions that the Gita had in view, war considered as an inevitable part of human life, but so restricted and regulated as to serve like other activities the ethical and spiritual development which was then regarded as the whole real object of life, war destructive within certain carefully fixed limits of the bodily life of individual men but constructive of their inner life and of the ethical elevation of the race. That war in the past has, when subjected to an ideal, helped in this elevation, as in the development of knighthood and chivalry, the Indian ideal of the Kshatriya, the Japanese ideal of the Samurai, can only be denied by the fanatics of pacifism. When it has fulfilled its function, it may well disappear; for if it tries to survive its utility, it will appear as an unrelieved brutality of violence stripped of its ideal and constructive aspects and will be rejected by the progressive mind of humanity; but its past service to the race must be admitted in any reasonable view of our evolution.

The physical fact of war, however, is only a special and outward manifestation of a general principle in life and the Kshatriya is only the outward manifestation and type of a general characteristic necessary to the completeness of human perfection. War typifies and embodies physically the aspect of battle and struggle which belongs to all life, both to our inner and our outer living, in a world whose method is a meeting and wrestling of forces which progress by mutual destruction towards a continually changing adjustment expressive of a progressive harmonizing and hopeful of a perfect harmony based upon some yet ungrasped potentiality of oneness. The Kshatriya is the type and embodiment of the fighter in man who accepts this principle in life and faces it as a warrior striving towards mastery, not shrinking from the destruction of bodies and forms, but through it all aiming at the realization of some principle of right, justice, law which shall be the basis of the harmony towards which the struggle tends. The Gita accepts this aspect of the world-energy and the physical fact of war which embodies it, and it addresses itself to the man of action, the striver and fighter, the Kshatriya,—war which is the extreme contradiction of the soul's high aspiration to peace within and harmlessness[1] without, the striver and fighter whose necessary turmoil of struggle and action seems to be the very contradiction of the soul's high ideal of calm mastery and self-possession,—and it seeks for an issue from the contradiction, a point at which its terms meet and a poise which shall be the first essential basis of harmony and transcendence.

Man meets the battle of life in the manner most consonant with the essential quality most dominant in his nature. There are, according to the Sankhya philosophy accepted in this respect by the Gita, three essential qualities or modes of the world-energy and therefore also of human nature, sattva, the mode of poise, knowledge and satisfaction, rajas, the mode of passion, action, and struggling emotion, tamas, the mode of ignorance and inertia. Dominated by tamas, man does not so much meet the rush and shock of the world-energies whirling about him and converging upon him as he succumbs to them, is overborne by them, afflicted, subjected; or at the most, helped by the other qualities, the tamasic man seeks only somehow to survive, to subsist so long as he may, to shelter himself in the fortress of an established routine of thought and action in which he feels himself to a certain extent protected from the battle, able to reject the demand which his higher nature makes upon him, excused from accepting the necessity of farther struggle and the ideal of an increasing effort and mastery. Dominated by rajas, man flings himself into the battle and attempts to use the struggle of forces for his own egoistic

1 ahimsa.

benefit, to slay, conquer, dominate, enjoy; or, helped by a certain measure of the sattwic quality, the rajasic man makes the struggle itself a means of increasing inner mastery, joy, power, possession. The battle of life becomes his delight and passion partly for its own sake, for the pleasure of activity and the sense of power, partly as a means of his increase and natural self-development. Dominated by sattva, man seeks in the midst of the strife for a principle of law, right, poise, harmony, peace, satisfaction. The purely sattwic man tends to seek this within, whether for himself alone or with an impulse to communicate it, when won, to other human minds, but usually by a sort of inner detachment from or else an outer rejection of the strife and turmoil of the active world-energy; but if the sattwic mind accepts partly the rajasic impulse, it seeks rather to impose this poise and harmony upon the struggle and apparent chaos, to vindicate a victory for peace, love and harmony over the principle of war, discord and struggle. All the attitudes adopted by the human mind towards the problem of life either derive from the domination of one or other of these qualities or else from an attempt at balance and harmony between them.

But there also comes a stage in which the mind recoils from the whole problem and, dissatisfied with the solutions given by the threefold mode of Nature, traigunya, seeks for some higher solution outside of it or else above it. It looks for an escape either into something which is outside and void of all qualities and therefore of all activity or in something which is superior to the three qualities and master of them and therefore at once capable of action and unaffected, undominated by its own action, in the nirguna or the trigunatıta. It aspires to an absolute peace and unconditioned existence or to a dominant calm and superior existence. The natural movement of the former attitude is towards the renunciation of the world, sannyasa; of the latter towards superiority to the claims of the lower nature and its whirl of actions and reactions, and its principle is equality and the inner renunciation of passion and desire. The former is the first impulse of Arjuna recoiling from the calamitous culmination of all his heroic activity in the great cataclysm of battle and massacre, Kurukshetra; losing his whole past principle of action, inaction and the rejection of life and its claims seem to him the only issue. But it is to an inner superiority and not to the physical renunciation of life and action that he is called by the voice of the divine Teacher.

Arjuna is the Kshatriya, the rajasic man who governs his rajasic action by a high sattwic ideal. He advances to this gigantic struggle, to this Kurukshetra with the full acceptance of the joy of battle, as to "a holiday of fight", but with a proud confidence in the righteousness of his cause; he advances in his rapid chariot tearing the hearts of his enemies with the victorious clamour of his war-conch; for he wishes to look upon all these Kings of men who have come here to champion against him the cause of unrighteousness and establish as a rule of life the disregard of law, justice and truth which they would replace by the rule of a selfish and arrogant egoism. When this confidence is shattered within him, when he is smitten down from his customary attitude and mental basis of life, it is by the uprush of the tamasic quality into the rajasic man, inducing a recoil of astonishment, grief, horror, dismay, dejection, bewilderment of the mind and the war of reason against itself, a collapse towards the principle of ignorance and inertia. As a result, he turns towards renunciation. Better the life of the mendicant living upon alms than this dharma of the Kshatriya, this battle and action culminating in undiscriminating massacre, this principle of mastery and glory and power which can only be won by destruction and bloodshed, this conquest of blood-stained enjoyments, this vindication of justice and right by a means which contradicts all righteousness and this affirmation of the social law by a war which destroys in its process and result all that constitutes society.

Sannyasa is the renunciation of life and action and of the

threefold modes of Nature, but it has to be approached through one or other of the three qualities. The impulse may be tamasic, a feeling of impotence, fear, aversion, disgust, horror of the world and life; or it may be the rajasic quality tending towards tamas, an impulse of weariness of the struggle, grief, disappointment, refusal to accept any longer this vain turmoil of activity with its pains and its eternal discontent. Or the impulse may be that of rajas tending towards sattwa, the impulse to arrive at something superior to anything life can give, to conquer a higher state, to trample down life itself under the feet of an inner strength which seeks to break all bonds and transcend all limits. Or it may be sattwic, an intellectual perception of the vanity of life and the absence of any real goal or justification for this ever-cycling world-existence or else a spiritual perception of the Timeless, the Infinite, the Silent, the nameless and formless Peace beyond. The recoil of Arjuna is the tamasic recoil from action of the sattwa-rajasic man. The Teacher may confirm it in its direction, using it as a dark entry to the purity and peace of the ascetic life; or he may purify it at once and raise it towards the rare altitudes of the sattwic tendency of renunciation. In fact, he does neither. He discourages the tamasic recoil and the tendency to renunciation and enjoins the continuance of action and even of the same fierce and terrible action, but he points the disciple towards another and inner renunciation which is the real issue from his crisis and the way towards the soul's superiority to the world-Nature and yet its calm and self-possessed action in the world. Not a physical asceticism, but an inner askesis is the teaching of the Gita.

VII

THE CREED OF THE ARYAN FIGHTER[1]

The Answer of the divine Teacher to the first flood of Arjuna's passionate self-questioning, his shrinking from slaughter, his sense of sorrow and sin, his grieving for an empty and desolate life, his forecast of evil results of an evil deed, is a strongly worded rebuke. All this, it is replied, is confusion of mind and delusion, a weakness of the heart, an unmanliness, a fall from the virility of the fighter and the hero. Not this was fitting in the son of Pritha, not thus should the champion and chief hope of a righteous cause abandon it in the hour of crisis and peril or suffer the sudden amazement of his heart and senses, the clouding of his reason and the downfall of his will to betray him into the casting away of his divine weapons and the refusal of his God-given work. This is not the way cherished and followed by the Aryan man; this mood came not from heaven, nor can it lead to heaven, and on earth it is the forfeiting of the glory that waits upon strength and heroism and noble works. Let him put from him this weak and self-indulgent pity, let him

Rise, and smite his enemies!

The answer of a hero to a hero, shall we say, but not that which we should expect from a divine Teacher from whom we

---

1 Gita, II. 1-38.

demand rather that he shall always encourage gentleness and saintliness and self-abnegation and the recoil from worldly aims and cessation from the ways of the world? The Gita expressly says that Arjuna has thus lapsed into unheroic weakness, "his eyes full and distressed with tears, his heart overcome by de-pression and discouragement," because he is invaded by pity, krpayavistam. Is this not then a divine weakness? Is not pity a divine emotion which should not thus be discouraged with harsh rebuke? Or are we in face of a mere gospel of war and heroic action, a Nietzschean creed of power and high-browed strength, of Hebraic or old Teutonic hardness which holds pity to be a weakness and thinks like the Norwegian hero who thanked God because He had given him a hard heart? But the teaching of the Gita springs from an Indian creed and to the Indian mind compassion has always figured as one of the largest elements of the divine nature. The Teacher himself enumerating in a later chapter the qualities of the godlike nature in many places among them compassion to creatures, gentleness, freedom from wrath and from the desire to slay and do hurt, no less than fearlessness and high spirit and energy. Harshness and hardness and fierce-ness and a satisfaction in slaying enemies and amassing wealth and unjust enjoyments are Asuric qualities; they come from the violent Titanic nature which denies the Divine in the world and the Divine in man and worships Desire only as its deity. It is not then from any such standpoint that the weakness of Arjuna merits rebuke.

"Whence has come to thee this dejection, this stain and darkness of the soul in the hour of difficulty and peril?" asks Krishna of Arjuna. The question points to the real nature of Arjuna's deviation from his heroic qualities. There is a divine compassion which descends to us from on high and for the man whose nature does not possess it, is not cast in its mould, to pretend to be the superior man, the master-man or the superman is a folly and an insolence, for he alone is the superman who most manifests the highest nature of the Godhead in humanity. This compassion observes with an eye of love and wisdom and calm strength the battle and the struggle, the strength and weakness of man, his virtues and sins, his joy and suffering, his knowledge and his ignorance, his wisdom and his folly, his aspiration and his failure and it enters into it all to help and to heal. In the saint and philanthropist, it may cast itself into the mould of a plenitude of love or charity; in the thinker and hero it assumes the largeness and the force of a helpful wisdom and strength. It is this compassion in the Aryan fighter, the soul of his chivalry, which will not break the bruised reed, but helps and protects the weak and the oppressed and the wounded and the fallen. But it is also the divine compassion that smites down the strong tyrant and the confident oppressor, not in wrath and with hatred,—for these are not the high divine qualities, the wrath of God against the sinner, God's hatred of the wicked are the fables of half-enlightened creeds, as much a fable as the eternal torture of the Hells they have invented,—but, as the old Indian spirituality clearly saw, with as much love and compassion for the strong Titan erring by his strength and slain for his sins as for the sufferer and the oppressed who have to be saved from his violence and injustice.

But such is not the compassion which actuates Arjuna in the rejection of his work and mission. That is not compassion but an impotence full of a weak self-pity, a recoil from the mental suffering which his act must entail on himself,—"I see not what shall thrust from me the sorrow that dries up the senses,"—and of all things self-pity is among the most ignoble and un-Aryan of moods. Its pity for others is also a form of self-indulgence; it is the physical shrinking of the nerves from the act of slaughter, the egoistic emotional shrinking of the heart from the destruction of the Dhritarashtrians because they are "one's own people" and without them life will be empty. This pity is a weakness of the mind and senses,—a weakness which may well be beneficial to men of a lower grade of development, who have to be weak because otherwise they will be hard and cruel; for they have to cure the harsher by the gentler forms of sensational egoism, they have to call in tamas, the debile principle, to help sattwa, the principle of light, in quelling the strength and excess of their rajasic passions. But this way is not for the developed Aryan man who has to grow not by weakness, but by an ascension from strength to strength. Arjuna is the divine man, the master-man in the making and as such he has been chosen by the gods. He has a work given to him, he has God beside him in his chariot, he has the heavenly bow Gandiva in his hand, he has the champions of unrighteousness, the opponents of the divine leading of the world in his front. Not his is the right to determine what he shall do or not do according to his emotions and his passions, or to shrink from a necessary destruction by the claim of his egoistic heart and reason, or to decline his work because it will bring sorrow and emptiness to his life or because its earthly result has no value to him in the absence of the thousands who must perish. All that is a weak falling from his higher nature. He has to see only the work that must be done, kartavyam karma, to hear only the divine command breathed through his warrior nature, to feel only for the world and the destiny of mankind calling to him as its god-sent man to assist its march and clear its path of the dark armies that beset it.

secondly, another and larger founded on a more intimate knowledge, opening into deeper truths of our being, which is the real starting-point of the teaching of the Gita. This first answer relies on the philosophic and moral conceptions of the Vedantic philosophy and the social idea of duty and honour which formed the ethical basis of Aryan society. Arjuna has sought to justify his refusal on ethical and rational grounds, but he has merely cloaked by words of apparent rationality the revolt of his ignorant and unchastened emotions. He has spoken of the physical life and the death of the body as if these were the primary realities; but they have no such essential value to the sage and the thinker. The sorrow for the bodily death of his friends and kindred is a grief to which wisdom and the true knowledge of life lend no sanction.

The enlightened man does not mourn either for the living or the dead, for he knows that suffering and death are merely incidents in the history of the soul. The soul, not the body, is the reality. All these kings of men for whose approaching death he mourns, have lived before, they will live again in the human body; for as the soul passes physically through childhood and youth and age, so it passes on to the changing of the body. The calm and wise mind, the dhıra, the thinker who looks upon life steadily and does not allow himself to be disturbed and blinded by his sensations and emotions, is not deceived by material appearances; he does not allow the clamour of his blood and his nerves and his heart to cloud his judgment or to contradict his knowledge. He looks beyond the apparent facts of the life of the body and senses to the real fact of his being and rises beyond the emotional and physical desires of the ignorant nature to the true and only aim of the human existence.

What is that real fact? that highest aim? This, that human life and death repeated through the aeons in the great cycles of the world are only a long progress by which the human being prepares and makes himself fit for immortality. And how shall he prepare himself? who is the man that is fit? The man who rises above the conception of himself as a life and a body, who does not accept the material and sensational touches of the world at their own value or at the value which the physical man attaches to them, who knows himself and all as souls, learns himself to live in his soul and not in his body and deals with others too as souls and not as mere physical beings. For by immortality is meant not the survival of death,—that is already given to every creature born with a mind,—but the transcendence of life and death. It means that ascension by which man ceases to live as a mind-informed body and lives at last as a spirit and in the Spirit. Whoever is subject to grief and sorrow, a slave to the sensations and emotions, occupied by the touches of things transient cannot become fit for immortality. These things must be borne until they are conquered, till they can give no pain to the liberated man, till he is able to receive all the material happenings of the world whether joyful or sorrowful with a wise and calm equality, even as the tranquil eternal Spirit secret within us receives them. To be disturbed by sorrow and horror as Arjuna has been disturbed, to be deflected by them from the path that has to be travelled, to be overcome by self-pity and intolerance of sorrow and recoil from the unavoidable and trivial circumstance of the death of the body, this is un-Aryan ignorance. It is not the way of the Aryan climbing in calm strength towards the immortal life.

There is no such thing as death, for it is the body that dies, and the body is not the man. That which really is, cannot go out of existence, though it may change the forms through which it appears, just as that which is non-existent cannot come into being. The soul is and cannot cease to be. This opposition of is and is not, this balance of being and becoming, which is the mind's view of existence, finds its end in the realization of the soul as the one imperishable self by whom all this universe has been extended. Finite bodies have an end, but that which possesses and uses the body, is infinite, illimitable, eternal, indestructible. It casts away old and takes up new bodies as a man changes worn-out raiment for new; and what is there in this to grieve at and recoil and shrink? This is not born, nor does it die, nor is it a thing that comes into being once and passing away will never come into being again. It is unborn, ancient, sempiternal; it is not slain with the slaying of the body. Who can slay the immortal spirit? Weapons cannot cleave it, nor do the fire burn, nor do the waters drench it, nor the wind dry. Eternally stable, immobile, all-pervading, it is forever and forever. Not manifested like the body, but greater than all manifestation, not to be analyzed by the thought, but greater than all mind, not capable of change and modification like the life and its organs and their objects but beyond the changes of mind and life and body, it is yet the Reality which all these strive to figure.

Even if the truth of our being were a thing less sublime, vast, intangible by death and life, if the self were constantly subject to birth and death, still the death of beings ought not to be a cause of sorrow. For that is an inevitable circumstance of the soul's self-manifestation. Its birth is an appearing out of some state in which it is not non-existent but unmanifest to our mortal senses, its death is a return to that unmanifest world or condition and out of it, it will again appear in the physical manifestation. The to-do made by the physical mind and senses about death and the horror of death whether on the sick-bed or the battlefield, is the most ignorant of nervous clamours. Our sorrow for the death of men is an ignorant grieving for those for whom there is no cause to grieve, since they have neither gone out of existence nor suffered any painful or terrible change of condition but are beyond death no less in being and no more unhappy in circumstance than in life. But in reality, the higher truth is the real truth. All are that Self, that One, that Divine whom we look on and speak and hear of as the wonderful beyond our com-prehension, for after all our seeking and declaring of knowledge and learning from those who have knowledge no human mind has ever known this Absolute. It is this which is here veiled by the world, the master of the body; all life is only its shadow; the coming of the soul into physical manifestation and our passing out of it by death is only one of its minor movements. When we have known ourselves as this, then to speak of ourselves as slayer or slain is an absurdity. One thing only is the truth in which we have to live, the Eternal manifesting itself as the soul of man in the great cycle of its pilgrimage with birth and death for milestones, with worlds beyond as resting places, with all the circumstances of life happy or unhappy as the means of our progress and battle and victory and with immortality as the home to which the soul travels.

Therefore, says the Teacher, put away this vain sorrow and shrinking, fight, O son of Bharata. But wherefore such a conclusion? This high and great knowledge, this strenuous self-discipline of the mind and soul by which it is to rise beyond the clamour of the emotions and the cheat of the senses to true self-knowledge, may well free us from grief and delusion; it may well cure us of the fear of death and the sorrow for the dead; it may well show us that those whom we speak of as dead are not dead at all nor to be sorrowed for, since they have only gone beyond; it may well teach us to look undisturbed upon the most terrible assaults of life and upon the death of the body as a trifle; it may exalt us to the conception of all life's circumstances as a manifestation of the One and as a means for our souls to raise themselves above appearances by an upward evolution until we know ourselves as the immortal Spirit. But how does it justify the action demanded of Arjuna and the slaughter of Kurukshetra? The answer is that this is the action required of Arjuna in the path he has to travel; it has come inevitably in the performance of the function demanded of him by his svadharma, his social duty, the law of his life and the law of his being. This world, this manifestation of the Self in the material universe is not only a cycle of inner development but a field in which the external circumstances of life have to be accepted as an environment and an occasion for that development. It is a world of mutual help and struggle; not a serene and peaceful gliding through easy joys is the progress it allows us, but every step has to be gained by heroic effort and through a clash of opposing forces. Those who take up the inner and the outer struggle even to the most physical clash of all, that of war, are the Kshatriyas, the mighty men; war, force, nobility, courage are their nature; protection of the right and an unflinching acceptance of the gage of battle is their virtue and their duty. For there is continually a struggle between right and wrong, justice and injustice, the force that protects and the force that violates and oppresses, and when this has once been brought to the issue of physical strife, the champion and standard-bearer of the Right must not shake and tremble at the violent and terrible nature of the work he has to do; he must not abandon his followers or fellow-fighters, betray his cause and leave the standard of Right and Justice to trail in the dust and be trampled into mire by the blood-stained feet of the oppressor, because of a weak pity for the violent and cruel and a physical horror of the vastness of the destruction decreed. His virtue and his duty lie in battle and not in abstention from battle; it is not slaughter, but non-slaying which would here be the sin.

The Teacher then turns aside for a moment to give another answer to the cry of Arjuna over the sorrow of the death of kindred which will empty his life of the causes and objects of living. What is the true object of the Kshatriya's life and his true happiness? Not self-pleasing and domestic happiness and a life of comfort and peaceful joy with friends and relatives, but to battle for the right is his true object of life and to find a cause for which he can lay down his life or by victory win the crown and glory of the hero's existence is his greatest happiness. "There is no greater good for the Kshatriya than righteous battle, and when such a battle comes to them of itself like the open gate of heaven, happy are the Kshatriyas then. If thou doest not this battle for the right, then hast thou abandoned thy duty and virtue and thy glory, and sin shall be thy portion." He will by such a refusal incur disgrace and the reproach of fear and weakness and the loss of his Kshatriya honour. For what is the worst grief for a Kshatriya? It is the loss of his honour, his fame, his noble station among the mighty men, the men of courage and power; that to him is much worse than death. Battle, courage, power, rule, the honour of the brave, the heaven of those who fall nobly, this is the warrior's ideal. To lower that ideal, to allow a smirch to fall on that honour, to give the example of a hero among heroes whose action lays itself open to the reproach of cowardice and weakness and thus to lower the moral standard of mankind, is to be false to himself and to the demand of the world on its leaders and kings. "Slain thou shalt win Heaven, victorious thou shalt enjoy the earth; therefore arise, O son of Kunti, resolved upon battle."

This heroic appeal may seem to be on a lower level than the

stoical spirituality which precedes and the deeper spirituality which follows; for in the next verse the Teacher bids him to make grief and happiness, loss and gain, victory and defeat equal to his soul and then turn to the battle,—the real teaching of the Gita. But Indian ethics has always seen the practical necessity of graded ideals for the developing moral and spiritual life of man. The Kshatriya ideal, the ideal of the four orders, is here placed in its social aspect, not as afterwards in its spiritual meaning. This, says Krishna in effect, is my answer to you if you insist on joy and sorrow and the result of your actions as your motive of action. I have shown you in what direction the higher knowledge of self and the world points you; I have now shown you in what direction your social duty and the ethical standard of your order point you, svadharmam api caveksya. Whichever you consider, the result is the same. But if you are not satisfied with your social duty and the virtue of your order, if you think that leads you to sorrow and sin, then I bid you rise to a higher and not sink to a lower ideal. Put away all egoism from you, disregard joy and sorrow, disregard gain and loss and all worldly results; look only at the cause you must serve and the work that you must achieve by divine command; "so thou shalt not incur sin." Thus, Arjuna's plea of sorrow, his plea of the recoil from slaughter, his plea of the sense of sin, his plea of the unhappy results of his action, are answered according to the highest knowledge and ethical ideals to which his race and age had attained.

It is the creed of the Aryan fighter. "Know God," it says, "know thyself, help man; protect the Right, do without fear or weakness or faltering thy work of battle in the world. Thou art the eternal and imperishable Spirit, thy soul is here on its upward path to immortality; life and death are nothing, sorrow and wounds and suffering are nothing, for these things have to be conquered and overcome. Look not at thy own pleasure and gain and profit, but above and around, above at the shining summits to which thou climbest, around at this world of battle and trial in which good and evil, progress and retrogression are locked in stern conflict. Men call to thee, their strong man, their hero for help; help then, fight. Destroy when by destruction the world must advance, but hate not that which thou destroyest, neither grieve for all those who perish. Know everywhere the oneself, know all to be immortal souls and the body to be but dust. Do they work with a calm, strong and equal spirit; fight and fall nobly or conquer mightily. For this is the work that God and thy nature have given to thee to accomplish."

VIII

SANKHYA AND YOGA

In the moment of his turning from this first and summary answer to Arjuna's difficulties and in the very first words which strike the keynote of a spiritual solution, the Teacher makes at once a distinction which is of the utmost importance for the understanding of the Gita,—the distinction of Sankhya and Yoga. "Such is the intelligence (the intelligent knowledge of things and will) declared to thee in the Sankhya, hear now this in the Yoga, for if thou art in Yoga by this intelligence, O son of Pritha, thou shalt cast away the bondage of works." That is the literal translation of the words in which the Gita announces the distinction it intends to make.

The Gita is in its foundation a Vedantic work; it is one of the three recognized authorities for the Vedantic teaching and, although not described as a revealed Scripture, although, that is to say, it is largely intellectual, ratiocinative, philosophical in its method, founded indeed on the Truth, but not the directly inspired Word which is the revelation of the Truth through the higher faculties of the seer, it is yet so highly esteemed as to be ranked almost as a thirteenth Upanishad. But still its Vedantic ideas are throughout and thoroughly coloured by the ideas of the Sankhya and the Yoga way of thinking and it derives from this colouring the peculiar synthetic character of its philosophy. It is in fact primarily a practical system of Yoga that it teaches, and it brings in metaphysical ideas only as explanatory of its practical system; nor does it merely declare Vedantic knowledge, but it founds knowledge and devotion upon works, even as it uplifts works to knowledge, their culmination, and informs them with devotion as their very heart and kernel of their spirit. Again, its Yoga is founded upon the analytical philosophy of the Sankhyas, takes that as a starting-point and always keeps it as a large element of its method and doctrine but still it proceeds far beyond it, negatives even some of its characteristic tendencies and finds a means of reconciling the lower analytical knowledge of Sankhya with the higher synthetic and Vedantic truth.

What, then, are the Sankhya and Yoga of which the Gita speaks? They are certainly not the systems which have come down to us under these names as enunciated respectively in the Sankhya Karika of Ishwara Krishna and the Yoga aphorisms of Patanjali. This Sankhya is not the system of the Karikas,—at least as that is generally understood; for the Gita nowhere for a moment admits the multiplicity of Purushas as a primal truth of being and it affirms emphatically what the traditional Sankhya strenuously denies, the One as Self and Purusha, that One again as the Lord, Ishwara or Purushottama, and Ishwara as the cause of the universe. The traditional Sankhya is, to use our modern distinctions, atheistic; the Sankhya of the Gita admits and subtly reconciles the theistic, pantheistic, and monistic views of the universe.

Nor is this Yoga the Yoga system of Patanjali; for that is a purely subjective method of Raja yoga, an internal discipline, limited, rigidly cut out, severely and scientifically graded, by which the mind is progressively stilled and taken up into Samadhi so that we may gain the temporal and eternal results of this self-exceeding, the temporal in a great expansion of the soul's knowledge and powers, the eternal in the divine union. But the Yoga of the Gita is a large, flexible, and many-sided system with various elements, which are all successfully harmonized by a sort of natural and living assimilation, and of these elements Raja yoga is only one and not the most important and vital. This Yoga does not adopt any strict and scientific gradation but is a process of natural soul-development; it seeks by the adoption of a few principles of subjective poise and action to bring about a renovation of the soul and a sort of change, ascension, or new birth out of the lower nature into the divine. Accordingly, its idea of Samadhi is quite different from the ordinary notion of the Yogic trance and while Patanjali gives to works only an initial importance for moral purification and religious concentration, the Gita goes so far as to make works the distinctive characteristic of Yoga. Action to Patanjali is only a preliminary, in the Gita it is a permanent foundation; in the Raja yoga it has practically to be put aside when its result has been attained or at any rate ceases very soon to be a means for the Yoga, for the Gita it is a means of the highest ascent and continues even after the complete liberation of the soul.

This much has to be said in order to avoid any confusion of thought that might be created by the use of familiar words in a connotation wider than the technical sense now familiar to us. Still, all that is essential in the Sankhya and Yoga systems, all in them that is large, catholic, and universally true, is admitted by the Gita, even though it does not limit itself by them like the opposing schools. Its Sankhya is the catholic and Vedantic Sankhya such as we find it in its first principles and elements in the great Vedantic synthesis of the Upanishads and in the later developments of the Puranas. Its idea of Yoga is that large idea of a principally subjective practice and inner change, necessary for the finding of the Self or the union with God, of which the Raja yoga is only one special application. The Gita insists that Sankhya and Yoga are not two different, incompatible, and discordant systems, but one in their principle and aim; they differ only in their method and starting point. The Sankhya also is a Yoga, but it proceeds by knowledge; it starts, that is to say, by intellectual discrimination and analysis of the principles of our being and attains its aim through the vision and possession of the Truth. Yoga, on the other hand, proceeds by works; it is in its first principle Karma yoga; but it is evident from the whole teaching of the Gita and its later definitions that the word karma is used in a very wide sense and that by Yoga is meant the selfless devotion of all the inner as well as the outer activities as a sacrifice to the Lord of all works, offered to the Eternal as Master of all the soul's energies and austerities. Yoga is the practice of the Truth of which knowledge gives the vision, and its practice has for its motor-power a spirit of illumined devotion, of calm or fervent consecration to that which knowledge sees to be the Highest.

But what are the truths of Sankhya? The philosophy drew its name from its analytical process. Sankhya is the analysis, the enumeration, the separative and discriminative setting forth of the principles of our being of which the ordinary mind sees only the combinations and results of combination. It did not seek at all to synthetize. Its original standpoint is in fact dualistic, not with the very relative dualism of the Vedantic schools which call themselves by that name, Dwaita but in a very absolute and trenchant fashion. For it explains existence not by one, but by two original principles whose interrelation is the cause of the universe, —Purusha, the inactive, Prakriti, the active. Purusha is the Soul, not in the ordinary or popular sense of the word, but of pure conscious Being immobile, immutable, and self-luminous. Prakriti is Energy and its process. Purusha does nothing, but it reflects the action of Energy and its processes; Prakriti is mechanical, but by being reflected in Purusha it assumes the appearance of consciousness in its activities and thus there are created those phenomena of creation, conservation, dissolution, birth and life and death, consciousness and unconsciousness, sense-knowledge and intellectual knowledge and ignorance, action and inaction, happiness and suffering which the Purusha under the influence of Prakriti attributes to itself although they belong not at all to itself but to the action or movement of Prakriti alone.

For Prakriti is constituted of three gunas or essential modes of energy, sattwa, the seed of intelligence, conserves the workings of energy; rajas, the seed of force and action, creates the workings of energy; tamas, the seed of inertia and non-intelligence, the denial of sattwa and rajas, dissolves what they create and conserve. When these three powers of the energy of Prakriti are in a state of equilibrium, all is in rest, there is no movement, action or creation and there is therefore nothing to be reflected in the immutable luminous being of the conscious Soul. But when the equilibrium is disturbed, then the three gunas fall into a state of inequality in which they strive with and act upon each other and the whole inextricable business of ceaseless creation, conservation and dissolution begins, un-rolling the phenomena of the cosmos. This continues so long as the Purusha consents to reflect the disturbance which obscures his eternal nature and attributes to it the nature of Prakriti; but when he withdraws his consent, the gunas fall into equilibrium and the soul returns to its eternal, unchanging immobility; it is delivered from phenomena. This reflection and this giving or withdrawal of consent seem to be the only powers of Purusha; he is the witness of Nature by virtue of reflection and the giver of the sanction, saksı and anumanta of the Gita, but not actively the Ishwara. Even his giving of consent is passive, and his withdrawing of consent is only another passivity. All action subjective or objective is foreign to the Soul; it has neither an active will nor an active intelligence. It cannot therefore be the sole cause of the cosmos and the affirmation of a second cause becomes necessary. Not Soul alone by its nature of conscious knowledge, will and delight is the cause of the universe, but Soul and Nature are the dual cause, a passive Consciousness, and an active Energy. So, the Sankhya explains the existence of the cosmos.

But whence then come this conscious intelligence and conscious will which we perceive to be so large a part of our being and which we commonly and instinctively refer not to the Prakriti, but to the Purusha? According to the Sankhya this intelligence and will are entirely a part of the mechanical energy of Nature and are not properties of the soul; they are the principle of Buddhi, one of the twenty-four tattvas, the twenty-four cosmic principles. Prakriti in the evolution of the world bases herself with her three gunas in her as the original substance of things, unmanifest, inconscient, out of which are evolved successively five elemental conditions of energy or matter,—for Matter and Force are the same in the Sankhya philosophy. These are called by the names of the five concrete elements of ancient thought, ether, air, fire, water, and earth; but it must be remembered that they are not elements in the modern scientific sense but subtle conditions of material energy and nowhere to be found in their purity in the gross material world. All objects are created by the combination of these five subtle conditions or elements. Again, each of these five is the base of one of five subtle properties of energy or matter, sound, touch, form, taste, and smell, which constitute the way in which the mind-sense perceives objects. Thus, by these five elements of Matter put forth from primary energy and these five sense relations through which Matter is known is evolved what we would call in modern language the objective aspect of cosmic existence.

Thirteen other principles constitute the subjective aspect of the cosmic Energy,—Buddhi or Mahat, Ahankara, Manas and its ten sense-functions, five of knowledge, five of action. Manas, mind, is the original sense which perceives all objects and reacts upon them; for it has at once an inferent and an efferent activity, receives by perception what the Gita calls the outward touches of things, bahya sparsa, and so forms its idea of the world and exercises its reactions of active vitality. But it specializes its most ordinary functions of reception by aid of the five perceptive senses of hearing, touch, sight, taste, and smell, which make the five properties of things their respective objects and specializes certain necessary vital functions of reaction by aid of the five active senses which operate for speech, locomotion, the seizing of things, ejection, and generation. Buddhi, the discriminating principle, is at once intelligence and will; it is that power in Nature which discriminates and coordinates. Ahankara, the ego-sense, is the subjective principle in Buddhi by which the Purusha is induced to identify himself with Prakriti and her activities. But these subjective principles are themselves as mechanical, as much a part of the inconscient energy as those which constitute her objective operations. If we find it difficult to realize how intelligence and will can be properties of the mechanical Inconscient and themselves mechanical (jada), we have only to remember that modern Science itself has been driven to the same conclusion. Even in the mechanical action of the atom there is a power which can only be called an inconscient will and in all the works of Nature that pervading will does inconsciently the works of intelligence. What we call mental intelligence is precisely the same thing in its essence as that which discriminates and coordinates subconsciously in all the activities of the material universe and conscious Mind itself, Science has tried to demonstrate, is only a result and transcript of the mechanical action of the inconscient. But Sankhya explains what modern Science leaves in obscurity, the process by which the mechanical and inconscient takes on the appearance of consciousness. It is because of the reflection of Prakriti in Purusha; the light of consciousness of the Soul is attributed to the workings of the mechanical energy and it is thus that the Purusha, observing Nature as the witness and forgetting himself, is deluded with the idea generated in her that it is he who thinks, feels, wills, acts, while all the time the operation of thinking, feeling, willing, acting is conducted really by her and her three modes and not by himself at all. To get rid of this delusion is the first step towards the liberation of the soul from Nature and her works.

There are certainly plenty of things in our existence which the Sankhya does not explain at all or does not explain satisfactorily, but if all we need is a rational explanation of the cosmic processes in their principles as a basis for the great object common to the ancient philosophies, the liberation of the soul from the obsession of cosmic Nature, then the Sankhya explanation of the world and the Sankhya way of liberation seem as good and as effective as any other. What we do not seize at first is why it should bring in an element of pluralism into its dualism by affirming one Prakriti, but many Purushas. It would seem that the existence of one Purusha and one Prakriti should be sufficient to account for the creation and procession of the universe. But the Sankhya was bound to evolve pluralism by its rigidly analytical observation of the principles of things. First, actually, we find that there are many conscious beings in the world, and each regards the same world in his own way and has his independent experience of its subjective and objective things, his separate dealings with the same perceptive and reactive processes. If there were only one Purusha, there would not be this central independence and separative-ness, but all would see the world in an identical fashion and with a common subjectivity and objectivity. Because Prakriti is one, all witness the same world; because her principles are everywhere the same, the general principles which constitute internal and external experience are the same for all; but the infinite difference of view and outlook and attitude, action and experience and escape from experience,—a difference not of the natural operations which are the same but of the witnessing consciousness,—are utterly inexplicable except on the supposition that there is a multiplicity of witnesses, many Purushas. The separative ego-sense, we may say, is a sufficient explanation? But the ego-sense is a common principle of Nature and need not vary; for by itself it simply induces the Purusha to identify himself with Prakriti, and if there is only one Purusha, all beings would be one, joined and alike in their egoistic consciousness; however different in detail might be the mere forms and combinations of their natural parts, there would be no difference of soul-outlook and soul-experience. The variations of Nature ought not to make all this central difference, this multiplicity of outlook and from beginning to end this separateness of experience in one Witness, one Purusha. Therefore, the pluralism of souls is a logical necessity to a pure Sankhya system divorced from the Vedantic elements of the ancient knowledge which first gave it birth. The cosmos and its process can be explained by the commerce of one Prakriti with one Purusha but not the multiplicity of conscious beings in the cosmos.

There is another difficulty quite as formidable. Liberation is the object set before itself by this philosophy as by others. This liberation is effected, we have said, by the Purusha's withdrawal of his consent from the activities of Prakriti which she conducts only for his pleasure; but, in sum, this is only a way of speaking. The Purusha is passive and the act of giving or withdrawing consent cannot really belong to it but must be a movement in Prakriti itself. If we consider, we shall see that it is, so far as it is an operation, a movement of reversal or recoil in the principle of Buddhi, the discriminative will. Buddhi has been lending itself to the perceptions of the mind-sense; it has been busy discriminating and coordinating the operations of the cosmic energy and by the aid of the ego-sense identifying the Witness with her works of thought, sense, and action. It arrives by the process of discriminating things at the acid and dissolvent realization that this identity is a delusion; it discriminates finally the Purusha from Prakriti and perceives that all is mere disturbance of the equilibrium of the gunas; the Buddhi, at once intelligence and will, recoils from the falsehood which it has been supporting and the Purusha, ceasing to be bound, no longer associates himself with the interest of the mind in the cosmic play. The ultimate result will be that Prakriti will lose her power to reflect herself in the Purusha; for the effect of the ego-sense is destroyed and the intelligent will becoming indifferent ceases to be the means of her sanction: necessarily then her gunas must fall into a state of equilibrium, the cosmic play must cease, the Purusha return to his immobile repose. But if there were only the one Purusha and this recoil of the discriminating principle from its delusions took place, all cosmos would cease. As it is, we see that nothing of the kind happens. A few beings among innumerable millions attain liberation or move towards it; the rest are in no way affected, nor is cosmic Nature in her play with them one whit inconvenienced by this summary rejection which should be the end of all her processes. Only by the theory of many independent Purushas can this fact be explained. The only at all logical ex-planation from the point of view of Vedantic monism is that of the Mayavada but there the whole thing becomes a dream, both bondage and liberation are circumstances of the unreality, the empirical blunderings of Maya; in reality there is none freed, none bound. The more realistic Sankhya view of things does not admit this phantasmagoric idea of existence and therefore cannot adopt this solution. Here too we see that the multiplicity of souls is an inevitable conclusion from the data of the Sankhya analysis of existence.

The Gita starts from this analysis and seems at first, even in its setting forth of Yoga, to accept it almost wholly. It accepts Prakriti and her three gunas and twenty-four principles; accepts the attribution of all action to the Prakriti and the passivity of the Purusha; accepts the multiplicity of conscious beings in the cosmos; accepts the dissolution of the identifying ego-sense, the discriminating action of the intelligent will and the transcendence of the action of the three modes of energy as the means of liberation. The Yoga which Arjuna is asked to practice from the outset is Yoga by the Buddhi, the intelligent will. But there is one deviation of capital importance,—the Purusha is regarded as one, not many; for the free, immaterial, immobile, eternal, immutable Self of the Gita, but for one detail, is a Vedantic description of the eternal, passive, immobile, immutable Purusha of the Sankhyas. But the capital difference is that there is One and not many. This brings in the whole difficulty which the Sankhya multiplicity avoids and necessitates a quite different solution. This the Gita provides by bringing into its Vedantic Sankhya the ideas and principles of Vedantic Yoga.

The first important new element we find is in the conception of Purusha itself. Prakriti conducts her activities for the pleasure of Purusha; but how is that pleasure determined? In the strict Sankhya analysis, it can only be by the passive consent of the silent Witness. Passively the Witness consents to the action of the intelligent will and the ego-sense, passively he consents to the recoil of that will from the ego-sense. He is Witness, source of the consent, by reflection upholder of the work of Nature, saksı Anumanta bharta, but nothing more. But the Purusha of the Gita is also the Lord of Nature; he is Ishwara. If the operation of the intelligent will belongs to Nature, the origination and power of the will proceed from the conscious Soul; he is the Lord of Nature. If the act of intelligence of the Will is the act of Prakriti, the source and light of the intelligence are actively contributed by the Purusha; he is not only the Witness, but the Lord and Knower, master of knowledge and will, jnata ısvarah. He is the supreme cause of the action of Prakriti, the supreme cause of its withdrawal from action. In the Sankhya analysis Purusha and Prakriti in their dualism are the cause of the cosmos; in this synthetic Sankhya Purusha by his Prakriti is the cause of the cosmos. We see at once how far we have travelled from the rigid purism of the traditional analysis.

But what of the oneself immutable, immobile, eternally free, with which the Gita began? That is free from all change or involution in change, avikarya, unborn, unmanifested, the Brahman, yet it is that "by which all this is extended." Therefore, it would seem that the principle of the Ishwara is in its being; if it is immobile, it is yet the cause and lord of all action and mobility. But how? And what of the multiplicity of conscious beings in the cosmos? They do not seem to be the Lord, but rather very much not the Lord, anısa, for they are subject to the action of the three gunas and the delusion of the ego-sense and if, as the Gita seems to say, they are all the oneself, how did this involution, subjection and delusion come about or how is it explicable except by the pure passivity of the Purusha? And whence the multiplicity? or how is it that the oneself in one body and mind attains liberation while in others it remains under the delusion of bondage? These are difficulties which cannot be passed by without a solution.

The Gita answers them in its later chapters by an analysis of Purusha and Prakriti which brings in new elements very proper to a Vedantic Yoga, but alien to the traditional Sankhya. It speaks of three Purushas or rather a triple status of the Purusha. The Upanishads in dealing with the truths of Sankhya seem sometimes to speak only of two Purushas. There is one unborn of three colours, says a text, the eternal feminine principle of Prakriti with its three gunas, ever creating; there are two unborn, two Purushas, of whom one cleaves to and enjoys her, the other abandons her because he has enjoyed all her enjoyments. In another verse they are described as two birds on one tree, eternally yoked companions, one of whom eats the fruits of the tree,—the Purusha in Nature enjoying her cosmos,—the other eats not but watches his fellow,—the silent Witness, withdrawn from the enjoyment; when the first sees the second and knows that all is his greatness, then he is delivered from sorrow. The point of view in the two verses is different, but they have a common implication. One of the birds is the eternally silent, unbound Self or Purusha by whom all this is extended, and he regards the cosmos he has extended, but is aloof from it; the other is the Purusha involved in Prakriti. The first verse indicates that the two are the same, represent different states, bound and liberated, of the same conscious being,—for the second Unborn has descended into the enjoyment of Nature and withdrawn from her; the other verse brings out what we would not gather from the former, that in its higher status of unity the self is forever free, inactive, unattached, though it descends in its lower being into the multiplicity of the creatures of Prakriti and withdraws from it by reversion in any individual creature to the higher status. This theory of the double status of the one conscious soul opens a door; but the process of the multiplicity of the One is still obscure.

To these two the Gita, developing the thought of other passages in the Upanishads,[1] adds yet another, the supreme, the Purushottama, the highest Purusha, whose greatness all this creation is. Thus, there are three, the Kshara, the Akshara, the Uttama. Kshara, the mobile, the mutable is Nature, svabhava, it is the various becoming of the soul; the Purusha here is the multiplicity of the divine Being; it is the Purusha multiple not apart from, but in Prakriti. Akshara, the immobile, the immutable, is the silent and inactive self, it is the unity of the divine Being, Witness of Nature, but not involved in its movement; it is the inactive Purusha free from Prakriti and her works. The Uttama is the Lord, the supreme Brahman, the supreme Self, who possesses both the immutable unity and the mobile multiplicity. It is by a large mobility and action of His nature, His energy, His will, and power, that He manifests Himself in the world and by a greater stillness and immobility of His being that He is aloof from it; yet is He as Purushottama above both the aloofness from Nature and the attachment to Nature. This idea of the Purushottama, though continually implied in the Upanishads, is disengaged, and definitely brought out by the Gita and has exercised a powerful influence on the later developments of the Indian religious consciousness. It is the foundation of the highest Bhakti yoga which claims to exceed the rigid definitions of monistic philosophy; it is at the back of the philosophy of the devotional Puranas.

The Gita is not content, either, to abide within the Sankhya analysis of Prakriti; for that makes room only for the ego-sense and not for the multiple Purusha, which is there not a part of Prakriti, but separate from her. The Gita affirms on the contrary

---

1 Purusah . . . aksarat paratah parah, — although the Akshara is supreme, there is a ... ..supreme Purusha higher than it, says the Upanishad.

that the Lord by His nature becomes the Jiva. How is that possible since there are only the twenty-four principles of the cosmic Energy and no others? Yes, says the divine Teacher in effect, that is a perfectly valid account for the apparent operations of the cosmic Prakriti with its three gunas and the relation attributed to Purusha and Prakriti there is also quite valid and of great use for the practical purposes of the involution and the withdrawal. But this is only the lower Prakriti of the three modes, the inconscient, the apparent; there is a higher, a supreme, a conscient and divine Nature, and it is that which has become the individual soul, the Jiva. In the lower nature each being appears as the ego, in the higher he is the individual Purusha. In other words, multiplicity is part of the spiritual nature of the One. This individual soul is myself, in the creation it is a partial manifestation of me, mamaiva amsah, and it possesses all my powers; it is witness, giver of the sanction, upholder, knower, lord. It descends into the lower nature and thinks itself bound by action, so to enjoy the lower being: it can draw back and know itself as the passive Purusha free from all action. It can rise above the three gunas and, liberated from the bondage of action, yet possess action, even as I do myself, and by adoration of the Purushottama and union with him it can enjoy wholly its divine Nature.

Such is the analysis, not confining itself to the apparent cosmic process but penetrating into the occult secrets of super-conscious Nature, uttamam rahasyam, by which the Gita founds its synthesis of Vedanta, Sankhya and Yoga, its synthesis of knowledge, works and devotion. By the pure Sankhya alone the combining of works and liberation is contradictory and impossible. By pure Monism alone the permanent continuation of works as a part of Yoga and the indulgence of devotion after perfect knowledge and liberation and union are attained, become impossible or at least irrational and otiose. The Sankhya knowledge of the Gita dissipates and the Yoga system of the Gita triumphs over all these obstacles.

IX

SANKHYA, YOGA AND VEDANTA

The Whole object of the first six chapters of the Gita is to synthetize in a large frame of Vedantic truth the two methods, ordinarily supposed to be diverse and even opposite, of the Sankhyas and the Yogins. The Sankhya is taken as the starting-point and the basis; but it is from the beginning and with a progressively increasing emphasis permeated with the ideas and methods of Yoga and remoulded in its spirit. The practical difference, as it seems to have presented itself to the religious minds of that day, lay first in this that Sankhya proceeded by knowledge and through the Yoga of the intelligence, while Yoga proceeded by works and the transformation of the active consciousness and, secondly,—a corollary of this first distinction,—that Sankhya led to entire passivity and the renunciation of works, sannyasa, while Yoga held to be quite sufficient the inner renunciation of desire, the purification of the subjective principle which leads to action and the turning of works Godwards, towards the divine existence and towards liberation. Yet both had the same aim, the transcendence of birth and of this terrestrial existence and the union of the human soul with the Highest. This at least is the difference as it is presented to us by the Gita.

The difficulty which Arjuna feels in understanding any possible synthesis of these oppositions is an indication of the hard line that was driven in between these two systems in the normal ideas of the time. The Teacher sets out by reconciling works and the Yoga of the intelligence: the latter, he says, is far superior to mere works; it is by the Yoga of the Buddhi, by knowledge raising man out of the ordinary human mind and its desires into the purity and equality of the Brahmic condition free from all desire that works can be made acceptable. Yet are works a means of salvation but works thus purified by knowledge.

Filled with the notions of the then prevailing culture, misled by the emphasis which the Teacher lays upon the ideas proper to Vedantic Sankhya, conquest of the senses, withdrawal from mind into the Self, ascent into the Brahmic condition, extinction of our lower personality in the Nirvana of impersonality,—for the ideas proper to Yoga are as yet subordinated and largely held back,—Arjuna is perplexed and asks, "If thou holdest the intelligence to be greater than works, why then dost thou appoint me to a terrible work? Thou seemest to bewilder my intelligence with a confused and mingled speech; tell me then decisively that one thing by which I may attain to my soul's weal."

In answer Krishna affirms that the Sankhya goes by knowledge and renunciation, the Yoga by works; but the real renunciation is impossible without Yoga, without works done as a sacrifice, done with equality and without desire of the fruit, with the perception that it is Nature which does the actions and not the soul; but immediately afterwards he declares that the sacrifice of knowledge is the highest, all work finds its consummation in knowledge, by the fire of knowledge all works are burnt up; therefore by Yoga works are renounced and their bondage overcome for the man who is in possession of his Self. Again, Arjuna is perplexed; here are desireless works, the principle of Yoga and renunciation of works, the principle of Sankhya, put together side by side as if part of one method, yet there is no evident reconciliation between them. For the kind of reconciliation which the Teacher has already given,—in outward inaction to see action still persisting and in apparent action to see a real inaction since the soul has renounced its illusion of the worker and given up works into the hands of the Master of sacrifice,—is for the practical mind of Arjuna too slight, too subtle and expressed almost in riddling words; he has not caught their sense or at least not penetrated into their spirit and reality. Therefore, he asks again, "Thou declarest to me the renunciation of works, O Krishna, and again thou declarest to me Yoga; which one of these is the better way, that tell me with a clear decisiveness."

The answer is important, for it puts the whole distinction Twofold, says Krishna, is the self-application of the soul by which it enters into the Brahmic condition: "that of the Sankhyas by the Yoga of knowledge, that of the Yogins by the Yoga of works." This identification of Sankhya with Jnana yoga and of Yoga with the way of works is interesting; for it shows that quite a different order of ideas prevailed at that time from those we now possess as the result of the great Vedantic development of Indian thought, subsequent evidently to the composition of the Gita, by which the other Vedic philosophies fell into desuetude as practical methods of liberation. To justify the language of the Gita we must suppose that at that time it was the Sankhya method which was very commonly[1] adopted by those who followed the path of knowledge. Subsequently, with the spread of Buddhism, the Sankhya method of knowledge must have been much overshadowed by the Buddhistic. Buddhism, like the Sankhya non-Theistic and anti-Monistic, laid stress on the impermanence of the results of the cosmic energy, which it presented not as Prakriti but as Karma because the Buddhists admitted neither the Vedantic Brahman nor the inactive Soul of the Sankhyas, and it made the recognition of this impermanence by the discriminating mind its means of

1 The systems of the Puranas and Tantras are full of the ideas of the Sankhya, though subordinated to the Vedantic idea and mingled with many others.

liberation. When the re-action against Buddhism arrived, it took up not the old Sankhya notion, but the Vedantic form popularized by Shankara who replaced the Buddhistic impermanence by the cognate Vedantic idea of illusion, Maya, and the Buddhistic idea of Non-Being, indefinable Nirvana, a negative Absolute, by the opposite and yet cognate Vedantic idea of the indefinable Being, Brahman, an ineffably positive Absolute in which all feature and action and energy cease because in That they never really existed and are mere illusions of the mind. It is the method of Shankara based upon these concepts of his philosophy, it is the renunciation of life as an illusion of which we ordinarily think when we speak now of the Yoga of knowledge. But in the time of the Gita Maya was evidently not yet quite the master word of the Vedantic philosophy, nor had it, at least with any decisive clearness, the connotation which Shankara brought out of it with such a luminous force and distinctness; for in the Gita there is little talk of Maya and much of Prakriti and, even, the former word is used as little more than an equivalent of the latter but only in its inferior status; it is the lower Prakriti of the three gunas, traigunyamayimaya. Prakriti, not illusive Maya, is in the teaching of the Gita the effective cause of cosmic existence.

Still, whatever the precise distinctions of their metaphysical ideas, the practical difference between the Sankhya and Yoga as developed by the Gita is the same as that which now exists between the Vedantic Yogas of knowledge and of works and the practical results of the difference are also the same. The Sankhya proceeded like the Vedantic Yoga of knowledge by the Buddhi, by the discriminating intelligence; it arrived by reflective thought, vicara, at right discrimination, viveka, of the true nature of the soul and of the imposition on it of the works of Prakriti through attachment and identification, just as the Vedantic method arrives by the same means at the right discrimination of the true nature of the Self and of the imposition on it of cosmic appearances by mental illusion which leads to egoistic identification and attachment. In the Vedantic method Maya ceases for the soul by its return to its true and eternal status as the oneself, the Brahman, and the cosmic action disappears; in the Sankhya method the working of the gunas falls to rest by the return of the soul to its true and eternal status as the inactive Purusha and the cosmic action ends. The Brahman of the Mayavadins is silent, immutable, and inactive; so too is the Purusha of the Sankhya; therefore, for both ascetic renunciation of life and works is a necessary means of liberation. But for the Yoga of the Gita, as for the Vedantic Yoga of works, action is not only a preparation but itself the means of liberation; and it is the justice of this view which the Gita seeks to bring out with such an unceasing force and insistence,—an insistence, unfortunately, which could not prevail in India against the tremendous tide of Buddhism,[2] was lost afterwards in the intensity of ascetic illusionism and the fervour of world-shunning saints and devotees and is only now beginning to exercise its real and salutary influence on the Indian mind. Renunciation is indispensable, but the true renunciation is the inner rejection of desire and egoism; without that the outer physical abandoning of works is a thing unreal and ineffective, with it, it ceases even to be necessary, although it is not forbidden. Knowledge is essential, there is no higher force for liberation, but works with knowledge are also needed; by the union of knowledge and works the soul dwells entirely in the Brahmic status not only in repose and inactive calm, but in the very midst and stress and violence of action. Devotion is all-important, but works with devotion are also important; by the union of knowledge, devotion and works the soul is taken up into the highest status of the Ishwara to dwell

2 At the same time the Gita seems to have largely influenced Mahayanist Buddhism and texts are taken bodily from it into the Buddhist Scriptures. It may therefore have helped largely to turn Buddhism, originally a school of quietistic and illuminated ascetics, into that religion of meditative devotion and compassionate action which has so powerfully influenced Asiatic culture.

there in the Purushottama who is master at once of the eternal spiritual calm and the eternal cosmic activity. This is the synthesis of the Gita.

But, apart from the distinction between the Sankhya way of knowledge and the Yoga way of works, there was another and similar opposition in the Vedanta itself, and this also the Gita has to deal with, to correct and to fuse into its large restatement of the Aryan spiritual culture. This was the distinction between Karmakanda and Jnanakanda, between the original thought that led to the philosophy of the Purva Mimansa, the Vedavada, and that which led to the philosophy of the Uttara Mimansa,[3] the Brahmavada, between those who dwelt in the tradition of the Vedic hymns and the Vedic sacrifice and those who put these aside as a lower knowledge and laid stress on the lofty metaphysical knowledge which emerges from the Upanishads.

For the pragmatic mind of the Vedavadins the Aryan religion of the Rishis meant the strict performance of the Vedic sacrifices and the use of the sacred Vedic mantras in order to possess all human desires in this world, wealth, progeny, victory, every kind of good fortune, and the joys of immortality in Paradise beyond. For the idealism of the Brahmavadins this was only a preliminary preparation and the real object of man, true purusartha, began with his turning to the knowledge of the Brahman which would give him the true immortality of an ineffable spiritual bliss far beyond the lower joys of this world or of any inferior heaven. Whatever may have been the true and original sense of the Veda, this was the distinction which had long established itself and with which therefore the Gita has to deal.

Almost the first word of the synthesis of works and knowledge

---

3 Jaimini's idea of liberation is the eternal Brahmaloka in which the soul that has come to know Brahman still possesses a divine body and divine enjoyments. For the Gita the Brahmaloka is not liberation; the soul must pass beyond to the supracosmic status.

is a strong, almost a violent censure and repudiation of the Vedavada, "this flowery word which they declare who have not clear discernment, devoted to the creed of the Veda, whose creed is that there is nothing else, souls of desire, seekers of Paradise,—it gives the fruits of the works of birth, it is multifarious with specialties of rites, it is directed to enjoyment and lordship as its goal." The Gita even seems to go on to attack the Veda itself which, though it has been practically cast aside, is still to Indian sentiment intangible, inviolable, the sacred origin and authority for all its philosophy and religion. "The action of the three gunas is the subject matter of the Veda; but do thou become free from the triple guna, O Arjuna." The Vedas in the widest terms, "all the Vedas",—which might well include the Upanishads also and seems to include them, for the general term Sruti is used later on,—are declared to be unnecessary for the man who knows. "As much use as there is in a well with water in flood on every side, so much is there in all the Vedas for the Brahmin who has the knowledge." Nay, the Scriptures are even a stumbling-block; for the letter of the Word— perhaps because of its conflict of texts and its various and mutually dissentient interpretations—bewilders the understanding, which can only find certainty and concentration by the light within. "When thy intelligence shall cross beyond the whorl of delusion, then shalt thou become indifferent to Scripture heard or that which thou hast yet to hear, gantasi nirvedam srotavyasya srutasya ca. When thy intelligence which is bewildered by the Sruti, srutivipratipanna, shall stand unmoving and stable in Samadhi, then shalt thou attain to Yoga." So offensive is all this to conventional religious sentiment that attempts are naturally made by the convenient and indispensable human faculty of text-twisting to put a different sense on some of these verses, but the meaning is plain and hangs together from beginning to end. It is confirmed and emphasized by a subsequent passage in which the knowledge of the knower is described as passing beyond the range of Veda and Upanishad, **sabdabrahmativartate.**

Let us see, however, what all this means; for we may be sure that a synthetic and catholic system like the Gita's will not treat such important parts of the Aryan culture in a spirit of mere negation and repudiation. The Gita has to synthetize the Yoga doctrine of liberation by works and the Sankhya doctrine of liberation by knowledge; it has to fuse karma with jnana. It has at the same time to synthetize the Purusha and Prakriti idea common to Sankhya and Yoga with the Brahmavada of the current Vedanta in which the Purusha, Deva, Ishwara,—supreme Soul, God, Lord,—of the Upanishads all became merged in the one all-swallowing concept of the immutable Brahman; and it has to bring out again from its overshadowing by that concept but not with any denial of it the Yoga idea of the Lord or Ishwara. It has too its own luminous thought to add, the crown of its synthetic system, the doctrine of the Purushottama and of the triple Purusha for which, though the idea is there, no precise and indisputable authority can be easily found in the Upanishads, and which seems indeed at first sight to be in contradiction with that text of the Sruti where only two Purushas are recognized. Moreover, in synthetizing works and knowledge it has to take account not only of the opposition of Yoga and Sankhya, but of the opposition of works to knowledge in Vedanta itself, where the connotation of the two words and therefore their point of conflict is not quite the same as the point of the Sankhya-Yoga opposition. It is not surprising at all, one may observe in passing, that with the conflict of so many philosophical schools all founding themselves on the texts of the Veda and Upanishads, the Gita should describe the understanding as being perplexed and confused, led in different directions by the Sruti, srutivipratipanna. What battles are even now delivered by Indian pundits and metaphysicians over the meaning of the ancient texts and to what different conclusions they lead! The understanding may well get disgusted and indifferent, gantasi nirvedam, refuse to hear any more texts new or old, srotavyasya srutasya ca and go into itself to discover the truth in the light of a deeper and inner and direct experience.

In the first six chapters the Gita lays a large foundation for its synthesis of works and knowledge, its synthesis of Sankhya, Yoga and Vedanta. But first it finds that karma, works, has a particular sense in the language of the Vedantins; it means the Vedic sacrifices and ceremonies or at most that and the ordering of life according to the Grihyasutras in which these rites are the most important part, the religious kernel of the life. By works the Vedantins understood these religious works, the sacrificial system, the yajna, full of a careful order, vidhi, of exact and complicated rites, kriya-visesa-bahulam. But in Yoga works had a much wider significance. The Gita insists on this wider significance; in our conception of spiritual activity all works have to be included, sarva-karmani. At the same time, it does not, like Buddhism, reject the idea of the sacrifice, it prefers to uplift and enlarge it. Yes, it says in effect, not only is sacrifice, yajna, the most important part of life, but all life, all works should be regarded as sacrifice, are yajna, though by the ignorant they are performed without the higher knowledge and by the most ignorant not in the true order, avidhi-purvakam. Sacrifice is the very condition of life; with sacrifice as their eternal companion the Father of creatures created the peoples. But the sacrifices of the Vedavadins are offerings of desire directed towards material rewards, desire eager for the result of works, desire looking to a larger enjoyment in Paradise as immortality and highest salvation. This the system of the Gita cannot admit; for that in its very inception starts with the renunciation of desire, with its rejection and destruction as the enemy of the soul. The Gita does not deny the validity even of the Vedic sacrificial works; it admits them, it admits that by these means one may get enjoyment here and Paradise beyond; it is I myself, says the divine Teacher, who accept these sacrifices and to whom they are offered, I who give these fruits in the form of the gods since so men choose to approach me. But this is not the true road, nor is the enjoyment of Paradise the liberation and fulfilment which man has to seek. It is the ignorant who worship the gods, not knowing whom they are worshipping ignorantly in these divine forms; for they are worshipping, though in ignorance, the One, the Lord, the only Deva, and it is he who accepts their offering. To that Lord must the sacrifice be offered, the true sacrifice of all the life's energies and activities, with devotion, without desire, for His sake and for the welfare of the peoples. It is because the Vedavada obscures this truth and with its tangle of ritual ties man down to the action of the three gunas that it has to be so severely censured and put roughly aside; but its central idea is not destroyed; transfigured and uplifted, it is turned into a most important part of the true spiritual experience and of the method of liberation.

The Vedantic idea of knowledge does not present the same difficulties. The Gita takes it over at once and completely and throughout the six chapters quietly substitutes the still immutable Brahman of the Vedantins, the One without a second immanent in all cosmos, for the still immutable but multiple Purusha of the Sankhyas. It accepts throughout these chapters' knowledge and realization of the Brahman as the most important, the indispensable means of liberation, even while it insists on desireless works as an essential part of knowledge. It accepts equally Nirvana of the ego in the infinite equality of the immutable, impersonal Brahman as essential to liberation; it practically identifies this extinction with the Sankhya return of the inactive immutable Purusha upon itself when it emerges out of identification with the actions of Prakriti; it combines and fuses the language of the Vedanta with the language of the Sankhya, as had already indeed been done by certain of the Upanishads.[4] But still there is a defect in the Vedantic position which has to be overcome. We may, perhaps, conjecture that at this time the Vedanta had not yet redeveloped the later theistic tendencies which in the Upanishads are already present as an element, but not so prominent as in the Vaishnava philosophies of the later Vedantins where they become indeed not only prominent but paramount. We may take it that the orthodox

4 Especially the Swetaswatara.

Vedanta was, at any rate in its main tendencies, pantheistic at the basis, monistic at the summit.[5] It knew of the Brahman, one without a second; it knew of the Gods, Vishnu, Shiva, Brahma and the rest, who all resolve themselves into the Brahman; but the one supreme Brahman as the one Ishwara, Purusha, Deva—words often applied to it in the Upanishads and justifying to that extent, yet passing beyond the Sankhya and the theistic conceptions—was an idea that had fallen from its pride of place;[6] the names could only be applied in a strictly logical Brahmavada to subordinate or inferior phases of the Brahman-idea. The Gita proposes not only to restore the original equality of these names and therefore of the conceptions they indicate, but to go a step farther. The Brahman in its supreme and not in any lower aspect has to be presented as the Purusha with the lower Prakriti for its Maya, so to synthetise thoroughly Vedanta and Sankhya, and as Ishwara, so to synthetise thoroughly both with Yoga; but the Gita is going to represent the Ishwara, the Purushottama, as higher even than the still and immutable Brahman and the loss of ego in the impersonal comes in at the beginning as only a great initial and necessary step towards union with the Purushottama. For the Purushottama is the supreme Brahman. It therefore passes boldly beyond the Veda and the Upanishads as they were taught by their best authorized exponents and affirms a teaching of its own which it has developed from them, but which may not be capable of being fitted in within the four corners of their meaning as ordinarily interpreted by the Vedantins.[7] In fact without this

---

5 The pantheistic formula is that God and the All are one, the monistic adds that God or Brahman alone exists, and the cosmos is only an illusory appearance or else a real but partial manifestation.

6 This is a little doubtful, but we may say at least that there was a strong tendency in that direction of which Shankara's philosophy was the last culmination.

7 In reality the idea of the Purushottama is already announced in the Upanishads, though in a more scattered fashion than in the Gita and,

free and synthetic dealing with the letter of the Scripture a work of large synthesis in the then state of conflict between numerous schools and with the current methods of Vedic exegesis would have been impossible.

The Gita in later chapters speaks highly of the Veda and the Upanishads. They are divine Scriptures; they are the Word. The Lord himself is the knower of Veda and the author of Vedanta, vedavid vedantakrt; the Lord is the one object of knowledge in all the Vedas, sarvair vedair aham eva vedyah, a language which implies that the word Veda means the book of knowledge and that these Scriptures deserve their appellation. The Purushottama from his high supremacy above the Immutable and the mutable has extended himself in the world and in the Veda. Still the letter of the Scripture binds and confuses, as the apostle of Christianity warned his disciples when he said that the letter killeth and it is the spirit that saves; and there is a point beyond which the utility of the Scripture itself ceases. The real source of knowledge is the Lord in the heart; "I am seated in the heart of every man and from me is knowledge," says the Gita; the Scripture is only a verbal form of that inner Veda, of that self-luminous Reality, it is sabdabrahma′: the mantra, says the Veda, has risen from the heart, from the secret place where is the seat of the truth, sadanad rtasya, guhayam. That origin is its sanction; but still the infinite Truth is greater than its word. Nor shall you say of any Scripture that it alone is all-sufficient, and no other truth can be admitted, as the Vedavadins said of the Veda, nanyad astıti vadinah. This is a saving and liberating word which must be applied to all the Scriptures of the world. Take all the Scriptures that are or have been, Bible and Koran and the books of the Chinese, Veda and

---

as in the Gita, the Supreme Brahman or Supreme Purusha is constantly described as containing in himself the opposition of the Brahman with qualities and without qualities, nirguno gunı. He is not one of these things to the exclusion of the other which seems to our intellect to be its contrary.

Upanishads and Purana and Tantra and Shastra and the Gita itself and the sayings of thinkers and sages, prophets, and Avatars, still you shall not say that there is nothing else or that the truth your intellect cannot find there is not true because you cannot find it there. That is the limited thought of the sectarian, or the composite thought of the eclectic religionist, not the untrammelled truth-seeking of the free and illumined mind and God-experienced soul. Heard or unheard before, that always is the truth which is seen by the heart of man in its illumined depths or heard within from the Master of all knowledge, the knower of the eternal Veda.

X

THE YOGA OF THE INTELLIGENT WILL

I have had to deviate in the last two essays and to drag the reader with me into the arid tracts of metaphysical dogma,—however cursorily and with a very insufficient and superficial treatment,—so that we might understand why the Gita follows the peculiar line of development it has taken, working out first a partial truth with only subdued hints of its deeper meaning, then returning upon its hints and bringing out their significance until it rises to its last great suggestion, its supreme mystery which it does not work out at all, but leaves to be lived out, as the later ages of Indian spirituality tried to live it out in great waves of love, of surrender, of ecstasy. Its eye is always on its synthesis and all its strains are the gradual preparation of the mind for its high closing note.

I have declared to you the poise of a self-liberating intelligence in Sankhya, says the divine Teacher to Arjuna. I will now declare to you another poise in Yoga. You are shrinking from the results of your works; you desire other results and turn from your right path in life because it does not lead you to them. But this idea of works and their result, desire of result as the motive, the work as a means for the satisfaction of desire, is the bondage of the ignorant who know not what works are, nor their true source, nor their real operation, nor their high utility. My Yoga will free you from all bondage of the soul to its works, karma-bandham prahasyasi. You are afraid of many things, afraid of sin, afraid of suffering, afraid of hell and punishment, afraid of God, afraid of this world, afraid of the hereafter, afraid of yourself. What is it that you are not afraid of at this moment, you the Aryan fighter, the world's chief hero? But this is the great fear which besieges humanity, its fear of sin and suffering now and hereafter, its fear in a world of whose true nature it is ignorant of a God who's true being also it has not seen and whose cosmic purpose it does not understand. My Yoga will deliver you from the great fear and even a little of it will bring deliverance. When you have once set out on this path, you will find that no step is lost; every least movement will be a gain; you will find there no obstacle that can baulk you of your advance. A bold and absolute promise and one to which the fearful and hesitating mind beset and stumbling in all its paths cannot easily lend an assured trust; nor is the large and full truth of it apparent unless with these first words of the message of the Gita we read also the last, "Abandon all laws of conduct and take refuge in Me alone; I will deliver you from all sin and evil; do not grieve."

But it is not with this deep and moving word of God to man, but rather with the first necessary rays of light on the path, directed not like that to the soul, but to the intellect, that the exposition begins. Not the Friend and Lover of man speaks first, but the guide and teacher who has to remove from him his ignorance of his true self and of the nature of the world and of the springs of his own action. For it is because he acts ignorantly, with a wrong intelligence and therefore a wrong will in these matters, that man is or seems to be bound by his works; otherwise works are no bondage to the free soul. It is because of this wrong intelligence that he has hope and fear, wrath and grief and transient joy; otherwise works are possible with a perfect serenity and freedom. Therefore, it is the Yoga of the buddhi, the intelligence, that is first enjoined on Arjuna. To act with right intelligence and, therefore, a right will, fixed in the One, aware of the oneself in all and acting out of its equal serenity, not running about in different directions under the thousand impulses of our superficial mental self, is the Yoga of the intelligent will.

There are, says the Gita, two types of intelligence in the human being. The first is concentrated, poised, one, homogeneous, directed singly towards the Truth; unity is its characteristic, concentrated fixity is its very being. In the other there is no single will, no unified intelligence, but only an endless number of ideas many-branching, coursing about, that is to say, in this or that direction in pursuit of the desires which are offered to it by life and by the environment. Buddhi, the word used, means, properly speaking, the mental power of understanding but it is evidently used by the Gita in a large philosophic sense for the whole action of the discriminating and deciding mind which determines both the direction and use of our thoughts and the direction and use of our acts; thought, intelligence, judgment, perceptive choice and aim are all included in its functioning: for the characteristic of the unified intelligence is not only concentration of the mind that knows, but especially concentration of the mind that decides and persists in the decision, vyavasaya, while the sign of the dissipated intelligence is not so much even discursiveness of the ideas and perceptions as discursiveness of the aims and desires, therefore of the will. Will, then, and knowledge are the two functions of the Buddhi. The unified intelligent will is fixed in the enlightened soul, it is concentrated in inner self-knowledge; the many-branching and multifarious, busied with many things, careless of the one thing needful is on the contrary subject to the restless and discursive action of the mind, dispersed in outward life and works and their fruits. “Works are far inferior,” says the Teacher, “to Yoga of the intelligence; desire rather refuge in the intelligence; poor and wretched souls are they who make the fruit of their works the object of their thoughts and activities.”

We must remember the psychological order of the Sankhya

which the Gita accepts. On one side there is the Purusha, the soul calm, inactive, immutable, one, not evolutive; on the other side there is Prakriti or Nature-force inert without the conscious Soul, active but only by juxtaposition to that consciousness, by contact with it, as we would say, not so much one at first as indeterminate, triple in its qualities, capable of evolution and involution. The contact of soul and nature generates the play of subjectivity and objectivity which is our experience of being what is to us the subjective first evolves, because the soul-consciousness is the first cause, inconscient Nature-force only the second and dependent cause but still it is Nature and not Soul which supplies the instruments of our subjectivity. First in order come Buddhi, discriminative or determinative power evolving out of Nature-force, and its subordinate power of self-discriminating ego. Then as a secondary evolution there arises out of these the power which seizes the discriminations of objects, sense-mind, or Manas,—we must record the Indian names because the corresponding English words are not real equivalents. As a tertiary evolution out of sense-mind we have the specializing organic senses, ten in number, five of perception, five of action; next the powers of each sense of perception, sound, form, scent, etc., which give their value to objects for the mind and make things what they are to our subjectivity,—and, as the substantial basis of these, the primary conditions of the objects of sense, the five elements of ancient philosophy or rather elementary conditions of Nature, panca bhuta, which constitute objects by their various combination.

Reflected in the pure consciousness of Purusha these degrees and powers of Nature-force become the material of our impure subjectivity, impure because its action is dependent on the perceptions of the objective world and on their subjective reactions. Buddhi, which is simply the determinative power that determines all inertly out of indeterminate inconscient Force, takes for us the form of intelligence and will. Manas, the inconscient force which seizes Nature's discriminations by objective action and reaction and grasps at them by attraction, becomes sense-perception and desire, the two crude terms or degradations of intelligence and will,—becomes the sense-mind sensational, emotive, volitional in the lower sense of wish, hope, longing, passion, vital impulsion, all the deformations (vikara) of will. The senses become the instruments of sense-mind, the perceptive five of our sense-knowledge, the active five of our impulsions and vital habits, mediators between the subjective and objective; the rest are the objects of our consciousness, visayas of the senses.

This order of evolution seems contrary to that which we perceive as the order of the material evolution; but if we remember that even Buddhi is in itself an inert action of inconscient Nature and that there is certainly in this sense an inconscient will and intelligence, a discriminative and determinative force even in the atom, if we observe the crude inconscient stuff of sensation, emotion, memory, impulsion in the plant and in the subconscient forms of existence, if we look at these powers of Nature-force assuming the forms of our subjectivity in the evolving consciousness of animal and man, we shall see that the Sankhya system squares well enough with all that modern enquiry has elicited by its observation of material Nature. In the evolution of the soul back from Prakriti towards Purusha, the reverse order has to be taken to the original Nature-evolution and that is how the Upanishads and the Gita following and almost quoting the Upanishads state the ascending order of our subjective powers. "Supreme, they say," beyond their objects "are the senses, supreme over the senses the mind, supreme over the mind the intelligent will: that which is supreme over the intelligent will, is he,"—is the conscious self, the Purusha. Therefore, says the Gita, it is this Purusha, this supreme cause of our subjective life which we have to understand and become aware of by the intelligence; in that we have to fix our will. So, holding our lower subjective self in Nature firmly poised and stilled by means of the greater really conscient self, we can destroy the restless ever-active enemy of our peace and self-mastery, the mind's desire.

For evidently there are two possibilities of the action of the intelligent will. It may take its downward and outward orientation towards a discursive action of the perceptions and the will in the triple play of Prakriti, or it may take its upward and inward orientation towards a settled peace and equality in the calm and immutable purity of the conscious silent soul no longer subject to the distractions of Nature. In the former alternative the subjective being is at the mercy of the objects of sense, it lives in the outward contact of things. That life is the life of desire. For the senses excited by their objects create a restless or often violent disturbance, a strong or even headlong outward movement towards the seizure of these objects and their enjoyment and they carry away the sense-mind, "as the winds carry away a ship upon the sea"; the mind subjected to the emotions, passions, longings, impulsions awakened by this outward movement of the senses carries away similarly the intelligent will, which loses therefore its power of calm discrimination and mastery. Subjection of the soul to the confused play of the three gunas of Prakriti in their eternal entangled twining and wrestling, ignorance, a false, sensuous, objective life of the soul, enslavement to grief and wrath and attachment and passion, are the results of the downward trend of the buddhi,—the troubled life of the ordinary, unenlightened, undisciplined man. Those who like the Vedavadins make sense-enjoyment the object of action and its fulfilment the highest aim of the soul, are misleading guides. The inner subjective self-delight independent of objects is our true aim and the high and wide poise of our peace and liberation.

Therefore, it is the upward and inward orientation of the intelligent will that we must resolutely choose with a settled concentration and perseverance, vyavasaya; we must fix it firmly in the calm self-knowledge of the Purusha. The first movement must be obviously to get rid of desire which is the whole root of the evil and suffering; and in order to get rid of desire, we must put an end to the cause of desire, the rushing out of the senses to seize and enjoy their objects. We must draw them back when they are inclined thus to rush out, draw them away from their objects,—as the tortoise draws in his limbs into the shell, so these into their source, quiescent in the mind, the mind quiescent in intelligence, the intelligence quiescent in the soul and its self-knowledge, observing the action of Nature but not subject to it, not desiring anything that the objective life can give.

It is not an external asceticism, the physical renunciation of the objects of sense that I am teaching, suggests Krishna immediately to avoid a misunderstanding which is likely at once to arise. Not the renunciation of the Sankhyas or the austerities of the rigid ascetic with his fasts, his maceration of the body, his attempt to abstain even from food; that is not the self-discipline or the abstinence which I mean, for I speak of an inner withdrawal, a renunciation of desire. The embodied soul, having a body, has to support it normally by food for its normal physical action; by abstention from food, it simply removes from itself the physical contact with the object of sense, but does not get rid of the inner relation which makes that contact hurtful. It retains the pleasure of the sense in the object, the rasa, the liking and disliking,—for rasa has two sides; the soul must, on the contrary, be capable of enduring the physical contact without suffering inwardly this sensuous reaction. Otherwise, there is nivrtti, cessation of the object, visaya vinivartante, but no subjective cessation, no nivrtti of the mind; but the senses are of the mind, subjective, and subjective cessation of the rasa is the only real sign of mastery. But how is this desireless contact with objects, this unsensuous use of the senses possible? It is possible, param drstva, by the vision of the supreme, — param, the Soul, the Purusha,—and by living in the Yoga, in union or oneness of the whole subjective being with that, through the Yoga of the intelligence; for the one Soul is calm, satisfied in its own delight, and that delight free from duality can take, once we see this supreme thing in us and fix the mind and will on that, the place of the sensuous object-ridden pleasures and repulsions of the mind. This is the true way of liberation.

Certainly self-discipline, self-control is never easy. All intelligent human beings know that they must exercise some control over themselves, and nothing is more common than this advice to control the senses but ordinarily it is only advised imperfectly and practiced imperfectly in the most limited and insufficient fashion. Even, however, the sage, the man of clear, wise, and discerning soul who really labours to acquire complete self-mastery finds himself hurried and carried away by the senses. That is because the mind naturally lends itself to the senses; it observes the objects of sense with an inner interest, settles upon them and makes them the object of absorbing thought for the intelligence and of strong interest for the will. By that attachment comes, by attachment desire, by desire distress, passion, and anger when the desire is not satisfied or is thwarted or opposed and by passion the soul is obscured, the intelligence and will forget to see and be seated in the calm observing soul; there is a fall from the memory of one's true self, and by that lapse the intelligent will is also obscured, destroyed even. For, for the time being, it no longer exists to our memory of ourselves, it disappears in a cloud of passion; we become passion, wrath, grief and cease to be self and intelligence and will. This then must be prevented and all the senses brought utterly under control; for only by an absolute control of the senses can the wise and calm intelligence be firmly established in its proper seat.

This cannot be done perfectly by the act of the intelligence itself, by a merely mental self-discipline; it can only be done by Yoga with something which is higher than itself and in which calm and self-mastery are inherent. And this Yoga can only arrive at its success by devoting, by consecrating, by giving up the whole self to the Divine, "to Me", says Krishna; for the Liberator is within us, but it is not our mind, nor our intelligence, nor our personal will,—they are only instruments. It is the Lord in whom, as we are told in the end, we have utterly to take refuge. And for that we must at first make him the object of our whole being and keep in soul-contact with him. This is the sense of the phrase "he must sit firm in Yoga, wholly given up to Me"; but as yet it is the merest passing hint after the manner of the Gita, three words only which contain in seed the whole gist of the highest secret yet to be developed. Yukta asıta matparah.

If this is done, then it becomes possible to move among the objects of sense, in contact with them, acting on them, but with the senses entirely under the control of the subjective self,—not at the mercy of the objects and their contacts and re-actions,—and that self again obedient to the highest self, the Purusha. Then, free from reactions, the senses will be delivered from the affections of liking and disliking, escape the duality of positive and negative desire, and calm, peace, clearness, happy tranquility, atmaprasada, will settle upon the man. That clear tranquility is the source of the soul's felicity; all grief begins to lose its power of touching the tranquil soul; the intelligence is rapidly established in the peace of the self; suffering is destroyed. It is this calm, desireless, griefless fixity of the buddhi in self-poise and self-knowledge to which the Gita gives the name of Samadhi.

The sign of the man in Samadhi is not that he loses consciousness of objects and surroundings and of his mental and physical self and cannot be recalled to it even by burning or torture of the body,—the ordinary idea of the matter; trance is a particular intensity, not the essential sign. The test is the expulsion of all desires, their inability to get at the mind, and it is the inner state from which this freedom arises, the delight of the soul gathered within itself with the mind equal and still and high-poised above the attractions and repulsions, the alternations of sunshine and storm and stress of the external life. It is drawn inward even when acting outwardly; it is concentrated in self even when gazing out upon things; it is directed wholly to the Divine even when to the outward vision of others busy and preoccupied with the affairs of the world. Arjuna, voicing the average human mind, asks for some outward, physical, practically discernible sign of this great Samadhi; how does such a man speak, how sit, how walk? No such signs can be given, nor does the Teacher attempt to supply them; for the only possible test of its possession is inward and that there are plenty of hostile psychological forces to apply. Equality is the great stamp of the liberated soul and of that equality even the most discernible signs are still subjective. "A man with mind untroubled by sorrows, who has done with desire for pleasures, from whom liking, and wrath and fear have passed away, such is the sage whose understanding has become founded in stability." He is "without the triple action of the qualities of Prakriti, without the dualities, ever based in his true being, without getting or having, possessed of his self." For what getting's and having's has the free soul? Once we are possessed of the Self, we are in possession of all things.

And yet he does not cease from work and action. There is the originality and power of the Gita, that having affirmed this static condition, this superiority to nature, this emptiness even of all that constitutes ordinarily the action of Nature for the liberated soul, it is still able to vindicate for it, to enjoin on it even the continuance of works and thus avoid the great defect of the merely quietistic and ascetic philosophies,—the defect from which we find them today attempting to escape. "Thou hast a right to action, but only to action, never to its fruits; let not the fruits of thy works be thy motive, neither let there be in thee any attachment to inactivity." Therefore, it is not the works practiced with desire by the Vedavadins, it is not the claim for the satisfaction of the restless and energetic mind by a constant activity, the claim made by the practical or the kinetic man, which is here enjoined. "Fixed in Yoga do thy actions, having abandoned attachment, having become equal in failure and success; for it is equality that is meant by Yoga." Action is distressed by the choice between a relative good and evil, the fear of sin and the difficult endeavour towards virtue? But the liberated who has united his reason and will with the Divine, casts away from him even here in this world of dualities both good doing and evil doing; for he rises to a higher law beyond good and evil, founded in the liberty of self-knowledge. Such desireless action can have no decisiveness, no effectiveness, no efficient motive, no large or vigorous creative power? Not so, action done in Yoga is not only the highest but the wisest, the most potent and efficient even for the affairs of the world; for it is informed by the knowledge and will of the Master of works: "Yoga is skill in works." But all action directed towards life leads away from the universal aim of the Yogin which is by common consent to escape from bondage to this distressed and sorrowful human birth? Not so, either; the sages who do works without desire for fruits and in Yoga with the Divine are liberated from the bondage of birth and reach that other perfect status in which there are none of the maladies which afflict the mind and life of a suffering humanity.

The status he reaches is the Brahmic condition; he gets to firm standing in the Brahman, brahmı sthiti. It is a reversal of the whole view, experience, knowledge, values, seeing's of earth-bound creatures. This life of the dualities which is to them their day, their waking, their consciousness, their bright condition of activity and knowledge, is to him a night, a troubled sleep and darkness of the soul; that higher being which is to them a night, a sleep in which all knowledge and will cease, is to the self-mastering sage his waking, his luminous day of true being, knowledge and power. They are troubled and muddy waters disturbed by every little inrush of desire; he is an ocean of wide being and consciousness which is ever being filled, yet ever motionless in its large poise of his soul; all the desires of the world enter into him as waters into the sea, yet he has no desire nor is troubled. For while they are filled with the troubling sense of ego and mine and thine, he is one with the oneself in all and has no "I" or "mine". He acts as others, but he has abandoned all desires and their longings. He attains to the great peace and is not bewildered by the shows of things; he has extinguished his individual ego in the One, lives in that unity and, fixed in that status at his end, can attain to extinction in the Brahman, Nirvana,—not the negative self-annihilation of the Buddhists, but the great immergence of the separate personal self into the vast reality of the one infinite impersonal Existence.

Such, subtly unifying Sankhya, Yoga and Vedanta, is the first foundation of the teaching of the Gita. It is far from being all, but it is the first indispensable practical unity of knowledge and work with a hint already of the third crowning intensest element in the soul's completeness, divine love, and devotion.

XI

WORKS AND SACRIFICE

The Yoga of the intelligent will and its culmination in the Brahmic status, which occupies all the close of the second chapter, contains the seed of much of the teaching of the Gita,—its doctrine of desireless works, of equality, of the rejection of outward renunciation, of devotion to the Divine; but as yet all this is slight and obscure. What is most strongly emphasized as yet is the withdrawal of the will from the ordinary motive of human activities, desire, from man's normal temperament of the sense-seeking thought and will with its passions and ignorance, and from its customary habit of troubled many-branching ideas and wishes to the desireless calm unity and passionless serenity of the Brahmic poise. So much Arjuna has understood. He is not unfamiliar with all this; it is the substance of the current teaching which points man to the path of knowledge and to the renunciation of life and works as his way of perfection. The intelligence withdrawing from sense and desire and human action and turning to the Highest, to the One, to the actionless Purusha, to the immobile, to the featureless Brahman, that surely is the eternal seed of knowledge. There is no room here for works, since works belong to the Ignorance; action is the very opposite of knowledge; its seed is desire, and its fruit is bondage. That is the orthodox philosophical doctrine, and Krishna seems quite to admit it when he says that works are far inferior to the Yoga of the intelligence. And yet works are insisted upon as part of the Yoga; so that there seems to be in this teaching a radical inconsistency. Not only so, for some kind of work no doubt may persist for a while, the minimum, the most inoffensive; but here is a work wholly inconsistent with knowledge, with serenity and with the motionless peace of the self-delighted soul,—a work terrible, even monstrous, a bloody strife, a ruthless battle, a giant massacre. Yet it is this that is enjoined, this that it is sought to justify by the teaching of inner peace and desireless equality and status in the Brahman! Here then is an unreconciled contradiction. Arjuna complains that he has been given a contradictory and confusing doctrine, not the clear, strenuously single road by which the human intelligence can move straight and trenchantly to the supreme good. It is in answer to this objection that the Gita begins at once to develop more clearly its positive and imperative doctrine of Works.

The Teacher first makes a distinction between the two means of salvation on which in this world men can concentrate separately, the Yoga of knowledge, the Yoga of works, the one implying, it is usually supposed, renunciation of works as an obstacle to salvation, the other accepting works as a means of salvation. He does not yet insist strongly on any fusion of them, on any reconciliation of the thought that divides them, but begins by showing that the renunciation of the Sankhyas, the physical renunciation, Sannyasa, is neither the only way, nor at all the better way. Naiskarmya, a calm voidness from works is no doubt that to which the soul, the Purusha has to attain; for it is Prakriti which does the work, and the soul has to rise above involution in the activities of the being and attain to a free serenity and poise watching over the operations of Prakriti, but not affected by them. That, and not cessation of the works of Prakriti, is what is really meant by the soul's naiskarmya. Therefore, it is an error to think that by not engaging in any kind of action this actionless state of the soul can be attained and enjoyed. Mere renunciation of works is not a sufficient, not even quite a proper means for salvation. "Not by abstention from works does a man enjoy actionlessness, nor by mere renunciation (of works) does he attain to his perfection,"—to siddhi, the accomplishment of the aims of his self-discipline by Yoga.

But at least it must be one necessary means, indispensable, imperative? For how, if the works of Prakriti continue, can the soul help being involved in them? How can I fight and yet in my soul not think or feel that I the individual am fighting, not desire victory nor be inwardly touched by defeat? This is the teaching of the Sankhyas that the intelligence of the man who engages in the activities of Nature, is entangled in egoism, ignorance and desire and therefore drawn to action; on the contrary, if the intelligence draws back, then the action must cease with the cessation of the desire and the ignorance. Therefore, the giving up of life and works is a necessary part, an inevitable circumstance, and an indispensable last means of the movement to liberation. This objection of a current logic,—it is not expressed by Arjuna, but it is in his mind as the turn of his subsequent utterances shows,—the Teacher immediately anticipates. No, he says, such renunciation, far from being indispensable, is not even possible. "For none stands even for a moment not doing work; everyone is made to do action helplessly by the modes born of Prakriti." The strong perception of the great cosmic action and the eternal activity and power of the cosmic energy which was so much emphasized afterwards by the teaching of the Tantric Shaktas who even made Prakriti or Shakti superior to Purusha, is a very remarkable feature of the Gita. Although here an undertone, it is still strong enough, coupled with what we might call the theistic and devotional elements of its thought, to bring in that activism which so strongly modifies in its scheme of Yoga the quietistic tendencies of the old metaphysical Vedanta. Man embodied in the natural world cannot cease from action, not for a moment, not for a second; his very existence here is an action; the whole universe is an act of God, mere living even is his movement.

Our physical life, its maintenance, its continuance is a journey, a pilgrimage of the body, sarira-yatra and that cannot be effected without action. But even if a man could leave his body unmaintained, otiose, if he could stand still always like a tree or sit inert like a stone, tisthati, that vegetable or material immobility would not save him from the hands of Nature; he would not be liberated from her workings. For it is not our physical movements and activities alone which are meant by works, by karma; our mental existence also is a great complex action, it is even the greater and more important part of the works of the unresting energy,—subjective cause and determinant of the physical. We have gained nothing if we repress the effect but retain the activity of the subjective cause. The objects of sense are only an occasion for our bondage, the mind's insistence on them is the means, the instrumental cause. A man may control his organs of action and refuse to give them their natural play, but he has gained nothing if his mind continues to remember and dwell upon the objects of sense. Such a man has bewildered him-self with false notions of self-discipline; he has not understood its object or its truth, nor the first principles of his subjective existence; therefore all his methods of self-discipline are false and null.[1] The body's actions, even the mind's actions are nothing in themselves, neither a bondage, nor the first cause of bondage. What is vital is the mighty energy of Nature which will have her way and her play in her great field of mind and life and body; what is dangerous in her, is the power of her three gunas, modes or qualities to confuse and bewilder the intelligence and so obscure the soul. That, as we shall see later, is the whole crux of action and liberation for the Gita. Be free from obscuration and bewilderment by the three gunas and action can

---

1 I cannot think that mithyacara means a hypocrite. How is a man a hypocrite who inflicts on himself so severe and complete a privation? He is mistaken and deluded, vimudhatma and his acara, his formally regulated method of self-discipline, is a false and vain method,—this surely is all that the Gita means.

continue, as it must continue and even the largest, richest, or most enormous and violent action; it does not matter, for nothing then touches the Purusha, the soul has naiskarmya.

But at present the Gita does not proceed to that larger point. Since the mind is the instrumental cause, since inaction is impossible, what is rational, necessary, the right way is a controlled action of the subjective and objective organism. The mind must bring the senses under its control as an instrument of the intelligent will and then the organs of action must be used for their proper office, for action, but for action done as Yoga. But what is the essence of this self-control, what is meant by action done as Yoga, Karmayoga? It is non-attachment; it is to do works without clinging with the mind to the objects of sense and the fruit of the works. Not complete inaction, which is an error, a confusion, a self-delusion, an impossibility, but action full and free done without subjection to sense and passion, desireless and unattached works, are the first secret of perfection. Do action thus self-controlled, says Krishna, niyatam kuru karma tvam: I have said that knowledge, the intelligence, is greater than works, jyayasi karmano buddhih, but I did not mean that inaction is greater than action; the contrary is the truth, karma jyayo akarmanah. For knowledge does not mean renunciation of works, it means equality and non-attachment to desire and the objects of sense; and it means the poise of the intelligent will in the Soul free and high-uplifted above the lower instrumentation of Prakriti and controlling the works of the mind and the senses and body in the power of self-knowledge and the pure objectless self-delight of spiritual realisation, niyatam karma.[2] Buddhiyoga is fulfilled by

2 Again, I cannot accept the current interpretation of niyatam˙ karma as if it meant fixed and formal works and were equivalent to the Vedic nityakarma, the regular works of sacrifice, ceremonial, and the daily rule of Vedic living. Surely, niyata simply takes up the niyamya of the last verse. Krishna makes a statement, "he who controlling the senses by the mind engages with the organs of action in Yoga of action, he excels," manasa niyamya arabhate karmayogam, and he immediately goes on to draw from the statement an

karmayoga; the Yoga of the self-liberating intelligent will finds its full meaning by the Yoga of desireless works. Thus, the Gita founds its teaching of the necessity of desireless works, niskama karma and unites the subjective practice of the Sankhyas— rejecting their merely physical rule—with the practice of Yoga.

But still there is an essential difficulty unsolved. Desire is the ordinary motive of all human actions, and if the soul is free from desire, then there is no farther rationale for action. We may be compelled to do certain works for the maintenance of the body, but even that is a subjection to the desire of the body which we ought to get rid of if we are to attain perfection. But granting that this cannot be done, the only way is to fix a rule for action outside ourselves, not dictated by anything in our subjectivity, the nityakarma of the Vedic rule, the routine of ceremonial sacrifice, daily conduct, and social duty, which the man who seeks liberation may do simply because it is enjoined upon him, without any personal purpose or subjective interest in them, with an absolute indifference to the doing, not because he is compelled by his nature but because it is enjoined by the Shastra. But if the principle of the action is not to be external to the nature but subjective, if the actions even of the liberated and the sage are to be controlled and determined by his nature, svabhava-niyatam, then the only subjective principle of action is desire of whatever kind, lust of the flesh or emotion of the heart or base or noble aim of the mind, but all subject to the gunas of Prakriti. Let us then interpret the niyata karma of the Gita as the nityakarma of the Vedic rule, its kartavya karma or work that has to be done as the Aryan rule of social duty and let us take too its work done as a sacrifice to simply

---

injunction, to sum it up and convert it into a rule. "Do thou do controlled action," niyatam˙ kuru karma tvam: niyatam takes up the niyamya, kuru karma takes up the arabhate karmayogam. Not formal works fixed by an external rule, but desireless works controlled by the liberated buddhi, is the Gita's teaching.

mean these Vedic sacrifices and this fixed social duty performed disinterestedly and without any personal object. This is how the Gita's doctrine of desireless work is often interpreted. But it seems to me that the Gita's teaching is not so crude and simple, not so local, and temporal and narrow as all that. It is large, free, subtle, and profound; it is for all time and for all men, not for a particular age and country. Especially, it is always breaking free from external forms, details, dogmatic notions and going back to principles and the great facts of our nature and our being. It is a work of large philosophic truth and spiritual practicality, not of constrained religious and philosophical formulas and stereotyped dogmas.

The difficulty is this, how, our nature being what it is and desire the common principle of its action, is it possible to institute a really desireless action? For what we call ordinarily disinterested action is not really desireless; it is simply a replacement of certain smaller personal interests by other larger desires which have only the appearance of being impersonal, virtue, country, mankind. All action, moreover, as Krishna insists, is done by the gunas of Prakriti, by our nature; in acting according to the Shastra we are still acting according to our nature,—even if this Shastric action is not, as it usually is, a mere cover for our desires, prejudices, passions, egoisms, our personal, national, sectarian vanities, sentiments, and preferences; but even otherwise, even at the purest, still we obey a choice of our nature, and if our nature were different and the gunas acted on our intelligence and will in some other combination, we would not accept the Shastra, but live according to our pleasure or our intellectual notions or else break free from the social law to live the life of the solitary or the ascetic. We cannot become impersonal by obeying something outside ourselves, for we cannot so get outside ourselves; we can only do it by rising to the highest in ourselves, into our free Soul and Self which is the same and one in all and has therefore no personal interests, to the Divine in our being who possesses

Himself transcendent of cosmos and is therefore not bound by His cosmic works or His individual action. That is what the Gita teaches and desire lessness is only a means to this end, not an aim in itself. Yes, but how is it to be brought about? By doing all works with sacrifice as the only object is the reply of the divine Teacher. "By doing works otherwise than for sacrifice, this world of men is in bondage to works; for sacrifice practice works, O son of Kunti, becoming free from all attachment." It is evident that all works and not merely sacrifice and social duties can be done in this spirit; any action may be done either from the ego-sense narrow or enlarged or for the sake of the Divine. All being and all action of Prakriti exist only for the sake of the Divine; from that it proceeds, by that it endures, to that it is directed. But so long as we are dominated by the ego-sense we cannot perceive or act in the spirit of this truth, but act for the satisfaction of the ego and in the spirit of the ego, otherwise than for sacrifice. Egoism is the knot of the bondage. By acting Godwards, without any thought of ego, we loosen this knot and finally arrive at freedom.

At first, however, the Gita takes up the Vedic statement of the idea of sacrifice and phrases the law of sacrifice in its current terms. This it does with a definite object. We have seen that the quarrel between renunciation and works has two forms, the opposition of Sankhya and Yoga which is already in principle reconciled and the opposition of Vedism and Vedantism which the Teacher has yet to reconcile. The first is a larger statement of the opposition in which the idea of works is general and wide. The Sankhya starts from the notion of the divine status as that of the immutable and inactive Purusha which each soul is in reality and makes an opposition between inactivity of Purusha and activity of Prakriti; so, its logical culmination is cessation of all works. Yoga starts from the notion of the Divine as Ishwara, lord of the operations of Prakriti and therefore superior to them, and its logical culmination is not cessation of works but the soul's superiority to them and freedom even though doing all works.

In the opposition of Vedism and Vedantism works, karma, are restricted to Vedic works and sometimes even to Vedic sacrifice and ritualized works, all else being excluded as not useful to salvation. Vedism of the Mimansakas insisted on them as the means, Vedantism taking its stand on the Upanishads looked on them as only a preliminary belonging to the state of ignorance and in the end to be overpassed and rejected, an obstacle to the seeker of liberation. Vedism worshipped the Devas, the gods, with sacrifice and held them to be the powers who assist our salvation. Vedantism was inclined to regard them as powers of the mental and material world opposed to our salvation (men, says the Upanishad, are the cattle of the gods, who do not desire man to know and be free); it saw the Divine as the immutable Brahman who has to be attained not by works of sacrifice and worship but by knowledge. Works only led to material results and to an inferior Paradise; therefore they have to be renounced.

The Gita resolves this opposition by insisting that the Devas are only forms of the one Deva, the Ishwara, the Lord of all Yoga and worship and sacrifice and austerity, and if it is true that sacrifice offered to the Devas leads only to material results and to Paradise, it is also true that sacrifice offered to the Ishwara leads beyond them to the great liberation. For the Lord and the immutable Brahman are not two different beings, but one and the same Being, and whoever strives towards either, is striving towards that one divine Existence. All works in their totality find their culmination and completeness in the knowledge of the Divine, sarvam karmakhilam partha jnane parisamapyate. They are not an obstacle, but the way to the supreme knowledge.

Thus, this opposition too is reconciled with the help of a large elucidation of the meaning of sacrifice. In fact, its conflict is only a restricted form of the larger opposition between Yoga and Sankhya. Vedism is a specialized and narrow form of Yoga; the principle of the Vedantists is identical with that of the Sankhyas, for to both the movement of salvation is the recoil of the intelligence, the buddhi, from the differentiating powers of Nature, from ego, mind, senses, from the subjective and the objective, and its return to the undifferentiated and the immutable. It is with this object of reconciliation in his mind that the Teacher first approaches his statement of the doctrine of sacrifice; but throughout, even from the very beginning, he keeps his eye not on the restricted Vedic sense of sacrifice and works, but on their larger and universal application,—that widening of narrow and formal notions to admit the great general truths they unduly restrict which is always the method of the Gita.

XII

THE SIGNIFICANCE OF SACRIFICE

The Gita's theory of sacrifice is stated in two separate passages; one we find in the third chapter, another in the fourth; the first gives it in language which might, taken by itself, seem to be speaking only of the ceremonial sacrifice; the second interpreting that into the sense of a large philosophical symbolism, transforms at once its whole significance and raises it to a plane of high psychological and spiritual truth. "With sacrifice the Lord of creatures of old created creatures and said, By this shall you bring forth (fruits or offspring), let this be your milker of desires. Foster by this the gods and let the gods foster you; fostering each other, you shall attain to the supreme good. Fostered by sacrifice the gods shall give you desired enjoyments, who enjoys their given enjoyments and has not given to them, he is a thief. The good who eat what is left from the sacrifice, are released from all sin; but evil are they and enjoy sin who cook (the food) for their own sake. From food creatures come into being, from rain is the birth of food, from sacrifice comes into being the rain, sacrifice is born of work; work know to be born of Brahman, Brahman is born of the Immutable; therefore, is the all-pervading Brahman established in the sacrifice. He who follows not here the wheel thus set in movement, evil is his being, sensual is his delight, in vain, O Partha, that man lives." Having thus stated the necessity of sacrifice,—we shall see hereafter in what sense we may understand a passage which seems at first sight to convey only a traditional theory of ritualism and the necessity of the ceremonial offering,—Krishna proceeds to state the superiority of the spiritual man to works. "But the man whose delight is in the Self and who is satisfied with the enjoyment of the Self and in the Self, he is content, for him there exists no work that needs to be done. He has no object here to be gained by action done and none to be gained by action undone; he has no dependence on all these existences for any object to be gained."

Here then are the two ideals, Vedist and Vedantist, standing as if in all their sharp original separation and opposition, on one side the active ideal of acquiring enjoyments here and the highest good beyond by sacrifice and the mutual dependence of the human being and the divine powers and on the other, facing it, the austerer ideal of the liberated man who, independent in the Spirit, has nothing to do with enjoyment or works or the human or the divine worlds, but exists only in the peace of the supreme Self, joys only in the calm joy of the Brahman. The next verses create a ground for the reconciliation between the two extremes; the secret is not inaction as soon as one turns towards the higher truth, but desireless action both before and after it is reached. The liberated man has nothing to gain by action, but nothing also to gain by inaction, and it is not at all for any personal object that he has to make his choice. "Therefore, without attachment perform ever the work that is to be done (done for the sake of the world, lokasangraha, as is made clear immediately afterward); for by doing work without attachment man attains to the highest. For it was even by works that Janaka and the rest attained to perfection." It is true that works and sacrifice are a means of arriving at the highest good, sreyah.

param avapsyatha; but there are three kinds of works, that done without sacrifice for personal enjoyment which is entirely selfish and egoistic and misses the true law and aim and utility of life, mogham partha sa jıvati, that done with desire, but with sacrifice and the enjoyment only as a result of sacrifice and therefore to that extent consecrated and sanctified, and that done without desire or attachment of any kind. It is the last which brings the soul of man to the highest, param apnoti purusah.

The whole sense and drift of this teaching turns upon the interpretation we are to give to the important words, yajna, karma, brahma, sacrifice, work, Brahman. If the sacrifice is simply the Vedic sacrifice, if the work from which it is born is the Vedic rule of works and if the brahman from which the work itself is born is the sabdabrahman in the sense only of the letter of the Veda, then all the positions of the Vedist dogma are conceded and there is nothing more. Ceremonial sacrifice is the right means of gaining children, wealth, enjoyment; by ceremonial sacrifice rain is brought down from heaven and the prosperity and continuity of the race assured; life is a continual transaction between the gods and men in which man offers ceremonial gifts to the gods from the gifts they have bestowed on him and in return is enriched, protected, fostered. Therefore, all human works have to be accompanied and turned into a sacrament by ceremonial sacrifice and ritualistic worship; work not so dedicated is accursed, enjoyment without previous ceremonial sacrifice and ritual consecration is a sin. Even salvation, even the highest good is to be gained by ceremonial sacrifice. It must never be abandoned. Even the seeker of liberation has to continue to do ceremonial sacrifice, although without attachment; it is by ceremonial sacrifice and ritualistic works done without attachment that men of the type of Janaka attained to spiritual perfection and liberation.

Obviously, this cannot be the meaning of the Gita, for it would be in contradiction with all the rest of the book. Even in the passage itself, without the illumining interpretation afterwards given to it in the fourth chapter, we have already an indication of a wider sense where it is said that sacrifice is born from work, work from brahman, brahman from the Akshara, and therefore the all-pervading Brahman, sarvagatam brahma, is established in the sacrifice. The connecting logic of the "there-fore" and the repetition of the word brahma are significant; for it shows clearly that the brahman from which all work is born has to be understood with an eye not so much to the current Vedic teaching in which it means the Veda as to a symbolical sense in which the creative Word is identical with the all-pervading Brah-man, the Eternal, the one Self present in all existences, sarva-bhutesu and present in all the workings of existence. The Veda is the knowledge of the Divine, the Eternal,—"I am He who is to be known in all the books of the Knowledge," vedais ca vedyah, Krishna will say in a subsequent chapter; but it is the knowledge of him in the workings of Prakriti, in the workings of the three gunas., first qualities or modes of Nature, traigunyavisaya.. vedah..

This Brahman or Divine in the workings of Nature is born, as we may say, out of the Akshara, the immutable Purusha, the Self who stands above all the modes or qualities or workings of Nature, nistraigunya. The Brahman is one but self-displayed in two aspects, the immutable Being and the creator and originator of works in the mutable becoming, atman, sarvabhutani; it is the immobile omnipresent Soul of things, and it is the spiritual principle of the mobile working of things, Purusha poised in himself and Purusha active in Prakriti; it is aksara and ksara. I both of these aspects the Divine Being, Purushottama, manifests himself in the universe; the immutable above all qualities is His poise of peace, self-possession, equality, samam brahma; from that proceeds His manifestation in the qualities of Prakriti and their universal workings; from the Purusha in Prakriti, from this Brahman with qualities, proceed all the works[1] of the universal

---

1 That this is the right interpretation results also from the opening of the eighth chapter where the universal principles are enumerated, aksara (brahma), svabhava, karma, ksara bhava, purusa, adhiyajna. Akshara is the immutable Brahman, spirit or self, Atman; swabhava is the principle of the self, adhyatma, operative as the original nature of the being, "own

energy, Karma, in man and in all existences; from that work proceeds the principle of sacrifice. Even the material interchange between gods and men proceeds upon this principle, as typified in the dependence of rain and its product food on this working and on them the physical birth of creatures. For all the working of Prakriti is in its true nature a sacrifice, yajna, with the Divine Being as the enjoyer of all energisms and works and sacrifice and the great Lord of all existences, bhoktaram yajnatapasam sarvaloka-mahesvaram and to know this Divine all-pervading and established in sacrifice, sarvagatam yajne pratisthitam, is the true, the Vedic knowledge.

But he may be known in an inferior action through the devas, the gods, the powers of the divine Soul in Nature and in the eternal interaction of these powers and the soul of man, mutually giving and receiving, mutually helping, increasing, raising each other's workings and satisfaction, a commerce in which man rises towards a growing fitness for the supreme good. He recognizes that his life is a part of this divine action in Nature and not a thing separate and to be held and pursued for its own sake. He regards his enjoyments and the satisfaction of his desires as the fruit of sacrifice and the gift of the gods in their divine universal workings and he ceases to pursue them in the false and evil spirit of sinful egoistic selfishness as if they were a good to be seized from life by his own unaided strength without return and without thankfulness. As this spirit increases in him, he subordinates his

---

way of becoming", and this proceeds out of the self, the Akshara; Karma proceeds from that and is the creative movement, visarga, which brings all natural beings and all changing subjective and objective shapes of being into existence; the result of Karma therefore is all this mutable becoming, the changes of nature developed out of the original self-nature, ksara bhava out of svabhava; Purusha is the soul, the divine element in the becoming, adhidaivata, by whose presence the workings of Karma become a sacrifice, yajna˜, to the Divine within; adhiyajna is this secret Divine who receives the sacrifice.

desires, becomes satisfied with sacrifice as the law of life and works and is content with whatever remains over from the sacrifice, giving up all the rest freely as an offering in the great and beneficent interchange between his life and the world-life. Whoever goes contrary to this law of action and pursues works and enjoyment for his own isolated personal self-interest, lives in vain; he misses the true meaning and aim and utility of living and the upward growth of the soul; he is not on the path which leads to the highest good. But the highest only comes when the sacrifice is no longer to the gods, but to the one all-pervading Divine established in the sacrifice, of whom the gods are inferior forms and powers, and when he puts away the lower self that desires and enjoys and gives up his personal sense of being the worker to the true executrix of all works, Prakriti, and his personal sense of being the enjoyer to the Divine Purusha, the higher and universal Self who is the real enjoyer of the works of Prakriti. In that Self and not in any personal enjoyment he finds now his sole satisfaction, complete content, pure delight; he has nothing to gain by action or inaction, depends neither on gods nor men for anything, seeks no profit from any, for the self-delight is all-sufficient to him, but does works for the sake of the Divine only, as a pure sacrifice, without attachment or desire. Thus, he gains equality and becomes free from the modes of Nature, nistraigunya; his soul takes its poise not in the insecurity of Prakriti, but in the peace of the immutable Brahman, even while his actions continue in the movement of Prakriti. Thus, is sacrifice his way of attaining the Highest.

That this is the sense of the passage is made clear in what follows, by the affirmation of lokasangraha as the object of works, of Prakriti as the sole doer of works and the divine Purusha as their equal upholder, to whom works have to be given up even in their doing,—this inner giving up of works and yet physical doing of them is the culmination of sacrifice,—and by the affirmation that the result of such active sacrifice with an equal and desireless mind is liberation from the bondage of works. "He who is satisfied with whatever gain comes to him and equal in failure and success, is not bound even when he acts. When a man liberated, free from attachment, acts for sacrifice, all his action is dissolved," leaves, that is to say, no result of bondage or after-impression on his free, pure, perfect, and equal soul. To these passages we shall have to return. They are followed by a perfectly explicit and detailed interpretation of the meaning of yajna in the language of the Gita which leaves no doubt at all about the symbolic use of the words and the psychological character of the sacrifice enjoined by this teaching. In the ancient Vedic system, there was always a double sense physical and psychological, outward, and symbolic, the exterior form of the sacrifice and the inner meaning of all its circumstances. But the secret symbolism of the ancient Vedic mystics, exact, curious, poetic, psychological, had been long forgotten by this time and it is now replaced by another, large, general, and philosophical in the spirit of Vedanta and a later Yoga. The fire of sacrifice, agni, is no material flame, but brahmagni, the fire of the Brahman, or it is the Brahman-ward energy, inner Agni, priest of the sacrifice, into which the offering is poured; the fire is self-control or it is a purified sense-action or it is the vital energy in that discipline of the control of the vital being through the control of the breath which is common to Raja yoga and Hathayoga, or it is the fire of self-knowledge, the flame of the supreme sacrifice. The food eaten as the leavings of the sacrifice is, it is explained, the nectar of immortality, amrta, left over from the offering; and here we have still something of the old Vedic symbolism in which the Soma-wine was the physical symbol of the amrta, the immortalizing delight of the divine ecstasy won by the sacrifice, offered to the gods, and drunk by men. The offering itself is whatever working of his energy, physical or psychological, is consecrated by him in action of body or action of mind to the gods or God, to the Self or to the universal powers, to one's own higher Self or to the Self in mankind and in all existences.

This elaborate explanation of the Yajna sets out with a vast and comprehensive definition in which it is declared that the act and energy and materials of the sacrifice, the giver and re-ceiver of the sacrifice, the goal and object of the sacrifice are all the one Brahman. "Brahman is the giving, Brahman is the food-offering, by Brahman it is offered into the Brahman-fire, Brahman is that which is to be attained by samadhi in Brahman-action." This then is the knowledge in which the liberated man has to do works of sacrifice. It is the knowledge declared of old in the great Vedantic utterances, "I am He", "All this verily is the Brahman, Brahman is this Self." It is the knowledge of the entire unity; it is the One manifest as the doer and the deed and the object of works, knower and knowledge and the object of knowledge. The universal energy into which the action is poured is the Divine; the consecrated energy of the giving is the Divine; whatever is offered is only some form of the Divine; the giver of the offering is the Divine himself in man; the action, the work, the sacrifice is itself the Divine in movement, in activity; the goal to be reached by sacrifice is the Divine. For the man who has this knowledge and lives and acts in it, there can be no binding works, no personal and egoistically appropriated action; there is only the divine Purusha acting by the divine Prakriti in His own being, offering everything into the fire of His self-conscious cosmic energy, while the knowledge and the possession of His divine existence and consciousness by the soul unified with Him is the goal of all this God-directed movement and activity. To know that and to live and act in this unifying consciousness is to be free.

But all even of the Yogins have not attained to this knowledge. "Some Yogins follow after the sacrifice which is of the gods; others offer the sacrifice by the sacrifice itself into the Brahman-fire." The former conceive of the Divine in various forms and powers and seek him by various means, ordinances, dharmas, laws or, as we might say, settled rites of action, self-discipline, consecrated works; for the latter, those who already know, the simple fact of sacrifice, of offering whatever work to the Divine itself, of casting all their activities into the unified divine consciousness and energy, is their one means, their one dharma. The means of sacrifice are various; the offerings are of many kinds. There is the psychological sacrifice of self-control and self-discipline which leads to the higher self-possession and self-knowledge. "Some offer their senses into the fires of control, others offer the objects of sense into the fires of sense, and others offer all the actions of the sense and all the actions of the vital force into the fire of the Yoga of self-control kindled by knowledge." There is, that is to say, the discipline which receives the objects of sense-perception without allowing the mind to be disturbed or affected by its sense-activities, the senses themselves becoming pure fires of sacrifice; there is the discipline which stills the senses so that the soul in its purity may appear from behind the veil of mind-action, calm and still; there is the discipline by which, when the self is known, all the actions of the sense-perceptions and all the action of the vital being are received into that one still and tranquil soul. The offering of the striver after perfection may be material and physical, dravya-yajna, like that consecrated in worship by the devotee to his deity, or it may be the austerity of his self-discipline and energy of his soul directed to some high aim, tapo-yajna or it may be some form of Yoga like the Pranayama of the Rajayogins and Hathayogins or any other yoga-yajna. All these tend to the purification of the being; all sacrifice is a way towards the attainment of the highest.

The one thing needful, the saving principle constant in all these variations, is to subordinate the lower activities, to diminish the control of desire and replace it by a superior energy, to abandon the purely egoistic enjoyment for that diviner delight which comes by sacrifice, by self-dedication, by self-mastery, by the giving up of one's lower impulses to a greater and higher aim. "They who enjoy the nectar of immortality left over from the sacrifice attain to the eternal Brahman." Sacrifice is the law of the world, and nothing can be gained without it, neither mastery here, nor the possession of heavens beyond, nor the supreme possession of all; "this world is not for him who doeth not sacrifice, how than any other world?" Therefore, all these and many other forms of sacrifice have been "extended in the mouth of the Brahman," the mouth of that Fire which receives all offerings; they are all means and forms of the one great Existence in activity, means by which the action of the human being can be offered up to That of which his outward existence is a part and with which his inmost self is one. They are "all born of work"; all proceed from and are ordained by the one vast energy of the Divine which manifests itself in the universal karma and makes all the cosmic activity a progressive offering to the One-self and Lord and of which the last stage for the human being is self-knowledge and the possession of the divine or Brahmic consciousness. "So, knowing thou shalt become free."

But there are gradations in the range of these various forms of sacrifice, the physical offering the lowest, the sacrifice of knowledge the highest. Knowledge is that in which all this action culminates, not any lower knowledge, but the highest, self-knowledge and God-knowledge, that which we can learn from those who know the true principles of existence, that by possessing which we shall not fall again into the bewilderment of the mind's ignorance and into its bondage to mere sense-knowledge and to the inferior activity of the desires and passions. The knowledge in which all culminates is that by which "thou shalt see all existences (becomings, bhutani) without exception in the Self, then in Me." For the Self is that one, immutable, all-pervading, all-containing, self-existent reality or Brahman hidden behind our mental being into which our consciousness widens out when it is liberated from the ego; we come to see all beings as becomings, bhutani, within that one self-existence.

But this Self or immutable Brahman we see too to be the self-presentation to our essential psychological consciousness of a supreme Being who is the source of our existence and of whom all that is mutable or immutable is the manifestation. He is God, the Divine, the Purushottama. To Him we offer everything as a sacrifice; into His hands we give up our actions; in His existence we live and move; unified with Him in our nature and with all existence in Him, we become one soul and one power of being with Him and with all beings; with His supreme reality we identify and unite our self-being. By works done for sacrifice, eliminating desire, we arrive at knowledge and at the soul's possession of itself; by works done in self-knowledge and God-knowledge we are liberated into the unity, peace, and joy of the divine existence.

XIII
THE LORD OF THE SACRIFICE

We have before we can proceed further, to gather up all that has been said in its main principles. The whole of the Gita's gospel of works rests upon its idea of sacrifice and contains in fact the eternal connecting truth of God and the world and works. The human mind seizes ordinarily only fragmentary notions and standpoints of a many-sided eternal truth of existence and builds upon them its various theories of life and ethics and religion, stressing this or that sign or appearance, but to some entirety of it, it must always tend to reawaken whenever it returns in an age of large enlightenment to any entire and synthetic relation of its world-knowledge with its God-knowledge and self-knowledge. The gospel of the Gita reposes upon this fundamental Vedantic truth that all being is the one Brahman and all existence the wheel of Brahman, a divine movement opening out from God and returning to God. All is the expressive activity of Nature and Nature a power of the Divine which works out the consciousness and will of the divine Soul master of her works and inhabitant of her forms. It is for his satisfaction that she descends into the absorption of the forms of things and the works of life and mind and returns again through mind and self-knowledge to the conscious possession of the Soul that dwells within her. There is first an involving of self and all it is or means in an evolution of phenomena; there is afterwards an evolution of self, a revelation of all it is and means, all that is hidden and yet suggested by the phenomenal creation. This cycle of Nature could not be what it is but for the Purusha assuming and maintaining simultaneously three eternal poises each of which is necessary to the totality of this action. It must manifest itself in the mutable, and there we see it as the finite, the many, all existences, sarvabhutani¯. It appears to us as the finite personality of these million creatures with their infinite diversities and various relations and it appears to us behind these as the soul and force of the action of the gods,—that is to say, the cosmic powers and qualities of the Divine which preside over the workings of the life of the universe and constitute to our perception different universal forms of the one Existence, or, it may be, various self-statements of personality of the one supreme Person. Then, secret behind and within all forms and existences, we perceive too an immutable, an infinite, a timeless, an impersonal, a one unchanging spirit of existence, an indivisible Self of all that is, in which all these many find themselves to be really one. And therefore, by returning to that the active, finite personality of the individual being discovers that it can release itself into a silent largeness of universality and the peace and poise of an immutable and unattached unity with all that proceeds from and is supported by this indivisible Infinite. Or he may even escape into it from individual existence. But the highest secret of all, uttamam rahasyam, is the Purushottama. This is the supreme Divine, God, who possesses both the infinite and the finite and in whom the personal and the impersonal, the oneself and the many existences, being and becoming, the world-action and the supracosmic peace, pravrtti and nivrtti, meet, are united, are possessed together and in each other. In God all things find their secret truth and their absolute reconciliation.

All truth of works must depend upon the truth of being. All active existence must be in its inmost reality a sacrifice of works offered by Prakriti to Purusha, Nature offering to the supreme and infinite Soul the desire of the multiple finite Soul within her. Life is an altar to which she brings her workings and the fruits of her workings and lays them before whatever aspect of the Divinity the consciousness in her has reached for whatever result of the sacrifice the desire of the living soul can seize on as its immediate or its highest good. According to the grade of consciousness and being which the soul has reached in Nature, will be the Divinity it worships, the delight which it seeks and the hope for which it sacrifices. And in the movement of the mutable Purusha in Nature all is and must be interchange for existence is one and its divisions must found themselves on some law of mutual dependence, each growing by each and living by all. Where sacrifice is not willingly given, Nature exacts it by force, she satisfies the law of her living. A mutual giving and receiving is the law of Life without which it cannot for one moment endure, and this fact is the stamp of the divine creative Will on the world it has manifested in its being, the proof that with sacrifice as their eternal companion the Lord of creatures has created all these existences. The universal law of sacrifice is the sign that the world is of God and belongs to God and that life is his dominion and house of worship and not a field for the self-satisfaction of the independent ego; not the fulfilment of the ego,—that is only our crude and obscure beginning,—but the discovery of God, the worship and seeking of the Divine and the Infinite through a constantly enlarging sacrifice culminating in a perfect self-giving founded on a perfect self-knowledge, is that to which the experience of life is at last intended to lead.

But the individual being begins with ignorance and persists long in ignorance. Acutely conscious of himself he sees the ego as the cause and whole meaning of life and not the Divine. He sees himself as the doer of works and does not see that all the workings of existence including his own internal and external activities are the workings of one universal Nature and nothing else. He sees himself as the enjoyer of works and imagines that for him all exists and him Nature ought to satisfy and obey his personal will; he does not see that she is not at all concerned with satisfying him or at all careful of his will, but obeys a higher universal will and seeks to satisfy a Godhead who transcends her and her works and creations; his finite being, his will and his satisfactions are hers and not his, and she offers them at every moment as a sacrifice to the Divine of whose purpose in her she makes all this the covert instrumentation. Because of this ignorance whose seal is egoism, the creature ignores the law of sacrifice and seeks to take all he can for himself and gives only what Nature by her internal and external compulsion forces him to give. He can really take nothing except what she allows him to receive as his portion, what the divine Powers within her yield to his desire. The egoistic soul in a world of sacrifice is as if a thief or robber who takes what these Powers bring to him and has no mind to give in return. He misses the true meaning of life and, since he does not use life and works for the enlargement and elevation of his being through sacrifice, he lives in vain.

Only when the individual being begins to perceive and acknowledge in his acts the value of the self in others as well as the power and needs of his own ego, begins to perceive universal Nature behind his own workings and through the cosmic godheads gets some glimpse of the One and the Infinite, is he on his way to the transcendence of his limitation by the ego and the discovery of his soul. He begins to discover a law other than that of his desires, to which his desires must be more and more subordinated and subjected; he develops the purely egoistic into the understanding and ethical being. He begins to give more value to the claims of the self in others and less to the claims of his ego; he admits the strife between egoism and altruism and by the increase of his altruistic tendencies he prepares the enlargement of his own consciousness and being. He begins to perceive Nature and divine Powers in Nature to whom he owes sacrifice, adoration, obedience, because it is by them and by their law that the workings both of the mental and the material world are controlled, and he learns that only by increasing their presence and their greatness in his thought and will and life can he himself increase his powers, knowledge, right action and the satisfactions which these things bring to him. Thus, he adds the religious and supraphysical to the material and egoistic sense of life and prepares himself to rise through the finite to the Infinite.

But this is only a long intermediate stage. It is still subject to the law of desire, to the centrality of all things in the conceptions and needs of his ego and to the control of his being as well as his works by Nature, though it is a regulated and governed desire, a clarified ego, and a Nature more and more subtilized and enlightened by the sattwic, the highest natural principle. All this is still within the domain, though the very much enlarged domain, of the mutable, finite, and personal. The real self-knowledge and consequently the right way of works lies beyond; for the sacrifice done with knowledge is the highest sacrifice and that alone brings a perfect working. That can only come when he perceives that the self in him and the self in others are one being and this self is something higher than the ego, an infinite, an impersonal, a universal existence in whom all move and have their being,—when he perceives that all the cosmic gods to whom he offers his sacrifice are forms of one infinite Godhead and when again, leaving all his limited and limiting conceptions of that one Godhead, he perceives him to be the supreme and ineffable Deity who is at once the finite and the infinite, the one self and the many, beyond Nature though manifesting himself through Nature, beyond limitation by qualities though formulating the power of his being through infinite quality. This is the Purushottama to whom the sacrifice has to be offered, not for any transient personal fruit of works, but for the soul's possession of God and in order to live in harmony and union with the Divine.

In other words, man's way to liberation and perfection lies

through an increasing impersonality. It is his ancient and constant experience that the more he opens himself to the im-personal and infinite, to that which is pure and high and one and common in all things and beings, the impersonal and infinite in Nature, the impersonal and infinite in life, the impersonal and infinite in his own subjectivity, the less he is bound by his ego and by the circle of the finite, the more he feels a sense of largeness, peace, pure happiness. The pleasure, joy, satisfaction which the finite by itself can give or the ego in its own right attain, is transitory, petty, and insecure. To dwell entirely in the ego-sense and its finite conceptions, powers, satisfactions is to find this world for ever full of transience and suffering, anityam asukham; the finite life is always troubled by a certain sense of vanity for this fundamental reason that the finite is not the whole or the highest truth of life; life is not entirely real until it opens into the sense of the infinite. It is for this reason that the Gita opens its gospel of works by insisting on the Brahmic consciousness, the impersonal life, that great object of the discipline of the ancient sages. For the impersonal, the infinite, the One in which all the impermanent, mutable, multiple activity of the world finds above itself its base of permanence, security, and peace, is the immobile Self, the Akshara, the Brahman. If we see this, we shall see that to raise one's consciousness and the poise of one's being out of limited personality into this infinite and impersonal Brahman is the first spiritual necessity. To see all beings in this oneself is the knowledge which raises the soul out of egoistic ignorance and its works and results; to live in it is to acquire peace and firm spiritual foundation.

The way to bring about this great transformation follows a double path; for there is the way of knowledge and there is the way of works, and the Gita combines them in a firm synthesis. The way of knowledge is to turn the understanding, the intelligent will away from its downward absorption in the workings of the mind and the senses and upward to the self, the Purusha or Brahman; it is to make it dwell always on the one idea of the oneself and not in the many-branching conceptions of the mind and many-streaming impulses of desire. Taken by itself this path would seem to lead to the complete renunciation of works, to an immobile passivity and to the severance of the soul from Nature. But in reality, such an absolute renunciation, passivity and severance are impossible. Purusha and Prakriti are twin principles of being which cannot be severed, and so long as we remain in Nature, our workings in Nature must continue, even though they may take a different form or rather a different sense from those of the unenlightened soul. The real renunciation—for renunciation, sannyasa, there must be—is not the fleeing from works, but the slaying of ego and desire. The way is to abandon attachment to the fruit of works even while doing them, and the way is to recognize Nature as the agent and leave her to do her works and to live in the soul as the witness and sustainer, watching and sustaining her, but not attached either to her actions or their fruits. The ego, the limited and troubled personality is then quieted and merged in the consciousness of the one impersonal Self, while the works of Nature continue to our vision to operate through all these "becoming's" or existences who are now seen by us as living and acting and moving, under her impulsion entirely, in this one infinite Being; our own finite existence is seen and felt to be only one of these and its workings are seen and felt to be those of Nature, not of our real self, which is the silent, impersonal unity. The ego claimed them as its own doings and therefore we thought them ours; but the ego is now dead and henceforth they are no longer ours, but Nature's. We have achieved by the slaying of ego impersonality in our being and consciousness; we have achieved by the renunciation of desire impersonality in the works of our nature. We are free not only in inaction, but in action; our liberty does not depend on a physical and temperamental immobility and vacancy, nor do we fall from freedom directly we act. Even in a full current of natural action the impersonal soul in us remains calm, still, and free.

The liberation given by this perfect impersonality is real, is complete, is indispensable; but is it the last word, the end of the whole matter? All life, all world-existence, we have said, is the sacrifice offered by Nature to the Purusha, the one and secret soul in Nature, in whom all her workings take place; but its real sense is obscured in us by ego, by desire, by our limited, active, multiple personality. We have risen out of ego and desire and limited personality and by impersonality, its great corrective, we have found the impersonal Godhead; we have identified our being with the oneself and soul in whom all exist. The sacrifice of works continues, conducted not by ourselves any longer, but by Nature,—Nature operating through the finite part of our being, mind, senses, body,—but in our infinite being. But to whom then is this sacrifice offered and with what object? For the impersonal has no activity and no desires, no object to be gained, no dependence for anything on all this world of creatures; it exists for itself, in its own self-delight, in its own immutable eternal being. We may have to do works without desire as a means in order to reach this impersonal self-existence and self-delight, but, that movement once executed, the object of works is finished; the sacrifice is no longer needed. Works may even then continue because Nature continues and her activities; but there is no longer any further object in these works. The sole reason for our continuing to act after liberation is purely negative; it is the compulsion of Nature on our finite parts of mind and body. But if that be all, then, first, works may well be whittled down and reduced to a minimum, may be confined to what Nature's compulsion absolutely will have from our bodies; and secondly, even if there is no reduction to a minimum,—since action does not matter and inaction also is no object,—then the nature of the works also does not matter. Arjuna, once having attained knowledge, may continue to fight out the battle of Kurukshetra, following his old Kshatriya nature, or he may leave it and live the life of the Sannyasin, following his new quietistic impulse. Which of these things he does, becomes quite indifferent; or rather the second is the better way, since it will discourage more quickly the impulses of Nature which still have a hold on his mind owing to past created tendency and, when his body has fallen from him, he will securely depart into the Infinite and Impersonal with no necessity of returning again to the trouble and madness of life in this transient and sorrowful world, anityam asukham imam lokam.

If this were so, the Gita would lose all its meaning; for its first and central object would be defeated. But the Gita insists that the nature of the action does matter and that there is a positive sanction for continuance in works, not only that one quite negative and mechanical reason, the objectless compulsion of Nature. There is still, after the ego has been conquered, a divine Lord and enjoyer of the sacrifice, bhoktaram yajnatapasam and there is still an object in the sacrifice. The impersonal Brahman is not the very last word, not the utterly highest secret of our being; for impersonal and personal, finite, and infinite turn out to be only two opposites, yet concomitant aspects of a divine Being unlimited by these distinctions who is both these things at once. God is an ever-unmanifest Infinite ever self-impelled to manifest himself in the finite; he is the great impersonal Person of whom all personalities are partial appearances; he is the Divine who reveals himself in the human being, the Lord seated in the heart of man. Knowledge teaches us to see all beings in the one impersonal self, for so we are liberated from the separative ego-sense and then through this delivering impersonality to see them in this God, atmani atho mayi, "in the Self and then in Me." Our ego, our limiting personalities stand in the way of our recognising the Divine who is in all and in whom all have their being; for, subject to personality, we see only such fragmentary aspects of Him as the finite appearances of things suffer us to seize. We have to arrive at him not through our lower personality, but through the high, infinite, and impersonal part of our being, and that we find by becoming this self-one in all in whose existence the whole world is comprised. This infinite containing, not excluding all finite appearances, this impersonal admitting, not rejecting all individualities and personalities, this immobile sustaining, pervading, containing, not standing apart from all the movement of Nature, is the clear mirror in which the Divine will reveal His being. Therefore, it is to the Impersonal that we have first to attain; through the cosmic deities, through the aspects of the finite alone the perfect knowledge of God cannot be totally obtained. But neither is the silent immobility of the impersonal Self, conceived as shut into itself and divorced from all that it sustains, contains, and pervades, the whole all-revealing all-satisfying truth of the Divine. To see that we have to look through its silence to the Purushottama, and he in his divine greatness possesses both the Akshara and the Kshara; he is seated in the immobility, but he manifests himself in the movement and in all the action of cosmic Nature; to him even after liberation the sacrifice of works in Nature continues to be offered.

The real goal of the Yoga is then a living and self-completing union with the divine Purushottama and is not merely a self-extinguishing immergence in the impersonal Being. To raise our whole existence to the Divine Being, to dwell in him (mayyeva nivasisyasi), to be at one with him, unify our consciousness with his, to make our fragmentary nature a reflection of his perfect nature, to be inspired in our thought and sense wholly by the divine knowledge, to be moved in will and action utterly and faultlessly by the divine will, to lose desire in his love and delight, is man's perfection; it is that which the Gita describes as the highest secret. It is the true goal and the last sense of human living and the highest step in our progressive sacrifice of works. For he remains to the end the Master of Works and the soul of sacrifice.

XIV

THE PRINCIPLE OF DIVINE WORKS

This then is the sense of the Gita's doctrine of sacrifice. Its full significance depends on the idea of the Purushottama which as yet is not developed,—we find it set forth clearly only much later in the eighteen chapters,—and therefore we have had to anticipate, at whatever cost of infidelity to the progressive method of the Gita's exposition, that central teaching. At present the Teacher simply gives a hint, merely adumbrates this supreme presence of the Purushottama and his relation to the immobile Self in whom it is our first business, our pressing spiritual need to find our poise of perfect peace and equality by attainment to the Brahmic condition. He speaks as yet not at all in set terms of the Purushottama, but of himself,—"I", Krishna, Narayana, the Avatar, the God in man who is also the Lord in the universe incarnated in the figure of the divine charioteer of Kurukshetra. "In the Self, then in Me," is the formula he gives, implying that the transcendence of the individual personality by seeing it as a "becoming" in the impersonal self-existent Being is simply a means of arriving at that great secret impersonal Personality, which is thus silent, calm, and uplifted above Nature in the impersonal Being, but also present and active in Nature in all these million becoming's. Losing our lower individual personality in the Impersonal, we arrive finally at union with that supreme Personality, which is not separate and individual, but yet assumes all individualities. Transcending the lower nature of the three gunas and seating the soul in the immobile Purusha beyond the three gunas, we can ascend finally into the higher nature of the infinite Godhead which is not bound by the three gunas even when it acts through Nature. Reaching the inner actionlessness of the silent Purusha, naiskarmya, and leaving Prakriti to do her works, we can attain supremely beyond to the status of the divine Mastery which is able to do all works and yet be bound by none. The idea of the Purushottama, seen here as the incarnate Narayana, Krishna, is therefore the key. Without it the withdrawal from the lower nature to the Brahmic condition leads necessarily to inaction of the liberated man, his indifference to the works of the world; with it the same withdrawal becomes a step by which the works of the world are taken up in the spirit, with the nature and in the freedom of the Divine. See the silent Brahman as the goal and the world with all its activities has to be forsaken; see God, the Divine, the Purushottama as the goal, superior to action yet its inner spiritual cause and object and original will, and the world with all its activities is conquered and possessed in a divine transcendence of the world. It can become instead of a prison-house an opulent kingdom, rajyam samrddham, which we have conquered for the spiritual life by slaying the limitation of the tyrant ego and overcoming the bondage of our gaoler desires and breaking the prison of our individualistic possession and enjoyment. The liberated universalized soul becomes svarat, samrat, self-ruler and emperor.

The works of sacrifice are thus vindicated as a means of liberation and absolute spiritual perfection, samsiddhi. So Janaka and other great Karmayogins of the mighty ancient Yoga attained to perfection, by equal and desireless works done as a sacrifice, without the least egoistic aim or attachment—karmanaiva hi samsiddhim asthita janakadayah. So too and with the same desire lessness, after liberation and perfection, works can and have to be continued by us in a large divine spirit, with the calm high nature of a spiritual royalty. "Thou shouldst do works also regarding the holding together of the peoples, lokasangraham evapi sampasyan kartum arhasi. Whatsoever the Best doeth, that the lower kind of man puts into practice; the standard he creates, the people follows. O son of Pritha, I have no work that I need to do in all the three worlds, I have nothing that I have not gained and have yet to gain, and I abide verily in the paths of action," varta eva ca karmani,—eva implying, I abide in it and do not leave it as the Sannyasin thinks himself bound to abandon works. "For if I did not abide sleeplessly in the paths of action, men follow in every way my path, these peoples would sink to destruction if I did not work, and I should be the creator of confusion and slay these creatures. As those who know not act with attachment to the action, he who knows should act without attachment, having for his motive to hold together the peoples. He should not create a division of their understanding in the ignorant who are attached to their works; he should set them to all actions, doing them himself with knowledge and in Yoga." There are few more important passages in the Gita than these seven striking couplets.

But let us clearly understand that they must not be interpreted, as the modern pragmatic tendency concerned much more with the present affairs of the world than with any high and far-off spiritual possibility seeks to interpret them, as no more than a philosophical and religious justification of social service, patriotic, cosmopolitan, and humanitarian effort, and attachment to the hundred eager social schemes and dreams which attract the modern intellect. It is not the rule of a large moral and intellectual altruism which is here announced, but that of a spiritual unity with God and with this world of beings who dwell in him and in whom he dwells. It is not an injunction to subordinate the individual to society and humanity or immolate egoism on the altar of the human collectivity, but to fulfil the individual in God and to sacrifice the ego on the one true altar of the all-embracing Divinity. The Gita moves on a plane of ideas and experiences higher than those of the modern mind which is at the stage indeed of a struggle to shake off the coils of egoism but is still mundane in its outlook and intellectual and moral rather than spiritual in its temperament. Patriotism, cosmopolitanism, service of society, collectivism, humanitarianism, the ideal or religion of humanity are admirable aids towards our escape from our primary condition of individual, family, social, national egoism into a secondary stage in which the individual realizes, as far as it can be done on the intellectual, moral and emotional level,—on that level he cannot do it entirely in the right and perfect way, the way of the integral truth of his being,—the oneness of his existence with the existence of other beings. But the thought of the Gita reaches beyond to a tertiary condition of our developing self-consciousness towards which the secondary is only a partial stage of advance.

The Indian social tendency has been to subordinate the individual to the claims of society, but Indian religious thought and spiritual seeking have been always loftily individualistic in their aims. An Indian system of thought like the Gita's cannot possibly fail to put first the development of the individual, the highest need of the individual, his claim to discover and exercise his largest spiritual freedom, greatness, splendour, royalty,—his aim to develop into the illumined seer and king in the spiritual sense of seerdom and kingship, which was the first great charter of the ideal humanity promulgated by the ancient Vedic sages. To exceed himself was their goal for the individual, not by losing all his personal aims in the aims of an organised human society, but by enlarging, heightening, aggrandizing himself into the consciousness of the Godhead. The rule given here by the Gita is the rule for the master man, the superman, the divinized human being, the Best, not in the sense of any Nietzschean, any one-sided and lopsided, any Olympian, Apollonian or Dionysian, any angelic or demoniac super manhood but in that of the man whose whole personality has been offered up into the being, nature and consciousness of the one transcendent and universal Divinity and by loss of the smaller self has found its greater self, has been divinized.

To exalt oneself out of the lower imperfect Prakriti, traigunyamayı maya, into unity with the divine being, consciousness and nature,[1] madbhavam agatah, is the object of the Yoga. But when this object is fulfilled, when the man is in the Brahmic status and sees no longer with the false egoistic vision himself and the world, but sees all beings in the Self, in God and the Self in all beings, God in all beings, what shall be the action,—since action there still is,—which results from that seeing, and what shall be the cosmic or individual motive of all his works? It is the question of Arjuna,[2] but answered from a stand-point other than that from which Arjuna had put it. The motive cannot be personal desire on the intellectual, moral, emotional level, for that has been abandoned,—even the moral motive has been abandoned, since the liberated man has passed beyond the lower distinction of sin and virtue, lives in a glorified purity beyond good and evil. It cannot be the spiritual call to his perfect self-development by means of disinterested works, for the call has been answered, the development is perfect and fulfilled. His motive of action can only be the holding together of the peoples, cikırsur lokasangraham. This great march of the peoples towards a far-off divine ideal has to be held together, prevented from falling into the bewilderment, confusion and utter discord of the understanding which would lead to dissolution and destruction and to which the world moving forward in the night or dark twilight of ignorance would be too easily prone if it were not held together, conducted, kept to the great lines of its discipline by the illumination, by the strength, by the rule and example, by the visible standard and the invisible influence of its Best. The best, the individuals who are in advance of the general line and above the general level of the collectivity, are the natural leaders of mankind, for it is they who can point to the race both the way they must follow and the standard or ideal

1 Sayujya, salokya and sadrsya or sadharmya. Sadharmya is becoming of one law of being and action with the Divine.

2 kim prabhaseta kim asıta vrajeta kim.

they have to keep to or to attain. But the divinized man is the Best in no ordinary sense of the word and his influence, his example must have a power which that of no ordinarily superior man can exercise. What example then shall he give? What rule or standard shall he uphold?

In order to indicate more perfectly his meaning, the divine Teacher, the Avatar gives his own example, his own standard to Arjuna. "I abide in the path of action," he seems to say, "the path that all men follow; thou too must abide in action. In the way I act, in that way thou too must act. I am above the necessity of works, for I have nothing to gain by them; I am the Divine who possess all things and all beings in the world, and I am myself beyond the world as well as in it and I do not depend upon anything or anyone in all the three worlds for any object; yet I act. This too must be thy manner and spirit of working. I, the Divine, am the rule and the standard; it is I who make the path in which men tread; I am the way and the goal. But I do all this largely, universally, visibly in part, but far more invisibly; and men do not really know the way of my workings. Thou, when thou knowest and seest, when thou hast become the divinised man, must be the individual power of God, the human yet divine example, even as I am in my avatars. Most men dwell in the ignorance, the God-seer dwells in the knowledge; but let him not confuse the minds of men by a dangerous example, rejecting in his superiority the works of the world; let him not cut short the thread of action before it is spun out, let him not perplex and falsify the stages and gradations of the ways I have hewn. The whole range of human action has been decreed by me with a view to the progress of man from the lower to the higher nature, from the apparent undivine to the conscious Divine. The whole range of human works must be that in which the God-knower shall move. All individual, all social action, all the works of the intellect, the heart and the body are still his, not any longer for his own separate sake but for the sake of God in the world, of God in all beings and that all those beings may move forward, as he has moved, by the path of works towards the discovery of the Divine in themselves. Outwardly his actions may not seem to differ essentially from theirs; battle and rule as well as teaching and thought, all the various commerce of man with man may fall in his range; but the spirit in which he does them must be very different, and it is that spirit which by its influence shall be the great attraction drawing men upwards to his own level, the great lever lifting the mass of men higher in their ascent."

The giving of the example of God himself to the liberated man is profoundly significant; for it reveals the whole basis of the Gita's philosophy of divine works. The liberated man is he who has exalted himself into the divine nature and according to that divine nature must be his actions. But what is the divine nature? It is not entirely and solely that of the Akshara, the immobile, inactive, impersonal self; for that by itself would lead the liberated man to actionless immobility. It is not characteristically that of the Kshara, the multitudinous, the personal, the Purusha self-subjected to Prakriti; for that by itself would lead him back into subjection to his personality and to the lower nature and its qualities. It is the nature of the Purushottama who holds both these together and by his supreme divinity reconciles them in a divine reconciliation which is the highest secret of his being, rahasyam hyetad uttamam. He is not the doer of works in the personal sense of our action involved in Prakriti; for God works through his power, conscious nature, effective force,—Shakti, Maya, Prakriti,—but yet above it, not involved in it, not subject to it, not unable to lift himself beyond the laws, workings, habits of action it creates, not affected or bound by them, not unable to distinguish himself, as we are unable, from the workings of life, mind and body. He is the doer of works who acts not, kartaram akartaram. "Know me," says Krishna, "for the doer of this (the fourfold law of human workings) who am yet the imperishable non-doer. Works fix not themselves on me (na limpanti), nor have I desire for the fruits of action." But neither is he the inactive, impassive, unpuissant Witness and nothing else; for it is he who works in the steps and measures of his power; every movement of it, every particle of the world of beings it forms is instinct with his presence, full of his consciousness, impelled by his will, shaped by his knowledge.

He is, besides, the Supreme without qualities who is possessed of all qualities, nirguno gunı.[3] He is not bound by any mode of nature or action, nor consists, as our personality consists, of a sum of qualities, modes of nature, characteristic operations of the mental, moral, emotional, vital, physical being, but is the source of all modes and qualities, capable of developing any he wills in whatever way and to whatever degree he wills; he is the infinite being of which they are ways of becoming, the immeasurable quantity and unbound ineffable of which they are measures, numbers and figures, which they seem to rhythmise and arithmise in the standards of the universe. Yet neither is he merely an impersonal indeterminate, nor a mere stuff of conscious existence for all determinations and personalizing's to draw upon for their material, but a supreme Being, the one original conscious Existent, the perfect Personality capable of all relations even to the most human, concrete and intimate; for he is friend, comrade, lover, playmate, guide, teacher, master, ministrant of knowledge or ministrant of joy, yet in all relations unbound, free and absolute. This too the divinised man becomes in the measure of his attainment, impersonal in his personality, unbound by quality or action even when maintaining the most personal and intimate relations with men, unbound by any dharma even when following in appearance this or that dharma. Neither the dynamism of the kinetic man nor the actionless light of the ascetic or quietist, neither the vehement personality of the man of action nor the indifferent impersonality of the philosophic sage is the complete divine ideal. These are the two conflicting standards of the man of this world and the ascetic or the quietist philosopher, one

3 Swetaswatara Upanishad.

immersed in the action of the Kshara, the other striving to dwell entirely in the peace of the Akshara; but the complete divine ideal proceeds from the nature of the Purushottama which transcends this conflict and reconciles all divine possibilities.

The kinetic man is not satisfied with any ideal which does not depend upon the fulfilment of this cosmic nature, this play of the three qualities of that nature, this human activity of mind and heart and body. The highest fulfilment of that activity, he might say, is my idea of human perfection, of the divine possibility in man; some ideal that satisfies the intellect, the heart, the moral being, some ideal of our human nature in its action can alone satisfy the human being; he must have something that he can seek in the workings of his mind and life and body. For that is his nature, his dharma, and how can he be fulfilled in something outside his nature? For to his nature each being is bound and within it he must seek for his perfection. According to our human nature must be our human perfection; and each man must strive for it according to the line of his personality, his svadharma, but in life, in action, not outside life and action. Yes, there is a truth in that, replies to the Gita; the fulfilment of God in man, the play of the Divine in life is part of the ideal perfection. But if you seek it only in the external, in life, in the principle of action, you will never find it; for you will then not only act according to your nature, which is in itself a rule of perfection, but you will be—and this is a rule of the imperfection—eternally subject to its modes, its dualities of liking and dislike, pain and pleasure and especially to the rajasic mode with its principle of desire and its snare of wrath and grief and longing,—the restless, all-devouring principle of desire, the insatiable fire which besieges your worldly action, the eternal enemy of knowledge by which it is covered over here in your nature as is a fire by smoke or a mirror by dust and which you must slay in order to live in the calm, clear, luminous truth of the spirit. The senses, mind and intellect are the seat of this eternal cause of imperfection and yet it is within this sense, mind and intellect, this play of the lower nature that you would limit your search for perfection! The effort is vain. The kinetic side of your nature must first seek to add to itself the quietistic; you must uplift yourself beyond this lower nature to that which is above the three gunas, that which is founded in the highest principle, in the soul. Only when you have attained to peace of soul, can you become capable of a free and divine action.

The quietist, the ascetic, on the other hand cannot see any possibility of perfection into which life and action enter. Are they not the very seat of bondage and imperfection? Is not all action imperfect in its nature, like a fire that must produce smoke, is not the principle of action itself rajasic, the father of desire, a cause that must have its effect of obscuration of knowledge, its round of longing and success and failure, its oscillations of joy and grief, its duality of virtue and sin? God may be in the world, but he is not of the world; he is a God of renunciation and not the Master or cause of our works; the master of our works is desire, and the cause of works is ignorance. If the world, the Kshara is in a sense a manifestation or a lila of the Divine, it is an imperfect play with the ignorance of Nature, an obscuration rather than a manifestation. That is surely evident from our very first glance at the nature of the world and does not the fullest experience of the world teach us always the same truth? is it not a wheel of the ignorance binding the soul to continual birth by the impulse of desire and action until at last that is exhausted or cast away? Not only desire, but action also must be flung away; seated in the silent self the soul will then pass away into the motionless, actionless, imperturbable, absolute Brahman. To this objection of the impersonalizing quietist the Gita is at more pains to answer than to that of the man of the world, the kinetic individual. For this quietism having hold of a higher and more powerful truth which is yet not the whole or the highest truth, its promulgation as the universal, complete, highest ideal of human life is likely to be more confusing and disastrous to the advance of the human race towards its goal than the error of an exclusive kinetism. A strong one-sided truth, when set forth as the whole truth, creates a strong light but also a strong confusion; for the very strength of its element of truth increases the strength of its element of error. The error of the kinetic ideal can only prolong the ignorance and retard the human advance by setting it in search of perfection where perfection cannot be found; but the error of the quietistic ideal contains in itself the very principle of world-destruction. Where I to act upon it, says Krishna, I should destroy the peoples and be the author of confusion; and though the error of an individual human being, even though a nearly divine man, cannot destroy the whole race, it may produce a widespread confusion which may be in its nature destructive of the principle of human life and disturbing to the settled line of its advance.

Therefore, the quietistic tendency in man must be got to recognize its own incompleteness and admit on an equality with itself the truth which lies behind the kinetic tendency,—the fulfilment of God in man and the presence of the Divine in all the action of the human race. God is there not only in the silence, but in the action; the quietism of the impassive soul unaffected by Nature and the kinetism of the soul giving itself to Nature so that the great world-sacrifice, the Purusha-Yajna, may be effected, are not a reality and a falsehood in perpetual struggle nor yet two hostile realities, one superior, the other inferior, each fatal to the other; they are the double term of the divine manifestation. The Akshara alone is not the whole key of their fulfilment, not the very highest secret. The double fulfilment, the reconciliation is to be sought in the Purushottama represented here by Krishna, at once supreme Being, Lord of the worlds and Avatar. The divinised man entering into his divine nature will act even as he acts; he will not give himself up to inaction. The Divine is at work in man in the ignorance and at work in man in the knowledge. To know Him is our soul's highest welfare and the condition of its perfection, but to know and realize Him as a transcendent peace and silence is not all; the secret that has to be learned is at once the secret of the eternal and unborn Divine and the secret of the divine birth and works, janma karma ca me divyam. The action which proceeds from that knowledge, will be free from all bondage; "he who so knoweth me," says the Teacher, "is not bound by works." If the escape from the obligation of works and desire and from the wheel of rebirth is to be the aim and the ideal, then this knowledge is to be taken as the true, the broad way of escape; for, says the Gita, "he who knows in their right principles my divine birth and works, comes when he leaves his body, not to rebirth, but to Me, O Arjuna." Through the knowledge and possession of the divine birth he comes to the unborn and imperishable Divine who is the self of all beings, ajo avyaya atma; through the knowledge and execution of divine works to the Master of works, the lord of all beings, bhutanam ısvara. He lives in that unborn being, his works are those of that universal Mastery.

XV

THE POSSIBILITY AND PURPOSE OF AVATARHOOD

In speaking of this Yoga in which action and knowledge become one, the Yoga of the sacrifice of works with knowledge, in which works are fulfilled in knowledge, knowledge supports, changes and enlightens works, and both are offered to the Purushottama, the supreme Divinity who becomes manifest within us as Narayana, Lord of all our being and action seated secret in our hearts forever, who becomes manifest even in the human form as the Avatar, the divine birth taking possession of our humanity, Krishna has declared in passing that this was the ancient and original Yoga which he gave to Vivasvan, the Sun-God, Vivasvan gave it to Manu, the father of men, Manu gave it to Ikshvaku, head of the Solar line, and so it came down from royal sage to royal sage till it was lost in the great lapse of Time and is now renewed for Arjuna, because he is the lover and devotee, friend and comrade of the Avatar. For this, he says, is the highest secret,—thus claiming for it a superiority to all other forms of Yoga, because those others lead to the impersonal Brahman or to a personal Deity, to a liberation in actionless knowledge or a liberation in absorbed beatitude, but this gives the highest secret and the whole secret; it brings us to divine peace and divine works, to divine knowledge, action and ecstasy unified in a perfect freedom; it unites into itself all the Yogic paths as the highest being of the Divine reconciles and makes one in itself all the different and even contrary powers and principles of its manifested being. Therefore, this Yoga of the Gita is not, as some contend, only the Karmayoga, one and the lowest, according to them, of the three paths, but a highest Yoga synthetic and integral directing Godward all the powers of our being.

Arjuna takes the declaration about the transmission of the Yoga in its most physical sense,—there is another significance in which it can be taken,—and asks how the Sun-God, one of the first-borns of beings, ancestor of the Solar dynasty, can have received the Yoga from the man Krishna who is only now born into the world. Krishna does not reply, as we might have expected him to have done, that it was as the Divine who is the source of all knowledge that he gave the Word to the Deva who is his form of knowledge, giver of all inner and outer light,—bhargah savitur devasya yo no dhiyah pracodayat; he accepts instead the opportunity which Arjuna gives him of declaring his concealed Godhead, a declaration for which he had prepared when he gave himself as the divine example for the worker who is not bound by his works, but which he has not yet quite explicitly made. He now openly announces himself as the incarnate Godhead, the Avatar.

We have had occasion already, when speaking of the divine Teacher, to state briefly the doctrine of Avatarhood as it appears to us in the light of Vedanta, the light in which the Gita presents it to us. We must now look a little more closely at this Avatarhood and at the significance of the divine Birth of which it is the outward expression; for that is a link of considerable importance in the integral teaching of the Gita. And we may first translate the words of the Teacher himself in which the nature and purpose of Avatarhood are given summarily and remind ourselves also of other passages or references which bear upon it. "Many are my lives that are past, and thine also, O Arjuna; all of them I know, but thou knowest not, O scourge of the foe. Though I am the unborn, though I am imperishable in my self-existence, though I am the Lord of all existences, yet I stand upon my own Nature, and I come into birth by my self-Maya. For whensoever there is the fading of the Dharma and the uprising of unrighteousness, then I loose myself forth into birth. For the deliverance of the good, for the destruction of the evildoers, for the enthroning of the Right I am born from age to age. He who knoweth thus in its right principles my divine birth and my divine work, when he abandons his body, comes not to rebirth, he comes to Me, O Arjuna. Delivered from liking and fear and wrath, full of me, taking refuge in me, many purified by austerity of knowledge have arrived at my nature of being (madbhavam, the divine nature of the Purushottama). As men approach me, so I accept them to my love (bhajami); men follow in every way my path, O son of Pritha."

But most men, the Gita goes on to say, desiring the fulfilment of their works, sacrifice to the gods, to various forms and personalities of the one Godhead, because the fulfilment (siddhi) that is born of works,—of works without knowledge,—is very swift and easy in the human world; it belongs indeed to that world alone. The other, the divine self-fulfillment in man by the sacrifice with knowledge to the supreme Godhead, is much more difficult; its results belong to a higher plane of existence, and they are less easily grasped. Men therefore have to follow the fourfold law of their nature and works and on this plane of mundane action they seek the Godhead through his various qualities. But, says Krishna, though I am the doer of the fourfold works and creator of its fourfold law, yet I must be known also as the non-doer, the imperishable, the immutable Self. "Works affect me not, nor have I desire for the fruit of works;" for God is the impersonal beyond this egoistic personality and this strife of the modes of Nature, and as the Purushottama also, the impersonal Personality, he possesses this supreme freedom even in works. Therefore, the doer of divine works even while following the fourfold law has to know and live in that which is beyond, in the impersonal Self and so in the supreme Godhead. "He who thus knows me is not bound by his works. So, knowing was work done by the men of old who sought liberation; do therefore, thou also, work of that more ancient kind done by ancient men."

The second portion of these passages which has here been given in substance, explains the nature of divine works, divyam karma, with the principle of which we have had to deal in the last essay; the first, which has been fully translated, explains the way of the divine birth, divyam janma, the Avatarhood. But we have to remark carefully that the upholding of Dharma in the world is not the only object of the descent of the Avatar, that great mystery of the Divine manifest in humanity; for the upholding of the Dharma is not an all-sufficient object in itself, not the supreme possible aim for the manifestation of a Christ, a Krishna, a Buddha, but is only the general condition of a higher aim and a more supreme and divine utility. For there are two aspects of the divine birth; one is a descent, the birth of God in humanity, the Godhead manifesting itself in the human form and nature, the eternal Avatar; the other is an ascent, the birth of man into the Godhead, man rising into the divine nature and consciousness, madbhavam agatah; it is the being born anew in a second birth of the soul. It is that new birth which Avatarhood and the upholding of the Dharma are intended to serve. This double aspect in the Gita's doctrine of Avatarhood is apt to be missed by the cursory reader satisfied, as most are, with catching a superficial view of its profound teachings, and it is missed too by the formal commentator petrified in the rigidity of the schools. Yet it is necessary, surely, to the whole meaning of the doctrine. Otherwise, the Avatar idea would be only a dogma, a popular superstition, or an imaginative or mystic deification of historical or legendary supermen, not what the Gita makes all its teaching, a deep philosophical and religious truth, and an essential part of or step to the supreme mystery of all, rahasyam uttamam.

If there were not this rising of man into the Godhead to be helped by the descent of God into humanity, Avatarhood for the sake of the Dharma would be an otiose phenomenon, since mere Right, mere justice or standards of virtue can always be upheld by the divine omnipotence through its ordinary means, by great men or great movements, by the life and work of sages and kings and religious teachers, without any actual incarnation. The Avatar comes as the manifestation of the divine nature in the human nature, the apocalypse of its Christhood, Krishnahood, Buddhahood, in order that the human nature may by moulding its principle, thought, feeling, action, being on the lines of that Christhood, Krishnahood, Buddhahood transfigure itself into the divine. The law, the Dharma which the Avatar establishes is given for that purpose chiefly; the Christ, Krishna, Buddha stands in its Centre as the gate, he makes through himself the way men shall follow. That is why each Incarnation holds before men his own example and declares of himself that he is the way and the gate; he declares too the oneness of his humanity with the divine being, declares that the Son of Man and the Father above from whom he has descended are one, that Krishna in the human body, manusım tanum asritam and the supreme Lord and Friend of all creatures are but two revelations of the same divine Purushottama, revealed there in his own being, revealed here in the type of humanity.

That the Gita contains as its kernel this second and real object of the Avatarhood, is evident even from this passage by itself rightly considered; but it becomes much clearer if we take it, not by itself,—always the wrong way to deal with the texts of the Gita,—but in its right close connection with other passages and with the whole teaching. We have to remember and take together its doctrine of the one Self in all, of the Godhead seated in the heart of every creature, its teaching about the relations between the Creator and his creation, its strongly emphasized idea of the Vibhuti,— noting too the language in which the Teacher gives his own divine example of selfless works which applies equally to the human Krishna and the divine Lord of the worlds, and giving their due weight to such passages as that in the ninth chapter, "Deluded minds despise me lodged in the human body because they know not my supreme nature of being, Lord of all existences"; and we have to read in the light of these ideas this passage we find before us and its declaration that by the knowledge of his divine birth and divine works men come to the Divine and by becoming full of him and even as he and taking refuge in him they arrive at his nature and status of being, madbhavam. For then we shall understand the divine birth and its object, not as an isolated and miraculous phenomenon, but in its proper place in the whole scheme of the world-manifestation; without that we cannot arrive at its divine mystery, but shall either scout it altogether or accept it ignorantly and, it may be, superstitiously or fall into the petty and superficial ideas of the modern mind about it by which it loses all its inner and helpful significance.

For to the modern mind Avatarhood is one of the most difficult to accept or to understand of all the ideas that are streaming in from the East upon the rationalized human consciousness. It is apt to take it at the best for a mere figure for some high manifestation of human power, character, genius, great work done for the world or in the world, and at the worst to regard it as a superstition,—to the heathen a foolishness and to the Greeks a stumbling-block. The materialist, necessarily, cannot even look at it, since he does not believe in God; to the rationalist or the Deist it is a folly and a thing of derision; to the thoroughgoing dualist who sees an unbridgeable gulf between the human and the divine nature, it sounds like a blasphemy. The rationalist objects that if God exists, he is extra cosmic or supracosmic and does not intervene in the affairs of the world, but allows them to be governed by a fixed machinery of law, —he is, in fact, a sort of far-off constitutional monarch or spiritual King Log, at the best an indifferent inactive Spirit behind the activity of Nature, like some generalized or abstract witness Purusha of the Sankhyas; he is pure Spirit and cannot put on a body, infinite and cannot be finite as the human being is finite, the ever unborn creator and cannot be the creature born into the world, —these things are impossible even to his absolute omnipotence. To these objections the thoroughgoing dualist would add that God is in his person, his role, and his nature different and separate from man; the perfect cannot put on human imperfection; the unborn personal God cannot be born as a human personality; the Ruler of the worlds cannot be limited in a nature-bound human action and in a perishable human body. These objections, so formidable at first sight to the reason, seem to have been present to the mind of the Teacher in the Gita when he says that although the Divine is unborn, imperishable in his self-existence, the Lord of all beings, yet he assumes birth by a supreme resort to the action of his Nature and by force of his self-Maya; that he whom the deluded despise because lodged in a human body, is verily in his supreme being the Lord of all; that he is in the action of the divine consciousness the creator of the fourfold Law and the doer of the works of the world and at the same time in the silence of the divine consciousness the impartial witness of the works of his own Nature,—for he is always, beyond both the silence and the action, the supreme Purushottama. And the Gita is able to meet all these oppositions and to reconcile all these contraries because it starts from the Vedantic view of existence, of God and the universe.

For in the Vedantic view of things all these apparently formidable objections are null and void from the beginning. The idea of the Avatar is not indeed indispensable to its scheme, but it comes in naturally into it as a perfectly rational and logical conception. For all here is God, is the Spirit or Self-existence, is Brahman, ekamevadvitıyam,—there is nothing else, nothing other and different from it and there can be nothing else, can be nothing other and different from it; Nature is and can be nothing else than a power of the divine consciousness; all beings are and can be nothing else than inner and outer, subjective and objective soul-forms and bodily forms of the divine being which exist in or result from the power of its consciousness. Far from the Infinite being unable to take on finiteness, the whole universe is nothing else but that; we can see, look as we may, nothing else at all in the whole wide world we inhabit. Far from the Spirit being incapable of form or disdaining to connect itself with form of matter or mind and to assume a limited nature or a body, all here is nothing but that, the world exists only by that connection, that assumption. Far from the world being a mechanism of law with no soul or spirit intervening in the movement of its forces or the action of its minds and bodies,—only some original indifferent Spirit passively existing somewhere outside or above it,—the whole world and every particle of it is on the contrary nothing but the divine force in action and that divine force determines and governs its every movement, inhabits its every form, possesses here every soul and mind; all is in God and in him moves and has its being, in all he is, acts and displays his being; every creature is the disguised Narayana.

Far from the unborn being unable to assume birth, all beings are even in their individuality unborn spirits, eternal without beginning or end, and in their essential existence and their universality all are the one unborn Spirit of whom birth and death are only a phenomenon of the assumption and change of forms. The assumption of imperfection by the perfect is the whole mystic phenomenon of the universe; but the imperfection appears in the form and action of the mind or body assumed, subsists in the phenomenon,—in that which assumes it there is no imperfection, even as in the Sun which illumines all there is no defect of light or of vision, but only in the capacities of the individual organ of vision. Nor does God rule the world from some remote heaven, but by his intimate omnipresence; each finite working of force is an act of infinite Force and not of a limited separate self-existent energy labouring in its own underived strength; in every finite working of will and knowledge we can discover, supporting it, an act of the infinite all-will and all-knowledge. God's rule is not an absentee, foreign and external government; he governs all because he exceeds all, but also because he dwells within all movements and is their absolute soul and spirit. Therefore, none of the objections opposed by our reason to the possibility of Avatarhood can stand in their principle; for the principle is a vain division made by the intellectual reason which the whole phenomenon and the whole reality of the world are busy every moment contradicting and disproving.

But still, apart from the possibility, there is the question of the actual divine working,—whether actually the divine consciousness does appear coming forward from beyond the veil to act at all directly in the phenomenal, the finite, the mental and material, the limited, the imperfect. The finite is indeed nothing but a definition, a face-value of the Infinite's self-representations to its own variations of consciousness; the real value of each finite phenomenon is an infinite value, is indeed the very Infinite. Each being is infinite in its self-existence, whatever it may be in the action of its phenomenal nature, its temporal self-representation. The man is not, when we look closely, himself alone, a rigidly separate self-existent individual, but humanity in a mind and body of itself; and humanity too is no rigidly separate self-existent species or genus, it is the All-existence, the universal Godhead figuring itself in the type of humanity; there it works out certain possibilities, develops, evolves, as we now say, certain powers of its manifestations. What it evolves, is itself, is the Spirit.

For what we mean by Spirit is self-existent being with an infinite power of consciousness and unconditioned delight in its being; it is either that or nothing, or at least nothing which has anything to do with man and the world or with which, therefore, man or the world has anything to do. Matter, body is only a massed motion of force of conscious being employed as a starting-point for the variable relations of consciousness working through its power of sense; nor is Matter anywhere really void of consciousness, for even in the atom, the cell there is, as is now made abundantly clear in spite of itself by modern Science, a power of will, an intelligence at work; but that power is the power of will and intelligence of the Self, Spirit or Godhead within it, it is not the separate, self-derived will or idea of the mechanical cell or atom. This universal will and intelligence, involved, develops its powers from form to form, and on earth at least it is in man that it draws nearest to the full divine and there first becomes, even in the outward intelligence in the form, obscurely conscious of its divinity. But still there too there is a limitation, there is that imperfection of the manifestation which prevents the lower forms from having the self-knowledge of their identity with the Divine. For in each limited being the limitation of the phenomenal action is accompanied by a limitation also of the phenomenal consciousness which defines the nature of the being and makes the inner difference between creature and creature. The Divine works behind indeed and governs its special manifestation through this outer and imperfect consciousness and will, but is itself secret in the cavern, guhayam, as the Veda puts it, or as the Gita expresses it, "In the heart of all existences the Lord abides turning all existences as if mounted on a machine by Maya." This secret working of the Lord hidden in the heart from the egoistic nature-consciousness through which he works, is God's universal method with creatures. Why then should we suppose that in any form he comes forward into the frontal, the phenomenal consciousness for a more direct and consciously divine action? Obviously, if at all, then to break the veil between himself and humanity which man limited in his own nature could never lift.

The Gita explains the ordinary imperfect action of the creature by its subjection to the mechanism of Prakriti and its limitation by the self-representations of Maya. These two terms are only complementary aspects of one and the same effective force of divine consciousness. Maya is not essentially illusion,—the element or appearance of illusion only enters in by the ignorance of the lower Prakriti, Maya of the three modes of Nature,—it is the divine consciousness in its power of various self-representation of its being, while Prakriti is the effective force of that consciousness which operates to work out each such self-representation according to its own law and fundamental idea, svabhava and svadharma, in its own proper quality and particular force of working, guna-karma. "Leaning — pressing down upon my own Nature (Prakriti) I create (loose forth into various being) all this multitude of existences, all helplessly subject to the control of Nature." Those who know not the Divine lodged in the human body, are ignorant of it because they are grossly subject to this mechanism of Prakriti, helplessly subject to its mental limitations and acquiescent in them, and dwell in an Asuric nature that deludes with desire and bewilders with egoism the will and the intelligence, mohinim prakrtim srit΄ah. For the Purushottama within is not readily manifest to any and every being; he conceals himself in a thick cloud of darkness or a bright cloud of light, utterly he envelops and wraps himself in his Yogamaya.[1] "All this world," says the Gita, "because it is bewildered by the three states of being determined by the modes of Nature, fails to recognize me, for this my divine Maya of the modes of Nature is hard to get beyond; those cross beyond it who approach Me; but those who dwell in the Asuric nature of being, have their knowledge reft from them by Maya." In other words, there is the inherent consciousness of the divine in all, for in all the Divine dwells; but he dwells there covered by his Maya and the essential self-knowledge of beings is reft from them, turned into the error of egoism by the action of Maya, the action of the mechanism of Prakriti. Still by drawing back from the mechanism of Nature to her inner and secret Master man can become conscious of the indwelling Divinity.

Now it is notable that with a slight but important variation

1 naham prakasah sarvasya yogamaya-samavrtah.

of language the Gita describes in the same way both the action of the Divine in bringing about the ordinary birth of creatures and his action in his birth as the Avatar. "Leaning upon my own Nature, prakrtim svam avastabhya," it will say later, "I loose forth variously, visrjami, this multitude of creatures helplessly subject owing to the control of Prakriti, avasam prakrter vasat."

"Standing upon my own Nature," it says here, "I am born by my self-Maya, prakrtim svam adhisthaya . . . atmamayaya, I loose forth myself, atmanam srjami." The action implied in the word avastabhya is a forceful downward pressure by which the object controlled is overcome, oppressed, blocked, or limited in its movement or working and becomes helplessly subject to the controlling power, avasam vasat; Nature in this action becomes mechanical and its multitude of creatures are held helpless in the mechanism, not lords of their own action. On the contrary the action implied in the word adhisthaya is a dwelling in, but also a standing upon and over the Nature, a conscious control and government by the indwelling Godhead, adhisthatri devata, in which the Purusha is not helplessly driven by the Prakriti through ignorance, but rather the Prakriti is full of the light and the will of the Purusha. Therefore, in the normal birth that which is loosed forth,—created, as we say,—is the multitude of creatures or becomings, bhutagramam; in the divine birth that which is loosed forth, self-created, is the self-conscious self-existent being, atmanam; for the Vedantic distinction between atma and Bhutani is that which is made in European philosophy between the Being and its becomings. In both cases Maya is the means of the creation or manifestation but in the divine birth it is by self-Maya, atmamayaya, not the involution in the lower Maya of the ignorance, but the conscious action of the self-existent Godhead in its phenomenal self-representation, well aware of its operation and its purpose,—that which the Gita calls elsewhere Yogamaya. In the ordinary birth Yogamaya is used by the Divine to envelop and conceal itself from the lower consciousness, so it becomes for us the means of the ignorance, avidya-maya; but it is by this same Yogamaya that self-knowledge also is made manifest in the return of our consciousness to the Divine, it is the means of the knowledge, vidya-maya and in the divine birth it so operates—as the knowledge controlling and enlightening the works which are ordinarily done in the Ignorance.

The language of the Gita shows therefore that the divine birth is that of the conscious Godhead in our humanity and essentially the opposite of the ordinary birth even though the same means are used, because it is not the birth into the Ignorance, but the birth of the knowledge, not a physical phenomenon, but a soul-birth. It is the Soul's coming into birth as the self-existent Being controlling consciously its becoming and not lost to self-knowledge in the cloud of the ignorance. It is the Soul born into the body as Lord of Nature, standing above and operating in her freely by its will, not entangled and helplessly driven round and round in the mechanism; for it works in the knowledge and not, as most do, in the ignorance. It is the secret Soul in all coming forward from its governing secrecy behind the veil to possess wholly in a human type, but as the Divine, the birth which ordinarily it possesses only from behind the veil as the Ishwara while the outward consciousness in front of the veil is rather possessed than in possession because there it is a partially conscious being, the Jiva lost to self-knowledge and bound in its works through a phenomenal subjection to Nature. The Avatar[2] therefore is a direct manifestation in humanity by Krishna the divine Soul of that divine condition of being to which Arjuna, the human soul, the type of a highest human being, a Vibhuti, is called upon by the Teacher to arise, and to which he can only arise by climbing out of the ignorance and limitation of his ordinary humanity. It is the manifestation from above of that which we have to develop from below; it is the descent of God into that divine birth of the

2 The word Avatara means a descent; it is a coming down of the Divine below the line which divides the divine from the human world or status.

human being into which we mortal creatures must climb; it is the attracting divine example given by God to man in the very type and form and perfected model of our human existence.

XVI

THE PROCESS OF AVATARHOOD

We see that the mystery of the divine Incarnation in man, the assumption by the Godhead of the human type and the human nature, is in the view of the Gita only the other side of the eternal mystery of human birth itself, which is always in its essence, though not in its phenomenal appearance, even such a miraculous assumption. The eternal and universal self of every human being is God; even his personal self is a part of the Godhead, mamaivamsah,—not a fraction or fragment, surely, since we cannot think of God as broken up into little pieces, but a partial consciousness of the one Consciousness, a partial power of the one Power, a partial enjoyment of world-being by the one and universal Delight of being, and therefore in manifestation or, as we say, in Nature a limited and finite being of the one infinite and illimitable Being. The stamp of that limitation is an ignorance by which he forgets, not only the Godhead from which he came forth, but the Godhead, which is always within him, there living in the secret heart of his own nature, there burning like a veiled Fire on the inner altar in his own temple-house of human consciousness.

He is ignorant because there is upon the eyes of his soul and all its organs the seal of that Nature, Prakriti, Maya, by which he has been put forth into manifestation out of God's eternal being; she has minted him like a coin out of the precious metal of the divine substance, but overlaid with a strong coating of the alloy of her phenomenal qualities, stamped with her own stamp and mark of animal humanity, and although the secret sign of the Godhead is there, it is at first indistinguishable and always with difficulty decipherable, not to be really discovered except by that initiation into the mystery of our own being which distinguishes a Godward from an earthward humanity. In the Avatar, the divinely-born Man, the real substance shines through the coating; the mark of the seal is there only for form, the vision is that of the secret Godhead, the power of the life is that of the secret Godhead, and it breaks through the seals of the assumed human nature; the sign of the Godhead, an inner soul-sign, not outward, not physical, stands out legible for all to read who care to see or who can see; for the Asuric nature is always blind to these things, it sees the body and not the soul, the external being and not the internal, the mask and not the Person. In the ordinary human birth, the Nature-aspect of the universal Divine assuming humanity prevails; in the incarnation the God-aspect of the same phenomenon takes its place. In the one he allows the human nature to take possession of his partial being and to dominate it; in the other he takes possession of his partial type of being and its nature and divinely dominates it. Not by evolution or ascent like the ordinary man, the Gita seems to tell us, not by a growing into the divine birth, but by a direct descent into the stuff of humanity and a taking up of its moulds.

But it is to assist that ascent or evolution the descent is made or accepted; that the Gita makes very clear. It is, we might say, to exemplify the possibility of the Divine manifest in the human being, so that man may see what that is and take courage to grow into it. It is also to leave the influence of that manifestation vibrating in the earth-nature and the soul of that manifestation presiding over its upward endeavour. It is to give a spiritual mould of divine manhood into which the seeking soul of the human being can cast itself. It is to give a dharma, a religion,—not a mere creed, but a method of inner and outer living,—a way, a rule and law of self-moulding by which he can grow towards divinity. It is too, since this growth, this ascent is no mere isolated and individual phenomenon, but like all in the divine world-activities a collective business, a work and the work for the race, to assist the human march, to hold it together in its great crises, to break the forces of the downward gravitation when they grow too insistent, to uphold or restore the great dharma of the Godward law in man's nature, to prepare even, however far off, the kingdom of God, the victory of the seekers of light and perfection, sadhunam and the overthrow of those who fight for the continuance of the evil and the darkness. All these are recognized objects of the descent of the Avatar, and it is usually by his work that the mass of men seek to distinguish him and for that that they are ready to worship him. It is only the spiritual who see that this external Avatarhood is a sign, in the symbol of a human life, of the eternal inner Godhead making himself manifest in the field of their own human mentality and corporeality so that they can grow into unity with that and be possessed by it. The divine manifestation of a Christ, Krishna, Buddha in external humanity has for its inner truth the same manifestation of the eternal Avatar within in our own inner humanity. That which has been done in the outer human life of earth, may be repeated in the inner life of all human beings.

This is the object of the incarnation, but what is the method? First, we have the rational or minimizing view of Avatarhood which sees in it only an extraordinary manifestation of the diviner qualities moral, intellectual and dynamic by which average humanity is exceeded. In this idea there is a certain truth. The Avatar is at the same time the Vibhuti. This Krishna who in his divine inner being is the Godhead in a human form, is in his outer human being the leader of his age, the great man of the Vrishni's. This is from the point of view of the Nature, not of the soul. The Divine manifests himself through infinite qualities of his nature and the intensity of the manifestation is measured by their power and their achievement. The vibhuti of the Divine is therefore, impersonally, the manifest power of his quality, it is his outflowing, in whatever form, of Knowledge, Energy, Love, Strength and the rest; personally, it is the mental form and the animate being in whom this power is achieved and does its great works. A pre-eminence in this inner and outer achievement, a greater power of divine quality, an effective energy is always the sign. The human vibhuti is the hero of the race's struggle towards divine achievement, the hero in the Carlylean sense of heroism, a power of God in man. "I am Vasudeva (Krishna) among the Vrishni's," says the Lord in the Gita, "Dhananjaya (Arjuna) among the Pandavas, Vyasa among the sages, the seer-poet Ushanas among the seer-poets," the first in each category, the greatest of each group, the most powerfully representative of the qualities and works in which its characteristic soul-power manifests itself. This heightening of the powers of the being is a very necessary step in the progress of the divine manifestation. Every great man who rises above our average level, raises by that very fact our common humanity; he is a living assurance of our divine possibilities, a promise of the Godhead, a glow of the divine Light and a breath of the divine Power.

It is this truth which lies behind the natural human tendency to the deification of great minds and heroic characters; it comes out clearly enough in the Indian habit of mind which easily sees a partial (amsa) Avatar in great saints, teachers, founders, or most significantly in the belief of southern Vaishnavas that some of their saints were incarnations of the symbolic living weapons of Vishnu,—for that is what all great spirits are, living powers and weapons of the Divine in the upward march and battle. This idea is innate and inevitable in any mystic or spiritual view of life which does not draw an inexorable line between the being and nature of the Divine and our human being and nature; it is the sense of the divine in humanity. But still the Vibhuti is not the Avatar; otherwise, Arjuna, Vyasa, Ushanas would be Avatars as well as Krishna, even if in a less degree of the power of Avatarhood. The divine quality is not enough; there must be the inner consciousness of the Lord and Self-governing the human nature by his divine presence. The heightening of the power of the qualities is part of the becoming, bhutagrama, an ascent in the ordinary manifestation; in the Avatar there is the special manifestation, the divine birth from above, the eternal and universal Godhead descended into a form of individual humanity, atmanam srjami, and conscious not only behind the veil but in the outward nature.

There is an intermediary idea, a more mystical view of Avatarhood which supposes that a human soul calls down this descent into himself and is either possessed by the divine consciousness or becomes an effective reflection or channel of it. This view rests upon certain truths of spiritual experience. The divine birth in man, his ascent, is itself a growing of the human into the divine consciousness, and in its intensest culmination is a losing of the separate self in that. The soul merges its individuality in an infinite and universal being or loses it in the heights of a transcendent being it becomes one with the Self, the Brahman, the Divine or, as it is sometimes more absolutely put, becomes the oneself, the Brahman, the Divine. The Gita itself speaks of the soul becoming the Brahman, brahmabhuta, and of its thereby dwelling in the Lord, in Krishna, but it does not, it must be marked, speak of it as becoming the Lord or the Purushottama, though it does declare that the Jiva himself is always Ishwara, the partial being of the Lord, mamaivamsah. For this greatest union, this highest becoming is still part of the ascent; while it is the divine birth to which every Jiva arrives, it is not the descent of the Godhead, not Avatarhood, but at most Buddhahood according to the doctrine of the Buddhists, it is the soul awakened from its present mundane individuality into an infinite super consciousness. That need not carry with it either the inner consciousness or the characteristic action of the Avatar.

On the other hand, this entering into the divine consciousness may be attended by a reflex action of the Divine entering or coming forward into the human parts of our being, pouring himself into the nature, the activity, the mentality, the corporeality even of the man; and that may well be at least a partial Avatarhood. The Lord stands in the heart, says the Gita,—by which it means of course the heart of the subtle being, the nodus of the emotions, sensations, mental consciousness, where the individual Purusha also is seated, — but he stands there veiled, enveloped by his Maya. But above, on a plane within us but now superconscient to us, called heaven by the ancient mystics, the Lord and the Jiva stand together revealed as of one essence of being, the Father and the Son of certain symbolisms, the Divine Being and the divine Man who comes forth from Him born of the higher divine Nature,[1] the virgin Mother, para prakrti, para maya, into the lower or human nature. This seems to be the inner doctrine of the Christian incarnation; in its Trinity the Father is above in this inner Heaven; the Son or supreme Prakriti become Jiva of the Gita descends as the divine Man upon earth, in the mortal body; the Holy Spirit, pure Self, Brahmic consciousness is that which makes them one and that also in which they communicate; for we hear of the Holy Spirit descending upon Jesus and it is the same descent which brings down the powers of the higher consciousness into the simple humanity of the Apostles.

But also, the higher divine consciousness of the Purushottama may itself descend into the humanity and that of the Jiva disappear into it. This is said by his contemporaries to have happened in the occasional transfigurations of Chaitanya when he who in his normal consciousness was only the lover and devotee of the Lord and rejected all deification, became in these abnormal

---

1 In the Buddhist legend the name of the mother of Buddha makes the symbolism clear; in the Christian the symbol seems to have been attached by a familiar mythopoeic process to the actual human mother of Jesus of Nazareth.

moments the Lord himself and so spoke and acted, with all the out-flooding light and love and power of the divine Presence. Supposing this to be the normal condition, the human receptacle to be constantly no more than a vessel of this divine Presence and divine Consciousness, we should have the Avatar according to this intermediary idea of the incarnation. That easily recommends itself as possible to our human notions; for if the human being can elevate his nature so as to feel a unity with the being of the Divine and himself a mere channel of its conscious-ness, light, power, love, his own will, and personality lost in that will and that being,—and this is a recognized spiritual status,—then there is no inherent impossibility of the reflex action of that Will, Being, Power, Love, Light, Consciousness occupying the whole personality of the human Jiva. And this would not be merely an ascent of our humanity into the divine birth and the divine nature, but a descent of the divine Purusha into humanity, an Avatar.

The Gita, however, goes much farther. It speaks clearly of the Lord himself being born; Krishna speaks of his many births that are past and makes it clear by his language that it is not merely the receptive human being but the Divine of whom he makes this affirmation, because he uses the very language of the Creator, the same language which he will employ when he has to describe his creation of the world. "Although I am the unborn Lord of creatures, I create (loose forth) myself by my Maya," presiding over the actions of my Prakriti. Here there is no question of the Lord and the human Jiva or of the Father and the Son, the divine Man, but only of the Lord and his Prakriti. The Divine descends by his own Prakriti into birth in its human form and type and brings into it the divine Consciousness and the divine Power, though consenting, though willing to act in the form, type, mould of humanity and he governs its actions in the body as the indwelling and over-dwelling Soul, adhisthaya. From above he governs always, indeed, for so he governs all nature, the human included; from within also he governs all nature, always, but hidden; the difference here is that he is manifest, that the nature is conscious of the divine Presence as the Lord, the Inhabitant, and it is not by his secret will from above, "the will of the Father which is in heaven," but by his quite direct and apparent will that he moves the nature. And here there seems to be no room for the human intermediary; for it is by resort to his own nature, prakrtim svam, and not the special nature of the Jiva that the Lord of all existence thus takes upon himself the human birth.

This doctrine is a hard saying, a difficult thing for the human reason to accept and for an obvious reason, because of the evident humanity of the Avatar. The Avatar is always a dual phenomenon of divinity and humanity; the Divine takes upon himself the human nature with all its outward limitations and makes them the circumstances, means, instruments of the divine consciousness and the divine power, a vessel of the divine birth and the divine works. But so surely it must be, since otherwise the object of the Avatar's descent is not fulfilled; for that object is precisely to show that the human birth with all its limitations can be made such a means and instrument of the divine birth and divine works, precisely to show that the human type of consciousness can be compatible with the divine essence of consciousness made manifest, can be converted into its vessel, drawn into nearer conformity with it by a change of its mould and a heightening of its powers of light and love and strength and purity; and to show also how it can be done. If the Avatar were to act in an entirely supernormal fashion, this object would not be fulfilled. A merely supernormal or miraculous Avatar would be a meaningless absurdity; not that there need be an entire absence of the use of supernormal powers such as Christ's so-called miracles of healing, for the use of supernormal powers is quite a possibility of human nature; but there need not be that at all, nor in any case is it the root of the matter, nor would it at all do if the life were nothing else but a display of supernormal fireworks. The Avatar does not come as a thaumaturgic magician, but as the divine leader of humanity and the exemplar of a divine humanity. Even human sorrow and physical suffering he must assume and use so as to show, first, how that suffering may be a means of redemption,—as did Christ,—secondly, to show how, having been assumed by the divine soul in the human nature, it can also be overcome in the same nature,—as did Buddha. The rationalist who would have cried to Christ, "If thou art the Son of God, come down from the cross," or points out sagely that the Avatar was not divine because he died and died too by disease,—as a dog dieth,—knows not what he is saying: for he has missed the root of the whole matter. Even, the Avatar of sorrow and suffering must come before there can be the Avatar of divine joy; the human limitation must be assumed in order to show how it can be overcome; and the way and the extent of the overcoming, whether internal only or external also, depends upon the stage of the human advance; it must not be done by a non-human miracle.

The question then arises, and it is the sole real difficulty, for here the intellect falters and stumbles over its own limits, how is this human mind and body assumed? For they were not created suddenly and all of a piece, but by some kind of evolution, physical or spiritual or both. No doubt, the descent of the Avatar, like the divine birth from the other side, is essentially a spiritual phenomenon, as is shown by the Gita's atmanam srjami, it is a soul-birth; but still there is here an attendant physical birth. How then were this human mind and body of the Avatar created? If we suppose that the body is always created by the hereditary evolution, by inconscient Nature and its immanent Life-spirit without the intervention of the individual soul, the matter becomes simple. A physical and mental body is prepared fit for the divine incarnation by a pure or great heredity and the descending Godhead takes possession of it. But the Gita in this very passage applies the doctrine of reincarnation, boldly enough, to the Avatar himself, and in the usual theory of reincarnation the reincarnating soul by its past spiritual and psychological evolution itself determines and in a way prepares its own mental and physical body. The soul prepares its own body, the body is not prepared for it without any reference to the soul. Are we then to suppose an eternal or continual Avatar himself evolving, we might say, his own fit mental and physical body according to the needs and pace of the human evolution and so appearing from age to age, yuge yuge? In some such spirit some would interpret the ten incarnations of Vishnu, first in animal forms, then in the animal man, then in the dwarf man-soul, Vamana, the violent Asuric man, Rama of the axe, the divinely-natured man, a greater Rama, the awakened spiritual man, Buddha, and, preceding him in time, but final in place, the complete divine manhood, Krishna,—for the last Avatar, Kalki, only accomplishes the work Krishna began,—he fulfils in power the great struggle which the previous Avatars prepared in all its potentialities. It is a difficult assumption to our modern mentality, but the language of the Gita seems to demand it. Or, since the Gita does not expressly solve the problem, we may solve it in some other way of our own, as that the body is prepared by the Jiva but assumed from birth by the Godhead or that it is prepared by one of the four Manus, catvaro manavah, of the

Gita, the spiritual Fathers of every human mind and body. This is going far into the mystic field from which the modern reason is still averse; but once we admit Avatarhood, we have already entered it and, once entered, may as well tread in it with firm footsteps.

There the Gita's doctrine of Avatarhood stands. We have had to advert to it at length in this aspect of its method, as we did to the question of its possibility, because it is necessary to look at it and face the difficulties which the reasoning mind of man is likely to offer to it. It is true that the physical Avatarhood does not fill a large space in the Gita, but still it does occupy a definite place in the chain of its teachings and is implied in the whole scheme, the very framework being the Avatar leading the Vibhuti, the man who has risen to the greatest heights of mere manhood, to the divine birth and divine works. No doubt, too, the inner descent of the Godhead to raise the human soul into himself is the main thing,— it is the inner Christ, Krishna or Buddha that matters. But just as the outer life is of immense importance for the inner development, so the external Avatarhood is of no mean importance for this great spiritual manifestation. The consummation in the mental and physical symbol assists the growth of the inner reality; afterwards the inner reality expresses itself with greater power in a more perfect symbolization of itself through the outer life. Between these two, spiritual reality and mental and physical expression, acting and returning upon each other constantly the manifestation of the Divine in humanity has elected to move always in the cycles of its concealment and its revelation.

XVII

THE DIVINE BIRTH AND DIVINE WORKS

The Work for which the Avatar descends has like his birth a double sense and a double form. It has an outward side of the divine force acting upon the external world in order to maintain there and to reshape the divine law by which the Godward effort of humanity is kept from decisive retrogression and instead decisively carried forward in spite of the rule of action and reaction, the rhythm of advance and relapse by which Nature proceeds. It has an inward side of the divine force of the Godward consciousness acting upon the soul of the individual and the soul of the race, so that it may receive new forms of revelation of the Divine in man and may be sustained, renewed, and enriched in its power of upward self-unfolding. The Avatar does not descend merely for a great outward action, as the pragmatic sense in humanity is too often tempted to suppose. Action and event have no value in themselves, but only take their value from the force which they represent and the idea which they symbolise and which the force is there to serve.

The crisis in which the Avatar appears, though apparent to the outward eye only as a crisis of events and great material changes, is always in its source and real meaning a crisis in the consciousness of humanity when it has to undergo some grand modification and effect some new development. For this action of change a divine force is needed; but the force varies always according to the power of consciousness which it embodies; hence the necessity of a divine consciousness manifesting in the mind and soul of humanity. Where, indeed, the change is mainly intellectual and practical, the intervention of the Avatar is not needed; there is a great uplifting of consciousness, a great manifestation of power in which men are for the time being exalted above their normal selves, and this surge of consciousness and power finds its wave-crests in certain exceptional individuals, Vibhuti's, whose action leading the general action is sufficient for the change intended. The Reformation in Europe and the French Revolution were crises of this character; they were not great spiritual events, but intellectual and practical changes, one in religious, the other in social and political ideas, forms and motives, and the modification of the general consciousness brought about was a mental and dynamic, but not a spiritual modification. But when the crisis has a spiritual seed or intention, then a complete or a partial manifestation of the God-consciousness in a human mind and soul comes as its originator or leader. That is the Avatar.

The outward action of the Avatar is described in the Gita as the restoration of the Dharma; when from age to age the Dharma fades, languishes, loses force and its opposite arises, strong and oppressive, then the Avatar comes and raises it again to power; and as these things in idea are always represented by things in action and by human beings who obey their impulsion, his mission is, in its most human and outward terms, to relieve the seekers of the Dharma who are oppressed by the reign of the reactionary darkness and to destroy the wrong-doers who seek to maintain the denial of the Dharma. But the language used can easily be given a poor and insufficient connotation which would deprive Avatarhood of all its spiritual depth of meaning. Dharma is a word which has an ethical and practical, a natural and philosophical and a religious and spiritual significance, and it may be used in any of these senses exclusive of the others, in a purely ethical, a purely philosophical or a purely religious sense. Ethically it means the law of righteousness, the moral rule of conduct, or in a still more outward and practical significance social and political justice, or even simply the observation of the social law. If used in this sense we shall have to understand that when unrighteousness, injustice and oppression prevail, the Avatar descends to deliver the good and destroy the wicked, to break down injustice and oppression and restore the ethical balance of mankind.

Thus, the popular and mythical account of the Krishna avatar is that the unrighteousness of the Kurus as incarnated in Duryodhana and his brothers became so great a burden to the earth that she had to call upon God to descend and lighten her load; accordingly, Vishnu incarnated as Krishna, delivered the oppressed Pandavas, and destroyed the unjust Kauravas. A similar account is given of the descent of the previous Vishnu avatars, of Rama to destroy the unrighteous oppression of Ravana, of Parashurama to destroy the unrighteous license of the military and princely caste, the Kshatriyas, of the dwarf Vamana to destroy the rule of the Titan Bali. But obviously the purely practical, ethical, or social and political mission of the Avatar which is thus thrown into popular and mythical form, does not give a right account of the phenomenon of Avatarhood. It does not cover its spiritual sense, and if this outward utility were all, we should have to exclude Buddha and Christ whose mission was not at all to destroy evil-doers and deliver the good, but to bring to all men a new spiritual message and a new law of divine growth and spiritual realization. On the other hand, if we give to the word dharma only its religious sense, in which it means a law of religious and spiritual life, we shall indeed get to the kernel of the matter, but we shall be in danger of excluding a most important part of the work done by the Avatar. Always we see in the history of the divine incarnations the double work, and inevitably, because the Avatar takes up the workings of God in human life, the way of the divine Will and Wisdom in the world, and that always fulfils itself externally as well as internally, by inner progress in the soul and by an outer change in the life.

The Avatar may descend as a great spiritual teacher and saviour, the Christ, the Buddha, but always his work leads, after he has finished his earthly manifestation, to a profound and powerful change not only in the ethical, but in the social and outward life and ideals of the race. He may, on the other hand, descend as an incarnation of the divine life, the divine personality and power in its characteristic action, for a mission ostensibly social, ethical, and political, as is represented in the story of Rama or Krishna; but always then this descent becomes in the soul of the race a permanent power for the inner living and the spiritual rebirth. It is indeed curious to note that the permanent, vital, universal effect of Buddhism and Christianity has been the force of their ethical, social and practical ideals and their influence even on the men and the ages which have rejected their religious and spiritual beliefs, forms and disciplines; later Hinduism which rejected Buddha, his sangha and his dharma, bears the ineffaceable imprint of the social and ethical influence of Buddhism and its effect on the ideas and the life of the race, while in modern Europe, Christian only in name, humanitarianism is the translation into the ethical and social sphere and the aspiration to liberty, equality and fraternity the translation into the social and political sphere of the spiritual truths of Christianity, the latter especially being effected by men who aggressively rejected the Christian religion and spiritual discipline and by an age which in its intellectual effort of emancipation tried to get rid of Christianity as a creed. On the other hand, the life of Rama and Krishna belongs to the prehistoric past which has come down only in poetry and legend and may even be regarded as myths; but it is quite immaterial whether we regard them as myths or historical facts, because their permanent truth and value lie in their persistence as a spiritual form, presence, influence in the inner consciousness of the race and the life of the human soul. Avatarhood is a fact of divine life and consciousness which may realize itself in an outward action, but must persist, when that action is over and has done its work, in a spiritual influence; or may realize itself in a spiritual influence and teaching but must then have its permanent effect, even when the new religion or discipline is exhausted, in the thought, temperament and outward life of mankind.

We must then, in order to understand the Gita's description of the work of the Avatar, take the idea of the Dharma in its fullest, deepest, and largest conception, as the inner and the outer law by which the divine Will and Wisdom work out the spiritual evolution of mankind and its circumstances and results in the life of the race. Dharma in the Indian conception is not merely the good, the right, morality and justice, ethics; it is the whole government of all the relations of man with other beings, with Nature, with God, considered from the point of view of a divine principle working itself out in forms and laws of action, forms of the inner and the outer life, orderings of relations of every kind in the world. Dharma[1] is both that which we hold to and that which holds together our inner and outer activities. In its primary sense it means a fundamental law of our nature which secretly conditions all our activities and in this sense, each being, type, species, individual, group has its own dharma. Secondly, there is the divine nature which has to develop and manifest in us, and in this sense, dharma is the law of the inner workings by which that grows in our being. Thirdly, there is the law by which we govern our outgoing thought and action and our relations with each other so as to help best both our own growth and that of the human race towards the divine ideal.

Dharma is generally spoken of as something eternal and unchanging, and so it is in the fundamental principle, in the ideal,

---

1 The word means "holding" from the root dhr, to hold.

but in its forms, it is continually changing and evolving, because man does not already possess the ideal or live in it, but aspires more or less perfectly towards it, is growing to-wards its knowledge and practice. And in this growth dharma is all that helps us to grow into the divine purity, largeness, light, freedom, power, strength, joy, love, good, unity, beauty and against it stands its shadow and denial, all that resists its growth and has not undergone its law, all that has not yielded up and does not will to yield up its secret of divine values, but presents a front of perversion and contradiction, of impurity, narrowness, bondage, darkness, weakness, vileness, discord and suffering and division, and the hideous and the crude, all that man has to leave behind in his progress. This is the adharma, not-dharma, which strives with and seeks to overcome the dharma, to draw backward and downward, the reactionary force which makes for evil, ignorance, and darkness. Between the two there is perpetual battle and struggle, oscillation of victory and defeat in which sometimes the upward and sometimes the downward forces prevail. This has been typified in the Vedic image of the struggle between the divine and the Titanic powers, the sons of the Light and the undivided Infinity and the children of the Darkness and Division, in Zoroastrianism by Ahuramazda and Ahriman, and in later religions in the contest between God and his angels and Satan or Iblis and his demons for the possession of human life and the human soul.

It is these things that condition and determine the work of the Avatar. In the Buddhistic formula the disciple takes refuge from all that opposes his liberation in three powers, the dharma, the sangha, the Buddha. So, in Christianity we have the law of Christian living, the Church, and the Christ. These three are always the necessary elements of the work of the Avatar. He gives a dharma, a law of self-discipline by which to grow out of the lower into the higher life and which necessarily includes a rule of action and of relations with our fellowmen and other beings, endeavour in the eightfold path or the law of faith, love, and purity or any other such revelation of the nature of the divine in life. Then because every tendency in man has its collective as well as its individual aspect, because those who follow one way are naturally drawn together into spiritual companionship and unity, he establishes the sangha˙, the fellowship and union of those whom his personality and his teaching unite. In Vaishnavism there is the same trio, bhagavata, bhakta, bhagavan,—the bhagavata, which is the law of the Vaishnava dispensation of adoration and love, the bhakta representing the fellowship of those in whom that law is manifest, bhagavan, the divine Lover and Beloved in whose being and nature the divine law of love is founded and fulfils itself. The Avatar represents this third element, the divine personality, nature and being who is the soul of the dharma and the sangha, informs them with himself, keeps them living and draws men towards the felicity and the liberation.

In the teaching of the Gita, which is more catholic and complex than other specialized teachings and disciplines, these things assume a larger meaning. For the unity here is the all-embracing Vedantic unity by which the soul sees all in itself and itself in all and makes itself one with all beings. The dharma is therefore the taking up of all human relations into a higher divine meaning; starting from the established ethical, social and religious rule which binds together the whole community in which the God-seeker lives, it lifts it up by informing it with the Brahmic consciousness; the law it gives is the law of one-ness, of equality, of liberated, desireless, God-governed action, of God-knowledge and self-knowledge enlightening and drawing to itself all the nature and all the action, drawing it towards divine being and divine consciousness, and of God-love as the supreme power and crown of the knowledge and the action. The idea of companionship and mutual aid in God-love and God-seeking which is at the basis of the idea of the sangha or divine fellowship, is brought in when the Gita speaks of the seeking of God through love and adoration, but the real sangha of this teaching is all humanity. The whole world is moving towards this dharma, each man according to his capacity, —"it is my path that men follow in every way,"—and the God-seeker, making himself one with all, making their joy and sorrow and all their life his own, the liberated made already oneself with all beings, lives in the life of humanity, lives for the one Self in humanity, for God in all beings, acts for lokasangraha, for the maintaining of all in their dharma and the Dharma, for the maintenance of their growth in all its stages and in all its paths towards the Divine. For the Avatar here, though he is manifest in the name and form of Krishna, lays no exclusive stress on this one form of his human birth, but on that which it represents, the Divine, the Purushottama, of whom all Avatars are the human births, of whom all forms and names of the Godhead worshipped by men are the figures. The way declared by Krishna here is indeed announced as the way by which man can reach the real knowledge and the real liberation, but it is one that is inclusive of all paths and not exclusive. For the Divine takes up into his universality all Avatars and all teachings and all dharmas.

The Gita lays stress upon the struggle of which the world is the theatre, in its two aspects, the inner struggle and the outer battle. In the inner struggle the enemies are within, in the individual, and the slaying of desire, ignorance, egoism is the victory. But there is an outer struggle between the powers of the Dharma and the Adharma in the human collectivity. The former is supported by the divine, the godlike nature in man, and by those who represent it or strive to realize it in human life, the latter by the Titanic or demoniac, the Asuric and Rakshasic nature whose head is a violent egoism, and by those who represent and strive to satisfy it. This is the war of the Gods and Titans, the symbol of which the old Indian literature is full, the struggle of the Mahabharata of which Krishna is the central figure being often represented in that image; the Pandavas who fight for the establishment of the kingdom of the Dharma, are the sons of the Gods, their powers in human form, their adversaries are incarnations of the Titanic powers, they are Asuras. This outer struggle to the Avatar comes to aid, directly or indirectly, to destroy the reign of the Asuras, the evildoers, and in them depress the power they represent and to restore the oppressed ideals of the Dharma. He comes to bring nearer the kingdom of heaven on earth in the collectivity as well as to build the kingdom of heaven within in the individual human soul.

The inner fruit of the Avatar's coming is gained by those who learn from it the true nature of the divine birth and the divine works and who, growing full of him in their consciousness and taking refuge in him with their whole being, manmaya mam upasritah, purified by the realizing force of their knowledge and delivered from the lower nature, attain to the divine being and divine nature, madbhavam. The Avatar comes to reveal the divine nature in man above this lower nature and to show what are the divine works, free, unegoistic, disinterested, impersonal, universal, full of the divine light, the divine power, and the divine love. He comes as the divine personality which shall fill the consciousness of the human being and replace the limited egoistic personality, so that it shall be liberated out of ego into infinity and universality, out of birth into immortality. He comes as the divine power and love which calls men to itself, so that they may take refuge in that and no longer in the insufficiency of their human wills and the strife of their human fear, wrath and passion, and liberated from all this unquiet and suffering may live in the calm and bliss of the Divine.[2] Nor does it matter essentially in what form and name or putting forward what aspect of the Divine he comes; for in all ways, varying with their nature, men are following the path set to them by the Divine which will in the end lead them to him and the aspect of him which suits their nature is that which they can

---

2 *janma karma ca me divyam evam yo vetti tattvatah,*
tyaktva deham punarjanma naiti mam eti so'rjuna.
vıtaragabhayakrodha manmaya mam upasritah
bahavo jnanatapasa puta madbhavam agatah.

best follow when he comes to lead them; in whatever way men accept, love and take joy in God, in that way God accepts, loves and takes joy in man. Ye yatha mam prapadyante tams tathaiva bhajamyaham.

XVIII

THE DIVINE WORKER

To Attain to the divine birth,—a divinizing new birth of the soul into a higher consciousness,—and to do divine works both as a means towards that before it is attained and as an expression of it after it is attained, is then all the Karmayoga of the Gita. The Gita does not try to define works by any outward signs through which it can be recognizable to an external gaze, measurable by the criticism of the world; it deliberately renounces even the ordinary ethical distinctions by which men seek to guide themselves in the light of the human reason. The signs by which it distinguishes divine works are all profoundly intimate and subjective; the stamp by which they are known is invisible, spiritual, supra-ethical.

They are recognizable only by the light of the soul from which they come. For, it says, "what is action and what is in-action, as to this even the sages are perplexed and deluded," because, judging by practical, social, ethical, intellectual standards, they discriminate by accidentals and do not go to the root of the matter; "I will declare to thee that action by the knowledge of which thou shalt be released from all ills. One has to under-stand about action as well as to understand about wrong action and about inaction one has to understand; thick and tangled is the way of works." Action in the world is like a deep forest, gahana, through which man goes stumbling as best he can, by the light of the ideas of his time, the standards of his personality, his environment, or rather of many times, many personalities, layers of thought and ethics from many social stages all inextricably confused together, temporal and conventional amidst all their claim to absoluteness and immutable truth, empirical and irrational in spite of their aping of right reason. And finally, the sage seeking in the midst of it all the highest foundation of fixed law and an original truth finds himself obliged to raise the last supreme question, whether all action and life itself are not a delusion and a snare and whether cessation from action, akarma, is not the last resort of the tired and disillusioned human soul. But, says Krishna, in this matter even the sages are perplexed and deluded. For by action, by works, not by inaction comes the knowledge and the release.

What then is the solution? what is that type of works by which we shall be released from the ills of life, from this doubt, this error, this grief, from this mixed, impure, and baffling result even of our purest and best-intentioned acts, from these million forms of evil and suffering? No outward distinctions need be made, is the reply; no work the world needs, be shunned; no limit or hedge set round our human activities; on the contrary, all actions should be done, but from a soul in Yoga with the Divine, yuktah krtsna-karma-krt. Akarma, cessation from action is not . . .the way; the man who has attained to the insight of the highest reason, perceives that such inaction is itself a constant action, a state subject to the workings of Nature and her qualities. The mind that takes refuge in physical inactivity, is still under the delusion that it and not Nature is the doer of works; it has mistaken inertia for liberation; it does not see that even in what seems absolute inertia greater than that of the stone or clod, Nature is at work, keeps unimpaired her hold. On the contrary, in the full flood of action the soul is free from its works, is not the doer, not bound by what is done, and he who lives in the freedom of the soul, not in the bondage of the modes of Nature, alone has release from works. This is what the Gita clearly means when it says that he who in action can see inaction and can see action still continuing in cessation from works, is the man of true reason and discernment among men. This saying hinges upon the Sankhya distinction between Purusha and Prakriti, between the free inactive soul, eternally calm, pure, and unmoved in the midst of works, and ever active Nature operative as much in inertia and cessation as in the overt turmoil of her visible hurry of labour. This is the knowledge which the highest effort of the discriminating reason, the buddhi, gives to us, and therefore whoever possesses it is the truly rational and discerning man, sa buddhiman¯ manusyesu,—not the perplexed thinker who judges.

life and works by the external, uncertain, and impermanent distinctions of the lower reason. Therefore, the liberated man is not afraid of action, he is a large and universal doer of all works, krtsna-karma-krt; not as others do them in subjection to Nature but poised in the silent calm of the soul, tranquilly in Yoga with the Divine. The Divine is the lord of his works, he is only their channel through the instrumentality of his nature conscious of and subject to her Lord. By the flaming intensity and purity of this knowledge all his works are burned up as in a fire and his mind remains without any stain or disfiguring mark from them, calm, silent, unperturbed, white, and clean and pure. To do all in this liberating knowledge, without the personal egoism of the doer, is the first sign of the divine worker.

The second sign is freedom from desire; for where there is not the personal egoism of the doer, desire becomes impossible; it is starved out, sinks for want of a support, dies of inanition. Outwardly the liberated man seems to undertake works of all kinds like other men, on a larger scale perhaps with a more powerful will and driving force, for the might of the divine will works in his active nature; but from all his inceptions and under-takings the inferior concept and nether will of desire is entirely banished, sarve samarambhah kamasankalpavarjitah. He has abandoned all attachment to the fruits of his works, and where one does not work for the fruit, but solely as an impersonal instrument of the Master of works, desire can find no place,—not even the desire to serve successfully, for the fruit is the Lord's and determined by him and not by the personal will and effort, or to serve with credit and to the Master's satisfaction, for the real doer is the Lord himself and all glory belongs to a form of his Shakti missioned in the nature and not to the limited human personality. The human mind and soul of the liberated man does nothing, na kincit karoti; even though through his nature he engages in action, it is the Nature, the executive Shakti, it is the conscious Goddess governed by the divine Inhabitant who does the work.

It does not follow that the work is not to be done perfectly, with success, with a right adaptation of means to ends on the contrary a perfect working is easier to action done tranquilly in Yoga than to action done in the blindness of hopes and fears, lamed by the judgments of the stumbling reason, running about amidst the eager trepidations of the hasty human will: Yoga, says the Gita elsewhere, is the true skill in works, yogah karmasu kausalam. But all this is done impersonally by the action of a great universal light and power operating through the individual nature. The Karmayogin knows that the power given to him will be adapted to the fruit decreed, the divine thought behind the work equated with the work he has to do, the will in him,—which will not be wish or desire, but an impersonal drive of conscious power directed towards an aim not his own,—subtly regulated in its energy and direction by the divine wisdom. The result may be success, as the ordinary mind understands it, or it may seem to that mind to be defeat and failure; but to him it is always the success intended, not by him, but by the all-wise manipulator of action and result, because he does not seek for victory, but only for the fulfilment of the divine will and wisdom which works out its ends through apparent failure as well as and often with greater force than through apparent triumph. Arjuna, bidden to fight, is assured of victory; but even if certain defeat were before him, he must still fight because that is the present work assigned to him as his immediate share in the great sum of energies by which the divine will is surely accomplished.

The liberated man has no personal hopes; he does not seize on things as his personal possessions; he receives what the divine Will brings him, covets nothing, is jealous of none: what comes to him he takes without repulsion and without attachment; what goes from him he allows to depart into the whirl of things without repining or grief or sense of loss. His heart and self are under perfect control; they are free from reaction and passion; they make no turbulent response to the touches of outward things. His action is indeed a purely physical action, sariram kevalam karma; for all else comes from above, is not generated on the human plane, is only a reflection of the will, knowledge, joy of the divine Purushottama. Therefore, he does not by a stress on doing and its objects bring about in his mind and heart any of those reactions which we call passion and sin. For sin consists not at all in the outward deed, but in an impure reaction of the personal will, mind and heart which accompanies it or causes it; the impersonal, the spiritual is always pure, apapaviddham, and gives to all that it does its own inalienable purity. This spiritual impersonality is a third sign of the divine worker. All human souls, indeed, who have attained to a certain greatness and largeness are conscious of an impersonal Force or Love or Will and Knowledge working through them, but they are not free from egoistic reactions, sometimes violent enough, of their human personality. But this freedom the liberated soul has attained; for he has cast his personality into the impersonal, where it is no longer his, but is taken up by the divine Person, the Purushottama, who uses all finite qualities infinitely and freely and is bound by none. He has become a soul and ceased to be a sum of natural qualities; and such appearance of personality as remains for the operations of Nature, is something unbound, large, flexible, universal; it is a free mould for the Infinite, it is a living mask of the Purushottama.

The result of this knowledge, this desirelessness and this impersonality is a perfect equality in the soul and the nature. Equality is the fourth sign of the divine worker. He has, says the Gita, passed beyond the dualities; he is dvandvatita. We have seen that he regards with equal eyes, without any disturbance of feeling, failure and success, victory, and defeat but not only these, all dualities are in him surpassed and reconciled. The outward distinctions by which men determine their psychological attitude towards the happenings of the world, have for him only a subordinate and instrumental meaning. He does not ignore them, but he is above them. Good happening and evil happening, so all-important to the human soul subject to desire, are to the desireless divine soul equally welcome since by their mingled strand are worked out the developing forms of the eternal good. He cannot be defeated, since all for him is moving towards the divine victory in the Kurukshetra of Nature, dharmaksetre kuruksetre, the field of doings which is the field of the evolving Dharma, and every turn of the conflict has been designed and mapped by the foreseeing eye of the Master of the battle, the Lord of works and Guide of the dharma. Honour and dishonour from men cannot move him, nor their praise nor their blame; for he has a greater clear-seeing judge and another standard for his action and his motive admits no dependence upon worldly rewards. Arjuna the Kshatriya prizes naturally honour and reputation and is right in shunning disgrace and the name of coward as worse than death; for to maintain the point of honour and the standard of courage in the world is part of his dharma: but Arjuna the liberated soul need care for none of these things, he has only to know the kartavyam karma, the work which the supreme Self demands from him, and to do that and leave the result to the Lord of his actions. He has passed even beyond that distinction of sin and virtue which is so all-important to the human soul while it is struggling to minimize the hold of its egoism and lighten the heavy and violent yoke of its passions,—

the liberated has risen above these struggles and is seated firmly in the purity of the witnessing and enlightened soul. Sin has fallen away from him, and not a virtue acquired and increased by good action and impaired or lost by evil action, but the inalienable and unalterable purity of a divine and selfless nature is the peak to which he has climbed and the seat upon which he is founded. There the sense of sin and the sense of virtue have no starting-point or applicability.

Arjuna, still in the ignorance, may feel in his heart the call of right and justice and may argue in his mind that abstention from battle would be a sin entailing responsibility for all the suffering that injustice and oppression and the evil karma of the triumph of wrong bring upon men and nations, or he may feel in his heart the recoil from violence and slaughter and argue in his mind that all shedding of blood is a sin which nothing can justify. Both of these attitudes would appeal with equal right to virtue and reason, and it would depend upon the man, the circumstances, and the time which of these might prevail in his mind or before the eyes of the world. Or he might simply feel constrained by his heart and his honour to support his friends against his enemies, the cause of the good and just against the cause of the evil and oppressive. The liberated soul looks beyond these conflicting standards; he sees simply what the supreme Self demands from him as needful for the maintenance or for the bringing forward of the evolving Dharma. He has no personal ends to serve, no personal loves and hatreds to satisfy, no rigidly fixed standard of action which opposes its rock-line to the flexible advancing march of the progress of the human race or stands up defiant against the call of the Infinite. He has no personal enemies to be conquered or slain but sees only men who have been brought up against him by circumstances and the will in things to help by their opposition the march of destiny. Against them he can have no wrath or hatred; for wrath and hatred are foreign to the divine nature. The Asura's desire to break and slay what opposes him, the Rakshasa's grim lust of slaughter are impossible to his calm and peace and his all-embracing sympathy and understanding. He has no wish to injure, but on the contrary a universal friendliness and compassion, maitrah karuna eva ca: but this compassion is that of a divine soul overlooking men, embracing all other souls in himself, not the shrinking of the heart and the nerves and the flesh which is the ordinary human form of pity: nor does he attach a supreme importance to the life of the body, but looks beyond to the life of the soul and attaches to the other only an instrumental value. He will not hasten to slaughter and strife, but if war comes in the wave of the Dharma, he will accept it with a large equality and a perfect understanding and sympathy for those whose power and pleasure of domination he has to break and whose joy of triumphant life he has to destroy.

For in all he sees two things, the Divine inhabiting every being equally, the varying manifestation unequal only in its temporary circumstances. In the animal and man, in the dog, the unclean outcaste and the learned and virtuous Brahmin, in the saint and the sinner, in the indifferent and the friendly and the hostile, in those who love him and benefit and those who hate him and afflict, he sees himself, he sees God and has at heart for all the same equal kindliness, the same divine affection. Circumstances may determine the outward clasp or the outward conflict, but can never affect his equal eye, his open heart, his inner embrace of all. And in all his actions there will be the same principle of soul, a perfect equality, and the same principle of work, the will of the Divine in him active for the need of the race in its gradually developing advance towards the Godhead.

Again, the sign of the divine worker is that which is central to the divine consciousness itself, a perfect inner joy and peace which depends upon nothing in the world for its source or its continuance; it is innate, it is the very stuff of the soul's consciousness, it is the very nature of divine being. The ordinary man depends upon outward things for his happiness; therefore, he has desire; therefore, he has anger and passion, pleasure and pain, joy, and grief; therefore, he measures all things in the balance of good fortune and evil fortune. None of these things can affect the divine soul; it is ever satisfied without any kind of dependence, nitya-trpto nirasrayah; for its delight, its divine ease, its happiness, its glad light are eternal within, ingrained in itself, atma-ratih, antah-sukho 'ntar-aramas tathantar-jyotir eva yah. What joy it takes in outward things is not for their sake, not for things which it seeks in them and can miss, but for the self in them, for their expression of the Divine, for that which is eternal in them and which it cannot miss. It is without attachment to their outward touches but finds everywhere the same joy that it finds in itself, because itself is theirs, has become oneself with the self of all beings, because it is united with the one and equal Brahman in them through all their differences, brahmayoga-yuktatma, sarvabhutatma-bhutatma. It does not rejoice in the touches of the pleasant or feel anguish in the touches of the unpleasant; neither the wounds of things, nor the wounds of friends, nor the wounds of enemies can disturb the firmness of its outgazing mind or bewilder its receiving heart; this soul is in its nature, as the Upanishad puts it, avranam, without wound or scar. In all things it has the same imperishable Ananda, sukham aksayam asnute.

That equality, impersonality, peace, joy, freedom do not depend on so outward a thing as doing or not doing works. The Gita insists repeatedly on the difference between the inward and the outward renunciation, tyaga and sannyasa. The latter, it says, is valueless without the former, hardly possible even to attain without it, and unnecessary when there is the inward freedom. In fact, tyaga itself is the real and sufficient Sannyasa. "He should be known as the eternal Sannyasin who neither hates nor desires; free from the dualities he is happily and easily released from all bondage." The painful process of outward Sannyasa, duhkham aptum, is an unnecessary process. It is perfectly true that all actions, as well as the fruit of action, have to be given up, to be renounced, but inwardly, not outwardly, not into the inertia of Nature, but to the Lord in sacrifice, into the calm and joy of the Impersonal from whom all action proceeds without disturbing his peace. The true Sannyasa of action is the reposing of all works on the Brahman. "He who, having abandoned attachment, acts reposing (or founding) his works on the Brahman, brahmanyadhaya karmani, is not stained by sin even as water clings not to the lotus-leaf." Therefore, the Yogins first "do works with the body, mind, understanding, or even merely with the organs of action, abandoning attachment, for self-purification, sangam tyaktvatmasuddhaye. By abandoning attachment to the fruits of works the soul in union with Brahman attains to peace of rapt foundation in Brahman, but the soul not in union is attached to the fruit and bound by the action of desire." The foundation, the purity, the peace once attained, the embodied soul perfectly controlling its nature, having renounced all its actions by the mind, inwardly, not outwardly, "sits in its nine-gated city neither doing nor causing to be done." For this soul is the one impersonal Soul in all, the all-pervading Lord, prabhu, vibhu, who, as the impersonal, neither creates the works of the world, nor the mind's idea of being the doer, na kartrtvam na karmani, nor the coupling of works to their fruits, the chain of cause and effect. All that is worked out by the Nature in the man, svabhava, his principle of self-becoming, as the word literally means. The all-pervading Impersonal accepts neither the sin nor the virtue of any: these are things created by the ignorance in the creature, by his egoism of the doer, by his ignorance of his highest self, by his involution in the operations of Nature, and when the self-knowledge within him is released from this dark envelope, that knowledge lights up like a sun the real self within him; he knows himself then to be the soul supreme above the instruments of Nature. Pure, infinite, inviolable, immutable, he is no longer affected; no longer does he imagine himself to be modified by her workings. By complete identification with the Impersonal he can, too, release himself from the necessity of returning by birth into her movement.

And yet this liberation does not at all prevent him from acting. Only, he knows that it is not he who is active, but the modes, the qualities of Nature, her triple gunas. "The man who knows the principles of things thinks, his mind in Yoga (with the inactive Impersonal), 'I am doing nothing'; when he sees, hears, touches, smells, eats, moves, sleeps, breathes, speaks, takes, ejects, opens his eyes, or closes them, he holds that it is only the senses acting upon the objects of the senses." He himself, safe in the immutable, unmodified soul, is beyond the grip of the three gunas, trigunatıta; he is neither sattwic, rajasic nor tamasic; he sees with a clear untroubled spirit the alter-nations of the natural modes and qualities in his action, their rhythmic play of light and happiness, activity and force, rest, and inertia. This superiority of the calm soul observing its action but not involved in it, this traigunatıtya, is also a high sign of the divine worker. By itself the idea might lead to a doctrine of the mechanical determinism of Nature and the perfect aloofness and irresponsibility of the soul; but the Gita effectively avoids this fault of an insufficient thought by its illumining supertheistic idea of the Purushottama. It makes it clear that it is not in the end Nature which mechanically determines its own action; it is the will of the Supreme which inspires her; he who has already slain the Dhritarashtrians, he of whom Arjuna is only the hu-man instrument, a universal Soul, a transcendent Godhead is the master of her labour. The reposing of works in the Impersonal is a means of getting rid of the personal egoism of the doer, but the end is to give up all our actions to that great Lord of all, sarva-loka-mahesvara. "With a consciousness identified with the Self, renouncing all thy actions into Me, mayi sarvani karmani sannyasyadhyatmacetasa, freed from personal hopes and desires, from the thought of 'I' and 'mine', delivered from the fever of the soul, fight," work, do my will in the world. The Divine motives, inspires, determines the entire action; the human soul impersonal in the Brahman is the pure and silent channel of his power; that power in the Nature executes the divine movement. Such only are the works of the liberated soul, muktasya karma, for in nothing does he act from a personal inception; such are the actions of the accomplished Karmayogin. They rise from a free spirit and disappear without modifying it, like waves that rise and disappear on the surface of conscious, immutable depths. Gata sangasya muktasya jnanavasthita-cetasah, yajnayacaratah karma samagram praviliyate.

XIX

EQUALITY

Since knowledge, desirelessness, impersonality, equality, the inner self-existent peace and bliss, freedom from or at least superiority to the tangled interlocking of the three modes of Nature are the signs of the liberated soul, they must accompany it in all its activities. They are the condition of that unalterable calm which this soul preserves in all the movement, all the shock, all the clash of forces which surround it in the world. That calm reflects the equable immutability of the Brah-man in the midst of all mutations, and it belongs to the indivisible and impartial Oneness which is forever immanent in all the multiplicities of the universe. For an equal and all-equalizing spirit is that Oneness is in the midst of the million differences and inequalities of the world; and equality of the spirit is the sole real equality. For in all else in existence there can only be similarity, adjustment, and balance; but even in the greatest similarities of the world we find difference of inequality and difference of unlikeness and the adjusted balancing's of the world can only come about by a poising of combined unequal weights.

Hence the immense importance attached by the Gita in its elements of Karmayoga to equality; it is the nodus of the free spirit's free relations with the world. Self-knowledge, desireless-ness, impersonality, bliss, freedom from the modes of Nature, when withdrawn into themselves, self-absorbed, inactive, have no need of equality; for they take no cognisance of the things in which the opposition of equality and inequality arises. But the moment the spirit takes cognisance of and deals with the multiplicities, personalities, differences, inequalities of the action of Nature, it has to effectuate these other signs of its free status by this one manifesting sign of equality. Knowledge is the consciousness of unity with the One; and in relation with the many different beings and existences of the universe it must show itself by an equal oneness with all. Impersonality is the one immutable spirit's superiority to the variations of its multiple personality in the world; in its dealings with the personalities of the universe it must show itself in the equal and impartial spirit of its action with regard to all, however various that action may be made by the variety of relations into which it is moulded or of the conditions under which it has to take place. So, Krishna in the Gita says that none is dear to him, none hated, to all he is equal in spirit; yet is the God-lover the special receiver of his grace, because the relation he has created is different and the one impartial Lord of all yet meets each soul according to its way of approach to him. Desirelessness is the illimitable Spirit's superiority to the limiting attraction of the separate objects of desire in the world; when it has to enter into relations with those objects, it must show it either by an equal and impartial indifference in their possession or by an equal and impartial unattached delight in all and love for all which, because it is self-existent, does not depend upon possession or non-possession, but is in its essence unperturbed and immutable. For the spirit's bliss is in itself, and if this bliss is to enter into relations with things and creatures, it is only in this way that it can manifest its free spirituality. Traigunatitya, transcendence of the gunas, is the unperturbed spirit's superiority to that flux of action of the modes of Nature which is in its constant character perturbed and unequal; if it has to enter into relations with the conflicting and unequal activities of Nature, if the free soul is to allow its nature any action at all, it must show its superiority by an impartial equality towards all activities, results, or happenings.

Equality is the sign and also for the aspirant the test. Where there is inequality in the soul, there there is in evidence some unequal play of the modes of Nature, motion of desire, play of personal will, feeling and action, activity of joy and grief or that disturbed and disturbing delight which is not true spiritual bliss but a mental satisfaction bringing in its train inevitably a counterpart or recoil of mental dissatisfaction. Where there is inequality of soul, there there is deviation from knowledge, loss of steadfast abiding in the all-embracing and all-reconciling oneness of the Brahman and unity of things. By his equality the Karmayogin knows in the midst of his action that he is free.

It is the spiritual nature of the equality enjoined, high and universal in its character and comprehension, which gives its distinctive note to the teaching of the Gita in this matter. For otherwise the mere teaching of equality in itself as the most desirable status of the mind, feelings, and temperament in which we rise superior to human weakness, is by no means peculiar to the Gita. Equality has always been held up to admiration as the philosophic ideal and the characteristic temperament of the sages. The Gita takes up indeed this philosophic ideal but carries it far beyond into a higher region where we find ourselves breathing a larger and purer air. The Stoic poise, the philosophic poise of the soul are only its first and second steps of ascension out of the whirl of the passions and the tossing's of desire to a serenity and bliss, not of the Gods, but of the Divine himself in his supreme self-mastery. The Stoic equality, making character its pivot, founds itself upon self-mastery by austere endurance; the happier and serener philosophic equality prefers self-mastery by knowledge, by detachment, by a high intellectual indifference seated above the disturbances to which our nature is prone, udasinavad asinah, as the Gita expresses it; there is also the religious or Christian equality which is a perpetual kneeling or a prostrate resignation and submission to the will of God. These are the three steps and means towards divine peace, heroic endurance, sage indifference, pious resignation, titiksa, udasinata, namas or nati. The Gita takes them all in its large synthetic manner and weaves them into its upward soul-movement, but it gives to each a profounder root, a larger outlook, a more universal and transcendent significance. For to each it gives the values of the spirit, its power of spiritual being beyond the strain of character, beyond the difficult poise of the understanding, beyond the stress of the emotions.

The ordinary human soul takes a pleasure in the customary disturbances of its nature-life: it is because it has this pleasure and because, having it, it gives a sanction to the troubled play of the lower nature that the play continues perpetually; for the Prakriti does nothing except for the pleasure and with the sanction of its lover and enjoyer, the Purusha. We do not recognize this truth because under the actual stroke of the adverse disturbance, smitten by grief, pain, discomfort, misfortune, failure, defeat, blame, dishonour, the mind shrinks back from the blow, while it leaps eagerly to the embrace of the opposite and pleasurable disturbances, joy, pleasure, satisfactions of all kinds, prosperity, success, victory, glory, praise; but this does not alter the truth of the soul's pleasure in life which remains constant behind the dualities of the mind. The warrior does not feel physical pleasure in his wounds or find mental satisfaction in his defeats; but he has a complete delight in the godhead of battle which brings to him defeat and wounds as well as the joy of victory, and he accepts the chances of the former and the hope of the latter as part of the mingled weft of war, the thing which the delight in him pursues. Even, wounds bring him a joy and pride in memory, complete when the pain of them has passed, but often enough present even while it is there and actually fed by the pain. Defeat keeps for him the joy and pride of indomitable resistance to a superior adversary, or, if he is of a baser kind, the passions of hatred and revenge which also have their darker and crueler pleasures. So, it is with the pleasure of the soul in the normal play of our life.

The mind recoils by pain and dislike from the adverse strokes of life; that is Nature's device for enforcing a principle of self-protection, jugupsa, so that the vulnerable nervous and bodily parts of us may not unduly rush upon self-destruction to embrace it: it takes joy in the favourable touches of life; that is Nature's lure of rajasic pleasure, so that the force in the creature may overcome the tamasic tendencies of inertia and inactivity and be impelled fully towards action, desire, struggle, success, and by its attachment to these things her ends may be worked out. Our secret soul takes a pleasure in this strife and effort, and even a pleasure in adversity and suffering, which can be complete enough in memory and retrospect, but is present too behind at the time and often even rises to the surface of the afflicted mind to support it in its passion; but what really attracts the soul is the whole mingled weft of the thing we call life with all its disturbance of struggle and seeking, its attractions and repulsions, its offer and its menace, its varieties of every kind. To the rajasic desire-soul in us a monotonous pleasure, success without struggle, joy without a shadow must after a time become fatiguing, insipid, cloying; it needs a background of darkness to give full value to its enjoyment of light: for the happiness it seeks and enjoys is of that very nature, it is in its very essence relative and dependent on the perception and experience of its opposite. The joy of the soul in the dualities is the secret of the mind's pleasure in living.

Ask it to rise out of all this disturbance to the unmingled joy of the pure bliss-soul which all the time secretly supports its strength in the struggle and makes its own continued existence possible,—it will draw back at once from the call. It does not believe in such an existence; or it believes that it would not be life, that it would not be at all the varied existence in the world around it in which it is accustomed to take pleasure; it would be something tasteless and without savour. Or it feels that the effort would be too difficult for it; it recoils from the struggle of the ascent, although in reality the spiritual change is not at all more difficult than the realisation of the dreams the desire-soul pursues, nor entails more struggle and labour in the attainment than the tremendous effort which the desire-soul expends in its passionate chase after its own transient objects of pleasure and desire. The true cause of its unwillingness is that it is asked to rise above its own atmosphere and breathe a rarer and purer air of life, whose bliss and power it cannot realize and hardly even conceives as real, while the joy of this lower turbid nature is to it the one thing familiar and palpable. Nor is this lower satisfaction in itself a thing evil and unprofitable; it is rather the condition for the upward evolution of our human nature out of the tamasic ignorance and inertia to which its material being is most subject; it is the rajasic stage of the graded ascent of man towards the supreme self-knowledge, power, and bliss. But if we rest eternally on this plane, the madhyama gatih of the Gita, our ascent remains unfinished, the evolution of the soul incomplete.

Through the sattwic being and nature to that which is beyond the three gunas lies the way of the soul to its perfection.

The movement which will lead us out of the disturbances of the lower nature must be necessarily a movement towards equality in the mind, in the emotional temperament, in the soul. But it is to be noted that, although in the end we must arrive at a superiority to all the three gunas of the lower nature, it is yet in its incipience by a resort to one or other of the three that the movement must begin. The beginning of equality may be sattwic, rajasic or tamasic; for there is a possibility in the human nature of a tamasic equality. It may be purely tamasic, the heavy equability of a vital temperament rendered inertly irresponsive to the shocks of existence by a sort of dull insensibility undesirous of the joy of life. Or it may result from a weariness of the emotions and desires accumulated by a surfeit and satiety of the pleasure or else, on the contrary, a disappointment and a disgust and shrinking from the pain of life, a lassitude, a fear and horror and dislike of the world: it is then in its nature a mixed movement, rajaso-tamasic, but the lower quality predominates. Or, approaching the sattwic principle, it may aid itself by the intellectual perception that the desires of life cannot be satisfied, that the soul is too weak to master life, that the whole thing is nothing but sorrow and transient effort and nowhere in it is there any real truth or sanity or light or happiness; this is the sattwo-tamasic principle of equality and is not so much equality, though it may lead to that, as indifference or equal refusal. Essentially, the movement of tamasic equality is a generalization of Nature's principle of jugupsa or self-protecting recoil extended from the shunning of particular painful effects to a shunning of the whole life of Nature itself as in sum leading to pain and self-tormenting and not to the delight which the soul demands.

In tamasic equality by itself there is no real liberation; but it can be made a powerful starting-point, if, as in Indian asceticism, it is turned into the sattwic by the perception of the greater existence, the truer power, the higher delight of the immutable Self above Nature. The natural turn of such a movement, however, is towards Sannyasa, the renunciation of life and works, rather than to that union of inner renunciation of desire with continued activity in the world of Nature which the Gita advocates. The Gita, however, admits and makes room for this movement; it allows as a recoiling starting-point the perception of the defects of the world-existence, birth and disease and death and old age and sorrow, the historic starting-point of the Buddha, janma-mrtyu-jara-vyadhi-duhkha-dosanudarsanam, and it accepts the . . .effort of those whose self-discipline is motived by a desire for release, even in this spirit, from the curse of age and death, jara-marana-moksaya mam asritya yatanti ye. But that, to be of any profit, must be accompanied by the sattwic perception of a higher state and the taking delight and refuge in the existence of the Divine, mam asritya. Then the soul by its recoil comes to a greater condition of being, lifted beyond the three gunas and free from birth and death and age and grief, and enjoys the immortality of its self-existence, janma-mrtyu-jara-duhkhair vimukto mrtam asnute. The tamasic unwillingness to accept the pain and effort of life is indeed by itself a weakening and degrading thing, and in this lies the danger of preaching to all alike the gospel of asceticism and world-disgust, that it puts the stamp of a tamasic weakness and shrinking on unfit souls, confuses their understanding, buddhibhedam janayet, diminishes the sustained aspiration, the confidence in living, the power of effort which the soul of man needs for its salutary, its necessary rajasic struggle to master its environment, without really opening to it—for it is yet incapable of that—a higher goal, a greater endeavour, a mightier victory. But in souls that are fit this tamasic recoil may serve a useful spiritual purpose by slaying their rajasic attraction, their eager preoccupation with the lower life which prevents the sattwic awakening to a higher possibility. Seeking then for a refuge in the void they have created, they are able to hear the divine call, "O soul that findest thyself in this transient and unhappy world, turn and put thy delight in Me," anityam asukham lokam imam prapya bhajasva mam.

Still, in this movement, the equality consists only in an equal recoil from all that constitutes the world; and it arrives at indifference and aloofness, but does not include that power to accept equally all the touches of the world pleasurable or painful without attachment or disturbance which is a necessary element in the discipline of the Gita. Therefore, even if we begin with the tamasic recoil,—which is not at all necessary,—it can only be as a first incitement to a greater endeavour, not as a permanent pessimism. The real discipline begins with the movement to mastery over these things from which we were first inclined merely to flee. It is here that the possibility of a kind of rajasic equality comes in, which is at its lowest the strong nature's pride in self-mastery, self-control, superiority to passion and weakness; but the Stoic ideal seizes upon this point of departure and makes it the key to an entire liberation of the soul from subjection to all weakness of its lower nature. As the tamasic inward recoil is a generalization of Nature's principle of jugupsa or self-protection from suffering, so the rajasic upward movement is a generalization of Nature's other principle of the acceptance of struggle and effort and the innate impulse of life towards mastery and victory; but it transfers the battle to the field where alone complete victory is possible. Instead of a struggle for scattered outward aims and transient successes, it proposes nothing less than the conquest of Nature and the world itself by a spiritual struggle and an inner victory. The tamasic recoil turns from both the pains and pleasures of the world to flee from them; the rajasic movement turns upon them to bear, master and rise superior to them. The Stoic self-discipline calls desire and passion into its embrace of the wrestler and crushes them between its arms, as did old Dhritarashtra in the epic the iron image of Bhima. It endures the shock of things painful and pleasurable, the causes of the physical and mental affections of the nature and breaks their effects to pieces; it is complete when the soul can bear all touches without being pained or attracted, excited or troubled. It seeks to make man the conqueror and king of his nature.

The Gita, making its call on the warrior nature of Arjuna, starts with this heroic movement. It calls on him to turn on the great enemy desire and slay it. Its first description of equality is that of the Stoic philosopher. "He whose mind is undisturbed in the midst of sorrows and amid pleasures is free from desire, from whom liking and fear and wrath have passed away, is the sage of settled understanding. Who in all things is without affection though visited by this good or that evil and neither hates nor rejoices, his intelligence sits firmly founded in wisdom." If one abstains from food, it says, giving a physical example, the object of sense ceases to affect, but the affection itself of the sense, the rasa, remains; it is only when, even in the exercise of the sense, it can keep back from seeking its sensuous aim in the object, artha, and abandon the affection, the desire for the pleasure of taste, that the highest level of the soul is reached. It is by using the mental organs on the objects, "ranging over them with the senses," visayan indriyais caran, but with senses subject to the self, freed from liking and disliking, that one gets into a large and sweet clearness of soul and temperament in which passion and grief find no place. All desires have to enter into the soul, as waters into the sea, and yet it has to remain immovable, filled but not disturbed so, in the end all desires can be abandoned. To be freed from wrath and passion and fear and attraction is repeatedly stressed as a necessary condition of the liberated status, and for this we must learn to bear their shocks, which cannot be done without exposing ourselves to their causes. "He who can bear here in the body the velocity of wrath and desire, is the Yogin, the happy man." Titiksa, the will and power to endure, is the means. "The material touches which cause heat and cold, happiness and pain, things transient which come and go, these learn to endure. For the man whom these do not trouble nor pain, the firm and wise who is equal in pleasure and suffering, makes himself apt for immortality." The equal-souled has to bear suffering and not hate, to receive pleasure and not rejoice. Even the physical affections are to be mastered by endurance and this too is part of the Stoic discipline. Age, death, suffering, pain are not fled from, but accepted and vanquished by a high indifference.[1] Not to flee appalled from Nature in her lower masks, but to meet and conquer her is the true instinct of the strong nature, purusarsabha, the leonine soul among men. Thus compelled, she throws aside her mask and reveals to him his true nature as the free soul, not her subject but her king and lord, svarat, samrat.

But the Gita accepts this Stoic discipline, this heroic philosophy, on the same condition that it accepts the tamasic recoil,—it must

1 Dhıras tatra na muhyati, says the Gita; the strong and wise soul is not perplexed, troubled, or moved by them. But still they are accepted only to be conquered, jara-marana-moksaya yatanti.

have above it the sattwic vision of knowledge, at its root the aim at self-realization and in its steps the ascent to the divine Nature. A Stoic discipline which merely crushed down the common affections of our human nature,—although less dangerous than a tamasic weariness of life, unfruitful pessimism, and sterile inertia, because it would at least increase the power and self-mastery of the soul,—would still be no unmixed good, since it might lead to insensibility and an inhuman isolation without giving the true spiritual release. The Stoic equality is justified as an element in the discipline of the Gita because it can be associated with and can help to the realization of the free immutable Self in the mobile human being, param drstva and to status in that new self-consciousness, esa brahmi sthitih.

"Awakening by the understanding to the Highest which is beyond even the discerning mind, put force on the self by the self to make it firm and still, and slay this enemy who is so hard to assail, Desire." Both the tamasic recoil of escape and the rajasic movement of struggle and victory are only justified when they look beyond themselves through the sattwic principle to the self-knowledge which legitimizes both the recoil and the struggle.

The pure philosopher, the thinker, the born sage not only relies upon the sattwic principle in him as his ultimate justification but uses it from the beginning as his instrument of self-mastery. He starts from the sattwic equality. He too observes the transitoriness of the material and external world and its failure to satisfy the desires or to give the true delight, but this causes him no grief, fear, or disappointment. He observes all with an eye of tranquil discernment and makes his choice without repulsion or perplexity. "The enjoyments born of the touches of things are causes of sorrow, they have a beginning and an end; therefore, the sage, the man of awakened understanding, budhah, does not place his delight in these." "The self in him is unattached to the touches of external things; he finds his happiness in himself." He sees, as the

Gita puts it, that he is himself his own enemy and his own friend, and therefore he takes care not to dethrone himself by casting his being into the hands of desire and passion, natmanam avasadayet, but delivers himself out of that imprisonment by his own inner power, uddhared atmanatmanam; for whoever has conquered his lower self, finds in his higher self his best friend and ally. He becomes satisfied with knowledge, master of his senses, a Yogin by sattwic equality,—for equality is Yoga, samatvam yoga ucyate,—regarding alike clod and stone and gold, tranquil and self-poised in heat and cold, suffering and happiness, honour, and disgrace. He is equal in soul to friend and enemy and to neutral and indifferent, because he sees that these are transitory relations born of the changing conditions of life. Even by the pretensions of learning and purity and virtue and the claims to superiority which men base upon these things, he is not led away. He is equal-souled to all men, to the sinner and the saint, to the virtuous, learned, and cultured Brahmin and the fallen outcaste. All these are the Gita's descriptions of the sattwic equality, and they sum up well enough what is familiar to the world as the calm philosophic equality of the sage.

Where then is the difference between this and the larger equality taught by the Gita? It lies in the difference between the intellectual and philosophic discernment and the spiritual, the Vedantic knowledge of unity on which the Gita found its teaching. The philosopher maintains his equality by the power of the buddhi, the discerning mind; but even that by itself is a doubtful foundation. For, though master of himself on the whole by a constant attention or an acquired habit of mind, in reality he is not free from his lower nature, and it does actually assert itself in many ways and may at any moment take a violent revenge for its rejection and suppression. For, always, the play of the lower nature is a triple play, and the rajasic and tamasic qualities are ever lying in wait for the sattwic man. "Even the mind of the wise man who labours for perfection is carried away by the vehement insistence of the senses." Perfect security can only be had by resorting to something higher than the sattwic quality, something higher than the discerning mind, to the Self,—not the philosopher's intelligent self, but the divine sage's spiritual self which is beyond the three gunas. All must be consummated by a divine birth into the higher spiritual nature.

And the philosopher's equality is like the Stoic's, like the world-fleeing ascetic's, inwardly a lonely freedom, remote and aloof from men; but the man born to the divine birth has found the Divine not only in himself, but in all beings. He has realized his unity with all, and his equality is therefore full of sympathy and oneness. He sees all as himself and is not intent on his lonely salvation; he even takes upon himself the burden of their happiness and sorrow by which he is not himself affected or subjected. The perfect sage, the Gita more than once repeats, is ever engaged with a large equality in doing good to all creatures and makes that his occupation and delight, sarvabhutahite ratah. The perfect Yogin is no solitary musing on the Self in his ivory tower of spiritual isolation, but yuktah krtsna-karma-krt, . . .a many-sided universal worker for the good of the world, for God in the world. For he is a bhakta, a lover and devotee of the Divine, as well as a sage and a Yogin, a lover who loves God wherever he finds Him and who finds Him everywhere; and what he loves, he does not disdain to serve, nor does action carry him away from the bliss of union, since all his acts proceed from the One in him and to the One in all they are directed. The equality of the Gita is a large synthetic equality in which all is lifted up into the integrality of the divine being and the divine nature.

XX

EQUALITY AND KNOWLEDGE

YOGA and knowledge are, in this early part of the Gita's teaching, the two wings of the soul's ascent. By Yoga is meant union through divine works done without desire, with equality of soul to all things and all men, as a sacrifice to the Supreme, while knowledge is that on which this desirelessness, this equality, this power of sacrifice is founded. The two wings indeed assist each other's flight; acting together, yet with a subtle alternation of mutual aid, like the two eyes in a man which see together because they see alternately, they increase one an-other mutually by interchange of substance. As the works grow more and more desireless, equal-minded, sacrificial in spirit, the knowledge increases; with the increase of the knowledge the soul becomes firmer in the desireless, sacrificial equality of its works. The sacrifice of knowledge says the Gita, therefore, is greater than any material sacrifice. "Even if thou art the greatest doer of sin beyond all sinners, thou shalt cross over all the crookedness of evil in the ship of knowledge. . . . There is nothing in the world equal in purity to knowledge." By knowledge desire and its first-born child, sin, are destroyed. The liberated man is able to do works as a sacrifice because he is freed from attachment through his mind, heart and spirit being firmly founded in self-knowledge, gata-sangasya jnanavasthita-cetasah. All his work disappears completely as soon as done, suffers laya, as one might say, in the being of the Brahman, praviliyate; it has no reactionary consequence on the soul of the apparent doer. The work is done by the Lord through his Nature, it is no longer personal to the human instrument. The work itself becomes but power of the nature and substance of the being of the Brahman.

It is in this sense that the Gita is speaking when it says that all the totality of work finds its completion, culmination, end in knowledge, sarvam karmakhilam jnane parisamapyate. "As a fire kindled turns to ashes its fuel, so the fire of knowledge turns all works to ashes." By this it is not at all meant that when knowledge is complete, there is cessation from works. What is meant is made clear by the Gita when it says that he who has destroyed all doubt by knowledge and has by Yoga given up all works and is in possession of the Self is not bound by his works, yoga-sannyasta-karmanam atmavantam na karmani nibadhnanti, and that he whose self has become the self of all existences, acts and yet is not affected by his works, is not caught in them, receives from them no soul-ensnaring reaction, kurvann api na lipyate. Therefore, it says, the Yoga of works is better than the physical renunciation of works, because, while Sannyasa is difficult for embodied beings who must do works so long as they are in the body, Yoga of works is entirely sufficient, and it rapidly and easily brings the soul to Brahman. That Yoga of works is, we have seen, the offering of all action to the Lord, which induces as its culmination an inner and not an outer, a spiritual, not a physical giving up of works into the Brahman, into the being of the Lord, brahmani adhaya karmani, mayi sannyasya. When works are thus "reposed on the Brahman," the personality of the instrumental doer ceases; though he acts, he does nothing; for he has given up not only the fruits of his works, but the works themselves and the doing of them to the Lord. The Divine then takes the burden of work from him; the Supreme becomes the doer and the act and the result.

This knowledge of which the Gita speaks, is not an intellectual activity of the mind; it is a luminous growth into the highest state of being by the outshining of the light of the divine sun of Truth, "that Truth, the Sun lying concealed in the dark-ness" of our ignorance of which the Rigveda speaks, tat satyam suryam tamasi ksiyantam. The immutable Brahman is there in the spirit's skies above this troubled lower nature of the dualities, untouched either by its virtue or by its sin, accepting neither our sense of sin nor our self-righteousness, untouched by its joy and its sorrow, indifferent to our joy in success and our grief in failure, master of all, supreme, all-pervading, prabhu vibhu, calm, strong, pure, equal in all things, the source of Nature, not the direct doer of our works, but the witness of Nature and her works, not imposing on us either the illusion of being the doer, for that illusion is the result of the ignorance of this lower Nature. But this freedom, mastery, purity we cannot see; we are bewildered by the natural ignorance which hides from us the eternal self-knowledge of the Brahman secret within our being. But knowledge comes to its persistent seeker and removes the natural self-ignorance; it shines out like a long-hidden sun and lights up to our vision that self-being supreme beyond the dualities of this lower existence, adityavat prakasayati tat param. By a long whole-hearted endeavour, by directing our whole conscious being to that, by making that our whole aim, by turning it into the whole object of our discerning mind and so seeing it not only in ourselves but everywhere, we become one thought and self with that, tad-buddhayas tad-atmanah, we are washed clean of all the darkness and suffering of the lower man by the waters of knowledge,[1] jnana-nirdhuta-kalmasah.

The result is, says the Gita, a perfect equality to all things and all persons; and then only can we repose our works completely in

1 The Rigveda so speaks of the streams of the Truth, the waters that have perfect knowledge, the waters that are full of the divine sunlight, rtasya dharah, apo vicetasah, svarvatır apah. What are here metaphors, are there concrete symbols.

the Brahman. For the Brahman is equal, samam brahma, and it is only when we have this perfect equality, samye sthitam manah, "seeing with an equal eye the learned and cultured Brahmin, the cow, the elephant, the dog, the outcaste" and knowing all as one Brahman, that we can, living in that oneness, see like the Brahman our works proceeding from the nature freely without any fear of attachment, sin, or bondage. Sin and stain then cannot be for we have overcome that creation full of desire and its works and reactions which belongs to the ignorance, tair jitah sargah and living in the supreme and divine Nature there is no longer fault or defect in our works; for these are created by the inequalities of the ignorance. The equal Brahman is faultless, nirdosam hi samam brahma, beyond the confusion of good and evil, and living in the Brahman we too rise beyond good and evil; we act in that purity, stainlessly, with an equal and single purpose of fulfilling the welfare of all existences, ksına-kalmasah sarvabhuta-hite ratah. The Lord in our hearts is in the ignorance also the cause of our actions, but through his Maya, through the egoism of our lower nature which creates the tangled web of our actions and brings back upon our egoism the recoil of their tangled reactions affecting us inwardly as sin and virtue, affecting us outwardly as suffering and pleasure, evil fortune and good fortune, the great chain of Karma. When we are freed by knowledge, the Lord, no longer hidden in our hearts, but manifest as our supreme self, takes up our works and uses us as faultless instruments, nimitta-matram, for the helping of the world. Such is the intimate union between knowledge and equality; knowledge here in the buddhi reflected as equality in the temperament; above, on a higher plane of consciousness, knowledge as the light of the Being, equality as the stuff of the Nature.

Always in this sense of a supreme self-knowledge is this word jnana used in Indian philosophy and Yoga; it is the light by which we grow into our true being, not the knowledge by which we increase our information and our intellectual riches; it is not scientific or psychological or philosophic or ethical or aesthetic or worldly and practical knowledge. These too no doubt help us to grow, but only in the becoming, not in the being; they enter into the definition of Yogic knowledge only when we use them as aids to know the Supreme, the Self, the Divine,—scientific knowledge, when we can get through the veil of processes and phenomena and see the one Reality behind which explains them all; psychological knowledge, when we use it to know ourselves and to distinguish the lower from the higher, so that this we may renounce and into that we may grow; philosophical knowledge, when we turn it as a light upon the essential principles of existence so as to discover and live in that which is eternal; ethical knowledge, when by it having distinguished sin from virtue we put away the one and rise above the other into the pure innocence of the divine Nature; aesthetic knowledge, when we discover by it the beauty of the Divine; knowledge of the world, when we see through it the way of the Lord with his creatures and use it for the service of the Divine in man. Even then they are only aids; the real knowledge is that which is a secret to the mind, of which the mind only gets reflections, but which lives in the spirit.

The Gita in describing how we come by this knowledge, says that we get first initiation into it from the men of knowledge who have seen, not those who know merely by the intellect, its essential truths; but the actuality of it comes from within ourselves: "the man who is perfected by Yoga, finds it of him-self in the self by the course of Time," it grows within him, that is to say, and he grows into it as he goes on increasing in desirelessness, in equality, in devotion to the Divine. It is only of the supreme knowledge that this can altogether be said; the knowledge which the intellect of man amasses, is gathered laboriously by the senses and the reason from outside. To get this other knowledge, self-existent, intuitive, self-experiencing, self-revealing, we must have conquered and controlled our mind and senses, samyatendriyah, so that we are no longer subject to their delusions, but rather the mind and senses become its pure mirror; we must have fixed our whole conscious being on the truth of that supreme reality in which all exists, tat-parah, so that it may display in us its luminous self-existence.

Finally, we must have a faith which no intellectual doubt can be allowed to disturb, sraddhavan labhate jnanam. "The ignorant who has not faith, the soul of doubt goeth to perdition; neither this world, nor the supreme world, nor any happiness is for the soul full of doubts." In fact, it is true that without faith nothing decisive can be achieved either in this world or for possession of the world above, and that it is only by laying hold of some sure basis and positive support that man can attain any measure of terrestrial or celestial success and satisfaction and happiness; the merely sceptical mind loses itself in the void. But still in the lower knowledge doubt and scepticism have their temporary uses; in the higher they are stumbling blocks: for there the whole secret is not the balancing of truth and error, but a constantly progressing realisation of revealed truth. In intellectual knowledge there is always a mixture of falsehood or incompleteness which has to be got rid of by subjecting the truth itself to sceptical inquiry; but in the higher knowledge falsehood cannot enter and that which intellect contributes by attaching itself to this or that opinion, cannot be got rid of by mere questioning, but will fall away of itself by persistence in realisation. Whatever incompleteness there is in the knowledge attained, it must be got rid of, not by questioning in its roots what has already been realized but by proceeding to further and more complete realisation through a deeper, higher, and wider living in the Spirit. And what is not yet realized must be prepared for by faith, not by sceptical questioning, because this truth is one which the intellect cannot give and which is indeed often quite opposed to the ideas in which the reasoning and logical mind gets entangled: it is not a truth which has to be proved, but a truth which has to be lived inwardly, a greater reality into which we have to grow. Finally, it is in itself a self-existent truth and would be self-evident if it were not for the sorceries of the ignorance in which we live; the doubts, the perplexities which prevent us from accepting and following it, arise from that ignorance, from the sense-bewildered, opinion-perplexed heart and mind, living as they do in a lower and phenomenal truth and therefore questioning the higher realities, ajnana-sambhutam hrtstham samsayam. They have to be cut away by the sword of knowledge, says the Gita, by the knowledge that realizes, by resorting constantly to Yoga, that is, by living out the union with the Supreme whose truth being known all is known, yasmin vijnate sarvam vijnatam.

The higher knowledge we then get is that which is to the knower of Brahman his constant vision of things when he lives uninterruptedly in the Brahman, brahmavid brahmani sthitah. That is not a vision or knowledge or consciousness of Brahman to the exclusion of all else, but a seeing of all in Brahman and as the Self. For, it is said, the knowledge by which we rise beyond all relapse back into the bewilderment of our mental nature, is "that by which thou shalt see all existences without exception in the Self, then in Me." Elsewhere the Gita puts it more largely, "Equal-visioned everywhere, he sees the Self in all existences and all existences in the Self. He who sees Me everywhere and all and each in Me, is never lost to Me nor I to him. He who has reached oneness and loves Me in all beings, that Yogin, howsoever he lives and acts, is living and acting in Me. O Arjuna, he who sees all equally everywhere as himself, whether it be happiness or suffering, I hold him to be the supreme Yogin." That is the old Vedantic knowledge of the Upanishads which the Gita holds up constantly before us; but it is its superiority to other later formulations of it that it turns persistently this knowledge into a great practical philosophy of divine living. It always insists on the relation between this knowledge of oneness and Karmayoga, and therefore on the knowledge of oneness as the basis of a liberated action in the world. Whenever it speaks of knowledge, it turns at once to speak of equality which is its result; whenever it speaks of equality, it turns to speak too of the knowledge which is its basis. The equality it enjoins does not begin and end in a static condition of the soul useful only for self-liberation; it is always a basis of works. The peace of the Brahman in the liberated soul is the foundation; the large, free, equal, world-wide action of the Lord in the liberated nature radiates the power which proceeds from that peace; these two made one synthesize divine works and God-knowledge.

We see at once what a profound extension we get here for the ideas which otherwise the Gita has in common with other systems of philosophic, ethical, or religious living. En-durance, philosophic indifference, resignation are, we have said, the foundation of three kinds of equality; but the Gita's truth of knowledge not only gathers them all up together, but gives them an infinitely profound, a magnificently ample significance. The Stoic knowledge is that of the soul's power of self-mastery by fortitude, an equality attained by a struggle with one's nature, maintained by a constant vigilance and control against its natural rebellions: it gives a noble peace, an austere happiness, but not the supreme joy of the liberated self-living not by a rule, but in the pure, easy, spontaneous perfection of its divine being, so that "however it may act and live, it acts and lives in the Divine," because here perfection is not only attained but possessed in its own right and has no longer to be maintained by effort, for it has become the very nature of the soul's being. The Gita accepts the endurance and fortitude of our struggle with the lower nature as a preliminary movement; but if a certain mastery comes by our individual strength, the freedom of mastery only comes by our union with God, by a merging or dwelling of the personality in the one divine Person and the loss of the personal will in the divine Will. There is a divine Master of Nature and her works, above her though inhabiting her, who is our highest being and our universal self; to be one with him is to make ourselves divine. By union with God, we enter into a supreme freedom and a supreme mastery. The ideal of the Stoic, the sage who is king because by self-rule he becomes master also of outward conditions, resembles superficially the Vedantic idea of the self-ruler and all-ruler, svarat samrat; but it is on a lower plane.

The Stoic kingship is maintained by a force put upon self and environment; the entirely liberated kingship of the Yogin exists naturally by the eternal royalty of the divine nature, a union with its unfettered universality, a finally unforced dwelling in its superiority to the instrumental nature through which it acts. His mastery over things is because he has become one soul with all things. To take an image from Roman institutions, the Stoic freedom is that of the libertus, the freedman, who is still really a dependent on the power that once held him enslaved; his is a freedom allowed by Nature because he has merited it. The freedom of the Gita is that of the freeman, the true freedom of the birth into the higher nature, self-existent in its divinity. Whatever he does and however he lives, the free soul lives in the Divine; he is the privileged child of the mansion, balavat, who cannot err or fall because all he is and does is full of the Perfect, the All-blissful, the All-loving, the All-beautiful. The kingdom which he enjoys, rajyam samrddham, is a sweet and happy dominion of which it may be said, in the pregnant phrase of the Greek thinker, "The kingdom is of the child."

The knowledge of the philosopher is that of the true nature of mundane existence, the transience of outward things, the vanity of the world's differences and distinctions, the superiority of the inner calm, peace, light, self-dependence. It is an equality of philosophic indifference; it brings a high calm, but not the greater spiritual joy; it is an isolated freedom, a wisdom like that of the Lucretian sage high in his superiority upon the cliff-top whence he looks down on men tossed still upon the tempestuous waters from which he has escaped,—in the end something after all aloof and ineffective. The Gita admits the philosophic motive of indifference as a preliminary movement; but the indifference to which it finally arrives, if indeed that inadequate word can be at all applied, has nothing in it of the philosophic aloofness. It is indeed a position as of one seated above, udasinavat, but as the Divine is seated above, having no need at all in the world, yet he does works always and is present everywhere supporting, helping, guiding the labour of creatures. This equality is founded upon oneness with all beings. It brings in what is wanting to the philosophic equality; for its soul is the soul of peace, but also it is the soul of love. It sees all beings without exception in the Divine, it is oneself with the Self of all existences and therefore it is in supreme sympathy with all of them. Without exception, asesena, not only with all that is good and fair and pleases; nothing and no one, however vile, fallen, criminal, repellent in appearance, can be excluded from this universal, this whole-souled sympathy and spiritual oneness. Here there is no room, not merely for hatred or anger or uncharitableness, but for aloofness, disdain, or any petty pride of superiority. A divine compassion for the ignorance of the struggling mind, a divine will to pour forth on it all light and power and happiness there will be, indeed, for the apparent man; but for the divine Soul within him there will be more, there will be adoration and love. For from all, from the thief and the harlot and the outcaste as from the saint and the sage, the Beloved looks forth and cries to us, "This is I." "He who loves Me in all beings,"—what greater word of power for the utmost intensities and profundities of divine and universal love, has been uttered by any philosophy or any religion?

Resignation is the basis of a kind of religious equality, submission to the divine will, a patient bearing of the cross, a submissive forbearance. In the Gita this element takes the more ample form of an entire surrender of the whole being to God. It is not merely a passive submission, but an active self-giving; not only a seeing and an accepting of the divine Will in all things, but a giving up of one's own will to be the instrument of the Master of works, and this not with the lesser idea of being a servant of

God, but, eventually at least, of such a complete renunciation both of the consciousness and the works to him that our being becomes one with his being and the impersonalized nature only an instrument and nothing else. All result good or bad, pleasing, or unpleasing, fortunate, or unfortunate, is accepted as belonging to the Master of our actions, so that finally not only are grief and suffering borne, but they are banished: a perfect equality of the emotional mind is established. There is no assumption of personal will in the instrument; it is seen that all is already worked out in the omniscient prescience and omnipotent effective power of the universal Divine and that the egoism of men cannot alter the workings of that Will. Therefore, the final attitude is that enjoined on Arjuna in a later chapter, "All has been already done by Me in my divine will and foresight; become only the occasion, O Arjuna," nimitta-matram bhava savyasacin. This attitude must lead finally to an absolute union of the personal with the Divine Will and, with the growth of knowledge, bring about a faultless response of the instrument to the divine Power and Knowledge. A perfect, an absolute equality of self-surrender, the mentality a passive channel of the divine Light and Power, the active being a mightily effective instrument for its work in the world, will be the poise of this supreme union of the Transcendent, the universal and the individual.

Equality too there will be with regard to the action of others upon us. Nothing that they can do will alter the inner oneness, love, sympathy which arises from the perception of the oneself in all, the Divine in all beings. But a resigned forbearance and submission to them and their deeds, a passive non-resistance, will be no necessary part of the action; it cannot be, since a constant instrumental obedience to the divine and universal Will must mean in the shock of opposite forces that fill the world a conflict with personal wills which seek rather their own egoistic satisfaction. Therefore, Arjuna is bidden to resist, to fight, to conquer; but, to fight without hatred or personal desire or personal enmity or antagonism, since to the liberated soul these feelings are impossible. To act for the lokasangraha, impersonally, for the keeping and leading of the peoples on the path to the divine goal, is a rule which rises necessarily from the oneness of the soul with the Divine, the universal Being, since that is the whole sense and drift of the universal action. Nor does it conflict with our oneness with all beings, even those who present themselves here as opponents and enemies. For the divine goal is their goal also, since it is the secret aim of all, even of those whose outward minds, misled by ignorance and egoism, would wander from the path, and resist the impulsion. Resistance and defeat are the best outward service that can be done to them. By this perception the Gita avoids the limiting conclusion which might have been drawn from a doctrine of equality impracticably overriding all relations and of a weakening love without knowledge, while it keeps the one thing essential unimpaired. For the soul oneness with all, for the heart calm universal love, sympathy, compassion, but for the hands freedom to work out impersonally the good, not of this or that person only without regard to or to the detriment of the divine plan, but the purpose of the creation, the progressing welfare and salvation of men, the total good of all existences.

Oneness with God, oneness with all beings, the realisation of the eternal divine unity everywhere and the drawing onwards of men towards that oneness are the law of life which arises from the teachings of the Gita. There can be none greater, wider, more profound. Liberated oneself, to live in this oneness, to help mankind on the path that leads towards it and meanwhile to do all works for God and help man also to do with joy and acceptance all the works to which he is called, krtsna-karma-krt, sarvakarmani josayan, no greater or more liberal rule of divine works can be given. This freedom and this oneness are the secret goal of our human nature, and the ultimate will in the existence of the race. It is that to which it must turn for the happiness all mankind is now vainly seeking, when once men lift their eyes and their hearts to see the Divine in them and around, in all and everywhere, sarvesu, sarvatra, and learn that it is in him they live, while this lower nature of division is only a prison-wall which they must break down or at best an infant-school which they must outgrow, so that they may become adult in nature and free in spirit. To be made oneself with God above and God in man and God in the world is the sense of liberation and the secret of perfection.

XXI

THE DETERMINISM OF NATURE

When we can live in the higher Self by the unity of works and self-knowledge, we become superior to the method of the lower workings of Prakriti. We are no longer enslaved to Nature and her gunas but one with the Ishwara, the master of our nature, we are able to use her without subjection to the chain of Karma, for the purposes of the Divine Will in us; for that is what the greater Self in us is, he is the Lord of her works and unaffected by the troubled stress of her reactions. The soul ignorant in Nature, on the contrary, is enslaved by that ignorance to her modes, because it is identified there, not felicitously with its true self, not with the Divine who is seated above her, but stupidly and unhappily with the ego-mind which is a subordinate factor in her operations in spite of the exaggerated figure it makes, a mere mental knot and point of reference for the play of the natural workings. To break this knot, no longer to make the ego the centre and beneficiary of our works, but to derive all from and refer all to the divine Super soul is the way to become superior to all the restless trouble of Nature's modes. For it is to live in the supreme consciousness, of which the ego-mind is a degradation, and to act in an equal and unified Will and Force and not in the unequal play of the gunas which is a broken seeking and striving, a disturbance, an inferior Maya.

The passages in which the Gita lays stress on the subjection of the ego-soul to Nature, have by some been understood as the enunciation of an absolute and a mechanical determinism which leaves no room for any freedom within the cosmic existence. Certainly, the language it uses is emphatic and seems very absolute. But we must take, here as elsewhere, the thought of the Gita as a whole and not force its affirmations in their solitary sense quite detached from each other,—as indeed every truth, however true in itself, yet, taken apart from others which at once limit and complete it, becomes a snare to bind the intellect and a misleading dogma; for in reality each is one thread of a complex weft, and no thread must be taken apart from the weft. Everything in the Gita is even so interwoven and must be understood in its relation to the whole. The Gita itself makes a distinction between those who have not the knowledge of the whole, akrtsnavidah, and are misled by the partial truths of existence, and the Yogin who has the synthetic knowledge of the totality, krtsna-vit. To see all existence steadily and see it whole and not be misled by its conflicting truths, is the first necessity for the calm and complete wisdom to which the Yogin is called upon to rise. A certain absolute freedom is one aspect of the soul's relations with Nature at one pole of our complex being a certain absolute determinism by Nature is the opposite aspect at its opposite pole; and there is also a partial and apparent, therefore an unreal eidolon of liberty which the soul receives by a contorted reflection of these two opposite truths in the developing mentality. It is the latter to which we ordinarily give, more or less inaccurately, the name of free will; but the Gita regards nothing as freedom which is not a complete liberation and mastery.

We have always to keep in mind the two great doctrines which stand behind all the Gita's teachings with regard to the soul and Nature,—the Sankhya truth of the Purusha and Prakriti corrected and completed by the Vedantic truth of the threefold Purusha and the double Prakriti of which the lower form is the Maya of the three gunas and the higher is the divine nature and the true soul-nature. This is the key which reconciles and explains what we might have otherwise to leave as contradictions and inconsistencies. There are, in fact, different planes of our conscious existence, and what is practical truth on one plane ceases to be true, because it assumes a quite different appearance as soon as we rise to a higher level from which we can see things more in the whole. Recent scientific discovery has shown that man, animal, plant and even the metal have essentially the same vital reactions and they would, therefore, if each has a certain kind of what for want of a better word we must call nervous consciousness, possess the same basis of mechanical psychology. Yet if each of these could give its own mental account of what it experiences, we should have four quite different and largely contradictory statements of the same reactions and the same natural principles, because they get, as we rise in the scale of being, a different meaning and value and have to be judged by a different outlook. So, it is with the levels of the human soul. What we now call in our ordinary mentality our free will and have a certain limited justification for so calling it yet appears to the Yogin who has climbed beyond and to whom our night is day and our day night, not free will at all, but a subjection to the modes of Nature. He regards the same facts, but from the higher outlook of the whole-knower, krtsna-vit, while we view it altogether from the more limited mentality of our partial knowledge, akrtsnavidah, which is an ignorance. What we vaunt of as our freedom is to him bondage. The perception of the ignorance of our assumption of freedom while one is all the time in the meshes of this lower nature, is the viewpoint at which the Gita arrives, and it is in contradiction to this ignorant claim that it affirms the complete subjection of the ego-soul on this plane to the gunas. "While the actions are being entirely done by the modes of Nature," it says, "he whose self is bewildered by egoism thinks that it is his 'I' which is doing them. But one who knows the true principles of the divisions of the modes and of works, realizes that it is the modes which are acting and reacting on each other and is not caught in them by attachment. Those who are bewildered by the modes, get attached to the modes and their works; dull minds, not knowers of the whole, let not the knower of the whole disturb them in their mental standpoint. Giving up thy works to Me, free from desire and egoism, fight delivered from the fever of thy soul." Here there is the clear distinction between two levels of consciousness, two standpoints of action, that of the soul caught in the web of its egoistic nature and doing works with the idea, but not the reality of free will, under the impulsion of Nature, and that of the soul delivered from its identification with the ego, observing, sanctioning, and governing the works of Nature from above her.

We speak of the soul being subject to Nature; but on the other hand, the Gita in distinguishing the properties of the soul and Nature affirms that while Nature is the executrix, the soul is always the lord, Isvara. It speaks here of the self being bewildered by egoism, but the real Self to the Vedantin is the divine, eternally free, and self-aware. What then is this self that is bewildered by Nature, this soul that is subject to her? The answer is that we are speaking here in the common parlance of our lower or mental view of things; we are speaking of the apparent self, of the apparent soul, not of the real self, not of the true Purusha. It is really the ego, which is subject to Nature, inevitably, because it is itself part of Nature, one functioning of her machinery; but when the self-awareness in the mind-consciousness identifies itself with the ego, it creates the appearance of a lower self, an ego-self. And so too what we think of ordinarily as the soul is really the natural personality, not the true Person, the Purusha, but the desire-soul in us which is a reflection of the consciousness of the Purusha in the workings of Prakriti: it is, in fact, itself only an action of the three modes and therefore a part of Nature. Thus, there are, we may say, two souls in us, the apparent or desire-soul, which changes with the mutations of the gunas and is entirely constituted and determined by them, and the free and eternal Purusha not limited by Nature and her gunas. We have two selves, the apparent self, which is only the ego, that mental centre in us which takes up this mutable action of Prakriti, this mutable personality, and which says "I am this personality, I am this natural being who am doing these works,"—but the natural being is simply Nature, a composite of the gunas,—and the true self which is, indeed, the upholder, the possessor and the lord of Nature and figured in her, but is not itself the mutable natural personality. The way to be free must then be to get rid of the desires of this desire-soul and the false self-view of this ego. "Having become free from desire and egoism," cries the Teacher, "fight with all the fever of thy soul passed away from thee,"— nirasir nirmamo bhutva.

This view of our being starts from the Sankhya analysis of the dual principle in our nature, Purusha, and Prakriti. Purusha is inactive, akarta; Prakriti is active, kartri: Purusha is the being full of the light of consciousness; Prakriti is the Nature, mechanical, reflecting all her works in the conscious witness, the Purusha. Prakriti works by the inequality of her three modes, gunas, in perpetual collision and intermixture and mutation with each other; and by her function of ego-mind she gets the Purusha to identify himself with all this working and so creates the sense of active, mutable, temporal personality in the silent eternity of the Self. The impure natural consciousness overclouds the pure soul-consciousness; the mind forgets the Person in the ego and the personality; we suffer the discriminating intelligence to be carried away by the sense-mind and its outgoing functions and by the desire of the life and the body. So long as the Purusha sanctions this action, ego and desire and ignorance must govern the natural being.

But if this were all, then the only remedy would be to withdraw altogether the sanction, suffer, or compel all our nature by this withdrawal to fall into a motionless equilibrium of the three gunas and so cease from all action. But this is precisely the remedy,—

though it is undoubtedly a remedy, one which abolishes, we might say, the patient along with the disease,—which the Gita constantly discourages. Especially, to resort to a tamasic inaction is just what the ignorant will do if this truth is thrust upon them; the discriminating mind in them will fall into a false division, a false opposition, buddhibheda; their active nature and their intelligence will be divided against each other and produce a disturbance and confusion without true issue, a false and self-deceiving line of action, mithyacara or else a mere tamasic inertia, cessation of works, diminution of the will to life and action, not therefore a liberation, but rather a subjection to the lowest of the three gunas, to tamas, the principle of ignorance and of inertia. Or else they will not be able to understand at all, they will find fault with this higher teaching, assert against it their present mental experience, their ignorant idea of free will and, yet more confirmed by the plausibility of their logic in their bewilderment and the deception of ego and desire, lose their chance of liberation in a deeper, more obstinate confirmation of the ignorance.

In fact, these higher truths can only be helpful, because there only they are true to experience and can be lived on a higher and vaster plane of consciousness and being. To view these truths from below is to mis-see, misunderstand and probably to misuse them. It is a higher truth that the distinction of good and evil is indeed a practical fact and law valid for the egoistic human life which is the stage of transition from the animal to the divine, but on a higher plane we rise beyond good and evil, are above their duality even as the Godhead is above it. But the unripe mind, seizing on this truth without rising from the lower consciousness where it is not practically valid, will simply make it a convenient excuse for indulging its Asuric propensities, denying the distinction between good and evil altogether and falling by self-indulgence deeper into the morass of perdition, sarva-jnana-vimudhan nastan acetasah. So too with this truth....of the determinism of Nature; it will be mis-seen and misused, as those misuse it who declare that a man is what his nature has made him and cannot do otherwise than as his nature compels him. It is true in a sense, but not in the sense, which is attached to it, not in the sense that the ego-self can claim irresponsibility and impunity for itself in its works; for it has will and it has desire and so long as it acts according to its will and desire, even though that be its nature, it must bear the reactions of its Karma. It is in a net, if you will, a snare which may well seem perplexing, illogical, unjust, terrible to its present experience, to its limited self-knowledge, but a snare of its own choice, a net of its own weaving.

The Gita says, indeed, "All existences follow their nature and what shall coercing it avail?" which seems, if we take it by itself, a hopelessly absolute assertion of the omnipotence of Nature over the soul; "even the man of knowledge acts according to his own nature." And on this it founds the injunction to follow faithfully in our action the law of our nature. "Better is one's own law of works, svadharma, though in itself faulty than an alien law well-wrought out; death in one's own law of being is better, perilous is it to follow an alien law." What is precisely meant by this svadharma, we have to wait to see until we get to the more elaborate disquisition in the closing chapters about Purusha and Prakriti and the gunas but certainly, it does not mean that we are to follow any impulse, even though evil, which what we call our nature dictates to us. For between these two verses the Gita throws in this further injunction, "In the object of this or that sense liking and disliking are set in ambush; fall not into their power, for they are the be setters of the soul in its path." And immediately after this, in answer to Arjuna's objection who asks him, if there is no fault in following our Nature, what are we then to say of that in us which drives a man to sin, as if by force, even against his own struggling will, the Teacher replies that this is desire and its companion wrath, children of rajas, the second guna, the principle of passion, and this desire is the soul's great enemy and has to be slain. Abstention from evildoing it declares to be the first condition for liberation, and always it enjoins self-mastery, self-control, samyama, control of the mind, senses, all the lower being.

There is therefore a distinction to be made between what is essential in the nature, its native and inevitable action, which it avails not at all to repress, suppress, coerce, and what is accidental to it, its wanderings, confusions, perversions, over which we must certainly get control. There is a distinction implied too between coercion and suppression, nigraha, and control with right use and right guidance, samyama. The former is a violence done to the nature by the will, which in the end depresses the natural powers of the being, atmanam avasadayet; the latter is the control of the lower by the higher self, which successfully gives to those powers their right action and their maximum efficiency,—yogah karmasu kausalam. This nature of samyama is made very clear by the Gita in the opening of its sixth chapter, "By the self thou shouldst deliver the self, thou shouldst not depress and cast down the self (whether by self-indulgence or suppression); for the self is the friend of the self and the self is the enemy. To the man is his self a friend in whom the (lower) self has been conquered by the (higher) self, but to him who is not in possession of his (higher) self, the (lower) self is as if an enemy and it acts as an enemy." When one has conquered one's self and attained to the calm of a perfect self-mastery and self-possession, then is the supreme self in a man founded and poised even in his outwardly conscious human being, samahita. In other words, to master the lower self by the higher, the natural self by the spiritual is the way of man's perfection and liberation.

Here then is a very great qualification of the determinism of Nature, a precise limitation of its meaning and scope. How the passage from subjection to mastery works out is best seen if we observe the working of the gunas in the scale of Nature from the bottom to the top. At the bottom are the existences in which the principle of tamas is supreme, the beings who have not yet attained to the light of self-consciousness and are utterly driven by the current of Nature. There is a will even in the atom, but we see clearly enough that it is not free will, because it is mechanical, and the atom does not possess the will but is possessed by it. Here the buddhi, the element of intelligence and will in Prakriti, is actually and plainly what the Sankhya asserts it to be, jada, a mechanical, even an inconscient principle in which the light of the conscious Soul has not at all struggled to the surface: the atom is not conscious of an intelligent will; tamas, the inert and ignorant principle, has its grip on it, contains rajas, conceals sattva within itself and holds a high holiday of mastery, Nature compelling this form of existence to act with a stupendous force indeed, but as a mechanical instrument, yantrarudham mayaya.

Next, in the plant the principle of rajas has struggled to the surface, with its power of life, with its capacity of the nervous reactions which in us are recognizable as pleasure and suffering, but sattva is quite involved, has not yet emerged to awaken the light of a conscious intelligent will; all is still mechanical, sub-conscient or half-conscient, tamas stronger than rajas, both gaolers of the imprisoned sattwa.

In the animal, though tamas is still strong, though we may still describe him as belonging to the tamasic creation, tamasa sarga, yet rajas prevails much more against tamas, brings with it its developed power of life, desire, emotion, passion, pleasure, suffering, while sattwa, emerging, but still dependent on the lower action, contributes to these the first light of the conscious mind, the mechanical sense of ego, conscious memory, a certain kind of thought, especially the wonders of instinct and animal intuition. But as yet the buddhi, the intelligent will, has not developed the full light of consciousness; therefore, no responsibility can be attributed to the animal for its actions. The tiger can be no more blamed for killing and devouring than the atom for its blind movements, the fire for burning and consuming or the storm for its destructions. If it could answer the question, the tiger would indeed say, like man, that it had free will, it would have the egoism of the doer, it would say, "I kill, I devour"; but we can see clearly enough that it is not really the tiger, but Nature in the tiger that kills, it is Nature in the tiger that devours; and if it refrains from killing or devouring, it is from satiety, from fear or from indolence, from another principle of Nature in it, from the action of the guna called tamas. As it was Nature in the animal that killed, so it is Nature in the animal that refrained from killing. Whatever soul is in it, sanctions passively the action of Nature, is as much passive in its passion and activity as in its indolence or inaction. The animal like the atom acts according to the mechanism of its Nature and not otherwise, sadrsam cestate svasyah prakrteh, as if mounted on a machine, yantrarudho mayaya.

Well, but in man at least there is another action, a free soul, a free will, a sense of responsibility, a real doer other than Nature, other than the mechanism of Maya? So, it seems, because in man there is a conscious intelligent will; buddhi is full of the light of the observing Purusha, who through it, it seems, observes, understands, approves, or disapproves, gives, or withholds the sanction, seems indeed at last to begin to be the lord of his nature. Man is not like the tiger or the fire or the storm; he cannot kill and say as a sufficient justification, "I am acting according to my nature", and he cannot do it, because he has not the nature and not, therefore, the law of action, svadharma, of the tiger, storm, or fire. He has a conscious intelligent will, a buddhi, and to that he must refer his actions. If he does not do so, if he acts blindly according to his impulses and passions, then the law of his being is not rightly worked out, svadharmah su-anusthitah, he has not acted according to the full measure of his humanity, but even as might the animal. It is true that the principle of rajas or the principle of tamas gets hold of his buddhi and induces it to justify any and every action he commits or any avoidance of action; but still the justification or at least the reference to the buddhi must be there either before or after the action is committed. And, besides, in man sattva is awake and acts not only as intelligence and intelligent will, but as a seeking for light, for right knowledge and right action according to that knowledge, as a sympathetic perception of the existence and claims of others, as an attempt to know the higher law of his own nature, which the sattwic principle in him creates, and to obey it, and as a conception of the greater peace and happiness which virtue, knowledge and sympathy bring in their train. He knows more or less imperfectly that he has to govern his rajasic and tamasic by his sattwic nature and that thither tends the perfection of his normal humanity.

But is the condition of the predominantly sattwic nature freedom and is this will in man a free will? That the Gita, from the standpoint of a higher consciousness in which alone is true freedom, denies. The buddhi or conscious intelligent will is still an instrument of Nature and when it acts, even in the most sattwic sense, it is still Nature which acts and the soul which is carried on the wheel by Maya. At any rate, at least nine-tenths of our freedom of will is a palpable fiction; that will is created and determined not by its own self-existent action at a given moment, but by our past, our heredity, our training, our environment, the whole tremendous complex thing we call Karma, which is, behind us, the whole past action of Nature on us and the world converging in the individual, determining what he is, determining what his will shall be at a given moment and determining, as far as analysis can see, even its action at that moment. The ego associates itself always with its Karma and it says, "I did" and "I will" and "I suffer", but if it looks at itself and sees how it was made, it is obliged to say of man as of the animal, "Nature did this in me, Nature wills in me", and if it qualifies by saying "my Nature", that only means "Nature as self-determined in this individual creature". It was the strong perception of this aspect of existence which compelled the Buddhists to declare that all is Karma and that there is no self in existence, that the idea of self is only a delusion of the ego-mind.

When the ego thinks "I choose and will this virtuous and not that evil action", it is simply associating itself, somewhat like the fly on the wheel, or rather as might a cog or other part of a mechanism if it were conscious, with a predominant wave or a formed current of the sattwic principle by which Nature chooses through the buddhi one type of action in preference to another. Nature forms itself in us and wills in us, the Sankhya would say, for the pleasure of the inactive observing Purusha.

But even if this extreme statement has to be qualified, and we shall see hereafter in what sense, still the freedom of our individual will, if we choose to give it that name, is very relative and almost infinitesimal, so much is it mixed up with other determining elements. Its strongest power does not amount to mastery. It cannot be relied upon to resist the strong wave of circumstance or of other nature which either overbears or modifies or mixes up with it or at the best subtly deceives and circumvents it. Even the most sattwic will is so overborne or mixed up with or circumvented by the rajasic and tamasic gunas as to be only in part sattwic, and thence arises that sufficiently strong element of self-deception, of a quite involuntary and even innocent make-believe and hiding from oneself which the merciless eye of the psychologist detects even in the best human action. When we think that we are acting quite freely, powers are concealed behind our action which escape the most careful self-introspection; when we think that we are free from ego, the ego is there, concealed, in the mind of the saint as in that of the sinner. When our eyes are really opened on our action and its springs, we are obliged to say with the Gita "guna gunesu vartante", "it was the modes of Nature that were acting upon the modes."

For this reason even a high predominance of the sattwic principle does not constitute freedom. For, as the Gita points out, the sattwa binds, as much as the other gunas, and binds just in the same way, by desire, by ego; a nobler desire, a purer ego,—but so long as in any form these two hold the being, there is no freedom. The man of virtue, of knowledge, has his ego of the virtuous man, his ego of knowledge, and it is that sattwic ego which he seeks to satisfy; for his own sake he seeks virtue and knowledge. Only when we cease to satisfy the ego, to think and to will from the ego, the limited "I" in us, then is there a real freedom. In other words, freedom, highest self-mastery begin when above the natural self we see and hold the supreme Self of which the ego is an obstructing veil and a blinding shadow. And that can only be when we see the oneself in us seated above Nature and make our individual being one with it in being and consciousness and in its individual nature of action only an instrument of a supreme Will, the one Will that is really free. For that we must rise high above the three gunas, become trigunatita; for that Self is beyond even the sattwic principle. We have to climb to it through the sattwa, but we attain to it only when we get beyond sattwa; we reach out to it from the ego but only reach it by leaving the ego. We are drawn towards it by the highest, most passionate, most stupendous and ecstatic of all desires; but we can securely live in it only when all desire drops away from us. We have at a certain stage to liberate ourselves even from the desire of our liberation.

XXII

BEYOND THE MODES OF NATURE

So far then extends the determinism of Nature, and what it amounts to is this that the ego from which we act is itself an instrument of the action of Prakriti and cannot therefore be free from the control of Prakriti; the will of the ego is a will determined by Prakriti, it is a part of the nature as it has been formed in us by the sum of its own past action and self-modification, and by the nature in us so formed and the will in it so formed our present action also is determined. It is said by some that the first initiating action is always free to our choice however much all that follows may be determined by that and in this power of initiation and its effect on our future lies our responsibility. But where is that first action in Nature which has no determining past behind it, where is that present condition of our nature which is not in sum and detail the result of the action of our past nature? We have that impression of a free initial act because we are living at every moment from our present on towards our future and we do not live back constantly from our present into our past, so that what is strongly vivid to our minds is the present and its consequences while we have a much less vivid hold of our present as entirely the consequence of our past; this latter we are apt to look on as if it were dead and done with. We speak and act as if we were perfectly free in the pure and virgin moment to do what we will with ourselves using an absolute inward independence of choice.

But there is no such absolute liberty, our choice has no such independence.

Certainly, the will in us has always to choose between a certain number of possibilities, for that is the way in which Nature always acts; even our passivity, our refusal to will, is itself a choice, itself an act of the will of Nature in us; even in the atom there is a will always at its work. The whole difference is the extent to which we associate our idea of self with the action of the will in Nature; when we so associate ourselves, we think of it as our will and say that it is a free will and that it is we who are acting. And error or not, illusion or not, this idea of our will, of our action is not a thing of no consequence, of no utility; everything in Nature has a consequence and a utility. It is rather that process of our conscious being by which Nature in us becomes more and more aware of and responsive to the presence of the secret Purusha within her and opens by that increase of knowledge to a greater possibility of action; it is by the aid of the ego-idea and the personal will that she raises herself to her own higher possibilities, rises out of the sheer or else the predominant passivity of the tamasic nature into the passion and the struggle of the rajasic nature and from the passion and the struggle of the rajasic nature to the greater light, happiness and purity of the sattwic nature. The relative self-mastery gained by the natural man over himself is the dominion achieved by the higher possibilities of his nature over its lower possibilities, and this is done in him when he associates his idea of self with the struggle of the higher guna to get the mastery, the predominance over the lower guna. The sense of free will, illusion or not, is a necessary machinery of the action of Nature, necessary for man during his progress, and it would be disastrous for him to lose it before he is ready for a higher truth. If it be said, as it has been said, that Nature deludes man to fulfil her behests and that the idea of a free individual will is the most powerful of these delusions, then it must also be said that the delusion is for his good and without it he could not rise to his full possibilities.

But it is not a sheer delusion, it is only an error of standpoint and an error of placement. The ego thinks that it is the real self and acts as if it were the true centre of action and as if all existed for its sake, and there it commits an error of standpoint and placement. It is not wrong in thinking that there is something or someone within ourselves, within this action of our nature, who is the true centre of its action and for whom all exists; but this is not the ego, it is the Lord secret within our hearts, the divine Purusha, and the Jiva, other than ego, who is a portion of his being. The self-assertion of ego-sense is the broken and distorted shadow in our minds of the truth that there is a real Self within us which is the master of all and for whom and at whose behest Nature goes about her works. So too the ego's idea of free will is a distorted and misplaced sense of the truth that there is a free Self within us and that the will in Nature is only a modified and partial reflection of its will, modified and partial because it lives in the successive moments of Time and acts by a constant series of modifications which forget much of their own precedents and are only imperfectly conscious of their own consequences and aims. But the Will within, exceeding the moments of Time, knows all these, and the action of Nature in us is an attempt, we might say, to work out under the difficult conditions of a natural and egoistic ignorance what is foreseen in full supramental light by the inner Will and Knowledge.

But a time must come in our progress when we are ready to open our eyes to the real truth of our being, and then the error of our egoistic free will must fall away from us. The rejection of the idea of egoistic free will does not imply a cessation of action, because Nature is the doer and carries out her action after this machinery is dispensed with even as she did before it came into usage in the process of her evolution. In the man who has rejected it, it may even be possible for her to develop a greater action; for his mind may be more aware of all that his nature is by the self-creation of the past, more aware of the powers that environ and are working upon it to help or to hinder its growth, more aware too of the latent greater possibilities which it contains by virtue of all in it that is unexpressed, yet capable of expression; and this mind may be a freer channel for the sanction of the Purusha to the greater possibilities that it sees and a freer instrument for the response of Nature, for her resultant attempt at their development and realisation. But the rejection of free will must not be a mere fatalism or idea of natural determinism in the understanding without any vision of the real Self in us; for then the ego still remains as our sole idea of self and, as that is always the instrument of Prakriti, we still act by the ego and with our will as her instrument, and the idea in us brings no real change, but only a modification of our intellectual attitude. We shall have accepted the phenomenal truth of the determination of our egoistic being and action by Nature, we shall have seen our subjection: but we shall not have seen the unborn Self within which is above the action of the gunas; we shall not have seen wherein lies our gate of freedom. Nature and ego are not all we are, there is the free soul, the Purusha.

But in what consists this freedom of the Purusha? The Purusha of the current Sankhya philosophy is free in the essence of his being, but because he is the non-doer, akarta; and in so far as he permits Nature to throw on the inactive Soul her shadow of action, he becomes bound phenomenally by the actions of the gunas and cannot recover his freedom except by dissociation from her and by cessation of her activities. If then a man casts from him the idea of himself as the doer or of the works as his, if, as the Gita enjoins, he fixes himself in the view of himself as the inactive non-doer, atmanam akartaram, and all action as not his own but Nature's, as the play of her gunas, will not a like result follow? The Sankhya Purusha is the giver of the sanction, but a passive sanction only, anumati, the work is entirely Nature's; essentially, he is the witness and sustainer, not the governing and active consciousness of the universal Godhead. He is the Soul that sees and accepts, as a spectator accepts the representation of a play he is watching, not the Soul that both governs and watches the play planned by himself and staged in his own being. If then he withdraws the sanction, if he refuses to acknowledge the illusion of doing by which the play continues, he ceases also to be the sustainer and the action comes to a stop, since it is only for the pleasure of the witnessing conscious Soul that Nature performs it and only by his support that she can maintain it. Therefore, it is evident that the Gita's conception of the relations of the Purusha and Prakriti are not the Sankhya's, since the same movement leads to a quite different result, in one case to cessation of works, in the other to a great, a selfless and desireless, a divine action. In the Sankhya Soul and Nature are two different entities, in the Gita they are two aspects, two powers of one self-existent being; the Soul is not only giver of the sanction, but lord of Nature, Ishwara, through her enjoying the play of the world, through her executing divine will and knowledge in a scheme of things supported by his sanction and existing by his immanent presence, existing in his being, governed by the law of his being and by the conscious will within it. To know, to respond to, to live in the divine being and nature of this Soul is the object of withdrawing from the ego and its action. One then rises above the lower nature of the gunas to the higher divine nature.

The movement by which this ascension is determined results from the complex poise of the Soul in its relations with Nature; it depends on the Gita's idea of the triple Purusha. The Soul that immediately informs the action, the mutations, the successive becomings of Nature, is the Kshara, that which seems to change with her changes, to move in her motion, the Person who follows in his idea of his being the changes of his personality brought about by the continuous action of her Karma. Nature here is Kshara, a constant movement and mutation in Time, a constant becoming. But this Nature is simply the executive power of the Soul itself; for only by what he is, can she become, only according to the possibilities of his becoming, can she act; she works out the becoming of his being. Her Karma is determined by Swabhava, the own nature, the law of self-becoming of the soul, even though, because it is the agent and executive of the becoming, the action rather seems often to determine the nature. According to what we are, we act, and by our action we develop, we work out what we are. Nature is the action, the mutation, the becoming, and it is the Power that executes all these; but the Soul is the conscious Being from which that Power proceeds, from whose luminous stuff of consciousness she has drawn the variable will that changes and expresses its changes in her actions. And this Soul is One and Many; it is the one Life-being out of which all life is constituted, and it is all these living beings; it is the cosmic Existent, and it is all this multitude of cosmic existences, sarvabhutani, for all these are One; all the many Purushas are in their original being the one and only Purusha. But the mechanism of the ego-sense in Nature, which is part of her action, induces the mind to identify the soul's consciousness with the limited becoming of the moment, with the sum of her active consciousness in a given field of space and time, with the result from moment to moment of the sum of her past actions. It is possible to realize in a way the unity of all these beings even in Nature herself and to become aware of a cosmic Soul which is manifest in the whole action of cosmic Nature, Nature manifesting the Soul, the Soul constituting the Nature. But this is to become aware only of the great cosmic Becoming, which is not false or unreal, but the knowledge of which alone does not give us the true knowledge of our Self; for our true Self is always something more than this and something beyond it.

For, beyond the soul manifest in Nature and bound up with its action, is another status of the Purusha, which is entirely a status and not at all an action; that is the silent, the immutable, the all-pervading, self-existent, motionless Self, sarvagatam acalam, immutable Being and not Becoming, the Akshara. In the Kshara the Soul is involved in the action of Nature, therefore it is concentrated, loses itself, as it were, in the moments of Time, in the waves of the Becoming, not really, but only in appearance and by following the current; in the Akshara Nature falls to silence and rest in the Soul, therefore it becomes aware of its immutable Being. The Kshara is the Sankhya's Purusha when it reflects the varied workings of the gunas of Nature, and it knows itself as the Saguna, the Personal; the Akshara is the Sankhya's Purusha when these gunas have fallen into a state of equilibrium, and it knows itself as the Nirguna, the Impersonal. Therefore, while the Kshara, associating itself with the work of Prakriti, seems to be the doer of works, karta, the Akshara dissociated from all the workings of the gunas is the inactive non-doer, akarta, and witness. The soul of man, when it takes the poise of the Kshara, identifies itself with the play of personality and readily clouds its self-knowledge with the ego-sense in Nature, so that he thinks of himself as the ego-doer of works; when it takes its poise in the Akshara, it identifies itself with the Impersonal and is aware of Nature as the doer and itself as the inactive witnessing Self, akartaram. The mind of man has to tend to one of these poises, it takes them as alternatives; it is bound by Nature to action in the mutations of quality and personality, or it is free from her workings in immutable impersonality.

But these two, the status and immutability of the Soul and the action of the Soul and its mutability in Nature, actually coexist. And this would be an anomaly irreconcilable except by some such theory as that of Maya or else of a double and divided being, if there were not a supreme reality of the Soul's existence of which these are the two contrary aspects, but which is limited by neither of them. We have seen that the Gita finds this in the Purushottama. The supreme Soul is the Ishwara, God, the Master of all being, sarvaloka-mahesvara. He puts forth his own active nature, his Prakriti,—svam prakrtim, says the Gita,—manifest in the Jiva, worked out by the svabhava, "own-becoming", of each Jiva according to the law of the divine being in it, the great lines of which each Jiva must follow, but worked out too in the egoistic nature by the bewildering play of the three gunas upon each other, guna gunesu vartante. That is the traigunyamayi maya, the Maya hard for man to get beyond, duratyaya,—yet can one get beyond it by transcending the three gunas. For while all this is done by the Ishwara through his Nature-Power in the Kshara, in the Akshara he is untouched, indifferent, regarding all equally, extended within all, yet above all. In all three he is the Lord, the supreme Ishwara in the highest, the presiding and all-pervading Impersonality, prabhu and vibhu, in the Akshara, and the immanent Will and present active Lord in the Kshara. He is free in his impersonality even while working out the play of his personality; he is not either merely impersonal or personal, but one and the same being in two aspects; he is the impersonal-personal, nirguno guni, of the Upanishad. By him all has been willed even before it is worked out,—as he says of the still living Dhartarashtrians, "already have they been slain by Me," maya nihatah purvam eva,—and the working out by Nature is only the result of his Will; yet by virtue of his impersonality behind he is not bound by his works, kartaram akartaram.

But man as the individual self, owing to his ignorant self-identification with the work and the becoming, as if that were all his soul and not a power of his soul, a power proceeding from it, is bewildered by the ego-sense. He thinks that it is he and others who are doing all; he does not see that Nature is doing all and that he is misrepresenting and disfiguring her works to himself by ignorance and attachment. He is enslaved by the gunas, now hampered in the dull case of tamas, now blown by the strong winds of rajas, now limited by the partial lights of sattwa, not distinguishing himself at all from the nature-mind which alone is thus modified by the gunas. He is therefore mastered by pain and pleasure, happiness and grief, desire and passion, attachment, and disgust: he has no freedom.

He must, to be free, get back from the Nature action to the status of the Akshara; he will then be trigunatita, beyond the gunas. Knowing himself as the Akshara Brahman, the unchanging Purusha, he will know himself as an immutable impersonal self, the Atman, tranquilly observing and impartially supporting the action, but himself calm, indifferent, untouched, motionless, pure, one with all beings in their self, not one with Nature and her workings. This self, though by its presence authorizing the works of Nature, though by its all-pervading existence supporting and consenting to them, prabhu vibhu, does not itself create works or the state of the doer or the joining of the works to their fruit, na kartrtvam na karmani srjati na karma-phala-samyogam, but only watches nature in the Kshara working out these things, svabhavas tu pravartate; it accepts neither the sin nor the virtue of the living creatures born into this birth as its own, nadatte kasyacit papam na caiva sukrtam; it preserves its spiritual purity. It is the ego bewildered by ignorance which attributes these things to itself, because it assumes the responsibility of the doer and chooses to figure as that and not as the instrument of a greater power, which is all that it really is; ajnanenavrtam jnanam tena muhyanti jantavah. By going back into the impersonal self, the soul gets back into a greater self-knowledge and is liberated from the bondage of the works of Nature, untouched by her gunas, free from her shows of good and evil, suffering and happiness. The natural being, the mind, body, life, still remain, Nature still works; but the inner being does not identify himself with these, nor while the gunas play in the natural being, does he rejoice or grieve. He is the calm and free immutable Self observing all.

Is this the last state, the utmost possibility, the highest secret? It cannot be, since this is a mixed or divided, not a perfectly harmonized status, a double, not a unified being, a freedom in the soul, an imperfection in the Nature. It can only be a stage. What then is there beyond it? One solution is that of the Sannyasin who rejects the nature, the action altogether, so far at least as action can be rejected, so that there may be an unmixed undivided freedom; but this solution, though admitted, is not preferred by the Gita. The Gita also insists on the giving up of actions, sarva-karmani sannyasya, but inwardly to the Brahman. Brahman in the Kshara supports wholly the action of Prakriti, Brahman in the Akshara, even while supporting, dissociates itself from the action, preserves its freedom; the individual soul, unified with the Brahman in the Akshara, is free and dissociated, yet unified with the Brahman in the Kshara, supports but is not affected. This it can do best when it sees that both are aspects of the one Purushottama. The Purushottama, inhabiting all existences as the secret Ishwara, controls the Nature and by his will, now no longer distorted and disfigured by the ego-sense, the Nature works out the actions by the swabhava; the individual soul makes the divinised natural being an instrument of the divine Will, nimitta-matram. He remains even in action trigunatita, beyond the gunas, free from the gunas, nistraigunya, he fulfils entirely at last the early injunction of the Gita, nistraigunyo bhavarjuna. He is indeed still the enjoyer of the gunas, as is the Brahman, though not limited by them, nirgunam˙ gunabhoktr ca, unattached, yet all-supporting, even as is that Brahman, asaktam˙ sarvabhrt but the action of the gunas within him is quite changed; it is lifted above their egoistic character and re-actions. For he has unified his whole being in the Purushottama, has assumed the divine being and the higher divine nature of becoming, madbhava, has unified even his mind and natural consciousness with the Divine, manmana maccittah. This change is the final evolution of the nature and the consummation of the divine birth, rahasyam uttamam. When it is accomplished, the soul is aware of itself as the master of its nature and, grown a light of the divine Light and will of the divine Will, is able to change its natural workings into a divine action.

XXIII

NIRVANA AND WORKS IN THE WORLD

THE UNION of the soul with the Purushottama by a Yoga of the whole being is the complete teaching of the Gita and not only the union with the immutable Self as in the narrower doctrine which follows the exclusive way of knowledge. That is why the Gita subsequently, after it has effected the reconciliation of knowledge and works, is able to develop the idea of love and devotion, unified with both works and knowledge, as the highest height of the way to the supreme secret. For if the union with the immutable Self were the sole secret or the highest secret, that would not at all be possible; for then at a given point our inner basis for love and devotion, no less than our inner foundation of works, would crumble away and collapse. Union utter and exclusive with the immutable Self alone means the abolition of the whole point of view of the mutable being, not only in its ordinary and inferior action but in its very roots, in all that makes its existence possible, not only in the works of its ignorance, but in the works of its knowledge. It would mean the abolition of all that difference in conscious poise and activity between the human soul and the Divine which makes possible the play of the Kshara; for the action of the Kshara would become then entirely a play of the ignorance without any root or basis of divine reality in it. On the contrary, union by Yoga with the Purushottama means the knowledge and enjoyment of our oneness with him in our self-existent being and of a certain differentiation in our active being. It is the persistence of the latter in a play of divine works which are urged by the motive power of divine love and constituted by a perfected divine Nature, it is the vision of the Divine in the world harmonized with a realisation of the Divine in the self which makes action and devotion possible to the liberated man and not only possible but inevitable in the perfect mode of his being.

But the direct way to union lies through the firm realisation of the immutable Self, and it is the Gita's insistence on this as a first necessity, after which alone works and devotion can acquire their whole divine meaning, that makes it possible for us to mistake its drift. For if we take the passages in which it insists most rigorously upon this necessity and neglect to observe the whole sequence of thought in which they stand, we may easily come to the conclusion that it does really teach actionless absorption as the final state of the soul and action only as a preliminary means towards stillness in the motionless Immutable. It is in the close of the fifth and throughout the sixth chapter that this insistence is strongest and most comprehensive. There we get the description of a Yoga which would seem at first sight to be incompatible with works and we get the repeated use of the word Nirvana to describe the status to which the Yogin arrives.

The mark of this status is the supreme peace of a calm self-extinction, santim nirvana-paramam and as if to make it quite clear that it is not the Buddhist's Nirvana in a blissful negation of being but the Vedantic loss of a partial in a perfect being that it intends, the Gita always uses the phrase brahma-nirvana, extinction in the Brahman; and the Brahman here certainly seems to mean the Immutable, to denote primarily at least the inner timeless Self withdrawn from active participation even though immanent in the externality of Nature. We have to see then what is the drift of the Gita here, and especially whether this peace is the peace of an absolute inactive cessation, whether the self-extinction in the Akshara means the absolute excision of all knowledge and consciousness of the Kshara and of all action in the Kshara. We are accustomed indeed to regard Nirvana and any kind of existence and action in the world as incompatible and we might be inclined to argue that the use of the word is by itself sufficient and decides the question. But if we look closely at Buddhism, we shall doubt whether the absolute incompatibility really existed even for the Buddhists; and if we look closely at the Gita, we shall see that it does not form part of this supreme Vedantic teaching.

The Gita after speaking of the perfect equality of the Brahman-knower who has risen into the Brahman-consciousness, brahmavid brahmani sthitah, develops in nine verses that follow its idea of Brahmayoga and of Nirvana in the Brahman. "When the soul is no longer attached to the touches of outward things," it begins, "then one finds the happiness that exists in the Self; such a one enjoys an imperishable happiness, because his self is in Yoga, yukta, by Yoga with the Brahman." The non-attachment is essential, it says, in order to be free from the attacks of desire and wrath and passion, a freedom without which true happiness is not possible. That happiness and that equality are to be gained entirely by man in the body: he is not to suffer any least remnant of the subjection to the troubled lower nature to remain in the idea that the perfect release will come by a putting off of the body; a perfect spiritual freedom is to be won here upon earth and possessed and enjoyed in the human life, prak sarıra-vimoksanat. It then continues, "He who has the inner happiness and the inner ease and repose and the inner light, that Yogin becomes the Brahman and reaches self-extinction in the Brahman, brahma-nirvanam."

Here, very clearly, Nirvana means the extinction of the ego in the higher spiritual, inner Self, that which is forever timeless, spaceless, not bound by the chain of cause and effect and the changes of the world-mutation, self-blissful, self-illumined and forever at peace. The Yogin ceases to be the ego, the little person limited by the mind and the body; he becomes the Brahman; he is unified in consciousness with the immutable divinity of the eternal Self which is immanent in his natural being.

But is this a going in into some deep sleep of samadhi away from all world-consciousness, or is it the preparatory movement for a dissolution of the natural being and the individual soul into some absolute Self who is utterly and forever beyond Nature and her works, laya, moksa? Is that withdrawal necessary before we can enter into Nirvana, or is Nirvana, as the context seems to suggest, a state which can exist simultaneously with world-consciousness and even in its own way include it? Apparently, the latter, for in the succeeding verse the Gita goes on to say,

"Sages win Nirvana in the Brahman, they in whom the stains of sin are effaced, and the knot of doubt is cut asunder, masters of their selves, who are occupied in doing good to all creatures, sarvabhuta-hite ratah." That would almost seem to mean that to be thus is to be in Nirvana. But the next verse is quite clear and decisive, "Yatis (those who practise self-mastery by Yoga and austerity) who are delivered from desire and wrath and have gained self-mastery, for them Nirvana in the Brahman exists all about them, encompasses them, they already live in it because they have knowledge of the Self." That is to say, to have knowledge and possession of the self is to exist in Nirvana. This is clearly a large extension of the idea of Nirvana. Freedom from all stain of the passions, the self-mastery of the equal mind on which that freedom is founded, equality to all beings, sarvabhutesu, and beneficial love for all, final destruction of that doubt and obscurity of the ignorance which keeps us divided from the all-unifying Divine and the knowledge of the One Self within us and in all are evidently the conditions of Nirvana which are laid down in these verses of the Gita, go to constitute it and are its spiritual substance.

Thus, Nirvana is clearly compatible with world-consciousness and with action in the world. For the sages who possess it are conscious of and in intimate relation by works with the Divine in the mutable universe; they are occupied with the good of all creatures, sarvabhuta-hite. They have not renounced the experiences of the Kshara Purusha, they have divinised them; for the Kshara, the Gita tells us, is all existences, sarvabhutani and the doing universal good to all is a divine action in the mutability of Nature. This action in the world is not inconsistent with living in Brahman, it is rather its inevitable condition and outward result because the Brahman in whom we find Nirvana, the spiritual consciousness in which we lose the separative ego-consciousness, is not only within us but within all these existences, exists not only above and apart from all these universal happenings, but pervades them, contains them, and is extended in them. Therefore by Nirvana in the Brahman must be meant a destruction or extinction of the limited separative consciousness, falsifying and dividing, which is brought into being on the surface of existence by the lower Maya of the three gunas, and entry into Nirvana is a passage into this other true unifying consciousness which is the heart of existence and its continent and its whole containing and supporting, its whole original and eternal and final truth. Nirvana when we gain it, enter into it, is not only within us, but all around, abhito vartate, because this is not only the Brahman-consciousness which lives secret within us, but the Brahman-consciousness in which we live. It is the Self which we are within, the supreme Self of our individual being but also the Self which we are without, the supreme Self of the universe, the self of all existences. By living in that self, we live in all and no longer in our egoistic being alone; by oneness with that self a steadfast oneness with all in the universe becomes the very nature of our being and the root status of our active consciousness and root motive of all our action.

But again, we get immediately afterwards two verses which might seem to lead away from this conclusion. "Having put outside of himself all outward touches and concentrated the vision between the eyebrows and made equal the prana and the apana moving within the nostrils, having controlled the senses, the mind and the understanding, the sage devoted to liberation, from whom desire, and wrath and fear have passed away is ever free." Here we have a process of Yoga that brings in an element which seems quite other than the Yoga of works and other even than the pure Yoga of knowledge by discrimination and contemplation; it belongs in all its characteristic features to the system, introduces the psycho-physical askesis of Rajayoga. There is the conquest of all the movements of the mind, cittavrtti-nirodha; there is the control of the breathing, Pranayama; there is the drawing in of the sense and the vision. All of them are processes which lead to the inner trance of Samadhi, the object of all of them moksa, and moksa signifies in ordinary parlance the renunciation not only of the separative ego-consciousness but of the whole active consciousness, a dissolution of our being into the highest Brahman. Are we to suppose that the Gita gives this process in that sense as the last movement of a release by dissolution or only as a special means and a strong aid to overcome the outward-going mind? Is this the finale, the climax, the last word? We shall find reason to regard it as both a special means, an aid, and at least one gate of a final departure, not by dissolution, but by an uplifting to the supracosmic existence. For even here in this passage this is not the last word; the last word, the finale, the climax comes in a verse that follows and is the last couplet of the chapter. "When a man has known Me as the Enjoyer of sacrifice and Tapasya (of all askesis and energisms), the mighty lord of all the worlds, the friend of all creatures, he comes by the peace." The power of the Karmayoga comes in again; the knowledge of the active Brahman, the cosmic super-soul, is insisted on among the conditions of the peace of Nirvana.

We get back to the great idea of the Gita, the idea of the Purushottama,—though that name is not given till close upon the end, it is always that which Krishna means by his "I" and "Me", the Divine who is there as the one self in our timeless immutable being, who is present too in the world, in all existences, in all activities, the master of the silence and the peace, the master of the power and the action, who is here incarnate as the divine charioteer of the stupendous conflict, the Transcendent, the Self, the All, the master of every individual being. He is the enjoyer of all sacrifice and of all Tapasya, therefore shall the seeker of liberation do works as a sacrifice and as a Tapasya; he is the lord of all the worlds, manifested in Nature and in these beings, therefore shall the liberated man still do works for the right government and leading on of the peoples in these worlds, loka-sangraha; he is the friend of all existences, therefore is the sage who has found Nirvana within him and all around, still and always occupied with the good of all creatures,—even as the Nirvana of Mahayana Buddhism took for its highest sign the works of a universal compassion. Therefore too, even when he has found oneness with the Divine in his timeless and immutable self, is he still capable, since he embraces the relations also of the play of Nature, of divine love for man and of love for the Divine, of bhakti.

That this is the drift of the meaning, becomes clearer when we have fathomed the sense of the sixth chapter which is a large comment on and a full development of the idea of these closing verses of the fifth,—that shows the importance which the Gita attaches to them. We shall therefore run as briefly as possible through the substance of this sixth chapter. First the Teacher emphasizes—and this is very significant—his often-repeated asseveration about the real essence of Sannyasa, that it is an inward, not an outward renunciation. "Whoever does the work to be done without resort to its fruits, he is the Sannyasin and the Yogin, not the man who lights not the sacrificial fire and does not the works. What they have called renunciation (Sannyasa), known to be in truth Yoga; for none becomes a Yogin who has not renounced the desire-will in the mind." Works are to be done, but with what purpose and in what order? They are first to be done while ascending the hill of Yoga, for then works are the cause, karanam. The cause of what? The cause of self-perfection, of liberation, of nirvana in the Brahman; for by doing works with a steady practice of the inner renunciation this perfection, this liberation, this conquest of the desire-mind and the ego-self and the lower nature are easily accomplished.

But when one has got to the top? Then works are no longer the cause; the calm of self-mastery and self-possession gained by works becomes the cause. Again, the cause of what? Of fixity in the Self, in the Brahman-consciousness and of the perfect equality in which the divine works of the liberated man are done. "For when one does not get attached to the objects of sense or to works and has renounced all will of desire in the mind, then is he said to have ascended to the top of Yoga." That, as we know already, is the spirit in which the liberated man does works; he does them without desire and attachment, without the egoistic personal will and the mental seeking which is the parent of desire. He has conquered his lower self, reached the perfect calm in which his highest self is manifest to him, that highest self always concentrated in its own being, samahita, in Samadhi, not only in the trance of the inward-drawn consciousness, but always, in the waking state of the mind as well, in exposure to the causes of desire and of the disturbance of calm, to grief and pleasure, heat and cold, honour, and disgrace, all the dualities, sitosna-sukhaduhkhesu tathamanapamanayoh. This higher self is the Akshara, kutastha, which stands above the changes and the perturbations of the natural being; and the Yogin is said to be in Yoga with it when he also is like it, kutastha, when he is

superior to all appearances and mutations, when he is satisfied with self-knowledge, when he is equal-minded to all things and happenings and persons.

But this Yoga is after all no easy thing to acquire, as Arjuna indeed shortly afterwards suggests, for the restless mind is always liable to be pulled down from these heights by the attacks of outward things and to fall back into the strong control of grief and passion and inequality. Therefore, it would seem, the Gita proceeds to give us in addition to its general method of knowledge and works a special process of Rajayogic meditation also, a powerful method of practice, abhyasa, a strong way to the complete control of the mind and all its workings. In this process the Yogin is directed to practise continually union with the Self so that that may become his normal consciousness. He is to sit apart and alone, with all desire and idea of possession banished from his mind, self-controlled in his whole being and consciousness. "He should set in a pure spot his firm seat, neither too high, nor yet too low, covered with a cloth, with a deerskin, with sacred grass, and there seated with a concentrated mind and with the workings of the mental consciousness and the senses un-der control he should practise Yoga for self-purification, atma-visuddhaye." The posture he takes must be the motionless erect posture proper to the practice of Rajayoga; the vision should be drawn in and fixed between the eyebrows, "not regarding the regions." The mind is to be kept calm and free from fear and the vow of Brahmacharya observed; the whole controlled mentality must be devoted and turned to the Divine so that the lower action of the consciousness shall be merged in the higher peace. For the object to be attained is the still peace of Nirvana. "Thus, always putting himself in Yoga by control of his mind the Yogin attains to the supreme peace of Nirvana which has its foundation in Me, santim nirvana-paramam matsamstham."

This peace of Nirvana is reached when all the mental consciousness is perfectly controlled and liberated from desire and remains still in the Self, when, motionless like the light of a lamp in a windless place, it ceases from its restless action, shut in from its outward motion and by the silence and stillness of the mind the Self is seen within, not disfigured as in the mind, but in the Self, seen, not as it is mistranslated falsely or partially by the mind and represented to us through the ego, but self-perceived by the Self, svaprakasa. Then the soul is satisfied and knows its own true and exceeding bliss, not that untranquil happiness which is the portion of the mind and the senses, but an inner and serene felicity in which it is safe from the mind's perturbations and can no longer fall away from the spiritual truth of its being. Not even the fieriest assault of mental grief can disturb it; for mental grief comes to us from outside, is a reaction to external touches, and this is the inner, the self-existent happiness of those who no longer accept the slavery of the unstable mental reactions to external touches. It is the putting away of the contact with pain, the divorce of the mind's marriage with grief, duhkha-samyoga-viyogam. The firm winning of this inalienable spiritual bliss is Yoga, it is the divine union; it is the greatest of all gains and the treasure beside which all others lose their value. There-fore is this Yoga to be resolutely practised without yielding to any discouragement by difficulty or failure until the release, until the bliss of Nirvana is secured as an eternal possession.

The main stress here has fallen on the stilling of the emotive mind, the mind of desire and the senses which are the recipients of outward touches and reply to them with our customary emotional reactions; but even the mental thought has to be stilled in the silence of the self-existent being. First, all the desires born of the desire-will have to be wholly abandoned without any exception or residue and the senses have to be held in by the mind so that they shall not run out to all sides after their usual disorderly and restless habit; but next the mind itself has to be seized by the buddhi and drawn inward. One should slowly cease from mental action by a buddhi held in the grasp of fixity and having fixed the mind in the higher self-one should not think of anything at all. Whenever the restless and unquiet mind goes forth, it should be controlled and brought into subjection in the Self. When the mind is thoroughly quieted, then there comes upon the Yogin the highest, stainless, passionless bliss of the soul that has become the Brahman. "Thus, freed from stain of passion and putting himself constantly into Yoga, the Yogin easily and happily enjoys the touch of the Brahman which is an exceeding bliss."

And yet the result is not, while one yet lives, a Nirvana which puts away every possibility of action in the world, every relation with beings in the world. It would seem at first that it ought to be so. When all the desires and passions have ceased, when the mind is no longer permitted to throw itself out in thought, when the practice of this silent and solitary Yoga has become the rule, what farther action or relation with the world of outward touches and mutable appearances is any longer possible? No doubt, the Yogin for a time still remains in the body, but the cave, the forest, the mountaintop seem now the fittest, the only possible scene of his continued living and constant trance of Samadhi his sole joy and occupation. But, first, while this solitary Yoga is being pursued, the renunciation of all other action is not recommended by the Gita. This Yoga, it says, is not for the man who gives up sleep and food and play and action, even as it is not for those who indulge too much in these things of the life and the body; but the sleep and waking, the food, the play, the putting forth of effort in works should all be yukta. This is generally interpreted as meaning that all should be moderate, regulated, done in fit measure, and that may indeed be the significance. But at any rate when the Yoga is attained, all this has to be yukta in another sense, the ordinary sense of the word everywhere else in the Gita. In all states, in waking and in sleeping, in food and play and action, the Yogin will then be in Yoga with the Divine, and all will be done by him in the consciousness of the Divine as the self and as the All and as that which supports and contains his own life and his action. Desire and ego and personal will and the thought of the mind are the motives of action only in the lower nature; when the ego is lost and the Yogin becomes Brahman, when he lives in and is, even, a transcendent and universal consciousness, action comes spontaneously out of that, luminous knowledge higher than the mental thought comes out of that, a power other and mightier than the personal will comes out of that to do for him his works and bring its fruits:1[1] personal action has ceased, all has been taken up into the Brahman and assumed by the Divine, mayi sannyasya karmani.

For when the Gita describes the nature of this self-realization and the result of the Yoga which comes by Nirvana of the separative ego-mind and its motives of thought and feeling and action into the Brahman-consciousness, it includes the cosmic sense, though lifted into a new kind of vision. "The man whose self is in Yoga, sees the self in all beings and all beings in the self, he sees all with an equal vision." All that he sees is to him the Self, all is his self, all is the Divine. But is there no danger, if he dwells at all in the mutability of the Kshara, of his losing all the results of this difficult Yoga, losing the Self, and falling back into the mind, of the Divine losing him and the world getting him, of his losing the Divine and getting back in its place the ego and the lower nature? No, says the Gita; "he who sees Me everywhere and sees all in Me, to him I do not get lost, nor does he get lost to Me." For this peace of Nirvana, though it is gained through the Akshara, is founded upon the being of the Purushottama, mat-samstham and that is extended, the Divine, the Brahman is extended too in the world of beings and, though transcendent of it, not imprisoned in its own transcendence. One has to see all things as He and live and act wholly in that vision; that is the perfect fruit of the Yoga.

But why act? Is it not safer to sit in one's solitude looking out upon the world, if you will, seeing it in Brahman, in the Divine, but not taking part in it, not moving in it, not living in it, not

1 yoga-ksemam vahamyaham.

acting in it, living rather ordinarily in the inner Samadhi? Should not that be the law, the rule, the dharma of this highest spiritual condition? No, again; for the liberated Yogin there is no other law, rule, dharma than simply this, to live in the Divine and love the Divine and be one with all beings; his freedom is an absolute and not a contingent freedom, self-existent and not dependent any longer on any rule of conduct, law of life or limitation of any kind. He no longer has any need of a process of Yoga because he is now perpetually in Yoga. "The Yogin who has taken his stand upon oneness and loves Me in all beings, however and in all ways, he lives and acts, lives and acts in Me." The love of the world spiritualized, changed from a sense-experience to a soul-experience, is founded on the love of God and in that love, there is no peril and no shortcoming. Fear and disgust of the world may often be necessary for the recoil from the lower nature, for it is really the fear and disgust of our own ego which reflects itself in the world. But to see God in the world is to fear nothing, it is to embrace all in the being of God; to see all as the Divine is to hate and loathe nothing but love God in the world and the world in God.

But at least the things of the lower nature will be shunned and feared, the things which the Yogin has taken so much trouble to surmount? Not this either; all is embraced in the equality of the self-vision. "He, O Arjuna, who sees with equality everything in the image of the Self, whether it be grief or it be happiness, him I hold to be the supreme Yogin." And by this it is not meant at all that he himself shall fall from the griefless spiritual bliss and feel again worldly unhappiness, even in the sorrow of others, but seeing in others the play of the dualities which he himself has left and surmounted, he shall still see all as himself, his self in all, God in all and, not disturbed or bewildered by the appearances of these things, moved only by them to help and heal, to occupy himself with the good of all beings, to lead men to the spiritual bliss, to work for the progress of the world Godwards, he shall live the divine life, so long as days upon earth are his portion. The God-lover who can do this, can thus embrace all things in God, can look calmly on the lower nature and the works of the Maya of the three gunas and act in them and upon them without perturbation or fall or disturbance from the height and power of the spiritual oneness, free in the largeness of the God-vision, sweet and great and luminous in the strength of the God-nature, may well be declared to be the supreme Yogin. He indeed has conquered the creation, jitah sargah.

The Gita brings in here as always bhakti as the climax of

the Yoga, sarvabhutasthitam yo mam bhajati ekatvam asthitah; that may almost be said to sum up the whole final result of the Gita's teaching—whoever loves God in all, and his soul is founded upon the divine oneness, however he lives and acts, lives, and acts in God. And to emphasize it still more, after an intervention of Arjuna and a reply to his doubt as to how so difficult a Yoga can be at all possible for the restless mind of man, the divine Teacher returns to this idea and makes it his culminating utterance. "The Yogin is greater than the doers of askesis, greater than the men of knowledge, greater than the men of works; become then the Yogin, O Arjuna," the Yogin, one who seeks for and attains, by works and knowledge and askesis or by whatever other means, not even spiritual knowledge or power or anything else for their own sake, but the union with God alone; for in that all else is contained and in that lifted beyond itself to a divinest significance. But even among Yogins the greatest is the Bhakta. "Of all Yogins he who with all his inner self given up to Me, for Me has love and faith, sraddhavan bhajate, him I hold to be the most united with Me in Yoga." It is this that is the closing word of these first six chapters and contains in itself the seed of the rest, of that which still remains unspoken and is nowhere entirely spoken; for it is always and remains something of a mystery and a secret, rahasyam, the highest spiritual mystery and the divine secret.

XXIV

THE GIST OF THE KARMAYOGA

The First six chapters of the Gita form a sort of pre-liminary block of the teaching; all the rest, all the other twelve chapters are the working out of certain unfinished figures in this block which here are seen only as hints behind the large-size execution of the main motives yet are in themselves of capital importance and are therefore reserved for a yet larger treatment on the other two faces of the work. If the Gita were not a great written Scripture which must be carried to its end, if it were actually a discourse by a living teacher to a disciple which could be resumed in good time, when the disciple was ready for farther truth, one could conceive of his stopping here at the end of the sixth chapter and saying, "Work this out first, there is plenty for you to do to realize it and you have the largest possible basis; as difficulties arise, they will solve themselves or I will solve them for you. But at present live out what I have told you; work in this spirit." True, there are many things here which cannot be properly understood except in the light thrown on them by what is to come after. In order to clear up immediate difficulties and obviate possible misunderstandings, I have had myself to anticipate a good deal, to bring in repeatedly, for example, the idea of the Purushottama, for without that it would have been impossible to clear up certain obscurities about the Self and action and the Lord of action, which the Gita deliberately accepts so that it may not disturb the firmness of the first steps by reaching out prematurely to things too great as yet for the mind of the human disciple.

Arjuna, himself, if the Teacher were to break off his discourse here, might well object: "You have spoken much of the destruction of desire and attachment, of equality, of the conquest of the senses and the stilling of the mind, of passionless and impersonal action, of the sacrifice of works, of the inner as preferable to the outer renunciation, and these things I understand intellectually, however difficult they may appear to me in practice. But you have also spoken of rising above the gunas, while yet one remains in action, and you have not told me how the gunas work, and unless I know that it will be difficult for me to detect and rise above them. Besides, you have spoken of bhakti as the greatest element in Yoga, yet you have talked much of works and knowledge, but very little or nothing of bhakti. And to whom is bhakti, this greatest thing, to be offered? Not to the still impersonal Self, certainly, but to you, the Lord. Tell me, then, what you are, who, as bhakti is greater even than this self-knowledge, are greater than the immutable Self, which is yet itself greater than mutable Nature and the world of action, even as knowledge is greater than works. What is the relation between these three things? between works and knowledge and divine love? between the soul in Nature and the immutable Self and that which is at once the changeless Self of all and the Master of knowledge and love and works, the supreme Divinity who is here with me in this great battle and massacre, my charioteer in the chariot of this fierce and terrible action?" It is to answer these questions that the rest of the Gita is written, and in a complete intellectual solution they have indeed to be taken up without delay and resolved. But in actual sadhana one has to advance from stage to stage, leaving many things, indeed the greatest things to arise subsequently and solve themselves fully by the light of the advance we have made in spiritual experience. The Gita follows to a certain extent this curve of experience and puts first a sort of large preliminary basis of works and knowledge which contains an element leading up to bhakti and to a greater knowledge, but not yet fully arriving. The six chapters present us with that basis.

We may then pause to consider how far they have carried the solution of the original problem with which the Gita started. The problem in itself, it may be useful again to remark, need not necessarily have led up to the whole question of the nature of existence and of the replacement of the normal by the spiritual life. It might have been dealt with on a pragmatical or an ethical basis or from an intellectual or an ideal standpoint or by a consideration of all of these together; that in fact would have been our modern method of solving the difficulty. By itself it raises in the first instance just this question, whether Arjuna should be governed by the ethical sense of personal sin in slaughter or by the consideration equally ethical of his public and social duty, the defence of the Right, the opposition demanded by conscience from all noble natures to the armed forces of injustice and oppression?

That question has been raised in our own time and the present hour, and it can be solved, as we solve it now, by one or other of very various solutions, but all from the standpoint of our normal life and our normal human mind. It may be answered as a question between the personal conscience and our duty to the society and the State, between an ideal and a practical morality, between "soul-force" and the recognition of the troublesome fact that life is not yet at least all soul and that to take up arms for the right in a physical struggle is sometimes inevitable. All these solutions are, however, intellectual, temperamental, emotional; they depend upon the individual standpoint and are at the best our own proper way of meeting the difficulty offered to us, proper because suitable to our nature and the stage of our ethical and intellectual evolution, the best we can, with the light we have, see, and do; it leads to no final solution. And this is so because it proceeds from the normal mind which is always a tangle of various tendencies of our being and can only arrive at a choice or an accommodation between them, between our reason, our ethical being, our dynamic needs, our life-instincts, our emotional being and those rarer movements which we may perhaps call soul-instincts or psychical preferences. The Gita recognizes that from this standpoint there can be no absolute, only an immediate practical solution and, after offering to Arjuna from the highest ideals of his age just such a practical solution, which he is in no mood to accept and indeed is evidently not intended to accept, it proceeds to quite a different standpoint and to quite another answer.

The Gita's solution is to rise above our natural being and normal mind, above our intellectual and ethical perplexities into another consciousness with another law of being and therefore another standpoint for our action; where personal desire and personal emotions no longer govern it; where the dualities fall away; where the action is no longer our own and where therefore the sense of personal virtue and personal sin is exceeded; where the universal, the impersonal, the divine spirit works out through us its purpose in the world; where we are ourselves by a new and divine birth changed into being of that Being, consciousness of that Consciousness, power of that Power, bliss of that Bliss, and, living no longer in our lower nature, have no works to do of our own, no personal aim to pursue of our own, but if we do works at all,—and that is the one real problem and difficulty left,—do only the divine works, those of which our outward nature is only a passive instrument and no longer the cause, no longer provides the motive; for the motive-power is above us in the will of the Master of our works. And this is presented to us as the true solution because it goes back to the real truth of our being and to live according to the real truth of our being is evidently the highest solution and the sole entirely true solution of the problems of our existence. Our mental and vital personality is a truth of our natural existence, but a truth of the ignorance, and all that attaches itself to it is also truth of that order, practically valid for the works of the ignorance, but no longer valid when we get back to the real truth of our being. But how can we actually be sure that this is the truth? We cannot so long as we remain satisfied with our ordinary mental experience; for our normal mental experience is wholly that of this lower nature full of the ignorance. We can only know this greater truth by living it, that is to say, by passing beyond the mental into the spiritual experience, by Yoga. For the living out of spiritual experience until we cease to be mind and become spirit, until, liberated from the imperfections of our present nature, we are able to live entirely in our true and divine being is what in the end we mean by Yoga.

This upward transference of our centre of being and the consequent transformation of our whole existence and consciousness, with a resultant change in the whole spirit and motive of our action, the action often remaining precisely the same in all its outward appearances, makes the gist of the Gita's Karmayoga. Change your being, be reborn into the spirit and by that new birth proceeds with the action to which the Spirit within has appointed you, may be said to be the heart of its message. Or again, put otherwise, with a deeper and more spiritual import,—make the work you have to do here your means of inner spiritual rebirth, the divine birth, and, having become divine, do still divine works as an instrument of the Divine for the leading of the peoples. Therefore, there are here two things which have to be clearly laid down and clearly grasped, the way to the change, to this upward transference, this new divine birth, and the nature of the work or rather the spirit in which it has to be done, since the outward form of it need not at all change, although really its scope and aim become quite different. But these two things are practically the same, for the elucidation of one elucidates the other. The spirit of our action arises from the nature of our being and the inner foundation it has taken, but also this nature is itself affected by the trend and spiritual effect of our action; a very great change in the spirit of our works changes the nature of our being and alters the foundation it has taken; it shifts the Centre of conscious force from which we act. If life and action were entirely illusory, as some would have it, if the Spirit had nothing to do with works or life, this would not be so; but the soul in us develops itself by life and works and, not indeed so much the action itself, but the way of our soul's inner force of working determines its relations to the Spirit. This is, indeed, the justification of Karmayoga as a practical means of the higher self-realization.

We start from this foundation that the present inner life of man, almost entirely dependent as it is upon his vital and physical nature, only lifted beyond it by a limited play of mental energy, is not the whole of his possible existence, not even the whole of his present real existence. There is within him a hidden Self, of which his present nature is either only an outer appearance or is a partial dynamic result. The Gita seems throughout to admit its dynamic reality and not to adopt the severer view of the extreme Vedantists that it is only an appearance, a view which strikes at the very roots of all works and action. Its way of formulating this element of its philosophical thought,—it might be done in a different way,—is to admit the Sankhya distinction between the Soul and Nature, the power that knows, supports, and informs and the power that works, acts, provides all the variations of instrument, medium and process. Only it takes the free and immutable Soul of the Sankhyas, calls it in Vedantic language the one immutable omnipresent Self or Brahman, and distinguishes it from this other soul involved in Nature, which is our mutable and dynamic being, the multiple soul of things, the basis of variation and personality. But in what then consists of this action of Nature?

It consists in a power of process, Prakriti, which is the interplay of three fundamental modes of its working, three qualities, gunas. And what is the medium? It is the complex system of existence created by a graded evolution of the instruments of Prakriti, which, as they are reflected here in the soul's experience of her workings, we may call successively the reason and the ego, the mind, the senses, and the elements of material energy which are the basis of its forms. These are all mechanical, a complex engine of Nature, yantra; and from our modern point of view, we may say that they are all involved in material energy and manifest themselves in it as the soul in Nature becomes aware of itself by an upward evolution of each instrument, but in the inverse order to that which we have stated, matter first, then sensation, then mind, next reason, last spiritual consciousness. Reason, which is at first only preoccupied with the workings of Nature, may then detect their ultimate character, may see them only as a play of the three gunas in which the soul is entangled, may distinguish between the soul and these workings; then the soul gets a chance of disentangling itself and of going back to its original freedom and immutable existence. In Vedantic language, it sees the spirit, the being; it ceases to identify itself with the instruments and workings of Nature, with its becoming; it identifies itself with its true Self and being and recovers its immutable spiritual self-existence. It is then from this spiritual self-existence, according to the Gita, that it can freely and as the master of its being, the Ishwara, support the action of its becoming.

Looking only at the psychological facts on which these philosophical distinctions are founded,—philosophy is only a way of formulating to ourselves intellectually in their essential significance the psychological and physical facts of existence and their relation to any ultimate reality that may exist,—we may say that there are two lives we can lead, the life of the soul engrossed in the workings of its active nature, identified with its psychological and physical instruments, limited by them, bound by its personality, subject to Nature, and the life of the Spirit, superior to these things, large, impersonal, universal, free, unlimited, transcendent, supporting with an infinite equality its natural being and action, but exceeding them by its freedom and infinity. We may live in what is now our natural being or we may live in our greater and spiritual being. This is the first great distinction on which the Karmayoga of the Gita is founded.

The whole question and the whole method lie then in the liberation of the soul from the limitations of our present natural being. In our natural life the first dominant fact is our subjection to the forms of material Nature, the outward touches of things. These present themselves to our life through the senses, and the life through the senses immediately returns upon these objects to seize upon them and deal with them, desires, attaches itself, seeks for results. The mind in all its inner sensations, reactions, emotions, habitual ways of perceiving, thinking and feeling obeys this action of the senses; the reason too carried away by the mind gives itself up to this life of the senses, this life in which the inner being is subject to the externality of things and cannot for a moment really get above it or outside the circle of its action upon us and its psychological results and reactions within us. It cannot get beyond them because there is the principle of ego by which the reason differentiates the sum of the action of Nature upon our mind, will, sense, body from her action in other minds, wills, nervous organisms, bodies; and life to us means only the way she affects our ego and the way our ego replies to her touches. We know nothing else; we seem to be nothing else; the soul itself seems then only a separate mass of mind, will, emotional and nervous reception and reaction. We may enlarge our ego, identify ourselves with the family, clan, class, country, nation, humanity even, but still the ego remains in all these disguises the root of our actions, only it finds a larger satisfaction of its separate being by these wider dealings with external things.

What acts in us is still the will of the natural being seizing upon the touches of the external world to satisfy the different phases of its personality, and the will in this seizing is always a will of desire and passion and attachment to our works and their results, the will of Nature in us; our personal will, we say, but our ego personality is a creation of Nature, it is not and cannot be our free self, our independent being. The whole is the action of the modes of Nature. It may be a tamasic action, and then we have an inert personality subject to and satisfied with the mechanical round of things, incapable of any strong effort at a freer action and mastery. Or it may be the rajasic action, and then we have the restless active personality which throws itself upon Nature and tries to make her serve its needs and desires but does not see that its apparent mastery is a servitude, since its needs and desires are those of Nature, and while we are subject to them, there can be for us no freedom. Or it may be a sattwic action, and then we have the enlightened personality which tries to live by reason or to realize some preferred ideal of good, truth or beauty; but this reason is still subject to the appearances of Nature and these ideals are only changing phases of our personality in which we find in the end no sure rule or permanent satisfaction. We are still carried on a wheel of mutation, obeying in our circling's through the ego some Power within us and within all this, but not ourselves that Power or in union and communion with it. Still there is no freedom, no real mastery.

Yet freedom is possible. For that we have to get first away into ourselves from the action of the external world upon our senses; that is to say, we have to live inwardly and be able to hold back the natural running of the senses after their external objects. A mastery of the senses, an ability to do without all that they hanker after, is the first condition of the true soul-life; only so can we begin to feel that there is a soul within us which is other than the mutations of mind in its reception of the touches of outward things, a soul which in its depths goes back to something self-existent, immutable, tranquil, self-possessed, grandiose, serene and august, master of itself and unaffected by the eager running's of our external nature. But this cannot be done so long as we are subject to desire. For it is desire, the principle of all our superficial life, which satisfies itself with the life of the senses and finds its whole account in the play of the passions. We must get rid then of desire and that propensity of our natural being destroyed, the passions which are its emotional results will fall into quietude; for the joy and grief of possession and of loss, success and failure, pleasant and unpleasant touches, which entertain them, will pass out of our souls. A calm equality will then be gained. And since we still have to live and act in the world and our nature in works is to seek for the fruits of our works, we must change that nature and do works without attachment to their fruits, otherwise desire and all its results remain. But how can we change this nature of the doer of works in us? By dissociating works from ego and personality, by seeing through the reason that all this is only the play of the gunas of Nature, and by dissociating our soul from the play, by making it first of all the observer of the workings of Nature and leaving those works to the Power that is really behind them, the something in Nature which is greater than ourselves, not our personality, but the Master of the universe. But the mind will not permit all this; its nature is to runout after the senses and carry the reason and will with it. Then we must learn to still the mind. We must attain that absolute peace and stillness in which we become aware of the calm, motionless, blissful Self within us which is eternally untroubled and unaffected by the touches of things, is sufficient to itself and finds there alone its eternal satisfaction.

This Self is our self-existent being. It is not limited by our personal existence. It is the same in all existences, pervasive, equal to all things, supporting the whole universal action with its infinity, but unlimited by all that is finite, unmodified by the changings of Nature and personality. When this Self is revealed within us, when we feel its peace and stillness, we can grow into that; we can transfer the poise of our soul from its lower immergence in Nature and draw it back into the Self. We can do this by the force of the things we have attained, calm, equality, passionless impersonality. For as we grow in these things, carry them to their fullness, subject all our nature to them, we are growing into this calm, equal, passionless, impersonal, all-pervading Self. Our senses fall into that stillness and receive the touches of the world on us with a supreme tranquility; our mind falls into stillness and becomes the calm, universal witness; our ego dissolves itself into this impersonal existence. All things we see in this self which we have become in ourself and we see this self in all; we become one being with all beings in the spiritual basis of their existence. By doing works in this selfless tranquility and impersonality, our works cease to be ours, cease to bind or trouble us with their reactions. Nature and her gunas weave the web of her works, but without affecting our griefless self-existent tranquility. All is given up into that one equal and universal Brahman.

But here there are two difficulties. First, there seems to be an antinomy between this tranquil and immutable Self and the action of Nature. How then does the action at all exist or how can it continue once we have entered into the immutable Self-existence? Where in that is the will to works which would make the action of our nature possible? If we say with the Sankhya that the will is in Nature and not in the Self, still there must be a motive in Nature and the power in her to draw the soul into its workings by interest, ego, and attachment and when these things cease to reflect themselves in the soul-consciousness, her power ceases and the motive of works ceases with it. But the Gita does not accept this view, which seems indeed to necessitate the existence of many Purushas and not one universal Purusha, otherwise the separate experience of the soul and its separate liberation while millions of others are still involved, would not be intelligible. Nature is not a separate principle, but the power of the Supreme going forth in cosmic creation. But if the Supreme is only this immutable Self and the individual is only something that has gone forth from him in the Power, then the moment it returns and takes its poise in the self, everything must cease except the supreme unity and the supreme calm. Secondly, even if in some mysterious way action still continues, yet since the Self is equal to all things, it cannot matter whether works are done or, if they are done, it cannot matter what work is done. Why then this insistence on the most violent and disastrous form of action, this chariot, this battle, this warrior, this divine charioteer?

The Gita answers by presenting the Supreme as something greater even than the immutable Self, more comprehensive, one who is at once this Self and the Master of works in Nature. But he directs the works of Nature with the eternal calm, the equality, the superiority to works and personality which belong to the immutable. This, we may say, is the poise of being from which he directs works and by growing into this we are growing into his being and into the poise of divine works. From this he goes forth as the Will and Power of his being in Nature, manifests himself in all existences, is born as Man in the world, is there in the heart of all men, reveals himself as the Avatar, the divine birth in man; and as man grows into his being, it is into the divine birth that he grows. Works must be done as a sacrifice to this Lord of our works, and we must by growing into the Self realize our oneness with him in our being and see our personality as a partial manifestation of him in Nature. One with him in being, we grow one with all beings in the universe and do divine works, not as ours, but as his workings through us for the maintenance and leading of the peoples.

This is the essential thing to be done and once this is done, the difficulties which present themselves to Arjuna will disappear. The problem is no longer one of our personal action, for that which makes our personality becomes a thing temporal and subordinate, the question is then only one of the workings of the divine Will through us in the universe. To understand that we must know what this supreme Being is in himself and in Nature, what the workings of Nature are and what they lead to and the intimate relation between the soul in Nature and this supreme Soul, of which bhakti with knowledge is the foundation. The elucidation of these questions is the subject of the rest of the Gita.

END OF THE FIRST SERIES

SECOND SERIES

PART I

THE SYNTHESIS OF WORKS, LOVE AND KNOWLEDGE

I

THE TWO NATURES[1]

The First six chapters of the Gita have been treated as a single block of teachings, its primary basis of practice and knowledge; the remaining twelve may be similarly treated as two closely connected blocks which develop the rest of the doctrine from this primary basis. The seventh to the twelfth chapters lay down a large metaphysical statement of the nature of the Divine Being and, on that foundation, closely relate and synthetise knowledge and devotion, just as the first part of the Gita related and synthetized works and knowledge. The vision of the World-Purusha intervenes in the eleventh chapter, gives a dynamic turn to this stage of the synthesis, and relates it vividly to works and life. Thus, again all is brought powerfully back to the original question of Arjuna round which the whole exposition revolves and completes its cycle. Afterwards the Gita proceeds by the differentiation of the Purusha and Prakriti to work out its ideas of the action of the gunas, of the ascension beyond the gunas and of the culmination of desireless works with knowledge where that coalesces with Bhakti,—knowledge, works and love made one,—and it rises thence to its great finale, the supreme secret of self-surrender to the Master of Existence.

1 Gita, VII. 1-14.

In this second part of the Gita, we come to a more concise and easy manner of statement than we have yet had. In the first six chapters the definitions have not yet been made which give the key to the underlying truth; difficulties are being met and solved; the progress is a little laboured and moves through several involutions and returns; much is implied the bearing of which is not yet clear. Here we seem to get on to clearer ground and to lay hold of a more compact and pointed expression. But because of this very conciseness we have to be careful always of our steps in order to avoid error and a missing of the real sense. For we are here no longer steadily on the safe ground of psychological and spiritual experience but have to deal with intellectual statements of spiritual and often of supracosmic truth. Metaphysical statement always has this peril and uncertainty about it that it is an attempt to define to our minds what is really infinite, an attempt which has to be made, but can never be quite satisfactory, quite final, or ultimate. The highest spiritual truth can be lived, can be seen, but can only be partially stated. The deeper method and language of the Upanishads with its free resort to image and symbol, its intuitive form of speech in which the hard limiting definiteness of intellectual utterance is broken down and the implications of words are allowed to roll out into an illimitable wave of suggestion, is in these realms the only right method and language. But the Gita cannot resort to this form because it is designed to satisfy an intellectual difficulty, answers a state of mind in which the reason, the arbiter to which we refer the conflicts of our impulses and sentiments, is at war with itself and impotent to arrive at a conclusion. The reason has to be led to a truth beyond itself, but by its own means and in its own manner. Offered a spiritually psychological solution, of the data of which it has no experience, it can only be assured of its validity if it is satisfied by an intellectual statement of the truths of being upon which the solution rests.

So far, the justifying truths that have been offered to it are those with which it is already familiar, and they are only sufficient as a starting-point. There is first the distinction between the Self and the individual being in Nature. The distinction has been used to point out that this individual being in Nature is necessarily subject, so long as he lives shut up within the action of the ego, to the workings of the three gunas which make up by their unstable movements the whole scope and method of the reason, the mind and the life and senses in the body. And within this circle there is no solution. Therefore, the solution has to be found by an ascent out of the circle, above this nature of the gunas, to the one immutable Self and silent Spirit, because then one gets beyond that action of the ego and desire which is the whole root of the difficulty. But since this by itself seems to lead straight towards inaction, as beyond Nature there is no instrumentality of action and no cause or determinant of action,—for the immutable self is inactive, impartial and equal to all things, all workings and all happenings,—the Yoga idea is brought in of the Ishwara, the Divine as master of works and sacrifice, and it is hinted but not yet expressly stated that this Divine exceeds even the immutable self and that in him lies the key to cosmic existence. Therefore, by rising to him through the Self it is possible to have spiritual freedom from our works and yet to continue in the works of Nature. But it has not yet been stated who is this Supreme, incarnate here in the divine teacher and charioteer of works, or what are his relations to the Self and to the individual being in Nature. Nor is it clear how the Will to works coming from him can be other than the will in the nature of the three gunas. And if it is only that, then the soul obeying it can hardly fail to be in subjection to the gunas in its action, if not in its spirit, and if so, at once the freedom promised becomes either illusory or incomplete. Will seems to be an aspect of the executive part of being, to be power and active force of nature, Shakti, Prakriti. Is there then a higher Nature than that of the three gunas? Is there a power of pragmatic creation, will, action other than that of ego, desire, mind, sense, reason, and the vital impulse?

Therefore, in this uncertainty, what has now to be done is to give more completely the knowledge on which divine works are to be founded. And this can only be the complete, the integral knowledge of the Divine who is the source of works and in who's being the worker becomes by knowledge free; for he knows the free Spirit from whom all works proceed and participates in his freedom. Moreover, this knowledge must bring a light that justifies the assertion with which the first part of the Gita closes. It must ground the supremacy of bhakti over all other motives and powers of spiritual consciousness and action; it must be a knowledge of the supreme Lord of all creatures to whom alone the soul can offer itself in the perfect self-surrender which is the highest height of all love and devotion. This is what the

The teacher proposes to give in the opening verses of the seventh chapter which initiate the development that occupies all the rest of the book. "Hear," he says, "how by practising Yoga with a mind attached to me and with me as asraya (the whole basis, lodgment, point of resort of the conscious being and action) thou shalt know me without any remainder of doubt, integrally, samagram mam. I will speak to thee without omission or remainder, asesatah," (for otherwise a ground of doubt may remain), "the essential knowledge, attended with all the comprehensive knowledge, by knowing which there shall be no other thing here left to be known." The implication of the phrase is that the Divine Being is all, vasudevah sarvam and therefore if he is known integrally in all his powers and principles, then all is known, not only the pure Self, but the world and action and Nature. There is then nothing else here left to be known because all is that Divine Existence. It is only because our view here is not thus integral, because it rests on the dividing mind and reason and the separative idea of the ego, that our mental perception of things is an ignorance. We have to get away from this mental and egoistic view to the true unifying knowledge, and that has two aspects, the essential, jnana and the comprehensive, vijnana, the direct spiritual awareness of the supreme Being and the right intimate knowledge of the principles of his existence, Prakriti, Purusha and the rest, by which all that is can be known in its divine origin and in the supreme truth of its nature. That integral knowledge, says the Gita, is a rare and difficult thing; "among thousands of men one here and there strives after perfection, and of those who strive and attain to perfection one here and there knows me in all the principles of my existence, tattvatah."

Then, to start with and in order to found this integral knowledge, the Gita makes that deep and momentous distinction, which is the practical basis of all its Yoga, the distinction between the two Natures, the phenomenal and the spiritual Nature. "The five elements (conditions of material being), mind, reason, ego, this is my eightfold divided Nature. But know my other Nature different from this, the supreme which becomes the Jiva and by which this world is upheld." Here is the first new metaphysical idea of the Gita which helps it to start from the notions of the Sankhya philosophy and yet exceed them and give to their terms, which it keeps and extends, a Vedantic significance. An eightfold Nature constituted of the five bhutas,—elements, as it is rendered, but rather elemental or essential conditions of material being to which are given the concrete names of earth, water, fire, air, and ether,—the mind with its various senses and organs, the reason-will and the ego, is the Sankhya description of Prakriti. The Sankhya stops there and because it stops there, it has to set up an unbridgeable division between the soul and Nature; it has to position them as two quite distinct primary entities. The Gita also, if it stopped there, would have to make the same incurable antinomy between the Self and cosmic Nature which would then be only the Maya of the three gunas and all this cosmic existence would be simply the result of this Maya; it could be nothing else. But there is something else, there is a higher principle, a nature of spirit, para prakrtir me. There is a supreme nature of the Divine which is the real source of cosmic existence and its fundamental creative force and effective energy and of which the other lower and ignorant Nature is only a derivation and a dark shadow. In this highest dynamis Purusha and Prakriti are one. Prakriti there is only the will and the executive power of the Purusha, his activity of being,—not a separate entity, but himself in Power.

This supreme Prakriti is not merely a presence of the power of spiritual being immanent in cosmic activities. For then it might be only the inactive presence of the all-pervading Self, immanent in all things or containing them, compelling in a way the world action but not itself active. Nor is this highest Prakriti the avyakta of the Sankhyas, the primary unmanifest seed-state of the manifest active eightfold nature of things, the one productive original force of Prakriti out of which her many instrumental and executive powers evolve. Nor is it sufficient to interpret that idea of avyakta in the Vedantic sense and say that this supreme Nature is the power involved and inherent in unmanifest Spirit or Self out of which cosmos comes and into which it returns. It is that, but it is much more; for that is only one of its spiritual states. It is the integral conscious-power of the supreme Being, cit-sakti, which is behind the self and cosmos. In the immutable

Self it is involved in the Spirit; it is there, but in nivrtti or a holding back from action: in the mutable self and the cosmos it comes out into action, pravrtti. There by its dynamic presence it evolves in the Spirit all existences and appears in them as their essential spiritual nature, the persistent truth behind their play of subjective and objective phenomena. It is the essential quality and force, svabhava, the self-principle of all their becoming, the inherent principle and divine power behind their phenomenal existence. The balance of the gunas is only a quantitative and quite derivative play evolved out of this supreme Principle. All this activity of forms, all this mental, sensuous, intelligential striving of the lower nature is only a phenomenon, which could not be at all except for this spiritual force and this power of being it comes from that, and it exists in that and by that solely. If we dwell in the phenomenal nature only and see things only by the notions it impresses on us, we shall not get at the real truth of our active existence. The real truth is this spiritual power, this divine force of being, this essential quality of the spirit in things or rather of the spirit in which things are and from which they draw all their potencies and the seeds of their movements. Get at that truth, power, quality, and we shall get at the real law of our becoming and the divine principle of our living, its source and sanction in the Knowledge and not only its process in the Ignorance.

This is to throw the sense of the Gita into language suited to our modern way of thinking; but if we look at its description of the Para Prakriti, we shall find that this is practically the substance of what it says. For first, this other higher Prakriti is, says Krishna, my supreme nature, prakrtim me param. And this "I" here is the Purushottama, the supreme Being, the supreme Soul, the transcendent and universal Spirit. The original and eternal nature of the Spirit and its transcendent and originating Shakti is what is meant by the Para Prakriti. For speaking first of the origin of the world from the point of view of the active power of his Nature, Krishna assevers, "This is the womb of all beings," etad-yonini bhutani. And in the next line of the couplet, again stating the same fact from the point of view of the originating Soul, he continues, "I am the birth of the whole world and so too its dissolution; there is nothing else supreme beyond Me." Here then the supreme Soul, Purushottama, and the supreme Nature, Para Prakriti, are identified: they are put as two ways of looking at one and the same reality. For when Krishna declares, I am the birth of the world and its dissolution, it is evident that it is this Para Prakriti, supreme Nature, of his being which is both these things. The Spirit is the supreme Being in his infinite consciousness and the supreme Nature is the infinity of power or will of being of the Spirit,—it is his infinite consciousness in its inherent divine energy and its supernal divine action. The birth is the movement of evolution of this conscious Energy out of the Spirit, para prakrtir jivabhuta, its activity in the mutable universe; the dissolution is the withdrawing of that activity by involution of the Energy into the immutable existence and self-gathered power of the Spirit. That then is what is initially meant by the supreme Nature.

The supreme Nature, para¯ prakrtih, is then the infinite timeless

conscious power of the self-existent Being out of which all existences in the cosmos are manifested and come out of timelessness into Time. But in order to provide a spiritual basis for this manifold universal becoming in the cosmos the supreme Nature formulates itself as the Jiva. To put it otherwise, the eternal multiple soul of the Purushottama appears as individual spiritual existence in all the forms of the cosmos. All existences are instinct with the life of the one indivisible Spirit; all are supported in their personality, actions, and forms by the eternal multiplicity of the one Purusha. We must be careful not to make the mistake of thinking that this supreme Nature is identical with the Jiva manifested in Time in the sense that there is nothing else or that it is only nature of becoming and not at all nature of being: that could not be the supreme nature of the Spirit. Even in Time it is something more; for otherwise the only truth of it in the cosmos would be nature of multiplicity and there would be no nature of unity in the world. That is not what the Gita says: it does not say that the supreme Prakriti is in its essence the Jiva, jıvatmikam but that it has become the Jiva, jıvabhutam; and it is implied in that expression that behind its manifestation as the Jiva here it is originally something else and higher, it is nature of the one supreme spirit. The Jiva, as we are told later on, is the Lord, isvara, but in his partial manifestation, mamaivamsah; even all the multiplicity of beings in the universe or in numberless universes could not be in their becoming the integral Divine, but only a partial manifestation of the infinite One. In them Brahman the one indivisible existence resides as if divided, avibhaktam ca bhutesu vibhaktam iva ca sthitam. The unity is the greater truth, the multiplicity is the lesser truth, though both are a truth and neither of them is an illusion.

It is by the unity of this spiritual nature that the world is sustained, yayedam dharyate jagat, even as it is that from which it is born with all its becoming's, etad-yonini bhutani sarvani and that also which withdraws the whole world and its existences into itself in the hour of dissolution, aham krtsnasya jagatah prabhavah pralayas tatha. But in the manifestation which is thus put forth in the Spirit, upheld in its action, withdrawn in its periodical rest from action, the Jiva is the basis of the multiple existence; it is the multiple soul, if we may so call it, or, if we prefer, the soul of the multiplicity we experience here. It is one always with the Divine in its being, different from it only in the power of its being,—different not in the sense that it is not at all the same power, but in this sense that it only supports the one power in a partial multiply individualized action. Therefore, all things are initially, ultimately and in the principle of their continuance too the Spirit. The fundamental nature of all is the nature of the Spirit and only in their lower differential phenomena do they seem to be something else, to be nature of body, life, mind, reason, ego, and the senses. But these are phenomenal derivatives, they are not the essential truth of our nature and our existence.

The supreme nature of spiritual being gives us then both an original truth and power of existence beyond cosmos and a first basis of spiritual truth for the manifestation in the cosmos. But where is the link between this supreme nature and the lower phenomenal nature? On me, says Krishna, all this, all that is here —sarvam idam, the common phrase in the Upanishads for the totality of phenomena in the mobility of the universe—is strung like pearls upon a thread. But this is only an image which we cannot press very far; for the pearls are only kept in relation to each other by the thread and have no other oneness or relation with the pearl-string except their dependence on it for this mutual connection. Let us go then from the image to that which it images. It is the supreme nature of Spirit, the infinite conscious power of its being, self-conscient, all-conscient, all-wise, which maintains these phenomenal existences in relation to each other, penetrates them, abides in, and supports them and weaves them into the system of its manifestation. This one supreme power manifests not only in all as the One, but in each as the Jiva, the individual spiritual presence; it manifests also as the essence of all quality of Nature. These are therefore the concealed spiritual powers behind all phenomena. This highest quality is not the working of the three gunas, which is phenomenon of quality and not its spiritual essence. It is rather the inherent, one, yet variable inner power of all these superficial variations. It is a fundamental truth of the Becoming, a truth that supports and gives a spiritual and divine significance to all its appearances. The workings of the gunas are only the superficial unstable becomings of reason, mind, sense, ego, life, and matter, sattvika bhava rajasas tamasas ca but this is rather the essential stable original intimate power of the becoming, svabhava. It is that which determines the primary law of all becoming and of each Jiva; it constitutes the essence and develops the movement of the nature. It is a principle in each creature that derives from and is immediately related to a transcendent divine Becoming, that of the Ishwara, madbhavah. In this relation of the divine bhava to the svabhava and of the svabhava to the superficial bhavah, of the divine Nature to the individual self-nature and of the self-nature in its pure and original quality to the phenomenal nature in all its mixed and confused play of qualities, we find the link between that supreme and this lower existence. The degraded powers and values of the inferior Prakriti derive from the absolute powers and values of the supreme Shakti and must go back to them to find their own source and truth and the essential law of their operation and movement. So too the soul or Jiva involved here in the shackled, poor, and inferior play of the phenomenal qualities, if he would escape from it and be divine and perfect, must by resort to the pure action of his essential quality of Swabhava go back to that higher law of his own being in which he can discover the will, the power, the dynamic principle, the highest working of his divine nature.

This is clear from the immediately subsequent passage in which the Gita gives a number of instances to show how the Divine in the power of his supreme nature manifests and acts within the animate and so-called inanimate existences of the universe. We may disentangle them from the loose and free order which the exigence of the poetical form imposes and put them in their proper philosophical series. First, the divine Power and Presence works within the five elemental conditions of matter. "I am taste in the waters, sound in ether, scent in earth, energy of light in fire," and, it may be added for more completeness, touch or contact in air. That is to say, the Divine himself in his Para Prakriti is the energy at the basis of the various sensory relations of which, according to the ancient Sankhya system, the ethereal, the radiant, electric, and gaseous, the liquid and the other elemental conditions of matter are the physical medium. The five elemental conditions of matter are the quantitative or material element in the lower nature and are the basis of material forms. The five Tanmatras—taste, touch, scent, and the others—are the qualitative element. These Tanmatras are the subtle energies whose action puts the sensory consciousness in relation to the gross forms of matter,—they are the basis of all phenomenal knowledge. From the material point of view matter is the reality and the sensory relations are derivative; but from the spiritual point of view the truth is the opposite. Matter and the material media are themselves derivative powers and at bottom are only concrete ways or conditions in which the workings of the quality of Nature in things manifest themselves to the sensory consciousness of the Jiva. The one original and eternal fact is the energy of Nature, the power and quality of being which so manifests itself to the soul through the senses. And what is essential in the senses, most spiritual, most subtle is itself stuff of that eternal quality and power. But energy, or power of being in Nature is the Divine himself in his Prakriti; each sense in its purity is therefore that Prakriti, each sense is the Divine in his dynamic conscious force.

This we gather better from the other terms of the series. "I am the light of sun and moon, the manhood in man, the intelligence of the intelligent, the energy of the energetic, the strength of the strong, the ascetic force of those who do askesis, tapasya." "I am life in all existences." In each case it is the energy of the essential quality on which each of these becomings depends for what it has become, that is given as the characteristic sign indicating the presence of the divine Power in their nature. Again, "I am pranava in all the Vedas," that is to say, the basic syllable OM, which is the foundation of all the potent creative sounds of the revealed word; OM is the one universal formulation of the energy of sound and speech, that which contains and sums up, synthesizes and releases all the spiritual power and all the potentiality of Vak and Shabda and of which the other sounds, out of whose stuff words of speech are woven, are supposed to be the developed evolutions. That makes it quite clear. It is not the phenomenal developments of the senses or of life or of light, intelligence, energy, strength, manhood, ascetic force that are proper to the supreme Prakriti. It is the essential quality in its spiritual power that constitutes the Swabhava. It is the force of spirit so manifesting; it is the light of its consciousness and the power of its energy in things revealed in a pure original sign that is the self-nature. That force, light, power is the eternal seed from which all other things are the developments and derivations and variabilities and plastic circumstances. Therefore, the Gita throws in as the most general statement in the series, "Know me to be the eternal seed of all existences, O son of Pritha." This eternal seed is the power of spiritual being, the conscious will in the being, the seed which, as is said elsewhere, the Divine casts into the great Brahman, into the supramental vastness, and from that all are born into phenomenal existence. It is that seed of spirit which manifests itself as the essential quality in all becoming's and constitutes their swabhava.

The practical distinction between this original power of essential quality and the phenomenal derivations of the lower nature, between the thing itself in its purity and the thing in its lower appearances, is indicated very clearly at the close of the series. "I am the strength of the strong devoid of desire and liking," stripped of all attachment to the phenomenal pleasure of things. "I am in beings the desire which is not contrary to their dharma." And as for the secondary subjective becoming's of Nature, bhavah (states of mind, affections of desire, movements of passion, the reactions of the senses, the limited and dual play of reason, the turns of the feeling and moral sense), which are sattwic, rajasic and tamasic, as for the working of the three gunas, they are, says the Gita, not themselves the pure action of the supreme spiritual nature, but are derivations from it; "they are verily from me," matta eva, they have no other origin, "but I am not in them, it is they that are in me." Here is indeed a strong and yet subtle distinction. "I am" says the Divine "the essential light, strength, desire, power, intelligence, but these derivations from them I am not in my essence, nor am I in them, yet are they all of them from me and they are all in my being." It is then upon the basis of these statements that we have to view the transition of things from the higher to the lower and again from the lower back to the higher nature.

The first statement offers no difficulty. The strong man in spite of the divine nature of the principle of strength in him falls into subjection to desire and to attachment, stumbles into sin, struggles towards virtue. But that is because he descends in all his derivative action into the grasp of the three gunas and does not govern that action from above, from his essential divine nature. The divine nature of his strength is not affected by these derivations, it remains the same in its essence in spite of every obscuration and every lapse. The Divine is there in that nature and supports him by its strength through the confusions of his lower existence till he is able to recover the light, illumine wholly his life with the true sun of his being and govern his will and its acts by the pure power of the divine will in his higher nature. But how can the Divine be desire, kama? for this desire, this kama has been declared to be our one great enemy who has to be slain. But that desire was the desire of the lower nature of the gunas which has its native point of origin in the rajasic being, rajoguna-samudbhavah; for this is what we usually mean when we speak of desire. This other, the spiritual, is a will not contrary to the dharma.

Is it meant that the spiritual kama is a virtuous desire, ethical in its nature, a sattwic desire,—for virtue is always sattwic in its origin and motive force? But then there would be here an obvious contradiction,—since in the very next line all sattwic affections are declared to be not the Divine, but only lower derivations. Undoubtedly sin has to be abandoned if one is to get anywhere near the Godhead; but so too has virtue to be overpassed if we are to enter into the Divine Being. The sattwic nature has to be attained, but it has then to be exceeded. Ethical action is only a means of purification by which we can rise towards the divine nature, but that nature itself is lifted beyond the dualities,—and indeed there could otherwise be no pure divine presence or divine strength in the strong man who is subjected to the rajasic passions. Dharma in the spiritual sense is not morality or ethics. Dharma, says the Gita elsewhere, is action governed by the swabhava, the essential law of one's nature. And this swabhava is at its core the pure quality of the spirit in its inherent power of conscious will and in its characteristic force of action. The desire meant here is therefore the purposeful will of the Divine in us searching for and discovering not the pleasure of the lower Prakriti, but the Ananda of its own play and self-fulfilling; it is the desire of the divine Delight of existence unrolling its own conscious force of action in accordance with the law of the swabhava.

But what again is meant by saying that the Divine is not in the becomings, the forms and affections of the lower nature, even the sattwic, though they all are in his being? In a sense he must evidently be in them, otherwise they could not exist. But what is meant is that the true and supreme spiritual nature of the Divine is not imprisoned there; they are only phenomena in his being created out of it by the action of the ego and the ignorance. The ignorance presents everything to us in an inverted vision and at least a partially falsified experience. We imagine that the soul is in the body, almost a result and derivation from the body; even we so feel it: but it is the body that is in the soul and a result and derivation from the soul. We think of the spirit as a small part of us—the Purusha who is no bigger than the thumb—in this great mass of material and mental phenomena: in reality, the latter for all its imposing appearance is a very small thing in the infinity of the being of the spirit. So, it is here; in much the same sense these things are in the Divine rather than the Divine in these things. This lower nature of the three gunas which creates so false a view of things and imparts to them an inferior character is a Maya, a power of illusion, by which it is not meant that it is all non-existent or deals with unrealities, but that it bewilders our knowledge, creates false values, envelops us in ego, mentality, sense, physicality, limited intelligence and there conceals from us the supreme truth of our existence. This illusive Maya hides from us the Divine that we are, the infinite and imperishable spirit. "By these three kinds of becoming which are of the nature of the gunas, this whole world is bewildered and does not recognize Me supreme beyond them and imperishable." If we could see that that Divine is the real truth of our existence, all else also would change to our vision, assume its true character and our life and action acquire the divine values and move in the law of the divine nature.

But why then, since the Divine is there after all and the divine nature at the root even of these bewildering derivations, since we are the Jiva and the Jiva is that, is this Maya so hard to overcome, maya duratyaya? Because it is still the Maya of the Divine, daivi hyesa gunamayi mama maya; "this is my divine Maya of the gunas." It is itself divine and a development from the nature of the Divine, but the Divine in the nature of the gods; it is daivi, of the godheads or, if you will, of the Godhead, but of the Godhead in its divided subjective and lower cosmic aspects, sattwic, rajasic and tamasic. It is a cosmic veil which the Godhead has spun around our understanding; Brahma, Vishnu and Rudra have woven its complex threads; the Shakti, the Supreme Nature is there at its base and is hidden in its every tissue. We have to work out this web in ourselves and turn through it and from it leaving it behind us when its use is finished, turn from the gods to the original and supreme Godhead in whom we shall discover at the same time the last sense of the gods and their works and the inmost spiritual verities of our own imperishable existence. "To Me who turn and come, they alone cross over beyond this Maya."

II

THE SYNTHESIS OF DEVOTION AND KNOWLEDGE[1]

The Gita is not a treatise of metaphysical philosophy, in spite of the great mass of metaphysical ideas which arise incidentally in its pages; for here no metaphysical truth is brought into expression solely for its own sake. It seeks the highest truth for the highest practical utility, not for intellectual or even for spiritual satisfaction, but as the truth that saves and opens to us the passage from our present mortal imperfection to an immortal perfection. Therefore, after giving us in the first fourteen verses of this chapter a leading philosophical truth of which we stand in need, it hastens in the next sixteen verses to make an immediate application of it. It turns it into a first starting-point for the unification of works, knowledge, and devotion,—for the preliminary synthesis of works and knowledge by themselves has already been accomplished.

We have before us three powers, the Purushottama as the supreme truth of that into which we have to grow, the Self and the Jiva. Or, as we may put it, there is the Supreme, there is the impersonal spirit, and there is the multiple soul, timeless

1 Gita, VII. 15-28.

foundation of our spiritual personality, the true and eternal individual, mamaivamsah sanatanah. All these three are divine, all three are the Divine. The supreme spiritual nature of being, the Para Prakriti free from any limitation by the conditioning Ignorance, is the nature of the Purushottama. In the impersonal Self there is the same divine nature, but here it is in its state of eternal rest, equilibrium, inactivity, nivritti. Finally, for activity, for pravritti, the Para Prakriti becomes the multiple spiritual personality, the Jiva. But the intrinsic activity of this supreme Nature is always a spiritual, a divine working. It is force of the supreme divine Nature; it is the conscious will of the being of the Supreme that throws itself out in various essential and spiritual power of quality in the Jiva: that essential power is the swabhava of the Jiva. All act and becoming which proceed directly from this spiritual force are a divine becoming and a pure and spiritual action. Therefore it follows that in action the effort of the human individual must be to get back to his true spiritual personality and to make all his works flow from the power of its supernal Shakti, to develop action through the soul and the inmost intrinsic being, not through the mental idea and vital desire, and to turn all his acts into a pure outflowing of the will of the Supreme, all his life into a dynamic symbol of the Divine Nature.

But there is also this lower nature of the three gunas whose character is the character of the ignorance and whose action is the action of the ignorance, mixed, confused, perverted; it is the action of the lower personality, of the ego, of the natural and not of the spiritual individual. It is in order to recede from that false personality that we have to resort to the impersonal Self and make ourselves one with it. Then, freed so from the ego personality, we can find the relation of the true individual to the Purushottama. It is one with him in being, even though necessarily partial and determinative, because individual, in action and temporal manifestation of nature. Freed too from the lower nature we can realize the higher, the divine, the spiritual. Therefore, to act from the soul does not mean to act from the desire soul; for that is not the high intrinsic being, but only the lower natural and superficial appearance. To act in accordance with the intrinsic nature, the swabhava, does not mean to act out of the passions of the ego, to enact with indifference or with desire sin and virtue according to the natural impulses and the unstable play of the gunas. Yielding to passion, an active or an inert indulgence of sin is no way either to the spiritual quietism of the highest impersonality or to the spiritual activity of the divine individual who is to be a channel for the will of the supreme Person, a direct power and visible becoming of the Purushottama.

The Gita has laid it down from the beginning that the very first precondition of the divine birth, the higher existence is the slaying of rajasic desire and its children, and that means the exclusion of sin. Sin is the working of the lower nature for the crude satisfaction of its own ignorant, dull, or violent rajasic and tamasic propensities in revolt against any high self-control and self-mastery of the nature by the spirit. And in order to get rid of this crude compulsion of the being by the lower Prakriti in its inferior modes we must have recourse to the highest mode of that Prakriti, the sattwic, which is seeking always for a harmonious light of knowledge and for a right rule of action. The Purusha, the soul within us which assents in Nature to the varying impulse of the gunas, has to give its sanction to that sattwic impulse and that sattwic will and temperament in our being which seeks after such a rule. The sattwic will in our nature has to govern us and not the rajasic and tamasic will. This is the meaning of all high reason in action as of all true ethical culture; it is the law of Nature in us striving to evolve from her lower and disorderly to her higher and orderly action, to act not in passion and ignorance with the result of grief and unquiet, but in knowledge and enlightened will with the result of inner happiness, poise, and peace. We cannot get beyond the three gunas, if we do not first develop within ourselves the rule of the highest guna, sattwa.

"The evildoers attain not to me," says the Purushottama, "souls bewildered, low in the human scale; for their knowledge is reft away from them by Maya and they resort to the nature of being of the Asura." This bewilderment is a befooling of the soul in Nature by the deceptive ego. The evildoer cannot attain to the Supreme because he is forever trying to satisfy the idol ego on the lowest scale of human nature; his real God is this ego. His mind and will, hurried away in the activities of the Maya of the three gunas, are not instruments of the spirit, but willing slaves or self-deceived tools of his desires. He sees this lower nature only and not his supreme self and highest being or the Godhead within himself and in the world: he explains all existence to his will in the terms of ego and desire and serves only ego and desire. To serve ego and desire without aspiration to a higher nature and a higher law is to have the mind and the temperament of the Asura. A first necessary step upward is to aspire to a higher nature and a higher law, to obey a better rule than the rule of desire, to perceive and worship a nobler godhead than the ego or than any magnified image of the ego, to become a right thinker and a right doer. This too is not in itself enough; for even the sattwic man is subject to the bewilderment of the gunas, because he is still governed by wish and disliking, iccha-dvesa.

He moves within the circle of the forms of Nature and has not the highest, not the transcendental and integral knowledge. Still by the constant upward aspiration in his ethical aim he in the end gets rid of the obscuration of sin which is the obscuration of rajasic desire and passion and acquires a purified nature capable of deliverance from the rule of the triple Maya. By virtue, alone man cannot attain to the highest, but by virtue[2] he can develop a first capacity for attaining to it, adhikara. For the crude rajasic or the dull tamasic ego is difficult to shake off and put below us; the

2 Obviously, by the true inner punya, a sattwic clarity in thought, feeling, temperament, motive and conduct, not a merely conventional or social virtue.

sattwic ego is less difficult and at last, when it sufficiently subtilizes and enlightens itself, becomes even easy to transcend, transmute or annihilate.

Man, therefore, has first of all to become ethical, sukrti, and then to rise to heights beyond any mere ethical rule of living, to the light, largeness, and power of the spiritual nature, where he gets beyond the grasp of the dualities and its delusion, dvandva-moha. There he no longer seeks his personal good or pleasure or shuns his personal suffering or pain, for by these things he is no longer affected, nor says any longer, "I am virtuous," "I am sinful," but acts in his own high spiritual nature by the will of the Divine for the universal good. We have already seen that for this end self-knowledge, equality, impersonality are the first necessities, and that that is the way of reconciliation between knowledge and works, between spirituality and activity in the world, between the ever-immobile quietism of the timeless self and the eternal play of the pragmatic energy of Nature. But the Gita now lays down another and greater necessity for the Karmayogin who has unified his Yoga of works with the Yoga of knowledge. Not knowledge and works alone are demanded of him now, but bhakti also, devotion to the Divine, love and adoration and the soul's desire of the Highest. This demand, not expressly made until now, had yet been prepared when the Teacher laid down as the necessary turn of his Yoga the conversion of all works into a sacrifice to the Lord of our being and fixed as its culmination the giving up of all works, not only into our impersonal Self, but through impersonality into the Being from whom all our will and power originate. What was there implied is now brought out and we begin to see more fully the Gita's purpose.

We have now set before us three interdependent movements of our release out of the normal nature and our growth into the divine and spiritual being. "By the delusion of the dualities which arises from wish and disliking, all existences in the creation are led into bewilderment," says the Gita. That is the ignorance, the egoism which fails to see and lay hold on the Divine everywhere, because it sees only the dualities of Nature and is constantly occupied with its own separate personality and its seeking's and shrinking's. For escape from this circle the first necessity in our works is to get clear of the sin of the vital ego, the fire of passion, the tumult of desire of the rajasic nature, and this has to be done by the steadying sattwic impulse of the ethical being. When that is done, yesam tvantagatam papam jananam punyakarmanam, . . .or rather as it is being done, for after a certain point all growth in the sattwic nature brings an increasing capacity for a high quietude, equality, and transcendence,—it is necessary to rise above the dualities and to become impersonal, equal, oneself with the Immutable, oneself with all existences. This process of growing into the spirit completes our purification. But while this is being done, while the soul is enlarging into self-knowledge, it has also to increase in devotion. For it has not only to act in a large spirit of equality, but to do also sacrifice to the Lord, to that Godhead in all beings which it does not yet know perfectly, but which it will be able so to know, integrally, samagram mam, when it has firmly the vision of the oneself everywhere and in all existences. Equality and vision of unity once perfectly gained, te dvandva-moha-nirmuktah, a supreme bhakti, an all-embracing devotion to the Divine, becomes the whole and the sole law of the being. All other law of conduct merges into that surrender, sarva-dharman parityajya. The soul then becomes firm in this bhakti and in the vow of self-consecration of all its being, knowledge, works; for it has now for its sure base, its absolute foundation of existence and action the perfect, the integral, the unifying knowledge of the all-originating Godhead, te bhajante mam drdha-vratah.

From the ordinary point of view any return towards bhakti or continuation of the heart's activities after knowledge and impersonality have been gained, might seem to be a relapse. For in bhakti there is always the element, the foundation even of personality, since its motive-power is the love and adoration of the individual soul, the Jiva, turned towards the supreme and universal Being. But from the standpoint of the Gita, where the aim is not inaction and immergence in the eternal Impersonal, but a union with the Purushottama through the integrality of our being, this objection cannot at all intervene. In this Yoga the soul escapes indeed its lower personality by the sense of its impersonal and immutable self-being but it still acts, and all action belongs to the multiple soul in the mutability of Nature. If we do not bring in as a corrective to an excessive quietism the idea of sacrifice to the Highest, we have to regard this element of action as something not at all ourselves, some remnant of the play of the gunas without any divine reality behind it, a last dis-solving form of ego, of I-ness, a continued impetus of the lower Nature for which we are not responsible since our knowledge rejects it and aims at escape from it into pure inaction. But by combining the tranquil impersonality of the oneself with the stress of the works of Nature done as a sacrifice to the Lord, we by this double key escape from the lower egoistic personality and grow into the purity of our true spiritual person. Then are we no longer the bound and ignorant ego in the lower, but the free Jiva in the supreme Nature. Then we no longer live in the knowledge of the one immutable and impersonal self and this mutable multiple Nature as two opposite entities but rise to the very embrace of the Purushottama discovered simultaneously through both of these powers of our being. All three are the spirit, and the two which are apparent opposites prove to be only confronting faces of the third which is the highest. "There is the immutable and impersonal spiritual being (Purusha)," says Krishna later on, "and there is the mutable and personal spiritual being. But there is too another Highest (uttama purusa) called the supreme self, Paramatman, he who has entered into this whole world and upbears it, the Lord, the imperishable. I am this Purushottama who am beyond the mutable and am greater and higher even than the immutable. He who has knowledge of me as the Purushottama, adores me (has bhakti for me, bhajati), with all-knowledge and in every way of his natural being." And it is this bhakti of an integral knowledge and integral self-giving which the Gita now begins to develop.

For note that it is bhakti with knowledge which the Gita demands from the disciple, and it regards all other forms of devotion as good in themselves but still inferior; they may do well by the way, but they are not the thing at which it aims in the soul's culmination. Among those who have put away the sin of the rajasic egoism and are moving towards the Divine, the Gita distinguishes between four kinds of bhaktas. There are those who turn to him as a refuge from sorrow and suffering in the world, arta. There are those who seek him as the giver of good in the world, artharthi. There are those who come to him in the desire for knowledge, jijnasu. And lastly there are those who adore him with knowledge, jnani. All are approved by the Gita, but only on the last does it lay the seal of its complete sanction. All these movements without exception are high and good, udarah sarva evaite, but the bhakti with knowledge excels them all, visisyate. We may say that these forms are successively the bhakti of the vital-emotional and affective nature,[3] that of the practical and dynamic nature, that of the reasoning intellectual nature and that of the highest intuitive being which takes up all the rest of the nature into unity with the Divine. Practically, however, the others may be regarded as preparatory movements. For the Gita itself here says that it is only at the end of many existences that one can, after possession of the integral knowledge and after working that out in oneself through many lives, attain at the long last to the Transcendent. For the knowledge of the Divine as all things that are is difficult to attain and rare on earth is the great soul, mahatma, who is capable of fully so seeing him and of entering into him with his whole

---

3 The later bhakti of ecstatic love is at its root's psychic in nature; it is vital-emotional only in its inferior forms or in some of its more outward manifestations.

being, in every way of his nature, by the wide power of this all-embracing knowledge, sarvavit sarvabhavena.

It may be asked how is that devotion high and noble, udara, which seeks God only for the worldly boons he can give or as a refuge in sorrow and suffering, and not the Divine for its own sake? Do not egoism, weakness, desire reign in such an adoration and does it not belong to the lower nature? Moreover, where there is not knowledge, the devotee does not approach the Divine in his integral all-embracing truth, vasudevah sarvam iti but constructs imperfect names and images of the Godhead which are only reflections of his own need, temperament, and nature and he worships them to help or appease his natural longings. He constructs for the Godhead the name and form of Indra or Agni, of Vishnu or Shiva, of a divinised Christ or Buddha, or else some composite of natural qualities, an indulgent God of love and mercy, or a severe God of righteousness and justice, or an awe-inspiring God of wrath and terror and flaming punishments, or some amalgam of any of these, and to that he raises his altars without and in his heart and mind and falls down before it to demand from it worldly good and joy or healing of his wounds or a sectarian sanction for an erring, dogmatic, intellectual, intolerant knowledge. All this up to a certain point is true enough. Very rare is the great soul who knows that Vasudeva the omnipresent Being is all that is, vasudevah sarvam iti sa mahatma sudurlabhah. Men are led away by various outer desires which take from them the working of the inner knowledge, kamais tais tair hrtajnanah. Ignorant, they resort to other godheads, imperfect forms of the deity which correspond to their desire, prapadyante 'nyadevatah. Limited, they set up this or that rule and cult, tam tam niyamam asthaya, which satisfies the need of their nature. And in all this it is a compelling personal determination, it is this narrow need of their own nature that they follow and take for the highest truth,—incapable yet of the infinite and its largeness. The Godhead in these forms gives them their desires if their faith is whole; but these fruits and gratifications are temporary, and it is a petty intelligence and unformed reason which makes the pursuit of them its principle of religion and life. And so far as there is a spiritual attainment by this way, it is only to the gods; it is only the Divine in formations of mutable nature and as the giver of her results that they realize. But those who adore the transcendent and integral Godhead embrace all this and transform it all, exalt the gods to their highest, Nature to her summits, and go beyond them to the very Godhead, realize and attain to the Transcendent. Devan deva-yajo yanti mad-bhakta yanti mam api.

Still the supreme Godhead does not at all reject these devotees because of their imperfect vision. For the Divine in his supreme transcendent being, unborn, imminuable, and superior to all these partial manifestations, cannot be easily known to any living creature. He is self-enveloped in this immense cloak of Maya, that Maya of his Yoga, by which he is one with the world and yet beyond it, immanent but hidden, seated in all hearts but not revealed to any and every being. Man in Nature thinks that these manifestations in Nature are all the Divine, when they are only his works and his powers and his veils. He knows all past and all present and future existences, but him none yet knoweth. If then after thus bewildering them with his workings in Nature, he were not to meet them in these at all, there would be no divine hope for man or for any soul in Maya. Therefore, according to their nature, as they approach him, he accepts their bhakti and answers to it with the reply of divine love and compassion. These forms are after all a certain kind of manifestation through which the imperfect human intelligence can touch him, these desires are first means by which our souls turn towards him: nor is any devotion worthless or ineffective, whatever its limitations. It has the one grand necessity, faith. "Whatever form of me any devotee with faith desires to worship, I make that faith of his firm and undeviating." By the force of that faith in his cult and worship he gets his desire and the spiritual realization for which he is at the moment fitted. By seeking all his good from the Divine, he shall come in the end to seek in the Divine all his good. By depending for his joys on the Divine, he shall learn to fix in the Divine all his joy. By knowing the Divine in his forms and qualities, he shall come to know him as the All and the Transcendent who is the source of all things.[4]

Thus, by spiritual development devotion becomes one with knowledge. The Jiva comes to delight in the one Godhead,—in the Divine known as all being and consciousness and delight and as all things and beings and happenings, known in Nature, known in the self, known for that which exceeds self and Nature. He is ever in constant union with him, nityayukta; his whole life and being are an eternal Yoga with the Transcendent than whom there is nothing higher, with the Universal besides whom there is no one else and nothing else. On him is concentred all his bhakti, ekabhaktih, not on any partial godhead, rule, or cult. This single devotion is his whole law of living, and he has gone beyond all creeds of religious belief, rules of conduct, personal aims of life. He has no griefs to be healed, for he is in possession of the All-blissful. He has no desires to hunger after, for he possesses the highest and the All and is close to the All-Power that brings all fulfilment. He has no doubts or baffled seeking's left, for all knowledge streams upon him from the Light in which he lives. He loves perfectly the Divine and is his beloved; for as he takes joy in the Divine, so too the Divine takes joy in him. This is the God-lover who has the knowledge, jnani bhakta. And this knower, says the Godhead in the Gita, is myself; the others seize only motives and aspects in Nature, but he the very self-being and all-being

4 There is a place also for the three lesser seeking's even after the highest attainment, but transformed, not narrowly personal,—for there can still be a passion for the removal of sorrow and evil and ignorance and for the increasing evolution and integral manifestation of the supreme good, power, joy, and knowledge in this phenomenal Nature.

of the Purushottama with which he is in union. His is the divine birth in the supreme Nature, integral in being, completed in will, absolute in love, perfected in knowledge. In him the Jiva's cosmic existence is justified because it has exceeded itself and so found its own whole and highest truth of being.

III

THE SUPREME DIVINE[1]

Already what has been said in the seventh chapter pro-vides us with the starting-point of our new and fuller position and fixes it with sufficient precision. Substantially it comes to this that we are to move inwardly towards a greater consciousness and a supreme existence, not by a total exclusion of our cosmic nature, but by a higher, a spiritual fulfilment of all that we now essentially are. Only there is to be a change from our mortal imperfection to a divine perfection of being. The first idea on which this possibility is founded, is the conception of the individual soul in man as in its eternal essence and its original power a ray of the supreme Soul and Godhead, here a veiled manifestation of him, a being of his being, a consciousness of his consciousness, a nature of his nature, but in the obscurity of this mental and physical existence self-forgetful of its source, its reality, its true character. The second idea is that of the double nature of the Soul in manifestation,—the original nature in which it is one with its own true spiritual being and the derived in which it is subject to the confusions of egoism and ignorance. The latter has to be cast away and the spiritual has to be inwardly recovered, fulfilled, made dynamic and active. Through an inner self-fulfillment, the opening of a new status, our birth into a new power, we return to the nature of the Spirit

1 Gita, VII. 29-30, VIII.

and re-become a portion of the Godhead from whom we have descended into this mortal figure of being.

There is here at once a departure from the general contemporary mind of Indian thought, a less negating attitude, a greater affirmation. In place of its obsessing idea of a self-annulment of Nature we get the glimpse of an ampler solution, the principle of a self-fulfillment in divine Nature. There is, even, at-least a foreshadowing of the later developments of the religions of Bhakti. Our first experience of what is beyond our normal status, concealed behind the egoistic being in which we live, is still for the Gita the calm of a vast impersonal immutable self in whose equality and oneness we lose our petty egoistic personality and cast off in its tranquil purity all our narrow motives of desire and passion. But our second completer vision reveals to us a living Infinite, a divine immeasurable Being from whom all that we are proceeds and to which all that we are belongs, self and nature, world, and spirit. When we are one with him in self and spirit, we do not lose ourselves, but rather recover our true selves in him poised in the supremacy of this Infinite. And this is done at one and the same time by three simultaneous movements,—an integral self-finding through works founded in his and our spiritual nature, an integral self-becoming through knowledge of the Divine Being in whom all exists and who is all, and—most sovereign and decisive movement of all—an integral self-giving through love and devotion of our whole being to this All and this Supreme, attracted to the Master of our works, to the Inhabitant of our hearts, to the continent of all our conscious existence. To him who is the source of all that we are, we give all that we are. Our persistent consecration turns into knowledge of him all our knowing and into light of his power all our action. The passion of love in our self-giving carries us up to him and opens the mystery of his deepest heart of being. Love completes the triple cord of the sacrifice, perfects the triune key of the highest secret, uttamam rahasyam.

An integral knowledge in our self-giving is the first condition of its effective force. And therefore, we have first of all to know this Purusha in all the powers and principles of his divine existence, tattvatah, in the whole harmony of it, in its eternal essence and living process. But to the ancient thought all the value of this knowledge, tattvajnana, lay in its power for release out of our mortal birth into the immortality of a supreme existence. The Gita therefore proceeds next to show how this liberation too in the highest degree is a final outcome of its own movement of spiritual self-fulfillment. The knowledge of the Purushottama, it says in effect, is the perfect knowledge of the Brahman. Those who have resort to Me as their refuge, mam asritya, their divine light, their deliverer, receiver, and harbourer of their souls, those who turn to Me in their spiritual effort towards release from age and death, from the mortal being and its limitations, says Krishna, come to know that Brahman and all the integrality of the spiritual nature and the entirety of Karma. And because they know Me and know at the same time the material and the divine nature of being and the truth of the Master of sacrifice, they keep knowledge of Me also in the critical moment of their departure from physical existence and have at that moment their whole consciousness in union with Me. Therefore, they attain to Me. No longer bound to the mortal existence, they reach the very highest status of the Divine quite as effectively as those who lose their separate personality in the impersonal and immutable Brahman. Thus, the Gita closes this important and decisive seventh chapter.

Here we have certain expressions which give us in their brief sum the chief essential truths of the manifestation of the supreme Divine in the cosmos. All the originative and effective aspects of it are there, all that concerns the soul in its return to integral self-knowledge. First there is that Brahman, tad brahma; adhyatma, second, the principle of the self in Nature; adhibhuta and adhidaiva next, the objective phenomenon and subjective phenomenon of being, adhiyajna last, the secret of the cosmic principle of works and sacrifice. I, the Purushottama (mam viduh), says in effect Krishna, I who am above all these things, must yet be sought and known through all together and by means of their relations,—that is the only complete way for the human consciousness which is seeking its path back towards Me. But these terms in themselves are not at first quite clear or at least they are open to different interpretations, they have to be made precise in their connotation, and Arjuna the disciple at once asks for their elucidation. Krishna answers very briefly,—nowhere does the Gita linger very long upon any purely meta-physical explanation; it gives only so much and in such a way as will make their truth just seizable for the soul to proceed on to experience. By that Brahman, a phrase which in the Upanishads is more than once used for the self-existent as opposed to the phenomenal being, the Gita intends, it appears, the immutable self-existence which is the highest self-expression of the Divine and on whose unalterable eternity all the rest, all that moves and evolves, is founded, aksaram paramam. By adhyatma it means svabhava, the spiritual way and law of being of the soul in the supreme Nature. Karma, it says, is the name given to the creative impulse and energy, visargah, which loses out things from this first essential self-becoming, this Swabhava, and effects, creates, works out under its influence the cosmic becoming of existences in Prakriti. By adhibhuta is to be understood all the result of mutable becoming, ksaro bhavah. By adhidaiva is intended the Purusha, the soul in Nature, the subjective being who observes and enjoys as the object of his consciousness all that is this mutable becoming of his essential existence worked out here by Karma in Nature. By adhiyajna, the Lord of works and sacrifice, I mean, says Krishna, myself, the Divine, the Godhead, the Purushottama here secret in the body of all these embodied existences. All that is, therefore, falls within this formula.

The Gita immediately proceeds from this brief statement to work out the idea of the final release by knowledge which it has suggested in the last verse of the preceding chapter. It will return indeed upon its thought hereafter to give such ulterior light as is needed for action and inner realisation, and we may wait till then for a fuller knowledge of all that these terms indicate. But before we proceed farther, it is necessary to bring out as much of the connection between these things as we are justified in understanding from this passage itself and from what has gone before. For here is indicated the Gita's idea of the process of the cosmos. First there is the Brahman, the highest immutable self-existent being which all existences are behind the play of cosmic Nature in time and space and causality, desa-kala-nimitta. For by that self-existence alone time and space and causality are able to exist and without that unchanging support omnipresent, yet indivisible they could not proceed to their di-visions and results and measures. But of itself the immutable Brahman does nothing, causes nothing, determines nothing; it is impartial, equal, all-supporting, but does not select or originate. What then originates, what determines, what gives the divine impulsion of the Supreme? what is it that governs Karma and actively unrolls the cosmic becoming in Time out of the eternal being? It is Nature as Swabhava. The Supreme, the Godhead, the Purushottama is there and supports on his eternal immutability the action of his higher spiritual Shakti. He displays the divine Being, Consciousness, Will or Power, yayedam dharyate jagat: that is the Para Prakriti. The self-awareness of the Spirit in this supreme Nature perceives in the light of self-knowledge the dynamic idea, the authentic truth of whatever he separates in his own being and expresses it in the Swabhava, the spiritual nature of the Jiva. The inherent truth and principle of the self of each Jiva, that which works itself out in manifestation, the essential divine nature in all which remains constant behind all conversions, perversions, reversions, that is the Swabhava. All that is in the Swabhava is loosed out into cosmic Nature for her to do what she can with it under the inner eye of the Purushottama. Out of the constant svabhava, out of the essential nature and self-principle of being of each becoming, she creates the varied mutations by which she strives to express it, unrolls all her changes in name and form, in time and space and those successions of condition developed one out of the other in time and space which we call causality, nimitta.

All this bringing out and continual change from state to state is Karma, is action of Nature, is the energy of Prakriti, the worker, the goddess of processes. It is first a losing forth of the svabhava into its creative action, visargah. The creation is of existences in the becoming, bhuta-karah and of all that they subjectively or otherwise become, bhava-karah. All taken together, it is a constant birth of things in Time, udbhava, of which the creative energy of Karma is the principle. All this mutable becoming emerges by a combination of the powers and energies of Nature, adhibhuta, which constitutes the world and is the object of the soul's consciousness. In it all the soul is the enjoying and observing Deity in Nature, the divine powers of mind and will and sense, all the powers of its conscious being by which it reflects this working of Prakriti are its godheads, adhidaiva. This soul in Nature is therefore the ksara purusa, it is the mutable soul, the eternal activity of the Godhead: the same soul in the Brahman drawn back from her is the aksara purusa, the immutable self, the eternal silence of the Godhead. But in the form and body of the mutable being inhabits the supreme Godhead. Possessing at once the calm of the immutable existence and the enjoyment of the mutable action their dwells in man the Purushottama. He is not only remote from us in some supreme status beyond, but he is here too in the body of every being, in the heart of man and in Nature. There he receives the works of Nature as a sacrifice and awaits the conscious self-giving of the human soul: but always even in the human creature's ignorance and egoism he is the Lord of his swabhava and the Master of all his works, who presides over the law of Prakriti and Karma. From him the soul came forth into the play of Nature's mutations; to him the soul returns through immutable self-existence to the highest status of the Divine, param dhama.

Man, born into the world, revolves between world and world in the action of Prakriti and Karma. Purusha in Prakriti is his formula: what the soul in him thinks, contemplates, and acts that always he becomes. All that he had been, determined his present birth; and all that he is, thinks, does in this life up to the moment of his death, determines what he will become in the worlds beyond and in lives yet to be. If birth is a becoming, death also is a becoming, not by any means a cessation. The body is abandoned, but the soul goes on its way, tyaktva kalevaram. Much then depends on what he is at the critical moment of his departure. For whatever form of becoming his consciousness is fixed on at the time of death and has been full of that always in his mind and thought before death, to that form he must attain, since the Prakriti by Karma works out the soul's thoughts and energies and that is in real fact her whole business. Therefore, if the soul in the human being desires to attain to the status of the Purushottama, there are two necessities, two conditions which must be satisfied before that can be possible. He must have moulded towards that ideal his whole inner life in his earthly living; and he must be faithful to his aspiration and will in his departing. "Whoever leaves his body and departs" says Krishna "remembering me at his time of end, comes to my bhava," that of the Purushottama, my status of being. He is united with the original being of the Divine and that is the ultimate becoming of the soul, paro bhavah, the last result of Karma in its return upon itself and towards its source. The soul which has followed the play of cosmic evolution that veils here its essential spiritual nature, its original form of becoming, svabhava, and has passed through all these other ways of becoming of its consciousness which are only its phenomena, tam tam bhavam, returns to that essential nature and, finding through this return its true self and spirit, comes to the original status of being which is from the point of view of the return a highest becoming, mad-bhavam. In a certain sense we may say that it becomes God, since it unites itself with nature of the Divine in a last transformation of its own phenomenal nature and existence.

The Gita here lays a great stress on the thought and state of mind at the time of death, a stress which will with difficulty be understood if we do not recognize what may be called the self-creative power of the consciousness. What the thought, the inner regard, the faith, sraddha, settles itself upon with a complete and definite insistence, into that our inner being tends to change. This tendency becomes a decisive force when we go to those higher spiritual and self-evolved experiences which are less dependent on external things than is our ordinary psychology, enslaved as that is to outward Nature. There we can see ourselves steadily becoming that on which we keep our minds fixed and to which we constantly aspire. Therefore, there any lapse of the thought, any infidelity of the memory always means a retardation of the change or some fall in its process and a going back towards what we were before,—at least so long as we have not substantially and irrevocably fixed our new becoming. When we have done that, when we have made it normal to our experience, the memory of it remains self-existently because that now is the natural form of our consciousness. In the critical moment of passing from the mortal plane of living, the importance of our then state of consciousness becomes evident. But it is not a death-bed remembrance at variance with or insufficiently prepared by the whole tenor of our life and our past subjectivity that can have this saving power. The thought of the Gita here is not on a par with the indulgences and facilities of popular religion; it has nothing in common with the crude fancies that make the absolution and last unction of the priest, an edifying "Christian" death after an unedifying profane life or the precaution or accident of a death in sacred Benares or holy Ganges a sufficient machinery of salvation. The divine subjective becoming on which the mind has to be fixed firmly in the moment of the physical death, yam smaran bhavam tyajati ante kalevaram, must have been one into which the soul was at each moment growing inwardly during the physical life, sada tad-bhava-bhavitah. "Therefore," says the divine Teacher, "at all times remember me and fight; for if thy mind and thy understanding are always fixed on and given up to Me, mayi arpita-mano-buddhih, to Me thou shalt surely come.

For it is by thinking always of him with a consciousness united with him in an undeviating Yoga of constant practice that one comes to the divine and supreme Purusha."

We arrive here at the first description of this supreme Purusha,—the Godhead who is even more and greater than the Immutable and to whom the Gita gives subsequently the name of Purushottama. He too in his timeless eternity is immutable and far beyond all this manifestation and here in Time there dawn on us only faint glimpses of his being conveyed through many varied symbols and disguises, avyakto aksarah. Still, he is not merely a featureless or indiscernible existence, anirdesyam; or he is indiscernible only because he is subtler than the last subtlety of which the mind is aware and because the form of the Divine is beyond our thought, anor aniyamsam acintya-rupam. This supreme Soul and Self is the Seer, the Ancient of Days and in his eternal self-vision and wisdom the Master and Ruler of all existence who sets in their place in his being all things that are kavim puranam anusasitaram sarvasya dhataram. This supreme Soul is the immutable self-existent Brahman of whom the Veda-knowers speak, and this is that into which the doers of askesis enter when they have passed beyond the affections of the mind of mortality and for the desire of which they practise the control of the bodily passions.[2] That eternal reality is the highest step, place, foothold of being (padam); therefore is it the supreme goal of the soul's movement in Time, itself no movement but a status original, sempiternal and supreme, param sthanam adyam.

The Gita describes the last state of the mind of the Yogin in which he passes from life through death to this supreme divine existence. A motionless mind, a soul armed with the strength of

2 The language here is taken bodily from the Upanishads.

Yoga, a union with God in bhakti,—the union by love is not here superseded by the featureless unification through knowledge, it remains to the end a part of the supreme force of the Yoga,—and the life-force entirely drawn up and set between the brows in the seat of mystic vision. All the doors of the sense are closed, the mind is shut in into the heart, the life-force taken up out of its diffused movement into the head, the intelligence concentrated in the utterance of the sacred syllable OM and its conceptive thought in the remembrance of the supreme Godhead, mam anusmaran. That is the established Yogic way of going, a last offering up of the whole being to the Eternal, the Transcendent. But still, that is only a process; the essential condition is the constant undeviating memory of the Divine in life, even in action and battle—mam anusmara yudhya ca—and the turning of the whole act of living into an uninterrupted Yoga, nitya-yoga. Whoever does that, finds Me easy to attain, says the Godhead; he is the great soul who reaches the supreme perfection.

The condition to which the soul arrives when it thus departs from life is supracosmic. The highest heavens of the cosmic plan are subject to a return to rebirth; but there is no rebirth imposed on the soul that departs to the Purushottama. Therefore, whatever fruit can be had from the aspiration of knowledge to the indefinable Brahman, is acquired also by this other and comprehensive aspiration through knowledge, works and love to the self-existent Godhead who is the Master of works and the Friend of mankind and of all beings. To know him so and so to seek him does not bind to rebirth or to the chain of Karma; the soul can satisfy its desire to escape permanently from the transient and painful condition of our mortal being. And the Gita here, in order to make more precise to the mind this circling round of births and the escape from it, adopts the ancient theory of the cosmic cycles which became a fixed part of Indian cosmological notions. There is an eternal cycle of alternating periods of cosmic manifestation and non-manifestation, each period called respectively a day and a night of the creator Brahma, each of equal length in Time, the long aeon of his working which endures for a thousand ages, the long aeon of his sleep of another thousand silent ages. At the coming of the Day all manifestations are born into being out of the unmanifest, at the coming of the Night all vanish or are dissolved into it. Thus, all these existences alternate helplessly in the cycle of becoming and non-becoming; they come into the becoming again and again, bhutva bhutva and they go back constantly into the unmanifest. But this unmanifest is not the original divinity of the Being; there is another status of his existence, bhavo 'nyo, a supracosmic unmanifest beyond this cosmic non-manifestation, which is eternally self-seated, is not an opposite of this cosmic status of manifestation but far above and unlike it, changeless, eternal, not forced to perish with the perishing of all these existences. "He is called the unmanifest immutable, him they speak of as the supreme soul and status, and those who attain to him return not; that is my supreme place of being, paramam dhama." For the soul attaining to it has escaped out of the cycle of cosmic manifestation and non-manifestation.

Whether we entertain or we dismiss this cosmological notion,—which depends on the value we are inclined to assign to the knowledge of "the knowers of day and night,"—the important thing is the turn the Gita gives to it. One might easily imagine that this eternally unmanifested Being whose status seems to have nothing to do with the manifestation or the non-manifestation, must be the ever undefined and indefinable Absolute, and the proper way to reach him is to get rid of all that we have become in the manifestation, not to carry up to it our whole inner consciousness in a combined concentration of the mind's knowledge, the heart's love, the Yogic will, the vital life-force. Especially, bhakti seems inapplicable to the Absolute who is void of every relation, avyavaharya. "But" insists the Gita,—although this condition is supracosmic and although it is eternally unmanifest,—still "that supreme Purusha has to be won by a bhakti which turns to him alone in whom all beings exist and by whom all this world has been extended in space." In other words, the supreme Purusha is not an entirely relation-less Absolute aloof from our illusions, but he is the Seer, Creator and Ruler of the worlds, kavim anusasitaram, dhataram, and it is by knowing and by loving Him as the One and the All, vasudevah sarvam iti, that we ought by a union with him of our whole conscious being in all things, all energies, all actions to seek the supreme consummation, the perfect perfection, the absolute release.

Then there comes a more curious thought which the Gita has adopted from the mystics of the early Vedanta. It gives the different times at which the Yogin has to leave his body according as he wills to seek rebirth or to avoid it. Fire and light and smoke or mist, the day and the night, the bright fortnight of the lunar month and the dark, the northern solstice and the southern, these are the opposites. By the first in each pair the knowers of the Brahman go to the Brahman; but by the second the Yogin reaches the "lunar light" and returns subsequently to human birth. These are the bright and the dark paths, called the path of the gods and the path of the fathers in the Upanishads, and the Yogin who knows them is not misled into any error. Whatever psycho-physical fact or else symbolism there may be behind this notion,[3]—it comes down from the age of the mystics who saw in every physical thing an effective symbol of the psychological and who traced everywhere an interaction and a sort of identity of the outward with the inward, light and knowledge, the fiery principle, and the spiritual energy,—we need observe only the turn by which the Gita closes the passage: "Therefore at all times be in Yoga."

3 Yogic experience shows in fact that there is a real psycho-physical truth, not indeed absolute in its application, behind this idea, viz., that in the inner struggle between the powers of the Light and the powers of the Darkness, the former tend to have a natural prevalence in the bright periods of the day or the year, the latter in the dark periods, and this balance may last until the fundamental victory is won.

For that is after all the essential, to make the whole being one with the Divine, so entirely and in all ways one as to be naturally and constantly fixed in union, and thus to make all living, not only thought and meditation, but action, labour, battle, a remembering of God. "Remember me and fight," means not to lose the ever-present thought of the Eternal for one single moment in the clash of the temporal which normally absorbs our minds and that seems sufficiently difficult, almost impossible. It is entirely possible indeed only if the other conditions are satisfied. If we have become in our consciousness oneself with all, one self which is always to our thought the Divine, and even our eyes and our other senses see and sense the Divine Being everywhere so that it is impossible for us at any time at all to feel or think of anything as that merely which the unenlightened sense perceives, but only as the Godhead at once concealed and manifested in that form, and if our will is one in consciousness with a supreme will and every act of will, of mind, of body is felt to come from it, to be its movement, instinct with it or identical, then what the Gita demands can be integrally done. The remembrance of the Divine Being becomes no longer an intermittent act of the mind, but the natural condition of our activities and in a way the very substance of the consciousness. The Jiva has become possessed of its right and natural, its spiritual relation to the Purushottama and all our life is a Yoga, an accomplished and yet an eternally self-accomplishing oneness.

IV

THE SECRET OF SECRETS

All the truth that has developed itself at this length step by step, each bringing forward a fresh aspect of the integral knowledge and finding on it some result of spiritual state and action, has now to take a turn of immense importance. The Teacher therefore takes care first to draw attention to the decisive character of what he is about to say, so that the mind of Arjuna may be awakened and attentive. For he is going to open his mind to the knowledge and sight of the integral Divinity and lead up to the vision of the eleventh book, by which the warrior of Kurukshetra becomes conscious of the author and upholder of his being and action and mission, the Godhead in man and the world, whom nothing in man and the world limits or binds, because all proceeds from him, is a movement in his infinite being, continues and is supported by his will, is justified in his divine self-knowledge, has him always for its origin, substance and end. Arjuna is to become aware of himself as existing only in God and as acting only by the power within him, his workings only an instrumentality of the divine action, his egoistic consciousness only a veil and to his ignorance a misrepresentation of the real being within him which is an immortal spark and portion of the supreme Godhead.

This vision is to remove whatever doubt may still remain within his mind; it is to make him strong for the action from which he has shrunk, but to which he is irrevocably commanded and can no more recoil from it,—for to recoil would be the negation and denial of the divine will and sanction within him already expressed in his individual consciousness but soon to assume the appearance of the greater cosmic sanction. For now, the world Being appears to him as the body of God ensouled by the eternal Time-spirit and with its majestic and dreadful voice missions him to the crash of the battle. He is called by it to the liberation of his spirit, to the fulfilment of his action in the cosmic mystery, and the two—liberation and action—are to be one movement. His intellectual doubts are clearing away as a greater light of self-knowledge and the knowledge of God and Nature is being unfolded before him. But intellectual clarity is not enough; he must see with the inner sight illumining his blind outward human vision, so that he may act with the consent of his whole being, with a perfect faith in all his members, sraddha, with a perfect devotion to the Self of his self and the Master of his being and to the same Self of the world and Master of all being in the universe.

All that has gone before laid the foundations of the knowledge or prepared its first necessary materials or scaffolding, but now the full frame of the structure is to be placed before his unsealed vision. All that is to come after will have its great importance because it will analyze parts of this frame, show in what this or that in it consists but in substance the integral knowledge of the Being who is speaking to him is to be now un-veiled to his eyes so that he cannot choose but see. What has gone before showed him that he is not bound fatally to the knot of the ignorance and egoistic action in which he had hitherto remained contented till its partial solutions sufficed no longer to satisfy his mind bewildered by the conflict of opposite appearances that make up the action of the world and his heart troubled by the entanglement of his works from which he feels himself unable to escape except by renunciation of life and works. He has been shown that there are two opposed ways of working and living, one in the ignorance of the ego, one in the clear self-knowledge of a divine being. He may act with desire, with passion, an ego driven by the qualities of the lower Nature, subject to the balance of virtue and sin, joy and sorrow, preoccupied with the fruits and consequences of his works, success and defeat, good result and evil result, bound on the world machine, caught up in a great tangle of action and inaction and perverse action which perplex the heart and mind and soul of man with their changing and contrary masks and appearances. But he is not utterly tied down to the works of the ignorance; he may do if he will the works of knowledge. He may act here as the higher thinker, the knower, the Yogin, the seeker of freedom first and afterwards the liberated spirit. To perceive that great possibility and to keep his will and intelligence fixed on the knowledge and self-vision which will realize and make it effectual, is the path of escape from his sorrow and bewilderment, the way out of the human riddle.

There is a spirit within us calm, superior to works, equal, not bound in this external tangle, surveying it as its supporter, source, immanent witness, but not involved in it. Infinite, containing all, oneself in all, it surveys impartially the whole action of nature, and it sees that it is only the action of Nature, not its own action. It sees that the ego and its will and its intelligence are all the machinery of Nature and that all their activities are determined by the complexity of her triple modes and qualities. The eternal spirit itself is free from these things. It is free from them because it knows; it knows that Nature and ego and the personal being of all these creatures do not make up the whole of existence. For existence is not merely a glorious or a vein, a wonderful or a dismal panorama of a constant mutation of becoming. There is something eternal, immutable, imperishable, a timeless self-existence; that is not affected by the mutations of Nature. It is their impartial witness, neither affecting nor affected, neither acting nor acted upon, neither virtuous nor sinful, but always pure, complete, great, and unwounded. Neither grieving nor rejoicing at all that afflicts and attracts the egoistic being, it is the friend of none, the enemy of none, but one equal self of all. Man is not now conscious of this self, because he is wrapped up in his outward-going mind, because he will not learn or has not learned to live within; he does not detach himself, draw back from his action and observe it as the work of Nature. Ego is the obstacle, the linchpin of the wheel of delusion, the loss of the ego in the soul's self the first condition of freedom. To become a spirit, no longer merely a mind and ego, is the opening word of this message of liberation.

Arjuna has been therefore called upon first to give up all desire of the fruits of his works and become simply the desireless impartial doer of whatever has to be done,—leaving the fruit to whatever power may be the master of the cosmic workings. For he very evidently is not the master; it is not for the satisfaction of his personal ego that Nature was set upon her ways, not for the fulfilment of his desires and preferences that the universal Life is living, not for the justification of his intellectual opinions, judgments and standards that the universal Mind is working, nor is it to that petty tribunal that it has to refer its cosmic aims or its terrestrial method and purposes. These claims can only be made by the ignorant souls who live in their personality and see everything from that poor and narrow standpoint. He must stand back first from his egoistic demand on the world and work only as one among the millions who contributes his share of effort and labour to a result determined not by himself, but by the universal action and purpose. But he has to do yet more, he has to give up the idea of being the doer and to see, freed from all personality, that it is the universal intelligence, will, mind, life that is at work in him and in all others. Nature is the universal worker; his works are hers, even as the fruits of her works in him are part of the grand sum of result guided by a greater Power than his own. If he can do these two things spiritually, then the tangle and bondage of his works will fall far away from him; for the whole knot of that bondage lay in his egoistic demand and participation. Passion and sin and personal joy and grief will fade away from his soul, which will now live within, pure, large, calm, equal to all persons and all things. Action will produce no subjective reaction and will leave no stain nor any mark on his spirit's purity and peace. He will have the inner joy, rest, ease, and inalienable bliss of a free unaffected being. Neither within nor without will he have any more the little old personality, for he will feel consciously oneself and spirit with all, even as his outer nature will have become to his consciousness an inseparable part of the universal mind, life and will. His separative egoistic personality will have been taken up and extinguished in the impersonality of spiritual being; his separative egoistic nature will be unified with the action of cosmic Nature.

But this liberation is dependent on two simultaneous, but not yet reconciled perceptions, the clear vision of spirit and the clear vision of Nature. This is not the scientific and intelligent detachment which is quite possible even to the materialistic philosopher who has some clear vision of Nature alone, but not the perception of his own soul and self-being. Nor is it the intellectual detachment of the idealistic sage who escapes from the more limiting and disturbing forms of his ego by a luminous use of the reason. This is a larger, more living, more perfect spiritual detachment which comes by a vision of the Supreme who is more than Nature and greater than mind and reason. But even this detachment is only the initial secret of freedom and of the clear vision of knowledge, it is not the whole clue to the divine mystery,—for by itself it would leave Nature unexplained and the natural active part of being isolated from the spiritual and quietistic self-existence. The divine detachment must be the foundation for a divine participation in Nature which will replace the old egoistic participation, the divine quietism must support a divine activism and kinetism. This truth which the Teacher has had in view all along and therefore insisted on the sacrifice of works, the recognition of the Supreme as the master of our works and the doctrine of the Avatar and the divine birth, has yet been at first kept subordinate to the primary necessity of a quietistic liberation. Only the truths which lead to spiritual calm, detachment, equality, and oneness, in a word, to the perception and becoming of the immutable self, have been fully developed and given their largest amplitude of power and significance. The other great and necessary truth, its complement, has been left in a certain obscurity of a lesser or relative light; it has been hinted at constantly, but not as yet developed. Now in these successive chapters it is being rapidly released into expression.

Throughout Krishna, the Avatar, the Teacher, the charioteer of the human soul in the world-action, has been preparing the revelation of the secret of himself, Nature's deepest secret. He has kept one note always sounding across his preparatory strain and insistently coming in as a warning and prelude of the larger ultimate harmony of his integral Truth. That note was the idea of a supreme Godhead which dwells within man and Nature, but is greater than man and Nature, is found by impersonality of the self, but of which impersonal self is not the whole significance. We now see the meaning of that strong recurring insistence. It was this one Godhead, the same in universal self and man and Nature who through the voice of the Teacher in the chariot was preparing for his absolute claim to the whole being of the awakened seer of things and doer of works. "I who am within thee," he was saying, "I who am here in this human body, I for whom all exists, acts, strives, am at once the secret of the self-existent spirit and of the cosmic action. This 'I' is the greater I of whom the largest human personality is only a partial and fragmentary manifestation, Nature itself only an inferior working. Master of the soul, master of all the works of the cosmos, I am the one Light, the sole Power, the only Being. This Godhead within thee is the Teacher, the Sun, the lifter of the clear blaze of knowledge in which thou becomest aware of the difference between thy immutable self and thy mutable nature. But look beyond the light itself to its source; then shalt thou know the supreme Soul in which is recovered the spiritual truth of personality and Nature. See then the oneself in all beings that thou mayst see me in all beings; see all beings in one spiritual self and reality, because that is the way to see all beings in me; know one Brahman in all that thou mayst see God who is the supreme Brahman. Know thyself, be thyself that thou mayst be united with me of whom this timeless self is the clear light or the transparent curtain. I the Godhead am the highest truth of self and spirit."

Arjuna has to see that the same Godhead is the higher truth too not only of self and spirit but of Nature and his own personality, the secret at once of the individual and the universe. That was the Will universal in Nature, greater than the acts of Nature which proceed from him, to whom belong her actions and man's and the fruits of them. Therefore, has he to do works as a sacrifice because that is the truth of his works and of all works. Nature is the worker and not ego, but Nature is only the power of the Being who is the sole master of all her works and energisms and of all the aeons of the cosmic sacrifice. Therefore since his works are that Being's, he has to give up all his actions to the Godhead in him and the world by whom they are done in the divine mystery of Nature. This is the double condition of the divine birth of the soul, of its release from the mortality of the ego and the body into the spiritual and eternal,—knowledge first of one's timeless immutable self and union through it with the timeless Godhead, but knowledge top of that which lives behind the riddle of cosmos, the Godhead in all existences and their workings. Thus, only can we aspire through the offering of all our nature and being to a living union with the One who has become in Time and Space all that is. Here is the place of bhakti in the scheme of the Yoga of an integral self-liberation. It is an adoration and aspiration towards that which is greater than imperishable self or changing Nature. All knowledge then becomes an adoration and aspiration, but all works to become an adoration and aspiration. Works of nature and freedom of soul are unified in this adoration and become one self-uplifting to the one Godhead. The final release, a passing away from the lower nature to the source of the higher spiritual becoming, is not an extinction of the soul,—only its form of ego becomes extinct,—but a departure of our whole self of knowledge, will and love to dwell no longer in his universal but in his supracosmic reality, a fulfilment, not an annullation.

Necessarily, to make this knowledge clear to the mind of Arjuna, the divine Teacher sets out by removing the source of two remaining difficulties, the antinomy between the impersonal self and the human personality and the antinomy between the self and Nature. While these two antinomies last, the Godhead in Nature and man remains obscure, irrational, and unbelievable. Nature has been represented as the mechanical bondage of the gunas, the soul as the egoistic being subject to that bondage. But if that be all their truth, they are not and cannot be divine. Nature, ignorant and mechanical, cannot be a power of God; for divine Power must be free in its workings, spiritual in its origin, spiritual in its greatness. The soul bound and egoistic in Nature, mental, vital, physical only, cannot be a portion of the Divine and itself a divine being; for such a divine being must be itself of the very nature of the Divine, free, spiritual, self-developing, self-existent, superior to mind, life, and body. Both these difficulties and the obscurities they bring in are removed by one illumining ray of truth. Mechanical Nature is only a lower truth; it is the formula of an inferior phenomenal action. There is a higher which is the spiritual and that is the nature of our spiritual personality, our true person. God is at once impersonal and personal. His impersonality is to our psychological realisation an infinite of timeless being, consciousness, bliss of existence; his personality represents itself here as a conscious power of being, a conscious centre of knowledge and will and the joy of multiple self-manifestation. We are that one impersonality in the static essence of our being; we are each of us the multitude of that essential power in our spiritual person. But the distinction is only for the purposes of self-manifestation; the divine impersonality is, when one goes behind it, at the same time infinite He, a supreme soul and spirit. It is the great "I"—so aham, I am He, from which all personality and nature proceed and disport themselves here diversely in the appearance of an impersonal world. Brahman is all this that is, says the Upanishad, for Brahman is oneself which sees itself in four successive positions of consciousness. Vasudeva, the eternal Being, is all, says the Gita. He is the Brahman, consciously supports and originates all from his higher spiritual nature, consciously here becomes all things in a nature of intelligence, mind, life and sense and objective phenomenon of material existence. The Jiva is he in that spiritual nature of the Eternal, his eternal multiplicity, his self-vision from many centres of conscious self-power. God, Nature, and Jiva are the three terms of existence and these three are one being. How does this Being manifest himself in cosmos? First as the immutable timeless self-omnipresent and all-supporting which is in its eternity being and not becoming. Then, held in that being there is an essential power or spiritual principle of self-becoming, svabhava, through which by spiritual self-vision it determines and expresses, creates by liberation all that is latent or contained in its own existence. The power or the energy of that self-becoming loses forth into universal action, Karma, all that is thus determined in the spirit. All creation is this action, is this working of the essential nature, is Karma. But it is developed here in a mutable Nature of intelligence, mind, life, sense, and form-objectivity of material phenomenon actually cut off from the absolute light and limited by the Ignorance. All its workings become there a sacrifice of the soul in Nature to the supreme Soul secret within her, and the supreme Godhead dwells therefore in all as the Master of their sacrifice, whose presence and power govern it and whose self-knowledge and delight of being receive it. To know this is to have the right knowledge of the universe and the vision of God in the cosmos and to find out the door of escape from the Ignorance. For this knowledge, made effective for man by the offering up of his works and all his consciousness to the

Godhead in all, enables him to return to his spiritual existence and through it to the supracosmic Reality eternal and luminous above this mutable Nature.

This truth is the secret of being which the Gita is now going to apply in its amplitude of result for our inner life and our outer works. What it is going to say is the most secret thing of all.[1] It is the knowledge of the whole Godhead, samagram mam, which the Master of his being has promised to Arjuna, that essential knowledge attended with the complete knowledge of it in all its principles which will leave nothing yet to be known. The whole knot of the ignorance which has bewildered his human mind and has made his will recoil from his divinely appointed work, will have been cut entirely asunder. This is the wisdom of all wisdoms, the secret of all secrets, the king's knowledge, the king-secret. It is a pure and supreme light which one can verify by direct spiritual experience and see in oneself as the truth: it is the right and just knowledge, the very law of being. It is easy to practise when one gets hold of it, sees it, tries faithfully to live in it.

But faith is necessary; if faith is absent, if one trusts to the critical intelligence which goes by outward facts and jealously questions the revelatory knowledge because that does not square with the divisions and imperfections of the apparent nature and seems to exceed it and state something which carries us beyond the first practical facts of our present existence, its grief, its pain, evil, defect, undivine error and stumbling, asubham, then there is no possibility of living out that greater knowledge. The soul that fails to get faith in the higher truth and law, must return into the path of ordinary mortal living subject to death and error and evil: it cannot grow into the Godhead which it denies. For this is a truth which has to be lived,—and lived in the soul's growing light, not argued out in the mind's darkness. One has to grow into it, one has to become it,—that is the only way to verify it. It is

1 Gita, IX. 1-3.

only by an exceeding of the lower self that one can become the real divine self and live the truth of our spiritual existence. All the apparent truths one can oppose to it are appearances of the lower Nature. The release from the evil and the defect of the lower Nature, asubham, can only come by accepting a higher knowledge in which all this apparent evil becomes convinced of ultimate unreality, is shown to be a creation of our darkness. But to grow thus into the freedom of the divine Nature one must accept and believe in the Godhead secret within our present limited nature. For the reason why the practice of this Yoga becomes possible and easy is that in doing it we give up the whole working of all that we naturally are into the hands of that inner divine Purusha. The Godhead works out the divine birth in us progressively, simply, infallibly, by taking up our being into his and by filling it with his own knowledge and power, jnanadipena bhasvata; he lays hands on our obscure ignorant nature and transforms it into his own light and wideness. What with entire faith and without egoism we believe in and impelled by him will to be, the God within will surely accomplish. But the egoistic mind and life we now and apparently are, must first surrender itself for transmutation into the hands of that inmost secret Divinity within us.

V

THE DIVINE TRUTH AND WAY

The Gita then proceeds to unveil the supreme and integral secret, the one thought and truth in which the seeker of perfection and liberation must learn to live and the one law of perfection of his spiritual members and of all their movements. This supreme secret is the mystery of the transcendent Godhead who is all and everywhere, yet so much greater and other than the universe and all its forms that nothing here contains him, nothing expresses him really, and no language which is borrowed from the appearances of things in space and time and their relations can suggest the truth of his unimaginable being. The consequent law of our perfection is an adoration by our whole nature and its self-surrender to its divine source and possessor. Our one ultimate way is the turning of our entire existence in the world, and not merely of this or that in it, into a single movement towards the Eternal. By the power and mystery of a divine Yoga we have come out of his in-expressible secrecies into this bounded nature of phenomenal things. By a reverse movement of the same Yoga, we must transcend the limits of phenomenal nature and recover the greater consciousness by which we can live in the Divine and the Eternal.

The supreme being of the Divine is beyond manifestation: the true sempiternal image of him is not revealed in matter, nor is it seized by life, nor is it cognizable by mind, acintya-rupa, avyaktamurti. What we see is only a self-created form, rupa, not the eternal form of the Divinity, svarupa. There is someone or there is something that is other than the universe, inexpressible, unimaginable, an ineffably infinite Godhead be-yond anything that our largest or subtlest conceptions of infinity can shadow. All this weft of things to which we give the name of universe, all this immense sum of motion to which we can fix no limits and vainly seek in its forms and movements for any stable reality, any status, level and point of cosmic leverage, has been spun out, shaped, extended by this highest Infinite, founded upon this ineffable supracosmic Mystery. It is founded upon a self-formulation which is itself unmanifest and unthinkable. All this mass of becomings always changing and in motion, all these creatures, existences, things, breathing and living forms cannot contain him either in their sum or in their separate existence. He is not in them; it is not in them or by them that he lives, moves, or has his being,—God is not the Becoming. It is they that are in him, it is they that live and move in him and draw their truth from him; they are his becoming's, he is their being.[1] In the unthinkable timeless and spaceless infinity of his existence he has extended this minor phenomenon of a boundless universe in an endless space and time.

And even to say of him that all exists in him is not the whole truth of the matter, not the entirely real relation: for it is to speak of him with the idea of space, and the Divine is spaceless and timeless. Space and time, immanence and pervasion and exceeding are all of them terms and images of his consciousness. There is a Yoga of divine Power, me yoga aisvarah, by which the Supreme creates phenomena of himself in a spiritual, not a material, self-formulation of his own extended infinity, an ex-tension of which the material is only an image. He sees himself as one with that, is identified with that and all it harbours. In that infinite self-seeing,

1 matsthani sarvabhutani na caham tesvavasthitah.

which is not his whole seeing,—the pantheist's identity of God and universe is a still more limited view,—he is at once one with all that is and yet exceeds it; but he is other also than this self or extended infinity of spiritual being which contains and exceeds the universe. All exists here in his world-conscious infinite, but that again is upheld as a self-conception by the supracosmic reality of the Godhead which exceeds all our terms of world and being and consciousness.

This is the mystery of his being that he is supracosmic, yet not in any exclusive sense extracosmic. For he pervades it all as itself; there is a luminous uninvolved presence of the self-being of God, mama atma, which is in constant relation with the becoming and brings all its existences into manifestation by his simple presence.[2] Therefore it is that we have these terms of Being and becoming, existence in itself, atman, and existences dependent upon it, bhutani, mutable beings and immutable being. But the highest truth of these two relations and the resolution of their antinomy must be found in that which exceeds it; it is the supreme Godhead who manifests both containing self and its contained phenomena by the power of his spiritual consciousness, yogamaya. And it is only through union with him in our spiritual consciousness that we can arrive at our real relations with his being.

Metaphysically stated, this is the intention of these verses of the Gita, but they rest founded not upon any intellectual speculation but on spiritual experience; they synthetise because they arise globally from certain truths of spiritual consciousness. When we attempt to put ourselves into conscious relations with whatever supreme or universal Being there exists concealed or manifest in the world, we arrive at a very various experience and one or other variant term of this experience is turned by different intellectual conceptions into their fundamental idea of existence. We have, to start with, the crude experience first of a Divine who is something

2 bhutabhrn na ca bhutastho mamatma bhutabhavanah.

quite different from and greater than ourselves, quite different from and greater than the universe in which we live and so it is and no more so long as we live only in our phenomenal selves and see around us only the phenomenal face of the world. For the highest truth of the Supreme is supracosmic and all that is phenomenal seems a thing other than the infinity of the self-conscious spirit, seems an image of a lesser truth if not an illusion. When we dwell in this difference only, we regard the Divine as if extracosmic. That he is only in this sense that he is not, being supracosmic, contained in the cosmos and its creations but not in the sense that they are outside his being: for there is nothing outside the one Eternal and Real. We realize this first truth of the Godhead spiritually when we get the experience that we live and move and have our being in him alone, that however different from him we may be, we depend on him for our existence and the universe itself is only a phenomenon and movement in the Spirit.

But again, we have the farther and more transcendent experience that our self-existence is one with his self-existence. We perceive a oneself of all and of that we have the consciousness and the vision: we can no longer say or think that we are entirely different from him, but that there is self and there is phenomenon of the self-existent; all is one in self, but all is variation in the phenomenon. By an exclusive intensity of union with the self we may even come to experience the phenomenon as a thing dreamlike and unreal. But again, by a double intensity we may have too the double experience of a supreme self-existent oneness with him and yet of ourselves as living with him and in many relations to him in a persistent form, an actual derivation of his being. The universe, and our existence in the universe, becomes to us a constant and real form of the self-aware existence of the Divine. In that lesser truth we have our relations of difference between us and him and all these other living or inanimate powers of the Eternal and our dealings with his cosmic self in the nature of the universe. These relations are other than the supracosmic truth, they are derivative creations of a certain power of consciousness of the spirit, and because they are other and because they are creations the exclusive seekers of the supracosmic Absolute tax them with an unreality relative or complete. Yet are they from him, they are existent forms derived from his being, not figments created out of nothing. For it is ever itself and figures of itself and not things quite other than itself that the Spirit sees everywhere. Nor can we say that there is nothing at all in the supracosmic that corresponds to these relations. We cannot say that they are derivations of consciousness sprung from that source but yet with nothing in the source which at all supports or justifies them, nothing that is the eternal reality and supernal principle of these forms of his being.

Again, if we press in yet another way the difference between the self and the forms of self, we may come to regard the Self as containing and immanent, we may admit the truth of omnipresent spirit, and yet the forms of spirit, the moulds of its presence may affect us not only as something other than it, not only as transient, but as unreal images. We have the experience of the Spirit, the Divine Being immutable and ever containing in his vision the mutabilities of the universe; we have too the separate, the simultaneous or the coincident experience of the Divine immanent in ourselves and in all creatures. And yet the universe may be to us only an empirical form of his and our consciousness, or only an image or a symbol of existence by which we have to construct our significant relations with him and to grow gradually aware of him. But on the other hand, we get another revealing spiritual experience in which we are forced to see as the very Divine all things, not only that Spirit which dwells immutable in the universe and in its countless creatures but all this inward and outward becoming. All is then to us a divine Reality manifesting himself in us and in the cosmos. If this experience is exclusive, we get the pantheistic identity, the One that is all: but the pantheistic vision is only a partial seeing. This extended universe is not all that the Spirit is, there is an Eternal greater than it by which alone its existence is possible. Cosmos is not the Divine in all his utter reality, but a single self-expression, a true but minor motion of his being. All these spiritual experiences, however different or opposed at first sight, are yet reconcilable if we cease to press on one or other exclusively and if we see this simple truth that the divine Reality is something greater than the universal existence, but yet that all universal and particular things are that Divine and nothing else,—significative of him, we might say, and not entirely That in any part or sum of their appearance, but still they could not be significative of him if they were something else and not term and stuff of the divine existence. That is the Real; but they are its expressive realities.[3]

This is what is intended by the phrase, vasudevah sarvam iti, the Godhead is all that is universe and all that is in the universe and all that is more than the universe. The Gita lays stress first on his supracosmic existence. For otherwise the mind would miss its highest goal and remain turned towards the cosmic only or else attached to some partial experience of the Divine in the cosmos. It lays stress next on his universal existence in which all moves and acts. For that is the justification of the cosmic effort and that is the vast spiritual self-awareness in which the Godhead self-seen as the Time-Spirit does his universal works. Next it insists with a certain austere emphasis on the acceptance of the Godhead as the divine inhabitant in the human body. For he is the Immanent in all existences, and if the indwelling divinity is not recognized, not

---

3 Even if in the mind we feel them to be comparatively unreal in face of the absolutely Real. Shankara's Mayavada apart from its logical scaffolding comes when reduced to terms of spiritual experience to no more than an exaggerated expression of this relative unreality. Beyond mind the difficulty disappears, for there it never existed. The separate experiences that lie behind the differences of religious sects and schools of philosophy or Yoga, transmuted, shed their divergent mental sequences, are harmonized and, when exalted to their highest common intensity, unified in the supramental infinite.

only will the divine meaning of individual existence be missed, the urge to our supreme spiritual possibilities deprived of its greatest force, but the relations of soul with soul in humanity will be left petty, limited, and egoistic. Finally, it insists at great length on the divine manifestation in all things in the universe and affirms the derivation of all that is from the nature, power, and light of the one Godhead. For that seeing too is essential to the God-knowledge; on it is founded the integral turn of the whole being and the whole nature God-wards, the acceptance by man of the works of the divine Power in the world and the possibility of remoulding his mentality and will into the type of the God-action, transcendent in initiation, cosmic in motive, transmitted through the individual, the Jiva.

The supreme Godhead, the Self immutable behind the cosmic consciousness, the individual Divinity in the human being and the Divine secretly conscious or partially manifested in cosmic Nature and all her works and creatures, are then one reality, one Godhead. But the truths that we can put forward the most confidently of one, are reversed or they alter their sense when we try to apply them to the other poises of the one Being. Thus, the Divine is always the Lord, Ishwara; but we cannot therefore crudely apply the idea of his essential lordship and mastery in exactly the same way without change in all four fields. As the Divine manifest in cosmic Nature, he acts in close identity with Nature. He is himself then Nature, so to speak, but with a spirit within her workings which foresees and fore-wills, understands and enforces, compels the action, overrules in the result. As the one silent self of all he is the non-doer, and Nature alone is the doer. He leaves all these works to be done by her according to the law of our being, svabhavas tu pravartate, and yet he is still the lord, prabhu vibhu, because he views and upholds our action and enables Nature to work by his silent sanction. He by his immobility transmits the power of the supreme Godhead through the compulsion of his pervading motionless Presence and supports its workings by the equal regard of his witness Self in all things. As the supreme supracosmic Godhead he originates all but is above all; he compels all to manifest but does not lose himself in what he creates or attach himself to the works of his Nature. His is the free presiding Will of being that is antecedent to all the necessities of the natural action. In the individual he is during the ignorance the secret Godhead in us who compels all to revolve on the machine of Nature on which the ego is carried round as part of the machinery, at once a clog and a convenience. But since all the Divine is within each being, we can rise above this relation by transcending the ignorance. For we can identify ourselves with the oneself supporter of all things and become the witness and non-doer. Or else we can put our individual being into the human soul's right relation with the supreme Godhead within us and make it in its parts of nature the immediate cause and instrument, nimitta, and in its spiritual self and person a high participant in the supreme, free, and unattached mastery of that inner Numen. This is a thing we have to see clearly in the Gita: we have to allow for this variation of the sense of the same truth according to the nodus of relation from which its application comes into force. Otherwise, we shall see mere contradiction and inconsistency where none exists or be baffled like Arjuna by what seems to us a riddling utterance.

Thus, the Gita begins by affirming that the Supreme contains all things in himself, but is not in any, matsthani sarva-bhutani, "all are situated in Me, not I in them," and yet it proceeds immediately to say, "and yet all existences are not situated in Me, my self is the bearer of all existences, and it is not situated in existences." And yet again it insists with an apparent self-contradiction that the Divine has lodged himself, has taken up his abode in the human body, manusim tanum asritam, and that the recognition of this truth is necessary for the soul's release by the integral way of works and love and knowledge. These statements are only in appearance inconsistent with each other. It is as the supracosmic

Godhead that he is not in existences, nor even they in him; for the distinction we make between Being and becoming applies only to the manifestation in the phenomenal universe. In the supracosmic existence all is eternal Being and all, if there too there is any multiplicity, are eternal beings; nor can the spatial idea of indwelling come in, since a supracosmic absolute being is not affected by the concepts of time and space which are created here by the Lord's Yogamaya. There is a spiritual, not a spatial or temporal coexistence, a spiritual identity and coincidence must be the foundation. But on the other hand, in the cosmic manifestation there is an extension of universe in space and time by the supreme unmanifest supracosmic Being, and in that extension, he appears first as a self who supports all these existences; bhuta-bhrt, he bears them in his all-pervading self-existence. And, even, through this omnipresent self the supreme Self too, the Paramatman, can be said to bear the universe; he is its invisible spiritual foundation and the hidden spiritual cause of the becoming of all existences. He bears the universe as the secret spirit in us bears our thoughts, works, movements. He seems to pervade and to contain mind, life, and body, to support them by his presence: but this pervasion is itself an act of consciousness, not material; the body itself is only a constant act of consciousness of the spirit.

This divine Self contains all existences; all are situated in him, not materially in essence, but in that extended spiritual conception of self-being of which our too rigid notion of a material and etheric space is only a rendering in the terms of the physical mind and senses. In reality all even here is spiritual coexistence, identity, and coincidence; but that is a fundamental truth which we cannot apply until we get back to the supreme consciousness. Till then such an idea would only be an intellectual concept to which nothing corresponds in our practical experience. We have to say, then, using these terms of relation in space and time, that the universe and all its beings exist in the divine Self-existent as everything else exists in the spatial primacy of ether. "It is as the great, the all-pervading aerial principle dwells in the etheric that all existences dwell in Me, that is how you have to conceive of it," says the Teacher here to Arjuna. The universal existence is all-pervading and infinite and the Self-existent too is all-pervading and infinite; but the self-existent infinity is stable, static, immutable, the universal is an all-pervading movement, sarvatragah. The Self is one, not many; but the universal expresses itself as all existence and is, as it seems, the sum of all existences. One is Being; the other is Power of Being which moves and creates and acts in the existence of the fundamental, supporting, immutable Spirit. The Self does not dwell in all these existences or in any of them; that is to say, he is not contained by any,—just as the ether here is not contained in any form, though all forms are derived ultimately from the ether. Nor is he contained in or constituted by all existences together—any more than the ether is contained in the mobile extension of the aerial principle or is constituted by the sum of its forms or its forces. But still in the movement also is the Divine; he dwells in the many as the Lord in each being. Both these relations are true of him at one and the same time. The one is a relation of self-existence to the universal movement; the other, the immanence, is a relation of the universal existence to its own forms. The one is a truth of being in its all-containing immutability, self-existent; the other is a truth of Power of the same being manifest in the government and information of its own self-veiling and self-revealing movements.

The Supreme from above cosmic existence leans, it is here said, or presses down upon his Nature to loose from it in an eternal cyclic recurrence all that it contains in it, all that was once manifest and has become latent. All existences act in the universe in subjection to this impelling movement and to the laws of manifested being by which is expressed in cosmic harmonies the phenomenon of the divine All-existence. The Jiva follows the cycle of it's becoming in the action of this divine Nature, prakrtim mamikam, svam prakrtim, the "own nature" of the Divine. It becomes in the turns of her progression this or that personality; it always follows the curve of its own law of being as a manifestation of the divine Nature, whether in her higher and direct or her lower and derived movement, whether in ignorance or in knowledge; it returns out of her action into her immobility and silence in the lapse of the cycle. Ignorant, it is subject to her cyclic whirl, not Master of Itself but dominated by her, avasah prakrter vasat; only by return to the divine consciousness can it attain to mastery and freedom. The Divine too follows the cycle, not as subject to it, but as its informing Spirit and guide, not with his whole being involved in it, but with his power of being accompanying and shaping it. He is the presiding control of his own action of Nature, adhyaksa,—not a spirit born in her, but the creative spirit who causes her to produce all that appears in the manifestation. If in his power he accompanies her and causes all her workings, he is outside it too, as if One seated above her universal action in the supracosmic mastery, not attached to her by any involving and mastering desire and not therefore bound by her works, because he infinitely exceeds them and precedes them, is the same before, during and after all their procession in the cycles of Time. All their mutations make no difference to his immutable being. The silent self that pervades and supports the cosmos is not affected by its changes because, though supporting, it does not participate in them. This greatest supreme supracosmic Self also is not affected because it exceeds and eternally transcends them.

But also, since this action is the action of the divine Nature, sva¯ prakrtih and the divine Nature can never be separate from the Divine, in everything she creates the Godhead must be immanent. That is a relation which is not the whole truth of his being, but neither is it a truth which we cannot at all afford to ignore. He is lodged in the human body. Those who ignore his presence, who despise because of its masks the divinity in the human form, are bewildered and be fooled by the appearances of Nature and they cannot realize that there is the secret Godhead within, whether conscious in humanity as in the Avatar or veiled by his Maya. Those who are great-souled, who are not shut up in their idea of ego, who open themselves to the indwelling Divinity, know that the secret spirit in man which appears here bounded by the limited human nature, is the same ineffable splendour which we worship beyond as the supreme Godhead. They become aware of the highest status of him in which he is master and lord of all existences and yet see that in each existence he is still the supreme Deity and the indwelling Godhead. All the rest is a self-limitation for the manifesting of the variations of Nature in the cosmos. They see too that as it is his Nature which has become all that is in the universe, everything here is in its inner fact nothing but one Divine, all is Vasudeva, and they worship him not only as the supreme Godhead beyond, but here in the world, in his oneness and in every separate being. They see this truth, and, in this truth, they live and act; him they adore, live, serve both as the Transcendent of things and as God in the world and as the Godhead in all that is, serve him with works of sacrifice, seek him out by knowledge, see nothing else but him everywhere and lift their whole being to him both in its self and in all its inward and outward nature. This they know to be the large and perfect way; for it is the way of the whole truth of the one supreme and universal and individual Godhead.[4]

---

4 Gita, IX. 4-11, 13-15, 34.

VI

WORKS, DEVOTION AND KNOWLEDGE

This then is the integral truth, the highest and widest knowledge. The Divine is supracosmic, the eternal Para-brahman who supports with his timeless and spaceless existence all this cosmic manifestation of his own being and nature in Space and Time. He is the supreme spirit who ensouls the forms and movements of the universe, Paramatman. He is the supernal Person of whom all self and nature, all being and becoming in this or any universe are the self-conception and the self-energizing, Purushottama. He is the ineffable Lord of all existence who by his spiritual control of his own manifested Power in Nature unrolls the cycles of the world and the natural evolution of creatures in the cycles, Parameshwara. From him the Jiva, individual spirit, soul in Nature, existent by his being, conscious by the light of his consciousness, empowered to knowledge, to will and to action by his will and power, enjoying existence by his divine enjoyment of the cosmos, has come here into the cosmic rounds.

The inner soul in man is here a partial self-manifestation of the Divine, self-limited for the works of his Nature in the universe, prakrtir jiva-bhuta. In his spiritual essence the individual is one with the Divine. In the works of the divine Prakriti, he is one with him, yet there is an operative difference and many deep relations with God in Nature and with God above cosmic Nature. In the works of the lower appearance of Prakriti he seems by an ignorance and egoistic separation to be quite other than the One and to think, will, act, enjoy in this separative consciousness for the egoistic pleasure and purpose of his personal existence in the universe and its surface relations with other embodied minds and lives. But in fact, all his being, all his thinking, all his willingness and action and enjoyment are only a reflection—egoistic and perverted so long as he is in the ignorance—of the Divine's being, the Divine's thought, will, action and enjoyment of Nature. To get back to this truth of himself is his direct means of salvation, his largest and nearest door of escape from subjection to the Ignorance. Since he is a spirit, a soul with a nature of mind and reason, of will and dynamic action, of emotion and sensation and life's seeking for the delight of existence, it is by turning all these powers Godwards that the return to the highest truth of himself can be made entirely possible. He must know with the knowledge of the supreme Self and Brahman; he must turn his love and adoration to the supreme Person; he must subject his will and works to the supreme Lord of cosmos. Then he passes from the lower to the divine Nature: he casts from him the thought and will and works of the Ignorance and thinks, wills, and works in his divine identity as soul of that Soul, power, and light of that Spirit; he enjoys all the inner infinite of the Divine and no longer only these outward touches, masks, and appearances. Thus, divinely living, thus directing his whole self and soul and nature Godwards, he is taken up into the truest truth of the supreme Brahman.

To know Vasudeva as all and live in that knowledge is the secret. He knows him as the Self, immutable, continent of all as well as immanent in all things. He draws back from the confused and perturbed whirl of the lower nature to dwell in the still and inalienable calm and light of the self-existent spirit. There he realizes a constant unity with this self of the Divine that is present in all existences and supports all cosmic movement and action and phenomenon. He looks upward from this eternal unchanging spiritual hypostasis of the mutable universe to the greater Eternal, the supracosmic, the Real. He knows him as the divine Inhabitant in all things that are, the Lord in the heart of man, the secret Ishwara, and removes the veil between his natural being and this inner spiritual Master of his being. He makes his will, thought, and works one in knowledge with the Ishwara's, attuned by an ever-present realisation to the sense of the indwelling Divinity, sees and adores him in all and changes the whole human action to the highest meaning of the divine nature. He knows him as the source and the substance of all that is around him in the universe. All things that are he sees as at once in their appearance the veils and in their secret trend the means and signs of self-manifestation of that one unthinkable Reality and everywhere discovers that oneness, Brahman, Purusha, Atman, Vasudeva, the Being that has become all these creatures. Therefore, too his whole inner existence comes into tune and harmony with the Infinite now self-revealed in all that lives or is within and around him and his whole outer existence turns into an exact instrumentation of the cosmic purpose. He looks up through the Self to the Parabrahman who there and here is the one and only existence. He looks up through the divine Inhabitant in all to that supernal Person who in his supreme status is beyond all habitation. He looks up through the Lord manifested in the universe to the Supreme who exceeds and rules all his manifestation. Thus, he arises through a limitless unfolding of knowledge and upward vision and aspiration to that to which he has turned with an all-compelling integrality, sarvabhavena.

This integral turning of the soul Godwards bases royally the Gita's synthesis of knowledge and works and devotion. To know God thus integrally is to know him as One in the self and in all manifestation and beyond all manifestation,—and all this unitedly and at once. And yet even so, to know him is not enough unless it is accompanied by an intense uplifting of the heart and soul Godwards, unless it kindles a one-pointed and at the same time all-embracing love, adoration, aspiration. Indeed, the knowledge which is not companioned by an aspiration and vivified by an uplifting is no true knowledge, for it can be only an intellectual seeing and a barren cognitive endeavour. The vision of God brings infallibly the adoration and passionate seeking of the Divine,—a passion for the Divine in his self-existent being, but also for the Divine in ourselves, and for the Divine in all that is. To know with the intellect is simply to understand and may be an effective starting-point,—or, too, it may not be, and it will not be if there is no sincerity in the knowledge, no urge towards inner realisation in the will, no power upon the soul, no call in the spirit: for that would mean that the brain has externally understood, but inwardly the soul has seen nothing. True knowledge is to know with the inner being, and when the inner being is touched by the light, then it arises to embrace that which is seen, it yearns to possess, it struggles to shape that in itself and itself to it, it labours to become one with the glory of its vision. Knowledge in this sense is an awakening to identity and, since the inner being realizes itself by consciousness and delight, by love, by possession and oneness with whatever of itself it has seen, knowledge awakened must bring an overmastering impulse towards this true and only perfect realisation. Here that which is known is not an externalized object but the divine Purusha, self, and lord of all that we are. An all-seizing delight in him and a deep and moved love and adoration of him must be the inevitable result and is the very soul of this knowledge. And this adoration is no isolated seeking of the heart, but an offering of the whole existence. Therefore, it must also take the form of a sacrifice; there is a giving of all our works to the Ishwara, there is a surrender of all our active inward and outward nature to the Godhead of our adoration in its every subjective and in its every objective movement. All our subjective workings move in him, and they seek him, the Lord and Self, as the source and goal of their power and endeavour. All our objective workings move out towards him in the world and make him their object, initiate a service of God in the world of which the controlling power is the Divinity within us in whom we are oneself with the universe and its creatures. For both world and self, Nature, and the soul in her are enlightened by the consciousness of the One, are inner and outer bodies of the transcendent Purushottama. So comes a synthesis of mind and heart and will in the oneself and spirit and with it the synthesis of knowledge, love and works in this integral union, this embracing God-realization, this divine Yoga.

But to arrive at this movement at all is difficult for the ego-bound nature. And to arrive at its victorious and harmonious integrality is not easy even when we have set our feet on the way finally and forever. Mortal mind is bewildered by its ignorant reliance upon veils and appearances; it sees only the outward human body, human mind, human way of living and catches no liberating glimpse of the Divinity who is lodged in the creature. It ignores the divinity within itself and cannot see it in other men, and even though the Divine manifest himself in humanity as Avatar and Vibhuti, it is still blind and ignores or despises the veiled Godhead, avajananti mam mudha manusim tanum asritam. And if it ignores him in the living creature, still less can it see him in the objective world on which it looks out from its prison of separative ego through the barred windows of the finite mind. It does not see God in the universe; it knows nothing of the supreme Divinity who is master of these planes full of various existences and dwells within them; it is blind to the vision by which all in the world grows divine and the soul itself awakens to its own inherent divinity and becomes of the Godhead, godlike. What it does see readily, and to that it attaches itself with passion, is only the life of the ego hunting after finite things for their own sake and for the satisfaction of the earthly hunger of the intellect, body, senses. Those who have given themselves up too entirely to this outward drive of the mentality, fall into the hands of the lower nature, cling to it and make it their foundation. They become a prey to the nature of the Rakshasa in man who sacrifices everything to a violent and inordinate satisfaction of his separate vital ego and makes that the dark godhead of his will and thought and action and enjoyment. Or they are hurried onward in a fruitless cycle by the arrogant self-will, self-sufficient thought, self-regarding act, self-satisfied and yet ever unsatisfied intellectualized appetite of enjoyment of the Asuric nature. But to live persistently in this separative ego-consciousness and make that the centre of all our activities is to miss altogether the true self-awareness. The charm it throws upon the misled instruments of the spirit is an enchantment that chains life to a profitless circling. All its hope, action, knowledge are vain things when judged by the divine and eternal standard, for it shuts out the great hope, excludes the liberating action, banishes the illuminating knowledge. It is a false knowledge that sees the phenomenon but misses the truth of the phenomenon, a blind hope that chases after the transient but misses the eternal, a sterile action whose every profit is annulled by loss and amounts to a perennial labour of Sisyphus.[1]

The great-souled who open themselves to the light and largeness of the diviner nature of which man is capable, are alone on the path narrow in the beginning, inexpressibly wide in the end that leads to liberation and perfection. The growth of the god in man is man's proper business; the steadfast turning of this lower Asuric and Rakshasic into the divine nature is the carefully hidden meaning of human life. As this growth increases, the veil falls, and the soul comes to see the greater significance of action and the real truth of existence. The eye opens to the Godhead in man, to the Godhead in the world; it sees inwardly and comes to know outwardly the infinite Spirit, the Imperishable from whom all existences originate and who exists in all and by him and in him all exist always. Therefore, when this vision, this knowledge seizes on the soul, its whole life-aspiration becomes a surpassing

1 Gita, IX. 11-12.

love and fathomless adoration of the Divine and Infinite. The mind attaches itself singly to the eternal, the spiritual, the living, the universal, the Real; it values nothing but for its sake, it delights only in the all-blissful Purusha. All the word and all the thought become one hymning of the universal greatness, Light, Beauty, Power and Truth that has revealed itself in its glory to the human spirit and a worship of the one supreme Soul and infinite Person. All the long stress of the inner self to break outward becomes a form now of spiritual endeavour and aspiration to possess the Divine in the soul and realize the Divine in the nature. All life becomes a constant Yoga and unification of that Divine and this human spirit. This is the manner of the integral devotion; it creates a single uplifting of our whole being and nature through sacrifice by the dedicated heart to the eternal Purushottama.2[2]

Those who lay a predominant stress on knowledge, arrive to the same point by an always increasing, engrossing, enforcing power of the vision of the Divine on the soul and the nature. Theirs is the sacrifice of knowledge and by an ineffable ecstasy of knowledge they come to the adoration of the Purushottama, jnana-yajnena yajanto mam upasate. This is a comprehension filled with Bhakti because it is integral in its instruments, integral in its objective. It is not a pursuit of the Supreme merely as an abstract unity or an indeterminable Absolute. It is a heart-felt seeking and seizing of the Supreme and the Universal, a pursuit of the Infinite in his infinity and of the Infinite in all that is finite, a vision and embracing of the One in his oneness and of the One in all his several principles, his innumerable visages, forces, forms, here, there, everywhere, timelessly and in time, multiply, multitudinously, in endless aspects of his Godhead, in beings without number, all his million universal faces fronting us in the world and its creatures, ekatvena prthaktvena bahudha visvatomukham. This knowledge easily becomes an adoration, a large devotion, a vast self-giving, an

2 IX. 13-14.

integral self-offering because it is the knowledge of a Spirit, the contact of a Being, the embrace of a supreme and universal Soul which claims all that we are even as it lavishes on us when we approach it all the treasures of its endless delight of existence.[3]

The way of works too turns into an adoration and a devotion of self-giving because it is an entire sacrifice of all our will and its activities to the one Purushottama. The outward Vedic rite is a powerful symbol, effective for a slighter though still a heavenward purpose; but the real sacrifice is that inner oblation in which the Divine, All becomes himself the ritual action, the sacrifice, and every single circumstance of the sacrifice. All the working and forms of that inner rite are the self-ordinance and self-expression of his power in us mounting by our aspiration towards the source of its energies. The Divine Inhabitant be-comes himself the flame and the offering, because the flame is the Godward will and that will is God himself within us. And the offering too is form and force of the constituent Godhead in our nature and being, all that has been received from him is given up to the service and the worship of its own Reality, its own supreme Truth and Origin. The Divine Thinker be-comes himself the sacred mantra; it is the Light of his being that expresses itself in the thought directed Godward and is effective in the revealing word of splendour that enshrines the thought's secret and in the rhythm that repeats for man the rhythms of the Eternal. The illumining Godhead is himself the Veda and that which is made known by the Veda. He is both the knowledge and the object of the knowledge. The Rik, the Yajur, the Sama, the word of illumination which lights up the mind with the rays of knowledge, the word of power for the right ordaining of action, the word of calm and harmonious attainment for the bringing of the divine desire of the spirit, are themselves the Brahman, the Godhead. The mantra of the divine Consciousness brings its light of revelation, the mantra of the divine Power its will of effectuation, the mantra of the divine

3 IX. 15.

Ananda its equal fulfilment of the spiritual delight of existence. All word and thought are an out-flowering of the great OM,—OM, the Word, the Eternal. Manifest in the forms of sensible objects, manifest in that conscious play of creative self-conception of which forms and objects are the figures, manifest behind in the self-gathered superconscient power of the Infinite, OM is the sovereign source, seed, womb of thing and idea, form and name,—it is itself, integrally, the supreme Intangible, the original Unity, the timeless Mystery self-existent above all manifestation in supernal being.[4] This sacrifice is therefore at once works and adoration and knowledge.[5]

To the soul that thus knows, adores, offers up all its workings in a great self-surrender of its being to the Eternal, God is all, and all is the Godhead. It knows God as the Father of this world who nourishes and cherishes and watches over his children. It knows God as the divine Mother who holds us in her bosom, lavishes upon us the sweetness of her love and fills the universe with her forms of beauty. It knows him as the first Creator from whom has originated all that originates and creates in space and time and relation. It knows him as the Master and ordainer of all universal and of every individual dispensation. The world and fate and uncertain eventuality cannot terrify, the aspect of suffering and evil cannot bewilder the man who has surrendered himself to the Eternal. God to the soul that sees is the path and God is the goal of his journey, a path in which there is no self-losing and a goal to which his wisely guided steps are surely arriving at every moment. He knows the Godhead as the master of his and all being, the upholder of his nature, the husband of the nature-soul, its lover and cherisher, the inner witness of all his thoughts and actions.

4 AUM, — A the spirit of the gross and external, Virat, U the spirit of the subtle and internal, Taijasa, M the spirit of the secret superconscient omnipotence, Prajna, OM the Absolute, Turiya. — Mandukya Upanishad.

5 IX. 16-17.

God is his house and country, the refuge of his seeking's and desires, the wise and close and benignant friend of all beings. All birth and status and destruction of apparent existences is to his vision and experience the One who brings forward, maintains, and withdraws his temporal self-manifestation in its system of perpetual recurrences. He alone is the imperishable seed and origin of all that seem to be born and perish and their eternal resting-place in their non-manifestation. It is he that burns in the heat of the sun and the flame; it is he who is the plenty of the rain and its withholding; he is all this physical Nature and her workings. Death is his mask and immortality is his self-revelation. All that we call existent is he and all that we look upon as non-existent still is their secret in the Infinite and is part of the mysterious being of the Ineffable.[6]

Nothing but the highest knowledge and adoration, no other way than an entire self-giving and surrender to this Highest who is all, will bring us to the Highest. Other religion, other worship, other knowledge, other seeking always has its fruits, but these are transient and limited to the enjoyment of divine symbols and appearances. There are always open for our following according to the balance of our mentality an outer and an inmost knowledge, an outer and an inmost seeking. Outward religion is the worship of an outward deity and the pursuit of an external beatitude: its devotees purify their conduct from sin and attain to an active ethical righteousness in order to satisfy the fixed law, the Shastra, the external dispensation; they perform the ceremonial symbol of the outer communion. But their object is to secure after the mortal pleasure and pain of earthly life the bliss of heavenly worlds, a greater happiness than earth can give but still a personal and mundane enjoyment though in a larger world than the field of this limited and suffering terrestrial nature. And to that to which they aspire, they attain by faith and right endeavour; for material existence and earthly activities are not the whole scope of our

6 IX. 17-19.

personal becoming or the whole formula of the cosmos. Other worlds there are of a larger felicity, svargalokam visalam. Thus, the Vedic ritualist of old learned the exoteric sense of the triple Veda, purified himself from sin, drank the wine of communion with the gods and sought by sacrifice and good deeds the rewards of heaven. This firm belief in a Beyond and this seeking of a diviner world secures to the soul in its passing the strength to attain to the joys of heaven on which its faith and seeking were centred but the return to mortal existence imposes itself because the true aim of that existence has not been found and realized. Here and not elsewhere the highest Godhead has to be found, the soul's divine nature developed out of the imperfect physical human nature and through unity with God and man and universe the whole large truth of being discovered and lived and made visibly wonderful. That completes the long cycle of our becoming and admits us to a supreme result; that is the opportunity given to the soul by the human birth and, until that is accomplished, it cannot cease. The God-lover advances constantly towards this ultimate necessity of our birth in cosmos through a concentrated love and adoration by which he makes the supreme and universal Divine the whole object of his living—not either egoistic terrestrial satisfaction or the celestial worlds—and the whole object of his thought and his seeing. To see nothing but the Divine, to be at every moment in union with him, to love him in all creatures and have the delight of him in all things is the whole condition of his spiritual existence. His God-vision does not divorce him from life, nor does he miss anything of the fullness of life; for God himself becomes the spontaneous bringer to him of every good and of all his inner and outer getting and having, yoga-ksemam vahamyaham. The joy of heaven and the joy of earth are only a small shadow of his possessions; for as he grows into the Divine, the Divine too flows out upon him with all the light, power, and joy of an infinite existence.7[7]

---

7 IX. 20-22.

Ordinary religion is a sacrifice to partial godheads other than the integral Divinity. The Gita takes its direct examples from the old Vedic religion on its exoteric side as it had then developed; it describes this outward worship as a sacrifice to other godheads, anya-devatah, to the gods, or to the divinized Ancestors or to elemental powers and spirits, devan, pitrn, Bhutani. Men consecrate their life and works ordinarily to partial powers or aspects of the divine Existence as they see or conceive them—mostly powers and aspects that ensoul to them things prominent in Nature and man or else reflect to them their own humanity in a divine exceeding symbol. If they do this with faith, then their faith is justified; for the Divine accepts whatever symbol, form, or conception of himself is present to the mind of the worshipper, yam yam tanum sraddhaya arcati, as it is said elsewhere and meets him according to the faith that is in him. All sincere religious belief and practice is really a seeking after the one supreme and universal Godhead; for he always is the sole master of man's sacrifice and askesis and infinite enjoyer of his effort and aspiration. However small or low the form of the worship, however limited the idea of the godhead, however restricted the giving, the faith, the effort to get behind the veil of one's own ego-worship and limitation by material Nature, it yet forms a thread of connection between the soul of man and the All-soul and there is a response. Still the response, the fruit of the adoration and offering is according to the knowledge, the faith and the work and cannot exceed their limitations, and therefore from the point of view of the greater God-knowledge, which alone gives the entire truth of being and becoming, this inferior offering is not given according to the true and highest law of the sacrifice. It is not founded on a knowledge of the supreme Godhead in his integral existence and the true principles of his self-manifestation, but attaches itself to external and partial appearances,—na mam abhijananti tattvena. Therefore, its sacrifice too is limited in its object, largely egoistic in its motive, partial and mistaken in its action and its giving, yajanti avidhi-purvakam. An entire seeing of the Divine is the condition of an entire conscious self-surrender; the rest attains to things that are incomplete and partial and has to fall back from them and return to enlarge it-self in a greater seeking and wider God-experience. But to follow after the supreme and universal Godhead alone and utterly is to attain all knowledge and result which other ways acquire, while yet one is not limited by any aspect, though one finds the truth of him in all aspects. This movement embraces all forms of divine being on its way to the supreme Purushottama.8[8]

This absolute self-giving, this one-minded surrender is the devotion which the Gita makes the crown of its synthesis. All action and effort are by this devotion turned into an offering to the supreme and universal Godhead. "Whatever thou doest, whatever thou enjoyest, whatever thou sacrificest, whatever thou givest, whatever energy of tapasya, of the soul's will or effort thou puttest forth, make it an offering unto Me." Here the least, the slightest circumstance of life, the most insignificant gift out of oneself or what one has, the smallest action assumes a divine significance and it becomes an acceptable offering to the Godhead who makes it a means for his possession of the soul and life of the God-lover. The distinctions made by desire and ego then disappear. As there is no straining after the good result of one's action, no shunning of unhappy result, but all action and result are given up to the Supreme to whom all work and fruit in the world belong forever, there is no farther bondage. For by an absolute self-giving all egoistic desire disappears from the heart and there is a perfect union between the Divine and the individual soul through an inner renunciation of its separate living. All will, all action, all result become that of the Godhead, work divinely through the purified and illumined nature and no longer belong to the limited personal ego. The finite nature thus surrendered becomes a free channel of the Infinite; the soul in its spiritual being, uplifted out of the ignorance and the limitation, returns to its oneness with the

8 IX. 23-25.

Eternal. The Divine Eternal is the inhabitant in all existences; he is equal in all and the equal friend, father, mother, creator, lover, supporter of all creatures. He is the enemy of none, and he is the partial lover of none; none has he cast out, none has he eternally condemned, none has he favoured by any despotism of arbitrary caprice: all at last equally come to him through their circling's in the ignorance. But it is only this perfect adoration that can make this indwelling of God in man and man in God a conscious thing and an engrossing and perfect union. Love of the Highest and a total self-surrender are the straight and swift way to this divine oneness.[9]

The equal Divine Presence in all of us makes no other preliminary condition, if once this integral self-giving has been made in faith and in sincerity and with a fundamental completeness. All have access to this gate; all can enter into this temple: our mundane distinctions disappear in the mansion of the All-lover. There the virtuous man is not preferred, nor the sinner shut out from the Presence; together by this road the Brahmin pure of life and exact in observance of the law and the outcaste born from a womb of sin and sorrow and rejected of men can travel and find an equal and open access to the supreme liberation and the highest dwelling in the Eternal. Man and woman find their equal right before God; for the divine Spirit is no respecter of persons or of social distinctions and restrictions: all can go straight to him without intermediary or shackling condition. "If" says the divine Teacher "even a man of very evil conduct turns to me with a sole and entire love, he must be regarded as a saint, for the settled will of endeavour in him is a right and complete will. Swiftly he becomes a soul of righteousness and obtains eternal peace." In other words, a will of entire self-giving opens wide all the gates of the spirit and brings in response an entire descent and self-giving of the Godhead to the human being, and that at once reshapes and assimilates everything in us to the law of the divine

9 IX. 26-29.

existence by a rapid transformation of the lower into the spiritual nature. The will of self-giving forces away by its power the veil between God and man; it annuls every error and annihilates every obstacle. Those who aspire in their human strength by effort of knowledge or effort of virtue or effort of laborious self-discipline, grow with much anxious difficulty towards the Eternal; but when the soul gives up its ego and its works to the Divine, God himself comes to us and takes up our burden. To the ignorant he brings the light of the divine knowledge, to the feeble the power of the divine will, to the sinner the liberation of the divine purity, to the suffering the infinite spiritual joy and Ananda. Their weakness and the stumbling's of their human strength make no difference. "This is my word of promise," cries the voice of the Godhead to Arjuna, "that he who loves me shall not perish." Previous effort and preparation, the purity and the holiness of the Brahmin, the enlightened strength of the king-sage great in works and knowledge have their value, because they make it easier for the imperfect human creature to arrive at this wide vision and self-surrender; but even without this preparation all who take refuge in the divine Lover of man, the Vaishya once preoccupied with the narrowness of wealth-getting and the labour of production, the Shudra hampered by a thousand hard restrictions, woman shut in and stunted in her growth by the narrow circle society has drawn around her self-expansion, those too, papa-yonayah, on whom their past Karma has imposed even the very worst of births, the outcaste, the Pariah, the Chandala, find at once the gates of God opening before them. In the spiritual life all the external distinctions of which men make so much because they appeal with an oppressive force to the outward mind, cease before the equality of the divine Light and the wide omnipotence of an impartial Power.10[10]

The earthly world preoccupied with the dualities and bound to the immediate transient relations of the hour and the moment

10 IX. 30-32.

is for man, so long as he dwells here attached to these things and while he accepts the law they impose on him for the law of his life, a world of struggle, suffering and sorrow. The way to liberation is to turn from the outward to the inward, from the appearance created by the material life which lays its burden on the mind and imprisons it in the grooves of the life and the body to the divine Reality which waits to manifest itself through the freedom of the spirit. Love of the world, the mask, must change into the love of God, the Truth. Once this secret and inner Godhead is known and is embraced, the whole being and the whole life will undergo a sovereign uplifting and a marvellous transmutation. In place of the ignorance of the lower Nature absorbed in its outward works and appearances the eye will open to the vision of God everywhere, to the unity and universality of the spirit. The world's sorrow and pain will disappear in the bliss of the All-blissful; our weakness and error and sin will be changed into the all-embracing and all-transforming strength, truth, and purity of the Eternal. To make the mind one with the divine consciousness, to make the whole of our emotional nature one love of God everywhere, to make all our works one sacrifice to the Lord of the worlds and all our worship and aspiration one adoration of him and self-surrender, to direct the whole self Godwards in an entire union is the way to rise out of a mundane into a divine existence. This is the Gita's teaching of divine love and devotion, in which knowledge, works and the heart's longing become one in a supreme unification, a merging of all their divergences, an intertwining of all their threads, a high fusion, a wide identifying movement.[11]

11 IX. 33-34.

VII

THE SUPREME WORD OF THE GITA

We have now got to the inmost kernel of the Gita's Yoga, the whole living and breathing centre of its teaching. We can see now quite clearly that the ascent of the limited human soul when it withdraws from the ego and the lower nature into the immutable Self calm, silent and stable, was only a first step, an initial change. And now too we can see why the Gita from the first insisted on the Ishwara, the Godhead in the human form, who speaks always of himself, "aham, mam," as of some great secret and omnipresent Being, lord of all the worlds and master of the human soul, one who is greater even than that immutable self-existence which is still and unmoved forever and abides forever untouched by the subjective and objective appearances of the natural universe.

All Yoga is a seeking after the Divine, a turn towards union with the Eternal. According to the adequacy of our perception of the Divine and the Eternal will be the way of the seeking, the depth and fullness of the union and the integrality of the realisation. Man, the mental being, approaches the Infinite through his finite mind and has to open some near gate of this finite upon that Infinite. He seeks for some conception on which his mind is able to seize, selects some power of his nature which by force of an absolute self-heightening can reach out and lay its touch on the infinite Truth that in itself is beyond his mental comprehension.

Some face of that infinite Truth—for because it is infinite, it has numberless faces, words of its meaning, self-suggestions—he attempts to see, so that by attaching himself to it he can arrive through direct experience to the immeasurable reality it figures. However narrow the gate may be, he is satisfied if it offers some prospect into the wideness which attracts him, if it sets him on the way to the fathomless profundity and unreachable heights of that which calls to his spirit. And as he approaches it, so it receives him, ye yatha mam prapadyante.

Philosophic mind attempts to attain to the Eternal by an abstractive knowledge. The business of knowledge is to comprehend and for the finite intellect that means to define and determine. But the only way to determine the indeterminable is by some kind of universal negation, neti neti. Therefore, the mind proceeds to exclude from the conception of the Eternal all that offers itself as limitable by the senses and the heart and the understanding. An entire opposition is made between the Self and the not-self, between an eternal, immutable, indefinable self-existence and all forms of existence,—between Brahman and Maya, between the ineffable Reality and all that undertakes to express, but cannot express the Ineffable,—between Karma and Nirvana, between the ever continuous but ever impermanent action and conception of the universal Energy and some absolute ineffable supreme Negation of its action and conception which is empty of all life and mentality and dynamic significance. That strong drive of knowledge towards the Eternal leads away from everything that is transient. It negates life in order to return to its source, cuts away from us all that we seem to be in order to get from it to the nameless and impersonal reality of our being. The desires of the heart, the works of the will and the conceptions of the mind are rejected; even in the end knowledge itself is negated and abolished in the Identical and Unknowable. By the way of an increasing quietude ending in an absolute passivity the Maya-created soul or the bundle of associations we call ourselves enters into annihilation of its idea of personality, makes an end of the lie of living, disappears into Nirvana.

But this difficult abstractive method of self-negation, however it may draw to it some exceptional natures, cannot satisfy universally the embodied soul in man, because it does not give an outlet to all the straining of his complex nature towards the perfect Eternal. Not only his abstracting contemplative intellect but his yearning heart, his active will, his positive mind in search of some Truth to which his existence and the existence of the world is a manifold key, have their straining towards the Eternal and Infinite and seek to find in it their divine Source and the justification of their being and their nature. From this need arise the religions of love and works, whose strength is that they satisfy and lead Godwards the most active and developed powers of our humanity,—for only by starting from these can knowledge be effective. Even Buddhism with its austere and uncompromising negation both of subjective self and objective things had still to found itself initially on a divine discipline of works and to admit as a substitute for bhakti the spiritualized emotionalism of a universal love and compassion, since so only could it become an effective way for mankind, a truly liberating religion. Even illusionist Mayavada with its ultra logical intolerance of action and the creations of mentality had to allow a provisional and practical reality to man and the universe and to God in the world in order to have a first foothold and a feasible starting-point; it had to affirm what it denied in order to give some reality to man's bondage and to his effort for liberation.

But the weakness of the kinetic and the emotional religions is that they are too much absorbed in some divine Personality and in the divine values of the finite. And, even when they have a conception of the infinite Godhead, they do not give us the full satisfaction of knowledge because they do not follow it out into its most ultimate and supernal tendencies. These religions fall short of a complete absorption in the Eternal and the perfect union by identity,—and yet to that identity in some other way, if not in the abstractive, since there all oneness has its basis, the spirit that is in man must one day arrive. On the other hand, the weakness of a contemplative quietistic spirituality is that it arrives at this result by a too absolute abstraction and in the end, it turns into a nothing or a fiction the human soul whose aspiration was yet all the time the whole sense of this attempt at union; for without the soul and its aspiration liberation and union could have no meaning. The little that this way of thinking recognizes of his other powers of existence, it relegates to an inferior preliminary action which never arrives at any full or satisfying realisation in the Eternal and Infinite. Yet these things too which it restricts unduly, the potent will, the strong yearning of love, the positive light and all-embracing intuition of the conscious mental being are from the Divine, represent essential powers of him and must have some justification in their Source and some dynamic way of self-fulfillment in him. No God-knowledge can be integral, perfect, or universally satisfying which leaves unfulfilled their absolute claim, no wisdom utterly wise which in its intolerant asceticism of search negates or in the pride of pure knowledge belittles the spiritual reality behind these ways of the Godhead.

The greatness of the central thought of the Gita in which all its threads are gathered up and united, consists in the synthetic value of a conception which recognizes the whole nature of the soul of man in the universe and validates by a large and wise unification its many-sided need of the supreme and infinite Truth, Power, Love, Being to which our humanity turns in its search for perfection and immortality and some highest joy and power and peace. There is a strong and wide endeavour towards a comprehensive spiritual view of God and man and universal existence. Not indeed that everything without any exception is seized in these eighteen chapters, no spiritual problem left for solution; but still so large a scheme is laid out that we have only to fill in, to develop, to modify, to stress, to follow out points, to work out hint and illuminate adumbration in order to find a clue to any further claim of our intelligence and need of our spirit. The Gita itself does not evolve any quite novel solution out of its own questionings. To arrive at the comprehensiveness at which it aims, it goes back behind the great philosophical systems to the original Vedanta of the Upanishads; for there we have the widest and profoundest extant synthetic vision of spirit and man and cosmos. But what is in the Upanishads undeveloped to the intelligence because wrapped up in a luminous kernel of intuitive vision and symbolic utterance, the Gita brings out in the light of a later intellectual thinking and distinctive experience.

In the frame of its synthesis, it admits the seeking of the abstractive thinkers for the Indefinable, anirdesyam, the ever unmanifest Immutable, avyaktam aksaram. Those who devote themselves to this search, find, they also, the Purushottama, the supreme Divine Person, mam, the Spirit and highest Soul and Lord of things. For his utmost self-existent way of being is indeed an unthinkable, acintyarupam, an unimaginable positive, an absolute quintessence of all absolutes far beyond the determination of the intelligence. The method of negative passivity, quietude, renunciation of life and works by which men feel after this intangible Absolute is admitted and ratified in the Gita's philosophy, but only with a minor permissive sanction. This negating knowledge approaches the Eternal by one side only of the truth and that side the most difficult to reach and follow for the embodied soul in Nature, duhkham dehavadbhir avapyate; it proceeds by a highly specialized, even an unnecessarily arduous way, "narrow and difficult to tread as a razor's edge." Not by denying all relations, but through all relations is the Divine Infinite naturally approachable to man and most easily, widely, intimately seizable. This seeing is not after all the largest or the truest truth that the Supreme is without any relations with the mental, vital, physical existence of man in the universe, avyavaharyam, nor that what is described as the empirical truth of things, the truth of relations, vyavahara, is altogether the opposite of the highest spiritual truth, paramartha. On the contrary there are a thousand relations by which the supreme Eternal is secretly in contact and union with our human existence and by all essential ways of our nature and of the world's nature, sarva-bhavena, can that contact be made sensible, and that union made real to our soul, heart, will, intelligence, spirit. Therefore, is this other way natural and easy for man, sukham aptum. God does not make himself difficult of approach to us; only one thing is needed, one demand made on us, the single indomitable will to break through the veil of our ignorance and the whole, the persistent seeking of the mind and heart and life for that which is all the time near to it, within it, its own soul of being and spiritual essence and the secret of its personality and its impersonality, its self and its nature. This is our one difficulty; the rest the Master of our existence will himself see to and accomplish, aham tvam moksayisyami ma sucah.

In the very part of its teaching in which the Gita's synthesis leans most towards the side of pure knowledge, we have seen that it constantly prepares for this fuller truth and more pregnant experience. Indeed, it is implied in the very form the Gita gives to the realisation of the self-existent Immutable. That immutable Self of all existences seems indeed to stand back from any active intervention in the workings of Nature; but it is not void of all relation whatever and remote from all connection. It is our witness and supporter; it gives a silent and impersonal sanction; it has even an impassive enjoyment. The many-sided action of Nature is still possible even when the soul is poised in that calm self-existence: for the witness soul is the immutable Purusha and Purusha has always some relation with Prakriti. But now the reason of this double aspect of silence and of activity is revealed in its entire significance,—because the silent all-pervading Self is only one side of the truth of the divine Being. He who pervades the world as the one unchanging self that supports all its mutations, is equally the Godhead in man, the Lord in the heart of every creature, the conscient Cause and Master of all our subjective becoming and all our inward-taking and outward-going objectivized action. The Ishwara of the Yogins is one with the Brahman of the seeker of knowledge, one supreme and universal Spirit, one supreme and universal Godhead.

This Godhead is not the limited personal God of so many exoteric religions; for those are all only partial and outward formations of this other, this creative and directive, this per-sonal side of his complete truth of existence. This is the one supreme Person, Soul, Being, Purusha of whom all godheads are aspects, all individual personality a limited development in cosmic Nature. This Godhead is not a particularized name and form of Divinity, ista-devata, constructed by the intelligence or embodying the special aspiration of the worshipper. All such names and forms are only powers and faces of the one Deva who is the universal Lord of all worshippers and all religions: but this is itself that universal Deity, deva-deva. This Ishwara is not a reflection of the impersonal and indeterminable Brahman in illusive Maya: for from beyond all cosmos as well as within it he rules and is the Lord of the worlds and their creatures. He is Parabrahman who is Parameshwara, supreme Lord because he is the supreme Self and Spirit, and from his highest original existence he originates and governs the universe, not self-deceived, but with an all-knowing omnipotence. Nor is the working of his divine Nature in the cosmos an illusion whether of his or our consciousness. The only illusive Maya is the ignorance of the lower Prakriti which is not a creator of non-existent things on the impalpable background of the One and Absolute, but because of its blind encumbered and limited working misrepresents to the human mind by the figure of ego and other inadequate figures of mind, life and matter the greater sense, the deeper realities of existence. There is a supreme, a divine Nature which is the true creatrix of the universe. All creatures and all objects are becoming's of the one divine Being; all life is a working of the power of the one Lord; all nature is a manifestation of the one Infinite. He is the Godhead in man; the Jiva is spirit of his Spirit. He is the Godhead in the universe; this world in Space and Time is his phenomenal self-extension.

In the unrolling of this comprehensive vision of existence and super-existence the Yoga of the Gita finds its unified significance and unexampled amplitude. This supreme Godhead is the one unchanging imperishable Self in all that is; therefore, to the spiritual sense of this unchanging imperishable self-man has to awake and to unify with it his inner impersonal being. He is the Godhead in man who originates and directs all his workings; therefore man has to awake to the Godhead within himself, to know the divinity he houses, to rise out of all that veils and obscures it and to become united with this inmost Self of his self, this greater consciousness of his consciousness, this hidden Master of all his will and works, this Being within him who is the fount and object of all his various becoming. He is the Godhead whose divine nature, origin of all that we are, is thickly veiled by these lower natural derivations; therefore, man has to get back from his lower apparent existence, imperfect and mortal, to his essential divine nature of immortality and perfection. This Godhead is one in all things that are, the self who lives in all and the self in whom all live and move; therefore, man has to discover his spiritual unity with all creatures, to see all in the self and the self in all beings, even to see all things and creatures as himself, atmaupamyena sarvatra and accordingly think, feel, and act in all his mind, will and living. This Godhead is the origin of all that is here or elsewhere and by his Nature he has become all these innumerable existences, abhut sarvani Bhutani, therefore man has to see and adore the One in all things animate and inanimate, to worship the manifestation in sun and star and flower, in man and every living creature, in the forms and forces, qualities and powers of Nature, vasudevah sarvam iti. He has to make himself by divine vision and divine sympathy and finally by a strong inner identity one universality with the universe. A passive relationless identity excludes love and action, but this larger and richer oneness fulfils itself by works and by a pure emotion: it becomes the source and continent and substance and motive and divine purpose of all our acts and feelings. Kasmai devaya havisa vidhema, to what Godhead shall we give all our life and activities as an offering? This is that Godhead, this the Lord who claims our sacrifice. A passive relationless identity excludes the joy of adoration and devotion; but bhakti is the very soul and heart and summit of this richer, completer, more intimate union. This Godhead is the fulfilment of all relations, father, mother, lover, friend, and refuge of the soul of every creature. He is the one supreme and universal Deva, Atman, Purusha, Brahman, Ishwara of the secret wisdom. He has manifested the world in himself in all these ways by his divine Yoga: its multitudinous existences are one in him, and he is one in them in many aspects. To awaken to the revelation of him in all these ways together is man's side of the same divine Yoga.

To make it perfectly and indisputably clear that this is the supreme and entire truth of his teaching, this the integral knowledge which he had promised to reveal, the divine Avatar declares, in a brief reiteration of the upshot of all that he has been saying, that this and no other is his supreme word, paramam vacah.

"Again, hearken to my supreme word," bhuya¯ eva srnu me

paramam vacah. This supreme word of the Gita is, we find,

first the explicit and unmistakable declaration that the highest worship and highest knowledge of the Eternal are the knowledge and the adoration of him as the supreme and divine Origin of all that is in existence and the mighty Lord of the world and its peoples of whose being all things are the becomings. It is, secondly, the declaration of a unified knowledge and bhakti as the supreme Yoga; that is the destined and the natural way given to man to arrive at union with the eternal Godhead. And to make more significant this definition of the way, to give an illuminating point to this highest importance of bhakti founded upon and opening to knowledge and made the basis and motive-power for divinely appointed works, the acceptance of it by the heart and mind of the disciple is put as a condition for the farther development by which the final command to action comes at last to be given to the human instrument, Arjuna. "I will speak this supreme word to thee" says the Godhead "from my will for thy soul's good, now that thy heart is taking delight in me," te priyamanaya vaksyami. For this delight of the heart in God is the whole constituent and essence of true bhakti, bhajanti priti-purvakam. As soon as the supreme word is given, Arjuna is made to utter his acceptance of it and to ask for a practical way of seeing God in all things in Nature and from that question immediately and naturally there develops the vision of the Divine as the Spirit of the universe and there arises the tremendous command to the world-action.[1]

The idea of the Divine on which the Gita insists as the secret of the whole mystery of existence, the knowledge that leads to liberation, is one that bridges the opposition between the cosmic procession in Time and a supracosmic eternity without denying either of them or taking anything from the reality of either. It harmonizes the pantheistic, the theistic and the highest transcendental terms of our spiritual conception and spiritual experience. The Divine is the unborn Eternal who has no origin; there is and can be nothing before him from which he proceeds, because he is one and timeless and absolute. "Neither the gods nor the great Rishis know any birth of me. . . . He who knows me as the unborn without origin . . . " are the opening utterances of this supreme word. And it gives the high promise that this knowledge, not limiting, not intellectual, but pure and spiritual,—for the form and nature, if we can use such language, of this transcendental Being, his svarupa, are necessarily unthinkable by the mind, acintyarupa,—liberates mortal man from all confusion of ignorance and from all bondage

1 Gita, X. 1-18.

of sin, suffering and evil, yo vetti asammudhah sa martyesu sarva-papaih pramuc-yate. The human soul that can dwell in the light of this supreme spiritual knowledge is lifted by it beyond the ideative or sensible formulations of the universe. It rises into the ineffable power of an all-exceeding, yet all-fulfilling identity, the same beyond and here. This spiritual experience of the transcendental Infinite breaks down the limitations of the pantheistic conception of existence. The infinite of a cosmic monism which makes God and the universe one, tries to imprison the Divine in his world manifestation and leaves us that as our sole possible means of knowing him; but this experience liberates us into the timeless and spaceless Eternal. "Neither the Gods nor the Titans know thy manifestation" cries Arjuna in his reply: the whole universe or even numberless universes cannot manifest him, cannot contain his ineffable light and infinite greatness. All other lesser God-knowledge has its truth only by dependence on the ever unmanifested and ineffable reality of the transcendent Godhead.

But at the same time the divine Transcendence is not a negation, nor is it an Absolute empty of all relation to the universe. It is a supreme positive, it is an absolute of all absolutes. All cosmic relations derive from this Supreme; all cosmic existences return to it and find in it alone their true and immeasurable existence. "For I am altogether and in every way the origin of the gods and the great Rishis." The gods are the great undying Powers and immortal Personalities who consciously inform, constitute, preside over the subjective and objective forces of the cosmos. The gods are spiritual forms of the eternal and original Deity who descend from him into the many processes of the world. Multitudinous, universal, the gods weave out of the primary principles of being and its thousand complexities the whole web of this diversified existence of the One. All their own existence, nature, power, process proceeds in every way, in every principle, in its every strand from the truth of the transcendent Ineffable. Nothing is independently created here, nothing is caused self-sufficiently by these divine agents; everything finds its origin, cause, first spiritual reason for being and will to be in the absolute and supreme Godhead,—aham adih sarvasah. Nothing in the universe has its real cause in the universe, all proceeds from this supernal Existence.

The great Rishis, called here as in the Veda the seven original Seers, maharsayah sapta purve, the seven Ancients of the world, are intelligence-powers of that divine Wisdom which has evolved all things out of its own self-conscious infinitude, prajna¯ purani,—developed them down the range of the seven principles of its own essence. These Rishis embody the all-upholding, all-illumining, all-manifesting seven Thoughts of the Veda, sapta dhiyah,—the Upanishad speaks of all things as being arranged in septettes, sapta sapta. Along with these are coupled the four eternal Manus, fathers of man,—for the active nature of the Godhead is fourfold and humanity expresses this nature in its fourfold character. These also, as their name implies, are mental beings. Creators of all this life that depends on manifest or latent mind for its action, from them are all these living creatures in the world; all are their children and offspring, yesam loka imah prajah. And these great Rishis and these Manus are themselves perpetual mental becoming's of the supreme Soul [2]and born out of his spiritual transcendence into cosmic Nature,—originators, but he the origin of all that originates in the universe. Spirit of all spirits, Soul of all souls, Mind of all mind, Life of all life, Substance of all form, this transcendent Absolute is no complete opposite of all we are, but on the contrary the originating and illuminating Absolute of all the principles and powers of our and the world's being and nature.

This transcendent Origin of our existence is not separated from us by any unbridgeable gulf and does not disown the creatures that derive from him or condemn them to be only the figments of an

---

2 mad-bhava manasa jatah.

illusion. He is the Being, all are his becomings. He does not create out of a void, out of a Nihil or out of an un-substantial matrix of dream. Out of himself he creates, in himself he becomes; all are in his being, and all is of his being. This truth admits and exceeds the pantheistic seeing of things. Vasudeva is all, vasudevah sarvam; but Vasudeva is all that appears in the cosmos because he is too all that does not appear in it, all that is never manifested. His being is in no way limited by his becoming; he is in no degree bound by this world of relations. Even in becoming all he is still a Transcendence; even in assuming finite forms he is always the Infinite. Nature, Prakriti, is in her essence his spiritual power, self-power, atmasakti; this spiritual self-power develops infinite primal qualities of becoming in the inwardness of things and turns them into an external surface of form and action. For in her essential, secret and divine order the spiritual truth of each and all comes first, a thing of her deep identities; their psychological truth of quality and nature is dependent on the spiritual for all in it that is authentic, it derives from the spirit; least in necessity, last in order the objective truth of form and action derives from inner quality of nature and depends on it for all these variable presentations of existence here in the external order. Or in other words, the objective fact is only an expression of a sum of soul factors, and these go back always to a spiritual cause of their appearance.

This finite outward becoming is an expressive phenomenon of the divine Infinite. Nature is, secondarily, the lower Nature, a subordinate variable development of a few selective combinations out of the many possibilities of the Infinite. Evolved out of essential and psychological quality of being and becoming, svabhava, these combinations of form and energy, action and movement exist for a quite limited relation and mutual experience in the cosmic oneness. And in this lower, outward, and apparent order of things Nature as an expressive power of the Godhead is disfigured by the perversions of an obscure cosmic Ignorance and her divine significances lost in the materialized, separative and egoistic mechanism of our mental and vital experience. But still here also all is from the supreme Godhead, a birth, a becoming, an evolution,[3] a process of development through action of Nature out of the Transcendent. Aham sarvasya prabhavo mattah sarvam pravartate; "I am the birth of everything and from me all proceeds into development of action and movement." Not only is this true of all that we call good or praise and recognize as divine, all that is luminous, sattwic, ethical, peace-giving, spiritually joy-giving, "understanding and knowledge and freedom from the bewilderment of the Ignorance, forgiveness and truth and self-government and calm of inner control, non-injuring and equality, contentment and austerity and giving." It is true also of the oppositions that perplex the mortal mind and bring in ignorance and its bewilderment, "grief and pleasure, coming into being and destruction, fear and fearlessness, glory and ingloriousness" with all the rest of the interplay of light and darkness, all the myriad mixed threads that quiver so painfully and yet with a constant stimulation through the entanglement of our nervous mind and its ignorant subjectivities. All here in their separate diversities are subjective becoming's of existences in the one great Becoming and they get their birth and being from Him who transcends them. The Transcendent knows and originates these things but is not caught as in a web in that diversified knowledge and is not overcome by his creation. We must observe here the emphatic collocation of the three words from the verb bhu, to become, bhavanti, bhavah, bhutanam. All existences are becomings of the Divine, bhutani; all subjective states and movements are his and their psychological becomings, bhavah. These even, our lesser subjective conditions and their apparent results no less than the highest spiritual states, are all becomings from the supreme Being,[4] bhavanti matta eva. The Gita recognises and stresses the distinction between Being and becoming but does not turn it into an opposition. For that would be to abrogate the universal oneness. The Godhead is one in his transcendence, one all-supporting Self of things, one in

3 prabhava, bhava, pravrtti.

4 Cf. the Upanishad, atma eva abhut¯ sarvani bhutani, the Self has become all existences, with this contained significance in the choice of the words, the Self-existent has become all these becomings.

the unity of his cosmic nature. These three are one Godhead; all derives from him, all becomes from his being, all is eternal portion or temporal ex-pression of the Eternal. In the Transcendence, in the Absolute, if we are to follow the Gita, we must look, not for a supreme negation of all things, but for the positive key of their mystery, the reconciling secret of their existence.

But there is another supreme reality of the Infinite that must also be recognized as an indispensable element of the liberating knowledge. This reality is that of the transcendent down look as well as the close immanent presence of the divine government of the universe. The Supreme who becomes all creation, yet infinitely transcends it, is not a will-less cause aloof from his creation. He is not an involuntary originator who disowns all responsibility for these results of his universal Power or casts them upon an elusive consciousness entirely different from his own or leaves them to a mechanical Law or to a Demiurge or to a Manichean conflict of Principles. He is not an aloof and indifferent Witness who waits impassively for all to abolish itself or return to its unmoved original principle. He is the mighty lord of the worlds and peoples, loka-mahesvara and governs all not only from within but from above, from his supreme transcendence. Cosmos cannot be governed by a Power that does not transcend cosmos. A divine government implies the free mastery of an omnipotent Ruler and not an automatic force or mechanical law of determinative becoming limited by the apparent nature of the cosmos. This is the theistic seeing of the universe, but it is no shrinking and gingerly theism afraid of the world's contradictions, but one which sees God as the omniscient and omnipotent, the sole original Being who manifests in him-self all, whatever it may be, good and evil, pain and pleasure, light, and darkness as stuff of his own existence and governs himself what in himself he has manifested. Unaffected by its oppositions, unbound by his creation, exceeding, yet intimately related to this Nature and closely one with her creatures, their Spirit, Self, highest Soul, Lord, Lover, Friend, Refuge, he is ever leading them from within them and from above through the mortal appearances of ignorance and suffering and sin and evil, ever leading each through his nature and all through universal Nature towards a supreme light and bliss and immortality and transcendence. This is the fullness of the liberating knowledge. It is a knowledge of the Divine within us and in the world as at the same time a transcendent Infinite. An Absolute who has become all that is by his divine Nature, his effective power of Spirit, he governs all from his transcendence. He is intimately present within every creature and the cause, ruler, director of all cosmic happenings and yet is he far too great, mighty, and infinite to be limited by his creation.

This character of the knowledge is emphasized in three separate verses of promise. "Whosoever knows me," says the Godhead, "as the unborn who is without origin, mighty lord of the worlds and peoples, lives unbewildered among mortals and is delivered from all sin and evil. . . .Whosoever knows in its right principles this my pervading lordship and this my Yoga (the divine Yoga, aisvara yoga, by which the Transcendent is one with all existences, even while more than them all, and dwells in them and contains them as becomings of his own Nature), unites himself to me by an untrembling Yoga. . . .The wise hold me for the birth of each and all, hold each and all as developing from me its action and movement, and so holding they love and adore me . . . and I give them the Yoga of the understanding by which they come to me and I destroy for them the darkness which is born of the ignorance." These results must arise inevitably from the very nature of the knowledge and from the very nature of the Yoga which converts that knowledge into spiritual growth and spiritual experience. For all the perplexity of man's mind and action, all the stumbling, insecurity and affliction of his mind, his will, his ethical turn, his emotional, sensational, and vital urgings can be traced back to the groping and bewildered cognition and volition natural to his sense-obscured mortal mind in the body, sammoha.

But when he sees the divine Origin of all things, when he looks steadily from the cosmic appearance to its transcendent Reality and back from that Reality to the appearance, he is then delivered from this bewilderment of the mind, will, heart and senses, he walks enlightened and free, asammudhah martyesu.

Assigning to everything its supernal and real and not any longer only its present and apparent value, he finds the hidden links and connections; he consciously directs all life and act to their high and true object and governs them by the light and power which comes to him from the Godhead within him. Thus, he escapes from the wrong cognition, the wrong mental and volitional reaction, the wrong sensational reception, and impulse which here originate sin and error and suffering, sarva-papaih pramucyate. For living thus in the transcendent and universal he sees his own and every other individuality in their greater values and is released from the falsehood and ignorance of his separative and egoistic will and knowledge. That is always the essence of the spiritual liberation.

The wisdom of the liberated man is not then, in the view of the Gita, a consciousness of abstracted and unrelated impersonality, a do-nothing quietude. For the mind and soul of the liberated man are firmly settled in a constant sense, an integral feeling of the pervasion of the world by the actuating and directing presence of the divine Master of the universe, etam vibhutim mama yo vetti. He is aware of his spirit's transcendence of the cosmic order, but he is aware also of his oneness with it by the divine Yoga, yogam ca mama. And he sees each aspect of the transcendent, the cosmic and the individual existence in its right relation to the supreme Truth and puts all in their right place in the unity of the divine Yoga. He no longer sees each thing in its separateness,—the separate seeing that leaves all either unexplained or one-sided to the experiencing consciousness. Nor does he see all confusedly together,—the confused seeing that gives a wrong light and a chaotic action. Secure in the transcendence, he is not affected by the cosmic stress and the turmoil of Time and circumstance. Untroubled in the midst of all this creation and destruction of things, his spirit adheres to an unshaken and untrembling, an unvacillating Yoga of union with the eternal and spiritual in the universe. He watches through it all the divine persistence of the Master of the Yoga and acts out of a tranquil universality and oneness with all things and creatures. And this close contact with all things implies no involution of soul and mind in the separative lower nature, because his basis of spiritual experience is not the inferior phenomenal form and movement but the inner All and the supreme Transcendence. He becomes of like nature and law of being with the Divine, sadharmyam agatah, transcendent even in universality of spirit, universal even in the individuality of mind, life, and body. By this Yoga once perfected, undeviating, and fixed, avikampena yogena yujyate, he is able to take up whatever poise of nature, assume whatever human condition, do whatever world-action without any fall from his oneness with the divine Self, without any loss of his constant communion with the Master of existence.5[5]

This knowledge translated into the affective, emotional, temperamental plane becomes a calm love and intense adoration of the original and transcendental Godhead above us, the ever-present Master of all things here, God in man, God in Nature. It is at first a wisdom of the intelligence, the buddhi; but that is accompanied by a moved spiritualized state of the affective nature,[6] bhava. This change of the heart and mind is the beginning of a total change of all the nature. A new inner birth and becoming prepares us for oneness with the supreme object of our love and adoration, madbhavaya. There is an intense delight of love in the greatness and beauty and perfection of this divine Being now seen everywhere in the world and above it, priti. That

---

5 sarvatha vartamano'pi sa yogi mayi vartate.

6 budha bhava-samanvitah.

deeper ecstasy assumes the place of the scattered and external pleasure of the mind in existence or rather it draws all other delight into it and transforms by a marvellous alchemy the minds and the heart's feelings and all sense movements. The whole consciousness becomes full of the Godhead and replete with his answering consciousness; the whole life flows into one sea of bliss-experience. All the speech and thought of such God-lovers becomes a mutual utterance and understanding of the Divine. In that one joy is concentrated all the contentment of the being, all the play and pleasure of the nature. There is a continual union from moment to moment in the thought and memory, there is an unbroken continuity of the experience of oneness in the spirit. And from the moment that this inner state begins, even in the stage of imperfection, the Divine confirms it by the perfect Yoga of the will and intelligence. He uplifts the blazing lamp of knowledge within us, he destroys the ignorance of the separative mind and will, he stands revealed in the human spirit. By the Yoga of the will and intelligence founded on an illumined union of works and knowledge the transition was affected from our lower troubled mind-ranges to the immutable calm of the witnessing Soul above the active nature. But now by this greater yoga of the Buddhi founded on an illumined union of love and adoration with an all-comprehending knowledge the soul rises in a vast ecstasy to the whole transcendental truth of the absolute and all-originating Godhead. The Eternal is fulfilled in the individual spirit and individual nature; the individual spirit is exalted from birth in time to the infinitudes of the Eternal.

VIII

GOD IN POWER OF BECOMING

A very important step has been reached, a decisive statement of its metaphysical and psychological synthesis has been added to the development of the Gita's gospel of spiritual liberation and divine works. The Godhead has been revealed in thought to Arjuna; he has been made visible to the mind's search and the heart's seeing as the supreme and universal Being, the supernal and universal Person, the inward-dwelling Master of our existence for whom man's knowledge, will and adoration were seeking through the mists of the Ignorance. There remains only the vision of the multiple Virat Purusha to complete the revelation on one more of its many sides.

The metaphysical synthesis is complete. Sankhya has been admitted for the separation of the soul from the lower nature,—a separation that must be affected by self-knowledge through the discriminating reason and by transcendence of our subjection to the three gunas constituent of that nature. It has been completed and its limitations exceeded by a large revelation of the unity of the supreme Soul and supreme Nature, para purusa, para prakrti. Vedanta of the philosophers has been admitted for the self-effacement of the natural separative personality built round the ego. Its method has been used to replace the little personal by the large impersonal being, to annul the separative illusion in the unity of the Brahman and to substitute for the blind seeing of the ego the truer vision of all things in oneself and oneself in all things. Its truth has been completed by the impartial revelation of the Parabrahman from whom originate both the mobile and the immobile, the mutable and the immutable, the action and the silence. Its possible limitations have been transcended by the intimate revelation of the supreme Soul and Lord who becomes here in all Nature, manifests himself in all personality and puts forth the power of his Nature in all action. Yoga has been admitted for the self-surrender of the will, mind, heart, all the psychological being to the Ishwara, the divine Lord of the nature. It has been completed by the revelation of the supernal Master of existence as the original Godhead of whom the Jiva is the partial being in Nature. Its possible limitations have been exceeded by the soul's seeing of all things as the Lord in the light of a perfect spiritual oneness.

There results an integral vision of the Divine Existent at once as the transcendent Reality, supracosmic origin of cosmos, as the impersonal Self of all things, calm continent of the cosmos, and as the immanent Divinity in all beings, personalities, objects, powers, and qualities, the Immanent who is the constituent self, the effective nature and the inward and outward becoming of all existences. The Yoga of knowledge has been fulfilled sovereignly in this integral seeing and knowing of the One. The Yoga of works has been crowned by the surrender of all works to their Master,—for the natural man is now only an instrument of his will. The Yoga of love and adoration has been declared in its amplest forms. The intense consummation of knowledge and works, love conducts to a crowning union of soul and Oversoul in a highest amplitude. In that union the revelations of knowledge are made real to the heart as well as to the intelligence. In that union the difficult sacrifice of self in an instrumental action becomes the easy, free, and blissful expression of a living oneness. The whole means of the spiritual liberation has been given; the whole foundation of the divine action has been constructed.

Arjuna accepts the entire knowledge that has thus been given to him by the divine Teacher. His mind is already delivered from its doubts and seeking's; his heart, turned now from the outward aspect of the world, from its baffling appearance to its supreme sense and origin and its inner realities, is already released from sorrow and affliction and touched with the ineffable gladness of a divine revelation. The language which he is made to use in voicing his acceptance is such as to emphasize and insist once again on the profound integrality of this knowledge and its all-embracing finality and fullness. He accepts first the Avatar, the Godhead in man who is speaking to him as the supreme

Brahman, as the supracosmic All and Absolute of existence in which the soul can dwell when it rises out of this manifestation and this partial becoming to its source, param brahma, param dhama. He accepts him as the supreme purity of the ever-free Existence to which one arrives through the effacement of ego in the self's immutable impersonality calm and still forever, pavitram paramam. He accepts him next as the one Permanent, the eternal Soul, the divine Purusha, purusam sasvatam divyam.

He acclaims in him the original Godhead, adores the Unborn who is the pervading, indwelling, self-extending master of all existence, adi-devam ajam vibhum. He accepts him therefore not only as that Wonderful who is beyond expression of any kind, for nothing is sufficient to manifest him,—"neither the Gods nor the Titans, O blessed Lord, know thy manifestation," na hi te bhagavan vyaktim vidur deva na danavah,—but as the lord of all existences and the one divine efficient cause of all their becoming, God of the gods from whom all godheads have sprung, master of the universe who manifests and governs it from above by the power of his supreme and his universal Nature, bhuta-bhavana bhutesa deva-deva jagat-pate. And lastly, he accepts him as that Vasudeva in and around us who is all things here by virtue of the world-pervading, all-inhabiting, all-constituting master powers of his becoming, vibhutayah, "the sovereign powers of thy becoming by which thou standest pervading these worlds," yabhir vibhutibhir lokan imams tvam vyapya tisthasi.[1]

He has accepted the truth with the adoration of his heart, the submission of his will and the understanding of his intelligence. He is already prepared to act as the divine instrument in this knowledge and with this self-surrender. But a desire for a deeper constant spiritual realisation has been awakened in his heart and will. This is a truth which is evident only to the supreme Soul in its own self-knowledge,—for, cries Arjuna, "thou alone, O Purushottama, knowest thyself by thyself," atmana atmanam vettha. This is a knowledge that comes by spiritual identity and the unaided heart, will, intelligence of the natural man cannot arrive at it by their own motion and can only get at imperfect mental reflections that reveal less than they conceal and disfigure. This is a secret wisdom which one must hear from the seers who have seen the face of this Truth, have heard its word, and have become one with it in self and spirit. "All the Rishis say this of thee and the divine seer Narada, Asita, Devala, Vyasa." Or else one must receive it from within by revelation and inspiration from the inner Godhead who lifts in us the blazing lamp of knowledge. Svayancaiva bravisi me, "and thou thyself sayest it to me." Once revealed, it has to be accepted by the assent of the mind, the consent of the will and the heart's delight and submission, the three elements of the complete mental faith, sraddha. It is so that Arjuna has accepted it; "all this that thou sayest, my mind holds for the truth." But still there will remain the need of that deeper possession in the very self of our being out from its most intimate psychic centre, the soul's demand for that inexpressible permanent spiritual realisation of which the mental is only a preliminary or a shadow and without which there cannot be a complete union

1 Gita, X. 12-15.

with the Eternal.

Now the way to arrive at that realisation has been given to Arjuna. And so far, as regards the great self-evident divine principles, these do not baffle the mind; it can open to the idea of the supreme Godhead, to the experience of the immutable Self, to the direct perception of the immanent Divinity, to the contact of the conscient universal Being. One can, once the mind is illumined with the idea, follow readily the way and, with whatever preliminary difficult effort to exceed the normal mental perceptions, come in the end to the self-experience of these essential truths that stand behind our and all existence, atmana atmanam. One can do it with this readiness because these, once conceived, are evidently divine realities; there is nothing in our mental associations to prevent us from admitting God in these high aspects. But the difficulty is to see him in the apparent truths of existence, to detect him in this fact of Nature and in these disguising phenomena of the world's becoming; for here all is opposed to the sublimity of this unifying conception. How can we consent to see the Divine as man and animal being and inanimate object, in the noble and the low, the sweet and the terrible, the good and the evil? If, assenting to some idea of God extended in the things of the cosmos, we see him in ideal light of knowledge and greatness of power and charm of beauty and beneficence of love and ample largeness of spirit, how shall we avoid the breaking of the unity by their opposites which in actual fact cling to these high things and envelop them and obscure? And if in spite of the limitations of human mind and nature we can see God in the man of God, how shall we see him in those who oppose him and represent in act and nature all that we conceive of as undivine? If Narayana is without difficulty visible in the sage and the saint, how shall he be easily visible to us in the sinner, the criminal, the harlot, and the outcaste? To all the differentiations of the world-existence the sage, looking everywhere for the supreme purity and oneness, returns the austere cry, "not this, not this," neti neti.

Even if to many things in the world we give a willing or reluctant assent and admit the Divine in the universe, still before most must not the mind persist in that cry "not this, not this"? Here constantly the assent of the understanding, the consent of the will and the heart's faith become difficult to a human mentality anchored always on phenomenon and appearance. At least some compelling indications are needed, some links and bridges, some supports to the difficult effort at oneness.

Arjuna, though he accepts the revelation of Vasudeva as all and though his heart is full of the delight of it,—for already he finds that it is delivering him from the perplexity and stum-bling differentiations of his mind which was crying for a clue, a guiding truth amid the bewildering problems of a world of oppositions, and it is to his hearing the nectar of immortality, amrtam,—yet feels the need of such supports and indices. He feels that they are indispensable to overcome the difficulty of a complete and firm realisation; for how else can this knowledge be made a thing of the heart and life? He requires guiding indications, asks Krishna even for a complete and detailed enumeration of the sovereign powers of his becoming and desires that nothing shall be left out of the vision, nothing remain to baffle him. "Thou shouldst tell me" he says "of thy divine self-manifestations in thy sovereign power of becoming, divya¯ atma-vibhutayah, all without exception,—asesena, nothing omitted,—thy Vibhutis by which thou pervadest these worlds and peoples. How shall I know thee, O Yogin, by thinking of thee everywhere at all moments and in what pre-eminent becomings should I think of thee?" This Yoga by which thou art one with all and one in all and all are becomings of thy being, all are pervading or pre-eminent or disguised powers of thy nature, tell me of it, he cries, in its detail and extent, and tell me ever more of it; it is nectar of immortality to me, and however much of it I hear, I am not satiated. Here we get an indication in the Gita of something which the Gita itself does not bring out expressly, but which occurs frequently in the Upanishads and was developed later on by Vaishnavism and Shaktism in a greater intensity of vision, man's possible joy of the Divine in the world-existence, the universal Ananda, the play of the Mother, the sweetness and beauty of God's Lila.[2]

The divine Teacher accedes to the request of the disciple, but with an initial reminder that a full reply is not possible. For God is infinite and his manifestation is infinite. The forms of his manifestation too are innumerable. Each form is a symbol of some divine power, vibhuti, concealed in it and to the seeing eye each finite carries in it its own revelation of the infinite. Yes, he says, I will tell thee of my divine Vibhutis, but only in some of my principal pre-eminences and as an indication and by the example of things in which thou canst most readily see the power of the Godhead, pradhanyatah, uddesatah. For there is no end to the innumerable detail of the Godhead's self-extension in the universe, nasti anto vistarasya me. This reminder begins the passage and is repeated at the end in order to give it a greater and unmistakable emphasis. And then throughout the rest of the chapter[3] we get a summary description of these principal indications, these pre-eminent signs of the divine force present in the things and persons of the universe. It seems at first as if they were given pell-mell, without any order but still there is a certain principle in the enumeration, which, if it is once disengaged, can lead by a helpful guidance to the inner sense of the idea and its consequences. The chapter has been called the Vibhuti-Yoga,—an indispensable yoga. For while we must identify ourselves impartially with the universal divine Becoming in all its extension, its good and evil, perfection and imperfection, light, and darkness, we must at the same time realize that there is an ascending evolutionary power in it, an increasing intensity of its revelation in things, a hierarchic secret something that carries us upward from the first concealing

2 X. 16-18.

3 X. 19-42.

appearances through higher and higher forms towards the large ideal nature of the universal Godhead.

This summary enumeration begins with a statement of the primal principle that underlies all the power of this manifestation in the universe. It is this that in every being and object God dwells concealed and discoverable; he is housed as in a crypt in the mind and heart of everything and creature, an inner self in the core of its subjective and its objective becoming, one who is the beginning and middle and end of all that is, has been or will be. For it is this inner divine Self hidden from the mind and heart which he inhabits, this luminous Inhabitant concealed from the view of the soul in Nature which he has put forth into Nature as his representative, who is all the time evolving the mutations of our personality in Time and our sensational existence in Space,—Time and Space that are the conceptual movement and extension of the Godhead in us. All is this self-seeing Soul, this self-representing Spirit. Forever from within all beings, from within all conscient and inconscient existences, this All-conscient develops his manifested self in quality and power, develops it in the forms of objects, in the instruments of our subjectivity, in knowledge and word and thinking, in the creations of the mind and in the passion and actions of the doer, in the measures of Time, in cosmic powers and godheads and in the forces of Nature, in plant life, in animal life, in human and superhuman beings.

If we look at things with this eye of vision unblinded by differentiations of quality and quantity or by difference of values and oppositions of nature, we shall see that all things are in fact and can be nothing but powers of his manifestation, Vibhuti's of this universal Soul and Spirit, Yoga of this great Yogin, self-creations of this marvellous self-Creator. He is the unborn and the all-pervading Master of his own innumerable becomings in the universe, ajo vibhuh; all things are his powers and effectuations in his self-Nature, Vibhuti's. He is the origin of all they are, their beginning; he is their support in their ever-changing status, their middle; he is their end too, the culmination or the disintegration of each created thing in its cessation or its disappearance. He brings them out from his consciousness and is hidden in them, he withdraws them into his consciousness, and they are hidden in him for a time or forever. What is apparent to us is only a power of becoming of the One: what disappears from our sense and vision is effect of that power of becoming of the One. All classes, genera, species, individuals are such Vibhuti's. But since it is through power in his becoming that he is apparent to us, he is especially apparent in whatever is of a pre-eminent value or seems to act with a powerful and pre-eminent force. And therefore, in each kind of being we can see him most in those in whom the power of nature of that kind reaches its highest, its leading, its most effectively self-revealing manifestation. These are in a special sense Vibhuti's. Yet the highest power and manifestation is only a very partial revelation of the Infinite; even the whole universe is informed by only one degree of his greatness, illumined by one ray of his splendour, glorious with a faint hint of his delight and beauty. This is in sum the gist of the enumeration, the result we carry away from it, the heart of its meaning.

God is imperishable, beginningless, unending Time; this is his most evident Power of becoming and the essence of the whole universal movement. Aham eva aksayah kalah. In that movement of Time and Becoming God appears to our conception or experience of him by the evidence of his works as the divine Power who ordains and sets all things in their place in the movement. In his form of Space, it is he who fronts us in every direction, million-bodied, myriad-minded, manifest in each existence; we see his faces on all sides of us. Dhata 'ham visvato-mukhah. For simultaneously in all these many million persons and things, sarva-bhutesu, there works the mystery of his self and thought and force and his divine genius of creation and his marvellous art of formation and his impeccable ordering of relations and possibilities and inevitable consequences. He appears to us too in the universe as the universal spirit of Destruction, who seems to create only to undo his creations in the end,—"I am all-snatching Death," aham mrtyuh sarva-harah. And yet his Power of becoming does not cease from its workings, for the force of rebirth and new creation ever keeps pace with the force of death and destruction,—"and I am too the birth of all that shall come into being." The divine Self in things is the sustaining Spirit of the present, the withdrawing Spirit of the past, the creative Spirit of the future.

Then among all these living beings, cosmic godheads, superhuman and human and subhuman creatures, and amid all these qualities, powers and objects, the chief, the head, the greatest in quality of each class is a special power of the becoming of the Godhead. I am, says the Godhead, Vishnu among the Adityas, Shiva among the Rudras, Indra among the gods, Prahlada among the Titans, Brihaspati the chief of the high priests of the world, Skanda the war-god, leader of the leaders of battle, Marichi among the Maruts, the lord of wealth among the Yakshas and Rakshasas, the serpent Ananta among the Nagas, Agni among the Vasus, Chitraratha among the Gandharvas, Kandarpa the love-God among the progenitors, Varuna among the peoples of the sea, Aryaman among the Fathers, Narada among the divine sages, Yama lord of the Law among those who maintain rule and law, among the powers of storm the Wind-God. At the other end of the scale, I am the radiant sun among lights and splendours, the moon among the stars of night, the ocean among the flowing waters, Meru among the peaks of the world, Himalaya among the mountain-ranges, Ganges among the rivers, the divine thunderbolt among weapons. Among all plants and trees, I am the Aswattha, among horses Indra's horse Uchchaihsravas, Airavata among the elephants, among the birds Garuda, Vasuki the snake-god among the serpents, Kamadhuk the cow of plenty among cattle, the alligator among fishes, the lion among the beasts of the forest. I am Margasirsha, first of the months; I am spring, the fairest of the seasons.

In living beings, the Godhead tells Arjuna, I am consciousness by which they are aware of themselves and their surroundings. I am mind among the senses, mind by which they receive the impressions of objects and react upon them. I am man's qualities of mind and character and body and action; I am glory and speech and memory and intelligence and steadfastness and forgiveness, the energy of the energetic and the strength of the mighty. I am resolution and perseverance and victory, I am the sattwic quality of the good, I am the gambling of the cunning; I am the mastery and power of all who rule and tame and vanquish and the policy of all who succeed and conquer; I am the silence of things secret, the knowledge of the knower, the logic of those who debate. I am the letter A among letters, the dual among compounds, the sacred syllable OM among words, the Gayatri among metres, the Samaveda among the Vedas, and the great Sama among the mantras. I am Time the head of all reckoning to those who reckon and measure. I am spiritual knowledge among the many philosophies, arts, and sciences. I am all the powers of the human being and all the energies of the universe and its creatures.

Those in whom my powers rise to the utmost heights of human attainment are myself always, my special Vibhuti's. I am among men the king of men, the leader, the mighty man, the hero. I am Rama among warriors, Krishna among the Vrishni's, Arjuna among the Pandavas. The illumined Rishi is my Vibhuti; I am Bhrigu among the great Rishis. The great seer, the inspired poet who sees and reveals the truth by the light of the idea and sound of the word, is myself luminous in the mortal; I am Ushanas among the seer-poets. The great sage, thinker, philosopher is my power among men, my own vast intelligence; I am Vyasa among the sages. But, with whatever variety of degree in manifestation, all beings are in their own way and nature powers of the Godhead;

nothing moving or unmoving, animate, or inanimate in the world can be without me. I am the divine seed of all existences and of that seed they are the branches and flowers; what is in the seed of self, that only they can develop in Nature. There is no numbering or limit to my divine Vibhutis; what I have spoken is nothing more than a summary development and I have given only the light of a few leading indications and a strong opening to endless verities. Whatever beautiful and glorious creature thou seest in the world, whatever being is mighty and forceful among men and above man and below him, known to be a very splendour, light, and energy of Me and born of a potent portion and intense power of my existence. But what need is there of a multitude of details for this knowledge? Take it thus, that I am here in this world and everywhere, I am in all, and I constitute all: there is nothing else than I, nothing without Me. I support this entire universe with a single degree of my illimitable power and an infinitesimal portion of my fathomless spirit; all these worlds are only sparks, hints, glinting's of the I Am eternal and immeasurable.

IX

THE THEORY OF THE VIBHUTI

The Importance of this chapter of the Gita is very much greater than appears at first view or to an eye of prepossession which is looking into the text only for the creed of the last transcendence and the detached turning of the human soul away from the world to a distant Absolute. The message of the Gita is the gospel of the Divinity in man who by force of an increasing union unfolds himself out of the veil of the lower Nature, reveals to the human soul his cosmic spirit, reveals his absolute transcendences, reveals himself in man and in all beings. The potential outcome here of this union, this divine Yoga, man growing towards the Godhead, the Godhead manifest in the human soul and to the inner human vision, is our liberation from limited ego and our elevation to the higher nature of a divine humanity. For dwelling in this greater spiritual nature and not in the mortal weft, the tangled complexity of the three gunas, man, one with God by knowledge, love and will and the giving up of his whole being into the Godhead, is able indeed to rise to the absolute Transcendence, but also to act upon the world, no longer in ignorance, but in the right relation of the individual to the Supreme, in the truth of the Spirit, fulfilled in immortality, for God in the world and no longer for the ego. To call Arjuna to this action, to make him aware of the being and power that he is and of the Being and Power whose will acts through him, is the purpose of the embodied Godhead. To this end the divine Krishna is his charioteer; to this end there came upon him that great discouragement and deep dissatisfaction with the lesser human motives of his work; to substitute for them the larger spiritual motive this revelation is given to him in the supreme moment of the work to which he has been appointed. The vision of the World-Purusha and the divine command to action is the culminating point to which he was being led. That is already imminent; but without the knowledge now given to him through the Vibhuti-Yoga it would not bring with it its full meaning.

The mystery of the world-existence is in part revealed by the Gita. In part, for who shall exhaust its infinite depths or what creed, or philosophy say that it has enlightened in a narrow space or shut up in a brief system all the significance of the cosmic miracle? But so far as is essential for the Gita's purpose, it is revealed to us. We have the way of the origination of the world from God, the immanence of the Divine in it and its immanence in the Divine, the essential unity of all existence, the relation of the human soul obscured in Nature to the Godhead, its awakening to self-knowledge, its birth into a greater consciousness, its ascension into its own spiritual heights. But when this new self-vision and consciousness have been acquired in place of the original ignorance, what will be the liberated man's view of the world around him, his attitude towards the cosmic manifestation of which he has now the central secret? He will have first the knowledge of the unity of existence and the regarding eye of that knowledge. He will see all around him as souls and forms and powers of the one divine Being. Henceforward that vision will be the starting-point of all the inward and outward operations of his consciousness; it will be the fundamental seeing, the spiritual basis of all his actions. He will see all things and every creature living, moving, and acting in the One, contained in the divine and eternal Existence. But he will also see that One as the Inhabitant in all, their Self, the essential Spirit within them without whose secret presence in their conscious nature they could not at all live, move or act and without whose will, power, sanction, or sufferance not one of their movements at any moment would be in the least degree possible. Themselves too, their soul, mind, life, and physical mould he will see only as a result of the power, will and force of this oneself and Spirit. All will be to him a becoming of this one universal Being. Their consciousness he will see to be derived entirely from its consciousness, their power and will to be drawn from and dependent on its power and will, their partial phenomenon of nature to be a resultant from its greater divine Nature, whether in the immediate actuality of things it strikes the mind as a manifestation or a disguise, a figure, or a disfigurement of the Godhead. No untoward or bewildering appearance of things will in any smallest degree diminish or conflict with the completeness of this vision. It is the essential foundation of the greater consciousness into which he has arisen, it is the indispensable light that has opened around him and the one perfect way of seeing, the one Truth that makes all others possible.

But the world is only a partial manifestation of the Godhead, it is not itself that Divinity. The Godhead is infinitely greater than any natural manifestation can be. By his very infinity, by its absolute freedom he exists beyond all possibility of integral formulation in any scheme of worlds or extension of cosmic Nature, however wide, complex, endlessly varied this and every world may seem to us,—nasti anto vistarasya me,—however to our finite view infinite. Therefore, beyond cosmos the eye of the liberated spirit will see the utter Divine. Cosmos he will see as a figure drawn from the Divinity who is beyond all figure, a constant minor term in the absolute existence. Every relative and finite he will see as a figure of the divine Absolute and Infinite, and both beyond all finites and through each finite he will arrive at that alone, always see that beyond each phenomenon and natural creature and relative action and every quality and every happening; looking at each of these things and beyond it, he will find in the Divinity its spiritual significance.

These things will not be to his mind intellectual concepts or this attitude to the world simply a way of thinking or a pragmatic dogma. For if his knowledge is conceptual only, it is a philosophy, an intellectual construction, not a spiritual knowledge and vision, not a spiritual state of consciousness. The spiritual seeing of God and world is not ideative only, not even mainly or primarily ideative. It is direct experience and as real, vivid, near, constant, effective, intimate as to the mind its sensuous seeing and feeling of images, objects, and persons. It is only the physical mind that thinks of God and spirit as an abstract conception which it cannot visualize or represent to itself except by words and names and symbolic images and fictions. Spirit sees spirit, the divinised consciousness sees God as directly and more directly, as intimately and more intimately than bodily consciousness sees matter. It sees, feels, thinks, senses the Divine. For to the spiritual consciousness all manifest existence appears as a world of spirit and not a world of matter, not a world of life, not a world even of mind; these other things are to its view only God-thought, God-force, God-form. That is what the Gita means by living and acting in Vasudeva, mayi vartate. The spiritual consciousness is aware of the Godhead with that close knowledge by identity which is so much more tremendously real than any mental perception of the thinkable or any sensuous experience of the sensible. It is so aware even of the Absolute who is behind and beyond all world-existence and who originates and surpasses it and is forever outside its vicissitudes. And of the immutable self of this Godhead that pervades and supports the world's mutations with his unchanging eternity, this consciousness is similarly aware, by identity, by the oneness of this self with our own timeless unchanging immortal spirit. It is aware again in the same manner of the divine Person who knows himself in all these things and persons and becomes all things and persons in his consciousness and shapes their thoughts and forms and governs their actions by his immanent will. It is intimately conscious of God absolute, God as self, God as spirit, soul, and nature. Even this external Nature it knows by identity and self-experience but an identity freely admitting variation, admitting relations, admitting greater and lesser degrees of the action of the one power of existence. For Nature is God's power of various self-becoming, atma-vibhuti.

But this spiritual consciousness of world-existence will not see Nature in the world as the normal mind of man sees it in the ignorance or only as it is in the effects of the ignorance. All in this Nature that is of the ignorance, all that is imperfect or painful or perverse and repellent, does not exist as an absolute opposite of the nature of the Godhead, but goes back to something behind itself, goes back to a saving power of spirit in which it can find its own true being and redemption. There is an original and originating Supreme Prakriti, in which the divine power and will to be enjoys its own absolute quality and pure revelation. There is found the highest, there the perfect energy of all the energies we see in the universe. That is what presents itself to us as the ideal nature of the Godhead, a nature of absolute knowledge, absolute power and will, absolute love and delight. And all the infinite variations of its quality and energy, ananta-guna, aganana-sakti, are there wonderfully various, admirably, and spontaneously harmonized free self-formulations of this absolute wisdom and will and power and delight and love. All is there a many-sided untrammelled unity of infinites. Each energy, each quality is in the ideal divine nature pure, perfect, self-possessed, harmonious in its action; nothing there strives for its own separate limited self-fulfillment, all act in an inexpressible oneness. There all dharmas, all laws of being—dharma, law of being, is only characteristic action of divine energy and quality, guna-karma,—are one free and plastic dharma. The one divine Power of being[1] works with an immeasurable liberty and, tied to no single excluding law, not limited by any binding system, rejoices in her own play of infinity, and never falters in her truth of self-expression perfect forever.

---

1 tapas, cit-sakti.

But in the universe in which we live, there is a separating principle of selection and differentiation. There we see each energy, each quality which comes out for expression labouring as if for its own hand, trying to get as much self-expression as it can in whatever way it can, and accommodating somehow as best or as worst it may that effort with the concomitant or rival effort of other energies and qualities for their separate self-expression. The Spirit, the Divine dwells in this struggling world-nature and imposes on it a certain harmony by the inalienable law of the inner secret oneness on which the action of all these powers is based. But it is a relative harmony which seems to result from an original division, to emerge from and subsist by the shock of divisions and not from an original oneness. Or at least the oneness seems to be suppressed and latent, not to find itself, never to put off its baffling disguises. And in fact, it does not find itself till the individual being in this world-nature discovers in himself the higher divine Prakriti from whom this lesser movement is a derivation. Nevertheless, the qualities and energies at work in the world, operating variously in man, animal, plant, inanimate thing, are, whatever forms they may take, always divine qualities and energies. All energies and qualities are powers of the Godhead. Each comes from the divine Prakriti there, works for its self-expression in the lower Prakriti here, increases its potency of affirmation and actualized values under these hampering conditions, and as it reaches its heights of self-power, comes near to the visible expression of the Divinity, and directs itself upward to its own absolute in the supreme, the ideal, the divine Nature. For each energy is being and power of the Godhead and the expansion and self-expression of energy is always the expansion and expression of the Godhead.

One might even say that at a certain point of intensity each force in us, force of knowledge, force of will, force of love, force of delight, can result in an explosion which breaks the shell of the lower formulation and liberates the energy from its separative action into union with the infinite freedom and power of the divine

Being. A highest Godward tension liberates the mind through an absolute seeing of knowledge, liberates the heart through an absolute love and delight, liberates the whole existence through an absolute concentration of will towards a greater existence. But the percussion and the delivering shock come by the touch of the Divine on our actual nature which directs the energy away from its normal limited separative action and objects towards the Eternal, Universal and Transcendent, orientates it towards the infinite and absolute Godhead. This truth of the dynamic omnipresence of the divine Power of being is the foundation of the theory of the Vibhuti.

The infinite divine Shakti is present everywhere and secretly supports the lower formulation, para prakrtir me yaya dharyate jagat but it holds itself back, hidden in the heart of each natural existence, sarvabhutanam hrddese, until the veil of Yogamaya is rent by the light of knowledge. The spiritual being of man, the Jiva, possesses the divine Nature. He is a manifestation of God in that Nature, para¯prakrtir jıva-bhuta, and he has latent in him all the divine energies and qualities, the light, the force, the power of being of the Godhead. But in this inferior Prakriti in which we live, the Jiva follows the principle of selection and finite determination, and their whatever nexus of energy, whatever quality, or spiritual principle he brings into birth with him or brings forward as the seed of his self-expression, becomes an operative portion of his swabhava, his law of self-becoming, and determines his swadharma, his law of action. And if that were all, there would be no perplexity or difficulty; the life of man would be a luminous unfolding of godhead. But this lower energy of our world is a nature of ignorance, of egoism, of the three gunas. Because this is a nature of egoism, the Jiva conceives of himself as the separative ego: he works out his self-expression egoistically as a separative will to be in conflict as well as in association with the same will to be in others. He attempts to possess the world by strife and not by unity and harmony; he stresses an ego-centric discord. Because this is a nature of ignorance, a blind seeing and an imperfect or partial self-expression, he does not know himself, does not know his law of being, but follows it instinctively under the ill-understood compulsion of the world-energy, with a struggle, with much inner conflict, with a very large possibility of deviation. Because this is a nature of the three gunas, this confused and striving self-expression takes various forms of incapacity, perversion, or partial self-finding. Dominated by the guna of tamas, the mode of darkness and inertia, the power of being works in a weak confusion, a prevailing incapacity, an unaspiring subjection to the blind mechanism of the forces of the Ignorance. Dominated by the guna of rajas, the mode of action, desire and possession, there is a struggle, there is an effort, there is a growth of power and capacity, but it is stumbling, painful, vehement, misled by wrong notions, methods, and ideals, impelled to a misuse, corruption and perversion of right notions, methods, or ideals and prone, especially, to a great, often an enormous exaggeration of the ego. Dominated by the guna of sattwa, the mode of light and poise and peace, there is a more harmonious action, a right dealing with the nature, but right only within the limits of an individual light and a capacity unable to exceed the better forms of this lower mental will and knowledge. To escape from this tangle, to rise beyond the ignorance, the ego and the gunas is the first real step towards divine perfection. By that transcendence the Jiva finds his own divine nature and his true existence.

The liberated eye of knowledge in the spiritual consciousness does not in its outlook on the world see this struggling lower Nature alone. If we perceive only the apparent outward fact of our nature and others' nature, we are looking with the eye of the ignorance and cannot know God equally in all, in the sattwic, the rajasic, the tamasic creature, in God and Titan, in saint and sinner, in the wise man and the ignorant, in the great and in the little, in man, animal, plant and inanimate existence. The liberated vision sees three things at once as the whole occult truth of the natural being.

First and foremost, it sees the divine Prakriti in all, secret, present, waiting for evolution; it sees her as the real power in all things, that which gives its value to all this apparent action of diverse quality and force, and it reads the significance of these latter phenomena not in their own language of ego and ignorance, but in the light of the divine Nature. There-fore it sees too, secondly, the differences of the apparent action in Deva and Rakshasa, man and beast and bird and reptile, good and wicked, ignorant, and learned, but as action of divine quality and energy under these conditions, under these masks. It is not deluded by the mask but detects behind every mask the Godhead. It observes the perversion or the imperfection, but it pierces to the truth of the spirit behind, it discovers it even in the perversion and imperfection self-blinded, struggling to find itself, groping through various forms of self-expression and experience towards complete self-knowledge, towards its own infinite and absolute. The liberated eye does not lay undue stress on the perversion and imperfection but is able to see all with a complete love and charity in the heart, a complete understanding in the intelligence, a complete equality in the spirit. Finally, it sees the upward urge of the striving powers of the Will to be towards Godhead; it respects, welcomes, encourages all high manifestations of energy and quality, the flaming tongues of the Divinity, the mounting greatnesses of soul and mind and life in their intensities uplifted from the levels of the lower nature towards heights of luminous wisdom and knowledge, mighty power, strength, capacity, courage, heroism, benignant sweetness and ardour and grandeur of love and self-giving, pre-eminent virtue, noble action, captivating beauty and harmony, fine and godlike creation. The eye of the spirit sees and marks out the rising godhead of man in the great Vibhuti.

This is a recognition of the Godhead as Power, but power in its widest sense, power not only of might, but of knowledge, will, love, work, purity, sweetness, beauty. The Divine is being, consciousness and delight, and in the world, all throws itself out and finds itself again by energy of being, energy of consciousness and energy of delight; this is a world of the works of the divine Shakti. That Shakti shapes herself here in innumerable kinds of beings and each of them has its own characteristic powers of her force. Each power is the Divine himself in that form, in the lion as in the hind, in the Titan as in the God, in the inconscient sun that flames through ether as in man who thinks upon earth. The deformation given by the gunas is the minor, not really the major aspect; the essential thing is the divine power that is finding self-expression. It is the Godhead who manifests himself in the great thinker, the hero, the leader of men, the great teacher, sage, prophet, religious founder, saint, lover of man, the great poet, the great artist, the great scientist, the ascetic self-tamer, the tamer of things and events and forces. The work itself, the high poem, the perfect form of beauty, the deep love, the noble act, the divine achievement is a movement of godhead; it is the Divine in manifestation.

This is a truth which all ancient cultures recognized and respected, but one side of the modern mind has singular repug nances to the idea, sees in it a worship of mere strength and power, an ignorant or self-degrading hero-worship or a doctrine of the Asuric superman. Certainly, there is an ignorant way of taking this truth, as there is an ignorant way of taking all truths but it has its proper place, its indispensable function in the divine economy of Nature. The Gita puts it in that right place and perspective. It must be based on the recognition of the divine self in all men and all creatures; it must be consistent with an equal heart to the great and the small, the eminent and the obscure manifestation. God must be seen and loved in the ignorant, the humble, the weak, the vile, the outcaste. In the Vibhuti himself it is not, except as a symbol, the outward individual that is to be thus recognized and set high, but the one Godhead who displays himself in the power. But this does not abrogate the fact that there is an ascending scale in manifestation and that Nature mounts upward in her degrees of self-expression from her groping, dark or suppressed symbols to the first visible expressions of the Godhead. Each great being, each great achievement is a sign of her power of self-exceeding and a promise of the final, the supreme exceeding. Man, himself is a superior degree of natural manifestation to the beast and reptile, though in both there is the one equal Brahman. But man has not reached his own highest heights of self-exceeding and meanwhile every hint of a greater power of the Will to be in him must be recognized as a promise and an indication. Respect for the divinity in man, in all men, is not diminished but heightened and given a richer significance by lifting our eyes to the trail of the great Pioneers who lead or point him by whatever step of attainment towards supermanhood.

Arjuna himself is a Vibhuti; he is a man high in the spiritual evolution, a figure marked out in the crowd of his contemporaries, a chosen instrument of the divine Narayana, the Godhead in humanity. In one place the Teacher speaking as the supreme and equal Self of all declares that there is none dear to him, none hated, but in others he says that Arjuna is dear to him and his bhakta and therefore guided and safe in his hands, chosen for the vision and the knowledge. There is here only an apparent inconsistency. The Power as the self of the cosmos is equal to all, therefore to each being he gives according to the workings of his nature; but there is also a personal relation of the Purushottama to the human being in which he is especially near to the man who has come near to him. All these heroes and men of might who have joined in battle on the plain of Kurukshetra are vessels of the divine Will and through each he works according to his nature but behind the veil of his ego. Arjuna has reached that point when the veil can be rent, and the embodied Godhead can reveal the mystery of his workings to his Vibhuti. It is even essential that there should be the revelation. He is the instrument of a great work, a work terrible in appearance but necessary for a long step forward in the march of the race, a decisive movement in its struggle towards the kingdom of the Right and the Truth, dharmarajya. The history of the cycles of man is a progress towards the unveiling of the Godhead in the soul and life of humanity; each high event and stage of it is a divine manifestation. Arjuna, the chief instrument of the hidden Will, the great protagonist, must become the divine man capable of doing the work consciously as the action of the Divine. So only can that action become psychically alive and receive its spiritual import and its light and power of secret significance. He is called to self-knowledge; he must see God as the Master of the universe and the origin of the world's creatures and happenings, all as the Godhead's self-expression in Nature, God in all, God in himself as man and as Vibhuti, God in the lownesses of being and on its heights, God on the topmost summits, man too upon heights as the Vibhuti and climbing to the last summits in the supreme liberation and union. Time in its creation and destruction must be seen by him as the figure of the Godhead in its steps,—steps that accomplish the cycles of the cosmos on whose spires of movement the divine spirit in the human body rises doing God's work in the world as his Vibhuti to the supreme transcendences. This knowledge has been given; the Time-figure of the Godhead is now to be revealed and from the million mouths of that figure will issue the command for the appointed action to the liberated Vibhuti.

X

THE VISION OF THE WORLD-SPIRIT

TIME THE DESTROYER

The Vision of the universal Purusha is one of the best known and most powerfully poetic passages in the Gita, but its place in the thought is not altogether on the surface. It is evidently intended for a poetic and revelatory symbol, and we must see how it is brought in and for what purpose and discover to what it points in its significant aspects before we can capture its meaning. It is invited by Arjuna in his desire to see the living image, the visible greatness of the unseen Divine, the very embodiment of the Spirit and Power that governs the universe. He has heard the highest spiritual secret of existence, that all is from God, and all is the Divine and in all things God dwells and is concealed and can be revealed in every finite appearance. The illusion which so persistently holds man's sense and mind, the idea that things at all exist in themselves or for themselves apart from God or that anything subject to Nature can be self-moved and self-guided, has passed from him,—that was the cause of his doubt and bewilderment and refusal of action. Now he knows what is the sense of the birth and passing away of existences. He knows that the imperishable greatness of the divine conscious Soul is the secret of all these appearances. All is a Yoga of this great eternal

Spirit in things and all happenings are the result and expression of that Yoga; all Nature is full of the secret Godhead and in labour to reveal him in her. But he would see too the very form and body of this Godhead if that be possible. He has heard of his attributes and understood the steps and ways of his self-revelation; but now he asks of this Master of the Yoga to discover his very imperishable Self to the eye of Yoga. Not, evidently, the formless silence of his actionless immutability, but the Supreme from whom is all energy and action, of whom forms are the masks, who reveals his force in the Vibhuti,—the Master of works, the Master of knowledge and adoration, the Lord of Nature and all her creatures. For this greatest all-comprehending vision, he is made to ask because it is so, from the Spirit revealed in the universe, that he must receive the command to his part in the world-action.

What thou hast to see, replies to the Avatar, the human eye cannot grasp,—for the human eye can see only the outward appearances of things or make out of them separate symbol forms, each of them significant of only a few aspects of the eternal Mystery. But there is a divine eye, an inmost seeing, by which the supreme Godhead in his Yoga can be beheld and that eye I now give to thee. Thou shalt see, he says, my hundreds and thousands of divine forms, various in kind, various in shape and hue; thou shalt see the Adityas and the Rudras and the Maruts and the Aswins; thou shalt see many wonders that none has beheld; thou shalt see today the whole world related and unified in my body and whatever else thou willest to behold. This then is the keynote, the central significance. It is the vision of the One in the many, the Many in the One,—and all are the One. It is this vision that to the eye of the divine Yoga liberates, justifies, explains all that is and was and shall be. Once seen and held, it lays the shining axe of God at the root of all doubts and perplexities and annihilates all denials and oppositions. It is the vision that reconciles and unifies. If the soul can arrive at unity with the Godhead in this vision,—Arjuna has not yet done that, therefore we find that he has fear when he sees,—all even that is terrible in the world loses its terror. We see that it too is an aspect of the Godhead and once we have found his meaning in it, not looking at it by itself alone, we can accept the whole of existence with an all-embracing joy and a mighty courage, go forward with sure steps to the appointed work and envisage beyond it the supreme consummation. The soul admitted to the divine knowledge which beholds all things in one view, not with a divided, partial, and therefore bewildered seeing, can make a new discovery of the world and all else that it wills to see, yac canyad drastum icchasi; it can move on the basis of this all-relating and all-unifying vision from revelation to completing revelation.

The supreme Form is then made visible. It is that of the infinite Godhead whose faces are everywhere and in whom are all the wonders of existence, who multiplies unendingly all the many marvellous revelations of his being, a world-wide Divinity seeing with innumerable eyes, speaking from innumerable mouths, armed for battle with numberless divine uplifted weapons, glorious with divine ornaments of beauty, robed in heavenly raiment of deity, lovely with garlands of divine flowers, fragrant with divine perfumes. Such is the light of this body of God as if a thousand suns had risen at once in heaven. The whole world multitudinously divided and yet unified is visible in the body of the God of Gods. Arjuna sees him, God magnificent and beautiful and terrible, the Lord of souls who has manifested in the glory and greatness of his spirit this wild and monstrous and orderly and wonderful and sweet and terrible world and overcome with marvel and joy and fear he bows down and adores with words of awe and with clasped hands the tremendous vision. "I see" he cries "all the gods in thy body, O God, and different companies of beings, Brahma the creating lord seated in the Lotus, and the Rishis and the race of the divine Serpents. I see numberless arms and bellies and eyes and faces, I see thy infinite forms on every side, but I see not thy end nor thy middle nor thy beginning, O Lord of the universe, O Form universal. I see thee crowned and with thy mace and thy discus, hard to discern because thou art a luminous mass of energy on all sides of me, an encompassing blaze, a sun-bright fire-bright Immeasurable. Thou art the supreme Immutable whom we have to know, thou art the high foundation and abode of the universe, thou art the imperishable guardian of the eternal laws, thou art the sempiternal soul of existence."

But in the greatness of this vision there is too the terrific image of the Destroyer. This Immeasurable without end or middle or beginning is he in whom all things begin and exist and end. This Godhead who embraces the worlds with his numberless arms and destroys with his million hands, whose eyes are suns and moons, has a face of blazing fire and is ever burning up the whole universe with the flame of his energy. The form of him is fierce and marvellous and alone it fills all the regions and occupies the whole space between earth and heaven. The companies of the gods enter it, afraid, adoring; the Rishis and the Siddhas crying "May there be peace and weal" praise it with many praises; the eyes of Gods and Titans and Giants are fixed on it in amazement. It has enormous burning eyes; it has mouths that gape to devour, terrible with many tusks of destruction; it has faces like the fires of Death and Time. The kings and the captains and the heroes on both sides of the world-battle are hastening into its tusked and terrible jaws and some are seen with crushed and bleeding heads caught between its teeth of power; the nations are rushing to destruction with helpless speed into its mouths of flame like many rivers hurrying in their course towards the ocean or like moths that cast themselves on a kindled fire. With those burning mouths the Form of Dread is licking all the regions around; the whole world is full of his burning energies and baked in the fierceness of his lustres. The world and its nations are shaken and in anguish with the terror of destruction and Arjuna shares in the trouble and panic around him; troubled and in pain is the soul within him and he finds no peace or gladness. He cries to the dreadful Godhead,

"Declare to me who thou art that wearest this form of fierceness. Salutation to thee, O thou great Godhead, turn thy heart to grace. I would know who thou art who wast from the beginning, for I know not the will of thy workings."

This last cry of Arjuna indicates the double intention in the vision. This is the figure of the supreme and universal Being, the Ancient of Days who is forever, sanatanam purusam puranam, this is he who forever creates, for Brahma the Creator is one of the Godheads seen in his body, he who keeps the world always in existence, for he is the guardian of the eternal laws, but who is always too destroying in order that he may new-create, who is Time, who is Death, who is Rudra the Dancer of the calm and awful dance, who is Kali with her garland of skulls trampling naked in battle and flecked with the blood of the slaughtered Titans, who is the cyclone and the fire and the earthquake and pain and famine and revolution and ruin and the swallowing ocean. And it is this last aspect of him which he puts forward at the moment. It is an aspect from which the mind in men willingly turns away and ostrich-like hides its head so that perchance, not seeing, it may not be seen by the Terrible. The weakness of the human heart wants only fair and comforting truths or in their absence pleasant fables; it will not have the truth in its entirety because there, there is much that is not clear and pleasant and comfortable, but hard to understand and harder to bear. The raw religionist, the superficial optimistic thinker, the sentimental idealist, the man at the mercy of his sensations and emotions agree in twisting away from the sterner conclusions, the harsher and fiercer aspects of universal existence. Indian religion has been ignorantly reproached for not sharing in this general game of hiding, because on the contrary it has built and placed before it the terrible as well as the sweet and beautiful symbols of the Godhead. But it is the depth and largeness of its long thought and spiritual experience that prevent it from feeling or from giving countenance to these feeble shrinking's.

Indian spirituality knows that God is Love and Peace and calm Eternity,—the Gita which presents us with these terrible images, speaks of the Godhead who embodies himself in them as the lover and friend of all creatures. But there is too the sterner aspect of his divine government of the world which meets us from the beginning, the aspect of destruction, and to ignore it is to miss the full reality of the divine Love and Peace and Calm and Eternity and even to throw on it an aspect of partiality and illusion, because the comforting exclusive form in which it is put is not borne out by the nature of the world in which we live. This world of our battle and labour is a fierce dangerous destructive devouring world in which life exists precariously and the soul and body of man move among enormous perils, a world in which by every step forward, whether we will it or no, something is crushed and broken, in which every breath of life is a breath too of death. To put away the responsibility for all that seems to us evil or terrible on the shoulders of a semi-omnipotent Devil, or to put it aside as part of Nature, making an unbridgeable opposition between world-nature and God-Nature, as if Nature were independent of God, or to throw the responsibility on man and his sins, as if he had a preponderant voice in the making of this world or could create anything against the will of God, are clumsily comfortable devices in which the religious thought of India has never taken refuge. We have to look courageously in the face of the reality and see that it is God and none else who has made this world in his being and that, so he has made it. We have to see that Nature devouring her children, Time eating up the lives of creatures, Death universal and ineluctable and the violence of the Rudra forces in man and Nature are also the supreme Godhead in one of his cosmic figures. We have to see that God the bountiful and prodigal creator, God the helpful, strong, and benignant preserver is also God the devourer and destroyer. The torment of the couch of pain and evil on which we are racked is his touch as much as happiness and sweetness and pleasure. It is only when we see with the eye of the complete union and feel this truth in the depths of our being that we can entirely discover behind that mask too the calm and beautiful face of the all-blissful Godhead and in this touch that tests our imperfection the touch of the friend and builder of the spirit in man. The discords of the worlds are God's discords, and it is only by accepting and proceeding through them that we can arrive at the greater concords of his supreme harmony, the summits and thrilled vastnesses of his transcendent and his cosmic Ananda.

The problem raised by the Gita and the solution it gives demand this character of the vision of the World-Spirit. It is the problem of a great struggle, ruin and massacre which has been brought about by the all-guiding Will and in which the eternal Avatar himself has descended as the charioteer of the protagonist in the battle. The seer of the vision is himself the protagonist, the representative of the battling soul of man who has to strike down tyrant and oppressive powers that stand in the path of his evolution and to establish and enjoy the kingdom of a higher right and nobler law of being. Perplexed by the terrible aspect of the catastrophe in which kindred smite at kindred, whole nations are to perish and society itself seems doomed to sink down in a pit of confusion and anarchy, he has shrunk back, refused the task of destiny, and demanded of his divine Friend and Guide because he is appointed to so dreadful a work, kim karmani ghore mam niyojayasi. He has been shown then how individually to rise above the apparent character of whatever work he may do, to see that Nature the executive force is the doer of the work, his natural being the instrument, God the master of Nature and of works to whom he must offer them without desire or egoistic choice as a sacrifice. He has been shown too that the Divine who is above all these things and untouched by them yet manifests himself in man and Nature and their action and that all is a movement in the cycles of this divine manifestation. But now when he is put face to face with the embodiment of this truth, he sees in it magnified by the image of the divine greatness this aspect of terror and destruction and is appalled and can hardly bear it. For why should it be thus that the

All-spirit manifests himself in Nature? What is the significance of this creating and devouring flame that is mortal existence, this world-wide struggle, these constant disastrous revolutions, this labour and anguish and travail and perishing of creatures? He puts the ancient question and breathes the eternal prayer, "Declare to me who art thou that comest to us in this form of fierceness. I would know who art thou who wast from the beginning, for I know not the will of thy workings. Turn thy heart to grace."

Destruction, replies the Godhead, is the will of my workings with which I stand here on this field of Kurukshetra, the field of the working out of the Dharma, the field of human action,—as we might symbolically translate the descriptive phrase, dharma-ksetre kuru-ksetre,—a world-wide destruction which has come in the process of the Time-Spirit. I have a foreseeing purpose which fulfils itself infallibly and no participation or abstention of any human being can prevent, alter, or modify it; all is done by me already in my eternal eye of will before it can at all be done by man upon earth. I as Time have to destroy the old structures and to build up a new, mighty, and splendid kingdom. Thou as a human instrument of the divine Power and Wisdom hast in this struggle which thou canst not prevent to battle for the right and slay and conquer its opponents. Thou too, the human soul in Nature, hast to enjoy in Nature the fruit given by me, the empire of right and justice. Let this be sufficient for thee,—to be one with God in thy soul, to receive his command, to do his will, to see calmly a supreme purpose fulfilled in the world. "I am Time the waster of the peoples arisen and increased whose will in my workings is here to destroy the nations. Even without thee all these warriors shall be not, who are ranked in the opposing armies. Therefore arise, get thee glory, conquer thy enemies, and enjoy an opulent kingdom. By me and none other already even are they slain, do thou become the occasion only, O Savyasachin. Slay, by me who are slain, Drona, Bhishma, Jayadratha, Karna, and other heroic fighters; be not pained and troubled. Fight, thou shalt conquer the adversary in the battle." The fruit of the great and terrible work is promised and prophesied, not as a fruit hungered for by the individual,—for to that there is to be no attachment,—but as the result of the divine will, the glory and success of the thing to be done accomplished, the glory given by the Divine to himself in his Vibhuti. Thus is the final and compelling command to action given to the protagonist of the world-battle.

It is the Timeless manifest as Time and World-Spirit from whom the command to action proceeds. For certainly the Godhead when he says, "I am Time the Destroyer of beings," does not mean either that he is the Time-Spirit alone or that the whole essence of the Time-Spirit is destruction. But it is this which is the present will of his workings, pravrtti. Destruction is always a simultaneous or alternate element which keeps pace with creation, and it is by destroying and renewing that the Master of Life does his long work of preservation. More, destruction is the first condition of progress. Inwardly, the man who does not destroy his lower self-formations, cannot rise to a greater existence. Outwardly also, the nation or community or race which shrinks too long from destroying and replacing its past forms of life, is itself destroyed, rots and perishes and out of its debris other nations, communities and races are formed. By destruction of the old giant occupant's man made himself a place upon earth. By destruction of the Titans the gods maintain the continuity of the divine Law in the cosmos. Whoever prematurely attempts to get rid of this law of battle and destruction, strives vainly against the greater will of the World-Spirit. Whoever turns from it in the weakness of his lower members, as did Arjuna in the beginning,—therefore was his shrinking condemned as a small and false pity, an inglorious, an un-Aryan and unheavenly feebleness of heart and impotence of spirit, klaibyam, ksudram hrdaya-daurbalyam,—is showing not true virtue, but a want of spiritual courage to face the sterner truths of Nature and of action and existence. Man can only exceed the law of battle by discovering the greater law of his immortality.

There are those who seek this where it always exists and must primarily be found, in the higher reaches of the pure spirit, and to find it turn away from a world governed by the law of Death. That is an individual solution which makes no difference to mankind and the world, or rather makes only this difference that they are deprived of so much spiritual power which might have helped them forward in the painful march of their evolution.

What then is the master man, the divine worker, the opened channel of the universal Will to do when he finds the World-Spirit turned towards some immense catastrophe, figured before his eyes as Time the destroyer arisen and increased for the destruction of the nations, and himself put there in the forefront whether as a fighter with physical weapons or a leader and guide or an inspirer of men, as he cannot fail to be by the very force of his nature and the power within him, svabhavajena svena karmana? To abstain, to sit silent, to protest by non-intervention? But abstention will not help, will not prevent the fulfilment of the destroying Will, but rather by the lacuna it creates increase confusion. Even without thee, cries the Godhead, my will of destruction would still be accomplished, rte'pi tvam. If Arjuna were to abstain or even if the battle of Kurukshetra were not to be fought, that evasion would only prolong and make worse the inevitable confusion, disorder, ruin that are coming. For these things are no accident, but an inevitable seed that has been sown and a harvest that must be reaped. They who have sown the wind, must reap the whirlwind. Nor indeed will his own nature allow him any real abstention, prakrtis tvam niyoksyati. This the Teacher tells Arjuna at the close, "That which in thy egoism thou thinkest saying, I will not fight, vain is this thy resolve: Nature shall yoke thee to thy work. Bound by thy own action, which is born of the law of thy being, what from delusion thou desirest not to do, that thou shalt do even perforce." Then to give another turn, to use some kind of soul force, spiritual method and power, not physical weapons? But that is only another form of the same action; the destruction will still take place, and the turn given too will be not what the individual ego, but what the World-Spirit wills. Even, the force of destruction may feed on this new power, may get a more formidable impetus and Kali arise filling the world with a more terrible sound of her laughter's. No real peace can be till the heart of man deserves peace; the law of Vishnu cannot prevail till the debt to Rudra is paid. To turn aside then and preach to a still unevolved mankind the law of love and oneness? Teachers of the law of love and oneness there must be, for by that way must come the ultimate salvation. But not till the Time-Spirit in man is ready, can the inner and ultimate prevail over the outer and immediate reality. Christ and Buddha have come and gone, but it is Rudra who still holds the world in the hollow of his hand. And meanwhile the fierce forward labour of mankind tormented and oppressed by the Powers that are profiteers of egoistic force and their servants' cries for the sword of the Hero of the struggle and the word of its prophet.

The highest way appointed for him is to carry out the will of God without egoism, as the human occasion and instrument of that which he sees to be decreed, with the constant supporting memory of the Godhead in himself and man, mam anusmaran and in whatever ways are appointed for him by the Lord of his Nature. Nimittamatram bhava savyasacin. He will not cherish personal enmity, anger, hatred, egoistic desire, and passion, will not hasten towards strife or lust after violence and destruction like the fierce Asura, but he will do his work, lokasangrahaya.

Beyond the action he will look towards that to which it leads, that for which he is warring. For God the Time-Spirit does not destroy for the sake of destruction, but to make the ways clear in the cyclic process for a greater rule and a progressing manifestation, rajyam samrddham. He will accept in its deeper sense, which the superficial mind does not see, the greatness of the struggle, the glory of the victory,—if need be, the glory of the victory which comes masked as defeat,—and lead man too in the enjoyment of his opulent kingdom. Not appalled by the face of the Destroyer, he will see within it the eternal Spirit imperishable in all these perishing bodies and behind it the face of the Charioteer, the Leader of man, the Friend of all creatures, suhrdam sarvabhutanam. This formidable World-Form once seen and acknowledged, it is to that reassuring truth that the rest of the chapter is directed; it discloses in the end a more intimate face and body of the Eternal.

XI

THE VISION OF THE WORLD-SPIRIT[1]

THE DOUBLE ASPECT

Even while the effects of the terrible aspect of this vision are still upon him, the first words uttered by Arjuna after the Godhead has spoken are eloquent of a greater uplifting and reassuring reality behind this face of death and this destruction. "Rightly and in good place," he cries, "O Krishna, does the world rejoice and take pleasure in thy name, the Rakshasas are fleeing from thee in terror to all the quarters and the companies of the Siddhas bow down before thee in adoration. How should they not do thee homage, O great Spirit? For thou art the original Creator and Doer of works and greater even than creative Brahma. O thou Infinite, O thou Lord of the gods, O thou abode of the universe, thou art the Immutable and thou art what is and is not and thou art that which is the Supreme. Thou art the ancient Soul and the first and original Godhead and the supreme resting-place of this All; thou art the knower and that which is to be known and the highest status; O infinite in form, by thee was extended the universe. Thou art Yama and Vayu and Agni and Soma and Varuna and Prajapati, father of creatures, and the great-grandsire. Salutation to thee a thousand times over and again and yet again salutation, in front

---

1 Gita, XI. 35-55.

and behind and from every side, for thou art each and all that is. Infinite in might and immeasurable in strength of action thou pervadest all and art everyone."

But this supreme universal Being has lived here before him with the human face, in the mortal body, the divine Man, the embodied Godhead, the Avatar, and till now he has not known him. He has seen the humanity only and has treated the Divine as a mere human creature. He has not pierced through the earthly mask to the Godhead of which the humanity was a vessel and a symbol, and he prays now for that Godhead's forgiveness of his unseeing carelessness and his negligent ignorance. "For whatsoever I have spoken to thee in rash vehemence, thinking of thee only as my human friend and companion, 'O Krishna, O Yadava, O comrade,' not knowing this thy greatness, in negligent error or in love, and for whatsoever disrespect was shown by me to thee in jest, on the couch and the seat and in the banquet, alone or in thy presence, I pray forgiveness from thee the immeasurable. Thou art the father of all this world of the moving and unmoving; thou art one to be worshipped and the most solemn object of veneration. None is equal to thee, how then another greater in all the three worlds, O incomparable in might? Therefore, I bow down before thee and prostrate my body and I demand grace of thee the adorable Lord. As a father to his son, as a friend to his friend and comrade, as one dear with him he loves, so shouldst thou, O Godhead, bear with me. I have seen what never was seen before and I rejoice, but my mind is troubled with fear. O Godhead, show me that other form of thine. I would see thee even as before crowned and with thy mace and discus. Assume thy four-armed shape, O thousand-armed, O Form universal."

From the first words there comes the suggestion that the hidden truth behind these terrifying forms is a reassuring, a heartening and delightful truth. There is something that makes the heart of the world to rejoice and take pleasure in the name and nearness of the Divine. It is the profound sense of that which makes us see in the dark face of Kali the face of the Mother and to perceive even in the midst of destruction the protecting arms of the Friend of creatures, in the midst of evil the presence of a pure unalterable Benignity and in the midst of death the Master of Immortality. From the terror of the King of the divine action the Rakshasas, the fierce giant powers of darkness, flee destroyed, defeated, and overpowered. But the Siddhas, but the complete and perfect who know and sing the names of the Immortal and live in the truth of his being, bow down before every form of Him and know what every form enshrines and signifies. Nothing has real need to fear except that which is to be destroyed, the evil, the ignorance, the veilers in Night, the Rakshasa powers. All the movement and action of Rudra the Terrible is towards perfection and divine light and completeness.

For this Spirit, this Divine is only in outward form the Destroyer, Time who undoes all these finite forms: but in himself he is the Infinite, the Master of the cosmic Godheads, in whom the world and all its action are securely seated. He is the original and ever originating Creator, one greater than that figure of creative Power called Brahma which he shows to us in the form of things as one aspect of his trinity, creation chequered by a balance of preservation and destruction. The real divine creation is eternal; it is the Infinite manifested sempiternally in finite things, the Spirit who conceals and reveals himself for ever in his innumerable infinity of souls and in the wonder of their actions and in the beauty of their forms. He is the eternal Immutable; he is the dual appearance of the Is and Is-not, of the manifest and the never manifested, of things that were and seem to be no more, are and appear doomed to perish, shall be and shall pass. But what he is beyond all these is That, the Supreme, who holds all things mutable in the single eternity of a Time to which all is ever present. He possesses his immutable self in a timeless eternity of which Time and creation are an ever-extending figure.

This is the Truth of him in which all is reconciled; a harmony of simultaneous and interdependent truths start from and amount to the one that is real. It is the truth of a supreme Soul of whose supreme nature the world is a derivation and an inferior figure of that Infinite; of the Ancient of Days who forever presides over the long evolutions of Time; of the original Godhead of whom Gods and men and all living creatures are the children, the powers, the souls, spiritually justified in their being by his truth of existence; of the Knower who develops in man the knowledge of himself and world and God; of the one Object of all knowing who reveals himself to man's heart and mind and soul, so that every new opening form of our knowledge is a partial unfolding of him, up to the highest by which he is intimately, profoundly, and integrally seen and discovered. This is the high supreme Stability who originates and supports and receives to himself all that are in the universe. By him in his own existence the world is extended, by his omnipotent power, by his miraculous self-conception and energy and Ananda of never-ending creation. All is an infinity of his material and spiritual forms. He is all the many gods from the least to the greatest; he is the father of creatures, and all are his children and his people. He is the origin of Brahma, the father to the first father of the divine creators of these different races of living things. On this truth there is a constant insistence. Again, it is repeated that he is the All, he is each and every one, sarvah. He is the infinite Universal and he is each individual and everything that is, the one Force and Being in every one of us, the infinite Energy that throws itself out in these multitudes, the immeasurable Will and mighty Power of motion and action that forms out of itself all the courses of Time and all the happenings of the spirit in Nature.

And from that insistence the thought naturally turns to the presence of this one great Godhead in man. There the soul of the seer of the vision is impressed by three successive suggestions. First, it is borne in upon him that in the body of this son of Man who moved beside him as a transient creature upon earth and sat by his side and lay with him on the same couch and ate with him in the banquet and was the object of jest and careless word, actor in war and council and common things, in this figure of mortal man was all the time something great, concealed of tremendous significance, a Godhead, an Avatar, a universal Power, a One Reality, a supreme Transcendence. To this occult divinity in which all the significance of man and his long race is wrapped and from which all world-existence receives its inner meaning of ineffable greatness, he had been blind. Now only he sees the universal Spirit in the individual frame, the Divine embodied in humanity, the transcendent Inhabitant of this symbol of Nature. He has seen now only this tremendous, infinite, immeasurable Reality of all these apparent things, this boundless universal Form which so exceeds every individual form and yet of whom each individual thing is a house for his dwelling. For that great Reality is equal and infinite and the same in the individual and in the universe. And at first his blindness, his treatment of this Divine as the mere outward man, his seeing of only the mental and physical relation seems to him a sin against the Mightiness that was there. For the being whom he called Krishna, Yadava, comrade, was this immeasurable Greatness, this incomparable Might, this Spirit one in all of whom all are the creations. That and not the veiling outward humanity, avajanan manusim tanum asritam, was what he should have seen with awe and with submission and veneration.

But the second suggestion is that what was figured in the human manifestation and the human relation is also a reality which accompanies and mitigates for our mind the tremendous character of the universal vision. The transcendence and cosmic aspect have to be seen, for without that seeing the limitations of humanity cannot be exceeded. In that unifying oneness all has to be included. But by itself that would set too great a gulf between the transcendent spirit and this soul bound and circumscribed in an inferior Nature. The infinite presence in its unmitigated splendour would be too overwhelming for the separate littleness of the limited, individual, and natural man. A link is needed by which he can see this universal Godhead in his own individual and natural being, close to him, not only omnipotently there to govern all he is by universal and immeasurable Power, but humanly figured to support and raise him to unity by an intimate individual relation. The adoration by which the finite creature bows down before the Infinite, receives all its sweetness and draws near to a closest truth of companionship and oneness when it deepens into the more intimate adoration which lives in the sense of the fatherhood of God, the friendhood of God, the attracting love between the Divine Spirit and our human soul and nature. For the Divine inhabits the human soul and body; he draws around him and wears like a robe the human mind and figure. He assumes the human relations which the soul affects in the mortal body, and they find in God their own fullest sense and greatest realisation. This is the Vaishnava bhakti of which the seed is here in the Gita's words, but which received afterwards a more deep, ecstatic, and significant extension.

And from this second suggestion a third immediately arises. The form of the transcendent and universal Being is to the strength of the liberated spirit a thing mighty, encouraging and fortifying, a source of power, an equalizing, sublimating, all-justifying vision; but to the normal man it is overwhelming, appalling, incommunicable. The truth that reassures, even when known, is grasped with difficulty behind the formidable and mighty aspect of all-destructive Time and an incalculable Will and a vast immeasurable inextricable working. But there is too the gracious mediating form of divine Narayana, the God who is so close to man and in man, the Charioteer of the battle and the journey, with his four arms of helpful power, a humanized symbol of Godhead, not this million-armed universality. It is this mediating aspect which man must have for his support constantly before him. For it is this figure of Narayana which symbolizes the truth that reassures.

It makes close, visible, living, seizable the vast spiritual joy in which for the inner spirit and life of man the universal workings behind all their stupendous circling, retrogression, progression sovereignly culminate, their marvellous and auspicious upshot. To this humanized embodied soul their end becomes here a union, a closeness, a constant companionship of man and God, man living in the world for God, God dwelling in man and turning to his own divine ends in him the enigmatic world-process. And beyond the end is a yet more wonderful oneness and in living in the last transfigurations of the Eternal.

The Godhead in answer to Arjuna's prayer reassumes his own normal Narayana image, svakam rupam, the desired form of grace and love and sweetness and beauty. But first he declares the incalculable significance of the other mighty Image which he is about to veil. "This that thou now seest," he tells him, "is my supreme shape, my form of luminous energy, the universal, the original which none but thou amongst men has yet seen. I have shown it by my self-Yoga. For it is an image of my very Self and Spirit, it is the very Supreme self-figured in cosmic existence and the soul in perfect Yoga with me sees it without any trembling of the nervous parts or any bewilderment and confusion of the mind because he descries not only what is terrible and overwhelming in its appearance but also its high and reassuring significance. And thou also shouldst so envisage it without fear, without confusion of mind, without any sinking of the members; but since the lower nature in thee is not yet prepared to look upon it with that high strength and tranquility, I will reassume again for thee my Narayana figure in which the human mind sees isolated and toned to its humanity the calm, helpfulness, and delight of a friendly Godhead. The greater Form"—and this is repeated again after it has disappeared—"is only for the rare highest souls. The gods themselves ever desire to look upon it. It cannot be won by Veda or austerities or gifts or sacrifice; it can be seen, known, entered into only by that bhakti which regards, adores, and loves

Me alone in all things."

But what then is the uniqueness of this Form by which it is lifted so far beyond cognizance that all the ordinary endeavour of human knowledge and even the inmost austerity of its spiritual effort are insufficient, unaided, to reach the vision? It is this that man can know by other means this or that exclusive aspect of the one existence, its individual, cosmic or world-excluding figures, but not this greatest reconciling Oneness of all the aspects of the Divinity in which at one and the same time and in one and the same vision all is manifested, all is exceeded, and all is consummated. For here transcendent, universal, and individual Godhead, Spirit, and Nature, Infinite and finite, space and time and timelessness, Being and Becoming, all that we can strive to think and know of the Godhead, whether of the absolute or the manifested existence, are wonderfully revealed in an ineffable oneness. This vision can be reached only by the ab-solute adoration, the love, the intimate unity that crowns at their summit the fullness of works and knowledge. To know, to see, to enter into it, to be one with this supreme form of the Supreme becomes then possible, and it is that end which the Gita proposes for its Yoga. There is a supreme consciousness through which it is possible to enter into the glory of the Transcendent and contain in him the immutable Self and all mutable Becoming,—it is possible to be one with all, yet above all, to exceed world and yet embrace the whole nature at once of the cosmic and the supracosmic Godhead. This is difficult indeed for limited man imprisoned in his mind and body: but, says the Godhead, "be a doer of my works, accept me as the supreme being and object, become my bhakta, be free from attachment and without enmity to all existences; for such a man comes to me." In other words, superiority to the lower nature, unity with all creatures, oneness with the cosmic Godhead and the Transcendence, oneness of will with the Divine in works, absolute love for the One and for God in all,—this is the way to that absolute spiritual self-exceeding and that unimaginable transformation.

XII

THE WAY AND THE BHAKTA

In The eleventh chapter of the Gita the original object of the teaching has been achieved and brought up to a certain completeness. The command to divine action done for the sake of the world and in union with the Spirit who dwells in it and in all its creatures and in whom all its working takes place, has been given and accepted by the Vibhuti. The disciple has been led away from the old poise of the normal man and the standards, motives, outlook, egoistic consciousness of his ignorance, away from all that had finally failed him in the hour of his spiritual crisis. The very action which on that standing he had rejected, the terrible function, the appalling labour, he has now been brought to admit and accept on a new inner basis. A reconciling greater knowledge, a diviner consciousness, a high impersonal motive, a spiritual standard of oneness with the will of the Divine acting on the world from the fountain light and with the motive power of the spiritual nature,—this is the new inner principle of works which is to transform the old ignorant action. A knowledge which embraces oneness with the Divine and arrives through the Divine at conscious oneness with all things and beings, a will emptied of egoism and acting only by the command and as an instrumentation of the secret Master of works, a divine love whose one aspiration is towards a close intimacy with the supreme Soul of all existence, accomplished by the unity of these three perfected powers an inner all-comprehending unity with the transcendent and universal Spirit and Nature and all creatures are the foundation offered for his activities to the liberated man. For from that foundation the soul in him can suffer the instrumental nature to act in safety; he is lifted above all cause of stumbling, delivered from egoism and its limitations, rescued from all fear of sin and evil and consequence, exalted out of that bondage to the outward nature and the limited action which is the knot of the Ignorance. He can act in the power of the Light, no longer in twilight or darkness, and a divine sanction upholds every step of his conduct. The difficulty which had been raised by the antinomy between the freedom of the Spirit and the bondage of the soul in Nature, has been solved by a luminous reconciliation of Spirit with Nature. That antinomy exists for the mind in the ignorance; it ceases to exist for the spirit in its knowledge.

But there is something more to be said in order to bring out all the meaning of the great spiritual change. The twelfth chapter leads up to this remaining knowledge and the last six that follow develop it to a grand final conclusion. This thing that remains still to be said turns upon the difference between the current Vedantic view of spiritual liberation and the larger comprehensive freedom which the teaching of the Gita opens to the spirit. There is now a pointed return to that difference. The current Vedantic way led through the door of an austere and exclusive knowledge. The Yoga, the oneness which it recognized as the means and the absorbing essence of the spiritual release, was a Yoga of pure knowledge and a still oneness with a supreme Immutable, an absolute Indefinable,—the unmanifested Brah-man, infinite, silent, intangible, aloof, far above all this universe of relations. In the way proposed by the Gita knowledge is indeed the indispensable foundation, but an integral knowledge. Impersonal integral works are the first indispensable means; but a deep and large love and adoration, to which a relationless Unmanifest, an aloof and immovable Brahman can return no answer, since these things ask for a relation and an intimate personal closeness, are the strongest and highest power for re-lease and spiritual perfection and the immortal Ananda. The Godhead with whom the soul of man has to enter into this closest oneness, is indeed in his supreme status a transcendent Unthinkable too great for any manifestation, Parabrahman; but he is at the same time the living supreme Soul of all things. He is the supreme Lord, the Master of works and universal nature. He at once exceeds and inhabits as itself the soul and mind and body of the creature. He is Purushottama, Parameshwara and Paramatman and in all these equal aspects the same single and eternal Godhead. It is an awakening to this integral reconciling knowledge that is the wide gate to the utter release of the soul and an unimaginable perfection of the nature. It is this Godhead in the unity of all his aspects to whom our works and our adoration and our knowledge have to be directed as a constant inner sacrifice. It is this supreme soul, Purushottama, transcendent of the universe, but also its containing spirit, inhabitant and possessor, even as it is mightily figured in the vision of Kurukshetra, into whom the liberated spirit has to enter once it has reached to the vision and knowledge of him in all the principles and powers of his existence, once it is able to grasp and enjoy his multitudinous oneness, jnatum drastum tattvena pravestum ca.

The liberation of the Gita is not a self-oblivious abolition of the soul's personal being in the absorption of the One, sayujya mukti; it is all kinds of union at once. There is an entire unification with the supreme Godhead in essence of being and intimacy of consciousness and identity of bliss, sayujya,—for one object of this Yoga is to become Brahman, brahmabhuta. There is an eternal ecstatic dwelling in the highest existence of the Supreme, salokya,—for it is said, "Thou shalt dwell in me," nivasisyasi mayyeva. There is an eternal love and adoration in a uniting nearness, there is an embrace of the liberated spirit by its divine Lover and the enveloping Self of its infinitudes, samipya. There is an identity of the soul's liberated nature with the divine nature, sadrsya mukti,—for the perfection of the free spirit is to become even as the Divine, madbhavam agatah, and to be one with him in the law of its being and the law of its works and nature, sadharmyam agatah. The orthodox Yoga of knowledge aims at a fathomless immergence in the one infinite existence, sayujya; it looks upon that alone as the entire liberation. The Yoga of adoration envisages an eternal habitation or nearness as the greater release, salokya, samipya. The Yoga of works leads to oneness in power of being and nature, sadrsya. But the Gita envelops them all in its catholic integrality and fuses them all into one greatest and richest divine freedom and perfection.

Arjuna is made to raise the question of this difference. It must be remembered that the distinction between the impersonal immutable Akshara Purusha and the supreme Soul that is at once impersonality and divine Person and much more than either—that this capital distinction implied in the later chapters and in the divine "I" of which Krishna has constantly spoken, aham, mam, has as yet not been quite expressly and definitely drawn. We have been throughout anticipating it in order to understand from the beginning the full significance of the Gita's message and not have to go back again, as we would otherwise be obliged, over the same ground newly seen and prospected in the light of this greater truth. Arjuna has been enjoined first to sink his separate personality in the calm impersonality of the one eternal and immutable self, a teaching which agreed well with his previous notions and offered no difficulties. But now he is confronted with the vision of this greatest transcendent, this widest universal Godhead and commanded to seek oneness with him by knowledge and works and adoration. Therefore, he asks the better to have a doubt cleared which might otherwise have arisen, "Those devotees who thus by a constant union seek after thee, tvam, and those who seek after the unmanifest Immutable, which of these have the greater knowledge of Yoga?" This recalls the distinction made in the beginning by such phrases as "in the self, then in me," atmani atho mayi: Arjuna points the distinction, tvam, aksaram avyaktam. Thou, he says in substance, art the supreme Source and Origin of all beings, a Presence immanent in all things, a Power pervading the universe with thy forms, a Person manifest in thy Vibhutis, manifest in creatures, manifest in Nature, seated as the Lord of works in the world and in our hearts by thy mighty world-Yoga. As such I have to know, adore, unite myself with thee in all my being, consciousness, thoughts, feelings, and actions, satata-yukta. But what then of this Immutable who never manifests, never puts on any form, stands back and apart from all action, enters into no relation with the universe or with anything in it, is eternally silent and one and impersonal and immobile? This eternal Self is the greater Principle according to all current notions and the Godhead in the manifestation is an inferior figure: the unmanifest and not the manifest is the eternal Spirit. How then does the union which admits the manifestation, admits the lesser thing, come yet to be the greater Yoga-knowledge?

To this question Krishna replies with an emphatic decisiveness. "Those who found their mind in Me and by constant union, possessed of a supreme faith, seek after Me, I hold to be the most perfectly in union of Yoga." The supreme faith is that which sees God in all and to its eye the manifestation and the non-manifestation are one Godhead. The perfect union is that which meets the Divine at every moment, in every action and with all the integrality of the nature. But those also who seek by a hard ascent after the indefinable unmanifest Immutable alone, arrive, says the Godhead, to Me. For they are not mistaken in their aim, but they follow a more difficult and a less complete and perfect path. At the easiest, to reach the unmanifest Absolute they have to climb through the manifest Immutable here. This manifest Immutable is my own all-pervading impersonality and silence; vast, unthinkable, immobile, constant, omnipresent, it supports the action of personality but does not share in it. It offers no hold to the mind; it can only be gained by a motionless spiritual impersonality and silence and those who follow after it alone have to restrain altogether and even draw in completely the action of the mind and senses. But still by the equality of their understanding and by their seeing of oneself in all things and by their tranquil benignancy of silent will for the good of all existences they too meet me in all objects and creatures. No less than those who unite themselves with the Divine in all ways of their existence, sarva-bhavena and enter largely and fully into the unthinkable living fountainhead of universal things, divyam purusam acintya-rupam, these seekers too who climb through this more difficult exclusive oneness towards a relationless un-manifest Absolute find in the end the same Eternal. But this is a less direct and more arduous way; it is not the full and natural movement of the spiritualized human nature.

And it must not be thought that because it is more arduous, therefore it is a higher and more effective process. The easier way of the Gita leads more rapidly, naturally, and normally to the same absolute liberation. For its acceptance of the divine Person does not imply any attachment to the mental and sensuous limitations of embodied Nature. On the contrary it brings a swift and effectual unchaining from the phenomenal bondage of death and birth. The Yogin of exclusive knowledge imposes on himself a painful struggle with the manifold demands of his nature; he denies them even their highest satisfaction and cuts away from him even the upward impulses of his spirit whenever they imply relations or fall short of a negating absolute. The living way of the Gita on the contrary finds out the most intense upward trend of all our being and by turning it Godwards uses knowledge, will, feeling and the instinct for perfection as so many puissant wings of a mounting liberation. The unmanifest Brahman in its indefinable unity is a thing to which embodied souls can only arrive and that hardly by a constant mortification, a suffering of all the repressed members, a stern difficulty and anguish of the nature, duhkham avapyate, kleso 'dhikataras tesam. The indefinable Oneness accepts all that climb to it but offers no help of relation and gives no foothold to the climber. All has to be done by a severe austerity and a stern and lonely individual effort. How different is it for those who seek after the Purushottama in the way of the Gita! When they meditate on him with a Yoga which sees no one else, because it sees all to be Vasudeva, he meets them at every point, in every movement, at all times, with innumerable forms and faces, holds up the lamp of knowledge within and floods with its divine and happy lustre the whole of existence. Illumined, they discern the supreme Spirit in every form and face, arrive at once through all Nature to the Lord of Nature, arrive through all beings to the Soul of all being, arrive through themselves to the Self of all that they are incontinently they break through a hundred opening issues at once into that from which everything has its origin. The other method of a difficult relationless stillness tries to get away from all action even though that is impossible to embodied creatures. Here the actions are all given up to the supreme Master of action and he as the supreme Will meets the will of sacrifice, takes from it its burden, and assumes to himself the charge of the works of the divine Nature in us. And when too in the high passion of love the devotee of the Lover and Friend of man and of all creatures' casts upon him all his heart of consciousness and yearning of delight, then swiftly the Supreme comes to him as the saviour and deliverer and exalts him by a happy embrace of his mind and heart and body out of the waves of the sea of death in this mortal nature into the secure bosom of the Eternal.

This then is the swiftest, largest, and greatest way. On me, says the Godhead to the soul of man, repose all thy mind and lodge all thy understanding in me: I will lift them up bathed in the supernal blaze of the divine love and will and knowledge to myself from whom these things flow. Doubt not that thou shalt dwell in me above this mortal existence. The chain of the limiting earthly nature cannot hold the immortal spirit exalted by the passion, the power, and the light of the eternal love, will and knowledge. No doubt, on this way too there are difficulties; for there is the lower nature with its fierce or dull downward gravitation which resists and battles against the motion of ascent and clogs the wings of the exaltation and the upward rapture. The divine consciousness even when it has been found at first in a wonder of great moments or in calm and splendid durations, cannot at once be altogether held or called back at will; there is felt often an inability to keep the personal consciousness fixed steadily in the Divine; there are nights of long exile from the Light, there are hours or moments of revolt, doubt, or failure. But still by the practice of union and by constant repetition of the experience, that highest spirit grows upon the being and takes permanent possession of the nature. Is this also found too difficult because of the power and persistence of the outward-going movement of the mind? Then the way is simple, to do all actions for the sake of the Lord of the action, so that every outward-going movement of the mind shall be associated with the inner spiritual truth of the being and called back even in the very movement to the eternal reality and connected with its source. Then the presence of the Purushottama will grow upon the natural man till he is filled with it and becomes a godhead and a spirit; all life will become a constant remembering of God and perfection too will grow and the unity of the whole existence of the human soul with the supreme Existence.

But it may be that even this constant remembering of God and lifting up of our works to him is felt to be beyond the power of the limited mind, because in its forgetfulness it turns to the act and its outward object and will not remember to look within and lay our every movement on the divine altar of the Spirit. Then the way is to control the lower self in the act and do works without desire of the fruit. All fruit has to be renounced, to be given up to the Power that directs the work and yet the work has to be done that is imposed by It on the nature. For by this means the obstacle steadily diminishes and easily disappears; the mind is left free to remember the Lord and to fix itself in the liberty of the divine consciousness. And here the Gita gives an ascending scale of potencies and assigns the palm of excellence to this Yoga of desireless action. Abhyasa, practice of a method, repetition of an effort and experience is a great and powerful thing; but better than this is knowledge, the successful and luminous turning of the thought to the Truth behind things. This thought-knowledge too is excelled by a silent complete concentration on the Truth so that the consciousness shall eventually live in it and be always one with it. But more powerful still is the giving up of the fruit of one's works because that immediately destroys all causes of disturbance and brings and automatically preserves an inner calm and peace and calm and peace are the foundation on which all else becomes perfect and secure in possession by the tranquil spirit. Then the consciousness can be at ease, happily fix itself in the Divine and rise undisturbed to perfection. Then too knowledge, will and devotion can lift their pinnacles from a firm soil of solid calm into the ether of Eternity.

What then will be the divine nature, what will be the greater state of consciousness and being of the bhakta who has followed this way and turned to the adoration of the Eternal? The Gita in a number of verses rings the changes on its first insistent demand, on equality, on desirelessness, on freedom of spirit. This is to be the base always,—and that was why so much stress was laid on it in the beginning. And in that equality bhakti, the love and adoration of the Purushottama must rear the spirit towards some greatest highest perfection of which this calm equality will be the wide foundation. Several formulas of this fundamental equal consciousness are given here. First, an absence of egoism, of I-ness and my-ness, nirmamo nirahankarah. The bhakta of the Purushottama is one who has a universal heart and mind which has broken down all the narrow walls of the ego. A universal love dwells in his heart, a universal compassion flows from it like an encompassing sea. He will have friendship and pity for all beings and hate for no living thing: for he is patient, long-suffering, enduring, a well of forgiveness. A desireless content is his, a tranquil equality to pleasure and pain, suffering and happiness, the steadfast control of self and the firm unshakable will and resolution of the Yogin and a love and devotion which gives up the whole mind and reason to the Lord, to the Master of his consciousness and knowledge. Or, simply, he will be one who is freed from the troubled agitated lower nature and from its waves of joy and fear and anxiety and resentment and desire, a spirit of calm by whom the world is not afflicted or troubled, nor is he afflicted or troubled by the world, a soul of peace with whom all are at peace.

Or he will be one who has given up all desire and action to the Master of his being, one pure and still, indifferent to whatever comes, not pained or afflicted by any result or happening, one who has flung away from him all egoistic, personal and mental initiative whether of the inner or the outer act, one who lets the divine will and divine knowledge flow through him undeflected by his own resolves, preferences and desires, and yet for that very reason is swift and skillful in all action of his nature because this flawless unity with the supreme will, this pure instrumentation is the condition of the greatest skill in works. Again, he will be one who neither desires the pleasant and rejoices at its touch nor abhors the unpleasant and sorrows at its burden. He has abolished the distinction between fortunate and unfortunate happenings, because his devotion receives all things equally as good from the hands of his eternal Lover and Master. The God-lover dear to God is a soul of wide equality, equal to friend and enemy, equal to honour and insult, pleasure and pain, praise and blame, grief and happiness, heat and cold, to all that troubles with opposite affections the normal nature. He will have no attachment to person or thing, place, or home; he will be content and well-satisfied with whatever surroundings, whatever relation men adopt to him, whatever station, or fortune. He will keep a mind firm in all things because it is constantly seated in the highest self and fixed for ever on the one divine object of his love and adoration. Equality, desirelessness and freedom from the lower egoistic nature and its claims are always the one perfect foundation demanded by the Gita for the great liberation. There is to the end an emphatic repetition of its first fundamental teaching and original desideratum, the calm soul of knowledge that sees the oneself in all things, the tranquil egoless equality that results from this knowledge, the desireless action offered in that equality to the Master of works, the surrender of the whole mental nature of man into the hands of the mightier indwelling spirit. And the crown of this equality is love founded on knowledge, fulfilled in instrumental action, extended to all things and beings, a vast absorbing and all-containing love for the divine Self who is Creator and Master of the universe, suhrdam sarva-bhutanam sarva-loka-mahesvaram.

This is the foundation, the condition, the means by which the supreme spiritual perfection is to be won, and those who have it in any way are all dear to me, says the Godhead, bhaktiman¯me priyah. But exceedingly dear, atıva¯me priyah, are those souls nearest to the Godhead whose love of me is completed by the still wider and greatest perfection of which I have just shown to you the way and the process. These are the bhaktas who make the Purushottama their one supreme aim and follow out with a perfect faith and exactitude the immortalizing Dharma described in this teaching. Dharma in the language of the Gita means the innate law of the being and its works and an action proceeding from and determined by the inner nature, svabhava-niyatam karma. In the lower ignorant consciousness of mind, life and body there are many dharmas, many rules, many standards and laws because there are many varying determinations and types of the mental, vital, and physical nature. The immortal Dharma is one; it is that of the highest spiritual divine consciousness and its powers, para¯ prakrtih. It is beyond the three gunas, and to reach it all these lower dharmas have to be abandoned, sarva-dharman parityajya.

Alone in their place the one liberating unifying consciousness and power of the Eternal has to become the infinite source of our action, its mould, determinant and exemplar. To rise out of our lower personal egoism, to enter into the impersonal and equal calm of the immutable eternal all-pervading Akshara Purusha, to aspire from that calm by a perfect self-surrender of all one's nature and existence to that which is other and higher than the Akshara, is the first necessity of this Yoga. In the strength of that aspiration one can rise to the immortal Dharma. There, made one in being, consciousness and divine bliss with the greatest Uttama Purusha, made one with his supreme dynamic nature-force, sva prakrtih, the liberated spirit can know infinitely, love illimitably, act unfalteringly in the authentic power of a highest immortality and a perfect freedom. The rest of the Gita is written to throw a fuller light on this immortal Dharma.

PART II

THE SUPREME SECRET

XIII

THE FIELD AND ITS KNOWER[1]

The Gita in its last six chapters, in order to found on a clear and complete knowledge the way of the soul's rising out of the lower into the divine nature, restates in another form the enlightenment the Teacher has already imparted to Arjuna. Essentially it is the same knowledge, but details and relations are now made prominent and assigned their entire significance, thoughts and truths brought out in their full value that were alluded to only in passing or generally stated in the light of another purpose. Thus, in the first six chapters the knowledge necessary for the distinction between the immutable self and the soul veiled in nature was accorded an entire prominence. The references to the supreme Self and Purusha were summary and not at all explicit; it was assumed in order to justify works in the world and it was affirmed to be the Master of being, but there was otherwise nothing to show what it was and its relations to the rest were not even hinted at, much less developed. The remaining chapters are devoted to the bringing out of this suppressed knowledge in a conspicuous light and strong pre-eminence. It is to the Lord, the Ishwara, it is to the distinction of the higher and the lower nature and to the vision

1 Gita, XIII.

of the all-originating and all-constituting Godhead in Nature, it is to the One in all beings that prominence has been assigned in the next six Adhyayas (7-12) in order to find a root-unity of works and love with knowledge. But now it is necessary to bring out more definitely the precise relations between the supreme Purusha, the immutable self, the Jiva, and Prakriti in her action and her gunas. Arjuna is therefore made to put a question which shall evoke a clearer elucidation of these still ill-lighted matters. He asks to learn of the Purusha and the Prakriti; he inquires of the field of being and the knower of the field and of knowledge and the object of knowledge. Here is contained the sum of all the knowledge of self and the world that is still needed if the soul is to throw off its natural ignorance and staying its steps on a right use of knowledge, of life, of works and of its own relations with the Divine in these things ascend into unity of being with the eternal Spirit of existence.

The essence of the Gita's ideas in these matters has already, anticipating the final evolution of its thought, been elucidated in a certain measure; but, following its example, we may state them again from the point of view of its present preoccupation. Action being admitted, a divine action done with self-knowledge as the instrument of the divine Will in the cosmos being accepted as perfectly consistent with the Brahmic status and an indispensable part of the Godward movement, that action being uplifted inwardly as a sacrifice with adoration to the Highest, how does this way practically affect the great object of spiritual life, the rising from the lower into the higher nature, from mortal into immortal being? All life, all works are a transaction between the soul and Nature. What is the original character of that transaction? what does it become at its spiritual culminating point? to what perfection does it lead the soul that gets free from its lower and external motives and grows inwardly into the very highest poise of the Spirit and deepest motive-force of the works of its energy in the universe? These are the questions involved,—there are others which the Gita does not raise or answer, for they were not pressingly present to the human mind of that day,—and they are replied to in the sense of the solution drawn from a large-sighted combination of the Vedantic, Sankhya and Yoga views of existence which is the starting-point of the whole thought of the Gita.

The Soul which finds itself here embodied in Nature has a triple reality to its own self-experience. First it is a spiritual being apparently subjected by ignorance to the outward workings of Prakriti and represented in her mobility as an acting, thinking, mutable personality, a creature of Nature, an ego. Next when it gets behind all this action and motion, it finds its own higher reality to be an eternal and impersonal self and immutable spirit which has no other share in the action and movement than to support it by its presence and regard it as an undisturbed equal witness. And last, when it looks beyond these two opposite selves, it discovers a greater ineffable Reality from which both proceed, the Eternal who is Self of the self and the Master of all Nature and all action, and not only the Master, but the origin and the spiritual support and scene of these workings of his own energy in Cosmos, and not only the origin and spiritual container but the spiritual inhabitant in all forces, in all things and in all beings, and not only the inhabitant but, by the developments of this eternal energy of his being which we call Nature, himself all energies and forces, all things and all beings. This Nature itself is of two kinds, one derived and inferior, another original and supreme. There is a lower nature of the cosmic mechanism by association with which the soul in Prakriti lives in a certain ignorance born of Maya, traigunyamayi maya, conceives of itself as an ego of embodied mind and life, works under the power of the modes of Nature, thinks itself bound, suffering, limited by personality, chained to the obligation of birth and the wheel of action, a thing of desires, transient, mortal, a slave of its own nature. Above this inferior power of existence there is a higher divine and spiritual nature of its own true being in which this soul is forever a conscious portion of the Eternal and Divine, blissful, free, superior to its mask of becoming, immortal, imperishable, a power of the Godhead. To rise by this higher nature to the Eternal through divine knowledge, love and works founded on a spiritual universality is the key of the complete spiritual liberation. This much has been made clear; and we have to see now more in detail what farther considerations this change of being involves and especially what is the difference between these two natures and how our action and our soul-status are affected by the liberation. For that purpose, the Gita enters largely into certain details of the highest knowledge which it had hitherto kept in the background. Especially it dwells on the relation between Being and becoming, Soul and Nature, the action of the three gunas, the highest liberation, the largest fullest self-giving of the human soul to the Divine Spirit. There is in all that it says in these closing six chapters much of the greatest importance, but it is the last thought with which it closes that is of supreme interest; for in it we shall find the central idea of its teaching, its great word to the soul of man, its highest message.

First, the whole of existence must be regarded as a field of the soul's construction and action in the midst of Nature. The Gita explains the ksetram, field, by saying that it is this body, which is called the field of the spirit, and in this body, there is someone who takes cognizance of the field, ksetrajna, the knower of Nature. It is evident, however, from the definitions that succeed that it is not the physical body alone which is the field, but all too that the body supports, the working of nature, the mentality, the natural action of the objectivity and subjectivity of our being.[2] This wider body too is only the individual field; there is a larger, a universal, a world-body, a world-field of the same Knower.

---

2 The Upanishad speaks of a fivefold body or sheath of Nature, a physical, vital, mental, ideal, and divine body; this may be regarded as the totality of the field, ksetram.

For in each embodied creature there is this one Knower: in each existence he uses mainly and centrally this single outward result of the power of his nature which he has formed for his habitation, isa¯vasyam sarvam yat kinca, makes each separate sustained knot of his mobile Energy the first base and scope of his developing harmonies. In Nature he knows the world as it affects and is reflected by the consciousness in this one limited body; the world exists to us as it is seen in our single mind,—and in the end, even, this seemingly small, embodied consciousness can so enlarge itself that it contains in itself the whole universe, atmani visva-darsanam. But physically, it is a microcosm in a macrocosm, and the macrocosm too, the large world too, is a body and field inhabited by the spiritual knower.

That becomes evident when the Gita proceeds to state the character, nature, source, deformations, powers of this sensible embodiment of our being. We see then that it is the whole working of the lower Prakriti that is meant by the ksetra. That totality is the field of action of the embodied spirit here within us, the field of which it takes cognizance. For a varied and detailed knowledge of all this world of Nature in its essential action as seen from the spiritual viewpoint we are referred to the verses of the ancient seers, the seers of the Veda and Upanishads, in which we get the inspired and intuitive account of these creations of the Spirit, and to the Brahma Sutras which will give us the rational and philosophic analysis. The Gita contents itself with a brief practical statement of the lower nature of our being in the terms of the Sankhya thinkers. First there is the indiscriminate unmanifest Energy; out of that has come the objective evolution of the five elemental states of matter; as also the subjective evolution of the senses, intelligence and ego; there are too five objects of the senses, or rather five different ways of sense cognizance of the world, powers evolved by the universal energy in order to deal with all the forms of things she has created from the five elemental states assumed by her original objective substance,—organic relations by which the ego endowed with intelligence and sense acts on the formations of the cosmos: this is the constitution of the kshetra. Then there is a general consciousness that first informs and then illumines the Energy in its works; there is a faculty of that consciousness by which the Energy holds together the relations of objects; there is too a continuity, a persistence of the subjective and objective relations of our consciousness with its objects. These are the necessary powers of the field; all these are common and universal powers at once of the mental, vital, and physical Nature. Pleasure and pain, liking and disliking are the principal deformations of the kshetra. From the Vedantic point of view we may say that pleasure and pain are the vital or sensational deformations given by the lower energy to the spontaneous Ananda or delight of the spirit when brought into contact with her workings. And we may say from the same viewpoint that liking and disliking are the corresponding mental deformations given by her to the reactive Will of the spirit that determines its response to her contacts. These dualities are the positive and negative terms in which the ego soul of the lower nature enjoys the universe. The negative terms, pain, dislike, sorrow, repulsion, and the rest, are perverse or at the best ignorantly reverse responses: the positive terms, liking, pleasure, joy, attraction, are ill-guided responses or at the best insufficient and in character inferior to those of the true spiritual experience.

All these things taken together constitute the fundamental character of our first transactions with the world of Nature, but it is evidently not the whole description of our being; it is our actuality but not the limit of our possibilities. There is something beyond to be known, jneyam and it is when the knower of the field turns from the field itself to learn of himself within it and of all that is behind its appearances that real knowledge begins, jnanam,—the true knowledge of the field no less than of the knower. That turning inward alone delivers from ignorance. For the farther we go inward, the more we seize on greater and fuller realities of things and grasp the complete truth both of

God and the soul and of the world and its movements. Therefore, says the divine Teacher, it is the knowledge at once of the field and its knower, ksetra-ksetrajnayor jnanam, a united and even unified self-knowledge and world-knowledge, which is the real illumination and the only wisdom. For both soul and nature are the Brahman, but the true truth of the world of Nature can only be discovered by the liberated sage who also possesses the truth of the spirit. One Brahman, one reality in Self and Nature is the object of all knowledge.

The Gita then tells us what is the spiritual knowledge or rather it tells us what are the conditions of knowledge, the marks, the signs of the man whose soul is turned towards the inner wisdom. These signs are the recognized and traditional characteristics of the sage,—his strong turning away of the heart from attachment to outward and worldly things, his inward and brooding spirit, his steady mind and calm equality, the settled fixity of his thought and will upon the greatest inmost truths, upon the things that are real and eternal. First, there comes a certain moral condition, a sattwic government of the natural being. There is fixed in him a total absence of worldly pride and arrogance, a candid soul, a tolerant, long-suffering and benignant heart, purity of mind and body, tranquil firmness and steadfastness, self-control and a masterful government of the lower nature and the heart's worship given to the Teacher, whether to the divine Teacher within or to the human Master in whom the divine Wisdom is embodied,—for that is the sense of the reverence given to the Guru. Then there is a nobler and freer attitude towards the outward world, an attitude of perfect detachment and equality, a firm removal of the natural being's attraction to the objects of the senses and a radical freedom from the claims of that constant clamorous ego-sense, ego-idea, ego-motive which tyrannizes over the normal man. There is no longer any clinging to the attachment and absorption of family and home. There is instead of these vital and animal movements an unattached will and sense and intelligence, a keen perception of the defective nature of the ordinary life of physical man with its aimless and painful subjection to birth and death and disease and age, a constant equalness to all pleasant or unpleasant happenings,—for the soul is seated within and impervious to the shocks of external events,—and a meditative mind turned towards solitude and away from the vain noise of crowds and the assemblies of men. Finally, there is a strong turn within towards the things that really matter, a philosophic perception of the true sense and large principles of existence, a tranquil continuity of inner spiritual knowledge and light, the Yoga of an unswerving devotion, love of God, the heart's deep and constant adoration of the universal and eternal Presence.

The one object to which the mind of spiritual knowledge must be turned is the Eternal by fixity in whom the soul clouded here and swathed in the mists of Nature recovers and enjoys its native and original consciousness of immortality and transcendence. To be fixed on the transient, to be limited in the phenomenon is to accept mortality; the constant truth in things that perish is that in them which is inward and immutable. The soul when it allows itself to be tyrannized over by the appearances of Nature, misses itself and goes whirling about in the cycle of the births and deaths of its bodies. There, passionately following without end the mutations of personality and its interests, it cannot draw back to the possession of its impersonal and unborn self-existence. To be able to do that is to find oneself and get back to one's true being, that which assumes these births but does not perish with the perishing of its forms. To enjoy the eternity to which birth and life are only outward circumstances, is the soul's true immortality and transcendence. That Eternal or that Eternity is the Brahman. Brahman is That which is transcendent and That which is universal: it is the free spirit who supports in front the play of soul with nature and assures behind their imperishable oneness; it is at once the mutable and the immutable, the All that is the One. In his highest supracosmic status Brahman is a transcendent Eternity without origin or change far above the phenomenal oppositions of existence and non-existence, persistence, and transience between which the outward world moves. But once seen in the substance and light of this eternity, the world also becomes other than it seems to the mind and senses; for then we see the universe no longer as a whirl of mind and life and matter or a mass of the determinations of energy and substance but as no other than this eternal Brahman. A spirit who immeasurably fills and surrounds all this movement with himself—for indeed the movement too is himself—and who throws on all that is finite the splendour of his garment of infinity, a bodiless and million-bodied spirit whose hands of strength and feet of swiftness are on every side of us, whose heads and eyes and faces are those innumerable visages which we see wherever we turn, whose ear is everywhere listening to the silence of eternity and the music of the worlds, is the universal Being in whose embrace we live.

All relations of Soul and Nature are circumstances in the eternity of Brahman; sense and quality, their reflectors, and constituents, are this supreme Soul's devices for the presentation of the workings that his own energy in things constantly liberates into movement. He is himself beyond the limitation of the senses, sees all things but not with the physical eye, hears all things but not with the physical ear, is aware of all things but not with the limiting mind—mind which represents but cannot truly know. Not determined by any qualities, he possesses and determines in his substance all qualities and enjoys this qualitative action of his own Nature. He is attached to nothing, bound by nothing, fixed to nothing that he does; calm, he supports in a large and immortal freedom all the action and movement and passion of his universal Shakti. He becomes all that is in the universe; that which is in us is he and all that we experience outside ourselves is he. The inward and the outward, the far and the near, the moving and the unmoving, all this he is at once. He is the subtlety of the subtle which is beyond our knowledge, even as he is the density of force and substance which offers itself to the grasp of our minds. He is indivisible and the One but seems to divide himself in forms and creatures and appears as all these separate existences. All things can get back in him, can return in the Spirit to the indivisible unity of their self-existence. All is eternally born from him, upborne in his eternity, taken eternally back into his oneness. He is the light of all lights and luminous beyond all the darkness of our ignorance. He is knowledge and the object of knowledge. The spiritual supramental knowledge that floods the illumined mind and transfigures it is this spirit manifesting himself in light to the force-obscured soul which he has put forth into the action of Nature. This eternal Light is in the heart of every being; it is he who is the secret knower of the field, ksetrajna, and presides as the Lord in the heart of things over this province and over all these kingdoms of his manifested becoming and action. When man sees this eternal and universal Godhead within himself, when he becomes aware of the soul in all things and discovers the spirit in Nature, when he feels all the universe as a wave mounting in this Eternity and all that is as the one existence, he puts on the light of Godhead and stands free in the midst of the worlds of Nature. A divine knowledge and a perfect turning with adoration to this Divine is the secret of the great spiritual liberation. Freedom, love, and spiritual knowledge raise us from mortal nature to immortal being.

The Soul and Nature are only two aspects of the eternal Brahman, an apparent duality which founds the operations of his universal existence. The Soul is without origin and eternal, Nature too is without origin and eternal; but the modes of Nature and the lower forms she assumes to our conscious experience have an origin in the transactions of these two entities. They come from her, wear by her the outward chain of cause and effect, doing and the results of doing, force, and its workings, all that is here transient and mutable. Constantly they change and the soul and Nature seem to change with them, but in themselves these two powers are eternal and always the same. Nature creates and acts, the Soul enjoys her creation and action but in this inferior form of her action she turns this enjoyment into the obscure and petty figures of pain and pleasure. Forcibly the soul, the individual Purusha, is attracted by her qualitative workings and this attraction of her qualities draws him constantly to births of all kinds in which he enjoys the variations and vicissitudes, the good and evil of birth in Nature. But this is only the outward experience of the soul mutable in conception by identification with mutable Nature. Seated in this body is her and our Divinity, the supreme Self, Paramatman, the supreme Soul, the mighty Lord of Nature, who watches her action, sanctions her operations, upholds all she does, commands her manifold creation, enjoys with his universal delight this play of her figures of his own being. That is the self-knowledge to which we have to accustom our mentality before we can truly know ourselves as an eternal portion of the Eternal. Once that is fixed, no matter how the soul in us may comport itself outwardly in its transactions with Nature, whatever it may seem to do or however it may seem to assume this or that figure of personality and active force and embodied ego, it is in itself free, no longer bound to birth because one through impersonality of self with the inner unborn spirit of existence. That impersonality is our union with the supreme egoless I of all that is in cosmos.

This knowledge comes by an inner meditation through which the eternal self becomes apparent to us in our own self-existence. Or it comes by the Yoga of the Sankhyas, the separation of the soul from nature. Or it comes by the Yoga of works in which the personal will is dissolved through the opening up of our mind and heart and all our active forces to the Lord who assumes to himself the whole of our works in nature. The spiritual knowledge may be awakened by the urging of the spirit within us, its call to this or that Yoga, this or that way of oneness. Or it may come to us by hearing of the truth from others and the moulding of the mind into the sense of that to which it listens with faith and concentration. But however, arrived at, it carries us beyond death to immortality. Knowledge shows us high above the mutable transactions of the soul with the mortality of nature our highest Self as the supreme Lord of her actions, one and equal in all objects and creatures, not born in the taking up of a body, not subject to death in the perishing of all these bodies. That is the true seeing, the seeing of that in us which is eternal and immortal. As we perceive more and more this equal spirit in all things, we pass into that equality of the spirit; as we dwell more and more in this universal being, we become ourselves universal beings; as we grow more and more aware of this eternal, we put on our own eternity and are forever. We identify ourselves with the eternity of the self and no longer with the limitation and distress of our mental and physical ignorance. Then we see that all our works are an evolution and operation of Nature and our real self not the executive doer, but the free witness and lord and unattached enjoyer of the action. All this surface of cosmic movement is a diverse becoming of natural existences in the one eternal Being, all is extended, manifested, rolled out by the universal Energy from the seeds of her Idea deep in his existence; but the spirit even though it takes up and enjoys her workings in this body of ours, is not affected by its mortality because it is eternal beyond birth and death, is not limited by the personalities which it multiply assumes in her because it is the one supreme self of all these personalities, is not changed by the mutations of quality because it is itself undetermined by quality, does not act even in action, kartaram api akartaram because it supports natural action in a perfect spiritual freedom from its effects, is the originator indeed of all activities, but in no way changed or affected by the play of its Nature. As the all-pervading ether is not affected or changed by the multiple forms it assumes, but remains always the same pure subtle original substance, even so this spirit when it has done and become all possible things, remains through it all the same pure immutable subtle infinite essence. That is the supreme status of the soul, para gatih, that is the divine being and nature, madbhava and whoever arrives at spiritual knowledge, rises to that supreme immortality of the Eternal.

This Brahman, this eternal and spiritual knower of the field of his own natural becoming, this Nature, his perpetual energy, which converts herself into that field, this immortality of the soul in mortal nature,—these things together make the whole reality of our existence. The spirit within, when we turn to it, illumines the entire field of Nature with its own truth in all the splendour of its rays. In the light of that sun of knowledge the eye of knowledge opens in us, and we live in that truth and no longer in this ignorance. Then we perceive that our limitation to our present mental and physical nature was an error of the darkness, then we are liberated from the law of the lower Prakriti, the law of the mind and body, then we attain to the supreme nature of the spirit. That splendid and lofty change is the last, the divine and infinite becoming, the putting off of mortal nature, the putting on of an immortal existence.

XIV

ABOVE THE GUNAS[1]

THE DISTINCTIONS between the Soul and Nature rapidly drawn in the verses of the thirteenth chapter by a few decisive epithets, a few briefs but packed characterizations

of their separate power and functioning, and especially the distinction between the embodied soul subjected to the action of Nature by its enjoyment of her gunas, qualities or modes and the Supreme Soul which dwells enjoying the gunas, but not subject because it is itself beyond them, are the basis on which the Gita rests its whole idea of the liberated being made one in the conscious law of its existence with the Divine. That liberation, that oneness, that putting on of the divine nature, sadharmya, it declares to be the very essence of spiritual freedom and the whole significance of immortality. This supreme importance assigned to sadharmya is a capital point in the teaching of the Gita.

To be immortal was never held in the ancient spiritual teaching to consist merely in a personal survival of the death of the body: all beings are immortal in that sense, and it is only the forms that perish. The souls that do not arrive at liberation, live through the returning aeons; all exist involved or secret in the Brahman during the dissolution of the manifest worlds and are born again in the

1 Gita, XIV.

appearance of a new cycle. Pralaya, the end of a cycle of aeons, is the temporary disintegration of a universal form of existence and of all the individual forms which move in its rounds, but that is only a momentary pause, a silent interval followed by an outburst of new creation, reintegration, and reconstruction in which they reappear and recover the impetus of their progression. Our physical death is also a pralaya,—the Gita will presently use the word in the sense of this death, pralayam yati deha-bhrt, "the soul bearing the body comes to a pralaya," to a disintegration of that form of matter with which its ignorance identified its being and which now dissolves into the natural elements. But the soul itself persists and after an interval resumes in a new body formed from those elements its round of births in the cycle, just as after the interval of pause and cessation the universal Being resumes his endless round of the cyclic aeons. This immortality in the rounds of Time is common to all embodied spirits.

To be immortal in the deeper sense is something different from this survival of death and this constant recurrence. Immortality is that supreme status in which the Spirit knows itself to be superior to death and birth, not conditioned by the nature of its manifestation, infinite, imperishable, immutably eternal,—immortal, because never being born it never dies. The divine Purushottama, who is the supreme Lord and supreme Brahman, possesses forever this immortal eternity and is not affected by his taking up a body or by his continuous assumption of cosmic forms and powers because he exists always in this self-knowledge. His very nature is to be unchangeably conscious of his own eternity; he is self-aware without end or beginning. He is here the Inhabitant of all bodies, but as the unborn in everybody, not limited in his consciousness by that manifestation, not identified with the physical nature which he assumes; for that is only a minor circumstance of his universal activised play of existence. Liberation, immortality is to live in this unchangeably conscious eternal being of the Purushottama.2[2] But to arrive here at this greater spiritual immortality the embodied soul must cease to live according to the law of the lower nature; it must put on the law of the Divine's supreme way of existence which is in fact the real law of its own eternal essence. In the spiritual evolution of its becoming, no less than in its secret original being, it must grow into the likeness of the Divine.

And this great thing, to rise from the human into the divine nature, we can only do by an effort of Godward knowledge, will and adoration. For the soul sent forth by the Supreme as his eternal portion, his immortal representative into the workings of universal Nature is yet obliged by the character of those workings, avasam prakrter vasat, to identify itself in its external consciousness with her limiting conditions, to identify itself with a life, mind and body that are oblivious of their inner spiritual reality and of the innate Godhead. To get back to self-knowledge and to the knowledge of the real as distinct from the apparent relations of the soul with Nature, to know God and ourselves, and the world with a spiritual and no longer with a physical or externalized experience, through the deepest truth of the inner soul-consciousness and not through the misleading phenomenal significances of the sense-mind and the outward understanding, is an indispensable means of this perfection. Perfection cannot come without self-knowledge and God-knowledge and a spiritual

---

2 Mark that nowhere in the Gita is there any indication that dissolution of the individual spiritual being into the unmanifest, indefinable or absolute Brahman, avyaktam anirdesyam, is the true meaning or condition of immortality or the true aim of Yoga. On the contrary it describes immortality later on as an indwelling in the Ishwara in his supreme status, mayi nivasisyasi, param dhama, and here as sadharmya, param siddhim, a supreme perfection, a becoming of one law of being and nature with the Supreme, persistent still in existence and conscious of the universal movement but above it, as all the sages still exist, munayah sarve, not bound to birth in the creation, not troubled by the dissolution of the cycles.

attitude towards our natural existence, and that is why the ancient wisdom laid so much stress on salvation by knowledge,—not an intellectual cognizance of things, but a growing of man the mental being into a greater spiritual consciousness. The soul's salvation cannot come without the soul's perfection, without its growing into the divine nature; the impartial Godhead will not effect, it for us by an act of caprice or an arbitrary sanad of his favour. Divine works are effective for salvation because they lead us towards this perfection and to a knowledge of self and nature and God by a growing unity with the inner Master of our existence. Divine love is effective because by it we grow into the likeness of the sole and supreme object of our adoration and call down the answering love of the Highest to flood us with the light of his knowledge and the uplifting power and purity of his eternal spirit. Therefore, says the Gita, this is the supreme knowledge and the highest of all knowing's because it leads to the highest perfection and spiritual status, param siddhim and brings the soul to likeness with the Divine, sadharmya. It is the eternal wisdom, the great spiritual experience by which all the sages attained to that highest perfection, grew into one law of being with the Supreme and live forever in his eternity, not born in the creation, not troubled by the anguish of the universal dissolution. This perfection, then, this sadharmya is the way of immortality and the indispensable condition without which the soul cannot consciously live in the Eternal.

The soul of man could not grow into the likeness of the Divine, if it were not in its secret essence imperishably one with the Divine and part and parcel of his divinity: it could not be or become immortal if it were merely a creature of mental, vital and physical Nature. All existence is a manifestation of the divine Existence and that which is within us is spirit of the eternal Spirit. We have come indeed into the lower material nature and are under its influence, but we have come there from the supreme spiritual nature: this inferior imperfect status is our apparent, but that our real being.

The Eternal puts all this movement forth as his self-creation. He is at once the Father and Mother of the universe; the substance of the infinite Idea, vijnana, the Mahad Brahman, is the womb into which he casts the seed of his self-conception. As the Over-Soul he casts the seed; as the Mother, the Nature-Soul, the Energy filled with his conscious power, he receives it into this infinite substance of being made pregnant with his illimitable, yet self-limiting Idea. He receives into this Vast of self-conception and develops there the divine embryo into mental and physical form of existence born from the original act of conceptive creation. All we see springs from that act of creation; but that which is born here is only finite idea and form of the unborn and infinite. The Spirit is eternal and superior to all its manifestation: Nature, eternal without beginning in the Spirit, proceeds for ever with the rhythm of the cycles by unending act of creation and unconcluding act of cessation; the Soul too which takes on this or that form in Nature, is no less eternal than she, anadi ubhav api. Even while in Nature it follows the unceasing round of the cycles, it is, in the Eternal from which it proceeds into them, forever raised above the terms of birth and death, and even in its apparent consciousness here it can become aware of that innate and constant transcendence.

What is it then that makes the difference, what is it that gets the soul into the appearance of birth and death and bondage,—for this is patent that it is only an appearance? It is a subordinate act or state of consciousness, it is a self-oblivious identification with the modes of Nature in the limited workings of this lower motivity and with this self-wrapped ego-bounded knot of action of the mind, life and body. To rise above the modes of Nature, to be traigunyatita, is indispensable, if we are to get back into our fully conscious being away from the obsessing power of the lower action and to put on the free nature of the spirit and its eternal immortality. That condition of the sadharmya is what the Gita next proceeds to develop. It has already alluded to it and laid it down with a brief emphasis in a previous chapter; but it has now to indicate more precisely what are these modes, these gunas, how they bind the soul and keep it back from spiritual freedom and what is meant by rising above the modes of Nature.

The modes of Nature are all qualitative in their essence and are called for that reason its gunas or qualities. In any spiritual conception of the universe this must be so because the connecting medium between spirit and matter must be psyche or soul power and the primary action psychological and qualitative, not physical, and quantitative; for quality is the immaterial, the more spiritual element in all the action of the universal Energy, her prior dynamics. The predominance of physical Science has accustomed us to a different view of Nature because there the first thing that strikes us is the importance of the quantitative aspect of her workings and her dependence for the creation of forms on quantitative combinations and dispositions. And yet even there the discovery that matter is rather substance or act of energy than energy a motive power of self-existent material substance or an inherent power acting in matter has led to some revival of an older reading of universal Nature. The analysis of the ancient Indian thinkers allowed for the quantitative action of Nature, matra; but that it regarded as proper to its more objective and formally executive working, while the innately ideative executive power which disposes things according to the quality of their being and energy, guna, svabhava, is the primary determinant and underlies all the outer quantitative dispositions. In the basis of the physical world this is not apparent only because there the underlying ideative spirit, the Mahad Brahman, is overlaid and hidden up by the movement of matter and material energy. But even in the physical world the miraculous varying results of different combinations and quantities of elements otherwise identical with each other admits of no conceivable explanation if there is not a superior power of variative quality of which these material dispositions are only the convenient mechanical devices. Or let us say at once, there must be a secret ideative capacity of the universal energy, vijnana,—even if we suppose that energy and its instrumental idea, buddhi, to be themselves mechanical in their nature,—which fixes the mathematics and decides the resultants of these outer dispositions: it is the omnipotent Idea in the spirit which invents and makes use of these devices. And in the vital and mental existence quality at once openly appears as the primary power and amount of energy is only a secondary factor. But in fact, the mental, the vital, the physical existence are all subject to the limitations of quality, all are governed by its determinations, even though that truth seems more and more obscured as we descend the scale of existence. Only the Spirit, which by the power of its idea-being and its idea-force called mahat and vijnana fixes these conditions, is not so determined, not subject to any limitations either of quality or quantity because its immeasurable and indeterminable infinity is superior to the modes which it develops and uses for its creation.

But, again, the whole qualitative action of Nature, so infinitely intricate in its detail and variety, is figured as cast into the mould of three general modes of quality everywhere present, intertwined, almost inextricable, sattva, rajas, tamas. These modes are described in the Gita only by their psychological action in man, or incidentally in things such as food according as they produce a psychological or vital effect on human beings. If we look for a more general definition, we shall perhaps catch a glimpse of it in the symbolic idea of Indian religion which attributes each of these qualities respectively to one member of the cosmic Trinity, sattwa to the preserver Vishnu, rajas to the creator Brahma, tamas to the destroyer Rudra. Looking behind this idea for the rationale of the triple ascription, we might define the three modes or qualities in terms of the motion of the universal Energy as Nature's three concomitant and inseparable powers of equilibrium, kinesis, and inertia. But that is only their appearance in terms of the external action of Force. It is otherwise if we regard consciousness and force as twin terms of the one Existence, always coexistent in the reality of being, however in the primal outward phenomenon of material Nature light of consciousness may seem to disappear in a vast action of nescient unillumined energy, while at an opposite pole of spiritual quiescence action of force may seem to disappear in the stillness of the observing or witness consciousness. These two conditions are the two extremes of an apparently separated Purusha and Prakriti, but each at its extreme point does not abolish but at the most only conceals its eternal mate in the depths of its own characteristic way of being. Therefore, since consciousness is always there even in an apparently inconscient Force, we must find a corresponding psychological power of these three modes which informs their more outward executive action. On their psychological side the three qualities may be defined, tamas as Nature's power of nescience, rajas as her power of active seeking ignorance enlightened by desire and impulsion, sattwa as her power of possessing and harmonizing knowledge.

The three qualitative modes of Nature are inextricably intertwined in all cosmic existence. Tamas, the principle of inertia, is a passive and inert nescience which suffers all shocks and contacts without any effort of mastering response and by itself would lead to a disintegration of the whole action of the energy and a radical dispersion of substance. But it is driven by the kinetic power of rajas and even in the nescience of Matter is met and embraced by an innate though unpossessed preserving principle of harmony and balance and knowledge. Material energy appears to be tamasic in its basic action, jada, nescient, mechanic and in movement disintegrative. But it is dominated by a huge force and impulsion of mute rajasic kinesis which drives it, even in and even by its dispersion and disintegration, to build and create and again by a sattwic ideative element in its apparently inconscient force which is always imposing a harmony and preservative order on the two opposite tendencies. Rajas, the principle of creative endeavour and motion and impulsion in Prakriti, kinesis, pravrtti, so seen in Matter, appears more evidently as a conscious or half-conscious passion of seeking and desire and action in the dominant character of Life,—for that passion is the nature of all vital existence. And it would lead by itself in its own nature to a persistent but always mutable and unstable life and activity and creation without any settled result. But met on one side by the disintegrating power of tamas with death and decay and inertia, its ignorant action is on the other side of its functioning settled and harmonized and sustained by the power of sattwa, subconscient in the lower forms of life, more and more conscient in the emergence of mentality, most conscious in the effort of the evolved intelligence figuring as will and reason in the fully developed mental being. Sattwa, the principle of understanding knowledge and of according to assimilation, measure, and equilibrium, which by itself would lead only to some lasting concord of fixed and luminous harmonies, is in the motions of this world impelled to follow the mutable strife and action of the eternal kinesis and constantly overpowered or hedged in by the forces of inertia and nescience. This is the appearance of a world governed by the interlocked and mutually limited play of the three qualitative modes of Nature.

The Gita applies this generalized analysis of the universal Energy to the psychological nature of man in relation to his bondage to Prakriti and the realisation of spiritual freedom. Sattwa, it tells us, is by the purity of its quality a cause of light and illumination and by virtue of that purity it produces no disease or morbidity or suffering in the nature. When into all the doors in the body there comes a flooding of light, as if the doors and windows of a closed house were opened to sunshine, a light of understanding, perception, and knowledge,—when the intelligence is alert and illumined, the senses quickened, the whole mentality satisfied and full of brightness and the nervous being calmed and filled with an illumined ease and clarity, prasada, one should understand that there has been a great increase and uprising of the sattwic guna in the nature. For knowledge and a harmonious ease and pleasure and happiness are the characteristic results of sattwa.

The pleasure that is sattwic is not only that contentment which an inner clarity of satisfied will and intelligence brings with it, but all delight and content produced by the soul's possession of itself in light or by an accord or an adequate and truthful adjustment between the regarding soul and the surrounding Nature and her offered objects of desire and perception.

Rajas, again, the Gita tells us, has for its essence attraction of liking and longing. Rajas is a child of the attachment of the soul to the desire of objects; it is born from the nature's thirst for an unpossessed satisfaction. It is therefore full of unrest and fever and lust and greed and excitement, a thing of seeking impulsions, and all this mounts in us when the middle guna increases. It is the force of desire which motives all ordinary personal initiative of action and all that movement of stir and seeking and propulsion in our nature which is the impetus towards action and works, pravrtti. Rajas, then, is evidently the kinetic force in the modes of Nature. Its fruit is the lust of action, but also grief, pain, all kinds of suffering; for it has no right possession of its object—desire in fact implies non-possession—and even its pleasure of acquired possession is troubled and unstable because it has not clear knowledge and does not know how to possess nor can it find the secret of accord and right enjoyment. All the ignorant and passionate seeking of life belongs to the rajasic mode of Nature.

Tamas, finally, is born of inertia and ignorance and its fruit too is inertia and ignorance. It is the darkness of tamas which obscures knowledge and causes all confusion and delusion. Therefore, it is the opposite of sattwa, for the essence of sattwa is enlightenment, prakasa and the essence of tamas is absence of light, nescience, aprakasa. But tamas brings incapacity and negligence of action as well as the incapacity and negligence of error, inattention and misunderstanding or non-understanding; indolence, languor and sleep belong to this guna. Therefore, it is the opposite too of rajas; for the essence of rajas is movement and impulsion and kinesis, pravrtti, but the essence of tamas is inertia, apravrtti. Tamas is inertia of nescience and inertia of inaction, a double negative.

These three qualities of Nature are evidently present and active in all human beings, and none can be said to be quite devoid of one and another or free from any one of the three; none is cast in the mould of one guna to the exclusion of the others. All men have in them in whatever degree the rajasic impulse of desire and activity and the sattwic boon of light and happiness, some balance, some adjustment of mind to itself and its surroundings and objects, and all have their share of tamasic incapacity and ignorance or nescience. But these qualities are not constant in any man in the quantitative action of their force or in the combination of their elements; for they are variable and in a continual state of mutual impact, displacement, and interaction. Now one leads, now another increases and predominates and each subject's us to its characteristic action and consequences. Only by a general and ordinary predominance of one or other of the qualities can a man be said to be either sattwic or rajasic or tamasic in his nature; but this can only be a general and not an exclusive or absolute description. The three qualities are a triple power which by their interaction determine the character and disposition and through that and its various motions the actions of the natural man. But this triple power is at the same time a triple cord of bondage. "The three gunas born of Prakriti" says the Gita "bind in the body the imperishable dweller in the body." In a certain sense we can see at once that there must be this bondage in following the action of the gunas; for they are all limited by their finite of quality and operation and cause limitation. Tamas is on both its sides an incapacity and therefore very obviously binds to limitation. Rajasic desire as an initiator of action is a more positive power but still, we can see well enough that desire with its limiting and engrossing hold on man must always be a bondage. But how does sattwa, the power of knowledge and happiness, become a chain? It so becomes because it is a principle of mental nature, a principle of limited and limiting knowledge and of a happiness which depends upon right following or attainment of this or that object or else on particular states of the mentality, on a light of mind which can be only a more or less clear twilight. Its pleasure can only be a passing intensity or a qualified ease. Other is the infinite spiritual knowledge and the free self-existent delight of our spiritual being.

But then there is the question, how does our infinite and imperishable spirit, even involved in Nature, come thus to confine itself to the lower action of Prakriti and undergo this bondage and how is it not, like the supreme spirit of which it is a portion, free in its infinity even while enjoying the self-limitations of its active evolution? The reason, says the Gita, is our attachment to the gunas and to the result of their workings. Sattwa, it says, attaches to happiness, rajas attaches to action, tamas covers up the knowledge and attaches to negligence of error and inaction. Or again, "sattwa binds by attachment to knowledge and attachment to happiness, rajas binds the embodied spirit by attachment to works, tamas binds by negligence and indolence and sleep." In other words, the soul by attachment to the enjoyment of the gunas and their results concentrates its consciousness on the lower and outward action of life, mind, and body in Nature, imprisons itself in the form of these things and becomes oblivious of its own greater consciousness behind in the spirit, unaware of the free power and scope of the liberating Purusha. Evidently, in order to be liberated and perfect, we must get back from these things, away from the gunas and above them and return to the power of that free spiritual consciousness above Nature.

But this would seem to imply a cessation of all doing, since all-natural action is done by the gunas, by Nature through her modes. The soul cannot act by itself, it can only act through Nature and her modes. And yet the Gita, while it demands freedom from the modes, insists upon the necessity of action. Here comes in the importance of its insistence on the abandonment of the fruits, for it is the desire of the fruits which is the most potent cause of the soul's bondage and by abandoning it the soul can be free in action. Ignorance is the result of tamasic action, pain the consequence of rajasic works, pain of reaction, disappointment, dissatisfaction, or transience and therefore in attachment to the fruits of this kind of activity attended as they are with these undesirable accompaniments there is no profit. But of works rightly done the fruit is pure and sattwic, the inner result is knowledge and happiness. Yet attachment even to these pleasurable things must be entirely abandoned, first, because in the mind they are limited and limiting forms and, secondly, because, since sattwa is constantly entangled with and besieged by rajas and tamas which may at any moment overcome it, there is a perpetual insecurity in their tenure. But, even if one is free from any clinging to the fruit, there may be an attachment to the work itself, either for its own sake, the essential rajasic bond, or owing to a lax subjection to the drive of Nature, the tamasic, or for the sake of the attracting rightness of the thing done, which is the sattwic attaching cause powerful on the virtuous man or the man of knowledge. And here evidently the resource is in that other injunction of the Gita, to give up the action itself to the Lord of works and be only a desireless and equal-minded instrument of his will. To see that the modes of Nature are the whole agency and because of our works and to know and turn to that which is supreme above the gunas, is the way to rise above the lower nature. Only so can we attain to the movement and status of the Divine, mad-bhava, by which free from subjection to birth and death and their concomitants, decay, old age and suffering, the liberated soul shall enjoy in the end immortality and all that is eternal.

But what, asks Arjuna, are the signs of such a man, what his action and how is he said even in action to be above the three gunas? The sign, says Krishna, is that equality of which I have so constantly spoken; the sign is that inwardly he regards happiness and suffering alike, gold and mud and stone as of equal value and that to him the pleasant and the unpleasant, praise and blame, honour and insult, the faction of his friends and the faction of his enemies are equal things. He is steadfast in a wise imperturbable and immutable inner calm and quietude. He initiates no action but leaves all works to be done by the gunas of Nature. Sattwa, rajas or tamas may rise or cease in his outer mentality and his physical movements with their results of enlightenment, of impulsion to works or of inaction and the clouding over of the mental and nervous being, but he does not rejoice when this comes or that ceases, nor on the other hand does he abhor or shrink from the operation or the cessation of these things. He has seated himself in the conscious light of another principle than the nature of the gunas and that greater consciousness remains steadfast in him, above these powers and unshaken by their motions like the sun above clouds to one who has risen into a higher atmosphere. He from that height sees that it is the gunas that are in process of action and that their storm and calm are not himself but only a movement of Prakriti; his self is immovable above and his spirit does not participate in that shifting mutability of things unstable. This is the impersonality of the Brahmic status; for that higher principle, that greater wide high-seated consciousness, kutastha, is the immutable Brahman.

But still there is evidently here a double status, there is a scission of the being between two opposites; a liberated spirit in the immutable Self or Brahman watches the action of an unliberated mutable Nature,—Akshara and Kshara. Is there no greater status, no principle of more absolute perfection, or is this division the highest consciousness possible in the body, and is the end of Yoga to drop the mutable nature and the gunas born of the embodiment in Nature and disappear into the impersonality and everlasting peace of the Brahman? Is that laya or dissolution of the individual Purusha the greatest liberation? There is, it would seem, something else; for the Gita says at the close, always returning to this one final note, “He also who loves and strives after Me with an undeviating love and adoration, passes beyond the three gunas and he too is prepared for becoming the Brahman.” This “I” is the Purushottama who is the foundation of the silent Brahman and of immortality and imperishable spiritual existence and of the eternal dharma and of an utter bliss of happiness. There is a status then which is greater than the peace of the Akshara as it watches unmoved the strife of the gunas. There is a highest spiritual experience and foundation above the immutability of the Brahman, there is an eternal dharma greater than the rajasic impulsion to works, pravrtti, there is an absolute delight which is untouched by rajasic suffering and beyond the sattwic happiness, and these things are found and possessed by dwelling in the being and power of the Purushottama. But since it is acquired by bhakti, its status must be that divine delight, Ananda, in which is experienced the union of utter love[3] and possessing oneness, the crown of bhakti. And to rise into that Ananda, into that imperishable oneness must be the completion of spiritual perfection and the fulfilment of the eternal immortalizing dharma.

3 niratisayapremaspadatvam anandatattvam.

XV

THE THREE PURUSHAS[1]

The Doctrine of the Gita from the beginning to the end converges on all its lines and through all the flexibility of its turns towards one central thought and to that it is arriving in all its balancing and reconciliation of the disagreements of various philosophic systems and its careful synthetizing of the truths of spiritual experience, lights often conflicting or at least divergent when taken separately and exclusively pursued along their outer arc and curve of radiation, but here brought together into one focus of grouping vision. This central thought is the idea of a triple consciousness, three and yet one, present in the whole scale of existence.

There is a spirit here at work in the world that is one in innumerable appearances. It is the developer of birth and action, the moving power of life, the inhabiting and associating consciousness in the myriad mutabilities of Nature; it is the constituting reality of all this stir in Time and Space; it is itself Time and Space and Circumstance. It is this multitude of souls in the worlds; it is the gods and men and creatures and things and forces and qualities and quantities and powers and presences. It is Nature, which is power of the Spirit, and objects, which are

1 Gita, XV.

its phenomena of name and idea and form, and existences, who are portions and births and becomings of this single self-existent spiritual entity, the One, the Eternal. But what we see obviously at work before us is not this Eternal and his conscious Shakti, but a Nature which in the blind stress of her operations is ignorant of the spirit within her action. Her work is a confused, ignorant, and limiting play of certain fundamental modes, qualities, principles of force in mechanical operation and the fixity or the flux of their consequences. And whatever soul comes to the surface in her action, is itself in appearance ignorant, suffering, bound to the incomplete and unsatisfying play of this inferior Nature. The inherent Power in her is yet other than what it thus seems to be; for, hidden in its truth, manifest in its appearances, it is the Kshara, the universal Soul, the spirit in the mutability of cosmic phenomenon and becoming, one with the Immutable and the Supreme. We have to arrive at the hidden truth behind its manifest appearances; we have to discover the Spirit behind these veils and to see all as the One, vasudevah sarvam iti, individual, universal, transcendent. But this is a thing impossible to achieve with any completeness of inner reality, so long as we live concentrated in the inferior Nature. For in this lesser movement Nature is an ignorance, a Maya; she shelters the Divine within its folds and conceals him from herself and her creatures. The Godhead is hidden by the Maya of his own all-creating Yoga, the Eternal figured in transience, Being absorbed, and covered up by its own manifesting phenomena. In the Kshara taken alone as a thing in itself, the mutable universal apart from the undivided Immutable and the Transcendent, there is no completeness of knowledge, no completeness of our being and therefore no liberation.

But then there is another spirit of whom we become aware and who is none of these things, but self and self only. This Spirit is eternal, always the same, never changed or affected by manifestation, the one, the stable, a self-existence undivided and not even seemingly divided by the division of things and powers in Nature, inactive in her action, immobile in her motion. It is the Self of all and yet unmoved, indifferent, intangible, as if all these things which depend upon it were not-self, not its own results and powers and consequences, but a drama of action developed before the eye of an unmoved unparticipating spectator. For the mind that stages and shares in the drama is other than the Self which indifferently contains the action. This spirit is timeless, though we see it in Time; it is unextended in space, though we see it as if pervading space. We become aware of it in proportion as we draw back from out inward or look behind the action and motion for something that is eternal and stable or get away from time and its creation to the uncreated, away from phenomenon to being, from the personal to impersonality, from becoming to unalterable self-existence. This is the Akshara, the immutable in the mutable, the immobile in the mobile, the imperishable in things perishable. Or rather, since there is only an appearance of pervasion, it is the immutable, immobile, and imperishable in which proceeds all the mobility of mutable and perishable things.

The Kshara spirit visible to us as all-natural existence and the totality of all existences moves and acts pervadingly in the immobile and eternal Akshara. This mobile Power of Self acts in that fundamental stability of Self, as the second principle of material Nature, Vayu, with its contactual force of aggregation and separation, attraction, and repulsion, supporting the formative force of the fiery (radiant, gaseous, and electric) and other elemental movements, ranges pervadingly in the subtly massive stability of ether. This Akshara is the self-higher than the buddhi—it exceeds even that highest subjective principle of Nature in our being, the liberating intelligence, through which man returning beyond his restless mobile mental to his calm eternal spiritual self is at last free from the persistence of birth and the long chain of action, of Karma. This self in its highest status, param dhama, is an unmanifest beyond even the unmanifest principle of the original cosmic Prakriti, Avyakta, and, if the soul turns to this

Immutable, the hold of cosmos and Nature falls away from it and it passes beyond birth to an unchanging eternal existence. These two then are the two spirits we see in the world; one emerges in front in its action, the other remains behind it steadfast in that perpetual silence from which the action comes and in which all actions cease and disappear into timeless being, Nirvana. Dvav imau purusau loke ksaras caksara eva ca.

The difficulty which baffles our intelligence is that these two seem to be irreconcilable opposites with no real nexus between them or any transition from the one to the other except by an intolerant movement of separation. The Kshara acts, or at least motives action, separately in the Akshara; the Akshara stands apart, self-centred, separate in its inactivity from the Kshara. At first sight it would almost seem better, more logical, more easy of comprehension, if we admitted with the Sankhyas an original and eternal duality of Purusha and Prakriti, if not even an eternal plurality of souls. Our experience of the Akshara would then be simply the withdrawal of each Purusha into himself, his turning away from Nature and therefore from all contact with other souls in the relations of existence; for each is self-sufficient and infinite and complete in his own essence. But after all the final experience is that of a unity of all beings which is not merely a community of experience, a common subjection to one force of Nature, but a oneness in the spirit, a vast identity of conscious being beyond all this endless variety of determination, behind all this apparent separativism of relative existence. The Gita takes its stand in that highest spiritual experience. It appears indeed to admit an eternal plurality of souls subject to and sustained by their eternal unity, for cosmos is forever and manifestation goes on in unending cycles; nor does it affirm anywhere or use any expression that would indicate an absolute disappearance, laya, the annullation of the individual soul in the Infinite. But at the same time, it affirms with a strong insistence that the Akshara is the oneself of all these many souls, and it is therefore evident that these two spirits are a dual status of one eternal and universal existence. That is a very ancient doctrine; it is the whole basis of the largest vision of the Upanishads,—as when the Isha tells us that Brahman is both the mobile and the immobile, is the One and the Many, is the Self and all existences, atman, sarvabhutani, is the Knowledge and the Ignorance, is the eternal unborn status and also the birth of existences and that to dwell only on one of these things to the rejection of its eternal counterpart is a darkness of exclusive knowledge or a darkness of ignorance. It too insists like the Gita that man must know and must embrace both and learn of the Supreme in his entirety—samagram mam, as the Gita puts it—in order to enjoy immortality and live in the Eternal. The teaching of the Gita and this side of the teaching of the Upanishads are so far at one; for they look at and admit both sides of the reality and still arrive at identity as the conclusion and the highest truth of existence.

But this greater knowledge and experience, however true and however powerful in its appeal to our highest seeing, has still to get rid of a very real and pressing difficulty, a practical as well as a logical contradiction which seems at first sight to persist up to the highest heights of spiritual experience. The Eternal is other than this mobile subjective and objective experience, there is a greater consciousness, na idam yad upasate:[2] and yet at the same time all this is the Eternal, all this is the perennial self-seeing of the Self, sarvam khalu idam brahma,[3] ayam atma brahma.[4] The Eternal has become all existences, atma abhut sarvani bhutani;[5] as the Swetaswatara puts it, "Thou art this boy and yonder girl

2 Kena Upanishad.

3 Chhandogya Upanishad: Verily all this that is, is the Brahman.

4 Mandukya Upanishad: The Self is the Brahman.

5 Isha Upanishad.

and that old man walking supported on his staff,"—even as in the Gita the Divine says that he is Krishna and Arjuna and Vyasa and Ushanas, and the lion and the aswattha tree and consciousness and intelligence and all qualities and the self of all creatures. But how are these two the same, when they seem not only so opposite in nature, but so difficult to unify in experience? For when we live in the mobility of the becoming, we may be aware of but hardly live in the immortality of timeless self-existence. And when we fix ourselves in timeless being, Time and Space and circumstance fall away from us and begin to appear as a troubled dream in the Infinite. The most persuasive conclusion would be, at first sight, that the mobility of the spirit in Nature is an illusion, a thing real only when we live in it, but not real in essence, and that is why, when we go back into self, it falls away from our incorruptible essence. That is the familiar cutting of the knot of the riddle, brahma satyam jagan mithya.

The Gita does not take refuge in this explanation which has enormous difficulties of its own, besides its failure to account for the illusion,—for it only says that it is all a mysterious and incomprehensible Maya and then we might just as well say that it is all a mysterious and incomprehensible double reality, spirit concealing itself from spirit. The Gita speaks of Maya but only as a bewildering partial consciousness which loses hold of the complete reality, lives in the phenomenon of mobile Nature and has no sight of the Spirit of which she is the active Power, me prakrtih. When we transcend this Maya, the world does not disappear, it only changes its whole heart of meaning. In the spiritual vision we find not that all this does not really exist, but rather that all is, but with a sense quite other than its present mistaken significance: all is self and soul and nature of the Godhead, all is Vasudeva. The world for the Gita is real, a creation of the Lord, a power of the Eternal, a manifestation from the Parabrahman and even this lower nature of the triple Maya is a derivation from the supreme divine Nature. Nor can we take refuge altogether in this distinction that there is a double, an inferior active and temporal and a superior calm, still and eternal reality beyond action and that our liberation is to pass from this partiality to that greatness, from the action to the silence. For the Gita insists that we can and should, while we live, be conscious in the self and its silence and yet act with power in the world of Nature. And it gives the example of the Divine himself who is not bound by necessity of birth, but free, superior to the cosmos, and yet abides eternally in action, varta eva ca karmani. Therefore, it is by putting on a likeness of the divine nature in its completeness that the unity of this double experience becomes entirely possible. But what is the principle of that oneness?

The Gita finds it in its supreme vision of the Purushottama; for that is the type, according to its doctrine, of the complete and the highest experience, it is the knowledge of the whole-knowers, krtsnavidah. The Akshara is para, supreme in relation to the elements and action of cosmic Nature. It is the immutable Self of all, and the immutable Self of all is the Purushottama. The Akshara is he in the freedom of his self-existence unaffected by the action of his own power in Nature, not impinged on by the urge of his own becoming, undisturbed by the play of his own qualities. But this is only one aspect though a great aspect of the integral knowledge. The Purushottama is at the same time greater than the Akshara, because he is more than this immutability and he is not limited even by the highest eternal status of his being, param dhama. Still, it is through whatever is immutable and eternal in us that we arrive at that highest status from which there is no returning to birth and that was the liberation, which was sought by the wise of old, the ancient sages. But when pursued through the Akshara alone, this attempt at liberation becomes the seeking of the Indefinable, a thing hard for our nature embodied as we are here in Matter. The Indefinable, to which the Akshara, the pure intangible self here in us rises in its separative urge, is some supreme Unmanifest, paro avyaktah and that highest unmanifest Akshara is still the Purushottama. Therefore, the Gita has said, those also who follow after the Indefinable, come to me, the eternal Godhead. But yet is he more even than a highest unmanifest Akshara, more than any negative Absolute, neti neti, because he is to be known also as the supreme Purusha who extends this whole universe in his own existence. He is a supreme mysterious All, an ineffable positive Absolute of all things here. He is the Lord in the Kshara, Purushottama not only there, but here in the heart of every creature, Ishwara. And there too even in his highest eternal status, paro avyaktah, he is the supreme Lord, Parameshwara, no aloof and unrelated Indefinable, but the origin and father and mother and first foundation and eternal abode of self and cosmos and Master of all existences and enjoyer of askesis and sacrifice. It is by knowing him at once in the Akshara and the Kshara, it is by knowing him as the Unborn who partially manifests himself in all birth and even himself descends as the constant Avatar, it is by knowing him in his entirety, samagram mam, that the soul is easily released from the appearances of the lower Nature and returns by a vast sudden growth and broad immeasurable ascension into the divine being and supreme Nature. For the truth of the Kshara too is a truth of the Purushottama. The Purushottama is in the heart of every creature and is manifested in his countless Vibhutis; the Purushottama is the cosmic spirit in Time, and it is he that gives the command to the divine action of the liberated human spirit. He is both Akshara and Kshara, and yet he is other because he is more and greater than either of these opposites. Uttamah purusas tvanyah paramatmetyudahrtah, yo lokatrayam avisya bibhartyavyaya isvarah, "But other than these two is that highest spirit called the supreme Self, who enters the three worlds and upbears them, the imperishable Lord." This verse is the keyword of the Gita's reconciliation of these two apparently opposite aspects of our existence.

The idea of the Purushottama has been prepared, alluded to, adumbrated, assumed even from the beginning, but it is only now in the fifteenth chapter that it is expressly stated, and the distinction illuminated by a name. And it is instructive to see how it is immediately approached and developed. To ascend into the divine nature, we have been told, one must first fix oneself in a perfect spiritual equality and rise above the lower nature of the three gunas. Thus, transcending the lower Prakriti, we fix ourselves in the impersonality, the imperturbable superiority to all action, the purity from all definition and limitation by quality which is one side of the manifested nature of the Purushottama, his manifestation as the eternity and unity of the self, the Akshara. But there is also an ineffable eternal multiplicity of the Purushottama, a highest truest truth behind the primal mystery of soul manifestation. The Infinite has an eternal power, an unbeginning and unending action of his divine Nature, and in that action the miracle of soul personality emerges from a play of apparently impersonal forces, prakrtir jıvabhuta. This is possible because personality too is a character of the Divine and finds in the Infinite its highest spiritual truth and meaning. But the Person in the Infinite is not the egoistic, separative, oblivious personality of the lower Prakriti; it is something exalted, universal, and transcendent, immortal, and divine. That mystery of the supreme Person is the secret of love and devotion. The spiritual person, purusa, the eternal soul in us offers itself and all it has and is to the eternal Divine, the supreme Person and Godhead of whom it is a portion, amsa. The completeness of knowledge finds itself in this self-offering, this uplifting of our personal nature by love and adoration to the ineffable Master of our personality and its acts; the sacrifice of works receives by it its consummation and perfect sanction. It is then through these things that the soul of man fulfils itself most completely in this other and dynamic secret, this other great and intimate aspect of the divine nature and possesses by that fulfilment the foundation of immortality, the supreme felicity, and the eternal Dharma. And having so stated this double requisite, equality in the oneself, adoration of the one Lord, at first separately as if they were two different ways of arriving at the Brahmic status, brahmabhuyaya,—one taking the form of quietistic sannyasa, the other a form of divine love and divine action,—the Gita proceeds now to unite the personal and the impersonal in the Purushottama and to define their relations. For the object of the Gita is to get rid of exclusions and separative exaggerations and fuse these two sides of knowledge and spiritual experience into a single and perfect way to the supreme perfection.

First there comes a description of cosmic existence in the Vedantic image of the aswattha tree. This tree of cosmic existence has no beginning and no end, nanto na cadih, in space or in time; for it is eternal and imperishable, avyaya. The real form of it cannot be perceived by us in this material world of man's embodiment, nor has it any apparent lasting foundation here; it is an infinite movement, and its foundation is above in the supreme of the Infinite. Its principle is the ancient sempiternal urge to action, pravrtti, which forever proceeds without beginning or end from the original Soul of all existence, adyam purusam yatah pravrttih prasrta purani. Therefore, its original source is above, beyond Time in the Eternal, but its branches stretch down below, and it extends and plunges its other roots, well-fixed and clinging roots of attachment and desire with their consequences of more and more desire and an endlessly developing action, plunges them downward here into the world of men. The hymns of the Veda are compared to its leaves and the man who knows this tree of the cosmos is the Veda-knower. And here we see the sense of that rather disparaging view of the Veda or at least of the Vedavada, which we had to notice at the beginning. For the knowledge the Veda gives us is a knowledge of the gods, of the principles and powers of the cosmos, and its fruits are the fruits of a sacrifice which is offered with desire, fruits of enjoyment and lordship in the nature of the three worlds, in earth and heaven and the world between earth and heaven. The branches of this cosmic tree extend both below and above, below in the material, above in the supraphysical planes; they grow by the gunas of Nature, for the triple guna is all the subject of the Vedas, traigunya-visaya vedah.

The Vedic rhythms, chandamsi, are the leaves and the sensible objects of desire supremely gained by a right doing of sacrifice are the constant budding of the foliage. Man, therefore, so long as he enjoys the play of the gunas and is attached to desire, is held in the coils of Pravritti, in the movement of birth and action, turns about constantly between the earth and the middle planes and the heavens and is unable to get back to his supreme spiritual infinitudes. This was perceived by the sages. To achieve liberation, they followed the path of Nivritti or cessation from the original urge to action, and the consummation of this way is the cessation of birth itself and a transcendent status in the highest supracosmic reach of the Eternal. But for this purpose, it is necessary to cut these long-fixed roots of desire by the strong sword of detachment and then to seek for that highest goal whence, once having reached it, there is no compulsion of return to mortal life. To be free from the bewilderment of this lower Maya, without egoism, the great fault of attachment conquered, all desires stilled, the duality of joy and grief cast away, always to be fixed in wide equality, always to be firm in a pure spiritual consciousness, these are the steps of the way to that supreme Infinite. There we find the timeless being which is not illumined by sun or moon or fire but is itself the light of the presence of the eternal Purusha. I turn away, says the Vedantic verse, to seek that original Soul alone and to reach him in the great passage. That is the highest status of the Purushottama, his supracosmic existence.

But it would seem that this can be attained very well, best even, pre-eminently, directly, by the quiescence of Sannyasa. Its appointed path would seem to be the way of the Akshara, a complete renunciation of works and life, an ascetic seclusion, an ascetic inaction. Where is the room here, or at least where is the call, the necessity, for the command to action, and what has all this to do with the maintenance of the cosmic existence, lokasangraha, the slaughter of Kurukshetra, the ways of the Spirit in Time, the vision of the million-bodied Lord and his high-voiced bidding,

"Arise, slay the foe, enjoy a wealthy kingdom"? And what then is this soul in Nature? This spirit too, this Kshara, this enjoyer of our mutable existence, is the Purushottama; it is he in his eternal multiplicity, that is the Gita's answer. "It is an eternal portion of me that becomes the Jiva in a world of Jivas." This is an epithet, a statement of immense bearing and consequence. For it means that each soul, each being in its spiritual reality is the very Divine, however partial its actual manifestation of him in Nature. And it means too, if words have any sense, that each manifesting spirit, each of the many, is an eternal individual, an eternal unborn and undying power of the one Existence. We call this manifesting spirit the Jiva, because it appears here as if a living creature in a world of living creatures, and we speak of this spirit in man as the human soul and think of it in the terms of humanity only. But in truth it is something greater than its present appearance and not bound to its humanity: it was a lesser manifestation than the human in its past, it can become something much greater than mental man in its future. And when this soul rises above all ignorant limitation, then it puts on its divine nature of which its humanity is only a temporary veil, a thing of partial and incomplete significance. The individual spirit exists and ever existed beyond in the Eternal, for it is itself everlasting, sanatana. It is evidently this idea of the eternal individual which leads the Gita to avoid any expression at all suggestive of a complete dissolution, laya, and to speak rather of the highest state of the soul as a dwelling in the Purushottama, nivasisyasi mayyeva. If when speaking of the oneself of all it seems to use the language of Adwaita, yet this enduring truth of the eternal individual, mamamsah sanatanah, adds something which brings in a qualification and appears almost to accept the seeing of the Visishtadwaita,—though we must not therefore leap at once to the conclusion that that alone is the Gita's philosophy or that its doctrine is identical with the later doctrine of Ramanuja. Still this much is clear that there is an eternal, a real and not only an illusive principle of multiplicity in the spiritual being of the one divine Existence.

This eternal individual is no other than or in any way really separate from the Divine Purusha. It is the Lord himself, the Ishwara who by virtue of the eternal multiplicity of his oneness—is not all existence a rendering of that truth of the Infinite?—exists for ever as the immortal soul within us and has taken up this body and goes forth from the transient framework when it is cast away to disappear into the elements of Nature. He brings in with him and cultivates for the enjoyment of the objects of mind and sense the subjective powers of Prakriti, mind and the five senses and in his going forth too he goes taking them as the wind takes the perfumes from a vase. But the identity of the Lord and the soul in mutable Nature is hidden from us by outward appearance and lost in the crowding mobile deceptions of that Nature. And those who allow themselves to be governed by the figures of Nature, the figure of humanity or any other form, will never see it, but will ignore and despise the Divine lodged in the human body. Their ignorance cannot perceive him in his coming in and his going forth or in his staying and enjoying and assumption of quality but sees only what is there visible to the mind and senses, not the greater truth which can only be glimpsed by the eye of knowledge. Never can they have sight of him, even if they strive to do so, until they learn to put away the limitations of the outward consciousness and build in themselves their spiritual being, create for it, as it were, a form in their nature. Man, to know himself, must be krtatma, formed and complete in the spiritual mould, enlightened in the spiritual vision. The Yogins who have this eye of knowledge, see the Divine Being we are in their own endless reality, their own eternity of spirit. Illumined, they see the Lord in themselves and are delivered from the crude material limitation, from the form of mental personality, from the transient life formulation: they dwell immortal in the truth of the self and spirit. But they see him too not only in themselves, but in all the cosmos. In the light of the sun that illumines all this world they witness the light of the Godhead which is in us; the light in the moon and in fire is the light of the Divine. It is the Divine who has entered into this form of earth and is the spirit of its material force and sustains by his might these multitudes. The Divine is the godhead of Soma who by the rasa, the sap in the Earthmother, nourishes the plants and trees that clothe her surface. The Divine and no other is the flame of life that sustains the physical body of living creatures and turns its food into sustenance of their vital force. He is lodged in the heart of every breathing thing; from him are memory and knowledge and the debates of the reason. He is that which is known by all the Vedas and by all forms of knowing; he is the knower of Veda and the maker of Vedanta. In other words, the Divine is at once the Soul of matter and the Soul of life and the Soul of mind as well as the Soul of the supramental light that is beyond mind and its limited reasoning intelligence.

Thus, the Divine is manifest in a double soul of his mystery, a twofold power, dvav imau purusau; he supports at once the spirit of mutable things that is all these existences, ksarah sarvani bhutani and the immutable spirit that stands above them in his imperturbable immobility of eternal silence and calm. And it is by the force of the Divine in them that the mind and heart and will of man are so powerfully drawn in different directions by these two spirits as if by opposing and incompatible attractions one insistent to annul the other. But the Divine is neither wholly the Kshara, nor wholly the Akshara. He is greater than the immutable Self and he is much greater than the Soul of mutable things. If he is capable of being both at once, it is because he is other than they, anyah, the Purushottama above all cosmos and yet extended in the world and extended in the Veda, in self-knowledge and in cosmic experience. And whoever thus knows and sees him as the Purushottama, is no longer bewildered whether by the world-appearance or by the separate attraction of these two apparent contraries. These at first confront each other here in him as a positive of the cosmic action and as its negative in the Self who has no part in an action that belongs or seems to belong entirely to the ignorance of Nature. Or again they challenge his consciousness as a positive of pure, indeterminable, stable, eternal self-existence and as its negative of a world of elusive determinations and relations, ideas, and forms, perpetual unstable becoming and the creating and uncreating tangle of action and evolution, birth and death, appearance, and disappearance. He embraces and escapes them, overcomes their opposition, and becomes all-knowing, sarvavid, a whole-knower. He sees the entire sense both of the self and of things; he restores the integral reality of the Divine;[6] he unites the Kshara and the Akshara in the Purushottama. He loves, worships, cleaves to, and adores the supreme Self of his and all existence, the one Lord of his and all energies, the close and far-off Eternal in and beyond the world. And he does this too with no single side or portion of himself, exclusive spiritualized mind, blinding light of the heart intense but divorced from largeness, or sole aspiration of the will in works, but in all the perfectly illumined ways of his being and his becoming, his soul, and his nature. Divine in the equality of his imperturbable self-existence, one in it with all objects and creatures, he brings that boundless equality, that deep oneness down into his mind and heart and life and body and founds on it in an indivisible integrality the trinity of divine love, divine works and divine knowledge. This is the Gita's way of salvation.

And is that not too after all the real Adwaita which makes no least scission in the one eternal Existence? This utmost un-dividing Monism sees the one as the one even in the multiplicities of Nature, in all aspects, as much in the reality of self and of cosmos as in that greatest reality of the supracosmic which is the source of self and the truth of the cosmos and is not bound either by any affirmation of universal becoming or by any universal or absolute negation. That at least is the Adwaita of the Gita. This is the most secret Shastra, says the Teacher to Arjuna; this is the supreme teaching and science which leads us into the heart of the highest mystery of existence. Absolutely to know it, to seize it in

---

6 samagram mam.

knowledge and feeling and force and experience is to be perfected in the transformed understanding, divinely satisfied in heart and successful in the supreme sense and objective of all will and action and works. It is the way to be immortal, to rise towards the highest divine nature and to assume the eternal Dharma.

XVI

THE FULLNESS OF SPIRITUAL ACTION

THE DEVELOPMENT of the idea of the Gita has reached a point at which one question alone remains for solution,

—the question of our nature bound and defective and how it is to effect, not only in principle but in all its movements, its evolution from the lower to the higher being and from the law of its present action to the immortal Dharma. The difficulty is one which is implied in certain of the positions laid down in the Gita, but has to be brought out into greater prominence than it gets there and to be put into a clearer shape before our intelligence. The Gita proceeded on a psychological knowledge which was familiar to the mind of the time, and in the steps of its thought it was well able to abridge its transitions, to take much for granted and to leave many things unexpressed which we need to have put strongly into light and made precise to us. Its teaching sets out at the beginning to propose a new source and level for our action in the world; that was the starting-point and that motives also the conclusion. Its initial object was not precisely to propose a way of liberation, moksa, but rather to show the compatibility of works with the soul's effort towards liberation and of spiritual freedom itself when once attained with continued action in the world, muktasya karma. Incidentally, a synthetic Yoga or psychological method of arriving at spiritual liberation and perfection has been developed and certain metaphysical affirmations have been put forward, certain truths of our being and nature on which the validity of this Yoga reposes. But the original preoccupation remains throughout, the original difficulty and problem, how Arjuna, dislodged by a strong revulsion of thought and feeling from the established natural and rational foundations and standards of action, is to find a new and satisfying spiritual norm of works, or how he is to live in the truth of the Spirit—since he can no longer act according to the partial truths of the customary reason and nature of man—and yet to do his appointed work on the battlefield of Kurukshetra. To live inwardly calm, detached, silent in the silence of the impersonal and universal Self and yet do dynamically the works of dynamic Nature, and more largely, to be one with the Eternal within us and to do all the will of the Eternal in the world expressed through a sublimated force, a divine height of the personal nature uplifted, liberated, universalized, made one with God-nature,—this is the Gita's solution.

Let us see what this comes to in the most plain and positive terms and from the standpoint of the problem which is at the root of Arjuna's difficulty and refusal. His duty as a human being and a social being is the discharge of the high function of the Kshatriya without which the frame of society cannot be maintained, the ideals of the race cannot be vindicated, the harmonious order of right and justice cannot be upheld against the anarchic violence of oppression, wrong and injustice. And yet the appeal to duty by itself can no longer satisfy the protagonist of the struggle because in the terrible actuality of Kurukshetra it presents itself in harsh, perplexed, and ambiguous terms. The discharge of his social duty has suddenly come to signify assent to an enormous result of sin and sorrow and suffering; the customary means of maintaining social order and justice is found to lead instead to a great disorder and chaos. The rule of just claim and interest, that which we call rights, will not serve him here; for the kingdom he has to win for himself and his brothers and his side in the war is indeed rightly theirs and its assertion an overthrow of Asuric tyranny and a vindication of justice but a blood-bespattered justice and a kingdom possessed in sorrow and with the stain on it of a great sin, a monstrous harm done to society, a veritable crime against the race. Nor will the rule of Dharma, of ethical right, serve any better; for there is here a conflict of dharmas. A new and greater yet unguessed rule is needed to solve the problem, but what is that rule?

For to withdraw from his work, to take refuge in a saintly inactivity and leave the imperfect world with its unsatisfying methods and motives to take care of itself is one possible solution easy to envisage, easy to execute, but this is the very cutting of the knot that has been insistently forbidden by the Teacher. Action is demanded of man by the Master of the world who is the master of all his works and whose world is a field of action, whether done through the ego and in the ignorance or partial light of the limited human reason or initiated from a higher and more largely seeing plane of vision and motive. Again, to abandon this particular action as evil would be another kind of solution, the ready resort of the shortsighted moralizing mind but to this evasion too the Teacher refuses his assent. Arjuna's abstention would work a much greater sin and evil: it would mean, if it had any effect at all, the triumph of wrong and injustice and the rejection of his own mission as an instrument of the divine workings. A violent crisis in the destinies of the race has been brought about not by any blind motion of forces or solely by the confused clash of human ideas, interests, passions, egoisms, but by a Will which is behind these outward appearances. This truth Arjuna must be brought to see; he must learn to act impersonally, imperturbably as the instrument not of his little personal desires and weak human shrinking's but of a vaster and more luminous Power, a greater all-wise divine and universal Will. He must act impersonally and universally in a high union of his soul with the inner and outer Godhead, yukta, in a calm Yoga with his own supreme Self and the informing Self of the universe.

But this truth cannot be rightly seen, and this kind of action cannot be rightly undertaken, cannot become real as long as man is governed by the ego, even by the half-enlightened unillumined sattwic ego of the reason and the mental intelligence. For this is a truth of the spirit, this is an action from a spiritual basis. A spiritual, not an intellectual knowledge is the indispensable requisite for this way of works, its sole possible light, medium, incentive. First, therefore, the Teacher points out that all these ideas and feelings which trouble, perplex and baffle Arjuna, joy and sorrow, desire and sin, the mind's turn towards governing action by the outward results of action, the human shrinking from what seems terrible and formidable in the dealings of the universal Spirit with the world, are things born of the subjection of our consciousness to a natural ignorance, the way of working of a lower nature in which the soul is involved and sees itself as a separate ego returning to the action of things upon its dual reactions of pain and pleasure, virtue, and vice, right and wrong, good happening and evil fortune. These reactions create a tangled web of perplexity in which the soul is lost and bewildered by its own ignorance; it has to guide itself by partial and imperfect solutions that serve ordinarily with a stumbling sufficiency in the normal life but fail when brought to the test of a wider seeing and a profounder experience. To understand the real sense of action and existence one must retreat behind all these appearances into the truth of the spirit; one must find self-knowledge before one can have the basis of a right world-knowledge.

The first requisite is to shake the wings of the soul free from desire and passion and troubling emotion and all this perturbed and distorting atmosphere of human mind and arrive into an ether of dispassionate equality, a heaven of impersonal calm, an egoless feeling and vision of things. For only in that lucid upper air, reaches free from all storm and cloud, can self-knowledge come, and the law of the world and the truth of Nature be seen steadily and with an embracing eye and in an undisturbed and all-comprehending and all-penetrating light. Behind this little personality which is a helpless instrument, a passive or vainly resistant puppet of Nature and a form figured in her creations, there is an impersonal self-one in all which sees and knows all things; there is an equal, impartial, universal presence and support of creation, a witnessing consciousness that suffers Nature to work out the becoming of things in their own type, svabhava but does not involve and lose itself in the action she initiates. To draw back from the ego and the troubled personality into this calm, equal, eternal, universal, impersonal Self is the first step towards a seeing action in Yoga done in conscious union with the divine Being and the infallible Will that, however obscure now to us, manifests itself in the universe.

When we live tranquilly poised in this self of impersonal wideness, then because that is vast, calm, quiescent, impersonal, our other little false self, our ego of action disappears into its largeness, and we see that it is Nature that acts and not we, that all action is the action of Nature and can be nothing else. And this thing we call Nature is a universal executive Power of eternal being in motion which takes different shapes and forms in this or that class of its creatures and in each individual of the species according to its type of natural existence and the resultant function and law of its works. According to its nature each creature must act, and it cannot act by anything else. Ego and personal will and desire are nothing more than vividly conscious forms and limited natural workings of a universal Force that is itself formless and infinite and far exceeds them; reason and intelligence and mind and sense and life and body, all that we vaunt or take for our own, are Nature's instruments and creations. But the impersonal Self does not act and is not part of Nature: it observes the action from behind and above and remains lord of itself and a free and impassive knower and witness. The soul that lives in this impersonality is not affected by the actions of which our nature is an instrument; it does not reply to them or their effects by grief and joy, desire and shrinking, attraction and repulsion or any of the hundred dualities that draw and shake and afflict us. It regards all men and all things and all happenings with equal eyes, watches the modes or qualities of Nature acting on the modes or qualities, sees the whole secret of the mechanism, but is itself beyond these modes and qualities, a pure absolute essential being, impassive, free, at peace. Nature works out her action and the soul impersonal and universal supports her but is not involved, is not attached, is not entangled, is not troubled, is not bewildered. If we can live in this equal self, we too are at peace; our works continue so long as Nature's impulsion prolongs itself in our instruments, but there is a spiritual freedom and quiescence.

This duality of Self and Nature, quiescent Purusha, active Prakriti, is not, however, the whole of our being; these are not really the two last words in the matter. If it were so, either all works would be quite indifferent to the soul and this or that action or refraining from action would take place by some ungoverned turn of the mobile variations of the gunas,—Arjuna would be moved to battle by rajasic impulse in the instruments or withheld from it by tamasic inertia or sattwic indifference,—or else, if it so is that he must act and act only in this way, it would be by some mechanical determinism of Nature. Moreover, since the soul in its retreat would come to live in the impersonal quiescent Self and cease to live at all in active Nature, the final result would be quiescence, cessation, inertia, not the action imposed by the Gita. And, finally, this duality gives no real explanation why the soul is at all called to involve itself in Nature and her works; for it cannot be that the one ever uninvolved self-conscient spirit gets itself involved and loses its self-knowledge and has to return to that knowledge. This pure Self, this Atman is on the contrary always there, always the same, always the one self-conscient impersonal aloof Witness or impartial supporter of the action. It is this lacuna, this impossible vacuum that compels us to suppose two Purushas or two poses of the one Purusha, one secret in the Self that observes all from its self-existence—or perhaps observes nothing, another self-projected into Nature that lends itself to her action and identifies itself with her creations. But even this dualism of Self and Prakriti or Maya corrected by the dualism of the two Purushas is not the whole philosophic creed of the Gita. It goes beyond them to the supreme all-embracing oneness of a highest Purusha, Purushottama.

The Gita affirms that there is a supreme Mystery, a highest Reality that upholds and reconciles the truth of these two different manifestations. There is an utmost supreme Self, Lord, and Brahman, one who is both the impersonal and the personal but other and greater than either of them and other and greater than both of them together. He is Purusha, Self, and soul of our being, but he is also Prakriti; for Prakriti is the power of the All-Soul, the power of the Eternal and Infinite self-moved to action and creation. The supreme Ineffable, the universal Person, he becomes by his Prakriti all these creatures. The supreme Atman and Brahman, he manifests by his Maya of self-knowledge and his Maya of ignorance the double truth of the cosmic riddle. The supreme Lord, master of his Force, his Shakti, he creates, impels, and governs all this Nature and all the personality, power and works of these innumerable existences. Each soul is a partial being of this self-existent One, an eternal soul of this All-Soul, a partial manifestation of this supreme Lord and his universal Nature. All here is this Divine, this Godhead, Vasudeva; for by Nature and the soul in Nature he becomes all that is, and everything proceeds from him and lives in or by him, though he himself is greater than any widest manifestation, any deepest spirit, any cosmic figure. This is the complete truth of existence and this all the secret of the universal action that we have seen disengaging itself from the later chapters of the Gita.

But how does this greater truth modify or how affect the principle of spiritual action? It modifies it to begin with in this fundamental matter that the whole meaning of the relation of Self and soul and Nature gets changed, opens out to a new vision, fills in the blanks that were left, acquires a greater amplitude, assumes a true and spiritually positive, a flawlessly integral significance. The world is no longer a purely mechanical qualitative action and determination of Nature set over against the quiescence of an impersonal self-existence which has no quality or power of self-determination, no ability or impulse to create. The chasm left by this unsatisfactory dualism is bridged and an uplifting unity revealed between knowledge and works, the soul and Nature. The quiescent impersonal Self is a truth,—it is the truth of the calm of the Godhead, the silence of the Eternal, the freedom of the Lord of all birth and becoming and action and creation, his calm infinite freedom of self-existence not bound, troubled, or affected by his creation, not touched by the action and reaction of his Nature. Nature itself is now no inexplicable illusion, no separated and opposite phenomenon, but a movement of the Eternal, all her stir and activity and multiplicity founded and supported on the detached and observing tranquility of an immutable self and spirit. The Lord of Nature remains that immutable self even while he is at the same time the one and multiple soul of the universe and becomes in a partial manifestation all these forces, powers, consciousnesses, gods, animals, things, men. Nature of the gunas is a lower self- limited action of his power; it is nature of imperfectly conscious manifestation and therefore of a certain ignorance. The truth of the self, even as the truth of the Divine, is held back from her surface force absorbed here in its outer action—much as man's deeper being is held back from the knowledge of his surface consciousness—until the soul in her turns to find out this hidden thing, gets inside itself and discovers its own real verities, its heights, and its depths. That is why it has to draw back from its little personal and egoistic to its large and impersonal, immutable, and universal Self in order to become capable of self-knowledge.

But the Lord is there, not only in that self, but in Nature. He is in the heart of every creature and guides by his presence the turnings of this great natural mechanism. He is present in all, all lives in him, all is himself because all is a becoming of his being, a portion, or a figure of his existence. But all proceeds here in a lower partial working that has come out of a secret, a higher and greater and completer nature of Divinity, the eternal infinite nature or absolute self-power of the Godhead, devatmasakti. The perfect, integrally conscious soul hidden in man, an eternal portion of Deity, a spiritual being of the eternal Divine Being, can open in us and can too open us to him if we live constantly in this true truth of his action and our existence. The seeker of Godhead has to get back to the reality of his immutable and eternal impersonal self and at the same time he has to see everywhere the Divine from whom he proceeds, to see him as all, to see him in the whole of this mutable Nature and in every part and result of her and in all her workings, and there too to make himself one with God, there too to live in him, to enter there too into the divine oneness. He unites in that integrality the divine calm and freedom of his deep essential existence with a supreme power of instrumental action in his divinized self of Nature.

But how is this to be done? It can be done first by a right spirit in our will of works. The seeker has to regard all his action as a sacrifice to the Lord of works who is the eternal and universal Being and his own highest Self and the Self of all others and the supreme all-inhabiting, all-containing, all-governing Godhead in the universe. The whole action of Nature is such a sacrifice,—offered at first indeed to the divine Powers that move her and move in her, but these powers are only limited forms and names of the One and Illimitable. Man, ordinarily offers his sacrifice openly or under a disguise to his own ego; his oblation is the false action of his own self-will and ignorance. Or he offers his knowledge, action, aspiration, works of energy and effort to the gods for partial, temporal, and personal aims. The man of knowledge, the liberated soul offers on the contrary all his activities to the one eternal Godhead without any attachment to their fruit or to the satisfaction of his lower personal desires. He works for God, not for himself, for the universal welfare, for the Soul of the world and not for any particular object which is of his own personal creation or for any construction of his mental will or object of his vital longings, as a divine agent, not as a principal and separate profiteer in the world-commerce. And this, it must be noted, is a thing that cannot be really done except in proportion as the mind arrives at equality, universality, wide impersonality, and a clear freedom from every disguise of the insistent ego: for without these things the claim to be thus acting is a pretension or an illusion. The whole action of the world is the business of the Lord of the universe, the concern of the self-existent Spirit of whom it is the unceasing creation, the progressive becoming, the significant manifestation and living symbol in Nature. The fruits are his, the results are those determined by him, and our personal action is only a minor contribution ruled or overruled, so far as its motive is an egoistic claim, by this Self and Spirit in us who is the Self and Spirit in all and governs things for the universal end and good and not for the sake of our ego. To work impersonally, desirelessly and without attachment to the fruits of our work, for the sake of God and the world and the greater Self and the fulfilment of the universal will,—this is the first step towards liberation and perfection.

But beyond this step there lies that other greater motion, the inner surrender of all our actions to the Divinity within us. For it is infinite Nature that impels our works and a divine Will in and above her that demands action of us; the choice and turn our ego gives to it is a contribution of our tamasic, rajasic, sattwic quality, a deformation in the lower Nature. The deformation comes by the ego thinking of itself as the doer; the character of the act takes the form of the limited personal nature, and the soul is bound up with that and its narrow figures and does not allow the act to proceed freely and purely from the infinite power within it. And the ego is chained to the act and its outcome; it must suffer the personal consequence and reaction even as it claims the responsible origination and personal will of the doing. The free perfect working comes first by referring and finally by surrendering altogether the action and its origination to the divine Master of our existence; for we feel it progressively taken up by a supreme Presence within us, the soul drawn into deep intimacy and close unity with an inner Power and Godhead and the work originated directly from the greater Self, from the all-wise, infinite, universal force of an eternal being and not from the ignorance of the little personal ego. The action is chosen and shaped according to the nature, but entirely by the divine Will in the nature, and it is therefore free and perfect within, whatever its outward appearance; it comes stamped with the inward spiritual seal of the Infinite as the thing to be done, the movement and the step of the movement decreed in the ways of the omniscient Master of action, kartavyam karma. The soul of the liberated man is free in its impersonality, even while he contributes to the action as its means and its occasion his instrumental personal self-creation and the special will and power in his nature. That will and power is now not separately, egoistically his own, but a force of the suprapersonal Divine who acts in this becoming of his own self, this one of his myriad personalities by means of the characteristic form of the natural being, the swabhava. This is the high secret and mystery, uttamam rahasyam, of the action of the liberated man. It is the result of a growing of the human soul into a divine Light and of the union of its nature with a highest universal nature.

This change cannot come about except by knowledge. There is necessary a right knowledge of self and God and world and a living and growing into the greater consciousness to which that knowledge admits us. We know now what the knowledge is. It is sufficient to remember that it reposes on another and wider vision than the human mental, a changed vision and experience by which one is first of all liberated from the limitations of the ego sense and its contacts and feels and sees the oneself in all, all in God, all beings as Vasudeva, all as vessels of the Godhead and one's self too as a significant being and soul-power of that one Godhead; it treats in a spiritual uniting consciousness all the happenings of the lives of others as if they were happenings of one's own life; it allows no wall of separation and lives in a universal sympathy with all existences, while amidst the world-movement one still does the work that has to be done for the good of all, sarva-bhuta-hite, according to the way appointed by the Divine and in the measures imposed by the command of the Spirit who is Master of Time. Thus, living and acting in this knowledge the soul of man becomes united with the Eternal in personality and in impersonality, lives in the Eternal though acting in Time, even as the Eternal acts, and is free, perfect, and blissful whatever may be the form and determination of the work done in Nature.

The liberated man has the complete and total knowledge, krtsnavid, and does all works without any of the restrictions made by the mind, krtsna-karma-krt, according to the force and freedom and infinite power of the divine will within him. And since he is united with the Eternal, he has too the pure spiritual and illimitable joy of his eternal existence. He turns with adoration to the Self of whom he is a portion, the Master of his works and divine Lover of his soul and nature. He is not an impassive calm spectator only; he lifts not only his knowledge and will to the Eternal, but his heart also of love and adoration and passion. For without that uplifting of the heart his whole nature is not fulfilled and united with God; the ecstasy of the spirit's calm needs to be transformed by the ecstasy of the soul's Ananda. Beyond the personal Jiva and the impersonal Brahman or Atman he reaches the supracosmic Purushottama who is immutable in impersonality and fulfils himself in personality and draws us to him through these two different attractions. The liberated seeker rises personally to that highest Numen by his soul's love and joy in God and the adoration of the will in him for the Master of its works; the peace and largeness of his impersonal universal knowledge is perfected by delight in the self-existent integral close and intimate reality of this surpassing and universal Godhead. This delight glorifies his knowledge and unites it with the eternal delight of the Spirit in itself and its manifestation; this perfects too his personality in the superperson of the divine Purusha and makes his natural being and action one with eternal beauty, eternal harmony, eternal love, and Ananda.

But all this change means a total passing from the lower human to the higher divine nature. It is a lifting of our whole being or at least of the whole mental being that wills, knows and feels beyond what we are into some highest spiritual consciousness, some satisfying fullest power of existence, some deepest widest delight of the spirit. And this may well be possible by a transcendence of our present natural life, it may well be possible in some celestial state beyond the earthly existence or still beyond in a supracosmic superconscience; it may happen by transition to an absolute and infinite power and status of the Spirit. But while we are here in the body, here in life, here in action, what in this change becomes of the lower nature? For at present all our activities are determined in their trend and shape by the nature, and this Nature here is the nature of the three gunas, and in all natural being and in all natural activities there is the triple guna, tamas with its ignorance and inertia, rajas with its kinesis and action, its passion and grief and perversion, sattwa with its light and happiness, and the bondage of these things. And granted that the soul becomes superior in the self to the three gunas, how does it escape in its instrumental nature from their working and result and bondage? For even the man of knowledge, says the Gita, must act according to his nature. To feel and bear the reactions of the gunas in the outer manifestation, but to be free from them and superior in the observing conscious self behind is not sufficient; for it leaves still a dualism of freedom and subjection, a contradiction between what we are within and what we are without, between our self and our power, what we know ourselves to be and what we will and do. Where is the release here, where the full elevation and transformation to the higher spiritual nature, the immortal Dharma, the law proper to the infinite purity and power of a divine being? If this change cannot be affected while in the body, then so it must be said, that the whole nature cannot be transformed and there must remain an unreconciled duality until the mortal type of existence drops off like a discarded shell from the spirit. But in that case the gospel of works cannot well be the right or at least cannot be the ultimate gospel: a perfect quiescence or at least as perfect a quiescence as possible, a progressive Sannyasa and renunciation of works would seem still to be the true counsel of perfection,—as indeed the Mayavadin contends, who says that the Gita's way is no doubt the right way so long as we remain in action, but still all works are an illusion and quiescence the highest path. To act in this spirit is well, but only as a transition to a renunciation of all works, to cessation, to an absolute quiescence.

This is the difficulty which the Gita has still to meet in order to justify works to the seeker after the Spirit. Otherwise, it must say to Arjuna, "Act temporarily in this fashion, but afterwards seek the higher way of renunciation of works." But on the contrary, it has said that not the cessation of works, but renunciation of desire is the better way; it has spoken of the action of the liberated man, muktasya karma. It has even insisted on doing all actions, sarvani karmani, krtsna-karma-krt; it has said that in whatever way the perfected Yogin lives and acts, he lives and acts in God. This can only be, if the nature also in its dynamics and workings becomes divine, a power imperturbable, intangible, inviolate, pure, and untroubled by the reactions of the inferior Prakriti. How and by what steps is this most difficult transformation to be effected? What is this last secret of the soul's perfection? what the principle or the process of this transmutation of our human and earthly nature?

XVII

DEVA AND ASURA[1]

The Practical difficulty of the change from the ignorant and shackled normal nature of man to the dynamic freedom of a divine and spiritual being will be apparent if we ask ourselves, more narrowly, how the transition can be affected from the fettered embarrassed functioning of the three qualities to the infinite action of the liberated man who is no longer subject to the gunas. The transition is indispensable; for it is clearly laid down that he must be above or else without the three gunas, trigunatita, nistraigunya. On the other hand, it is no less clearly, no less emphatically laid down that in every natural existence here on earth the three gunas are there in their inextricable working and it is even said that all action of man or creature or force is merely the action of these three modes upon each other, a functioning in which one or other predominates and the rest modify its operation and results, guna gunesu vartante. How then can there be another dynamic and kinetic nature or any other kind of works? To act is to be subject to the three qualities of Nature; to be beyond these conditions of her working is to be silent in the Spirit. The Ishwara, the Supreme who is master of all her works and functions and guides and determines them by his divine will, is indeed above this mechanism of quality, not touched or limited by her modes, but still, it would seem that

1 Gita, XVI.

he acts always through them, always shapes by the power of the swabhava and through the psychological machinery of the gunas. These three are fundamental properties of Prakriti, necessary operations of the executive Nature-force which takes shape here in us, and the Jiva himself is only a portion of the Divine in this Prakriti. If then the liberated man still does works, still moves in the kinetic movement, it must be so that he moves and acts, in Nature and by the limitation of her qualities, subject to their reactions, not, in so far as the natural part of him persists, in the freedom of the Divine. But the Gita has said exactly the opposite, that the liberated Yogin is delivered from the guna reactions and whatever he does, however he lives, moves, and acts in God, in the power of his freedom and immortality, in the law of the supreme eternal Infinite, sarvatha vartamano'pi sa yogi mayi vartate. There seems here to be a contradiction, an impasse.

But this is only when we knot ourselves up in the rigid logical oppositions of the analytic mind, not when we look freely and subtly at the nature of spirit and at the spirit in Nature. What moves the world is not really the modes of Prakriti,—these are only the lower aspect, the mechanism of our normal nature. The real motive power is a divine spiritual Will which uses at present these inferior conditions, but is itself not limited, not dominated, not mechanized, as is the human will, by the gunas. No doubt, since these modes are so universal in their action, they must proceed from something inherent in the power of the Spirit; there must be powers in the divine Will-force from which these aspects of Prakriti have their origin. For everything in the lower normal nature is derived from the higher spiritual power of being of the Purushottama, mattah pravartate; it does not come into being de novo and without a spiritual cause. Something in the essential power of the spirit there must be from which the sattwic light and satisfaction, the rajasic kinesis, the tamasic inertia of our nature are derivations and of which they are the imperfect or degraded forms. But once we get back to these sources in their purity above this imperfection and degradation of them in which we live, we shall find that these motions put on a quite different aspect as soon as we begin to live in the spirit. Being and action and the modes of being and action become altogether different things, far above their present limited appearance.

For what is behind this troubled kinesis of the cosmos with all its clash and struggle? What is it that when it touches the mind, when it puts on mental values, creates the reactions of desire, striving, straining, error of will, sorrow, sin, pain? It is a will of the spirit in movement, it is a large divine will in action which is not touched by these things; it is a power[2] of the free and infinite conscious Godhead which has no desire because it exercises a universal possession and a spontaneous Ananda of its movements. Wearied by no striving and straining, it enjoys a free mastery of its means and its objects; misled by no error of the will, it holds a knowledge of self and things which is the source of its mastery and its Ananda; overcome by no sorrow, sin, or pain, it has the joy and purity of its being and the joy and purity of its power. The soul that lives in God acts by this spiritual will and not by the normal will of the unliberated mind: its kinesis takes place by this spiritual force and not by the rajasic mode of Nature, precisely because it no longer lives in the lower movement to which that deformation belongs but has got back in the divine nature to the pure and perfect sense of the kinesis.

And again what is behind the inertia of Nature, behind this Tamas which, when complete, makes her action like the blind driving of a machine, a mechanical impetus unobservant of anything except the groove in which it is set to spin and not conscious even of the law of that motion,—this Tamas that turns cessation of the accustomed action into death and disintegration and becomes in the mind a power for inaction and ignorance? This tamas is an obscurity which mistranslates, we may say, into

---

2 tapas, cit-sakti.

inaction of power and inaction of knowledge the Spirit's eternal principle of calm and repose—the repose which the Divine never loses even while he acts, the eternal repose which supports his integral action of knowledge, and the force of his creative will both there in its own infinities and here in an apparent limitation of its working and self-awareness. The peace of the Godhead is not a disintegration of energy or a vacant inertia; it would keep all that Infinity has known and done gathered up and concentratedly conscious in an omnipotent silence even if the Power everywhere ceased for a time actively to know and create. The Eternal does not need to sleep or rest; he does not get tired and flag; he has no need of a pause to refresh and recreate his exhausted energies; for his energy is inexhaustibly the same, indefatigable, and infinite. The Godhead is calm and at rest in the midst of his action; and on the other hand, his very cessation of action would retain in it the full power and all the potentialities of his kinesis. The liberated soul enters into this calm and participates in the eternal repose of the spirit. This is known to everyone who has had any taste at all of the joy of liberation, that it contains an eternal power of calm. And that profound tranquility can remain in the very heart of action, can persevere in the most violent motion of forces. There may be an impetuous flood of thought, doing, will, movement, an overflowing rush of love, the emotion of the self-existent spiritual ecstasy at its strongest intensity, and that may extend itself to a fiery and forceful spiritual enjoyment of things and beings in the world and in the ways of Nature, and yet this tranquility and repose would be behind the surge and in it, always conscious of its depths, always the same. The calm of the liberated man is not an indolence, incapacity, insensibility, inertia; it is full of immortal power, capable of all action, attuned to deepest delight, open to profoundest love and compassion and to every manner of intensest Ananda.

And so too beyond the inferior light and happiness of that purest quality of Nature, Sattwa, the power that makes for assimilation and equivalence, right knowledge and right dealing, fine harmony, firm balance, right law of action, right possession and brings so full a satisfaction to the mind, beyond this highest thing in the normal nature, admirable in itself so far as it goes and while it can be maintained but precarious, secured by limitation, dependent on rule and condition, there is at its high and distant source a greater light and bliss free in the free spirit. That is not limited nor dependent on limitation or rule or condition but self-existent and unalterable, not the result of this or that harmony amid the discords of our nature but the fount of harmony and able to create whatever harmony it will. That is a luminous spiritual and in its native action a direct supramental force of knowledge, jyotih, not our modified and derivative mental light, prakasa. That is the light and bliss of widest self-existence, spontaneous self-knowledge, intimate universal identity, deepest self-interchange, not of acquisition, assimilation, adjustment, and laboured equivalence. That light is full of a luminous spiritual will and there is no gulf or disparateness between its knowledge and its action. That delight is not our paler mental happiness, sukham but a profound concentrated intense self-existent bliss extended to all that our being does, envisages, creates, a fixed divine rapture, Ananda. The liberated soul participates more and more profoundly in this light and bliss and grows the more perfectly into it, the more integrally it unites itself with the Divine. And while among the gunas of the lower Nature there is a necessary disequilibrium, a shifting inconstancy of measures and a perpetual struggle for domination, the greater light and bliss, calm, will of kinesis of the Spirit do not exclude each other, are not at war, are not even merely in equilibrium, but each an aspect of the two others and in their fullness, all are inseparable and one. Our mind when it approaches the Divine may seem to enter into one to the exclusion of another, may appear for instance to achieve calm to the exclusion of kinesis of action, but that is because we approach him first through the selecting spirit in the mind. Afterwards when we are able to rise above even the spiritual mind, we can see that each divine power contains all the rest and can get rid of this initial error.[3]

We see then that action is possible without the subjection of the soul to the normal degraded functioning of the modes of Nature. That functioning depends on the mental, vital, and physical limitation into which we are cast; it is a deformation, an incapacity, a wrong or depressed value imposed on us by the mind and life in matter. When we grow into the spirit, this dharma or inferior law of Nature is replaced by the immortal dharma of the spirit; there is the experience of a free immortal action, a divine illimitable knowledge, a transcendent power, an unfathomable repose. But still there remains the question of the transition; for there must be a transition, a proceeding by steps since nothing in God's workings in this world is done by an abrupt action without procedure or basis. We have the thing we seek in us, but we have in practice to evolve it out of the inferior forms of our nature.[4] Therefore in the action of the modes itself there must be some means, some leverage, some point d'appui, by which we can effect this transformation. The Gita finds it in the full development of the sattwic guna till that in its potent expansion reaches a point at which it can go beyond itself and disappear into its source.

---

3 The account given here of the supreme spiritual and supramental forms of highest Nature action corresponding to the gunas is not derived from the Gita but introduced from spiritual experience. The Gita does not describe in any detail the action of the highest Nature, rahasyam uttamam; it leaves that for the seeker to discover by his own spiritual experience. It only points out the nature of the high sattwic temperament and action through which this supreme mystery has to be reached and insists at the same time on the overpassing of Sattwa and transcendence of the three gunas.

4 This is from the point of view of our nature ascending upwards by self-conquest, effort, and discipline. There must also intervene more and more a descent of the divine Light, Presence and Power into the being to transform it; otherwise, the change at the point of culmination and beyond it cannot take place. That is why there comes in as the last movement the necessity of an absolute self-surrender.

The reason is evident, because sattwa is a power of light and happiness, a force that makes for calm and knowledge, and at its highest point it can arrive at a certain reflection, almost a mental identity with the spiritual light and bliss from which it derives. The other two gunas cannot get this transformation, rajas into the divine kinetic will or tamas into the divine repose and calm, without the intervention of the sattwic power in Nature. The principle of inertia will always remain an inert inaction of power or an incapacity of knowledge until its ignorance disappears in illumination and its torpid incapacity is lost in the light and force of the omnipotent divine will of repose. Then only can we have the supreme calm. Therefore, tamas must be dominated by sattwa. The principle of rajas for the same reason must remain always a restless, troubled, feverish, or unhappy working because it has not right knowledge; its native movement is a wrong and perverse action, perverse through ignorance. Our will must purify itself by knowledge; it must get more and more to a right and luminously informed action before it can be converted into the divine kinetic will. That again means the necessity of the intervention of sattwa. The sattwic quality is a first mediator between the higher and the lower nature. It must indeed at a certain point transform or escape from itself and break up and dissolve into its source; its conditioned derivative seeking light and carefully constructed action must change into the free direct dynamics and spontaneous light of the spirit. But meanwhile a high increase of sattwic power delivers us largely from the tamasic and the rajasic disqualification; and its own disqualification, once we are not pulled too much downward by rajas and tamas, can be surmounted with a greater ease. To develop sattwa till it becomes full of spiritual light and calm and happiness is the first condition of this preparatory discipline of the nature.

That, we shall find, is the whole intention of the remaining chapters of the Gita. But first it prefaces the consideration of this enlightening movement by a distinction between two kinds of being, the Deva and the Asura; for the Deva is capable of a high self-transforming sattwic action, the Asura incapable. We must see what is the object of this preface, and the precise bearing of this distinction. The general nature of all human beings is the same, it is a mixture of the three gunas; it would seem then that in all there must be the capacity to develop and strengthen the sattwic element and turn it upward towards the heights of the divine transformation. That our ordinary turn is actually towards making our reason and will the servants of our rajasic or tamasic egoism, the ministers of our restless and ill-balanced kinetic desire or our self-indulgent indolence and static inertia, can only be, one would imagine, a temporary characteristic of our undeveloped spiritual being, a rawness of its imperfect evolution and must disappear when our consciousness rises in the spiritual scale. But we actually see that men, at least men above a certain level, fall very largely into two classes, those who have a dominant force of sattwic nature turned towards knowledge, self-control, beneficence, perfection, and those who have a dominant force of rajasic nature turned towards egoistic greatness, satisfaction of desire, the indulgence of their own strong will and personality which they seek to impose on the world, not for the service of man or God, but for their own pride, glory, and pleasure. These are the human representatives of the Devas and Danavas or Asuras, the Gods and the Titans. This distinction is a very ancient one in Indian religious symbolism. The fundamental idea of the Rig Veda is a struggle between the Gods and their dark opponents, between the Masters of Light, sons of Infinity, and the children of Division and Night, a battle in which man takes part and which is reflected in all his inner life and action. This was also a fundamental principle of the religion of Zoroaster. The same idea is prominent in later literature. The Ramayana is in its ethical intention the parable of an enormous conflict between the Deva in human form and the incarnate Rakshasa, between the representative of a high culture and Dharma and a huge, unbridled force and gigantic civilization of the exaggerated

Ego. The Mahabharata, of which the Gita is a section, takes for its subject a lifelong clash between human Devas and Asuras, the men of power, sons of the Gods, who are governed by the light of a high ethical Dharma and others who are embodied Titans, the men of power who are out for the service of their intellectual, vital, and physical ego. The ancient mind, more open than ours to the truth of things behind the physical veil, saw behind the life of man great cosmic Powers or being's representative of certain turns or grades of the universal Shakti, divine, titanic, gigantic, demoniac, and men who strongly represented in themselves these types of nature were themselves considered as Devas, Asuras, Rakshasas, Pisachas. The Gita for its own purposes takes up this distinction and develops the difference between these two kinds of beings, dvau bhutasargau. It has spoken previously of the nature which is Asuric and Rakshasic and obstructs God-knowledge, salvation, and perfection; it now contrasts it with the Daivic nature which is turned to these things.

Arjuna, says the Teacher, is of the Deva nature. He need not grieve with the thought that by acceptance of battle and slaughter he will be yielding to the impulses of the Asura. The action on which all turns, the battle which Arjuna has to fight with the incarnate Godhead as his charioteer at the bidding of the Master of the world in the form of the Time-Spirit, is a struggle to establish the kingdom of the Dharma, the empire of Truth, Right and Justice. He himself is born in the Deva kind; he has developed in himself the sattwic being, until he has now come to a point at which he is capable of a high transformation and liberation from the traigunya and therefore even from the sattwic nature. The distinction between the Deva and the Asura is not comprehensive of all humanity, not rigidly applicable to all its individuals, neither is it sharp and definite in all stages of the moral or spiritual history of the race or in all phases of the individual evolution. The tamasic man who makes so large a part of the whole, falls into neither category as it is here described, though he may have both elements in him in a low degree and for the most part serves tepidly the lower qualities. The normal man is ordinarily a mixture; but one or the other tendency is more pronounced, tends to make him predominantly rajaso-tamasic or sattwo-rajasic and can be said to be preparing him for either culmination, for the divine clarity or the titanic turbulence. For here what is in question is a certain culmination in the evolution of the qualitative nature, as will be evident from the descriptions given in the text. On one side there can be a sublimation of the sattwic quality, the culmination or manifestation of the unborn Deva, on the other a sublimation of the rajasic turn of the soul in nature, the entire birth of the Asura. The one leads towards that movement of liberation on which the Gita is about to lay stress; it makes possible a high self-exceeding of the sattwa quality and a transformation into the likeness of the divine being, vimoksaya. The other leads away from that universal potentiality and precipitates towards an exaggeration of our bondage to the ego. This is the point of the distinction.

The Deva nature is distinguished by an acme of the sattwic habits and qualities; self-control, sacrifice, the religious habit, cleanness and purity, candour and straightforwardness, truth, calm and self-denial, compassion to all beings, modesty, gentleness, forgivingness, patience, steadfastness, a deep sweet and serious freedom from all restlessness, levity and inconstancy are its native attributes. The Asuric qualities, wrath, greed, cunning, treachery, willful doing of injury to others, pride and arrogance and excessive self-esteem have no place in its composition. But its gentleness and self-denial and self-control are free too from all weakness: it has energy and soul force, strong resolution, the fearlessness of the soul that lives in the right and according to the truth as well as its harmlessness, tejah, abhayam, dhrtih, ahimsa, satyam. The whole being, the whole temperament is integrally pure; there is a seeking for knowledge and a calm and fixed abiding in knowledge. This is the wealth, the plenitude of the man born into the Deva nature.

The Asuric nature has too its wealth, its plenitude of force, but it is of a very different, a powerful and evil kind. Asuric men have no true knowledge of the way of action or the way of abstention, the fulfilling or the holding in of the nature. Truth is not in them, nor clean doing, nor faithful observance. They see naturally in the world nothing but a huge play of the satisfaction of self; theirs is a world with Desire for its cause and seed and governing force and law, a world of Chance, a world devoid of just relation and linked Karma, a world without God, not true, not founded in Truth. Whatever better intellectual or higher religious dogma they may possess, this alone is the true creed of their mind and will in action; they always follow the cult of Desire and Ego. On that way of seeing life, they lean in reality and by its falsehood they ruin their souls and their reason. The Asuric man becomes the centre or instrument of a fierce, Titanic, violent action, a power of destruction in the world, a fount of injury and evil. Arrogant, full of self-esteem and the drunkenness of their pride, these misguided souls delude themselves, persist in false and obstinate aims and pursue the fixed impure resolution of their longings. They imagine that desire and enjoyment are all the aim of life and in their inordinate and insatiable pursuit of it they are the prey of a devouring, a measurelessly unceasing care and thought and endeavour and anxiety till the moment of their death. Bound by a hundred bonds, devoured by wrath and lust, unweariedly occupied in amassing unjust gains which may serve their enjoyment and the satisfaction of their craving, always they think, "Today I have gained this object of desire, tomorrow I shall have that other; today I have so much wealth, more I will get tomorrow. I have killed this my enemy, the rest too I will kill. I am a lord and king of men, I am perfect, accomplished, strong, happy, fortunate, a privileged enjoyer of the world; I am wealthy, I am of high birth; who is there like unto me? I will sacrifice, I will give, I will enjoy." Thus, occupied by many egoistic ideas, deluded, doing works, but doing them wrongly, acting mightily but for themselves, for desire, for enjoyment, not for God in themselves and God in man, they fall into the unclean hell of their own evil. They sacrifice and give, but from a self-regarding ostentation, from vanity and with a stiff and foolish pride. In the egoism of their strength and power, in the violence of their wrath and arrogance they hate, despise, and belittle the God hidden in themselves and the God in man. And because they have this proud hatred and contempt of good and of God, because they are cruel and evil, the Divine casts them down continually into more and more Asuric births. Not seeking him, they find him not, and at last, losing the way to him altogether, sink down into the lowest status of soul-nature, adhamam gatim.

This graphic description, even giving its entire value to the distinction it implies, must not be pressed to carry more in it than it means. When it is said that there are two creations of beings in this material world, Deva and Asura,[5] it is not meant that human souls are so created by God from the beginning each with its own inevitable career in Nature, nor is it meant that there is a rigid spiritual predestination and those rejected from the beginning by the Divine are blinded by him so that they may be thrust down to eternal perdition and the impurity of Hell. All souls are eternal portions of the Divine, the Asura as well as the Deva, all can come to salvation: even the greatest sinner can turn to the Divine. But the evolution of the soul in Nature is an adventure of which Swabhava and the Karma governed by the swabhava are ever the chief powers; and if an excess in the manifestation of the swabhava, the self-becoming of the soul, a disorder in its play turns the law of being to the perverse side, if the rajasic qualities are given the upper hand, cultured to the diminution of sattwa, then the trend of Karma and its results necessarily culminate not in the sattwic

5 The distinction between the two creations has its full truth in supraphysical planes where the law of spiritual evolution does not govern the movement. There are worlds of the Devas, worlds of the Asuras, and there are in these worlds behind us constant types of beings which support the complex divine play of creation indispensable to the march of the universe and cast their influence also on the earth and on the life and nature of man in this physical plane of existence.

height which is capable of the movement of liberation but in the highest exaggeration of the perversities of the lower nature. The man, if he does not stop short and abandon his way of error, has eventually the Asura full-born in him, and once he has taken that enormous turn away from the Light and Truth, he can no more reverse the fatal speed of his course because of the very immensity of the misused divine power in him until he has plumbed the depths to which it falls, found bottom and seen where the way has led him, the power exhausted and misspent, himself down in the lowest state of the soul nature, which is Hell. Only when he understands and turns to the Light, does that other truth of the Gita come in, that even the greatest sinner, the most impure and violent evildoer is saved the moment he turns to adore and follow after the Godhead within him. Then, simply by that turn, he gets very soon into the sattwic way which leads to perfection and freedom.

The Asuric Prakriti is the rajasic at its height; it leads to the slavery of the soul in Nature, to desire, wrath, and greed, the three powers of the rajasic ego, and these are the three-fold doors of Hell, the Hell into which the natural being falls when it indulges the impurity and evil and error of its lower or perverted instincts. These three are again the doors of a great darkness, they fold back into tamas, the characteristic power of the original Ignorance; for the unbridled force of the rajasic nature, when exhausted, falls back into the weakness, collapse, darkness, incapacity of the worst tamasic soul-status. To escape from this downfall, one must get rid of these three evil forces and turn to the light of the sattwic quality, live by the right, in the true relations, according to the Truth and the Law; then one follows one's own higher good and arrives at the highest soul-status. To follow the law of desire is not the true rule of our nature; there is a higher and juster standard of its works. But where is it embodied or how is it to be found? In the first place, the human race has always been seeking for this just and high Law and whatever it has discovered is embodied in its Shastra, its rule of science and knowledge, rule of ethics, rule of religion, rule of best social living, rule of one's right relations with man and God and Nature. Shastra does not mean a mass of customs, some good, some bad, unintelligently followed by the customary routine mind of the tamasic man. Shastra is the knowledge and teaching laid down by intuition, experience and wisdom, the science and art and ethic of life, the best standards available to the race. The half-awakened man who leaves the observance of its rule to follow the guidance of his instincts and desires, can get pleasure but not happiness; for the inner happiness can only come by right living. He cannot move to perfection, cannot acquire the highest spiritual status. The law of instinct and desire seems to come first in the animal world, but the manhood of man grows by the pursuit of truth and religion and knowledge and a right life. The Shastra, the recognized Right that he has set up to govern his lower members by his reason and intelligent will, must therefore first be observed and made the authority for conduct and works and for what should or should not be done, till the instinctive desire nature is schooled and abated and put down by the habit of self-control and man is ready first for a freer intelligent self-guidance and then for the highest supreme law and supreme liberty of the spiritual nature.

For the Shastra in its ordinary aspect is not that spiritual law, although at its loftiest point, when it becomes a science and art of spiritual living, Adhyatma-shastra,—the Gita itself describes its own teaching as the highest and most secret Shastra,—it formulates a rule of the self-transcendence of the sattwic nature and develops the discipline which leads to spiritual transmutation. Yet all Shastra is built on a number of preparatory conditions, dharmas; it is a means, not an end. The supreme end is the freedom of the spirit when abandoning all dharmas the soul turns to God for its sole law of action, acts straight from the divine will and lives in the freedom of the divine nature, not in the Law, but in the Spirit. This is the development of the teaching which is prepared by the next question of Arjuna.

XVIII

THE GUNAS, FAITH AND WORKS[1]

The Gita has made a distinction between action according to the licence of personal desire and action done according to the Shastra. We must understand by the latter the recognized science and art of life which is the outcome

of mankind's collective living, its culture, religion, science, its progressive discovery of the best rule of life,—but mankind still walking in the ignorance and proceeding in a half-light towards knowledge. The action of personal desire belongs to the unregenerated state of our nature and is dictated by ignorance or false knowledge and an unregulated or ill-regulated kinetic or rajasic egoism. The action controlled by Shastra is an outcome of intellectual, ethical, aesthetic, social and religious culture; it embodies an attempt at a certain right living, harmony and right order and is evidently an effort, more or less advanced according to circumstances, of the sattwic element in man to overtop, regulate and control or guide, where it must be admitted, his rajasic and tamasic egoism. It is the means to a step-in advance and therefore mankind must first proceed through it and make this Shastra its law of action rather than obey the impulsion of its

1 Gita, XVII

personal desires. This is a general rule which humanity has always recognized wherever it has arrived at any kind of established and developed society; it has an idea of an order, a law, a standard of its perfection, something other than the guidance of its desires or the crude direction of its raw impulses. This greater rule the individual finds usually outside himself in some more or less fixed outcome of the experience and wisdom of the race, which he accepts, to which his mind and the leading parts of his being give their assent or sanction and which he tries to make his own by living it in his mind, will and action.

And this assent of the being, its conscious acceptance and will to believe and realize, may be called by the name which the Gita gives to it, his faith, sraddha. The religion, the philosophy, the ethical law, the social idea, the cultural idea in which I put my faith, gives me a law for my nature and its works, an idea of relative right or an idea of relative or absolute perfection and in proportion as I have a sincerity and completeness of faith in it and an intensity of will to live according to that faith, I can become what it proposes to me, I can shape myself into an image of that right or an exemplar of that perfection.

But we see also that there is a freer tendency in man other than the leading of his desires and other than his will to accept the Law, the fixed idea, the safe governing rule of the Shastra. The individual frequently enough, the community at any moment of its life is seen to turn away from the Shastra, becomes impatient of it, loses that form of its will and faith, and goes in search of another law which it is now more disposed to accept as the right rule of living and regard as a more vital or higher truth of existence. This may happen when the established Shastra ceases to be a living thing and degenerates or stiffens into a mass of customs and conventions. Or it may come because it is found that the Shastra is imperfect or no longer useful for the progress demanded; a new truth, a more perfect law of living has become imperative. If that does not exist, it has to be discovered by the effort of the race or by some great and illumined individual mind who embodies the desire and seeking of the race. The Vedic law becomes a convention, and a Buddha appears with his new rule of the eightfold path and the goal of Nirvana; and it may be remarked that he propounds it not as a personal invention, but as the true rule of Aryan living constantly rediscovered by the Buddha, the enlightened mind, the awakened spirit. But this practically means that there is an ideal, an eternal Dharma which religion, philosophy, ethics, and all other powers in man that strive after truth and perfection are constantly endeavouring to embody in new statements of the science and art of the inner and outer life, a new Shastra. The Mosaic law of religious, ethical and social righteousness is convicted of narrowness and imperfection and is now besides a convention; the law of Christ comes to replace it and claims at once to abrogate and to fulfil, to abrogate the imperfect form and fulfil in a deeper and broader light and power the spirit of the thing which it aimed at, the divine rule of living. And the human search does not stop there, but leaves these formulations too, goes back to some past truth it had rejected or breaks forward to some new truth and power but is always in search of the same thing, the law of its perfection, its rule of right living, its complete, highest, and essential self and nature.

This movement begins with the individual, who is no longer satisfied with the law because he finds that it no longer corresponds to his idea and largest or intensest experience of himself and existence and therefore he can no longer bring to it the will to believe and practise. It does not correspond to his inner way of being, it is not to him sat, the thing that truly is, the right, the highest or best or really good; it is not the truth and law of his or of all being. The Shastra is something impersonal to the individual, and that gives it its authority over the narrow personal law of his members; but at the same time, it is personal to the collectivity and is the outcome of its experience, its culture, or its nature. It is not in all its form and spirit the ideal rule of fulfilment of the Self or the eternal law of the Master of our nature, although it may contain in itself in small or larger measure indications, preparations, illuminating glimpses of that far greater thing. And the individual may have gone beyond the collectivity and be ready for a greater truth, a wider walk, a deeper intention of the Life-Spirit. The leading in him that departs from the Shastra may not indeed be always a higher movement; it may take the form of a revolt of the egoistic or rajasic nature seeking freedom from the yoke of something which it feels to be cramping to its liberty of self-fulfillment and self-finding. But even then, it is often justified by some narrowness or imperfection of the Shastra or by the degradation of the current rule of living into a merely restricting or lifeless convention. And so far, it is legitimate, it appeals to a truth, it has a good and just reason for existence: for though it misses the right path, yet the free action of the rajasic ego, because it has more in it of liberty and life, is better than the dead and hidebound tamasic following of a convention. The rajasic is always stronger, always more forcefully inspired and has more possibilities in it than the tamasic nature. But also, this leading may be sattwic at its heart; it may be a turn to a larger and greater ideal which will carry us nearer to a more complete and ample truth of our self and universal existence than has yet been seen and nearer therefore to that highest law which is one with the divine freedom. And in effect this movement is usually an attempt to lay hold on some forgotten truth or to move on to a yet undiscovered or unlived truth of our being. It is not a mere licentious movement of the unregulated nature; it has its spiritual justification and is a necessity of our spiritual progress. And even if the Shastra is still a living thing and the best rule for the human average, the exceptional man, spiritual, inwardly developed, is not bound by that standard. He is called upon to go beyond the fixed line of the Shastra. For this is a rule for the guidance, control and relative perfection of the normal imperfect man and he has to go on to a more absolute perfection: this is a system of fixed dharmas, and he has to learn to live in the liberty of the Spirit.

But what then shall be the secure base of an action which departs both from the guidance of desire and from the normal law? For the rule of desire has an authority of its own, no longer safe or satisfactory to us as it is to the animal or as it might have been to a primitive humanity, but still, so far as it goes, founded on a very living part of our nature and fortified by its strong indications; and the law, the Shastra has behind it all the authority of long established rule, old successful sanctions and a secure past experience. But this new movement is of the nature of a powerful adventure into the unknown or partly known, a daring development and a new conquest, and what then is the clue to be followed, the guiding light on which it can depend or its strong basis in our being? The answer is that the clue and support is to be found in man's sraddha, his faith, his will to believe, to live what he sees or thinks to be the truth of himself and of existence. In other words, this movement is man's appeal to himself or to something potent and compelling in himself or in universal existence for the discovery of his truth, his law of living, his way to fullness and perfection. And everything depends on the nature of his faith, the thing in himself or in the universal soul—of which he is a portion or manifestation—to which he directs it and on how near he gets by it to his real self and the Self or true being of the universe. If he is tamasic, obscure, clouded, if he has an ignorant faith, an inept will, he will reach nothing true and will fall away to his lower nature. If he is lured by false rajasic lights, he can be carried away by self-will into bypaths that may lead to morass or precipice. In either case his only chance of salvation lies in a return of sattwa upon him to impose a new enlightened order and rule upon his members which will liberate him from the violent error of his self-will or the dull error of his clouded ignorance. If on the other hand he has the sattwic nature and a sattwic faith and direction for his steps, he will arrive in sight of a higher yet unachieved ideal rule which may lead him even in rare instances beyond the sattwic light some way at least towards a highest divine illumination and divine way of being and living. For if the sattwic light is so strong in him as to bring him to its own culminating point, then he will be able advancing from that point to make out his gate of entrance into some first ray of that which is divine, transcendent, and absolute. In all effort at self-finding these possibilities are there; they are the conditions of this spiritual adventure.

Now we have to see how the Gita deals with this question on its own line of spiritual teaching and self-discipline. For Arjuna puts immediately a suggestive query from which the problem or one aspect of it arises. When men, he says, sacrifice to God or the gods with faith, sraddha, but abandon the rule of the Shastra, what is that concentrated will of devotion in them, nistha, which gives them this faith and moves them to this kind of action? Is it sattwa, rajas or tamas? to which strand of our nature does it belong? The answer of the Gita first states the principle that the faith in us is of a triple kind like all things in Nature and varies according to the dominating quality of our nature. The faith of each man takes the shape, hue, quality given to it by his stuff of being, his constituting temperament, his innate power of existence, sattvanurupa sarvasya sraddha. And then there comes a remarkable line in which the Gita tells us that this Purusha, this soul in man, is, as it were, made of sraddha, a faith, a will to be, a belief in itself and existence, and whatever is that will, faith or constituting belief in him, he is that and that is he. Sraddhamayo 'yam puruso yo yac-chraddhah sa eva sah. If we look into this pregnant saying a little closely, we shall find that this single line contains implied in its few forceful words almost the whole theory of the modern gospel of pragmatism. For if a man or the soul in a man consists of the faith which is in him, taken in this deeper sense, then it follows that the truth which he sees and wills to live is for him the truth of his being, the truth of himself that he has created or is creating and there can be for him no other real truth. This truth is a thing of his inner and outer action, a thing of his becoming, of the soul's dynamics, not of that in him which never changes. He is what he is today by some past will of his nature sustained and continued by a present will to know, to believe and to be in his intelligence and vital force, and whatever new turn is taken by this will and faith active in his very substance, that he will tend to become in the future. We create our own truth of existence in our own action of mind and life, which is another way of saying that we create our own selves, are our own makers.

But very obviously this is only one aspect of the truth and all one-aspected statements are suspect to the thinker. Truth is not merely whatever our own personality is or creates; that is only the truth of our becoming, one point or line of emphasis in a movement of widest volume. Beyond our personality there is, first, a universal being as well as a universal becoming of which ours is a little movement; and beyond that too there is the eternal Being out of which all becoming derives and to which it owes its potentialities, elements, original and final motives. We may say indeed that all becoming is only an act of universal consciousness, is Maya, is a creation of the will to become, and the only other reality, if there is any, is a pure eternal existence beyond consciousness, featureless, unexpressed and inexpressible. That is practically the standpoint taken by the Mayavadin's Adwaita and the sense of the distinction he makes between pragmatic truth which to his mind is illusory or at least only temporarily and partly real—while modern pragmatism takes it to be the true truth or at least the only recognizable reality because the only reality that we can act and know,—between that pragmatic illusion and on the other side of creative Maya the lonely Absolute featureless and inexpressible. But for the Gita absolute Brahman is also supreme Purusha, and Purusha is always conscious Soul, though its highest consciousness, its super-consciousness, if we will,—as, one may add, its lowest which we call the Inconscient,—is something very different from our mind consciousness to which alone we are accustomed to give the name. There is in that highest superconscience a highest truth and dharma of immortality, the greatest divine way of being, a way of the eternal and infinite. That eternal way of existence and divine manner of being exists already in the eternity of the Purushottama, but we are now attempting to create it here too in our becoming by Yoga; our endeavour is to become the Divine, to be as He, madbhava. That also depends on sraddha. It is by an act of our conscious substance and a belief in its truth, an inmost will to live it or be it that we come by it; but this does not mean that it does not already exist beyond us. Though it may not exist for our outward mind until we see and create ourselves anew into it, it is still there in the Eternal, and we may say even that it is already there in our own secret self; for in us also, in our depths the Purushottama always is. Our growing into that, our creation of it is his and its manifestation in us. All creation indeed since it proceeds from the conscious substance of the Eternal, is a manifestation of him and proceeds by a faith, acceptance, will to be in the originating consciousness, Chit-Shakti.

We are concerned at present, however, not with the metaphysical issue, but with the relation of this will or faith in our being to our possibility of growth into the perfection of the divine nature. This power, this sraddha is in any case our basis. When we live, when we are and do according to our desires, that is a persistent act of sraddha belonging mostly to our vital and physical, our tamasic and rajasic nature. And when we try to be, to live and to do according to the Shastra, we proceed by a persistent act of sraddha which belongs, supposing it to be not a routine faith, to a sattwic tendency that is constantly labouring to impose itself on our rajasic and tamasic parts. When we leave both these things and try to be, to live and to do according to some ideal or novel conception of truth of our own finding or our own individual acceptance, that too is a persistent act of sraddha which may be dominated by any one of these three qualities that constantly govern our every thought, will, feeling and act. And again, when we try to be, to live and to do according to the divine nature, then too we must proceed by a persistent act of sraddha, which must be according to the Gita the faith of the sattwic nature when it culminates and is preparing to exceed its own clear-cut limits. But all and any of these things implies some kinesis or displacement of nature, all suppose an inner or outer or ordinarily both an inner and an outer action. And what then will be the character of this action? The Gita states three main elements of the work we have to do, kartavyam karma and these three are sacrifice, giving and askesis. For when questioned by Arjuna on the difference between the outer and inner renunciation, sannyasa and tyaga, Krishna insists that these three things ought not to be renounced at all but ought altogether to be done, for they are the work before us, kartavyam karma and they purify the wise. In other words, these acts constitute the means of our perfection. But at the same time, they may be done unwisely or less wisely by the unwise. All dynamic action may be reduced in its essential parts to these three elements. For all dynamic action, all kinesis of the nature involves a voluntary or an involuntary Tapasya or askesis, an energism and concentration of our forces or capacities or of some capacity which helps us to achieve, to acquire or to become something, tapas. All action involves a giving of what we are or have, an expenditure which is the price of that achievement, acquisition or becoming, dana. All action involves too a sacrifice to elemental or to universal powers or to the supreme Master of our works. The question is whether we do these things inconsciently, passively, or at best with an unintelligent ignorant half-conscient will, or with an unwisely or perversely conscient energism, or with a wisely conscient will root in knowledge, in other words, whether our sacrifice, giving and askesis are tamasic, rajasic or sattwic in nature.

For everything here, including physical things, partakes of this triple character. Our food, for example, the Gita tells us, is either sattwic, rajasic or tamasic according to its character and effect on the body. The sattwic temperament in the mental and physical body turns naturally to the things that increase the life, increase the inner and outer strength, nourish at once the mental, vital, and physical force, and increase the pleasure and satisfaction and happy condition of mind and life and body, all that is succulent and soft and firm and satisfying. The rajasic temperament prefers naturally food that is violently sour, pun-gent, hot, acrid, rough, and strong and burning, the aliments that increase ill-health and the distempers of the mind and body. The tamasic temperament takes a perverse pleasure in cold, impure, stale, rotten or tasteless food or even accepts like the animals the remnants half-eaten by others. All-pervading is the principle of the three gunas. The gunas apply at the other end in the same way to the things of the mind and spirit, to sacrifice, giving and askesis, and the Gita distinguishes under each of these three heads between the three kinds in the customary terms of these things as they were formulated by the symbolism of the old Indian culture. But, remembering the very wide sense which the Gita itself gives to the idea of sacrifice, we may well enlarge the surface meaning of these hints and open them to a freer significance. And it will be convenient to take them in the reverse order, from tamas to sattwa, since we are considering how we go upward out of our lower nature through a certain sattwic culmination and self-exceeding to a divine nature and action beyond the three gunas.

The tamasic sacrifice is work which is done without faith, without, that is to say, any full conscious idea and acceptance and will towards the thing Nature yet compels us to execute. It is done mechanically, because the act of living demands it, because it comes in our way, because others do it, to avoid some other greater difficulty which may arise from not doing it, or from any other tamasic motive. And it is apt to be done, if we have in the full this kind of temperament, carelessly, perfunctorily, in the wrong way. It will not be performed by the Vidhi or right rule of the Shastra, will not be led in its steps according to the right method laid down by the art and science of life and the true science of the thing to be done. There will be no giving of food in the sacrifice,—and that act in the Indian ritual is symbolic of the element of helpful giving inherent in every action that is real sacrifice, the indispensable giving to others, the fruitful help to others, to the world, without which our action becomes a wholly self-regarding thing and a violation of the true universal law of solidarity and interchange. The work will be done without the Dakshina, the much-needed giving or self-giving to the leaders of the sacrificial action, whether to the outward guide and helper of our work or to the veiled or manifest godhead within us. It will be done without the mantra, without the dedicating thought which is the sacred body of our will and knowledge lifted upwards to the godheads we serve by our sacrifice. The tamasic man does not offer his sacrifice to the gods, but to inferior elemental powers or to those grosser spirits behind the veil who feed upon his works and dominate his life with their darkness.

The rajasic man offers his sacrifice to lower godheads or to perverse powers, the Yakshas, the keepers of wealth, or to the Asuric and the Rakshasic forces. His sacrifice may be performed outwardly according to the Shastra, but its motive is ostentation, pride, or a strong lust after the fruit of his action, a vehement demand for the reward of his works. All work therefore that proceeds from violent or egoistic personal desire or from an arrogant will intent to impose itself on the world for personal objects is of the rajasic nature, even if it mask itself with the insignia of the light, even if it be done outwardly as a sacrifice. Although it is ostensibly given to God or to the gods, it remains essentially an Asuric action. It is the inner state, motive and direction which give their value to our works, and not merely the apparent outer direction, the divine names we may call to sanction them or even the sincere intellectual belief which seems to justify us in the performance. Wherever there is a dominating egoism in our acts, there our work becomes a rajasic sacrifice. The true sattwic sacrifice on the other hand is distinguished by three signs that are the quiet seal of its character. First, it is dictated by the effective truth, executed according to the Vidhi, the right principle, the exact method and rule, the just rhythm and law of our works, their true functioning, their dharma; that means that the reason and enlightened will are the guides and determinants of their steps and their purpose. Secondly, it is executed with a mind concentrated and fixed on the idea of the thing to be done as a true sacrifice imposed on us by the divine law that governs our life and therefore performed out of a high inner obligation or imperative truth and without desire for the personal fruit,—the more impersonal the motive of the action and the temperament of the force put out in it, the more sattwic is its nature. And finally, it is offered to the gods without any reservation; it is acceptable to the divine powers by whom—for they are his masks and personalities—the Master of existence governs the universe.

This sattwic sacrifice comes then very near to the ideal and leads directly towards the kind of action demanded by the Gita; but it is not the last and highest ideal, it is not yet the action of the perfected man who lives in the divine nature. For it is carried out as a fixed dharma and it is offered as a sacrifice or service to the gods, to some partial power or aspect of the Divine manifested in ourselves or in the universe. Work done with a disinterested religious faith or selflessly for humanity or impersonally from devotion to the Right or the Truth is of this nature and action of that kind is necessary for our perfection; for it purifies our thought and will and our natural substance. The culmination of the sattwic action at which we have to arrive is of a still larger and freer kind; it is the high last sacrifice offered by us to the supreme Divine in his integral being and with a seeking for the Purushottama or with the vision of Vasudeva in all that is, the action done impersonally, universally, for the good of the world, for the fulfilment of the divine will in the universe. That culmination leads to its own transcending, to the immortal Dharma. For then comes a freedom in which there is no personal action at all, no sattwic rule of dharma, no limitation of Shastra; the inferior reason and will are themselves overpassed and it is not they but a higher wisdom that dictates and guides the work and commands its objective. There is no question of personal fruit; for the will that works is not our own but a supreme Will of which the soul is the instrument. There is no self-regarding and no selflessness; for the Jiva, the eternal portion of the Divine, is united with the highest Self of his existence and he and all are one in that Self and Spirit. There is no personal action, for all actions are given up to the Master of our works and it is he that does the action through the divinized Prakriti. There is no sacrifice,—unless we can say that the Master of sacrifice is offering the works of his energy in the Jiva to himself in his own cosmic form. This is the supreme self-surpassing state arrived at by the action that is sacrifice, this the perfection of the soul that has come to its full consciousness in the divine nature.

Tamasic tapasya is that which is pursued under a clouded and deluded idea hard and obstinate in its delusion, maintained by an ignorant faith in some cherished falsehood, performed with effort and suffering imposed on oneself in pursuit of some narrow and vulgar egoistic object empty of relation to any true or great aim or else with a concentration of the energy in a will to do hurt to others. That which makes this kind of energism tamasic is not any principle of inertia, for inertia is foreign to tapasya, but a darkness in the mind and nature, a vulgar narrowness and ugliness in the doing or a brutish instinct or desire in the aim or in the motive feeling. Rajasic energisms of askesis are those which are undertaken to get honour and worship from men, for the sake of personal distinction and outward glory and greatness or from some other of the many motives of egoistic will and pride. This kind of askesis is devoted to fleeting particular objects which add nothing to the heavenward growth and perfection of the soul; it is a thing without fixed and helpful principle, an energy bound up with changeful and passing occasion and itself of that nature. Or even if there is ostensibly a more inward and noble object and the faith and will are of a higher kind, yet if any kind of arrogance or pride or any great strength of violent self-will or desire enters into the askesis or if it drives some violent, lawless or terrible action contrary to the Shastra, opposed to the right rule of life and works and afflicting to oneself and to others, or if it is of the nature of self-torture and hurts the mental, vital and physical elements or violates the God within us who is seated in the inner subtle body, then too it is an unwise, an Asuric, a rajasic or rajaso-tamasic tapasya.

Sattwic tapasya is that which is done with a highest enlightened faith, as a duty deeply accepted or for some ethical or spiritual or other higher reason and with no desire for any external or narrowly personal fruit in the action. It is of the character of self-discipline and asks for self-control and a harmonizing of one's nature. The Gita describes three kinds of sattwic askesis. First comes the physical, the askesis of the outward act; under this head are especially mentioned worship and reverence of those deserving reverence, cleanness of the person, the action and the life, candid dealing, sexual purity, and avoidance of killing and injury to others. Next is askesis of speech, and that consists in the study of Scripture, kind, true and beneficent speech, and a careful avoidance of words that may cause fear, sorrow, and trouble to others. Finally, there is the askesis of mental and moral perfection, and that means the purifying of the whole temperament, gentleness and a clear and calm gladness of mind, self-control, and silence. Here comes in all that quiets or disciplines the rajasic and egoistic nature and all that replaces it by the happy and tranquil principle of good and virtue. This is the askesis of the sattwic dharma so highly prized in the system of the ancient Indian culture. Its greater culmination will be a high purity of the reason and will, an equal soul, a deep peace and calm, a wide sympathy and preparation of oneness, a reflection of the inner soul's divine gladness in the mind, life, and body. There at that lofty point the ethical is already passing away into the spiritual type and character. And this culmination too can be made to transcend itself, can be raised into a higher and freer light, can pass away into the settled godlike energy of the supreme nature. And what will remain then will be the spirit's immaculate Tapas, a highest will and luminous force in all the members acting in a wide and solid calm and a deep and pure spiritual delight, Ananda. There will then be no farther need of askesis, no tapasya, because all is naturally and easily divine, all is that, Tapas. There will be no separate labour of the lower energism because the energy of Prakriti will have found its true source and base in the transcendent will of the Purushottama. Then, because of this high initiation, the acts of this energy on the lower planes also will proceed naturally and spontaneously from an innate perfect will and by an inherent perfect guidance. There will be no limitation by any of the present dharmas; for there will be a free action far above the rajasic and tamasic nature, but also far beyond the too careful and narrow limits of the sattwic rule of action.

As with tapasya, all giving also is of an ignorant tamasic, an ostentatious rajasic or a disinterested and enlightened sattwic character. The tamasic gift is offered ignorantly with no consideration of the right conditions of time, place, and object; it is a foolish, inconsiderate and in reality, a self-regarding movement, an ungenerous and ignoble generosity, the gift offered without sympathy or true liberality, without regard for the feelings of the recipient and despised by him even in the acceptance. The rajasic kind of giving is that which is done with regret, unwillingness, or violence to oneself or with a personal and egoistic object or in the hope of a return of some kind from whatever quarter or a corresponding or greater benefit to oneself from the receiver. The sattwic way of giving is to bestow with right reason and goodwill and sympathy in the right conditions of time and place and on the right recipient who is worthy or to whom the gift can be really helpful. Its act is performed for the sake of the giving and the beneficence, without any view to a benefit already done or yet to be done to oneself by the receiver of the benefit and without any personal object in the action.

The culmination of the sattwic way of dana¯ will bring into the action an increasing element of that wide self-giving to others and to the world and to God, atma-dana, atma-samarpana, which is the high consecration of the sacrifice of works enjoined by the Gita. And the transcendence in the divine nature will be the greatest completeness of self-offering founded on the largest meaning of existence. All this manifold universe comes into birth and is constantly maintained by God's giving of himself and his powers and the lavish outflow of his self and spirit into all these existences; universal being, says the Veda, is the sacrifice of the Purusha. All the action of the perfected soul will be even such a constant divine giving of itself and its powers, an outflowing of the knowledge, light, strength, love, joy, helpful shakti which it possesses in the Divine and by his influence and effluence on all around it according to their capacity of reception or on all this world and its creatures. That will be the complete result of the complete self-giving of the soul to the Master of our existence.

The Gita closes this chapter with what seems at first sight a recondite utterance. The formula OM, Tat, Sat, is, it says, the triple definition of the Brahman, by whom the Brahmanas, the Vedas and sacrifices were created of old and in it resides all their significance. Tat, That, indicates the Absolute. Sat indicates the supreme and universal existence in its principle. OM is the symbol of the triple Brahman, the outward-looking, the inward or subtle and the superconscient causal Purusha. Each letter A, U, M indicates one of these three in ascending order and the syllable as a whole brings out the fourth state, Turiya, which rises to the Absolute. OM is the initiating syllable pronounced at the outset as a benedictory prelude and sanction to all act of sacrifice, all act of giving and all act of askesis; it is a reminder that our work should be made an expression of the triple Divine in our inner being and turned towards him in the idea and motive. The seekers of liberation indeed do these actions without desire of fruit and only with the idea, feeling, Ananda of the absolute Divine behind their nature. It is that which they seek by this purity and impersonality in their works, this high desirelessness, this vast emptiness of ego and plenitude of Spirit. Sat means good and it means existence. Both these things, the principle of good and the principle of reality, must be there behind all the three kinds of action. All good works are Sat, for they prepare the soul for the higher reality of our being; all firm abiding in sacrifice, giving and askesis and all works done with that central view, as sacrifice, as giving, as askesis, are Sat, for they build the basis for the highest truth of our spirit. And because sraddha is the central principle of our existence, any of these things done without sraddha is a falsity and has no true meaning or true substance on earth or beyond, no reality, no power to endure or create in life here or after the mortal life in greater regions of our conscious spirit. The soul's faith, not a mere intellectual belief, but its concordant will to know, to see, to believe and to do and be according to its vision and knowledge, is that which determines by its power the measure of our possibilities of becoming, and it is this faith and will turned in all our inner and outer self, nature and action towards all that is highest, most divine, most real and eternal that will enable us to reach the supreme perfection.

XIX

THE GUNAS, MIND AND WORKS[1]

The Gita has not yet completed its analysis of action in the light of this fundamental idea of the three gunas and the transcendence of them by a self-exceeding culmination of the highest sattwic discipline. Faith, sraddha, the will to believe and to be, know, live, and enact the Truth that we have seen is the principal factor, the indispensable force be-hind a self-developing action, most of all behind the growth of the soul by works into its full spiritual stature. But there are also the mental powers, the instruments and the conditions which help to constitute the momentum, direction and character of the activity and are therefore of importance for a full understanding of this psychological discipline. The Gita enters into a summary psychological analysis of these things before it proceeds to its great finale, the culmination of all it teaches, the highest secret which is that of a spiritual exceeding of all dharmas, a divine transcendence. And we have to follow it in its brief descriptions, summarily, expanding just enough to seize fully the main idea; for these are secondary things but yet each of great consequence in its own place and for its own purpose. It is their action cast in the type of the gunas that we have to bring out from the brief descriptions in the text; the nature of the culmination of any or each of them beyond the gunas will automatically follow

1 Gita, XVIII. 1-39.

from the character of the general transcendence.

This part of the subject is introduced by a last question of Arjuna regarding the principle of Sannyasa and the principle of Tyaga and their difference. The frequent harping, the reiterated emphasis of the Gita on this crucial distinction has been amply justified by the subsequent history of the later Indian mind, its constant confusion of these two very different things and its strong bent towards belittling any activity of the kind taught by the Gita as at best only a preliminary to the supreme inaction of Sannyasa. As a matter of fact, when people talk of Tyaga, of renunciation, it is always the physical renunciation of the world which they understand by the word or at least on which they lay emphasis, while the Gita takes absolutely the opposite view that the real Tyaga has action and living in the world as its basis and not a flight to the monastery, the cave, or the hilltop. The real Tyaga is action with a renunciation of desire and that too is the real Sannyasa.

The liberating activity of the sattwic self-discipline must no doubt be pervaded by a spirit of renunciation,—that is an essential element: but what renunciation and in what manner of the spirit? Not the renunciation of work in the world, not any outward asceticism or any ostentation of a visible giving up of enjoyment, but a renunciation, a leaving, tyaga, of vital desire and ego, a total laying aside, sannyasa, of the separate personal life of the desire soul and ego-governed mind and rajasic vital nature. That is the true condition for entering into the heights of Yoga whether through the impersonal self and Brahmic oneness or through universal Vasudeva or inwardly into the supreme Purushottama. More conventionally taken, Sannyasa in the standing terminology of the sages means the physical depositing or laying aside of desirable actions: Tyaga—this is the Gita's distinction—is the name given by the wise to a mental and spiritual renunciation, an entire abandonment of all attached clinging to the fruit of our works, to the action itself or to its personal initiation or rajasic impulse. In that sense Tyaga, not Sannyasa, is the better way. It is not the desirable actions that must be laid aside but the desire which gives them that character has to be put away from us. The fruit of the action may come in the dispensation of the Master of works, but there is to be no egoistic demand for that as a reward and condition of doing works. Or the fruit may not at all come and still the work has to be performed as the thing to be done, kartavyam karma, the thing which the Master within demands of us. The success, the failure are in his hands, and he will regulate them according to his omniscient will and inscrutable purpose. Action, all action has indeed to be given up in the end, not physically by abstention, by immobility, by inertia but spiritually to the Master of our being by whose power alone can any action be accomplished. There has to be a renunciation of the false idea of ourselves as the doer; for in reality, it is the universal Shakti that works through our personality and our ego. The spiritual transference of all our works to the Master and his Shakti is the real Sannyasa in the teaching of the Gita.

The question still arises, what works are to be done? Those even who stand for a final physical renunciation are not at one in this difficult matter. Some would have it that all works must be excised from our life, as if that were possible. But it is not possible so long as we are in the body and alive; nor can salvation consist in reducing our active selves by trance to the lifeless immobility of the clod and the pebble. The silence of Samadhi does not abrogate the difficulty, for as soon as the breath comes again into the body, we are once more in action and have toppled down from the heights of this salvation by spiritual slumber. But the true salvation, the release by an inner renunciation of the ego and union with the Purushottama remains steady in whatever state, persists in this world or out of it or in whatever world or out of all world, is self-existent, sarvatha vartamano'pi, and does not depend upon inaction or action. What then are the actions to be done? The thoroughgoing ascetic answer, not noted by the Gita—it was perhaps not altogether current at the time—might be that solely begging, eating and meditation are to be permitted among voluntary activities and otherwise only the necessary actions of the body. But the more liberal and comprehensive solution was evidently to continue the three most sattwic activities, sacrifice, giving and askesis. And these certainly are to be done, says the Gita, for they purify the wise. But more generally, and understanding these three things in their widest sense, it is the rightly regulated action, niyatam karma, that has to be done, action regulated by the Shastra, the science and art of right knowledge, right works, right living, or regulated by the essential nature, svabhava-niyatam karma or finally and best of all, regulated by the will of the Divine within and above us. The last is the true and only action of the liberated man, muktasya karma. To renounce these works is not a right movement—the Gita lays that down plainly and trenchantly in the end, niyatasya tu sannyasah karmano nopapadyate. To renounce them from an ignorant confidence in the sufficiency of that withdrawal for the true liberation is a tamasic renunciation. The gunas follow us, we see, into the renunciation of works as well as into works. A renunciation with attachment to inaction, sango akarmani, would be equally a tamasic withdrawal. And to give them up because they bring sorrow or are a trouble to the flesh and a weariness to the mind or in the feeling that all is vanity and vexation of spirit, is a rajasic renunciation and does not bring the high spiritual fruit; that too is not the true Tyaga. It is a result of intellectual pessimism or vital weariness; it has its roots in ego. No freedom can come from a renunciation governed by this self-regarding principle.

The sattwic principle of renunciation is to withdraw not from action, but from the personal demand, the ego factor behind it. It is to do works not dictated by desire but by the law of right living or by the essential nature, its knowledge, its ideal, its faith in itself and the Truth it sees, its sraddha. Or else, on a higher spiritual plane, they are dictated by the will of the Master and done with the mind in Yoga, without any personal attachment either to the action or to the fruit of the action. There must be a complete renunciation of all desire and of all self-regarding egoistic choice and impulse and finally of that much subtler egoism of the will which either says, "The work is mine, I am the doer", or even "The work is God's, but I am the doer." There must be no attachment to pleasant, desirable, lucrative, or successful work and no doing of it because it has that nature; but that kind of work too has to be done,—done totally, selflessly, with the assent of the spirit,—when it is the action demanded from above and from within us, kartavyam karma. There must be no aversion to unpleasant, undesirable, or ungratifying action or work that brings or is likely to bring with it suffering, danger, harsh conditions, inauspicious consequences; for that too has to be accepted, totally, selflessly, with a deep understanding of its need and meaning, when it is the work that should be done, kartavyam˙ karma. The wise man puts away the shrinking's and hesitations of the desire-soul and the doubts of the ordinary human intelligence, that measure by little personal, conventional, or otherwise limited standards. He follows in the light of the full sattwic mind and with the power of an inner renunciation lifting the soul to impersonality, towards God, towards the universal and eternal the highest ideal law of his nature or the will of the Master of works in his secret spirit. He will not do action for the sake of any personal result or for any reward in this life or with any attachment to success, profit, or consequence: neither will his works be undertaken for the sake of a fruit in the invisible hereafter or ask for a reward in other births or in worlds beyond us, the prizes for which the half-baked religious mind hungers. The three kinds of result, pleasant, unpleasant, and mixed, in this or other worlds, in this or another life are for the slaves of desire and ego; these things do not cling to the free spirit. The liberated worker who has given up his works by the inner sannyasa to a greater Power is free from Karma. Action he will do, for some kind of action, less or more, small, or great, is inevitable, natural, right for the embodied soul,—action is part of the divine law of living, it is the high dynamics of the spirit. The essence of renunciation, the true Tyaga, the true Sannyasa is not any rule of thumb of inaction but a disinterested soul, a selfless mind, the transition from ego to the free impersonal and spiritual nature. The spirit of this inner renunciation is the first mental condition of the highest culminating sattwic discipline.

The Gita then speaks of the five causes or indispensable requisites for the accomplishment of works as laid down by the Sankhya. These five are, first, the frame of body, life and mind which are the basis or standing-ground of the soul in Nature, adhisthana, next, the doer, karta, third, the various instrumentation of Nature, karana, fourth, the many kinds of effort which make up the force of action, cestah, and last, Fate, daivam, that is to say, the influence of the Power or powers other than the human factors, other than the visible mechanism of Nature, that stand behind these and modify the work and dispose its fruits in the steps of act and consequence. These five elements make up among them all the efficient causes, karana, that determine the shaping and outcome of whatever work man undertakes with mind and speech and body.

The doer is ordinarily supposed to be our surface personal ego, but that is the false idea of the understanding that has not arrived at knowledge. The ego is the ostensible doer, but the ego and its will are creations and instruments of Nature with which the ignorant understanding wrongly identifies our self, and they are not the only determinants even of human action, much less of its turn and consequence. When we are liberated from ego, our real self behind comes forward, impersonal and universal, and it sees in its self-vision of unity with the universal Spirit universal Nature as the doer of the work and the Divine Will behind as the master of universal Nature. Only so long as we have not this knowledge, are we bound by the character of the ego and its will as the doer and do good and evil and have the satisfaction of our tamasic, rajasic or sattwic nature. But once we live in this greater knowledge, the character and consequences of the work can make no difference to the freedom of the spirit. The work may be outwardly a terrible action like this great battle and slaughter of Kurukshetra; but although the liberated man takes his part in the struggle and though he slay all these peoples, he slays no man and he is not bound by his work, because the work is that of the Master of the Worlds and it is he who has already slain in his hidden omnipotent will all these armies. This work of destruction was needed that humanity might move forward to another creation and a new purpose, might get rid as in a fire of its past karma of unrighteousness and oppression and injustice and move towards a kingdom of the Dharma. The liberated man does all his appointed work as the living instrument one in spirit with the universal Spirit. And knowing that all this must be and looking beyond the outward appearance he acts not for self but for God and man and the human and cosmic order,[2] not in fact himself acting, but conscious of the presence and power of the divine Force in his deeds and their issue. He knows that the supreme Shakti is doing in his mental, vital, and physical body, adhisthana, as the sole doer the thing appointed by a Fate which is in truth not Fate, not a mechanical dispensation, but the wise and all-seeing Will that is at work behind human Karma. This "terrible work" on which the whole teaching of the Gita turns, is an extreme example of action inauspicious in appearance, akusalam, though a great good lies beyond the appearance. Impersonally has it to be done by the divinely ap-pointed man for the holding together of the world purpose, loka-sangrahartham without personal aim or desire, because it is the appointed service.

---

2 The cosmic order comes into question, because the triumph of the Asura in humanity means to that extent the triumph of the Asura in the balance of the world-forces.

It is clear then that the work is not the sole thing that matters; the knowledge in which we do works makes an immense spiritual difference. There are three things, says the Gita, which go to constitute the mental impulsion to works, and they are the knowledge in our will, the object of knowledge and the knower; and into the knowledge there always comes the working of the three gunas. It is this element of the gunas that makes all the difference to our view of the thing known and to the spirit in which the knower does his work. The tamasic ignorant knowledge is a small and narrow, a lazy or dully obstinate way of looking at things which has no eye for the real nature of the world or of the thing done or its field or the act or its conditions. The tamasic mind does not look for real cause and effect but absorbs itself in one movement or one routine with an obstinate attachment to it, can see nothing but the little section of personal activity before its eyes and does not know in fact what it is doing but blindly lets natural impulsion work out through its deed results of which it has no conception, foresight or comprehending intelligence. The rajasic knowledge is that which sees the multiplicity of things only in their separateness and variety of operation in all these existences and is unable to discover a true principle of unity or rightly coordinate its will and action, but follows the bent of ego and desire, the activity of its many-branching egoistic will and various and mixed motive in response to the solicitation of internal and environing impulsions and forces. This knowing is a jumble of sections of knowledge, often inconsistent knowledge, put forcefully together by the mind in order to make some kind of pathway through the confusion of our half-knowledge and half-ignorance. Or else it is a restless kinetic multiple action with no firm governing higher ideal and self-possessed law of true light and power within it. The sattwic knowledge on the contrary sees existence as one indivisible whole in all these divisions, one imperishable being in all becomings; it masters the principle of its action and the relation of the particular action to the total purpose of existence; it puts in the right place each step of the complete process. At the highest top of knowledge this seeing becomes the knowledge of the one spirit in the world, one in all these many existences of the one Master of all works, of the forces of cosmos as expressions of the Godhead and of the work itself as the operation of his supreme will and wisdom in man and his life and essential nature. The personal will has come to be entirely conscious, illumined, spiritually awake, and it lives and works in the One, obeys more and more perfectly his supreme mandate and grows more and more a faultless instrument of his light and power in the human person. The supreme liberated action arrives through this culmination of the sattwic knowledge.

There are again three things, the doer, the instrument, and the work done, that hold the action together and make it possible. And here again it is the difference of the gunas that determines the character of each of these elements. The sattwic mind that seeks always for a right harmony and right knowledge is the governing instrument of the sattwic man and moves all the rest of the machine. An egoistic will of desire supported by the desire-soul is the dominant instrument of the rajasic worker. An ignorant instinct or the unenlightened impulsion of the physical mind and the crude vital nature is the chief instrumental force of the tamasic doer of action. The instrument of the liberated man is a greater spiritual light and power, far higher than the highest sattwic intelligence, and it works in him by an enveloping descent from a supraphysical Centre and uses as a clear channel of its force a purified and receptive mind, life, and body.

Tamasic action is that done with a confused, deluded, and ignorant mind, in mechanical obedience to the instincts, impulsions and unseeing ideas, without regarding the strength or capacity or the waste and loss of blind misapplied effort or the antecedent and consequence and right conditions of the impulse, effort or labour. Rajasic action is that which a man undertakes under the dominion of desire, with his eyes fixed on the work and its hoped-for fruit and nothing else, or with an egoistic sense of his own personality in the action, and it is done with inordinate effort, with a passionate labour, with a great heaving and straining of the personal will to get at the object of its desire. Sattwic action is that which a man does calmly in the clear light of reason and knowledge and with an impersonal sense of right or duty or the demand of an ideal, as the thing that ought to be done whatever may be the result to himself in this world or another, a work performed without attachment, without liking or disliking for its spur or its drag, for the sole satisfaction of his reason and sense of right, of the lucid intelligence and the enlightened will and the pure disinterested mind and the high contented spirit. At the line of culmination of sattwa it will be transformed and become a highest impersonal action dictated by the spirit within us and no longer by the intelligence, an action moved by the highest law of the nature, free from the lower ego and its light or heavy baggage and from limitation even by best opinion, noblest desire, purest personal will or loftiest mental ideal. There will be none of these impedimenta; in their place there will stand a clear spiritual self-knowledge and illumination and an imperative intimate sense of an infallible power that acts and of the work to be done for the world and for the world's Master.

The tamasic doer of action is one who does not put himself really into the work, but acts with a mechanical mind, or obeys the most vulgar thought of the herd, follows the common routine, or is wedded to a blind error and prejudice. He is obstinate in stupidity, stubborn in error and takes a foolish pride in his ignorant doing; a narrow and evasive cunning replaces true intelligence; he has a stupid and insolent contempt for those with whom he has to deal, especially for wiser men and his betters. A dull laziness, slowness, procrastination, looseness, want of vigour or of sincerity mark his action. The tamasic man is ordinarily slow to act, dilatory in his steps, easily depressed, ready soon to give up his task if it taxes his strength, his diligence, or his patience.

The rajasic doer of action on the contrary is one eagerly attached to the work, bent on its rapid completion, passionately desirous of fruit and reward and consequence, greedy of heart, impure of mind, often violent and cruel and brutal in the means he uses; he cares little whom he injures or how much he injures others so long as he gets what he wants, satisfies his passions and will, vindicates the claims of his ego. He is full of an incontinent joy in success and bitterly grieved and stricken by failure. The sattwic doer is free from all this attachment, this egoism, this violent strength, or passionate weakness; his is a mind and will be unelated by success, undepressed by failure, full of a fixed impersonal resolution, a calm rectitude of zeal or a high and pure and selfless enthusiasm in the work that has to be done. At and beyond the culmination of sattwa this resolution, zeal, enthusiasm become the spontaneous working of the spiritual Tapas and at last a highest soul-force, the direct God-Power, the mighty and steadfast movement of a divine energy in the human instrument, the self-assured steps of the Seer-will, the gnostic intelligence and with it the wide delight of the free spirit in the works of the liberated nature.

The reason armed with the intelligent will works in man in whatever manner or measure he may possess these human gifts and it is accordingly right or perverted, clouded, or luminous, narrow, and small or large and wide like the mind of its possessor. It is the understanding power of his nature, buddhi, that chooses the work for him or, more often, approves and sets its sanction on one or other among the many suggestions of his complex instincts, impulsions, ideas, and desires. It is that which determines for him what is right or wrong, to be done or not to be done, Dharma or Adharma. And the persistence of the will[3] is that continuous force of mental Nature which sustains the work and gives it consistence and persistence. Here again there is the incidence of the gunas. The tamasic reason is a false, ignorant, and darkened instrument

3 dhrti.

which chains us to see all things in a dull and wrong light, a cloud of misconceptions, a stupid ignoring of the values of things and people. This reason calls light darkness and darkness light, takes what is not the true law and upholds it as the law, persists in the thing which ought not to be done and holds it up to us as the one right thing to be done. Its ignorance is invincible and its persistence of will is a persistence in the satisfaction and dull pride of its ignorance. That is on its side of blind action; but it is pursued also by a heavy stress of inertia and impotence, a persistence in dullness and sleep, an aversion to mental change and progress, a dwelling on the fears and pains and depressions of mind which deter us in our path or keep us to base, weak and cowardly ways. Timidity, shirking, evasion, indolence, the justification by the mind of its fears and false doubts and cautions and refusals of duty and its lapses and turnings from the call of our higher nature, a safe following of the line of least resistance so that there may be the least trouble and effort and peril in the winning of the fruit of our labour,—rather no fruit or poor result, it says, than a great and noble toil or a perilous and exacting endeavour and adventure,—these are characteristics of the tamasic will and intelligence.

The rajasic understanding, when it does not knowingly choose error and evil for the sake of the error and evil, can make distinctions between right and wrong, between what should or should not be done, but not rightly, rather with a pulling awry of their true measures and a constant distortion of values. And this is because its reason and will are a reason of the ego and a will of desire, and these powers misrepresent and distort the truth and the right to serve their own egoistic purpose. It is only when we are free from ego and desire and look steadily with a calm, pure, disinterested mind concerned only with the truth and its sequences that we can hope to see things rightly and in their just values. But the rajasic will fixes its persistent attention on the satisfaction of its own attached clinging's and desires in its pursuit of interest and pleasure and of what it thinks or chooses to think right and justice, Dharma. Always it is apt to put on these things the construction which will most flatter and justify its desires and to uphold as right or legitimate the means which will best help it to get the coveted fruits of its work and endeavour. That is the cause of three fourths of the falsehood and misconduct of the human reason and will. Rajas with its vehement hold on the vital ego is the great sinner and positive misleader.

The sattwic understanding sees in its right place, right form, right measure the movement of the world, the law of action and the law of abstention from action, the thing that is to be done and the thing that is not to be done, what is safe for the soul and what is dangerous, what is to be feared and shunned and what is to be embraced by the will, what binds the spirit of man and what sets it free. These are the things that it follows or avoids by the persistence of its conscious will according to the degree of its light and the stage of evolution it has reached in its upward ascent to the highest self and Spirit. The culmination of this sattwic intelligence is found by a high persistence of the aspiring buddhi when it is settled on what is beyond the ordinary reason and mental will, pointed to the summits, turned to a steady control of the senses and the life and a union by Yoga with man's highest Self, the universal Divine, the transcendent Spirit. It is there that arriving through the sattwic guna one can pass beyond the gunas, can climb beyond the limitations of the mind and its will and intelligence and sattwa itself disappear into that which is above the gunas and beyond this instrumental nature. There the soul is enshrined in light and enthroned in firm union with the Self and Spirit and Godhead. Arrived upon that summit we can leave the Highest to guide Nature in our members in the free spontaneity of a divine action: for there; there is no wrong or confused working, no element of error or impotence to obscure or distort the luminous perfection and power of the Spirit. All these lower conditions, laws, dharmas cease to have any hold on us; the Infinite acts in the liberated man and there is no law but the immortal truth and right of the free spirit, no Karma, no kind of bondage.

Harmony and order are the characteristic qualities of the sattwic mind and temperament, quiet happiness, a clear and calm content and an inner ease and peace. Happiness is indeed the one thing which is openly or indirectly the universal pursuit of our human nature,—happiness or its suggestion or some counterfeit of it, some pleasure, some enjoyment, some satisfaction of the mind, the will, the passions, or the body. Pain is an experience our nature has to accept when it must, involuntarily as a necessity, an unavoidable incident of universal Nature, or voluntarily as a means to what we seek after but not a thing desired for its own sake,—except when it is so sought in perversity or with an ardour of enthusiasm in suffering for some touch of fierce pleasure it brings or the intense strength it engenders. But there are various kinds of happiness or pleasure according to the guna which dominates in our nature. Thus, the tamasic mind can remain well-pleased in its indolence and inertia, its stupor and sleep, its blindness, and its error. Nature has armed it with the privilege of a smug satisfaction in its stupidity and ignorance, its dim lights of the cave, its inert contentment, its petty or base joys and its vulgar pleasures. Delusion is the beginning of this satisfaction and delusion is its consequence but still there is given a dull, a by no means admirable but a sufficient pleasure in his delusions to the dweller in the cave. There is a tamasic happiness founded in inertia and ignorance.

The mind of the rajasic man drinks of a fierier and more intoxicating cup; the keen, mobile, active pleasure of the senses and the body and the sense-entangled or fierily kinetic will and intelligence are to him all the joy of life and the very significance of living. This joy is nectar to the lips at the first touch, but there is a secret poison in the bottom of the cup and after it the bitterness of disappointment, satiety, fatigue, revolt, disgust, sin, suffering, loss, transience. And it must be so because these pleasures in their external figure are not the things which the spirit in us truly demands from life; there is something behind and beyond the transience of the form, something that is lasting, satisfying, self-sufficient. What the sattwic nature seeks, there-fore, is the satisfaction of the higher mind and the spirit and when it once gets this large object of its quest, there comes in a clear, pure happiness of the soul, a state of fullness, an abiding ease and peace. This happiness does not depend on outward things but on ourselves alone and on the flowering of what is best and most inward within us. But it is not at first our normal possession; it has to be conquered by self-discipline, a labour of the soul, a high and arduous endeavour. At first this means much loss of habitual pleasure, much suffering and struggle, a poison born of the churning of our nature, a painful conflict of forces, much revolt and opposition to the change due to the ill-will of the members or the insistence of vital movements, but in the end the nectar of immortality rises in the place of this bitterness and as we climb to the higher spiritual nature we come to the end of sorrow, the euthanasia of grief and pain. That is the surpassing happiness which descends upon us at the point or line of culmination of the sattwic discipline.

The self-exceeding of the sattwic nature comes when we get beyond the great but still inferior sattwic pleasure, beyond the pleasures of mental knowledge and virtue and peace to the eternal calm of the self and the spiritual ecstasy of the divine oneness. That spiritual joy is no longer the sattwic happiness, sukham, but the absolute Ananda. Ananda is the secret delight from which all things are born, by which all is sustained in existence and to which all can rise in the spiritual culmination. Only then can it be possessed when the liberated man, free from ego and its desires, lives at last one with his highest self, one with all beings and one with God in an absolute bliss of the spirit.

XX

SWABHAVA AND SWADHARMA[1]

It is then by a liberating development of the soul out of this lower nature of the triple gunas into the supreme divine nature beyond the three gunas that we can best arrive at spiritual perfection and freedom. And this again can best be brought about by an anterior development of the predominance of the highest sattwic quality to a point at which sattwa also is overpassed, mounts beyond its own limitations and breaks up into a supreme freedom, absolute light, serene power of the conscious spirit in which there is no determination by conflicting gunas. A highest sattwic faith and aim new shaping what we are according to the highest mental conception of our inner possibilities that we can form in the free intelligence, is changed by this transition into a vision of our own real being, a spiritual self-knowledge. A loftiest ideality or standard of dharma, a pursuit of the right law of our natural existence, is transformed into a free assured self-existent perfection in which all dependence on standards is transcended and the spontaneous law of the immortal self and spirit displaces the lower rule of the instruments and members. The sattwic mind and will change into that spiritual knowledge and dynamic power of identical existence in which the whole nature puts off its disguise and becomes a free self-expression of the godhead within it. The sattwic doer becomes

1 Gita, XVIII. 40-48.

the Jiva in contact with his source, united with the Purushottama; he is no longer the personal doer of the act, but a spiritual channel of the works of the transcendent and universal Spirit. His natural being transformed and illumined remains to be the instrument of a universal and impersonal action, the bow of the divine Archer. What was sattwic action becomes the free activity of the perfected nature in which there is no longer any personal limitation, any tethering to this or that quality, any bondage of sin and virtue, self, and others or any but a supreme spiritual self-determination. That is the culmination of works uplifted to the sole Divine Worker by a God-seeking and spiritual knowledge.

But there is still an incidental question of great importance in the old Indian system of culture and, even apart from that antique view, of considerable general importance, on which we have had some passing pronouncements already by the Gita and which now falls into its proper place. All action on the normal level is determined by the gunas; the action, which is to be done, kartavyam karma, takes the triple form of giving, askesis and sacrifice and any or all of these three may assume the character of any of the gunas. Therefore, we have to proceed by the raising of these things to the highest sattwic height of which they are capable and go yet farther beyond to a largeness in which all works become a free self-giving, an energy of the divine Tapas, a perpetual sacrament of the spiritual existence. But this is a general law and all these considerations have been the enunciation of quite general principles and refer indiscriminately to all actions and to all men alike. All can eventually arrive by spiritual evolution to this strong discipline, this large perfection, this highest spiritual state. But while the general rule of mind and action is the same for all men, we see too that there is a constant law of variation and each individual acts not only according to the common laws of the human spirit, mind, will, life, but according to his own nature; each man fulfils different functions or follows a different bent according to the rule of his own circumstances, capacities, turn, character, powers. What place is to be assigned to this variation, this individual rule of nature in the spiritual discipline?

The Gita has laid some stress on this point and even assigned to it a great preliminary importance. At the very start it has spoken of the nature, rule, and function of the Kshatriya as Arjuna's own law of action, svadharma;[2] it has proceeded to lay it down with a striking emphasis that one's own nature, rule, function should be observed and followed,—even if defective, it is better than the well-performed rule of another's nature. Death in one's own law of nature is better for a man than victory in an alien movement. To follow the law of another's nature is dangerous to the soul,[3] contradictory, as we may say, to the natural way of his evolution, a thing mechanically imposed and therefore imported, artificial and sterilizing to one's growth towards the true stature of the spirit. What comes out of the being is the right and healthful thing, the authentic movement, not what is imposed on it from outside or laid on it by life's compulsions or the mind's error. This swadharma is of four general kinds formulated outwardly in the action of the four orders of the old Indian social culture, caturvarnya. That system corresponds, says the Gita, to a divine law, it "was created by me according to the divisions of the gunas and works,"—created from the beginning by the Master of existence. In other words, there are four distinct orders of the active nature, or four fundamental types of the soul in nature, svabhava, and the work and proper function of each human being corresponds to his type of nature. This is now finally explained in preciser detail. The works of Brahmins, Kshatriyas, Vaishyas and Shudras, says the Gita, are divided according to the qualities (gunas) born of their own inner nature, spiritual temperament, essential character (svabhava). Calm, self-control, askesis, purity, long-suffering, candour, knowledge, acceptance of spiritual truth

---

2 II. 31. svadharmam api caveksya.

3 III. 35.

are the work of the Brahmin, born of his swabhava. Heroism, high spirit, resolution, ability, not fleeing in the battle, giving, lordship (isvara-bhava, the temperament of the ruler and leader) are the natural work of the Kshatriya. Agriculture, cattle-keeping, trade inclusive of the labour of the craftsman and the artisan are the natural work of the Vaishya. All work of the character of service falls within the natural function of the Shudra. A man, it goes on to say, who devotes himself to his own natural work in life acquires spiritual perfection, not indeed by the mere act itself, but if he does it with right knowledge and the right motive, if he can make it a worship of the Spirit of this creation and dedicate it sincerely to the Master of the universe from whom is all impulse to action. All labour, all action and function, whatever it be, can be consecrated by this dedication of works, can convert the life into a self-offering to the Godhead within and without us and is itself converted into a means of spiritual perfection. But a work not naturally one's own, even though it may be well performed, even though it may look better from the outside when judged by an external and mechanical standard or may lead to more success in life, is still inferior as a means of subjective growth precisely because it has an external motive and a mechanical impulsion. One's own natural work is better, even if it looks from some other point of view defective. One does not incur sin or stain when one acts in the true spirit of the work and in agreement with the law of one's own nature. All action in the three gunas is imperfect, all human work is subject to fault, defect, or limitation but that should not make us abandon our own proper work and natural function. Action should be rightly regulated action, niyatam karma but intrinsically one's own, evolved from within, in harmony with the truth of one's being, regulated by the Swabhava, svabhava-niyatam karma.

What precisely is the intention of the Gita? Let us take it first in its more outward meaning and consider the tinge given to the principle it enounces by the ideas of the race and the time—

the hue of the cultural environment, the ancient significance. These verses and the earlier pronouncements of the Gita on the same subject have been seized upon in current controversies on the caste question and interpreted by some as a sanction of the present system, used by others as a denial of the hereditary basis of caste. In point of fact the verses in the Gita have no bearing on the existing caste system because that is a very different thing from the ancient social ideal of caturvarna, the four clear-cut orders of the Aryan community, and in no way corresponds with the description of the Gita. Agriculture, cattle-keeping and trade of every kind are said here to be the work of the Vaishya; but in the later system the majority of those concerned in trade and in cattle-keeping, artisans, small craftsmen and others are actually classed as Shudras,—where they are not put altogether outside the pale,—and, with some exceptions, the merchant class is alone and that too not everywhere ranked as Vaishya. Agriculture, government, and service are the professions of all classes from the Brahmin down to the Shudra. And if the economical divisions of function have been confounded beyond any possibility of rectification, the law of the guna or quality is still less a part of the later system. There all is rigid custom, acara, with no reference to the need of the individual nature. If again we take the religious side of the contention advanced by the advocates of the caste system, we can certainly fasten no such absurd idea on the words of the Gita as that it is a law of a man's nature that he shall follow without regard to his personal bent and capacities the profession of his parents or his immediate or distant ancestors, the son of a milkman be a milkman, the son of a doctor a doctor, the descendants of shoemakers remain shoemakers to the end of measurable time, still less that by doing so, by this unintelligent and mechanical repetition of the law of another's nature without regard to his own individual call and qualities a man automatically farthers his own perfection and arrives at spiritual freedom. The Gita's words refer to the ancient system of caturvarna, as it existed or was supposed to exist in its ideal purity,—there is some controversy whether it was ever anything more than an ideal or general norm more or less loosely followed in practice,—and it should be considered in that connection alone. Here too there is considerable difficulty as to the exact outward significance.

The ancient system of the four orders had a triple aspect; it took a social and economic, a cultural and a spiritual appearance. On the economic side it recognized four functions of the social man in the community, the religious and intellectual, the political, the economic and the servile functions. There are thus four kinds of work, the work of religious ministration, letters, learning and knowledge, the work of government, politics, administration and war, the work of production, wealth-making and exchange, the work of hired labour and service. An endeavour was made to found and stabilize the whole arrangement of society on the partition of these four functions among four clearly marked classes. This system was not peculiar to India but was with certain differences the dominating feature of a stage of social evolution in other ancient or mediaeval societies. The four functions are still inherent in the life of all normal communities, but the clear divisions no longer exist anywhere. The old system everywhere broke down and gave place to a more fluid order or, as in India, to a confused and complex social rigidity and economic immobility degenerating towards a chaos of castes. Along with this economic division there existed the association of a cultural idea which gave to each class its religious custom, its law of honour, ethical rule, suitable education and training, type of character, family ideal and discipline. The facts of life did not always correspond to the idea,—there is always a certain gulf found between the mental ideal and the vital and physical practice,—but there was a constant and strenuous endeavour to keep up as much as possible a real correspondence. The importance of this attempt and of the cultural ideal and atmosphere it created in the past training of the social man, can hardly be put too high; but at the present day it has little more than a historical, a past and evolutionary significance.

Finally, wherever this system existed, it was given more or less a religious sanction (more in the East, very little in Europe) and in India a profounder spiritual use and significance. This spiritual significance is the real kernel of the teaching of the Gita.

The Gita found this system in existence and its ideal in possession of the Indian mind and it recognized and accepted both the ideal and system and its religious sanction. "The four-fold order was created by me," says Krishna, "according to the divisions of quality and active function." On the mere strength of this phrase, it cannot altogether be concluded that the Gita regarded this system as an eternal and universal social order. Other ancient authorities did not so regard it; rather they distinctly state that it did not exist in the beginning and will collapse in a later age of the cycle. Still, we may understand from the phrase that the fourfold function of social man was considered as normally inherent in the psychological and economic needs of every community and therefore a dispensation of the Spirit that expresses itself in the human corporate and individual existence. The Gita's line is in fact an intellectual rendering of the well-known symbol in the Vedic Purusha-Sukta. But what then should be the natural basis and form of practice of these functions? The practical basis in ancient times came to be the hereditary principle. A man's social function and position were no doubt determined originally, as they are still in freer, less closely ordered communities by environment, occasion, birth, and capacity; but as there set in a more fixed stratification, his rank came practically to be regulated by birth mainly or alone and in the later system of caste birth came to be the sole rule of status. The son of a Brahmin is always a Brahmin in status, though he may have nothing of the typical Brahmin qualities or character, no intellectual training or spiritual experience or religious worth or knowledge, no connection whatever with the right function of his class, no Brahminhood in his work and no Brahminhood in his nature.

This was an inevitable evolution, because the external signs are the only ones which are easily and conveniently determinable and birth was the most handy and manageable in an increasingly mechanized, complex, and conventional social order. For a time, the possible disparity between the hereditary fiction and the individual's real inborn character and capacity was made up or minimized by education and training: but eventually this effort ceased to be sustained and the hereditary convention held absolute rule. The ancient lawgivers, while recognising the hereditary practice, insisted that quality, character, and capacity were the one sound and real basis and that without them the hereditary social status became an unspiritual falsehood because it had lost its true significance. The Gita too, as always, founds its thought on the inner significance. It speaks indeed in one verse of the work born with a man, sahajam karma but this does not in itself imply a hereditary basis. According to the Indian theory of rebirth, which the Gita recognizes, a man's inborn nature and course of life are essentially determined by his own past lives, are the self-development already effected by his past actions and mental and spiritual evolution and cannot depend solely on the material factor of his ancestry, parentage, physical birth, which can only be of subordinate moment, one effective sign perhaps, but not the dominant principle. The word sahaja means that which is born with us, whatever is natural, inborn, innate; its equivalent in all other passages is svabhavaja. The work or function of a man is determined by his qualities, karma is determined by guna; it is the work born of his Swabhava, svabhavajam karma and regulated by his Swabhava, svabhava-niyatam karma. This emphasis on an inner quality and spirit which finds expression in work, function and action is the whole sense of the Gita's idea of Karma.

And from this emphasis on the inner truth and not on the outer form arises the spiritual significance and power which the Gita assigns to the following of the Swadharma. That is the really important bearing of the passage. Too much has been made of its connection with the outer social order, as if the object of the Gita were to support that for its own sake or to justify it by a religio-philosophical theory. In fact, it lays very little stress on the external rule and a very great stress on the internal law which the Varna system attempted to put into regulated outward practice. And it is on the individual and spiritual value of this law and not on its communal and economic or other social and cultural importance that the eye of the thought is fixed in this passage. The Gita accepted the Vedic theory of sacrifice, but gave it a profound turn, an inner, subjective, and universal meaning, a spiritual sense, and direction which alters all its values. Here too and in the same way it accepts the theory of the four orders of men but gives to it a profound turn, an inner, subjective, and universal meaning, a spiritual sense, and direction. And immediately the idea behind the theory changes its values and becomes an enduring and living truth not bound up with the transience of a particular social form and order. What the Gita is concerned with is not the validity of the Aryan social order now abolished or in a state of deliquescence,—if that were all, its principle of the Swabhava and Swadharma would have no permanent truth or value,—but the relation of a man's outward life to his inward being, the evolution of his action from his soul and inner law of nature.

And we see in fact that the Gita itself indicates very clearly its intention when it describes the work of the Brahmin and the Kshatriya not in terms of external function, not defined as learning, priest-work and letters or government, war, and politics but entirely in terms of internal character. The language reads a little curiously to our ear. Calm, self-control, askesis, purity, long-suffering, candour, knowledge, acceptance, and practice of spiritual truth would not ordinarily be described as a man's function, work, or life occupation. Yet this is precisely what the Gita means and says,—that these things, their development, their expression in conduct, their power to cast into form the law of the sattwic nature are the real work of the Brahmin: learning, religious ministration and the other outer functions are only its most suitable field, a favourable means of this inner development, its appropriate self-expression, its way of fixing itself into firmness of type and externalized solidity of character. War, government, politics, leadership, and rule are a similar field and means for the Kshatriya, but his real work is the development, the expression in conduct, the power to cast into form and dynamic rhythm of movement the law of the active battling royal or warrior spirit. The work of the Vaishya and Shudra is expressed in terms of external function, and this opposite turn may have some significance. For the temperament moved to production and wealth-getting or limited in the circle of labour and service, the mercantile and the servile mind, are usually turned outward, more occupied with the external values of their work than its power for character, and this disposition is not so favourable to a sattwic or spiritual action of the nature. That too is the reason why a commercial and industrial age or a society preoccupied with the idea of work and labour creates around it an atmosphere more favourable to the material than the spiritual life, more adapted to vital efficiency than to the subtler perfection of the high-reaching mind and spirit. Nevertheless, this kind of nature too and its functions have their inner significance, their spiritual value and can be made a means and power for perfection. As has been said elsewhere, not alone the Brahmin with his ideal of spirituality, ethical purity and knowledge and the Kshatriya with his ideal of nobility, chivalry, and high character, but the wealth-seeking Vaishya, the toil-imprisoned Shudra, woman with her narrow, circumscribed, and subject life, the very outcaste born from a womb of sin, papayonayah, can by this road rise at once towards the highest inner greatness and spiritual freedom, towards perfection, towards the liberation and fulfilment of the divine element in the human being.

Three propositions suggest themselves even at the first view and may be taken as implicit in all that the Gita says in this passage. First, all action must be determined from within because each man has in him something his own, some characteristic principle and inborn power of his nature. That is the efficient power of his spirit, that creates the dynamic form of his soul in nature and to express and perfect it by action, to make it effective in capacity and conduct and life is his work, his true Karma: that points him to the right way of his inner and outer living and is the right starting-point for his farther development. Next, there are broadly four types of nature each with its characteristic function and ideal rule of work and character and the type indicates the man's proper field and should trace for him his just circle of function in his outer social existence. Finally, whatever work a man does, if done according to the law of his being, the truth of his nature, can be turned Godwards and made an effective means of spiritual liberation and perfection. The first and last of these propositions are suggestions of an evident truth and justice. The ordinary way of man's individual and social living seems indeed to be a contradiction of these principles; for certainly we bear a terrible weight of external necessity, rule and law and our need for self-expression, for the development of our true person, our real soul, our inmost characteristic law of nature in life is at every turn interfered with, thwarted, forced from its course, given a very poor chance and scope by environmental influences. Life, State, society, family, all surrounding powers seem to be in a league to lay their yoke on our spirit, compel us into their moulds, impose on us their mechanical interest and rough immediate convenience. We become parts of a machine; we are not, are hardly allowed to be men in the true sense, manusya, purusa, souls, minds, free children of the spirit empowered to develop the highest characteristic perfection of our being and make it our means of service to the race. It would seem that we are not what we make ourselves, but what we are made. Yet the more we advance in knowledge, the more the truth of the Gita's rule is bound to appear. The child's education ought to be an outbringing of all that is best, most powerful, most intimate and living in his nature; the mould into which the man's action and development ought to run is that of his innate quality and power. He must acquire new things, but he will acquire them best, most vitally on the basis of his own developed type and inborn force. And so too the functions of a man ought to be determined by his natural turn, gift, and capacities. The individual who develops freely in this manner will be a living soul and mind and will have a much greater power for the service of the race. And we are able now to see more clearly that this rule is true not only of the individual but of the community and the nation, the group soul, the collective man. The second proposition of the four types and their functions is more open to dispute. It may be said that it is too simple and positive, that it takes no sufficient account of the complexity of life and the plasticity of human nature, and, whatever the theory or its intrinsic merits, the outward social application must lead precisely to that tyranny of a mechanical rule which is the flat contradiction of all law of Swadharma. But it has a profounder meaning under the surface which gives it a less disputable value. And even if we reject it, the third proposition will yet stand in its general significance. Whatever a man's work and function in life, he can, if it is determined from within or if he is allowed to make it a self-expression of his nature, turn it into a means of growth and of a greater inner perfection. And whatever it be, if he performs his natural function in the right spirit, if he enlightens it by the ideal mind, if he turns its action to the uses of the Godhead within, serves with it the Spirit manifested in the universe or makes it a conscious instrumentation for the purposes of the Divine in humanity, he can transmute it into a means towards the highest spiritual perfection and freedom.

But the Gita's teaching here has a still profounder significance if we take it not as a detached quotation self-contained in meaning, as is too often done, but as we should do, in connection with all that it has been saying throughout the work and especially in the last twelve chapters. The Gita's philosophy of life and works is that all proceeds from the Divine Existence, the transcendent and universal Spirit. All is a veiled manifestation of the Godhead, Vasudeva, yatah pravrttir bhutanam yena sar-vam idam tatam and to unveil the Immortal within and in the world, to dwell in unity with the Soul of the universe, to rise in consciousness, knowledge, will, love, spiritual delight to oneness with the supreme Godhead, to live in the highest spiritual nature with the individual and natural being delivered from shortcoming and ignorance and made a conscious instrument for the works of the divine Shakti is the perfection of which humanity is capable and the condition of immortality and freedom. But how is this possible when in fact we are enveloped in natural ignorance, the soul shut up in the prison of ego, overcome, beset, hammered, and moulded by the environment, mastered by the mechanism of Nature, cut off from our hold on the reality of our own secret spiritual force? The answer is that all this natural action, however now enveloped in a veiled and contrary working, still contains the principle of its own evolving freedom and perfection. A Godhead is seated in the heart of every man and is the Lord of this mysterious action of Nature. And though this Spirit of the universe, this One who is all, seems to be turning us on the wheel of the world as if mounted on a machine by the force of Maya, shaping us in our ignorance as the potter shapes a pot, as the weaver a fabric, by some skillful mechanical principle, yet is this spirit our own greatest self and it is according to the real idea, the truth of ourselves, that which is growing in us and finding always new and more adequate forms in birth after birth, in our animal and human and divine life, in that which we were, that which we are, that which we shall be,—it is in accordance with this inner soul-truth that, as our opened eyes will discover, we are progressively shaped by this spirit within us in its all-wise omnipotence. This machinery of ego, this tangled complexity of the three gunas, mind, body, life, emotion, desire, struggle, thought, aspiration, endeavour, this locked interaction of pain and pleasure, sin and virtue, striving and success and failure, soul and environment, myself and others, is only the outward imperfect form taken by a higher spiritual Force in me which pursues through its vicissitudes the progressive self-expression of the divine reality and greatness I am secretly in spirit and shall overtly become in nature. This action contains in itself the principle of its own success, the principle of the Swabhava and Swadharma.

The Jiva is in self-expression a portion of the Purushottama. He represents in Nature the power of the supreme Spirit; he is in his personality that Power; he brings out in an individual existence the potentialities of the Soul of the universe. This Jiva itself is spirit and not the natural ego; the spirit and not the form of ego is our reality and inner soul principle. The true force of what we are and can be is there in that higher spiritual Power and this mechanical Maya of the three gunas is not the inmost and fundamental truth of its movements; it is only a present executive energy, an apparatus of lower convenience, a scheme of outward exercise and practice. The spiritual Nature which has become this multiple personality in the universe, para prakrtir jıva-bhuta, is the basic stuff of our existence: all the rest is lower derivation and outer formation from a highest hidden activity of the spirit. And in Nature each of us has a principle and will of our own becoming; each soul is a force of self-consciousness that formulates an idea of the Divine in it and guides by that its action and evolution, its progressive self-finding, its constant varying self-expression, its apparently uncertain but secretly inevitable growth to fullness. That is our Swabhava, our own real nature; that is our truth of being which is finding now only a constant partial expression in our various becoming in the world. The law of action determined by this Swabhava is our right law of self-shaping, function, working, our Swadharma.

This principle obtains throughout cosmos; there is everywhere the one Power at work, one common universal Nature, but in each grade, form, energy, genus, species, individual creature she follows out a major Idea and minor ideas and principles of constant and complex variation that found both the permanent dharma of each and its temporary dharmas. These fix for it the law of its being in becoming, the curve of its birth and persistence and change, the force of its self-preservation and self-increasing, the lines of its stable and evolving self-expression and self-finding, the rules of its relations to all the rest of the expression of the Self in the universe. To follow the law of its being, Swadharma, to develop the idea in its being, Swabhava, is its ground of safety, its right walk and procedure. That does not in the end chain down the soul to any present formulation but rather by this way of development it enriches itself most surely with new experiences assimilated to its own law and principle and can most powerfully grow and break at its hour beyond present moulds to a higher self-expression. To be unable to maintain its own law and principle, to fail to adapt itself to its environment in such a way as to adapt the environment to itself and make it useful to its own nature is to lose itself, forfeit its right of self, deviate from its way of self, is perdition, vinasti, is falsehood, death, anguish of decay and dissolution and necessity of painful self-recovery often after eclipse and disappearance, is the vain circuit of the wrong road retarding our real progress. This law obtains in one form or another in all Nature; it underlies all that action of law of universality and law of variation revealed to us by science. The same law obtains in the life of the human being, his many lives in many human bodies. Here it has an outward play and an inward spiritual truth, and the outward play can only put on its full and real meaning when we have found the inward spiritual truth and enlightened all our action with the values of the spirit. This great and desirable transformation can be affected with rapidity and power in proportion to our progress in self-knowledge.

And first we have to see that the Swabhava means one thing in the highest spiritual nature and takes quite another form and significance in the lower nature of the three gunas. There too it acts, but is not in full possession of itself, is seeking as it were for its own true law in a half light or a darkness and goes on its way through many lower forms, many false forms, endless imperfections, perversions, self-losings, self-findings, seeking's after norm and rule before it arrives at self-discovery and perfection. Our nature here is a mixed weft of knowledge and ignorance, of truth and falsehood, of success and failure, of right and wrong, of finding and losing, of sin and virtue. It is always the Swabhava that is looking for self-expression and self-finding through all these things, svabhavas tu pravartate, a truth which should teach us universal charity and equality of vision, since we are all subject to the same perplexity and struggle. These motions belong, not to the soul, but to the nature. The Purushottama is not limited by this ignorance; he governs it from above and guides the soul through its changes. The pure immutable self is not touched by these movements; it witnesses and supports by its intangible eternity this mutable Nature in her vicissitudes. The real soul of the individual, the central being in us, is greater than these things, but accepts them in its outward evolution in Nature. And when we have got at this real soul, at the changeless universal self-sustaining us and at the Purushottama, the Lord within us who presides over and guides the whole action of Nature, we have found all the spiritual meaning of the law of our life. For we become aware of the Master of existence expressing himself for ever in his infinite quality, anantaguna, in all beings. We become aware of a fourfold presence of the Divinity, a Soul of self-knowledge and world-knowledge, a Soul of strength and power that seeks for and finds and uses its powers, a Soul of mutuality and creation and relation and interchange between creature and creature, a Soul of works those labours in the universe and serves all in each and turns the labour of each to the service of all others. We become aware too of the individual Power of the Divine in us, that which directly uses these fourfold powers, assigns our strain of self-expression, determines our divine work and office, and raises us through it all to his universality in manifoldness till we can find by it our spiritual oneness with him and with all that he is in the cosmos.

The external idea of the four orders of men in life is concerned only with the more outward working of this truth of the divine action; it is limited to one side of its operation in the functioning of the three gunas. It is true that in this birth men fall very largely into one of four types, the man of knowledge, the man of power, the productive vital man, the man of rude labour and service. These are not fundamental divisions, but stages of self-development in our manhood. The human being starts with a sufficient load of ignorance and inertia; his first state is one of rude toil enforced on his animal indolence by the needs of the body, by the impulsion of life, by necessity of Nature and, beyond a certain point of need, by some form of direct or indirect compulsion which society lays upon him, and those who are still governed by this tamas are the Shudras, the serfs of society who give it their toil and can contribute nothing or very little else in comparison with more developed men to its manifold play of life. By kinetic action man develops the rajasic guna in him and we get a second type of man who is driven by a constant instinct for useful creation, production, having, acquisition, holding and enjoying, the middle economic and vital man, the Vaishya. At a higher elevation of the rajasic or kinetic quality of our one common nature we get the active man with a more dominant will, with bolder ambitions, with the instinct to act, battle, and enforce his will, at the strongest to lead, command, rule, carry masses of men in his orbit, the fighter, leader, ruler, prince, king, Kshatriya. And where the sattwic mind predominates, we get the Brahmin, the man with a turn for knowledge, who brings thought, reflection, the seeking for truth and an intelligent or at the highest a spiritual rule into life and illumines by it his conception and mode of existence.

There is always in human nature something of all these four personalities developed or undeveloped, wide, or narrow, suppressed or rising to the surface, but in most men one or the other tends to predominate and seems to take up sometimes the whole space of action in the nature. And in any society, we should have all four types,—even, for an example, if we create a purely productive and commercial society such as modern times have attempted, or for that matter a Shudra society of labour, of the proletariate such as attracts the most modern mind and is now being attempted in one part of Europe and advocated in others. There would still be the thinkers moved to find the law and truth and guiding rule of the whole matter, the captains and leaders of industry who would make all this productive activity an excuse for the satisfaction of their need of adventure and battle and leadership and dominance, the many typical purely productive and wealth-getting men, the average workers satisfied with a modicum of labour and the reward of their labour. But these are quite outward things, and if that were all, this economy of human type would have no spiritual significance. Or it would mean at most, as has been sometimes held in India, that we have to go through these stages of development in our births; for we must perforce proceed progressively through the tamasic, the rajaso-tamasic, the rajasic or rajaso-sattwic to the sattwic nature, ascend and fix ourselves in an inner Brahminhood, brahmanya, and then seek salvation from that basis. But in that case, there would be no logical room for the Gita's assertion that even the Shudra or Chandala can by turning his life Godwards climb straight to spiritual liberty and perfection.

The fundamental truth is not this outward thing, but a force of our inner being in movement, the truth of the fourfold active power of the spiritual nature. Each Jiva possesses in his spiritual nature these four sides, is a soul of knowledge, a soul of strength and of power, a soul of mutuality and interchange, a soul of works and service, but one side or other predominates in the action and expressive spirit and tinges the dealings of the soul with its embodied nature; it leads and gives its stamp to the other powers and uses them for the principal strain of action, tendency, experience. The Swabhava then follows, not crudely and rigidly as put in the social demarcation, but subtly and flexibly the law of this strain and develops in developing it the other three powers. Thus, the pursuit of the impulse of works and service rightly done develops knowledge, increases power, trains closeness or balance of mutuality and skill and order of relation.

Each front of the fourfold godhead moves through the enlargement of its own dominant principle of nature and enrichment by the other three towards a total perfection. This development undergoes the law of the three gunas. There is possible a tamasic and rajasic way of following even the dharma of the soul of knowledge, a brute tamasic and a high sattwic way of following the dharma of power, a forceful rajasic or a beautiful and noble sattwic way of following the dharma of works and service. To arrive at the sattwic way of the inner individual Swadharma and of the works to which it moves us on the ways of life is a preliminary condition of perfection. And it may be noted that the inner Swadharma is not bound to any outward social or other form of action, occupation, or function. The soul of works or that element in us that is satisfied to serve, can, for example, make the life of the pursuit of knowledge, the life of struggle and power or the life of mutuality, production and interchange a means of satisfying its divine impulse to labour and to service.

And in the end to arrive at the divinest figure and most dynamic soul-power of this fourfold activity is a wide doorway to a swiftest and largest reality of the highest spiritual perfection. This we can do if we turn the action of the Swadharma into a worship of the inner Godhead, the universal Spirit, the transcendent Purushottama and, eventually, surrender the whole action into his hands, mayi sannyasya karmani. Then as we get beyond the limitation of the three gunas, so also do we get beyond the division of the fourfold law and beyond the limitation of all distinctive dharmas, sarvadharman parityajya. The Spirit takes up the individual into the universal Swabhava, perfects and unifies the fourfold soul of nature in us and does its self-determined works according to the divine will and the accomplished power of the godhead in the creature.

The Gita's injunction is to worship the Divine by our own work, sva-karmana; our offering must be the works determined by our own law of being and nature. For from the Divine all movement of creation and impulse to act originates and by him all this universe is extended and for the holding together of the worlds he presides over and shapes all action through the Swabhava. To worship him with our inner and outer activities, to make our whole life a sacrifice of works to the Highest is to prepare ourselves to become one with him in all our will and substance and nature. Our work should be according to the truth within us, it should not be an accommodation with outward and artificial standards: it must be a living and sincere expression of the soul and its inborn powers. For to follow out the living inmost truth of this soul in our present nature will help us eventually to arrive at the immortal truth of the same soul in the now superconscious supreme nature. There we can live in oneness with God and our true self and all beings and, perfected, become a faultless instrument of divine action in the freedom of the immortal Dharma.

XXI

TOWARDS THE SUPREME SECRET[1]

The Teacher has completed all else that he needed to say, he has worked out all the central principles and the supporting suggestions and implications of his message and elucidated the principal doubts and questions that might rise around it and now all that rests for him to do is to put into decisive phrase and penetrating formula the one last word, the heart itself of the message, the very core of his gospel. And we find that this decisive, last and crowning word is not merely the essence of what has been already said on the matter, not merely a concentrated description of the needed self-discipline, the Sadhana, and of that greater spiritual consciousness which is to be the result of all its effort and askesis; it sweeps out, as it were, yet farther, breaks down every limit and rule, canon and formula and opens into a wide and illimitable spiritual truth with an infinite potentiality of significance. And that is a sign of the profundity, the wide reach, the greatness of spirit of the Gita's teaching. An ordinary religious teaching or philosophical doctrine is well enough satisfied to seize on certain great and vital aspects of truth and turn them into utilizable dogma and instruction, method, and practice for the guidance of man in his inner life and the law and form of his action; it does not go farther, it does not open doors out of the circle of its

1 Gita, XVIII. 49-56.

own system, does not lead us out into some widest freedom and unimprisoned largeness. This limitation is useful and indeed for a time indispensable. Man bounded by his mind and will has need of a law and rule, a fixed system, a definite practice selective of his thought and action; he asks for the single unmistakable hewn path hedged, fixed and secure to the tread, for the limited horizons, for the enclosed resting-places. It is only the strong and few who can move through freedom to freedom. And yet in the end the free soul ought to have an issue out of the forms and systems in which the mind finds its account and takes its limited pleasure. To exceed our ladder of ascent, not to stop short even on the topmost stair but move untrammelled and at large in the wideness of the spirit is a release important for our perfection; the spirit's absolute liberty is our perfect status. And this is how the Gita leads us: it lays down a firm and sure but very large way of ascent, a great Dharma, and then it takes us out beyond all that is laid down, beyond all dharmas, into infinitely open spaces, divulges to us the hope, lets us into the secret of an absolute perfection founded in an absolute spiritual liberty, and that secret, guhyatamam, is the substance of what it calls its supreme word, that the hidden thing, the inmost knowledge.

And first the Gita restates the body of its message. It summarizes the whole outline and essence in the short space of fifteen verses, lines of a brief and concentrated expression and significance that miss nothing of the kernel of the matter, couched in phrases of the most lucid precision and clearness. And they must therefore be scanned with care, must be read deeply in the light of all that has gone before, because here it is evidently intended to extract what the Gita itself considers to be the central sense of its own teaching. The statement sets out from the original starting-point of the thought in the book, the enigma of human action, the apparently insuperable difficulty of living in the highest self and spirit while yet we continue to do the works of the world. The easiest way is to give up the problem as insoluble, life and action as an illusion or an inferior movement of existence to be abandoned as soon as we can rise out of the snare of the world into the truth of spiritual being. That is the ascetic solution, if it can be called a solution; at any rate it is a decisive and effective way out of the enigma, a way to which ancient Indian thought of the highest and most meditative kind, as soon as it commenced to turn at a sharp incline from its first large and free synthesis, had moved with an always increasing preponderance. The Gita like the Tantra and on certain sides the later religions attempts to preserve the ancient balance: it maintains the substance and foundation of the original synthesis, but the form has been changed and renovated in the light of a developing spiritual experience. This teaching does not evade the difficult problem of reconciling the full active life of man with the inner life in the highest self and spirit; it advances what it holds to be the real solution. It does not at all deny the efficacy of the ascetic renunciation of life for its own purpose, but it sees that that cuts instead of loosening the knot of the riddle and therefore it accounts it an inferior method and holds its own for the better way. The two paths both lead us out of the lower ignorant normal nature of man to the pure spiritual consciousness and so far, both must be held to be valid and even one in essence but where one stops short and turns back, the other advances with a firm subtlety and high courage, opens a gate on unexplored vistas, completes man in God and unites and reconciles in the spirit soul and Nature.

And therefore, in the first five of these verses the Gita so phrases its statement that it shall be applicable to both the way of the inner and the way of the outer renunciation and yet in such a manner that one has only to assign to some of their common expressions a deeper and more inward meaning in order to get the sense and thought of the method favoured by the Gita. The difficulty of human action is that the soul and nature of man seem fatally subjected to many kinds of bondage, the prison of the ignorance, the meshes of the ego, the chain of the passions, the hammering insistence of the life of the moment, an obscure and limited circle without an issue. The soul shut up in this circle of action has no freedom, no leisure or light of self-knowledge to make the discovery of itself and the true value of life and meaning of existence. It has indeed such hints of its being as it can get from its active personality and dynamic nature, but the standards of perfection it can erect there are much too temporal, restricted, and relative to be a satisfactory key to its own riddle. How, while absorbed and continually forced outward by the engrossing call of its active nature, is it to get back to its real self and spiritual existence? The ascetic renunciation and the way of the Gita are both agreed that it must first of all renounce this absorption, must cast from it the external solicitation of out-ward things and separate silent self from active nature; it must identify itself with the immobile Spirit and live in the silence. It must arrive at an inner inactivity, naiskarmya. It is therefore this saving inner passivity that the Gita puts here as the first object of its Yoga, the first necessary perfection in it or Siddhi. "An understanding without attachment in all things, a soul self-conquered and empty of desire, man attains by renunciation a supreme perfection of naiskarmya."

This ideal of renunciation, of a self-conquered stillness, spiritual passivity and freedom from desire is common to all the ancient wisdom. The Gita gives us its psychological foundation with an unsurpassed completeness and clearness. It rests on the common experience of all seekers of self-knowledge that there are two different natures and as it were two selves in us. There is the lower self of the obscure mental, vital, and physical nature subject to ignorance and inertia in the very stuff of its conscious-ness and especially in its basis of material substance, kinetic and vital indeed by the power of life but without inherent self-possession and self-knowledge in its action, attaining in the mind to some knowledge and harmony, but only with difficult effort and by a constant struggle with its own disabilities. And there is the higher nature and self of our spiritual being, self-possessed and self-luminous but in our ordinary mentality inaccessible to our experience. At times we get glimpses of this greater thing within us, but we are not consciously within it, we do not live in its light and calm and illimitable splendour. The first of these two very different things is the Gita's nature of the three gunas. Its seeing of itself is centred in the ego idea, its principle of action is desire born of ego, and the knot of ego is attachment to the objects of the mind and sense and the life's desire. The inevitable constant result of all these things is bondage, settled subjection to a lower control, absence of self-mastery, absence of self-knowledge. The other greater power and presence is discovered to be nature and being of the pure spirit unconditioned by ego, that which is called in Indian philosophy self and impersonal Brahman. Its principle is an infinite and an impersonal existence one and the same in all: and, since this impersonal existence is without ego, without conditioning quality, without desire, need or stimulus, it is immobile and immutable; eternally the same, it regards and supports but does not share or initiate the action of the universe. The soul when it throws itself out into active Nature is the Gita's Kshara, its mobile or mutable Purusha; the same soul gathered back into pure silent self and essential spirit is the Gita's Akshara, immobile or immutable Purusha.

Then evidently the straight and simplest way to get out of the close bondage of the active nature and back to spiritual freedom is to cast away entirely all that belongs to the dynamics of the ignorance and to convert the soul into a pure spiritual existence. That is what is called becoming Brahman, brahma-bhuya. It is to put off the lower mental, vital, physical existence and to put on the pure spiritual being. This can best be done by the intelligence and will, buddhi, our present topmost principle. It has to turn away from the things of the lower existence and first and foremost from its effective knot of desire, from our attachment to the objects pursued by the mind and the senses. One must become an understanding unattached in all things, asakta-buddhih sarvatra. Then all desire passes away from the soul in its silence; it is free from all longings, vigata-sprhah. That brings with it, or it makes possible the subjection of our lower and the possession of our higher self, a possession dependent on complete self-mastery, secured by a radical victory and conquest over our mobile nature, jitatma. And all this amounts to an absolute inner renunciation of the desire of things, sannyasa. Renunciation is the way to this perfection and the man who has thus inwardly renounced all is described by the Gita as the true Sannyasin. But because the word usually signifies as well an outward renunciation or sometimes even that alone, the Teacher uses another word, tyaga, to distinguish the inward from the outward withdrawal and says that Tyaga is better than Sannyasa. The ascetic way goes much farther in its recoil from the dynamic Nature. It is enamoured of renunciation for its own sake and insists on an outward giving up of life and action, a complete quietism of soul and nature. That, the Gita replies, is not possible entirely so long as we live in the body. As far as it is possible, it may be done, but such a rigorous diminution of works is not indispensable: it is not even really or at least ordinarily advisable. The one thing needed is a complete inner quietism and that is all the Gita's sense of naiskarmya.

If we ask why this reservation, why this indulgence to the dynamic principle when our object is to become the pure self and the pure self is described as inactive, akarta, the answer is that that inactivity and divorce of self from Nature are not the whole truth of our spiritual release. Self and Nature are in the end one thing; a total and perfect spirituality makes us one with all the Divine in self and in nature. In fact, this becoming Brahman, this assumption into the self of eternal silence, brahma-bhuya, is not all our objective, but only the necessary immense base for a still greater and more marvellous divine becoming, mad-bhava. And to get to that greatest spiritual perfection we have indeed to be immobile in the self, silent in all our members, but also to act in the power, Shakti, Prakriti, the true and high force of the Spirit. And if we ask how a simultaneity of what seem to be two opposites is possible, the answer is that that is the very nature of a complete spiritual being; always it has this double poise of the Infinite. The impersonal self is silent; we too must be inwardly silent, impersonal, withdrawn into the spirit. The impersonal self looks on all action as done not by it but by Prakriti; it regards with a pure equality all the working of her qualities, modes, and forces: the soul impersonalized in the self must similarly regard all our actions as done not by itself but by the qualities of Prakriti; it must be equal in all things, sarvatra. And at the same time in order that we may not stop here, in order that we may eventually go forward and find a spiritual rule and direction in our works and not only a law of inner immobility and silence, we are asked to impose on the intelligence and will the attitude of sacrifice, all our action inwardly changed and turned into an offering to the Lord of Nature, to the Being of whom she is the self-power, sva prakrtih, the supreme Spirit. Even we have eventually to renounce all into his hands, to abandon all personal initiation of action, sarvarambhah, to keep our natural selves only as an instrument of his works and his purpose. These things have been already explained fully and the Gita does not here insist, but uses simply without farther qualification the common terms, sannyasa and naiskarmya.

A completest inner quietism once admitted as our necessary means towards living in the pure impersonal self, the question how practically it brings about that result is the next issue that arises. "How, having attained this perfection, one thus attains to the Brahman, hear from me, O son of Kunti,—that which is the supreme concentrated direction of the knowledge." The knowledge meant here is the Yoga of the Sankhyas,—the Yoga of pure knowledge accepted by the Gita, jnana-yogena sankhyanam, so far as it is one with its own Yoga which also includes the way of works of the Yogins, karma-yogena yoginam. But all mention of works is kept back for the moment. For by Brahman here is meant at first the silent, the impersonal, the immutable. The Brahman indeed is both for the Upanishads and the Gita all that is and lives and moves; it is not solely an impersonal Infinite or an unthinkable and incommunicable Absolute, acintyam avyavaharyam. All this is Brahman, says the Upanishad; all this is Vasudeva, says the Gita,—the supreme Brahman is all that moves or is stable and his hands and feet and eyes and heads and faces are on every side of us. But still there are two aspects of this All,—his immutable eternal self that supports existence and his self of active power that moves abroad in the world movement. It is only when we lose our limited ego personality in the impersonality of the self that we arrive at the calm and free oneness by which we can possess a true unity with the universal power of the Divine in his world movement. Impersonality is a denial of limitation and division, and the cult of impersonality is a natural condition of true being, an indispensable preliminary of true knowledge and therefore a first requisite of true action. It is very clear that we cannot become oneself with all or one with the universal Spirit and his vast self-knowledge, his complex will and his widespread world-purpose by insisting on our limited personality of ego; for that divides us from others and it makes us bound and self-centred in our view and in our will to action.

Imprisoned in personality we can only get at a limited union by sympathy or by some relative accommodation of ourselves to the viewpoint and feeling and will of others. To be one with all and with the Divine and his will in the cosmos we must become at first impersonal and free from our ego and its claims and from the ego's way of seeing ourselves and the world and others. And we cannot do this if there is not something in our being other than the personality, other than the ego, an impersonal self-one with all existences. To lose ego and be this impersonal self, to become this impersonal Brahman in our consciousness is therefore the first movement of this Yoga.

How then is this to be done? First, says the Gita, through a union of our purified intelligence with the pure spiritual substance in us by the yoga of the buddhi, buddhya visuddhaya yuktah. This spiritual turning of the buddhi from the outward and downward to the inward and upward look is the essence of the Yoga of knowledge. The purified understanding has to control the whole being, atmanam niyamya; it must draw us away from attachment to the outward-going desires of the lower nature by a firm and a steady will, dhrtya, which in its concentration faces entirely towards the impersonality of the pure spirit. The senses must abandon their objects, the mind must cast away the liking and disliking which these objects excite in it,—for the impersonal self has no desires and repulsions; these are vital reactions of our personality to the touches of things and the corresponding response of the mind and senses to the touches is their support and their basis. An entire control has to be acquired over the mind, speech, and body, over even the vital and physical reactions, hunger and cold and heat and physical pleasure and pain; the whole of our being must become indifferent, unaffected by these things, equal to all outward touches and to their inward reactions and responses. This is the most direct and powerful method, the straight and sharp way of Yoga. There has to be a complete cessation of desire and attachment, vairagya; a strong resort to impersonal solitude, a constant union with the inmost self by meditation is demanded of the seeker. And yet the object of this austere discipline is not to be self-centred in some supreme egoistic seclusion and tranquility of the sage and thinker averse to the trouble of participation in the world-action; the object is to get rid of all ego. One must put away utterly first the rajasic kind of egoism, egoistic strength and violence, arrogance, desire, wrath, the sense and instinct of possession, the urge of the passions, the strong lusts of life. But afterwards must be discarded egoism of all kinds, even of the most sattwic type; for the aim is to make soul and mind and life free in the end from all imprisoning I-ness and my-ness, nirmama. The extinction of ego and its demands of all sorts is the method put before us. For the pure impersonal self which, unshaken, supports the universe has no egoism and makes no demand on thing or person; it is calm and luminously impassive and silently regards all things and persons with an equal and impartial eye of self-knowledge and world-knowledge. Then clearly it is by living inwardly in a similar or identical impersonality that the soul within, released from the siege of things, can best become capable of oneness with this immutable Brahman which regards and knows but is not affected by the forms and mutations of the universe.

This first pursuit of impersonality as enjoined by the Gita brings with it evidently a certain completest inner quietism and is identical in its inmost parts and principles of practice with the method of Sannyasa. And yet there is a point at which its tendency of withdrawal from the claims of dynamic Nature and the external world is checked and a limit imposed to prevent the inner quietism from deepening into refusal of action and a physical withdrawal. The renunciation of their objects by the senses, visayams tyaktva, is to be of the nature of Tyaga; it must be a giving up of all sensuous attachment, rasa, not a refusal of the intrinsic necessary activity of the senses. One must move among surrounding things and act on the objects of the sense-field with a pure, true, and intense, a simple and absolute operation of the senses for their utility to the spirit in divine action, kevalair indriyais caran and not at all for the fulfilment of desire. There is to be vairagya, not in the common significance of disgust of life or distaste for the world action, but renunciation of raga, as also of its opposite, dvesa. There must be a withdrawal from all mental and vital liking as from all mental and vital disliking whatsoever. And this is asked not for extinction, but in order that there may be a perfect enabling equality in which the spirit can give an unhampered and unlimited assent to the integral and comprehensive divine vision of things and to the integral divine action in Nature. A continual resort to meditation, dhyana-yoga-paro nityam, is the firm means by which the soul of man can realize itself of Power and itself of silence. And yet there must be no abandonment of the active life for a life of pure meditation; action must always be done as a sacrifice to the supreme Spirit. This movement of recoil in the path of Sannyasa prepares an absorbed disappearance of the individual in the Eternal, and renunciation of action and life in the world is an indispensable step in the process. But in the Gita's path of Tyaga it is a preparation rather for the turning of our whole life and existence and of all action into an integral oneness with the serene and immeasurable being, consciousness and will of the Divine, and it preludes and makes possible a vast and total passing upward of the soul out of the lower ego to the inexpressible perfection of the supreme spiritual nature, para prakrti.

This decisive departure of the Gita's thought is indicated in the next two verses, of which the first runs with a significant sequence, "When one has become the Brahman, when one neither grieves nor desires, when one is equal to all beings, then one gets the supreme love and devotion to Me." But in the narrow path of knowledge bhakti, devotion to the personal Godhead, can be only an inferior and preliminary movement; the end, the climax is the disappearance of personality in a featureless oneness with the impersonal Brahman in which there can be no place for bhakti: for there is none to be adored and none to adore; all else is lost in the silent immobile identity of the Jiva with the Atman. Here there is given to us something yet higher than the Impersonal,—here there is the supreme Self who is the supreme Ishwara, here there is the supreme Soul and its supreme nature, here there is the Purushottama who is beyond the personal and impersonal and reconciles them on his eternal heights. The ego personality still disappears in the silence of the Impersonal, but at the same time there remains even with this silence at the back the action of a supreme Self, one greater than the Impersonal. There is no longer the lower blind and limping action of the ego and the three gunas, but instead the vast self-determining movement of an infinite spiritual Force, a free immeasurable Shakti. All Nature becomes the power of the one Divine and all action his action through the individual as channel and instrument. In place of the ego there comes forward conscious and manifest the true spiritual individual in the freedom of his real nature, in the power of his supernal status, in the majesty and splendour of his eternal kinship to the Divine, an imperishable portion of the supreme Godhead, an indestructible power of the supreme Prakriti, mamaivamsah sanatanah, para prakrtir jıva-bhuta. The soul of man then feels itself to be one in a supreme spiritual impersonality with the Purushottama and in its universalized personality a manifest power of the Godhead. Its knowledge is a light of his knowledge; its will is a force of his will; its unity with all in the universe is a play of his eternal oneness. It is in this double realisation, it is in this union of two sides of an ineffable Truth of existence by either and both of which man can approach and enter into his own infinite being, that the liberated man has to live and act and feel and determine or rather have determined for him by the greatest power of his supreme self his relations with all and the inner and outer workings of his spirit. And in that unifying realization adoration, love and devotion are not only still possible, but are a large, an inevitable and a crowning portion of the highest experience. The One who eternally becomes the Many, the Many who in their apparent division are still eternally one, the Highest who displays in us this secret and mystery of existence, not dispersed by his multiplicity, not limited by his oneness,—this is the integral knowledge, this is the reconciling experience which makes one capable of liberated action, muktasya karma.

This knowledge comes, says the Gita, by a highest bhakti. It is attained when the mind exceeds itself by a supramental and high spiritual seeing of things and when the heart too rises in unison beyond our more ignorant mental forms of love and devotion to a love that is calm and deep and luminous with widest knowledge, to a supreme delight in God and an illimitable adoration, the unperturbed ecstasy, the spiritual Ananda. When the soul has lost its separative personality, when it has become the Brahman, it is then that it can live in the true Person and can attain to the supreme revealing bhakti for the Purushottama and can come to know him utterly by the power of its profound bhakti, its heart's knowledge, bhaktya mam abhijanati. That is the integral knowledge, when the heart's fathomless vision completes the mind's absolute experience,—samagram mam jnatva. "He comes to know Me," says the Gita, "who and how much I am and in all the reality and principles of my being, yavan yas casmi tattvatah." This integral knowledge is the knowledge of the Divine present in the individual; it is the entire experience of the Lord secret in the heart of man, revealed now as the supreme Self of his existence, the Sun of all his illumined consciousness, the Master and Power of all his works, the divine Fountain of all his soul's love and delight, the Lover and Beloved of his worship and adoration. It is the knowledge too of the Divine extended in the universe, of the Eternal from whom all proceeds and in whom all lives and has its being, of the Self and Spirit of the cosmos, of Vasudeva who has become all this that is, of the Lord of cosmic existence who reigns over the works of Nature. It is the knowledge of the divine Purusha luminous in his transcendent eternity, the form of whose being escapes from the thought of the mind but not from its silence; it is the entire living experience of him as absolute Self, supreme Brahman, supreme Soul, supreme Godhead: for that seemingly incommunicable Absolute is at the same time and even in that highest status the originating Spirit of the cosmic action and Lord of all these existences. The soul of the liberated man thus enters by a reconciling knowledge, penetrates by a perfect simultaneous delight of the transcendent Divine, of the Divine in the individual and of the Divine in the universe into the Purushottama, mam visate tadanantaram. He becomes one with him in his self-knowledge and self-experience, one with him in his being and consciousness and will and world-knowledge and world-impulse, one with him in the universe and in his unity with all creatures in the universe and one with him beyond world and individual in the transcendence of the eternal Infinite, sasvatam padam avyayam. This is the culmination of the supreme bhakti that is at the core of the supreme knowledge.

And it then becomes evident how action continual and unceasing and of all kinds without diminution or abandonment of any part of the activities of life can be not only quite consistent with a supreme spiritual experience, but as forceful a means of reaching this highest spiritual condition as bhakti or knowledge. Nothing can be more positive than the Gita's statement in this matter. "And by doing also all actions always lodged in Me he attains by my grace the eternal and imperishable status." This liberating action is of the character of works done in a profound union of the will and all the dynamic parts of our nature with the Divine in ourself and the cosmos. It is done first as a sacrifice with the idea still of our self as the doer. It is done next without that idea and with a perception of the Prakriti as the sole doer. It is done last with the knowledge of that Prakriti as the supreme power of the Divine and a renunciation, a surrender of all our actions to him with the individual as a channel only and an instrument. Our works then proceed straight from the Self and Divine within us, are a part of the indivisible universal action, are initiated and performed not by us but by a vast transcendent Shakti. All that we do is done for the sake of the Lord seated in the heart of all, for the Godhead in the individual and for the fulfilment of his will in us, for the sake of the Divine in the world, for the good of all beings, for the fulfilment of the world action and the world purpose, or in one word for the sake of the Purushottama and done really by him through his universal Shakti. These divine works, whatever their form or outward character, cannot bind but are rather a potent means for rising out of this lower Prakriti of the three gunas to the perfection of the supreme, divine, and spiritual nature. Disengaged from these mixed and limited dharmas we escape into the immortal Dharma which comes upon us when we make ourselves one in all our consciousness and action with the Purushottama. That oneness here brings with it the power to rise there into the immortality beyond Time. There we shall exist in his eternal transcendence. Thus, these eight verses carefully read in the light of the knowledge already given by the Teacher are a brief, but still a comprehensive indication of the whole essential idea, the entire central method, all the kernel of the complete Yoga of the Gita.

XXII

THE SUPREME SECRET[1]

The Essence of the teaching and the Yoga has thus been given to the disciple on the field of his work and battle and the divine Teacher now proceeds to apply it to his action, but in a way that makes it applicable to all action. Attached to a crucial example, spoken to the protagonist of Kurukshetra, the words bear a much wider significance and are a universal rule for all who are ready to ascend above the ordinary mentality and to live and act in the highest spiritual consciousness. To break out of ego and personal mind and see everything in the wideness of the self and spirit, to know God and adore him in his integral truth and in all his aspects, to surrender all oneself to the transcendent Soul of nature and existence, to possess and be possessed by the divine consciousness, to be one with the One in universality of love and delight and will and knowledge, one in him with all beings, to do works as an adoration and a sacrifice on the divine foundation of a world in which all is God and in the divine status of a liberated spirit, is the sense of the Gita's Yoga. It is a transition from the apparent to the supreme spiritual and real truth of our being, and one enters into it by putting off the many limitations of the separative consciousness and the mind's attachment to the passion and unrest and ignorance, the lesser light and knowledge,

---

1 Gita, XVIII. 57-66, 73.

the sin and virtue, the dual law and standard of the lower nature. Therefore, says the Teacher, "devoting all thyself to me, giving up in thy conscious mind all thy actions into Me, resorting to Yoga of the will and intelligence be always one in heart and consciousness with Me. If thou art that at all times, then by my grace thou shalt pass safe through all difficult and perilous passages but if from egoism thou hear not, thou shalt fall into perdition. Vain is this thy resolve, that in thy egoism thou thinkest, saying 'I will not fight'; thy nature shall appoint thee to thy work. What from delusion thou desirest not to do, that helplessly thou shalt do bound by thy own work born of thy swabhava. The Lord is stationed in the heart of all existences, O Arjuna, and turns them all round and round mounted on a machine by his Maya. In him take refuge in every way of thy being and by his grace thou shalt come to the supreme peace and the eternal status."

These are lines that carry in them the innermost heart of this Yoga and lead to its crowning experience and we must understand them in their innermost spirit and the whole vastness of that high summit of experience. The words express the most complete, intimate, and living relation possible between God and man; they are instinct with the concentrated force of religious feeling that springs from the human being's absolute adoration, his upward surrender of his whole existence, his unreserved and perfect self-giving to the transcendent and universal Divinity from whom he comes and in whom he lives. This stress of feeling is in entire consonance with the high and enduring place that the Gita assigns to bhakti, to the love of God, to the adoration of the Highest, as the inmost spirit and motive of the supreme action and the crown and core of the supreme knowledge. The phrases used and the spiritual emotion with which they vibrate seem to give the most intense prominence possible and an utmost importance to the personal truth and presence of the Godhead. It is no abstract Absolute of the philosopher, no indifferent impersonal Presence or ineffable Silence intolerant of all relations to whom this complete surrender of all our works can be made and this closeness and intimacy of oneness with him in all the parts of our conscious existence imposed as the condition and law of our perfection or of whom this divine intervention and protection and deliverance are the promise. It is a Master of our works, a Friend and Lover of our soul, an intimate Spirit of our life, an indwelling and over-dwelling Lord of all our personal and impersonal self and nature who alone can utter to us this near and moving message. And yet this is not the common relation established by the religions between man living in his sattwic or other ego-mind and some personal form and aspect of the Deity, ista-deva, constructed by that mind or offered to it to satisfy its limited ideal, aspiration or desire. That is the ordinary sense and actual character of the normal mental being's religious devotion; but here there is something wider that passes beyond the mind and its limits and its dharmas. It is something deeper than the mind that offers and something greater than the Ishta-deva that receives the surrender.

That which surrenders here is the Jiva, the essential soul, the original central and spiritual being of man, the individual Purusha. It is the Jiva delivered from the limiting and ignorant ego-sense who knows himself not as a separate personality but as an eternal portion and power and soul-becoming of the Divine, amsa sanatana, the Jiva released and uplifted by the passing away of ignorance and established in the light and freedom of his own true and supreme nature which is one with that of the Eternal. It is this central spiritual being in us who thus enters into a perfect and closely real relation of delight and union with the origin and continent and governing Self and Power of our existence. And he who receives our surrender is no limited Deity but the Purushottama, the one eternal Godhead, the one supreme Soul of all that is and of all Nature, the original transcendent Spirit of existence. An immutable impersonal self-existence is his first obvious spiritual self-presentation to the experience of our liberated knowledge, the first sign of his presence, the first touch and impression of his substance. A universal and transcendent infinite Person or Purusha is the mysterious hidden secret of his very being, unthinkable in form of mind, acintya-rupa but very near and present to the powers of our consciousness, emotion, will and knowledge when they are lifted out of themselves, out of their blind and petty forms into a luminous spiritual, an immeasurable supramental Ananda and power and gnosis. It is He, ineffable Absolute but also Friend and Lord and Enlightener and Lover, who is the object of this most complete devotion and approach and this most intimate inner becoming and surrender. This union, this relation is a thing lifted beyond the forms and laws of the limiting mind, too high for all these inferior dharmas; it is a truth of our self and spirit. And yet or rather therefore, because it is the truth of our self and spirit, the truth of its oneness with that Spirit from which all comes and by it and as its derivations and suggestions all exists and travails, it is not a negation but a fulfilment of all that mind and life point to and bear in them as their secret and unaccomplished significance. Thus, it is not by a nirvana, an exclusion and negating extinction of all that we are here, but by a nirvana, an exclusion and negating extinction of ignorance and ego and a consequent ineffable fulfilment of our knowledge and will and heart's aspiration, an uplifted and limitless living of them in the Divine, in the Eternal, nivasisyasi mayyeva, a transfigurement and transference of all our consciousness to a greater inner status that there comes this supreme perfection and release in the spirit.

The crux of the spiritual problem, the character of this transition of which it is so difficult for the normal mind of man to get a true apprehension, turns altogether upon the capital distinction between the ignorant life of the ego in the lower nature and the large and luminous existence of the liberated Jiva in his own true spiritual nature. The renunciation of the first must be complete, the transition to the second absolute. This is the distinction on which the Gita dwells here with all possible emphasis. On the one side is this poor, trepidant, braggart egoistic condition of consciousness, ahankrta bhava, the crippling narrowness of this little helpless separative personality according to whose viewpoint we ordinarily think and act, feel and respond to the touches of existence. On the other are the vast spiritual reaches of immortal fullness, bliss, and knowledge into which we are admitted through union with the divine Being, of whom we are then a manifestation and expression in the eternal light and no longer a disguise in the darkness of the ego-nature. It is the completeness of this union which is indicated by the Gita's satatam mac-cittah. The life of the ego is founded on a construction of the apparent mental, vital, and physical truth of existence, on a nexus of pragmatic relations between the individual soul and Nature, on an intellectual, emotional, and sensational interpretation of things used by the little limited I in us to maintain and satisfy the ideas and desires of its bounded separate personality amid the vast action of the universe. All our dharmas, all the ordinary standards by which we determine our view of things and our knowledge and our action, proceed upon this narrow and limiting basis, and to follow them even in the widest wheeling's round our ego Centre does not carry us out of this petty circle. It is a circle in which the soul is a contented or struggling prisoner, forever subject to the mixed compulsions of Nature.

For Purusha veils himself in this round, veils his divine and immortal being in ignorance and is subject to the law of an insistent limiting Prakriti. That law is the compelling rule of the three gunas. It is a triple stair that stumbles upward to-wards the divine light but cannot reach it. At its base is the law or dharma of inertia: the tamasic man inertly obeys in a customary mechanical action the suggestions and impulses, the round of will of his material and his half-intellectualized vital and sensational nature. In the middle intervenes the kinetic law or dharma; the rajasic man, vital, dynamic, active, attempts to impose himself on his world and environment, but only increases the wounding weight and tyrant yoke of his turbulent passions, desires and egoisms, the burden of his restless self-will, the yoke of his rajasic nature. At the top presses down upon life the harmonic regulative law or dharma; the sattwic man attempts to erect and follow his limited personal standards of reasoning knowledge, enlightened utility, or mechanized virtue, his religions and philosophies and ethical formulas, mental systems and constructions, fixed channels of idea and conduct which do not agree with the totality of the meaning of life and are constantly being broken in the movement of the wider universal purpose. The dharma of the sattwic man is the highest in the circle of the gunas; but that too is a limited view and a dwarfed standard. Its imperfect indications lead to a petty and relative perfection; temporarily satisfying to the enlightened personal ego, it is not founded either on the whole truth of the self or on the whole truth of Nature.

And in fact, the actual life of man is not at any time one of these things alone, neither a mechanical routine execution of the first crude law of Nature, nor the struggle of a kinetic soul of action, nor a victorious emergence of conscious light and reason and good and knowledge. There is a mixture of all these dharmas out of which our will and intelligence make a more or less arbitrary construction to be realized as best it can, but never in fact realized except by compromise with other compelling things in the universal Prakriti. The sattwic ideals of our enlightened will and reason are either themselves compromises, at best progressive compromises, subject to a constant imperfection and flux of change, or if absolute in their character, they can be followed only as a counsel of perfection ignored for the most part in practice or successful only as a partial influence. And if sometimes we imagine we have completely realized them, it is because we ignore in ourselves the subconscious or half-conscious mixture of other powers and motives that are usually as much or more than our ideals the real force in our action. That self-ignorance constitutes the whole vanity of human reason and self-righteousness; it is the dark secret lining behind the spotless white outsides of human sainthood and alone makes possible the specious egoisms of knowledge and virtue. The best human knowledge is a half knowledge and the highest human virtue a thing of mixed quality and, even when most sincerely absolute in standard, sufficiently relative in practice. As a general law of living the absolute sattwic ideals cannot prevail in conduct; indispensable as a power for the betterment and raising of personal aspiration and conduct, their insistence modifies life but cannot wholly change it, and their perfect fulfilment images itself only in a dream of the future or a world of heavenly nature free from the mixed strain of our terrestrial existence. It cannot be otherwise because neither the nature of this world nor the nature of man is or can be one single piece made of the pure stuff of sattwa.

The first door of escape we see out of this limitation of our possibilities, out of this confused mixture of dharmas is in a certain high trend towards impersonality, a movement inwards towards something large and universal and calm and free and right and pure hidden now by the limiting mind of ego. The difficulty is that while we can feel a positive release into this impersonality in moments of the quiet and silence of our being, an impersonal activity is by no means so easy to realise. The pursuit of an impersonal truth or an impersonal will in our conduct is vitiated so long as we live at all in our normal mind by that which is natural and inevitable to that mind, the law of our personality, the subtle urge of our vital nature, the colour of ego. The pursuit of impersonal truth is turned by these influences into an unsuspected cloak for a system of intellectual preferences supported by our mind's limiting insistence; the pursuit of a disinterested impersonal action is converted into a greater authority and apparent high sanction for our personal will's interested selections and blind arbitrary persistence's. On the other hand, an absolute impersonality would seem to impose an equally absolute quietism, and this would mean that all action is bound to the machinery of the ego and the three gunas and to recede from life and its works the only way out of the circle. This impersonal silence however is not the last word of wisdom in the matter, because it is not the only way and crown or not all the way and the last crown of self-realization open to our endeavour. There is a mightier fuller more positive spiritual experience in which the circle of our egoistic personality and the round of the mind's limitations vanish in the unwalled infinity of a greatest self and spirit and yet life and its works not only remain still acceptable and possible but reach up and out to their widest spiritual completeness and assume a grand ascending significance.

There have been different gradations in this movement to bridge the gulf between an absolute impersonality and the dynamic possibilities of our nature. The thought and practice of the Mahayana approached this difficult reconciliation through the experience of a deep desirelessness and a large dissolving freedom from mental and vital attachment and sanskaras and on the positive side a universal altruism, a fathomless compassion for the world and its creatures which became as it were the flood and outpouring of the high Nirvanic state on life and action.

That reconciliation was equally the sense of yet another spiritual experience, more conscious of a world significance, more profound, kindling, richly comprehensive on the side of action, a step nearer to the thought of the Gita: this experience we find or can at least read behind the utterances of the Taoist thinkers. There, there seems to be an impersonal ineffable Eternal who is spirit and at the same time the one life of the universe: it supports and flows impartially in all things, samam brahma; it is a One that is nothing, Asat, because other than all that we perceive and yet the totality of all these existences. The fluid personality that forms like foam on this Infinite, the mobile ego with its attachments and repulsions, its likings and disliking's, its fixed mental distinctions, is an effective image that veils and deforms to us the one reality,

Tao, the supreme All and Nothing. That can be touched only by losing personality and its little structural forms in the unseizable universal and eternal Presence and, this once achieved, we live in that a real life and have another greater consciousness which makes us penetrate all things, ourselves penetrable to all eternal influences. Here, as in the Gita, the highest way would seem to be a complete openness and self-surrender to the Eternal. "Your body is not your own," says the Taoist thinker, "it is the delegated image of God: your life is not your own, it is the delegated harmony of God: your individuality is not your own, it is the delegated adaptability of God." And here too a vast perfection and liberated action are the dynamic result of the soul's surrender. The works of ego personality are a separative running counter to the bias of universal nature. This false movement must be replaced by a wise and still passivity in the hands of the universal and eternal Power, a passivity that makes us adaptable to the infinite action, in harmony with its truth, plastic to the shaping breath of the Spirit. The man who has this harmony may be motionless within and absorbed in silence, but his Self will appear free from disguises, the divine Influence will be at work in him and while he abides in tranquility and an inward inaction, naiskarmya, yet he will act with an irresistible power and myriads of things and beings will move and gather under his influence. The impersonal force of the Self takes up his works, movements no longer deformed by ego and sovereignly acts through him for the keeping together and control of the world and its peoples, loka-sangraharthaya.

There is little difference between these experiences and the first impersonal activity inculcated by the Gita. The Gita also demands of us renunciation of desire, attachment, and ego, transcendence of the lower nature and the breaking up of our personality and its little formations. The Gita also demands of us to live in the Self and Spirit, to see the Self and Spirit in all and all in the Self and Spirit and all as the Self and Spirit. It demands of us like the Taoist thinker to renounce our natural personality and its works into the Self, the Spirit, the Eternal, the Brahman, atmani sannyasya, brahmani. And there is this coincidence because that is always man's highest and freest possible experience of a quietistic inner largeness and silence reconciled with an outer dynamic active living, the two coexistent or fused together in the impersonal infinite reality and illimitable action of the one immortal Power and sole eternal Existence. But the Gita adds a phrase of immense import that alters everything, atmani atho mayi. The demand is to see all things in the self and then in "Me" the Ishwara, to renounce all action into the Self, Spirit, Brahman and thence into the supreme Person, the Purushottama. There is here a still greater and profounder complex of spiritual experience, a larger transmutation of the significance of human life, a more mystic and heart-felt sweep of the return of the stream to the ocean, the restoration of personal works and the cosmic action to the Eternal Worker. The stress on pure impersonality has this difficulty and incompleteness for us that it reduces the inner person, the spiritual individual, that persistent miracle of our inmost being, to a temporary, illusive, and mutable formation in the Infinite. The Infinite alone exists and except in a passing play has no true regard on the soul of the living creature. There can be no real and permanent relation between the soul in man and the Eternal, if that soul is even as the always renewable body no more than a transient phenomenon in the Infinite.

It is true that the ego and its limited personality are even such a temporary and mutable formation of Nature and therefore it must be broken and we must feel ourselves one with all and infinite. But the ego is not the real person; when it has been dissolved there still remains the spiritual individual, there is still the eternal Jiva. The ego limitation disappears and the soul lives in a profound unity with the One and feels its universal unity with all things. And yet it is still our own soul that enjoys this expanse and oneness. The universal action, even when it is felt as the action of one and the same energy in all, even when it is experienced as the initiation and movement of the Ishwara, still takes different forms in different souls of men, amsah sanatanah, and a different turn in their nature. The light of spiritual knowledge, the manifold universal Shakti, the eternal delight of being stream into us and around us, concentrate in the soul and flow out on the surrounding world from each as from a centre of living spiritual consciousness whose circumference is lost in the infinite. More, the spiritual individual remains as a little universe of divine existence at once independent and inseparable from the whole infinite universe of the divine self-manifestation of which we see a petty portion around us. A portion of the Transcendent, creative, he creates his own world around him even while he retains this cosmic consciousness in which are all others. If it be objected that this is an illusion which must disappear when he retreats into the transcendent Absolute, there is after all no very certain certainty in that matter. For it is still the soul in man that is the enjoyer of this release, as it was the living spiritual centre of the divine action and manifestation; there is something more than the mere self-breaking of an illusory shell of individuality in the Infinite. This mystery of our existence signifies that what we are is not only a temporary name and form of the One, but as we may say, a soul and spirit of the Divine Oneness. Our spiritual individuality of which the ego is only a misleading shadow and projection in the ignorance has or is a truth that persists beyond the ignorance; there is something of us that dwells forever in the supreme nature of the Purushottama, nivasisyasi mayi. This is the profound comprehensiveness of the teaching of the Gita that while it recognizes the truth of the universalized impersonality into which we enter by the extinction of ego, brahma-nirvana,—for indeed without it there can be no liberation or at least no absolute release,—it recognizes too the persistent spiritual truth of our personality as a factor of the highest experience. Not this natural but that divine and central being in us is the eternal Jiva. It is the Ishwara, Vasudeva who is all things, that takes up our mind and life and body for the enjoyment of the lower Prakriti; it is the supreme Prakriti, the original spiritual nature of the supreme Purusha that holds together the universe and appears in it as the Jiva. This Jiva then is a portion of the Purushottama's original divine spiritual being, a living power of the living Eternal. He is not merely a temporary form of lower Nature, but an eternal portion of the Highest in his supreme Prakriti, an eternal conscious ray of the divine existence and as everlasting as that supernal Prakriti. One side of the highest perfection and status of our liberated consciousness must then be to assume the true place of the Jiva in a supreme spiritual Nature, there to dwell in the glory of the supreme Purusha and there to have the joy of the eternal spiritual oneness.

This mystery of our being implies necessarily a similar supreme mystery of the being of the Purushottama, rahasyam uttamam. It is not an exclusive impersonality of the Absolute that is the highest secret. This highest secret is the miracle of a supreme Person and apparent vast Impersonal that are one, an immutable transcendent Self of all things and a Spirit that manifests itself here at the very foundation of cosmos as an infinite and multiple personality acting everywhere,—a Self and Spirit revealed to our last, closest, profoundest experience as an illimitable Being who accepts us and takes us to him, not into a blank of featureless existence, but most positively, deeply, wonderfully into all Himself and in all the ways of his and our conscious existence. This highest experience and this largest way of seeing open a profound, moving, and endless significance to our parts of nature, our knowledge, will, heart's love and adoration, which is lost or diminished if we put an exclusive stress on the impersonal, because that stress suppresses or minimizes or does not allow of the intensest fulfilment of movements and powers that are a portion of our deepest nature, intensities and luminosities that are attached to the closest essential fibres of our self-experience. It is not the austerity of knowledge alone that can help us; there is room and infinite room for the heart's love and aspiration illumined and uplifted by knowledge, a more mystically clear, a greater calmly passionate knowledge. It is by the perpetual unified closeness of our heart-consciousness, mind-consciousness, all consciousness, satatam maccittah, that we get the widest, the deepest, the most integral experience of our oneness with the Eternal. A nearest oneness in all the being, profoundly individual in a divine passion even in the midst of universality, even at the top of transcendence is here enjoined on the human soul as its way to reach the Highest and its way to possess the perfection and the divine consciousness to which it is called by its nature as a spirit. The intelligence and will have to turn the whole existence in all its parts to the Ishwara, to the divine Self and Master of that whole existence, buddhi-yogam upasritya. The heart has to cast all other emotion into the delight of oneness with him and the love of Him in all creatures. The sense spiritualized has to see and hear and feel him everywhere. The life has to be utterly his life in the Jiva. All the actions have to proceed from his sole power and sole initiation in the will, knowledge, organs of action, senses, vital parts, body. This way is deeply impersonal because the separateness of ego is abolished for the soul universalized and restored to transcendence. And yet it is intimately personal because it soars to a transcendent passion and power of indwelling and oneness. A featureless extinction may be a rigorous demand of the mind's logic of self-annulment; it is not the last word of the supreme mystery, rahasyam uttamam.

The refusal of Arjuna to persevere in his divinely appointed work proceeded from the ego sense in him, ahankara. Behind it was a mixture and confusion and tangled error of ideas and impulsions of the sattwic, rajasic, tamasic ego, the vital nature's fear of sin and its personal consequences, the heart's recoil from individual grief and suffering, the clouded reason's covering of egoistic impulses by self-deceptive specious pleas of right and virtue, our nature's ignorant shrinking from the ways of God because they seem other than the ways of man and impose things terrible and unpleasant on his nervous and emotional parts and his intelligence. The spiritual consequences will be infinitely worse now than before, now that a higher truth and a greater way and spirit of action have been revealed to him, if yet persisting in his egoism he perseveres in a vain and impossible refusal. For it is a vain resolution, a futile recoil, since it springs only from a temporary failure of strength, a strong but passing deviation from the principle of energy of his inmost character and is not the true will and way of his nature. If now he casts down his arms, he will yet be compelled by that nature to resume them when he sees the battle and slaughter go on without him, his abstention a defeat of all for which he has lived, the cause for whose service he was born weakened and bewildered by the absence or inactivity of its protagonist, vanquished and afflicted by the cynical and unscrupulous strength of the champions of a self-regarding unrighteousness and injustice. And in this return, there will be no spiritual virtue. It was a confusion of the ideas and feelings of the ego mind that impelled his refusal; it will be his nature working through a restoration of the characteristic ideas and feelings of the ego mind that will compel him to annul his refusal. But whatever the direction, this continued subjection to the ego will mean a worse, a more fatal spiritual refusal, a perdition, vinasti; for it will be a definite falling away from a greater truth of his being than that which he has followed in the ignorance of the lower nature. He has been admitted to a higher consciousness, a new self-realization, he has been shown the possibility of a divine instead of an egoistic action; the gates have been opened before him of a divine and spiritual in place of a merely intellectual, emotional, sensuous, and vital life. He is called to be no longer a great blind instrument, but a conscious soul and an enlightened power and vessel of the Godhead.

For there is this possibility within us: there is open to us even at our human highest this consummation and transcendence. The ordinary mind and life of man is a half-enlightened and mostly an ignorant development and a partial uncompleted manifestation of something concealed within him. There is a godhead there concealed from himself, subliminal to his consciousness, immobilized behind the obscure veil of a working that is not wholly his own and the secret of which he has not yet mastered. He finds himself in the world thinking and willing and feeling and acting and he takes himself instinctively or intellectually conceives of himself or at least conducts his life as a separate self-existent being who has the freedom of his thought and will and feeling and action. He bears the burden of his sin and error and suffering and takes the responsibility and merit of his knowledge and virtue; he claims the right to satisfy his sattwic, rajasic or tamasic ego and arrogates the power to shape his own destiny and to turn the world to his own uses. It is this idea of himself through which Nature works in him, and she deals with him according to his own conception but fulfils all the time the will of the greater Spirit within her. The error of this self-view of man is like most of his errors the distortion of a truth, a distortion that creates a whole system of erroneous and yet effective values. What is true of his spirit he attributes to his ego-personality and gives it a false application, a false form, and a mass of ignorant consequences. The ignorance lies in this fundamental deficiency of his surface consciousness that he identifies himself only with the outward mechanical part of him which is a convenience of Nature and with so much only of the soul as reflects and is reflected in these workings. He misses the greater inner spirit within which gives to all his mind and life and creation and action an unfulfilled promise and a hidden significance. A universal Nature here obeys the power of the Spirit who is the master of the universe, shapes each creature and determines its action according to the law of its own nature, Swabhava, shapes man too and determines his action according to the general law of nature of his kind, the law of a mental being emmeshed and ignorant in the life and the body, shapes too each man and determines his individual action according to the law of his own distinct type and the variations of his own original swabhava. It is this universal Nature that forms and directs the mechanical workings of the body and the instinctive operations of our vital and nervous parts; and there our subjection to her is very obvious. And she has formed and directs the action too, hardly less mechanical as things now are, of our sense-mind and will and intelligence. Only, while in the animal the mind workings are a wholly mechanical obedience to Prakriti, man has this distinction that he embodies a conscious development in which the soul more actively participates, and that gives to his outward mentality the sense, useful to him, indispensable, but very largely a misleading sense, of a certain freedom and increasing mastery of his instrumental nature. And it is especially misleading because it blinds him to the hard fact of his bondage and his false idea of freedom prevents him from finding a true liberty and lordship. For the freedom and mastery of man over his nature are hardly even real and cannot be complete until he becomes aware of the Divinity within him and is in possession of his own real self and spirit other than the ego, atmavan. It is that which Nature is labouring to express in mind and life and body; it is that which imposes on her this or that law of being and working, Swabhava; it is that which shapes the outward destiny and the evolution of the soul within us. It is therefore only when he is in possession of his real self and spirit that his nature can become a conscious instrument and enlightened power of the godhead.

For then, when we enter into that inmost self of our existence, we come to know that in us and in all is the one Spirit and Godhead whom all Nature serves and manifests and we ourselves are soul of this Soul, spirit of this Spirit, our body his delegated image, our life a movement of the rhythm of his life, our mind a sheath of his consciousness, our senses his instruments, our emotions and sensations the seeking's of his delight of being, our actions a means of his purpose, our freedom only a shadow, suggestion or glimpse while we are ignorant, but when we know him and ourselves a prolongation and effective channel of his immortal freedom. Our masteries are a reflection of his power at work, our best knowledge a partial light of his knowledge, the highest most potent will of our spirit a projection and delegation of the will of this Spirit in all things who is the Master and Soul of the universe. It is the Lord seated in the heart of every creature who has been turning us in all our inner and outer action during the ignorance as if mounted on a machine on the wheel of this Maya of the lower Nature. And whether obscure in the Ignorance or luminous in the Knowledge, it is for him in us and him in the world that we have our existence. To live consciously and integrally in this knowledge and this truth is to escape from ego and break out of Maya. All other highest dharmas are only a preparation for this Dharma, and all Yoga is only a means by which we can come first to some kind of union and finally, if we have the full light, to an integral union with the Master and supreme Soul and Self of our existence. The greatest Yoga is to take refuge from all the perplexities and difficulties of our nature with this indwelling Lord of all Nature, to turn to him with our whole being, with the life and body and sense and mind and heart and understanding, with our whole dedicated knowledge and will and action, sarva-bhavena, in every way of our conscious self and our instrumental nature. And when we can at all times and entirely do this, then the divine Light and Love and Power takes hold of us, fills both self and instruments and leads us safe through all the doubts and difficulties and perplexities and perils that beset our soul and our life, leads us to a supreme peace and the spiritual freedom of our immortal and eternal status, param santim, sthanam sasvatam.

For after giving out all the laws, the dharmas, and the deepest essence of its Yoga, after saying that beyond all the first secrets revealed to the mind of man by the transforming light of spiritual knowledge, guhyat, this is a still deeper more secret truth, guhyataram, the Gita suddenly declares that there is yet a supreme word that it has to speak, paramam vacah, and a most secret truth of all, sarva-guhyatamam. This secret of secrets the Teacher will tell Arjuna as his highest good because he is the chosen and beloved soul, ista. For evidently, as had already been declared by the Upanishad, it is only the rare soul chosen by the Spirit for the revelation of his very body, tanum svam, who can be admitted to this mystery, because he alone is near enough in heart and mind and life to the Godhead to respond truly to it in all his being and to make it a living practice. The last, the closing supreme word of the Gita expressing the highest mystery is spoken in two brief, direct and simple slokas and these are left without farther comment or enlargement to sink into the mind and reveal their own fullness of meaning in the soul's experience. For it is alone this inner incessantly extending experience that can make evident the infinite deal of meaning with which are forever pregnant these words in themselves apparently so slight and simple. And we feel, as they are being uttered, that it was this for which the soul of the disciple was being prepared all the time and the rest was only an enlightening and enabling discipline and doctrine. Thus runs this secret of secrets, the highest most direct message of the Ishwara. "Become my-minded, my lover and adorer, a sacrificer to me, bow thyself to me, to me thou shalt come, this is my pledge and promise to thee, for dear art thou to me. Abandon all dharmas and take refuge in me alone. I will deliver thee from all sin and evil, do not grieve."

The Gita throughout has been insisting on a great and well-built discipline of Yoga, a large and clearly traced philosophical system, on the Swabhava and the Swadharma, on the sattwic law of life as leading out of itself by a self-exceeding exaltation to a free spiritual dharma of immortal existence utterly wide in its spaces and high-lifted beyond the limitation of even this highest guna, on many rules and means and injunctions and conditions of perfection, and now suddenly it seems to break out of its own structure and says to the human soul, "Abandon all dharmas, give thyself to the Divine alone, to the supreme Godhead above and around and within thee: that is all that thou needest, that is the truest and greatest way, that is the real deliverance." The Master of the worlds in the form of the divine Charioteer and Teacher of Kurukshetra has revealed to man the magnificent realities of God and Self and Spirit and the nature of the complex world and the relation of man's mind and life and heart and senses to the Spirit and the victorious means by which through his own spiritual self-discipline and effort he can rise out of mortality into immortality and out of his limited mental into his infinite spiritual existence. And now speaking as the Spirit and Godhead in man and in all things, he says to him,

"All this personal effort and self-discipline will not in the end be needed, all following, and limitation of rule and dharma can at last be thrown away as hampering encumbrances if thou canst make a complete surrender to Me, depend alone on the Spirit and Godhead within thee and all things and trust to his sole guidance. Turn all thy mind to me and fill it with the thought of me and my presence. Turn all thy heart to me, make thy every action, whatever it be, a sacrifice and offering to me. That done, leave me to do my will with thy life and soul and action; do not be grieved or perplexed by my dealings with thy mind and heart and life and works or troubled because they do not seem to follow the laws and dharmas man imposes on himself to guide his limited will and intelligence. My ways are the ways of a perfect wisdom and power and love that knows all things and combines all its movements in view of a perfect eventual result; for it is refining and weaving together the many threads of an integral perfection. I am here with thee in thy chariot of battle revealed as the Master of Existence within and without thee and I repeat the absolute assurance, the infallible promise that I will lead thee to myself through and beyond all sorrow and evil. Whatever difficulties and perplexities arise, be sure of this that I am leading thee to a complete divine life in the universal and an immortal existence in the transcendent Spirit."

The secret thing, guhyam, that all deep spiritual knowledge

reveals to us, mirrored in various teachings, and justified in the soul's experience, is for the Gita the secret of the spiritual self-hidden within us of which mind and external Nature are only manifestations or figures. It is the secret of the constant relations between soul and Nature, Purusha and Prakriti, the secret of an indwelling Godhead who is the lord of all existence and veiled from us in its forms and movements. These are the truths taught in many ways by Vedanta and Sankhya and Yoga and synthetized in the earlier chapters of the Gita. And amidst all their apparent distinctions they are one truth, and all the different ways of Yoga are various means of spiritual self-discipline by which our unquiet mind and blinded life are stilled and turned towards this many-aspected One and the secret truth of self and God made so real to us and intimate that we can either consciously live and dwell in it or lose our separate selves in the Eternal and no longer be compelled at all by the mental Ignorance.

The more secret thing, guhyataram, developed by the Gita is the profound reconciling truth of the divine Purushottama, at once self and Purusha, supreme Brahman, and a sole, intimate, mysterious, ineffable Godhead. That gives to the thought a larger and more deeply understanding foundation for an ultimate knowledge and to the spiritual experience a greater and more fully comprehending and comprehensive Yoga. This deeper mystery is founded on the secret of the supreme spiritual Prakriti and of the Jiva, an eternal portion of the Divine in that eternal and this manifested Nature and of one spirit and essence with him in his immutable self-existence. This profounder knowledge escapes from the elementary distinction of spiritual experience between the Beyond and what is here. For the Transcendent beyond the worlds is at the same time Vasudeva who is all things in all worlds; he is the Lord standing in the heart of every creature and the self of all existences and the origin and supernal meaning of everything that he has put forth in his Prakriti. He is manifested in his Vibhuti's, and he is the Spirit in Time who compels the action of the world and the Sun of all knowledge and the Lover and Beloved of the soul and the Master of all works and sacrifice. The result of an inmost opening to this deeper, truer, more secret mystery is the Gita's Yoga of integral knowledge, integral works, and integral bhakti. It is the simultaneous experience of spiritual universality and a free and perfected spiritual individuality, of an entire union with God and an entire dwelling in him as at once the frame of the soul's immortality and the support and power of our liberated action in the world and the body.

And now there comes the supreme word and most secret thing of all, guhyatamam, that the Spirit and Godhead is an Infinite free from all dharmas and though he conducts the world according to fixed laws and leads man through his dharmas of ignorance and knowledge, sin, and virtue, right and wrong, liking and disliking and indifference, pleasure and pain, joy and sorrow and the rejection of these opposites, through his physical and vital, intellectual, emotional, ethical and spiritual forms and rules and standards, yet the Spirit and Godhead transcends all these things, and if we too can cast away all dependence on dharmas, surrender ourselves to this free and eternal Spirit and, taking care only to keep ourselves absolutely and exclusively open to him, trust to the light and power and delight of the Divine in us and, unafraid and ungrieving, accept only his guidance, then that is the truest, the greatest release and that brings the absolute and inevitable perfection of our self and nature. This is the way offered to the chosen of the Spirit,—to those only in whom he takes the greatest delight because they are nearest to him and most capable of oneness and of being even as he, freely consenting and concordant with Nature in her highest power and movement, universal in soul consciousness, transcendent in the spirit.

For a time comes in spiritual development when we become aware that all our effort and action are only our mental and vital reactions to the silent and secret insistence of a greater Presence in and around us. It is borne in upon us that all our Yoga, our aspiration and our endeavour are imperfect or narrow forms, because disfigured or at least limited by the mind's associations, demands, prejudgments, predilections, mistranslations, or half translations of a vaster truth. Our ideas and experiences and efforts are mental images only of greatest things which would be done more perfectly, directly, freely, largely, more in harmony with the universal and eternal will by that Power itself in us if we could only put ourselves passively as instruments in the hands of a supreme and absolute strength and wisdom. That Power is not separate from us; it is our own self one with the self of all others and at the same time a transcendent Being and an immanent Person. Our existence, our action taken up into this greatest Existence would be no longer, as it seems to us now, individually our own in a mental separation. It would be the vast movement of an Infinity and an intimate ineffable Presence; it would be the constant spontaneity of formation and expression in us of this deep universal self and this transcendent Spirit. The Gita indicates that in order that that may wholly be, the surrender must be without reservations; our Yoga, our life, our state of inner being must be determined freely by this living Infinite, not predetermined by our mind's insistence on this or that dharma or any dharma. The divine Master of the Yoga, yogesvarah krsnah, will then himself take up our Yoga and raise us to our utmost possible perfection, not the perfection of any external or mental standard or limiting rule but vast and comprehensive, to the mind incalculable. It will be a perfection developed by an all-seeing Wisdom according to the whole truth, first indeed of our human swabhava, but afterwards of a greater thing into which it will open, a spirit and power illimitable, immortal, free and all-transmuting, the light and splendour of a divine and infinite nature.

All must be given as material of that transmutation. An omniscient consciousness will take up our knowledge and our ignorance, our truth, and our error, cast away their forms of insufficiency, sarva-dharman parityajya, and transform all into its infinite light. An almighty Power will take up our virtue and sin, our right and wrong, our strength and our weakness, cast away their tangled figures, sarva-dharman parityajya, and transform all into its transcendent purity and universal good and infallible force. An ineffable Ananda will take up our petty joy and sorrow, our struggling pleasure and pain, cast away their discordances and imperfect rhythms, sarva-dharman parityajya, and transform all into its transcendent and universal unimaginable delight. All that all the Yogas can do will be done and more; but it will be done in a greater seeing way, with a greater wisdom and truth than any human teacher, saint or sage can give us. The inner spiritual state to which this supreme Yoga will take us, will be above all that is here and yet comprehensive of all things in this and other worlds, but with a spiritual transformation of all, without limitation, without bondage, sarva-dharman parityajya. The infinite existence, consciousness, and delight of the Godhead in its calm silence and bright boundless activity will be there, will be its essential, fundamental, universal stuff, mould and character. And in that mould of infinity the Divine made manifest will overtly dwell, no longer concealed by his Yogamaya, and whenever and as he wills build in us whatever shapes of the Infinite, translucent forms of knowledge, thought, love, spiritual joy, power, and action according to his self-fulfilling will and immortal pleasure. And there will be no binding effect on the free soul and the unaffected nature, no unescapable crystallizing into this or that inferior formula. For all the action will be executed by the power of the Spirit in a divine freedom, sarva-dharman parityajya. An unfallen abiding in the transcendent Spirit, param dhama, will be the foundation and the assurance of this spiritual state. An intimate understanding oneness with universal being and all creatures, released from the evil and suffering of the separative mind but wisely regardful of true distinctions, will be the conditioning power. A constant delight, oneness, and harmony of the eternal individual here with the Divine and all that he is will be the effect of this integral liberation. The baffling problems of our human existence of which Arjuna's difficulty stands as an acute example, are created by our separative personality in the Ignorance. This Yoga because it puts the soul of man into its right relation with God and world-existence and makes our action God's, the knowledge and will shaping and moving it his and our life the harmony of a divine self-expression, is the way to their total disappearance.

The whole Yoga is revealed, the great word of the teaching is given, and Arjuna the chosen human soul is once more turned, no longer in his egoistic mind but in this greatest self-knowledge, to the divine action. The Vibhuti is ready for the divine life in the human, his conscious spirit for the works of the liberated soul, muktasya karma. Destroyed is the illusion of the mind; the soul's memory of its self and its truth concealed so long by the misleading shows and forms of our life has returned to it and become its normal consciousness: all doubt and perplexity gone, it can turn to the execution of the command and do faithfully whatever work for God and the world may be appointed and apportioned to it by the Master of our being, the Spirit and Godhead self-fulfilled in Time and universe.

XXIII

THE CORE OF THE GITA'S MEANING

What then is the message of the Gita and what its working value, its spiritual utility to the human mind of the present day after the long ages that have elapsed since it was written and the great subsequent transformations of thought and experience? The human mind moves always for-ward, alters its viewpoint, and enlarges its thought substance, and the effect of these changes is to render past systems of thinking obsolete or, when they are preserved, to extend, to modify and subtly or visibly to alter their value. The vitality of an ancient doctrine consists in the extent to which it naturally lends itself to such a treatment; for that means that whatever may have been the limitations or the obsolescence's of the form of its thought, the truth of substance, the truth of living vision and experience on which its system was built is still sound and retains a permanent validity and significance. The Gita is a book that has worn extraordinarily well, and it is almost as fresh and still in its real substance quite as new, because always renewable in experience, as when it first appeared in or was written into the frame of the Mahabharata. It is still received in India as one of the great bodies of doctrine that most authoritatively govern religious thinking and its teaching acknowledged as of the highest value if not wholly accepted by almost all shades of religious belief and opinion. Its influence is not merely philosophic or academic but immediate and living, an influence both for thought and action, and its ideas are actually at work as a powerful shaping factor in the revival and renewal of a nation and a culture. It has even been said recently by a great voice that all we need of spiritual truth for the spiritual life is to be found in the Gita. It would be to encourage the superstition of the book to take too literally that utterance. The truth of the spirit is infinite and cannot be circumscribed in that manner. Still, it may be said that most of the main clues are there and that after all the later developments of spiritual experience and discovery we can still return to it for a large inspiration and guidance. Outside India too it is universally acknowledged as one of the world's great scriptures, although in Europe its thought is better understood than its secret of spiritual practice. What is it then that gives this vitality to the thought and the truth of the Gita?

The central interest of the Gita's philosophy and Yoga is its attempt, the idea with which it sets out, continues, and closes, to reconcile and even effect a kind of unity between the inner spiritual truth in its most absolute and integral realisation and the outer actualities of man's life and action. A compromise between the two is common enough, but that can never be a final and satisfactory solution. An ethical rendering of spirituality is also common and has its value as a law of conduct; but that is a mental solution which does not amount to a complete practical reconciliation of the whole truth of spirit with the whole truth of life and it raises as many problems as it solves. One of these is indeed the starting-point of the Gita; it sets out with an ethical problem raised by a conflict in which we have on one side the dharma of the man of action, a prince and warrior and leader of men, the protagonist of a great crisis, of a struggle on the physical plane, the plane of actual life, between the powers of right and justice and the powers of wrong and injustice, the demand of the destiny of the race upon him that he shall resist and give battle and establish even though through a terrible physical struggle and a giant slaughter a new era and reign of truth and right and justice, and on the other side the ethical sense which condemns the means and the action as a sin, recoils from the price of individual suffering and social strife, unsettling and disturbance and regards abstention from violence and battle as the only way and the one right moral attitude. A spiritualized ethics insists on Ahinsa, on non-injuring and non-killing as the highest law of spiritual conduct. The battle, if it is to be fought out at all, must be fought on the spiritual plane and by some kind of non-resistance or refusal of participation or only by soul resistance, and if this does not succeed on the external plane, if the force of injustice conquers, the individual will still have preserved his virtue and vindicated by his example the highest ideal. On the other hand, a more insistent extreme of the inner spiritual direction, passing beyond this struggle between social duty and an absolutist ethical ideal, is apt to take the ascetic turn and to point away from life and all its aims and standards of action towards another and celestial or supracosmic state in which alone beyond the perplexed vanity and illusion of man's birth and life and death there can be a pure spiritual existence. The Gita rejects none of these things in their place,—for it insists on the performance of the social duty, the following of the dharma for the man who has to take his share in the common action, accepts Ahinsa as part of the highest spiritual-ethical ideal and recognizes the ascetic renunciation as a way of spiritual salvation. And yet it goes boldly beyond all these conflicting positions; greatly daring, it justifies all life to the spirit as a significant manifestation of the one Divine Being and asserts the compatibility of a complete human action and a complete spiritual life lived in union with the Infinite, consonant with the highest Self, expressive of the perfect Godhead.

All the problems of human life arise from the complexity of our existence, the obscurity of its essential principle and the secrecy of the inmost power that makes out its determinations and governs its purpose and its processes. If our existence were of one piece, solely material-vital or solely mental or solely spiritual, or even if the others were entirely or mainly involved in one of these or were quite latent in our subconscient or our superconscient parts, there would be nothing to perplex us; the material and vital law would be imperative or the mental would be clear to its own pure and unobstructed principle or the spiritual self-existent and self-sufficient to spirit. The animals are aware of no problems; a mental god in a world of pure mentality would admit none or would solve them all by the purity of a mental rule or the satisfaction of a rational harmony; a pure spirit would be above them and self-content in the infinite. But the existence of man is a triple web, a thing mysteriously physical-vital, mental, and spiritual at once and he knows not what are the true relations of these things, which the real reality of his life and his nature, whither the attraction of his destiny and where the sphere of his perfection.

Matter and life are his actual basis, the thing from which he starts and on which he stands and whose requirement and law he has to satisfy if he would exist at all on earth and in the body. The material and vital law is a rule of survival, of struggle, of desire and possession, of self-assertion and the satisfaction of the body, the life, and the ego. All the intellectual reasoning in the world, all the ethical idealism and spiritual absolutism of which the higher faculties of man are capable cannot abolish the reality and claim of our vital and material base or prevent the race from following under the imperative compulsion of Nature its aims and the satisfaction of its necessities or from making its important problems a great and legitimate part of human destiny and human interest and endeavour. And the intelligence of man even, failing to find any sustenance in spiritual or ideal solutions that solve everything else but the pressing problems of our actual human life, often turns away from them to an exclusive acceptance of the vital and material existence and the reasoned or instinctive pursuit of its utmost possible efficiency, well-being, and organized satisfaction. A gospel of the will to live or the will to power or of a rationalized vital and material perfection becomes the recognized dharma of the human race and all else is considered either a pretentious falsity or a quite subsidiary thing, a side issue of a minor and dependent consequence.

Matter and life however in spite of their insistence and great importance are not all that man is, nor can he wholly accept mind as nothing, but a servant of the life and body admitted to certain pure enjoyments of its own as a sort of reward for its service or regard it as no more than an extension and flower of the vital urge, an ideal luxury contingent upon the satisfaction of the material life. The mind much more intimately than the body and the life is the man, and the mind as it develops insists more and more on making the body and the life an instrument—an indispensable instrument and yet a considerable obstacle, otherwise there would be no problem—for its own characteristic satisfactions and self-realization. The mind of man is not only a vital and physical, but an intellectual, aesthetic, ethical, psychic, emotional and dynamic intelligence, and in the sphere of each of its tendencies its highest and strongest nature is to strain towards some absolute of them which the frame of life will not allow it to capture wholly and embody and make here entirely real. The mental absolute of our aspiration remains as a partly grasped shining or fiery ideal which the mind can make inwardly very present to itself, inwardly imperative on its effort and can even effectuate partly, but not compel all the facts of life into its image. There is thus an absolute, a high imperative of intellectual truth and reason sought for by our intellectual being; there is an absolute, an imperative of right and conduct aimed at by the ethical conscience; there is an absolute, an imperative of love, sympathy, compassion, oneness yearned after by our emotional and psychic nature; there is an absolute, an imperative of delight and beauty quivered to by the aesthetic soul; there is an absolute, an imperative of inner self-mastery and control of life laboured after by the dynamic will; all these are there together and impinge upon the absolute, the imperative of possession and pleasure and safe embodied existence insisted on by the vital and physical mind. And the human intelligence, since it is not able to realise entirely any of these things, much less all of them together, erects in each sphere many standards and dharmas, standards of truth and reason, of right and conduct, of delight and beauty, of love, sympathy, and oneness, of self-mastery and control, of self-preservation and possession and vital efficiency and pleasure, and tries to impose them on life. The absolute shining ideals stand far above and beyond our capacity and rare individuals approximate to them as best they can: the mass follow or profess to follow some less magnificent norm, some established possible and relative standard. Human life as a whole undergoes the attraction and yet rejects the ideal. Life resists in the strength of some obscure infinite of its own and wears down or breaks down any established mental and moral order. And this must be either because the two are quite different and disparate though meeting and interacting principles or because mind has not the clue to the whole reality of life. The clue must be sought in something greater, an unknown something above the mentality and morality of the human creature.

The mind itself has the vague sense of some surpassing factor of this kind and in the pursuit of its absolutes frequently strikes against it. It glimpses a state, a power, a presence that is near and within and inmost to it and yet immeasurably greater and singularly distant and above it; it has a vision of something more essential, more absolute than its own absolutes, intimate, infinite, one, and it is that which we call God, Self or Spirit. This then the mind attempts to know, enter, touch, and seize wholly, to approach it or become it, to arrive at some kind of unity or lose itself in a complete identity with that mystery, ascaryam. The difficulty is that this spirit in its purity seems something yet farther than the mental absolutes from the actualities of life, something not translatable by mind into its own terms, much less into those of life and action. Therefore, we have the intransigent absolutists of the spirit who reject the mental and condemn the material being and yearn after a pure spiritual existence happily purchased by the dissolution of all that we are in life and mind, a Nirvana. The rest of spiritual effort is for these fanatics of the Absolute a mental preparation or a compromise, a spiritualizing of life and mind as much as possible. And because the difficulty most constantly insistent on man's mentality in practice is that presented by the claims of his vital being, by life and conduct and action, the direction taken by this preparatory endeavour consists mainly in a spiritualizing of the ethical supported by the psychical mind—or rather it brings in the spiritual power and purity to aid these in enforcing their absolute claim and to impart a greater authority than life allows to the ethical ideal of right and truth of conduct or the psychic ideal of love and sympathy and oneness. These things are helped to some highest expression, given their broadest luminous basis by an assent of the reason and will to the underlying truth of the absolute oneness of the spirit and therefore the essential oneness of all living creatures. This kind of spirituality linked on in some way to the demands of the normal mind of man, persuaded to the acceptance of useful social duty and current law of social conduct, popularised by cult and ceremony and image is the outward substance of the world's greater religions. These religions have their individual victories, call in some ray of a higher light, impose some shadow of a larger spiritual or semi-spiritual rule, but cannot affect a complete victory, end flatly in a compromise and in the act of compromise are defeated by life. Its problems remain and even recur in their fiercest forms—even such as this grim problem of Kurukshetra. The idealizing intellect and ethical mind hope always to eliminate them, to discover some happy device born of their own aspiration and made effective by their own imperative insistence, which will annihilate this nether untoward aspect of life; but it endures and is not eliminated. The spiritualized intelligence on the other hand offers indeed by the voice of religion the promise of some victorious millennium hereafter, but meanwhile half convinced of terrestrial impotence, persuaded that the soul is a stranger and intruder upon earth, declares that after all not here in the life of the body or in the collective life of mortal man but in some immortal Beyond lies the heaven or the Nirvana where alone is to be found the true spiritual existence.

It is here that the Gita intervenes with a restatement of the truth of the Spirit, of the Self, of God and of the world and Nature. It extends and remoulds the truth evolved by a later thought from the ancient Upanishads and ventures with assured steps on an endeavour to apply its solving power to the problem of life and action. The solution offered by the Gita does not disentangle all the problem as it offers itself to modern mankind; as stated here to a more ancient mentality, it does not meet the insistent pressure of the present mind of man for a collective advance, does not respond to its cry for a collective life that will at last embody a greater rational and ethical and if possible, even a dynamic spiritual ideal. Its call is to the individual who has become capable of a complete spiritual existence; but for the rest of the race it prescribes only a gradual advance, to be wisely affected by following out faithfully with more and more of intelligence and moral purpose and with a final turn to spirituality the law of their nature. Its message touches the other smaller solutions but, even when it accepts them partly, it is to point them beyond themselves to a higher and more integral secret into which as yet only the few individuals have shown themselves fit to enter.

The Gita's message to the mind that follows after the vital and material life is that all life is indeed a manifestation of the universal Power in the individual, a derivation from the Self, a ray from the Divine, but actually it figures the Self and the Divine veiled in a disguising Maya, and to pursue the lower life for its own sake is to persist in a stumbling path and to enthrone our nature's obscure ignorance and not at all to find the true truth and complete law of existence. A gospel of the will to live, the will to power, of the satisfaction of desire, of the glorification of mere force and strength, of the worship of the ego and its vehement acquisitive self-will and tireless self-regarding intellect is the gospel of the Asura and it can lead only to some gigantic ruin and perdition. The vital and material man must accept for his government a religious and social and ideal dharma by which, while satisfying desire and interest under right restrictions, he can train and subdue his lower personality and scrupulously attune it to a higher law both of the personal and the communal life.

The Gita's message to the mind occupied with the pursuit of intellectual, ethical and social standards, the mind that insists on salvation by the observance of established dharmas, the moral law, social duty and function or the solutions of the liberated intelligence, is that this is indeed a very necessary stage, the dharma has indeed to be observed and, rightly observed, can raise the stature of the spirit and prepare and serve the spiritual life, but still it is not the complete and last truth of existence. The soul of man has to go beyond to some more absolute dharma of man's spiritual and immortal nature. And this can only be done if we repress and get rid of the ignorant formulations of the lower mental elements and the falsehood of egoistic personality, impersonalize the action of the intelligence and will, live in the identity of the oneself in all, break out of all ego-moulds into the impersonal spirit. The mind moves under the limiting compulsion of the triple lower nature, it erects its standards in obedience to the tamasic, rajasic or at highest the sattwic qualities; but the destiny of the soul is a divine perfection and liberation and that can only be based in the freedom of our highest self, can only be found by passing through its vast impersonality and universality beyond mind into the integral light of the immeasurable Godhead and supreme Infinite who is beyond all dharmas.

The Gita's message to those, absolutist seekers of the Infinite, who carry impersonality to an exclusive extreme, entertain an intolerant passion for the extinction of life and action and would have as the one ultimate aim and ideal an endeavour to cease from all individual being in the pure silence of the ineffable Spirit, is that this is indeed one path of journey and entry into the Infinite, but the most difficult, the ideal of inaction a dangerous thing to hold up by precept or example before the world, this way, though great, yet not the best way for man and this knowledge, though true, yet not the integral knowledge. The Supreme, the all-conscious Self, the Godhead, the Infinite is not solely a spiritual existence remote and ineffable; he is here in the universe at once hidden and expressed through man and the gods and through all beings and in all that is. And it is by finding him not only in some immutable silence but in the world and its beings and in all self and in all Nature, it is by raising to an integral as well as to a highest union with him all the activities of the intelligence, the heart, the will, the life that man can solve at once his inner riddle of self and God and the outer problem of his active human existence. Made Godlike, God-becoming, he can enjoy the infinite breadth of a supreme spiritual consciousness that is reached through works no less than through love and knowledge. Immortal and free, he can continue his human action from that highest level and transmute it into a supreme and all-embracing divine activity,—that indeed is the ultimate crown and significance here of all works and living and sacrifice and the world's endeavour.

This highest message is first for those who have the strength to follow after it, the master men, the great spirits, the God-knowers, God-doers, God-lovers who can live in God and for God and do their work joyfully for him in the world, a divine work uplifted above the restless darkness of the human mind and the false limitations of the ego. At the same time, and here we get the gleam of a larger promise which we may even extend to the hope of a collective turn towards perfection,—for if there is hope for man, why should there not be hope for mankind?

—the Gita declares that all can if they will, even to the lowest and sinfullest among men, enter into the path of this Yoga. And if there is a true self-surrender and an absolute unegoistic faith in the indwelling Divinity, success is certain in this path. The decisive turn is needed; there must be an abiding belief in the Spirit, a sincere and insistent will to live in the Divine, to be in self-one with him and in Nature—where too we are an eternal portion of his being—one with his greater spiritual Nature, God-possessed in all our members and Godlike.

The Gita in the development of its idea raises many issues, such as the determinism of Nature, the significance of the universal manifestation and the ultimate status of the liberated soul, questions that have been the subject of unending and inconclusive debate. It is not necessary in this series of essays of which the object is a scrutiny and positive affirmation of the substance of the Gita and a disengaging of its contribution to the abiding spiritual thought of humanity and its kernel of living practice, to enter far into these discussions or to consider where we may differ from its standpoint or conclusions, make any reserves in our assent or even, strong in later experience, go beyond its metaphysical teaching or its Yoga. It will be sufficient to close with a formulation of the living message it still brings for man the eternal seeker and discoverer to guide him through the present circuits and the possible steeper ascent of his life up to the luminous heights of his spirit.

XXIV

THE MESSAGE OF THE GITA

"The Secret of action," so we might summarize the message of the Gita, the word of its divine Teacher, "is one with the secret of all life and existence. Existence is not merely a machinery of Nature, a wheel of law in which the soul is entangled for a moment or for ages; it is a constant manifestation of the Spirit. Life is not for the sake of life alone, but for God, and the living soul of man is an eternal portion of the Godhead. Action is for self-finding, for self-fulfillment, for self-realization and not only for its own external and apparent fruits of the moment or the future. There is an inner law and meaning of all things dependent on the supreme as well as the manifested nature of the self; the true truth of works lies there and can be represented only incidentally, imperfectly and disguised by ignorance in the outer appearances of the mind and its action. The supreme, the faultless largest law of action is therefore to find out the truth of your own highest and inmost existence and live in it and not to follow any outer standard and dharma. All life and action must be till then an imperfection, a difficulty, a struggle, and a problem. It is only by discovering your true self and living according to its true truth, its real reality that the problem can be finally solved, the difficulty and struggle overpassed, and your doings perfected in the security of the discovered self and spirit turn into a divinely authentic action. Know then yourself; know your true self to be God and one with the self of all others; know your soul to be a portion of God. Live in what you know; live in the self, live in your supreme spiritual nature, be united with God and Godlike. Offer, first, all your actions as a sacrifice to the Highest and the One in you and to the Highest and the One in the world; deliver last all you are and do into his hands for the supreme and universal spirit to do through you his own will and works in the world. This is the solution that I present to you and in the end, you will find that there is no other."

Here it is necessary to state the Gita's view of the funda-mental opposition on which like all Indian teaching it takes its position. This finding of the true self, this knowledge of the Godhead within us and all is not an easy thing; nor is it an easy thing either to turn this knowledge, even though seen by the mind, into the stuff of our consciousness and the whole condition of our action. All action is determined by the effective state of our being, and the effective state of our being is determined by the state of our constant self-seeing will and active consciousness and by its basis of kinetic movement. It is what we see and believe with our whole active nature ourselves to be and our relations with the world to mean, it is our faith, our sraddha, that makes us what we are. But the consciousness of man is of a double kind and corresponds to a double truth of existence; for there is a truth of the inner reality and a truth of the outer appearance. According as he lives in one or the other, he will be a mind dwelling in human ignorance or a soul founded in divine knowledge.

In its outer appearance the truth of existence is solely what we call Nature or Prakriti, a Force that operates as the whole law and mechanism of being, creates the world which is the object of our mind and senses and creates too the mind and senses as a means of relation between the creature and the objective world in which he lives. In this outer appearance man in his soul, his mind, his life, his body seems to be a creature of Nature differentiated from others by a separation of his body, life, and mind and especially by his ego-sense—that subtle mechanism constructed for him that he may confirm and centralize his consciousness of all this strong separateness and difference. All in him, his soul of mind and its action as well as the functioning of his life and body, is very evidently determined by the law of his nature, cannot get outside of it, cannot operate otherwise. He attributes indeed a certain freedom to his personal will, the will of his ego; but that in reality amounts to nothing, since his ego is only a sense which makes him identify himself with the creation that Nature has made of him, with the varying mind and life and body she has constructed. His ego is itself a product of her workings, and as is the nature of his ego, so will be the nature of its will and according to that he must act, and he can no other.

This then is man's ordinary consciousness of himself, this his faith in his own being, that he is a creature of Nature, a separate ego establishing whatever relations with others and with the world, making whatever development of himself, satisfying whatever will, desire, idea of his mind may be permissible in her circle and consonant with her intention or law in his existence.

There is, however, something in man's consciousness which does not fall in with the rigidity of this formula; he has a faith, which grows greater as his soul develops, in another and an inner reality of existence. In this inner reality the truth of existence is no longer Nature but Soul and Spirit, Purusha rather than Prakriti. Nature herself is only a power of Spirit, Prakriti the force of the Purusha. A Spirit, a Self, a Being one in all is the master of this world which is only his partial manifestation. That Spirit is the upholder of Nature and her action and the giver of the sanction by which alone her law becomes imperative and her force and its ways operative. That Spirit within her is the Knower who illuminates her and makes her conscient in us; his is the immanent and superconscient Will that inspires and motives her workings. The soul in man, a portion of this Divinity, shares his nature. Our nature is our soul's manifestation, operates by its sanction and embodies its secret self-knowledge and self-consciousness and its will of being in her motions and forms and changes.

The real soul and self of us is hidden from our intelligence by its ignorance of inner things, by a false identification, by an absorption in our outward mechanism of mind, life, and body. But if the active soul of man can once draw back from this identification with its natural instruments, if it can see and live in the entire faith of its inner reality, then all is changed to it, life and existence take on another appearance, action a different meaning and character. Our being then becomes no longer this little egoistic creation of Nature but the largeness of a divine, immortal, and spiritual Power. Our consciousness becomes no longer that of this limited and struggling mental and vital creature, but an infinite, divine and spiritual consciousness.

And our will and action too are no longer that of this bounded personality and its ego, but a divine and spiritual will and action, the will and power of the Universal, the Supreme, the All-Self and Spirit acting freely through the human figure.

"This is the great change and transfiguration," runs the message of the Godhead in man, the Avatar, the divine Teacher, "to which I call the elect, and the elect are all who can turn their will away from the ignorance of the natural instruments to the soul's deepest experience, its knowledge of the inner self and spirit, its contact with the Godhead, its power to enter into the Divine. The elect are all who can accept this faith and this greater law. It is difficult indeed to accept for the human intellect attached always to its own cloud-forms and half lights of ignorance and to the yet obscurer habits of man's mental, nervous, and physical parts; but once received it is a great and sure and saving way, because it is identical with the true truth of man's being and it is the authentic movement of his inmost and supreme nature.

"But the change is a very great one, an enormous transformation, and it cannot be done without an entire turning and conversion of your whole being and nature. There will be needed a complete consecration of yourself and your nature and your life to the Highest and to nothing else but the Highest; for all must be held only for the sake of the Highest, nothing accepted except as it is in God and a form of God and for the sake of the Divine. There will be needed an admission of new truth, an entire turn and giving of your mind to a new knowledge of self and others and world and God and soul and Nature, a knowledge of oneness, a knowledge of universal Divinity, which will be at first an acceptance by the understanding but must become in the end a vision, a consciousness, a permanent state of the soul and the frame of its movements.

"There will be needed a will that shall make this new knowledge, vision, consciousness a motive of action and the sole motive. And it must be the motive not of an action grudging, limited, confined to a few necessary operations of Nature or to the few things that seem helpful to a formal perfection, apposite to a religious turn or to an individual salvation, but rather all action of human life taken up by the equal spirit and done for the sake of God and the good of all creatures. There will be needed an uplifting of the heart in a single aspiration to the Highest, a single love of the Divine Being, a single God-adoration. And there must be a widening too of the calmed and enlightened heart to embrace God in all beings. There will be needed a change of the habitual and normal nature of man as he is now to a supreme and divine spiritual nature. There will be needed in a word a Yoga which shall be at once a Yoga of integral knowledge, a Yoga of the integral will and its works, a Yoga of integral love, adoration and devotion and a Yoga of an integral spiritual perfection of the whole being and of all its parts and states and powers and motions.

"What then is this knowledge that will have to be admitted by the understanding, supported by the soul's faith, and made real and living to the mind, heart, and life? It is the knowledge of the supreme Soul and Spirit in its oneness and its wholeness. It is the knowledge of One who is forever, beyond Time and Space and name and form and world, high beyond his own personal and impersonal levels and yet from whom all this proceeds, One whom all manifests in manifold Nature and her multitude of figures. It is the knowledge of him as an impersonal eternal immutable Spirit, the calm and limitless thing we call Self, infinite, equal and always the same, unaffected, and unmodified and unchanged amid all this constant changing and all this multitude of individual personalities and soul powers and Nature powers and the forms and forces and eventualities of this transitory and apparent existence. It is the knowledge of him at the same time as the Spirit and Power who seems ever mutable in Nature, the Inhabitant who shapes himself to every form and modifies himself to every grade and degree and activity of his power, the Spirit who, becoming all that is even while he is forever infinitely more than all that is, dwells in man and animal and thing, subject and object, soul and mind and life and matter, every existence and every force and every creature.

"It is not by insisting on this or that side only of the truth that you can practise this Yoga. The Divine whom you have to seek, the Self whom you have to discover, the supreme Soul of whom your soul is an eternal portion, is simultaneously all these things; you have to know them simultaneously in a supreme oneness, enter into all of them at once and in all states and all things see Him alone. If he were solely the Spirit mutable in Nature, there would be only an eternal and universal becoming. If you limit your faith and knowledge to that one aspect, you will never go beyond your personality and its constant changeful figures; on such a foundation you would be bound altogether in the revolutions of Nature. But you are not merely a succession of soul moments in Time. There is an impersonal self in you which supports the stream of your personality and is one with God's vast and impersonal spirit. And incalculable beyond this impersonality and personality, dominating these two constant poles of what you are here, you are eternal and transcendent in the Eternal Transcendence.

"If, again, there were only the truth of an eternal impersonal self that neither acts nor creates, then the world and your soul would be illusions without any real basis. If you limit your faith and knowledge to this one lonely aspect, the renunciation of life and action is your only resource. But God in the world and you in the world are realities; the world and you are true and actual powers and manifestations of the Supreme. Therefore, accept life and action and do not reject them. One with God in your impersonal self and essence, an eternal portion of the Godhead turned to him by the love and adoration of your spiritual personality for its own Infinite, make of your natural being what it is intended to be, an instrument of works, a channel, a power of the Divine. That it always is in its truth, but now unconsciously and imperfectly, through the lower nature, doomed to a disfigurement of the Godhead by your ego. Make it consciously and perfectly and without any distortion by ego a power of the Divine in his supreme spiritual nature and a vehicle of his will and his works. In this way you will live in the integral truth of your own being and you will possess the integral God-union, the whole and flawless Yoga.

"The Supreme is the Purushottama, eternal beyond all manifestation, infinite beyond all limitation by Time or Space or Causality or any of his numberless qualities and features. But this does not mean that in his supreme eternity he is unconnected with all that happens here, cut off from world and Nature, aloof from all these beings. He is the supreme ineffable Brahman, he is impersonal self, he is all personal existences. Spirit here and life and matter, soul and Nature and the works of Nature are aspects and movements of his infinite and eternal existence. He is the supreme transcendent Spirit, and all comes into manifestation from him and are his forms and his self-powers. As the oneself he is here all-pervasive and equal and impersonal in man and animal and thing and object and every force of Nature. He is the supreme Soul, and all souls are tireless flames of this one Soul. All living beings are in their spiritual personality deathless portions of the one Person or Purusha. He is the eternal Master of all manifested existence, Lord of the worlds and their creatures. He is the omnipotent originator of all actions, not bound by his works, and to him go all action and effort and sacrifice. He is in all, and all are in him; he has become all and yet too he is above all and not limited by his creations. He is the transcendent Divine; he descends as the Avatar; he is manifest by his power in the Vibhuti; he is the Godhead secret in every human being. All the gods whom men worship are only personalities and forms and names and mental bodies of the one Divine Existence.

"The Supreme has manifested the world from his spiritual essence and in his own infinite existence and manifested himself too variously in the world. All things are his powers and figures and to the powers and figures of him there is no end because he himself is infinite. As a pervading and containing impersonal self-existence he informs and sustains equally and without any partiality, preference or attachment to any person or thing or happening or feature all this infinite manifestation in Time and the universe. This pure and equal Self does not act but supports impartially all the action of things. And yet it is the Supreme, but as the cosmic Spirit and the Time Spirit, who wills and conducts and determines the action of the world through his multitudinous power-to-be, that power of the Spirit which we call Nature. He creates, sustains, and destroys his creations. He is seated too in the heart of every living creature and from there as a secret Power in the individual, no less than from his universal presence in the Cosmos, he originates by force of Nature, manifests some line of his mystery in quality of nature and in executive energy of nature, shapes each thing and being separately according to its kind and initiates and upholds all action. It is this transcendent first origination from the Supreme and this constant universal and individual manifestation of Him in things and beings which makes the complex character of the cosmos.

"There are always these three eternal states of the Divine Being. There is always and forever this one eternal immutable self-existence which is the basis and support of existent things. There is always and forever this Spirit mutable in Nature manifested by her as all these existences. There is always and forever this transcendent Divine who can be both of these others at once, can be a pure and silent Spirit and at the same time the active soul and life of the cycles of the universe, because he is something other and more than these two whether taken separately or together. In us is the Jiva, a spirit of this Spirit, a conscious power of the Supreme. He is one who carries in his deepest self the whole of the immanent Divine and in Nature lives in the universal Divine,—no temporary creation but an eternal soul acting and moving in the eternal Self, in the eternal Infinite.

"This conscient soul in us can adopt either of these three states of the Spirit. Man can live here in the mutability of Nature and in that alone. Ignorant of his real self, ignorant of the Godhead within him, he knows only Nature: he sees her as a mechanical executive and creative Force and sees himself and others as her creations,—egos, separated existences in her universe. It is thus, superficially, that he now lives and, while it is so and until he exceeds this outer consciousness and knows what is within him, all his thought and science can only be a shadow of light thrown upon screens and surfaces. This ignorance is possible, is even imposed, because the Godhead within is hidden by the veil of his own power. His greater reality is lost to our view by the completeness with which he has identified himself in a partial appearance with his creations and images and absorbed the created mind in the deceptive workings of his own Nature. And it is possible also because the real, the eternal, the spiritual Nature which is the secret of things in themselves is not manifest in their outward phenomena. The Nature which we see when we look outwards, the Nature which acts in our mind and body and senses is a lower Force, a derivation, a Magician who creates figures of the Spirit but hides the Spirit in its figures, conceals the truth and makes men look upon masks, a Force which is only capable of a sum of secondary and depressed values, not of the full power and glory and ecstasy and sweetness of the manifestation of the Divine. This Nature in us is a Maya of the ego, a tangle of the dualities, a web of ignorance and the three gunas. And so long as the soul of man lives in the surface fact of mind and life and body and not in his self and spirit, he cannot see God and himself and the world as they really are, cannot overcome this Maya, but must do what he can with its terms and figures.

"It is possible by drawing back from the lower turn of his nature in which man now lives, to awake from this light that is darkness and live in the luminous truth of the eternal and immutable self-existence. Man, then is no longer bound up in his narrow prison of personality, no longer sees himself as this little I that thinks and acts and feels and struggles and labours for a little. He is merged in the vast and free impersonality of the pure spirit; he becomes the Brahman; he knows himself as one with the oneself in all things. He is no longer aware of ego, no longer troubled by the dualities, no longer feels anguish of grief or disturbance of joy, is no longer shaken by desire, is no longer troubled by sin, or limited by virtue. Or if the shadows of these things remain, he sees and knows them only as Nature working in her own qualities and does not feel them to be the truth of himself in which he lives. Nature alone acts and works out her mechanical figures: but the pure spirit is silent, inactive, and free. Calm, untouched by her workings, it regards them with a perfect equality and knows itself to be other than these things. This spiritual state brings with it a still peace and freedom but not the dynamic divinity, not the integral perfection; it is a great step, but it is not the integral God-knowledge and self-knowledge.

"A perfect perfection comes only by living in the supreme and the whole Divine. Then the soul of man is united with the Godhead of which it is a portion; then it is one with all beings in the self and spirit, one with them both in God and in Nature; then it is not only free but complete, plunged in the supreme felicity, ready for its ultimate perfection. He still sees the self as an eternal and changeless Spirit silently supporting all things; but he sees also Nature no longer as a mere mechanical force that works out things according to the mechanism of the gunas, but as a power of the Spirit and the force of God in manifestation. He sees that the lower Nature is not the inmost truth of the spirit's action; he becomes aware of a highest spiritual nature of the Divine in which is contained the source and the yet to be realized greater truth of all that is imperfectly figured now in mind, life, and body. Arisen from the lower mental to this supreme spiritual nature, he is delivered there from all ego. He knows himself as a spiritual being, in his essence one with all existences and in his active nature a power of the one Godhead and an eternal soul of the transcendent Infinite. He sees all in God and God in all; he sees all things as Vasudeva. He is delivered from the dualities of joy and grief, from the pleasant and the unpleasant, from desire and disappointment, from sin and virtue. All henceforth is to his conscious sight and sense the will and working of the Divine. He lives and acts as a soul and portion of the universal consciousness and power; he is filled with the transcendent divine delight, a spiritual Ananda. His action becomes the divine action and his status the highest spiritual status.

"This is the solution, this the salvation, this the perfection that I offer to all those who can listen to a divine voice within them and are capable of this faith and knowledge. But to climb to this pre-eminent condition the first necessity, the original radical step is to turn away from all that belongs to your lower Nature and fix yourself by concentration of the will and intelligence on that which is higher than either will or intelligence, higher than mind and heart and sense and body. And first of all, you must turn to your own eternal and immutable self, impersonal and the same in all creatures. So long as you live in ego and mental personality, you will always spin endlessly in the same rounds and there can be no real issue. Turn your will inward beyond the heart and its desires and the sense and its attractions; lift it up-ward beyond the mind and its associations and attachments and its bounded wish and thought and impulse. Arrive at something within you that is eternal, ever unchanged, calm, unperturbed, equal, impartial to all things and persons and happenings, not affected by any action, not altered by the figures of Nature. Be that, be the eternal self, be the Brahman. If you can become that by a permanent spiritual experience, you will have an assured basis on which you can stand delivered from the limitations of your mind-created personality, secure against any fall from peace and knowledge, free from ego.

"Thus, to impersonalize your being is not possible so long as you nurse and cherish and cling to your ego or anything that belongs to it. Desire and the passions that arise from desire are the principal sign and knot of ego. It is desire that makes you go on saying I and mine and subjects you through a persistent egoism to satisfaction and dissatisfaction, liking and disliking, hope and despair, joy, and grief, to your petty loves and hatreds, to wrath and passion, to your attachment to success and things pleasant and to the sorrow and suffering of failure and of things unpleasant. Desire always brings confusion of mind and limitation of the will, an egoistic and distorted view of things, a failure and clouding of knowledge. Desire and its preferences and violences are the first strong root of sin and error. There can be while you cherish desire no assured stainless tranquility, no settled light, no calm pure knowledge. There can be no right being—for desire is a perversion of the spirit—and no firm foundation for right thought, action and feeling. Desire, if permitted to remain under whatever colour, is a perpetual menace even to the wisest and can at any moment subtly or violently cast down the mind from even its firmest and most surely acquired foundation. Desire is the chief enemy of spiritual perfection.

"Slay then desire; put away attachment to the possession and enjoyment of the outwardness of things. Separate yourself from all that comes to you as outward touches and solicitations, as objects of the mind and senses. Learn to bear and reject all the rush of the passions and to remain securely seated in your inner self even while they rage in your members, until at last they cease to affect any part of your nature. Bear and put away similarly the forceful attacks and even the slightest insinuating touches of joy and sorrow. Cast away liking and disliking, destroy preference and hatred, root out shrinking and repugnance. Let there be a calm indifference to these things and to all the objects of desire in all your nature. Look on them with the silent and tranquil regard of an impersonal spirit.

"The result will be an absolute equality and the power of unshakable calm that the universal spirit maintains in front of its creations, facing ever the manifold action of Nature. Look with equal eyes; receive with an equal heart and mind all that comes to you, success and failure, honour and dishonour, the esteem and love of men and their scorn and persecution and hatred, every happening that would be to others a cause of joy and every happening that would be to others a cause of sorrow. Look with equal eyes on all persons, on the good and the wicked, on the wise and the foolish, on the Brahmin and the outcaste, on man at his highest and every pettiest creature. Meet equally all men whatever their relations to you, friend and ally, neutral and indifferent, opponent and enemy, lover and hater. These things touch the ego and you are called to be free from ego. These are personal relations and you have to observe all with the deep regard of the impersonal spirit. These are temporal and personal differences which you have to see but not be influenced by them; for you must fix not on these differences but on that which is the same in all, on the one self which all are, on the Divine in every creature and on the one working of Nature which is the equal will of God in men and things and energies and happenings and in all endeavour and result and whatever outcome of the world's labour.

"Action will still be done in you because Nature is always at work; but you must learn and feel that your self is not the doer of the action. Observe simply, observe unmoved the working of Nature and the play of her qualities and the magic of the gunas. Observe unmoved this action in yourself; look on all that is being done around you and see that it is the same working in others. Observe that the result of your works and theirs is constantly other than you or they desired or intended, not theirs, not yours, but omnipotently fixed by a greater Power that wills and acts here in universal Nature. Observe too that even the will in your works is not yours but Nature's. It is the will of the ego sense in you and is determined by the predominant quality in your composition which she has developed in the past or else brings forward at the moment. It depends on the play of your natural personality and that formation of Nature is not your true person. Draw back from this external formation to your inner silent self; you will see that you the Purusha are inactive, but Nature continues to do always her works according to her gunas. Fix yourself in this inner inactivity and stillness: no longer regard yourself as the doer. Remain seated in yourself above the play, free from the perturbed action of the gunas. Live secure in the purity of an impersonal spirit, live untroubled by the mortal waves that persist in your members.

"If you can do this, then you will find yourself uplifted into a great release, a wide freedom and a deep peace. Then you will be aware of God and immortal, possessed of your dateless self-existence, independent of mind and life and body, sure of your spiritual being, untouched by the reactions of Nature, unstained by passion and sin and pain and sorrow. Then you will depend for your joy and desire on no mortal or outward or worldly thing, but will possess inalienably the self-sufficient delight of a calm and eternal spirit. Then you will have ceased to be a mental creature and will have become spirit illimitable, the Brahman. And into this eternity of the silent self, rejecting from your mind all seed of thought and all root of desire, rejecting the figure of birth in the body, you can pass at your end by concentration in the pure Eternal and a mighty transference of your consciousness to the Infinite, the Absolute.

"This however is not all the truth of the Yoga and this end and way of departure, though a great end and a great way, is not the thing I propose to you. For I am the eternal Worker within you, and I ask of your works. I demand of you not a passive consent to a mechanical movement of Nature from which in yourself you are wholly separated, indifferent and aloof but action complete and divine, done as the willing and understanding instrument of the Divine, done for God in you and others and for the good of the world. This action I propose to you, first no doubt as a means of perfection in the supreme spiritual Nature, but as a part too of that perfection. Action is a part of the integral knowledge of God, of his greater mysterious truth and of an entire living in the Divine; action can and should be continued even after perfection and freedom are won. I ask of you the action of the Jivanmukta, the works of the Siddha. Something has to be added to the Yoga already described,—for that was only a first Yoga of knowledge. There is also a Yoga of action in the illumination of God-experience; works can be made one spirit with knowledge. For works done in a total self-vision and God-vision, a vision of God in the world and of the world in God are themselves a movement of knowledge, a movement of light, an indispensable means, and an intimate part of spiritual perfection.

"Therefore, now to the experience of a high impersonality add too this knowledge that the Supreme whom one meets as the pure silent Self can be met also as a vast dynamic Spirit who originates all works and is Lord of the worlds and the Master of man's action and endeavour and sacrifice. This apparently self-acting mechanism of Nature conceals an immanent divine Will that compels and guides it and shapes its purposes. But you cannot feel or know that Will while you are shut up in your narrow cell of personality, blinded and chained to your viewpoint of the ego and its desires. For you can wholly respond to it only when you are impersonalized by knowledge and widened to see all things in the self and in God and the self and God in all things. All becomes here by the power of the Spirit; all do their works by the immanence of God in things and his presence in the heart of every creature. The Creator of the worlds is not limited by his creations; the Lord of works is not bound by his works; the divine Will is not attached to its labour and the results of its labour: for it is omnipotent, all-possessing and all-blissful. But still the Lord looks down on his creations from his transcendence; he descends as the Avatar; he is here in you; he rules from within all things in the steps of their nature. And you too must do works in him, after the way and in the steps of the divine nature, untouched by limitation, attachment, or bondage. Act for the best good of all, act for the maintenance of the march of the world, for the support or the leading of its peoples. The action asked of you is the action of the liberated Yogin; it is the spontaneous output of a free and God-held energy, it is an equal-minded movement, it is a selfless and desireless labour.

"The first step on this free, this equal, this divine way of action is to put from you attachment to fruit and recompense and to labour only for the sake of the work itself that has to be done. For you must deeply feel that the fruits belong not to you but to the Master of the world. Consecrate your labour and leave its returns to the Spirit who manifests and fulfils himself in the universal movement. The outcome of your action is determined by his will alone and whatever it be, good or evil fortune, success, or failure, it is turned by him to the accomplishment of his world purpose. An entirely desireless and disinterested working of the personal will and the whole instrumental nature is the first rule of Karmayoga. Demand no fruit, accept whatever result is given to you; accept it with equality and a calm gladness: successful or foiled, prosperous, or afflicted, continue unafraid, untroubled, and unwavering on the steep path of the divine action.

"This is no more than the first step on the path. For you must be not only unattached to results, but unattached also to your labour. Cease to regard your works as your own; as you have abandoned the fruits of your work, so you must surrender the work also to the Lord of action and sacrifice. Recognize that your nature determines your action; your nature rules the immediate motion of your Swabhava and decides the expressive turn and development of your spirit in the paths of the executive force of Prakriti. Bring in no longer any self-will to confuse the steps of your mind in following the Godward way. Accept the action proper to your nature. Make of all you do from the greatest and most unusual effort to the smallest daily act, make of each act of your mind, each act of your heart, each act of your body, of every inner and outer turn, of every thought and will and feeling, of every step and pause and movement, a sacrifice to the Master of all sacrifice and Tapasya.

"Next know that you are an eternal portion of the Eternal, and the powers of your nature are nothing without him, nothing if not his partial self-expression. It is the Divine Infinite that is being progressively fulfilled in your nature. It is the supreme power-to-be, it is the Shakti of the Lord that shapes and takes shape in your swabhava. Give up then all sense that you are the doer; see the Eternal alone as the doer of the action. Let your natural being be an occasion, an instrument, a channel of power, a means of manifestation. Offer up your will to him and make it one with his eternal will: surrender all your actions in the silence of yourself and spirit to the transcendent Master of your nature. This cannot be really done or done perfectly so long as there is any ego sense in you or any mental claim or vital clamour. Action done in the least degree for the sake of the ego or tinged with the desire and will of the ego is not a perfect sacrifice. Nor can this great thing be well and truly done so long as there is inequality anywhere or any stamp of ignorant shrinking and preference. But when there is a perfect equality to all works, results, things and persons, a surrender to the Highest and not to desire or ego, then the divine Will determines without stumbling or deflection and the divine Power executes freely without any nether interference or perverting reaction all works in the purity and safety of your transmuted nature. To allow your every act to be shaped through you by the divine Will in its immaculate sovereignty is the highest degree of the perfection that comes by doing works in Yoga. That done, your nature will follow its cosmic walk in a complete and constant union with the Supreme, express the highest Self, obey the Ishwara.

"This way of divine works is a far better release and a more perfect way and solution than the physical renunciation of life and works. A physical abstention is not entirely possible and is not in the measure of its possibility indispensable to the spirit's freedom; it is besides a dangerous example, for it exerts a misleading influence on ordinary men. The best, the greatest set the standard which the rest of humanity strive to follow. Then since action is the nature of the embodied spirit, since works are the will of the eternal Worker, the great spirits, the master minds should set this example. World-workers should they be, doing all works of the world without reservation, God-workers free, glad and desireless, liberated souls and natures.

"The mind of knowledge and the will of action are not all; there is within you a heart whose demand is for delight. Here too in the heart's power and illumination, in its demand for delight, for the soul's satisfaction your nature must be turned, transformed, and lifted to one conscious ecstasy with the Divine. The knowledge of the impersonal self brings its own Ananda; there is a joy of impersonality, a singleness of joy of the pure spirit. But an integral knowledge brings a greater triple delight. It opens the gates of the Transcendent's bliss; it releases into the limitless delight of a universal impersonality; it discovers the rapture of all this multitudinous manifestation: for there is a joy of the Eternal in Nature. This Ananda in the Jiva, a portion here of the Divine, takes the form of an ecstasy founded in the Godhead who is his source, in his supreme self, in the Master of his existence. An entire God-love and adoration extends to a love of the world and all its forms and powers and creatures; in all the Divine is seen, is found, is adored, is served, or is felt in oneness. Add to knowledge and works this crown of the eternal triune delight; admit this love, learn this worship; make it one spirit with works and knowledge. That is the apex of the perfect perfection.

"This Yoga of love will give you a highest potential force for spiritual largeness and unity and freedom. But it must be a love which is one with God-knowledge. There is a devotion which seeks God in suffering for consolation and succour and deliverance; there is a devotion which seeks him for his gifts, for divine aid and protection and as a fountain of the satisfaction of desire; there is a devotion that, still ignorant, turns to him for light and knowledge. And so long as one is limited to these forms, there may persist even in their highest and noblest Godward turn a working of the three gunas. But when the God-lover is also the God-knower, the lover becomes oneself with the Beloved; for he is the chosen of the Most High and the elect of the Spirit. Develop in yourself this

God-engrossed love; the heart spiritualised and lifted beyond the limitations of its lower nature will reveal to you most intimately the secrets of God's immeasurable being, bring into you the whole touch and influx and glory of his divine Power and open to you the mysteries of an eternal rapture. It is perfect love that is the key to a perfect knowledge.

"This integral God-love demands too an integral work for the sake of the Divine in yourself and in all creatures. The ordinary man does works in obedience to some desire sinful or virtuous, some vital impulse low or high, some mental choice common or exalted or from some mixed mind and life motive. But the work done by you must be free and desireless; work done without desire creates no reaction and imposes no bondage. Done in a perfect equality and an unmoved calm and peace, but without any divine passion, it is at first the fine yoke of a spiritual obligation, kartavyam˙ karma, then the uplifting of a divine sacrifice; at its highest it can be the expression of a calm and glad acquiescence in active oneness. The oneness in love will do much more: it will replace the first impassive calm by a strong and deep rapture, not the petty ardour of egoistic desire but the ocean of an infinite Ananda. It will bring the moving sense and the pure and divine passion of the presence of the Beloved into your works; there will be an insistent joy of labour for God in yourself and for God in all beings. Love is the crown of works and the crown of knowledge.

"This love that is knowledge, this love that can be the deep heart of your action, will be your most effective force for an utter consecration and complete perfection. An integral union of the individual's being with the Divine Being is the condition of a perfect spiritual life. Turn then altogether towards the Divine; make one with him by knowledge, love and works all your nature. Turn utterly towards him and give up ungrudgingly into his hands your mind and your heart and your will, all your consciousness and even your very senses and body. Let your consciousness be sovereignly moulded by him into a flawless mould of his divine consciousness. Let your heart become a lucid or flaming heart of the Divine. Let your will be an impeccable action of his will. Let your very sense and body be the rapturous sensation and body of the Divine. Adore and sacrifice to him with all you are; remember him in every thought and feeling, every impulsion and act. Persevere until all these things are wholly his and he has taken up even in most common and outward things as in the inmost sacred chamber of your spirit his constant transmuting presence.

"This triune way is the means by which you can rise entirely out of your lower into your supreme spiritual nature. That is the hidden superconscient nature in which the Jiva, a portion of the high Infinite and Divine and intimately one in law of being with him, dwells in his Truth and not any longer in an externalized Maya. This perfection, this unity can be enjoyed in its own native status, aloof in a supreme supracosmic existence: but here also you may and should realise it, here in the human body and physical world. It is not enough for this end to be calm, inactive, and free from the gunas in the inner self and to watch and allow indifferently their mechanical action in the outer members. For the active nature as well as the self has to be given to the Divine and to become divine. All that you must grow into one law of being with the Purushottama, sadharmya; all must be changed into my conscious spiritual becoming, mad-bhava. A completest surrender must be there. Take refuge with Me in all the many ways and along all the living lines of your nature; for that alone will bring about this great change and perfection.

"This high consummation of the Yoga will at once solve or rather it will wholly remove and destroy at its roots the problem of action. Human action is a thing full of difficulties and perplexities, tangled and confused like a forest with a few more or less obscure paths cut into it rather than through it; but all this difficulty and entanglement arises from the single fact that man lives imprisoned in the ignorance of his mental, vital, and physical nature. He is compelled by its qualities and yet afflicted with responsibility in his will because something in him feels that he is a soul who ought to be what now he is not at all or very little, master and ruler of his nature. All his laws of living, all his dharmas must be under these conditions imperfect, temporary, and provisional and at best only partly right or true. His imperfections can cease only when he knows himself, knows the real nature of the world in which he lives and, most of all, knows the Eternal from whom he comes and in whom and by whom he exists. When he has once achieved a true consciousness and knowledge, there is no longer any problem; for then he acts freely out of himself and lives spontaneously in accordance with the truth of his spirit and his highest nature. At its fullest, at the highest height of this knowledge it is not he who acts but the Divine, the One eternal and infinite who acts in him and through him in his liberated wisdom and power and perfection.

"Man in his natural being is a sattwic, rajasic and tamasic creature of Nature. According as one or other of her qualities predominates in him, he makes and follows this or that law of his life and action. His tamasic, material, sensational mind subject to inertia and fear and ignorance either obeys partly the compulsion of its environment and partly the spasmodic impulses of its desires or finds a protection in the routine following of a dull customary intelligence. The rajasic mind of desire struggles with the world in which it lives and tries to possess always new things, to command, battle, conquer, create, destroy, accumulate. Always it goes forward tossed between success and failure, joy and sorrow, exultation, or despair. But in all, whatever law it may seem to admit, it follows really only the law of the lower self and ego, the restless, untired, self-devouring and all-devouring mind of the Asuric and Rakshasic nature. The sattwic intelligence surmounts partly this state, sees that a better law than that of desire and ego must be followed and erects and imposes on itself a social, an ethical, a religious rule, a Dharma, a Shastra. This is as high as the ordinary mind of man can go, to erect an ideal or practical rule for the guidance of the mind and will and as faithfully as possible observe it in life and conduct. This sattwic mind must be developed to its highest point where it succeeds in putting away the mixture of ego motive altogether and observes the Dharma for its own sake as an impersonal social, ethical, or religious ideal, the thing disinterestedly to be done solely because it is right, kartavyam karma.

"The real truth of all this action of Prakriti is, however, less outwardly mental, and more inwardly subjective. It is this that man is an embodied soul involved in material and mental nature, and he follows in it a progressive law of his development determined by an inner law of his being; his cast of spirit makes out his cast of mind and life, his swabhava. Each man has a swadharma, a law of his inner being which he must observe, find out and follow. The action determined by his inner nature, that is his real Dharma. To follow it is the true law of his development; to deviate from it is to bring in confusion, retardation, and error. That social, ethical, religious, or other law and ideal is best for him always which helps him to observe and follow out his Swadharma.

"All this action however is even at its best subject to the ignorance of the mind and the play of the gunas. It is only when the soul of man finds itself that he can overpass and erase from his consciousness the ignorance and the confusion of the gunas. It is true that even when you have found yourself and live in yourself, your nature will still continue on its old lines and act for a time according to its inferior modes. But now you can follow that action with a perfect self-knowledge and can make of it a sacrifice to the Master of your existence. Follow then the law of your Swadharma, do the action that is demanded by your Swabhava whatever it may be. Reject all motive of egoism, all initiation by self-will, all rule of desire, until you can make the complete surrender of all the ways of your being to the Supreme.

"And when you are once able to do that sincerely, that will be the moment to renounce the initiation of your acts without exception into the hands of the supreme Godhead within you. Then you will be released from all laws of conduct, liberated from all dharmas. The Divine Power and Presence within you will free you from sin and evil and lift you far above human standards of virtue. For you will live and act in the absolute and spontaneous right and purity of the spiritual being and the immaculate force of the divine nature. The Divine and not you will enact his own will and works through you, not for your lower personal pleasure and desire, but for the world-purpose and for your divine good and the manifest or secret good of all. Inundated with light, you will see the form of the Godhead in the world and in the works of Time, know his purpose and hear his command. Your nature will receive as an instrument his will only whatever it may be and do it without question because there will come with each initiation of your acts from above and within you an imperative knowledge and an illumined assent to the divine wisdom and its significance. The battle will be his, his the victory, his the empire.

"This will be your perfection in the world and the body, and beyond these worlds of temporal birth the supreme eternal superconsciousness will be yours and you will dwell forever in the highest status of the Supreme Spirit. The cycles of incarnation and the fear of mortality will not distress you; for here in life, you will have accomplished the expression of the Godhead, and your soul, even though it has descended into mind and body, will already be living in the vast eternity of the Spirit.

"This then is the supreme movement, this complete sur-render of your whole self and nature, this abandonment of all dharmas to the Divine who is your highest Self, this absolute aspiration of all your members to the supreme spiritual nature. If you can once achieve it, whether at the outset or much later on the way, then whatever you are or were in your outward nature, your way is sure and your perfection inevitable. A supreme Presence within you will take up your Yoga and carry it swiftly along the lines of your swabhava to its consummate completion. And afterwards whatever your way of life and mode of action, you will be consciously living, acting, and moving in him and the Divine Power will act through you in your every inner and outer motion. This is the supreme way because it is the highest secret and mystery and yet an inner movement progressively realizable by all. This is the deepest and most intimate truth of your real, your spiritual existence."

THE END

LIST OF TITLES WITH ISBN NO.

ISBN	TITLE
9788194914129	1984
9789390575220	1984 & Animal Farm (2In1)
9789390575572	1984 & Animal Farm (2In1): The International Best-Selling Classics
9789390575848	35 Sonnets
9789390575329	A Clergyman's Daughter
9789390575923	A Study In Scarlet
9789390896097	A Tale Of Two Cities
9789390896837	Abide in Christ
9789390896202	Abraham Lincoln
9789390896912	Absolute Surrender
9789390896608	African American Classic Collection
9789390575305	Aldous Huxley: The Collected Works
9789390896141	An Autobiography of M. K. Gandhi
9789390575886	Animal Farm
9789390575619	Animal Farm & The Great Gatsby (2In1)
9789390575626	Animal Farm & We
9789390896158	Anna Karenina
9789390575534	Antic Hay
9789390896165	Antony & Cleopatra
9789390896172	As I Lay Dying
9789390896226	As You like it
9789390575671	At Your Command
9789390575350	Awakened Imagination
9789390575114	Be What You Wish
9789390896233	Believe In yourself
9789390896998	Best of Charles Darwin: The Origin of Species & Autobiography
9789390896684	Best Of Horror : Dracula And Frankenstein
9789390575503	Best Of Mark Twain (The Adventures of Tom Sawyer AND The Adventures of Huckleberry Finn)
9789390896769	Black History Collection
9789390575756	Brave New World, Animal Farm & 1984 (3in1)

9789390896240	Brother Karamzov
9789390575053	Bulleh Shah Poetry
9789390575725	Burmese Days
9789390896257	Bushido
9789390896066	Can't Hurt Me
9788194914112	Chanakya Neeti: With The Complete Sutras
9789390896042	Crime and Punishment
9789390575527	Crome Yellow
9789390575046	Down and Out in Paris and London
9789390896844	Dracula
9789390575442	Emersons Essays: The Complete First & Second Series (Self-Reliance & Other Essays)
9789390575749	Emma
9789390575817	Essential Tozer Collection - The Pursuit of God & The Purpose of Man
9789390896578	Fascism What It Is and How to Fight It
9789390575688	Feeling is the Secret
9789390575190	Five Lessons
9789390575954	Frankenstein
9789390575237	Franz Kafka: Collected Works
9789390575282	Franz Kafka: Short Stories
9789390575060	George Orwell Collected Works
9789390575077	George Orwell Essays
9789390575213	George Orwell Poems
9788194914150	Greatest Poetry Ever Written Vol 1
9788194914143	Greatest Poetry Ever Written Vol 1
9789390896301	Gulliver's Travel
9789390575961	Gunaho Ka Devta
9789390575893	H. P. Lovecraft Selected Stories Vol 1
9789390575978	H. P. Lovecraft Selected Stories Vol 2
9789390896059	Hamlet
9789390575022	His Last Bow: Some Reminiscences of Sherlock Holmes
9789390896134	History of Western Philosophy
9789390575121	Homage To Catalonia

9789390896219	How to develop self-confidence and Improve public Speaking
9789390896295	How to enjoy your life and your Job
9789390575633	How to own your own mind
9789390896318	How to read Human Nature
9789390896325	How to sell your way through the life
9789390896370	How to use the laws of mind
9789390896387	How to use the power of prayer
9789390896028	How to win friends & Influence People
9788194824176	How To Win Friends and Influence People
9789390896103	Humility The Beauty of Holiness
9789390896653	Imperialism the Highest Stage of Capitalism
9789390575084	In Our Time
9789390575169	In Our Time & Three Stories and Ten poems
9789390575145	James Allen: The Collected Works
9789390896189	Jesus Himself
9789390575480	Jo's Boys
9789390896394	Julius Caesar
9789390575404	Keep the Aspidistra Flying
9789390896400	Kidnapped
9789390896424	King Lear
9789390575824	Lady Susan
9789390896455	Law of Success
9789390896264	Lincoln The Unknown
9789390575565	Little Men
9789390575640	Little Women
9788194914174	Lost Horizon
9789390896462	Macbeth
9789390896929	Man Eaters of Kumaon
9789390896523	Man The Dwelling Place of God
9789390896349	Man The Dwelling Place of God
9789390575909	Mansfield Park
9788194914136	Manto Ki 25 Sarvshreshth Kahaniya
9789390896509	Marxism, Anarchism, Communism
9789390575664	Mathematical Principles of Natural Philosophy

9788194914198	Meditations
9789390575800	Mein Kampf
9789390575794	Memory How To Develop, Train, And Use It
9789390896486	Mind Power
9789390896585	Money
9789390575039	Mortal Coils
9789390575770	My Life and Work
9789390896035	Narrative of the Life of Frederick Douglass
9789390575152	Neville Goddard: The Collected Works
9789390575985	Northanger Abbey
9789390896530	Notes From Underground
9789390896547	Oliver Twist
9789390575459	On War
9789390575541	One, None and a Hundred Thousand
9789390896554	Othelo
9789390575435	Out Of This World
9789390575015	Persuasion
9789390575510	Prayer The Art Of Believing
9789390575091	Pride and Prejudice
9789390896561	Psychic Perception
9789390575381	Rabindranath Tagore - 5 Best Short Stories Vol 2
9789390575367	Rabindranath Tagore - Short Stories (Masters Collections Including The Childs Return)
9789390575374	Rabindranath Tagore 5 Best Short Stories Vol 1 (Including The Childs Return
9789390896622	Romeo & Juliet
9789390896127	Sanatana Dharma
9789390575596	Seedtime & Harvest
9789390896639	Selected Stories of Guy De Maupassant
9789390575206	Self-Reliance & Other Essays
9789390575176	Sense and Sensibility
9789390575299	Shyamchi Aai
9789390896738	Socialism Utopian and Scientific
9789390896646	Success Through a Positive Mental Attitude
9789390575428	The Adventures of Huckleberry Finn

9789390575183	The Adventures of Sherlock Holmes
9789390575343	The Adventures of Tom Sawyer
9789390896691	The Alchemy Of Happiness
9789390575862	The Art Of Public Speaking
9789390896288	The Autobiography Of Charles Darwin
9788194914181	The Best of Franz Kafka: The Metamorphosis & The Trial
9789390575008	The Call Of Cthulhu and Other Weird Tales
9789390575107	The Case-Book of Sherlock Holmes
9789390896110	The Castle Of Otranto
9789390896745	The Communist Manifesto
9789390575589	The Complete Fiction of H. P. Lovecraft
9789390575497	The Complete Works of Florence Scovel Shinn
9789390896820	The Conquest of Breard
9789390896813	The Diary of a Young Girl
9789390896332	The Diary of a Young Girl The Definitive Edition of the Worlds Most Famous Diary
9789390575701	The Great Gatsby, Animal Farm & 1984 (3In1)
9789390575312	The Greatest Works Of George Orwell (5 Books) Including 1984 & Non-Fiction
9789390575992	The Hound of Baskervilles
9789390896707	The Idiot
9789390896714	The Invisible Man
9789390575657	The Knowledge of the holy
9789390575558	The Law & the Promise
9789390896721	The Law Of Attraction
9789390896776	The Leader in you
9789390896363	The Life of Christ
9789390896196	The Man-Eating Leopard of Rudraprayag
9789390896783	The Master Key to Riches
9789390575268	The Memoirs Of Sherlock Holmes
9789390896479	The Midsummer Night's Dream
9789390575466	The Mill On The Floss
9789390896790	The Miracles of your mind
9789390896660	The Mutual Aid A Factor in Evolution
9789390896448	The Origin of Species

9789390896905	The Peter Kropotkin Anthology The Conquest of Bread & Mutual Aid A Factor of Evolution
9789390896806	The Picture of Dorian Gray
9789390896271	The Picture of Dorian Gray
9789390575275	The Power Of Awareness
9789390896356	The Power of Concentration
9788194824169	The Power of Positive Thinking
9789390575411	The Power of the Spoken Word
9788194914105	The Power Of Your Subconscious Mind
9789390896899	The Power of Your Subconscious Mind
9789390896417	The Principles of Communism
9789390575787	The Psychology Of Mans Possible Evolution
9789390896615	The Psychology of Salesmanship
9789390575732	The Pursuit of God
9789390575398	The Pursuit of Happiness
9789390896851	The Quick and Easy Way to effective Speaking
9789390575947	The Return Of Sherlock Holmes
9789390575138	The Road To Wigan Pier
9789390896981	The Root of the Righteous
9789390575855	The Science Of Being Well
9788194914167	The Science Of Getting Rich, The Science Of Being Great & The Science Of Being Well (3In1)
9789390896011	The Screwtape Letters
9789390896073	The Screwtape Letters
9789390575336	The Secret Door to Success
9789390575695	The Secret Of Imagining
9789390896868	The Secret Of Success
9789390896431	The Seven Last Words
9789390575930	The Sign of the Four
9789390896004	The Sonnets
9789390896516	The Souls of Black Folk
9789390896875	The Sound and The Fury
9789390575244	The State and Revolution
9789390896882	The Story of My Life
9789390896936	The Story Of Oriental Philosophy

9789390896752	The Strange Case of Dr. Jekyll and Mr. Hyde
9789390896943	The Tempest
9789390575916	The Valley Of Fear
9789390575879	The Wind in the willows
9789390896080	The Wind in the willows
9789390575763	Their eyes were watching gofd
9789390575831	Three Stories
9789390896950	Twelfth Night
9789390896592	Twelve Years a Slave
9789390896677	Up from Slavery
9789390896974	Value Price and Profit
9789390896967	Wake Up and Live
9789390896493	With Christ in the School of Prayer
9789390575602	Your Faith is Your Fortune
9789390575473	Your Infinite Power To Be Rich
9789390575251	Your Word is Your Wand
9789390575718	Youth
9789391316099	A Christmas Carol
9789391316105	A Doll's House
9789391316501	A Passage to India
9789391316709	A Portrait of the Artist as a Young Man
9789391316112	A Tale of Two Cities
9789391316747	A Tear and a Smile
9789391316167	Agnes Gray
9789391316174	Alice's Adventures in Wonderland
9789391316136	Anandamath
9789391316181	Anne Of Green Gables
9789391316754	Anthem
9789391316198	Around The World in 80 Days
9789391316013	As A Man Thinketh
9789391316242	Autobiography of a Yogi
9789391316266	Beyond Good and Evil
9789391316761	Bleak House
9789391316778	Chitra, a Play in One Act
9789391316310	David Copperfield

9789391316075	Demian
9789391316785	Dubliners
9789391316051	Favourite Tales from the Arabian Nights
9789391316235	Gitanjali
9789391316068	Gravity
9789391316150	Great Speeches of Abraham Lincoln
9789391316662	Guerilla Warfare
9789391316839	Kim
9789391316822	Mother
9789391316211	My Childhood
9789391316846	Nationalism
9789391316327	Oliver Twist
9789391316853	Pygmalion
9789391316334	Relativity: The Special and the General Theory
9789391316389	Scientific Healing Affirmation
9789391316341	Sons and Lovers
9789391316587	Tales from India
9789391316372	Tess of The D'Urbervilles
9789391316396	The Awakening and Selected Stories
9789391316402	The Bhagvad Gita
9789391316303	The Book of Enoch
9789391316228	The Canterville Ghost
9789391316907	The Dynamic Laws of Prosperity
9789391316006	The Great Gatsby
9789391316860	The Hungry Stones and Other Stories
9789391316433	The Idiot
9789391316440	The Importance of Being Earnest
9789391316297	The Light of Asia
9789391316914	The Madman His Parables and Poems
9789391316457	The Odyssey
9789391316921	The Picture of Dorian Gray
9789391316464	The Prince
9789391316938	The Prophet
9789391316945	The Republic
9789391316518	The Scarlet Letter

9789391316143	The Seven Laws of Teaching
9789391316525	The Story of My Experiments with Truth
9789391316532	The Tales of the Mother Goose
9789391316549	The Thirty Nine Steps
9789391316594	The Time Machine
9789391316600	The Turn of the Screw
9789391316983	The Upanishads
9789391316617	The Yellow Wallpaper
9789391316426	The Yoga Sutras of Patanjali
9789391316990	Ulysses
9789391316624	Utopia
9789391316679	Vanity Fair
9789391316020	What Is To Be Done
9789391316686	Within A Budding Grove
9789391316693	Women in Love